Virtual Community Practices and Social Interactive Media:
Technology Lifecycle and Workflow Analysis

Demosthenes Akoumianakis
Technological Education Institution of Crete, Greece

INFORMATION SCIENCE REFERENCE

Hershey · New York

Director of Editorial Content: Kristin Klinger
Senior Managing Editor: Jamie Snavely
Managing Editor: Jeff Ash
Assistant Managing Editor: Carole Coulson
Typesetter: Carole Coulson
Cover Design: Lisa Tosheff
Printed at: Yurchak Printing Inc.

Published in the United States of America by
        Information Science Reference (an imprint of IGI Global)
        701 E. Chocolate Avenue
        Hershey PA 17033
        Tel: 717-533-8845
        Fax: 717-533-8661
        E-mail: cust@igi-global.com
        Web site: http://www.igi-global.com/reference

and in the United Kingdom by
        Information Science Reference (an imprint of IGI Global)
        3 Henrietta Street
        Covent Garden
        London WC2E 8LU
        Tel: 44 20 7240 0856
        Fax: 44 20 7379 0609
        Web site: http://www.eurospanbookstore.com

Library of Congress Cataloging-in-Publication Data

Virtual community practices and social interactive media : technology lifecycle and workflow analysis / Demosthenes Akoumianakis, editor.
        p. cm.

Includes bibliographical references and index.

Summary: "This book makes a step toward an improved understanding of existing literature, prevalent practice and future trends related to community thinking, virtual practices and their intertwining with new technologies and social media"--Provided by publisher.

ISBN 978-1-60566-340-1 (hardcover) -- ISBN 978-1-60566-341-8 (ebook) 1. Online social networks--Case studies. 2. Internet--Social aspects--Case studies. I. Akoumianakis, Demosthenes, 1966-

  HM742.V57 2009
  302.30285--dc22

                            2008047747

British Cataloguing in Publication Data
A Cataloguing in Publication record for this book is available from the British Library.

Table of Contents

Detailed Table of Contents

Section A
Introduction

This chapter aims to provide an introductory tutorial to the key topics and themes suggested in the chapter's title and further developed by authors in the four main parts of this volume. It was considered important to provide this introductory account for two main reasons. First, it serves the purpose of sketching the boundaries of the volume by establishing an early focus on the concepts being addressed and highlighting the volume's orientation. This is expected to help the reader clarify the difference between this edited collection of chapters and other relevant literature. Secondly, the tutorial will hopefully unfold the rationale behind the structure of the volume into parts as well as the contributions selected in each part.

Section B
Communities of Practice

Communities of practice (CoPs) have been taken into account by both practitioners and academics during the last ten years. From a strategic point of view, CoPs have shown their importance for the management of organizational knowledge by offering repositories of knowledge, improved capacity of making knowledge actionable and operational (Brown & Duguid, 1998) and by facilitating maintenance, reproduction, and extension of knowledge (Brown & Durguid, 2001). CoPs are also reported to achieve value creation and competitive advantages (Davenport & Prusak, 1998), learning at work (Swan et alt., 2002) that promotes organizational competitiveness (Furlong & Johnson, 2003), innovation, even a radical type (Swan et alt., 2002), responsiveness, improved staff skills and reduced duplication (du Plessis, 2008). This impressive list of achievements is not for free; some authors have pointed out the limits of CoP's (Duguid, 2005; Roberts, 2006; Amin & Roberts, 2008) from diverse points of view, including diversity of working environments, size, spatial or relational proximity, but mainly emphasizing the specificity of CoPs as a social practice paradigm, as it was defined by Wenger (1999, 2000) credited as the "inventor" of the term "CoP" (Lave & Wenger, 1991). This chapter focuses on the consideration of CoPs as an organizational reality than can be managed (Thompson, 2005), the contradictions that the idea of managing them generates, and how these controversial points can be overcome in a sound and honest way. To do so, the authors review different cases of CoP's within organizations intended for the managerial team to achieve important organizational goals. Their analysis provides: (a) a reflection regarding the Key Success Factors in the process of integrating communities of practice, (b) insight to the structure of a model of cultivation, intended as a guideline for new experiences in this area, and (c) an informative account of this model's adaptation to the studied organizations.

Chapter III

Richard Ribeiro, University of York, UK
Chris Kimble, Euromed Marseille École de Management, France

This chapter examines the possibility of discovering a "hidden" (potential) Community of Practice (CoP) inside electronic networks, and then using this knowledge to nurture it into a fully functioning Virtual Community of Practice (VCoP). Starting from the standpoint of the need to manage knowledge and create innovation, the chapter discusses several issues related to this subject. It begins by examining Nonaka's SECI model and his notion of Knowledge Transfer; the authors follow this by an investigation of the links between Communities of Practice (CoPs) and Knowledge Management; the chapter concludes by examining the relation between Nonaka's Communities of Interaction and CoPs. Having established this they start their examination of the characteristics of "hidden" Communities of Practice. Following on from the previous discussion, they look at what is meant by "hidden" CoPs and what their value might be. The authors also look at the distinction between Distributed CoPs (DCoPs) and Virtual CoPs (VCoPs) and the issues raised when moving from "hidden" CoPs to fully functioning VCoPs. The chapter concludes with some preliminary findings from a semi-structured interview conducted in the Higher Education Academy Psychology Network (UK). These findings are contrasted against the theory and some further proposals are made.

Chapter IV

Kam Hou VAT, University of Macau, Macau

The chapter investigates an actionable framework of knowledge sharing, from the perspective of appreciative inquiry. This framework should accommodate the creation of appreciative processes that would encourage or better institutionalize knowledge sharing among people of interest in an organization. The idea is extensible to the building of communities in cyberspace so much facilitated in today's Internet and World Wide Web, and it is increasingly visible that such a model of knowledge sharing is quite promising for today's virtual enterprises. The premise in our exploration is that organizations were beginning to understand the power of unleashing knowledge among individuals. What they struggled with was how exactly to unleash that power, albeit that the very behavior of hoarding knowledge is what makes employees successful. The presence of an explicitly appreciative format rendered by the enterprise should allow many to say what is on their mind without being questioned, critiqued or put on the defense. And it could be done using the many electronic services of technology-enabled appreciative systems made available. However, the task of identifying what to watch in building a knowledge-sharing community online is not at all straightforward. For example, community can be examined by focusing on how users or participants work with and learn from the experience of community participation, or on the nature of collective imagination and feelings of identity as a tool for understanding belonging and attachment to particular virtual communities. Our investigation should provide a basis to think about the generative potential of some appreciative processes on a virtual community's knowledge activities. The design and refinement of technology as the conduit for extending and enhancing an organization's appreciative systems is an essential issue, but the role of the individuals as participants in a virtual community is as important. The emergent challenge is to de-marginalize the concept of appreciative sharing of knowledge among members of the organization, expositing on the effective meaning behind the organization's creation of the appreciative framework for knowledge work through which purposeful individual or organizational activities could be supported with the elaboration of suitable information technologies.

Chapter V

The main goal of this chapter is to demonstrate how purposeful participatory design can be used to construct a virtual knowledge commons that both serves and is defined by communities. Other than the proposition that participatory design is a technique to guide participation within a community, the chapter also explores how this technique can be used to nurture and sustain a shared knowledge commons in the virtual environment. To this end, the conditions and consequences of the virtual environment are discussed, illustrating how with participation, the virtual commons is possibly sustainable. The chapter also raises the role of cultural institutions and examines a number of contemporary examples, resulting in a preliminary spectrum of participation by which practices of participation in the virtual knowledge commons by cultural institutions can be mapped. More research and fieldwork needs to be done to refine this model and generate exemplary practices for policy development and best practices in cultural institutions.

This chapter proposes and discusses the "social" experience factory (SEF). The SEF provides a general model and architecture supporting information-based product assembly by cross-organization communities of practice using interactive toolkits and practice-specific technologies. In terms of engineering ground, the SEF builds on two prevalent research tracks, namely experience-based and reuse-oriented proposals for the management of virtual assets and automated software assembly as conceived and facilitated by recent advances on software factories. In our account of the SEF, the authors will focus on functions facilitating electronic squads (i.e., cross-organization virtual community management) and workflows (i.e., practice management) which collectively define the scope of collaboration using the SEF. Further technical details on operational aspects of the SEF as deployed in the tourism sector to facilitate vacation package assembly are presented in Chapter XXI in this volume.

Section C
Social Media and Tools

Chapter VII

Evangelia Mantzari, Athens University of Economics and Business, Greece
George Lekakos, University of the Aegean, Greece
Adam Vrechopoulos, Athens University of Economics and Business, Greece

Until recently, television viewing was perceived as a passive experience that aimed in satisfying a person's or a group's need for entertainment, information and, in some cases, education. However, the development of Interactive Digital Television (iDTV) and the significant change of society's expectations due to the appearance of the World Wide Web brought new dynamics on the medium. To that end, nowadays, iDTV adopts a more social role (Social TV) in order to satisfy the individuals' request for active participation, communication and (virtual) community formulation. This chapter aims at describing the characteristics of Social TV, while providing information about its systems and business models. Similarly, the present study attempts to explain if and how Social TV can become a new setting for virtual communities and what are the potential implications for its viewers.

Chapter VIII

Diana Schimke, University of Regensburg, Germany
Heidrun Stoeger, University of Regensburg, Germany
Albert Ziegler, Ulm University, Germany

Participation and system usage is crucial for virtual communities to develop and sustain. However, many communities report very low participation rates of members. Finding and studying strategies for fostering participation in virtual communities is therefore a growing field of research and different approaches for strengthening participation in virtual communities exist – among them social visualization. While many tools for visualizing social interactions have been developed, not much empirical evidence about their actual effectiveness exists. To find out more about the effectiveness of social visualization on the participation rate (number of logins, forum posts, personal messages, and chat posts) the authors conducted an empirical study within CyberMentor – a virtual community for high school girls interested in science and technology. In our sample of N=231 girls the authors did not find a significant difference between the number of logins in the phases before and after the introduction of the visualization tool. The number of forum post, chat posts and personal messages however increased significantly after the incorporation of the visualization tool. Long-term effects were found for one-to-many communication technologies (forum, chat), but not for personal messages (one-to-one).

Chapter IX

The authors have been running the second decade since the time that pioneers in Grid started to work on a technology which seemed similar to its predecessors but in reality it was envisioned totally divergent from them. Many years later, the grid technology has gone through various development stages yielding common solution mechanisms for similar categories of problems across interdisciplinary fields. Several new concepts like the Virtual Organization and Semantic Grid have been perfected bringing closer the day when the scientific communities will collaborate as if all their members were at the same location, working with the same laboratory equipment and running the same algorithms. Many production-scale standard-based middlewares have been developed to an excellent degree and have already started to produce significant scalability gains, which in the past, were considered unthinkable.

Chapter X

Massive Multiplayer Online Games (MMOG) allows a large number of players to cooperate, compete and interact meaningfully in the online environment. Gamers are able to form social network with fellow gamers and create a unique virtual community. Although research has discussed the importance of social interaction in MMOG, it fails to articulate how social interaction takes place in the game. The current chapter aims to depict how gamers interact and socialize with each other in a popular MMOG, World of Warcraft. Through virtual ethnography, specific interaction patterns and communication behaviors within the community are discussed. It is concluded that the types of social interaction taken place in the gaming world is influenced by the temporal and spatial factors of the game as well as the game mechanisms.

In this chapter the authors aim to portray the social aspects of the World Wide Web and the current and emerging trends in "Social Web". The Social Web (or Web 2.0) is the term that is used frequently to characterize Web sites that feature user provided content as their primary data source and leverage the creation of online communities based on shared interests or other socially driven criteria. The need for adding more meaning and semantics to these social Web sites has been identified and to this end the Semantic Web initiative is described and its methodologies, standards, and architecture are examined in the context of the "Semantic Social Web". Finally the embellishment of Web Services with semantic annotations and semantic discovery functionality is described and the relevant technologies are explored.

Section D
Practice Toolkits and Design Perspectives

Chapter XII

George Triantafyllidis, Technological Education Institution of Crete, Greece
Nikolaos Grammalidis, Centre for Research and Technology Hellas, Greece
Dimitiros Tzovaras, Centre for Research and Technology Hellas, Greece

Extending visual communications to the third dimension (3D) has been a dream over decades. The ultimate goal of the viewing experience is to create the illusion of a real environment in its absence. However limitations of visual quality and user acceptance prevented the development of relevant mass markets so far. Recent achievements in research and development triggered an increasing interest in 3D visual technologies. From technological point of view, this includes improvements over the whole 3D technology chain, including image acquisition, 3D representation, compression, transmission, signal processing, interactive rendering and 3D display. In the center of all these different areas, the visualization of 3D information stands as the major aspiration to be satisfied, since 3D enriches the interaction experience. This enhanced user experience that 3D imaging offers compared to 2D, is the main reason behind the rapid increase of the virtual communities using and managing 3D data: Archaeological site 3D reproductions, virtual museums (in the field of cultural heritage); 3D plays, special effects (in the field of entertainment); virtual classes (in the field of learning) are only some examples of the potentialities of 3D data. It's clear that 3D imaging technologies provide a new and powerful mechanism for collaborative practicing. In this context, this chapter focuses on the utilization of 3D imaging technology and computer graphics, in various virtual communities in the domains of education, cultural heritage, protection, health and entertainment.

Chapter XIII

Theodor G. Wyeld, Flinders University, Norway
Ekaterina Prasolova-Førland, Norwegian University of Science and Technology, Norway

Remote, collaborative work practices are increasingly common in a globalised society. Simulating these environments in a pedagogical setting allows students to engage in cross-cultural exchanges encountered in the profession. However, identifying the pedagogical benefits of students collaborating remotely on a single project presents numerous challenges. Activity Theory (AT) provides a means for monitoring and making sense of their activities as individuals and as a collective. AT assists in researching the personal and social construction of students' intersubjective cognitive representations of their own learning activities. Moreover, AT makes the socially constructed cultural scripts captured in their cross-cultural exchanges analysable. Students' reflection on these scripts and their roles in them helps them better understand the heterogeneity of the cultures encountered. In this chapter Engestrom's (1999) simple AT triangular relationship of activity, action and operation is used to analyze and provide insights into how students cooperate with each other across different cultures in a 3D collaborative virtual environment.

Chapter XIV

This chapter draws upon contemporary social theory to make an argument about the ways that teachers create personalized communities of practice at The Math Forum, an online educational resource center. The discussion of social networks and personalized community is brought into dialogue with sociologically oriented strands of math education research to suggest that the collaborative community building work that Math Forum teachers do online allows them to not only form a learning community but allows them to overcoming tensions around mathematical identity formation which are important for advancing one's thinking as a math teacher. The chapter discusses some of the interview data conducted with math forum teachers and the importance of that information for the future of teacher professional development and the way an online community can support teacher learning.

Chapter XV

This chapter concentrates on the development of practice-specific toolkits for managing on-line practices in the context of virtual communities of practice. The authors describe two case studies in different application domains each presenting alternative but complementary insights to the design of computer-mediated practice vocabularies. The first case study describes how established practices in music performance are encapsulated in a suitably augmented music toolkit so as to facilitate the learning objectives of virtual teams engaged in music master classes. The second case study is slightly different in orientation as it seeks to establish a toolkit for engaging in new coordinative practices in the course of building information-based products such as vacation packages for tourists. This time the virtual team is a cross-organization virtual community of practice with members streamlining their efforts by internalizing and performing in accordance with the new practice. Collectively, the case studies provide insight to building novel practice-specific toolkits to either encapsulate existing or support novel practices.

Chapter XVI

Josefina Guerrero García, Université catholique de Louvain, Louvain School of Management (LSM), Belgium

Jean Vanderdonckt, Université catholique de Louvain, Louvain School of Management (LSM), Belgium

Juan Manuel González Calleros, Université catholique de Louvain, Louvain School of Management (LSM), Belgium

Technology to support groups is rapidly growing in use. In recent years, the Web has become a privileged platform for implementing community-oriented workflows, giving rise to a new generation of workflow information systems. Specifically, the Web provides ubiquitous access to information, supports explicit distribution of business process across workers, workplaces, and computing platforms. These processes could be all supported by platform-independent user interfaces. This chapter presents a model-driven engineering method that provides designers with methodological guidance on how to systematically derive user interfaces of workflow information systems from a series of models. For this purpose, the workflow is recursively decomposed into processes which are in turn decomposed into tasks. Each task gives rise to a task model whose structure, ordering, and connection with the domain model allows the automated generation of corresponding user interfaces in a transformational approach. The various models involved in the method can be edited in a workflow editor based on Petri nets and simulated interactively.

Section E
Practice Domains and Case Studies

Chapter XVII

Manolis Tsiknakis, Institute of Computer Science, FORTH, Greece

This chapter provides an overview and discussion of virtual communities in health and social care. The available literature indicates that a virtual community in health or social care can be defined as a group of people using telecommunications with the purposes of delivering health care and education, and/or providing support. Such communities cover a wide range of clinical specialties, technologies and stakeholders. Examples include peer-to-peer networks, virtual health care delivery and E-Science research teams. Virtual communities may empower patients and enhance coordination of care services; however, there is not sufficient systematic evidence of the effectiveness of virtual communities on clinical outcomes. When practitioners utilize virtual community tools to communicate with patients or colleagues they have to maximize sociability and usability of this mode of communication, while addressing concerns for privacy and the fear of de-humanizing practice, and the lack of clarity or relevance of current legislative frameworks. Furthermore, the authors discuss in this context ethical, legal considerations and the current status of research in this domain. Ethical challenges including the concepts of identity and deception, privacy and confidentiality and technical issues, such as sociability and usability are introduced and discussed.

This chapter examines a community of professionals, created by a government agency and charged with conducting country-wide, cross-disciplinary, and cross-sectoral research and innovation in the area of water. The analysis describes the structure of the community and places it in the context of existing project practices and institutional arrangements. Under challenging conditions, the professionals in the area recruit team members from their trusted long-term collaborators, work independently on projects, use standard communication technologies and prefer informal face-to-face contacts. Out of these practices emerge a sparsely connected community with permeable boundaries interspersed with foci of intense collaboration and exchange of ideas. In this community, professionals collaborate and exchange of ideas with the same colleagues. Both collaboration and exchanges of ideas tend to involve professionals from different disciplines and, to a lesser extent, from a different sectors and locations.

Chapter XIX

The chapter provides an overview of virtual music communities focusing on novel collaboration environments aiming to support networked and geographically dispersed music performance. A key objective of the work reported is to investigate online collaborative practices during virtual music performances in community settings. To this effect, the first part of the chapter is devoted to reviewing different kind of communities and their corresponding practices as manifested through social interaction. The second part of the chapter presents a case study, which elaborates on the realization of virtual music communities using a generic technological platform, namely DIAMOUSES. DIAMOUSES was designed to provide a host for several types of virtual music communities, intended for music rehearsals, live performances and music learning. Our recent experiments provide useful insights to the distinctive features of these alternative community settings as well as the practices prevailing in each case. The chapter is concluded by discussing open research issues and challenges relevant to virtual music performance communities.

Knowledge acquisition in E-Learning environments requires both, individualization of content, and social interaction based on relevant learning items. So far few e-learning systems support an integrated didactic and social perspective on knowledge transfer. Intelligibility Catchers (ICs) are E-Learning components designed for establishing sustainable communities of E-Learning practice. They encapsulate didactic and communication-centered concepts for effective collaborative and reflective generation and exchange of knowledge. Due to their open nature, they can be created dynamically, for any domain and on different levels of granularity. By intertwining content and communication, context can be kept for learning and exploration, even bound to specific community members.

Chapter XXI

Nikolas Vidakis, Technological Education Institution of Crete, Greece
Dimitrios Kotsalis, Technological Education Institution of Crete, Greece
Giannis Milolidakis, Technological Education Institution of Crete, Greece
George Vellis, Technological Education Institution of Crete, Greece
Anargyros Plemenos, Technological Education Institution of Crete, Greece
Emmanouela Robogiannaki, Technological Education Institution of Crete, Greece
Kyriakos Paterakis, Technological Education Institution of Crete, Greece
Demosthenes Akoumianakis, Technological Education Institution of Crete, Greece

This chapter describes recent work and experience in setting up and supporting cross-organization virtual communities of practice to facilitate new product development. The authors' reference domain is tourism and the community's joint enterprise is assembly of vacation packages. The chapter contrasts existing practices involved in building vacation packages against the computer-mediated practices flourishing in an electronic village of local interest on regional tourism. The electronic village is considered as an aggregation of thematic virtual communities (i.e., neighborhoods) each with own rules, policies and primitive offerings covering tourism services such as accommodation, transportation, cultural resources, and so forth. Electronic squads are formed as cross-neighborhood communities of practice to engage in computer-mediated assembly of vacation packages. The chapter presents key tasks involved in managing both electronic squads and the workflows through which the shared resources are combined and transformed into new collective offerings.

Chapter XXII

Demosthenes Akoumianakis, Technological Education Institution of Crete, Greece

This chapter attempts to consolidate concepts, ideas and results reported in this volume in an effort to synthesize an agenda and sketch a roadmap for future research and development on virtual community practices facilitated by synergistic combination of social interactive media. In this endeavor, the author revisits the notions of new media, communities and social practice, in the light of the preceding chapters and with the intention to pickup seemingly heterogeneous concepts and sketch the puzzle of social interactive media and virtual community practice. Their ultimate target is to make inroads towards a reference model for understanding and framing online social practice under the different regimes constituted by new media and social computing.

Preface

This volume is the result of nearly two years of intensive work to define relevant terms and scope, invite contributions, initiate and facilitate revisions, and finally edit a collection of chapters which will hopefully make a step towards an improved understanding of existing literature, prevalent practice and future trends related to community thinking, virtual practices and their intertwining with new technologies and social media.

This collection of chapters appears at a moment that virtual communities have already started to dominate our daily residential and business activities, acting as amplifiers of human intellect and making tremendous inroads in expanding our social substance and professional competence, both as individuals and members of society. The popular press provides subtle evidence. More than 15 out of the top 20 most popular Web sites are either social network sites per se, or have embedded social networking functions. Furthermore, numerous studies indicate the increasing engagement of users, especially young people in blogging activities, making Weblog hosting sites such as Myspace and Xanga among the most active sites on the Web with millions of daily visits.

Examining critically this new situation, one may pose several questions, recurring with every novel idea, new virtuality and technological trajectory:

- What is the innovative ground upon which it is based?
- Is it the result of advances in scientific endeavor, technical progress or incremental response to the end-users' ever increasing demand for information processing?
- Why does it happen when it does and what implications it bares upon human activities?
- How far-reaching are its effects and do they constitute a paradigm shift?

These are only a few of the questions one may ask when observing the new reality at home, in the office, the university and the variety of physical and virtual social gathering places. At the core of these new experiences are novel practices which increasingly determine how we think about ourselves as individuals and as members of wider social groupings. Some of these practices, such as for example social networking have matured to the point that they are already part of our culture. Others put into question our very existence as social creatures. For instance, multiple identity management in our virtual endeavors challenges our traditional means of presenting our selves to colleagues and peers.

Against these developments, the current volume aims to investigate critically some of the forces shaping present and future virtual community life, driving developments in new media and enabling either reproductions of existing practices or the emergence of totally new virtualities. The term virtuality refers to any kind of technological construction or mediation, which allows humans to attain business, residential, social or communication-oriented activities in a virtual space.

KEY THEMES AND ORIENTATION

In recent years, virtual communities of various sorts and types such as "place"-based online communities, virtual social networks, intra- and inter-organization distributed communities of practice, to mention a few, have stimulated a truly interdisciplinary thematic domain of discourse attracting the attention of scientists and researchers across a variety of disciplines, including the social sciences (e.g., sociology, cognitive psychology, anthropology, management science) and several engineering disciplines such as software engineering, telecommunications and multimedia. As in many other cases, the cross-disciplinary nature of the innovation creates the potential for a new virtuality, which as it turns out, it brings about a wider impact and has far-reaching effects than initially intended or anticipated.

Communities are not just aggregates of people, temporarily interacting; they are dynamic entities whose added value results from their continuous evolution. Their inherent complexity becomes evident from the variety of definitions attempted and the different connotations assigned to this social phenomenon. Community has been defined as a group of people who share social interactions, social ties, and a common "space"; as a social network of relationships that provide sociability support, information, and a sense of belonging, and as a set of relationships where people interact socially for mutual benefit. The key seems to be strong and lasting interactions that bind community members and that take place in some form of common space.

Accordingly, their virtual counterparts, in whatever way they are coined, are complex social systems enabled by a complex set of information technologies. Despite their infant stage, they have already shown the potential to provide the new virtuality, which in an increasingly networked society, can augment "collective" human intellect and set new standards for individuals and organizations. Stated differently, this new virtuality can re-shape the conduct of social activities, deepen professional knowledge and practice and create new grounds for knowledge management.

In the early 1990's when the first theoretical works on virtual communities appeared many scholars seemed to converge on the idea that the only difference between traditional and virtual communities is that the later exists in cyberspace. However, recent empirical studies indicate that this is no longer a valid assumption or sufficient distinction. In fact, virtuality brings new vocabulary and expands the community's language in many different ways. Consequently, the challenge is not only reproducing established practices online, but more importantly, it is gaining the required insight and understanding to design for new practices, specific to the new media, and viable only in virtual settings. This last point is intended to provide a preamble of this volume's orientation and point of departure from other relevant contributions found in the literature. Specifically, chapters within the volume aim to explore the intertwining between virtual communities, new media and the social practices emerging or reproduced as a result of new technology.

OBJECTIVE AND PERSPECTIVES

In light of the above, the objective of the volume is not simply to compile and disseminate state of the art knowledge on a truly multidisciplinary area, but also to highlight issues, which will further catalyze developments in the years to come. To this end, the scope of the volume is broad and covers the theoretical foundations of virtual communities, technological and engineering perspectives on the construction of community-based virtualities as well as the type, nature and scope of reconstructed or novel practices emerging in specific applications domains.

An explicit effort has been made to solicit contributions on current theoretical community thinking as advanced by developmental perspectives in social and management sciences, as well as contributions which improve our understanding of the engineering base of virtual practices as shaped by the synergistic fusion of emerging technologies. As for practical insights, the last part of the volume brings together results from recent and on-going research and development projects and case studies in various practice domains such as science and engineering, education and learning, collaborative music performance, tourism, health, entertainment and gaming.

The contributions in this volume come from professionals across a range of scientific and engineering disciplines, unfolding a variety of perspectives relevant to the study of the core subject matter. Depending on their interest, readers will find useful contributions rooted in developmental social sciences, management science, information management science, human-computer interaction, computer-supported cooperative work, computer science, biomedical engineering, to name a few. In terms of specific design methods and techniques, chapters provide details on the application of activity theory, online ethnography, distributed cognition and situated action models, structuration theory and symbolic interactionism in the design of virtual communities. Equally rich is the insight provided on new media, architectural models and tools. There are chapters reporting on architectural models for supporting communities of practice, emerging Grid infrastructures, the social Semantic Web and social TV, as well as chapters dedicated to specific practice-oriented toolkits and technologies such as social visualization, games, 3D imaging, and so forth.

STRUCTURE OF THE VOLUME

The volume is split into five sections. Section A is the *Introduction* and includes one chapter by the editor providing an overview and setting the context of the volume. Subsequent parts focus on clusters of on-going research and development activities.

Section B is concentrated on *Communities of Practice* and contains five chapters. The chapter by Edurne Loyarte and Olga Rivera (Spain) investigates conditions and key success factors for the management of communities of practice as revealed by recent theory and the authors' empirical work across a range of communities of practice. Richard Ribeiro (UK) and Chris Kimble (France) concentrate on a relatively unexplored issue regarding communities of practice, namely the search for "hidden" virtual communities of practice. Their chapter is motivated by the need for managing organizational knowledge and presents results of a recent case study focusing of identifying a "hidden" community in a virtual setting. Vat, H. Kam (China) elaborates on appreciative inquiry and its potential for managing knowledge in communities of practice within organizations. Natalie Pang (Australia) considers the broad topic of virtual knowledge commons and motivates the use of participatory design approaches to establishing sense of community and collective memories. The last chapter in this part is by Demosthenes Akoumianakis (Greece) detailing the components of the "Social Experience Factory" and how it may be used to facilitate mission-driven collaboration in communities of practice tasked to assembly information-based products and services.

Section C is entitled *Social Media and Tools* and contains five chapters. The chapter by Evangelia Mantzari, George Lekakos and Adam Vrechopoulos (Greece) reviews virtual communities formed around an emerging medium, namely Social TV, and outlines issues relevant to the enhancement of the users' viewing experience. Diana Schimke, Heidrun Stoeger, and Albert Ziegler (Germany) describe the relevance of social visualization to virtual communities and provide empirical evidence indicating how this technology may be used to strengthen sense of community amongst members. Ioannis Barbounakis and Michalis Zervakis (Greece) explore the new opportunities for virtual communities offered by computational and data grids as well as how the underlying component technologies can be exploited in support of the concept of "virtual organizations". Vivian Hsueh-hua Chen and Henry Been-Lirn Duh (Singapore) provide an interesting account of social interaction taking place in a virtual gaming community. Their chapter, informed by symbolic interactionism, details a virtual enthographic study of social interaction in World of Warcraft. The last chapter in this part by Stelios Sfakianakis (Greece) and elaborates on the promises and challenges of the social Semantic Web and Semantic Web services for virtual communities.

Section D is entitled *Practice Toolkits and Design Perspectives*. It contains five chapters reporting on a variety of practice-oriented technologies and how their design may be informed by established and emerging design techniques. The chapter by George Triantafyllidis, Nikolaos Grammalidis and Dimitrios Tovaras (Greece) investigates the new possibilities for virtual community practicing offered by 3D imaging technology. Their chapter reviews key components of this technology and presents recent examples of virtual collaborative activities in a variety of community settings. Theodor G Wyeld (Australia) and Ekaterina Prasolova-Førland (Norway) concentrate on online 3D learning communities and how learning materials and the learning experience can be informed by the activity theoretic perspective of cultural-historical psychology. Wes Shumar (USA) reviews the Math Forum and offers an informative account of how it fosters interaction, imagination and community building. The final two contributions in this section bring to the surface human-computer interaction issues related to the design of community workflows. The chapter by Demosthenes Akoumianakis, Giannis Milolidakis, George Vellis and Dimitrios Kotsalis (Greece) discusses design issues relevant to building practice-oriented interactive toolkits for communities of practice, either as facilitators of existing practices or as new practice enablers. Finally, Josefina Guerrero, Jean Vanderdonckt and Juan Manuel González Calleros (Belgium) describe a methodology for building user interfaces for community-oriented workflow information systems which exploits model-based user interface engineering techniques.

Section E, entitled *Practice Domains and Case Studies*, provides informative accounts of virtual community practices through recent case studies in a variety of application domains. The chapter by Manolis Tsiknakis (Greece) reviews virtual community in E-Health and the emerging practices with a strong insight to the ethical and legal issues involved. Dimitrina (Dima) Dimitrova (Canada) and Emmanue Koku (USA) provide a contextual account of professional research communities focusing on trust, independence and the role of technology. Chrisoula Alexandraki and Nikolas Valsamakis (Greece) explore virtual music communities, the variety of purposes they may serve, as well as the authors' recent work on collaborative music performance in virtual community settings. Chris Stary (Austria) offers an enlightening account of sustainable virtual communities in desktop-based and mobile device E-Learning contexts. Finally, Nikolas Vidakis, Dimitrios Kotsalis, Giannis Milolidakis, George Vellis, Anargyros Plemenos, Emmanouela Robogiannaki, Kyriakos Paterakis & Demosthenes Akoumianakis (Greece) present their recent experiences on developing a new computer-mediated virtual practice to support information-based product assembly by cross-organization virtual communities of practice in E-Tourism.

The volume is concluded by a chapter entitled *Social Interactive Media and Virtual Community Practices: Retrospective and an R&D Agenda* which reflects the editor's attempt to consolidate the contributions to the volume and to sketch a possible roadmap for future research and development on virtual community practices.

Acknowledgment

First, the editor would like to thank the authors of the chapters for their kind efforts, patience, understanding and commitment to completing this volume. Special thanks are due to those authors, who have reviewed chapters submitted by other authors, during the internal review process. Secondly, I would like to acknowledge the valuable efforts invested by external reviewers to ensure high quality of the accepted chapters. Thirdly, I must also thank the Publisher for giving me the opportunity to work on this volume and staff at IGI Global for their guidance and support as well as for their prompt response to the issues raised throughout this effort. Finally, a special note of thanks is due to my family, Maria, Giannis and Baggelis, for their patience during a difficult 18-month period.

Section A
Introduction

Chapter I
New Media, Communities, and Social Practice:
An Introductory Tutorial

Demosthenes Akoumianakis
Technological Education Institution of Crete, Greece

ABSTRACT

This chapter aims to provide an introductory tutorial to the key topics and themes suggested in the chapter's title and further developed by authors in the four main parts of this volume. It was considered important to provide this introductory account for two main reasons. First, it serves the purpose of sketching the boundaries of the volume by establishing an early focus on the concepts being addressed and highlighting the volume's orientation. This is expected to help the reader clarify the difference between this edited collection of chapters and other relevant literature. Secondly, the tutorial will hopefully unfold the rationale behind the structure of the volume into parts as well as the contributions selected in each part.

INTRODUCTION

This volume is primarily concerned with the design of virtual community practices enabled or facilitated by new media (i.e., social software, collaborative practice toolkits and emerging infrastructures such as Grids and Web 2.0) and performed by human collaborators in a variety of community settings (i.e., online communities, virtual communities of practice, cross-organization communities of practice, etc). Three key concepts stand out very promptly as primary challenges motivated by a variety of theoretical and / or engineering perspectives. These are the concepts of 'new media', 'community' and 'social practice'. Each by itself is a challenging concept in the sense that, despite years of study by researchers across different disciplines, common ground in terms of a consolidated body of knowledge is yet to be established. Furthermore, it is also striking that very few studies have attempted to explore how these three constituents are intertwined and how such intertwining gives rise to the new virtualities manifested through novel social practice toolkits and technologies. The above provide a sketch of the broad area covered by the authors contributing to this volume.

In order to bring these three concepts into perspective, this introductory chapter attempts to provide the necessary background information which is needed to gain better insight into the structure of the volume into parts and the individual contributions within these parts. Our objective is therefore to provide a tutorial which on the one hand will define the concepts of new media, community and social practice and on the other hand it will bring to the surface the distinct issues and challenges resulting from their intertwining.

The chapter is structured as follows. The next section sets the scene by providing a contextual account of the global challenges considered relevant, thus motivating the volume's organization and selected contributions. Our intention is not to preoccupy the research orientations of the individual contributions, but rather to provide an abstract and synthetic account of their common ground in the context of this volume. The next three sections are devoted to exploring the cornerstones of such common ground, namely new media, communities and social practices. This serves the purpose of both defining the concepts as well as outlining open research areas in an increasingly networked society. The last section summarizes and concludes the chapter.

MOTIVATION AND RESEARCH FOCUS

To set the context for our analysis, we will first consolidate our current understanding regarding how new media, community thinking and computer-mediated social practice are interrelated to facilitate the emergence of new virtualities. Specifically, our running hypothesis can be formulated as follows:

New social media (i.e., practice-specific toolkits, games, Social TV) and infrastructures (i.e., grids, Web 2.0) enable a variety of virtual community types (i.e., online communities, communities of practice, virtual cross-organization communities of practice, networks of practice, etc) in a variety of domains (i.e., organizational knowledge management, learning, music performance, tourism, health, eScience), resulting in the reproduction of existing or the incremental formation of new social practices as a result of the new virtualities.

In light of the above, one may pose several challenging questions, but for our purposes two of them stand out very promptly: (a) 'What is it that actually drives new virtualities in an increasingly networked society?' and (b) 'What determines the success or failure of new virtualities?' There are various perspectives from which these two questions could be addressed. Scientists would certainly bring to the forefront advances in the natural sciences which clearly have contributed to reshaping society over the centuries. Technologists would argue on the value of appropriating the benefits of scientific endeavors and making them available as integrated products and services. Social scientists would stress the human needs driving technical changes and resulting into new experiences of the world surrounding us. Innovation management scientists seem to unify these perspectives by distinguishing and classifying innovations as technology-push (i.e., radical technical change), demand-pull (i.e., incremental advances led by the market or creative users) and fusion-based (i.e., innovation resulting from appropriating intertwining technical achievements of different sectors).

Contextualizing the above to the aims and scope of this volume, one could easily explain why technological advances in the new media sectors create new opportunities for more effective, efficient and enjoyable human activities. In a similar vein, one would find it difficult to disagree with the view that sense of community and socialization is part of the human DNA. How easy, however, is it to explain some of the negative side effects resulting from (some sorts of) socializing in virtual space and how these side effects gain in popularity, mature and become common practices? This brings to surface the long-standing issue of deciding what society or communities we want to live in and how they are to be designed for the benefit of human kind. To respond to these issues one would definitely need a detailed understanding of the competing forces, as well as the dynamics which progressively influence the ultimate outcome.

The remaining sections of this chapter are devoted to briefly considering each of the three core concepts, namely new media, community and social practice, involved in shaping, structuring and managing collaborative practices and their subsuming activities in virtual space. We approach this either by elaborating on established notions from the relevant literature or by reference to specific chapters in this volume. As pointed out earlier, our interest is not to provide an exhaustive treatment of the three concepts, but rather to introduce them and establish links with chapters in this volume.

NEW MEDIA

Communities are frequently characterized by the medium around which they are formed and the specific situated practices it affords. For in-

stance, paper-based media such as newspapers or magazines designate community of people having common interests or sharing similar values. As for the practices afforded, they are highly individualistic, task-based and widely followed. Nevertheless, such media do not foster mutual engagement, social tights and interaction between the members, thereby facilitating a weak and passive sense of community. In this volume, we are not interesting in such media per se or the communities formed around them. Instead, we are keen to investigate and understand networked social media (of various types) which give rise to novel forms of virtual practicing, support rich interactions and foster social ties between community members.

Social media are empowered by a variety of technologies such as email, instant messaging, Web conferencing systems, Blogs, multimedia, music-sharing, voice over IP, to name a few, and facilitate novel applications and services such as virtual reference commons (i.e., Wikipedia, Google Groups), social networking (i.e., MySpace, Facebook, YouTube, Avatars United, Google Groups), music, video and photo sharing (i.e., Last. fm, YouTube, Flickr). Many of these social media services can be integrated via social network aggregation platforms like Mybloglog and Plaxo. In this context, it is worth comparing social media against traditional media to gain some insight into what makes the difference and why social media gain in popularity.

Social media and their applications have a number of characteristics that make them fundamentally different from traditional media such as newspapers, television, books, and radio. First, social media is not finite as there are no predetermined limits on pages or time. Secondly, in contrast with traditional media where users are the consumers of content, in social media it is users that are the content which is provided through active participation manifested as adding comments or even editing the stories themselves. Consequently, value in the social media results primarily, from the social interactions between people, as the discussion and integration of words builds shared-meaning, using technology as a conduit.

Social Interaction

Informally stated, social media may be conceived of as tools and/or artifacts allowing users to engage in some sort of social interaction. Giddens et al (2005) discuss social interaction, as the process by which we act and react to those around us and includes all forms of communication, verbal and nonverbal. Interactive computer-mediated tools and environments may form new social media allowing online socializing.

Socializing online is a multifaceted issue. People go online for a variety of purposes such as to chat, to find like-minded people, to debate issues, to play games, to share and seek for information, to find support, to shop, or just to hang-out with others. Respectively, there are tools such as chat-rooms, instant messaging software, bulletin boards and discussion forums, allowing people to join as members of groups or to create their own groups.

Consequently, online socialization may be framed to the users' conscious actions in a virtual setting. It can also be related to collective wisdom and experience codified as artifacts / objects used for representing common ground, rules and policies, aggregating contributions as expressed by participants, extracting tendencies within a group, revealing roles and role-undertaking, conveying awareness at various levels, such as task, activity and social. Finally, examining online socializing as a dynamic process it is useful to relate it to progressive attainment of a goal, change of perspective, view or opinion, level of stabilization and transitions from one level to another.

Then, it stands to argue that social software refers to any type of technology-enabled tool or systems that allow humans to attain online socializing. More specifically, social software is defined as technology-enabled tools and systems that foster and facilitate humane interaction, dialogue, collaboration and negotiation between members of a social network irrespective of their physical proximity. Therefore, the term is assigned a broad connotation intended to include all types of media supporting the range of social interactions that normally occur in a face-to-face setting (i.e., discussion, sharing, peer review and group activities) and which are substantiated through cognitive outcomes such as enhancement of elaboration and retention, increase of motivation and participation, clarification and negotiation of understanding, team building and exploration and discovery. For the purposes of the present analysis, such media are classified in two overlapping categories namely networked communication media and social practice toolkits (including emerging infrastructures for distributed collaborative computing).

Networked Communication Media

Networked communication media such as the Web, Web radio, Web TV, Blogs, Wikis, online community portals offer interactive media for online socializing and community engagement. However, their current structure and use is not yet appropriate for appropriating the benefits of social interaction.

A frequently cited shortcoming of the Web is that it is lacking cues and browsing mechanisms to turn online social spaces from abstract and informational experiences to 'places' inviting for social interaction (Lee et al., 2004). In other words, online social spaces fail to convey traces of life, character, relationships, and the social cues which are important for social interaction. Making the comparison with the social spaces found in the physical world, where such traces are predominant, in the networked communication media social information and patterns exist, but they are buried in the content-centric information.

In terms of the users' experience, the prevalent use of networked communication media is such that they are seen more as supplements to real world interactions, and often as a means of sustaining activities and relationships at home, among friends, and with the workplace. In other words, users don't think in terms of technologies, relationships or communication, they think in terms of consuming information.

Another distinction—for some a shortcoming—of networked communication media is that there is no 'civil inattention', which is typical and common in more traditional community media. Specifically, traditional media have the benefit of not requiring the user's explicit declaration to establish their social sphere. For instance, readers of a newspaper do not have to make their presence known to become part of the community; in spaces for social gathering in the physical world, you can see another person and have them know that you did so, without declaring it. There is no such thing online; an explicit assumption of networked communication media is that users are required to make their presence known. As a consequence users are forced to think primarily in terms of relationships and communication in addition to content.

Social Media

Networked communication media, while important and useful tend to be generic and neutral of domain of practice. A recent trend, which is expected to continue, is to augment popular networked communication media with social technologies so as to catalyze the 'social life' in virtual communities and communities of practice. Social media are dedicated interactive software tools and middleware technologies which provide the 'place' for engaging in the practice the community is about. Early efforts in this direction were inspired by CSCW and groupware and delivered a variety of computer conferencing systems, asynchronous discussion forums and

media spaces for dialog and collaborative work. Despite the widespread use of these technologies, users express numerous problems including the difficulties in adjusting to the technology, the extended time it takes to feel comfortable using it, information overload from having to dig through large amounts of postings, the large percentage of posting content that is off topic or irrelevant, the bandwidth and time requirements of opening numerous postings and the implications of the inherent time lag in computer conferencing (i.e., discussions may lose momentum and seem fragmented).

More recent efforts concentrate on social media and tools which exploit a wide range of emerging technologies such as social visualizations, Human-Computer Interaction and user interface software technologies, computational and data grids, as well as the technologies driving the evolution of the social Semantic Web. Chapters in this volume provide informative accounts of these novel approaches by elaborating the promises and challenges of a broad range of underlying technologies. Figure 1 depicts graphically some of the technologies reviewed in this volume.

Social visualization techniques might be useful to convey information about the online world and its participants. Specifically, it can be used to allow participants to explore structural and relational properties of a social network. Systems such as Conversation Map (Sack, 2000), Netscan (Smith & Fiore, 2001) and Personal Map (Farnham et al 2003) serve this purpose facilitating users in exploring social information in small- and large-scale conversation spaces. Additionally social visualization can be used to provide insights to task and activity-specific indicators such as amount of past or ongoing activity within the network, peak and slow times, who tends to answer particular types of questions (Donath 2002; Erickson et al. 2002; Erickson and Kellogg 2002), who is taking initiatives, type of contributions made, etc. As suggested by Donath (2002) such systems as well as earlier efforts including Comic Chat (Kurlander

Figure 1. Community tools and technology lifecycle trends

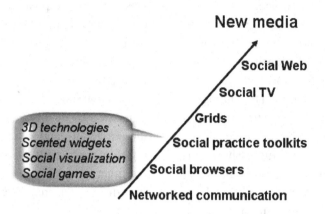

et al., 1996) and Chat Circle (Viegas & Donath, 1999) are valuable in giving the participants a better grasp of their online social space.

Human Computer Interaction (HCI) is another emerging technology which may provide substantial contribution to building social practice toolkits, either generic or domain-specific. Recently, there have been cutting edge developments in user interface software technologies conveying social information and navigation data. Scented widgets (Willett et al., 2007) are a representative example. Scented widgets are graphical user interface controls enhanced with embedded visualizations that facilitate navigation in information spaces. The idea of a scented widget, which is inspired from the concept of information scent – a user's "(imperfect) perception of the value, cost, or access path of information sources obtained from proximal cues" (Pirolli & Card, 1999) is to add visual cues to common user interface widgets such as radio buttons, sliders, and combo boxes so as to convey social information. The work by Willett et al. (2007) revealed how scented widgets can be used within applications with minimal modifications to existing source code.

Another HCI-inspired idea of a generic social practice toolkit is found in social browsers (Lee et al., 2004) which visualize a particular community property or characteristic of human interaction over time and support exploration and discovery of the social context information for its Web site. Two representative examples are the CHIplace and eTree social browsers. The CHIplace People browser provides a community map of the site members' different roles. The Portkey eTree browser portrays the participants and the extent of discussion participation through a visual ecosystem metaphor. Both social browsers make use of visualizations that evolve and dynamically adjust to reflect the activities in the community space, while they offer supplemental functionality (such as dynamic query) and information visualization techniques (such as animation, overview, and detail). These properties enable users to extract certain social information by observing patterns, human presence, and/or social activities and organizations in temporal context.

Grids and the technologies supporting the transition to Social Semantic Web constitute another important trend of great potential and promise in the context of establishing networked media for community practice, including social interaction. Computational and data grids promise to change the engineering foundations of large-scale communities, whether scientific or business-sponsored. Concepts such as the virtual organization and Semantic grids promise to provide the foundations for a new model of large-scale community collaboration. Sophisticated and standards-based middleware toolkits progressively establish a virtuality whereby community members collaborate as if they were at the same location, working with the same laboratory equipment and running the same algorithms.

The Social Web (or Web 2.0) is the term that is used frequently to characterize Web sites that feature user provided content as their primary data source and leverage the creation of online communities based on shared interests or other socially driven criteria. The need for adding more meaning and semantics to these social Web sites has been identified and to this end the Semantic Web initiative advances methodologies, standards, and architecture which will make possible the incremental transition to the "Semantic Social Web". To this effect, advances in Web Services (i.e., Semantic annotations and Semantic discovery functionality) constitute on-going areas of research and development.

COMMUNITIES

Since the late part of the 19th century, community as a social phenomenon has been, and continuous to be the subject of considerable debate for sociologists. In this debate two main traditions of theoretical thinking have emerged. The first considers community from a process oriented perspective accounting for the processes of social solidarity, material processes of production and consumption, law making and symbolic processes of collective experience and cultural meaning, The second tradition considers community in terms of place-based social interaction, collective value and shared symbol systems that create a normative structure typified by organic traditions, collective rituals, fellowship and consensus building (Fernback, 2007).

Recently, scholars within both traditions have provided valuable insight into how the term 'community' may be interpreted in the context of computer-supported social networks (Wellman, et al., 1996) to foster new virtualities such as online (virtual) communities (Rheingold, 1994), distributed communities (Gochenour, 2006), networks of practice (Brown and Duguid, 2000), knowledge communities (Lindkvist, 2005) and value-creating networks (Buchel & Raub, 2002). Although, these efforts are in pursue of seemingly similar targets, their underlying baseline as well as the resulting / proposed models have unique characteristics and distinct implications.

Figure 2, in an attempt to consolidate the prevailing concepts depicts as a continuum the types of communities reported in the relevant literature, their respective focus and reference models. As shown, today's online communities

Figure 2. Community types and focus

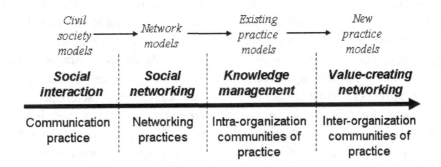

(located in the left hand side of the figure) are virtual encapsulations or either communication or networking practices rooted either in civil society models (i.e., virtual places or spaces) and network models, respectively. Such types of communities are clearly distinguished from more advanced forms such as intra- or inter-organization virtual CoP and value creating networks. The basic difference is that the later types, one way or another, seek to deepen professional knowledge. In light of the above, it stands to argue that the farther a community shifts to the right hand side of the plateau in Figure 2, the more compelling the need to articulate some sort of domain-oriented and practice-specific vocabulary. In turn, this may be designed either to reproduce virtually an existing practice, as the case may be with online communities or intra-organization CoP or as new practice per se, as in the case of cross-organization CoP. In this context, new practice implies an abstraction to which all members adhere irrespective of local sub-practices and procedures.

In the following, an attempt is made to further qualify the above distinctions, thus offering a means for differentiating community types on the grounds of the underlying virtuality supported, the kind of practice facilitated and the degree to which it is reproductions of established practices or new practice enabled and enacted virtually.

Virtual Communities

The term 'virtual community' was initially introduced in Howard Rheingold's seminal book in 1994 as a result of investigations in online virtual spaces such as MUDs, MOOs, IRC channels and bulletin boards (Rheingold, 1994). Since then, many authors have provided important insights to this new virtuality, resulting in consensus as to the meaning of the term. Specifically, in recent writings the term online or virtual community is coined with groups of people with a common interest or a shared purpose whose interactions are governed by policies in the form of tacit assumptions, rituals, protocols, rules, and laws and who use computer systems to support and mediate social interaction and facilitate a sense of togetherness (Preece, 2000).

Virtual communities offer a powerful model for improving knowledge-based assets and organizational competence building by fostering a social view on learning, knowledge creation (Kimble and Hildreth, 2005; Brown and Duguid, 2000; Erickson and Kellogg, 2001) and innovation (Fuller et al., 2006). The underlying assumption is that knowledge is deeply embedded in the collaborative artifacts as well as the technological practices and social context of the community which creates and manages it. In this volume, we have examined virtual communities in a variety of domains such as entertainment and games (Chen & Duh, in this volume), health and social support (Tsikankis, in this volume), eScience (Dimitrova & Koku, in this volume), tourism (Akoumianakis et al., in this volume) and learning (Wyeld & Prasolova-Førland, in this volume; Stary, in this volume).

The essence in all these virtual community cases is the variety of communicators, minimum level of interaction and a common interest that brings them together. Although there is little published work on motivations to participate, there is some evidence, also indicated by contributions in this volume, that motivation to contribute is not work driven, but arises from interest in the common themes and fulfills social, psychological, functional and hedonic needs.

These characteristics are frequently used to distinguish virtual communities from communities of practice or virtual communities of practice (Rebeiro & Kimble, in this volume). Moreover, differences are to be found in the intended scope, the social mechanisms undermining success (i.e., identity and engagement) as well as in structural and behavioral characteristics of the community members. As a result there is a growing literature addressing explicitly and distinctively the concept of a community of practice from various perspectives and settings. In the following we attempt a brief and non-exhaustive review of the basic concept and how it is both challenged and extended by recent works.

(Virtual) Communities of Practice

Community of practice (CoP) is a term typically coined with 'tightly knit' groups that have been practicing together long enough to develop into a cohesive community with relationships of mutuality and shared understandings (Brown and Duguid, 1998). Since the early 90s, when the term was introduced in the literature by the seminal works of Lave & Wegner (1991) and Brown & Druid (1991), many researchers across several disciplines have contributed to lively debates on what the term implies, how it relates to concepts such as online communities, knowledge communities, social networks, practice networks, as well as the new challenges posed for organizations and institutions. Recent works revisit the original concept based on criteria such as virtuality, organizational boundaries or innovativeness (Roberts, 2006), offering new stimulated insights and useful (re)interpretations. Today, theoretical thinking on communities of practice is advanced by researchers in the social sciences (sociology, anthropology, developmental psychology, management science, particularly knowledge management and learning), as well as by researchers in engineering disciplines such as information management science, human-computer interaction and computer-supported cooperative work. Occasionally, there are useful contributions rooted in economic geography, design sciences and the practice movement, which offer valuable insight to specific properties and characteristics of CoP.

Despite the wide appreciation of CoP and their stimulating influence on a number of scientific fields of inquiry, the usage of the term is diverse and standing to critique. As Cox (2005) states:

...sometimes the term [communities of practice] is used as a conceptual lens through which to examine the situated social construction of meaning; at other times it is used to refer to a virtual community or informal group sponsored by an organization to facilitate knowledge sharing or learning.

Furthermore, Swan et al (2002) criticize the concept of a CoP as neglecting or not appropriately addressing the management of innovation. Lindkvist (2005) also argues that CoP do not fit squarely with how temporary organizations or project organizations operate. His analysis leads to the distinction between knowledge communities – a concept inspired from the communities of practice literature – and collectivity of practice, which is conceived as knowledge collectivity. He also outlines some new options for organizational analysis made possible by recognizing these as two different and complementary notions. In a similar vein, Roberts (2006) summarizes and provides an informative review of extant critiques, limitations and new challenges posed.

Nevertheless, communities of practice remain an actively researched topic with recent contributions focusing on a variety of research lines aiming either to strengthening the available empirical base (Loyarte & Revera, in this volume) or refining and further qualifying the basic concept (Rebeiro & Kimble, in this volume) or even expanding and extending it (Kam, in this volume) to cover new ground.

SOCIAL (VIRTUAL) PRACTICES

Since social media afford rich virtual spaces, it is important to gain insight to the prevalent situated virtual practices, how they emerge, what is their nature and character and what social implications they bare. In light of this, practice-based approaches aiming to unfold what virtual community practices are, how they are enacted using the new media, how they are reproduced in community settings and how they are intertwined with knowledge are especially relevant. Once again, exploring this line of research is far from easy, as there are different connotations assigned to the term 'practice' from various scholars (e.g., Chia and Holt 2006; Giddens 1984; Jarzabkowski 2005; Lave and Wenger 1991; Orlikowski 2000) following established traditions in social sciences such as ethnomethodology, ethnography, cultural-historical psychology, organization and management science, philosophy as well as engineering disciplines such as design science.

Amin and Roberts (2008) in their recent analysis of knowing in action discuss key differences in task-based, epistemic or high creativity, professional and virtual knowing, reaching the conclusion that '*It is time that a more hetero-geneous lexicon for different types of situated practice was developed. This will help to reiterate that knowing in action always defies easy codi-fication and standardization in being a situated, embodied, practiced, experimental, and always provisional activity, but it will also allow the process of naming the many shapes and sizes of knowing in action to begin*' (p. 365). Although we share this view, for the purposes of our current analysis, we will make a reconciliation of the term 'practice' emphasizing commonalities in perspectives rather than variants.

Common Ground in Practice-Oriented Thinking

Independently of theoretical standpoint, there are some issues that seem to be common concerns for practice-oriented researchers and particularly relevant to the aims and objectives of this volume. In what follows, an attempt is made to extract the prominent commonalities found in the works of practice scholars, without claiming however, that our account is exhaustive. Our aim is to motivate our subsequent discussion which seeks to devise a reference context for framing practice.

Firstly, practice is conceived of as subsuming activities or as arrays of human activity (Barnes, 2001; Jarzabkowski 2005; Lounsbury and Crumley, 2007) which in turn have to be meaningful for the people or the practice being analyzed. An activity entails situated routine acts devoid of deeper social meaning, such as text editing, page formatting, etc., while practice, such as professional journalism or academic writing, provides order and meaning to a set of otherwise banal activities. An implication is that activities obtain their meaning from the practice in which they are subsumed. Consequently, an activity's object of reference, its symbolic manifestation and relational properties must be clearly defined and labeled so as to make sense for the practice in which these activities are embedded. Activity theorists have pursued this point further and have established useful ground on how culturally defined tools, or artifacts, mediate all human activities in a designated practice domain. The chapter by Wyeld and Prasolova-Førland (2009) in this volume provides a typical account in the context of online learning communities.

Secondly, activities embedded in or subsumed by practice are built on knowledge, skills or competences of those performing the activities or of the community in which the activities are performed. Wenger (2000) referring to communities of practice, claims that every practice in some sense is 'a form of knowledge, while knowing is participating in that practice' (p. 141). Similarly, Brown and Duguid (2001) use the notion of 'practice' to refer both 'to the way in which work is done and knowledge is created' (p. 200). In turn, knowledge may be expressed and contributed either through communication acts or by being codified into routines, procedures or patterns through which the world is made sense of.

Thirdly, any practice involves human agents and by this account, practice is an inherently social construct which is shared, negotiated and continuously refined by the engaged parties using practice-specific tools. Nevertheless, practitioners may share, obey and adhere to a designated practice without necessarily enacting it in the same manner. As a consequence practice interpretation and articulation may vary according to cultural background, folklore knowledge and experience. This implies that whereas communities of any type should be facilitated (by organizations, new media and tools), practices – and especially virtual or online practices – should be designed so as to be meaningful and appropriate to those engaging in them.

The next relevant issue, which seems to be common ground amongst practice scholars, is that the design of practices should not only be concerned with usability or performance-oriented targets such as efficiency and effectiveness. The primary challenge amounts to designing practices in such a way so as to foster community coherence. Wenger (1998, pp. 72–84) identified three dimensions of the relation by which practice is the source of coherence of a community. Mutual engagement describes how community members interact with each other in the practice. Joint enterprise embodies the shared interest of community members and the goal of the community as a whole, and symbolizes what the community is about. Shared repertoire consists of "routines, words, tools, ways of doing things, stories, gestures, symbols, genres, actions, or concepts that the community has produced or adopted in the course of its existence, and which have become part of its practice" (Wenger, 1998, pp. 83).

It is worth noticing that in none of these three dimensions is Wegner explicitly concerned with the processes, tools and artifacts facilitating the ultimate goal in each dimension. In terms of tools, Wegner's account seems to imply that social interaction tools constitute the primary means through which these goals are achieved, without however, making explicit what type of social software is considered appropriate or even whether existing tools are sufficient. Chapters in this volume take this issue further by suggesting that social interaction is intertwined and influenced

by the mechanics of the practice toolkit used. Thus, for instance the social interaction taking place in Chen's (2009) online gaming communities (see this volume) are not the same as social interaction taking place in traditional networked communication media and social software tools such as Facebook or Myspace. If this is the case, then community practice can no longer be solely framed in the social interactions between community members, but also in the mechanics (i.e., process, tool, artifacts) of the practice toolkit. Consequently, the question that stands out very promptly is *'what is the appropriate level for framing practice in community settings so as to design suitable practice toolkits?'*

(Re)framing Practice in Community Settings

To understand the problem of framing practice, we will make distinctions between creative versus technical practice and engineering versus social practice. Creative practice tends to avoid detail and value abstraction. It also tends to embrace ambiguity as enabling richness of meaning and bring into play our intuition and imagination. In terms of artifacts, creative practice tends to explore visual, spatial, textural and audio representations. A technical practice, by contrast, will try to eliminate ambiguity, seek certainty and pursue correctness, completeness and detail. To this end, it tends to use formalism, symbolic representations and logical reasoning.

Traditionally, engineering practice is framed in processes, tools and artifacts, while it is transmitted verbally using some sort of language. Its social character results not so much from the situational engagement in the practice or cultural reconstruction but from the fact that it is so well established that it is universally codified, accepted and used by many practitioners. Engineering disciplines and the natural sciences are mainly grounded upon such practices. Consequently, such practices have precise meaning which is typically decoupled from cultural interpretation and are instituted as blueprints for others to follow. In such practice domains, computer-mediation serves the purpose of easing the enactment, transmission and the reconstruction of practice, rather than changing the practice itself.

In contrast social practices are much more different as they are spontaneous, culturally interpreted, locally reconstructed and sometimes unpredictable. They are framed primarily in the interpersonal interactions between members and are transmitted both verbally and non-verbally. For instance, the 'practice of presence' entails making oneself physically available at a specific place for a specific purpose (i.e., socializing with co-present peers) and for a specific time interval. The social character of this practice results from the individual's situational engagement in the practice which entails social awareness (i.e., paying attention to what is happening, searching for people/artifacts), communicating acts such as meeting and addressing colleagues, passing on and exchanging information by expressing opinion, responding to comments), coordinative acts (i.e., knowing when and how to intervene to an event) as well as acts of civil inattention (i.e., non verbal acts which imply awareness of a social event, which for some reason is not temporarily worth of being addressed). In such cases, com-

puter-mediation is as much about reconstructing practices as it is about improvising and defining new practice elements. For instance, in online discussions or meeting there is no such thing as being physically co-located with participants. In a similar vein, there is no such a thing as civic inattention – one is made known when he/she declares his presence.

From the above, it stands to argue that new media bring about and afford new social practices which are progressively internalized by community members and become part of the community's culture. Nevertheless, it is not clear how such new social practices are designed in the first place. They could be direct online reconstructions of established non-virtual practices, or the result of demand-pull innovations driven by creative end users who can translate their creativity into novel products and services or even the derivatives of radical technical change.

The above distinctions can be summarized in Figure 3, which indicates the pathways through which novel practices may emerge as a result of research and technological development. The diagram also serves the purpose of distinguishing the variety of systems available today by taking account of the basic practice being served. Thus, in early virtual communities built around MUDs, MOOs, IRC channels and bulletin boards the

Figure 3. The practice grid and pathways of innovation

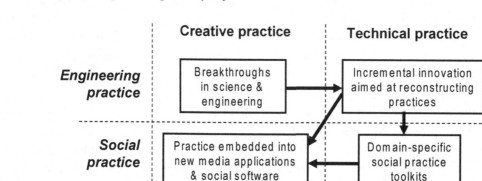

basic practice supported is that of communicating. Phrased differently communication serves as a constitutive practice of community. Systems adhering to this design objective emphasize the notion of a common virtual place resembling the meeting spaces encountered in civil society models. Moreover, the prevalent technical practices are effectively reproductions of interpersonal communication practices. Consequently, systems within this tradition are primarily incremental innovations aimed at reconstructing practice and resulting from technical advance (or breakthrough in science and engineering).

Subsequent efforts progressively shift away from the metaphor of a meeting 'place' to supporting reproductions of social networking practices with adaptations resulting from the intrinsic properties of the digital medium (see earlier discussion). These systems are transitions either along the technical practice dimension or in the diagonal dimension as indicated in Figure 3. A typical example of the former transition is mySpace which may be conceived of as the online practice of presence. Many other systems of the same tradition help people engage in a new practice of identity management by facilitating multiple online identities. As Turkle posits '... *today, people are being helped to develop ideas about identity as multiplicity by a new practice of identity as multiplicity in online life ...*' (1995, p. 260). We can therefore understand these developments as shifts towards building toolkits for engaging in the practice the community or the social network is about.

Another comment worth making regarding such turn into practice-toolkits relates to the boundary objects they support. Wenger & Snyder (2000) discuss three characteristics for objects to work as boundary bridges. First, everybody must be able to use them. This reflects the need to represent knowledge that is embedded in practice. Second, they must show real differences as well as common ground. Real differences are needed to make the object interesting; common ground is needed because otherwise the object will not be understood at all by one of the parties. Third, both groups must depend in some way on the knowledge transferred by the boundary objects so that there is the incentive for adjusting experiences and competences. In light of this, we can consider social practice toolkits as interactive software implementing and managing boundary

Figure 4. Levels for framing practice

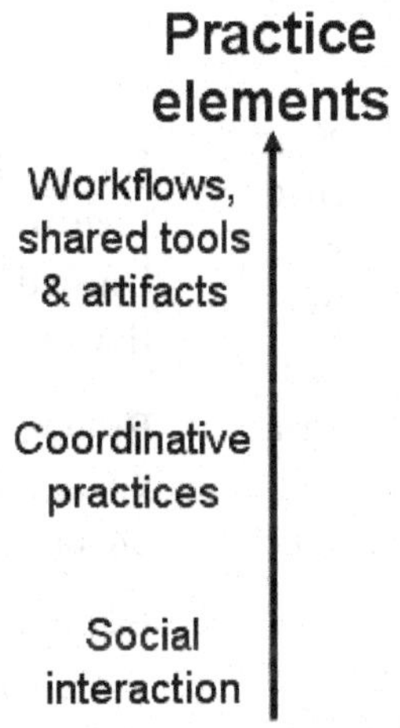

Practice elements

Workflows, shared tools & artifacts

Coordinative practices

Social interaction

objects. For instance, in popular social networking sites, identity management functions, such as building and maintaining user profiles, are seen as boundary object management tasks. It is likely that in the future social practice toolkits will increasingly need to support more complex and domain-specific boundary objects as vocabularies of a community's language. Moreover, the focus of designing such objects will progressively shift from the physical level (of interaction elements and widget-level components) to the coordinative practices supported, the underlying shared processes and workflows represented. This transition is schematically depicted in Figure 4 indicating the range and scope of practices to be designed when building practice-oriented toolkits.

SUMMARY AND CONCLUSION

In the previous sections, we have attempted to provide a tutorial account of concepts relevant to this volume, as a whole. Our intention was not to prescribe a single definition for any of the three subject matters, but to clarify their meaning and connotation as documented in the relevant literature. The reader will find further details and more elaborate accounts of these concepts in the chapters making up the four main parts of the volume. Concluding this introductory tutorial, it is worth making some important remarks which are repeatedly highlighted in many of the chapters in this volume.

Firstly, new media, communities and social practice are three concepts extensively researched and widely studied by scholars in social sciences and engineering disciplines. Our current reading of the state of practice is that whereas there is a plethora of generic social media, fostering a variety of virtual communities, these communities do not always have the appropriate tools for engaging in the practice they are about.

Secondly, there are practice domains and specific practices which cannot be effectively framed only in the social interactions between the members. In such cases, the challenge is to devise suitable boundary processes, tools and artifacts to enable sense of community and truly collaborative endeavors. Practice-oriented toolkits can provide a critical technology for addressing this challenge and establishing virtual places for engaging in the practice a community is formed to serve.

Thirdly, designing virtual places for engaging in practice entails an effort to understand and facilitate both a community's joint enterprise and the shared repertoire of resources. This makes 'one-size-fits-all' solutions inappropriate or partially useful. A more encompassing approach would be to invest on designing practice-oriented tools to foster community management (i.e., discovery, formation, maintenance and sustainability) on the grounds of value-creating participation.

REFERENCES

Akoumianakis, D., & Stephanidis, C. (2003). Multiple Metaphor|Environments: Designing for diversity. *Ergonomics*, *46*(1-3), 88-113.

Amin, A., & Roberts, J. (2008). Knowing in action: Beyond communities of practice. *Research policy*, *37*, 353–369.

Barnes, B. (2001). Practice as collective action. In T. Schatzki, K. K. Cetina, & E. Von Savigny (Eds.), *The practice turn in contemporary theory* (pp. 17-28). London: Routledge.

Brown, J. S., & Duguid, P. (1991). Organizational Learning and Communities of Practice: Toward a Unified View of Working, Learning, and Innovation. *Knowledge and Communities, 2*(1), 40-57.

Brown, J. S., & Duguid, P. (1998). Organizing knowledge. *California Management Review*, *40*, 90–111.

Brown, J. S., & Duguid, P. (2000). *The Social Life of Information*. Boston: Harvard Business School Press.

Buchel, B., & Raub, S. (2002). Building Knowledge-creating Value Networks. *European Management Journal, 20*(6), 587–596.

Chia, R., & Robin, H. (2006). Strategy as practical coping: A Heideggerian perspective. *Organization Studies, 27*, 635–655.

Cox, A. (2005). What are communities of practice? A comparative review of four seminal works. *Journal of Information Science, 31*(6), 527–540.

Denning, P., & Dunham, R. (2006). Innovation as language action. *Communications of the ACM, 49*(5), 47-52.

Donath, S. J. (2002). A Semantic Approach to Visualizing Online Conversations. *Communications of the ACM, 45*(4), 45-49.

Erickson, T., & Kellogg, W. (2001). Knowledge Communities: Online Environments for Supporting Knowledge Management and its Social Context. In M. Ackerman, P. Volkmar, and V. Wulf (Eds.), *Beyond Knowledge Management: Sharing Expertise*, (pp. 299-325), Cambridge, MA: MIT Press.

Farnham, S., et al. (2003): Personal Map: Automatically Modeling the User's Online Social Network, *Human–Computer Interaction* (INTERACT 03), (pp. 567-574), Amsterdam: IOS Press.

Fernback, J. (2007). Beyond the diluted community concept: a symbolic interactionist perspective on online social relations. *New Media & Society, 9*(1), 49–69.

Fuller, J., Bartl, M., Ernst, H., & Muhlbacher, H. (2006). Community based innovation: How to integrate members of virtual communities into new product development. *Electronic Commerce Research, 6*, 57–73.

Giddens, A. (1984). *The constitution of society, Outline of the theory of structuration*. Cambridge: Polity Press.

Giddens, A., Duneier, M., & Applebaum, R. P. (2005). *Introduction to sociology*. W.W. Norton & Company: College Books.

Gochenour, H. P. (2006). Distributed communities and nodal subjects. *New Media & Society, 8*(1), 33-51.

Jarzabkowski, P. (2005). *Strategy as practice: An activity-based approach*. London: Sage.

Kimble, C., & Hildreth P. (2005). Dualities, Distributed Communities of Practice and Knowledge Management. *Journal of Knowledge Management, 9*(4), 102-113.

Kurlander, D., Skelly, T., & Salesin, D. (1996). Comic Chat. In *Proceedings of the ACM SIGGRAPH 96*, (pp. 225-236). New York: ACM Press.

Lave, J., & Wegner, E. (1991). *Situated Learning – Legitimate peripheral participation*. Cambridge, MA: Cambridge University Press.

Lee, A., Girgensohn, A., & Zhang, J. (2004). Browsers to Support Awareness and Social Interaction. *IEEE Computer Graphics and Applications*, September/October, (pp. 66-75).

Lindkvist, L. (2005). Knowledge Communities and Knowledge Collectivities: A Typology of Knowledge Work in Groups. *Journal of Management Studies, 42*(6), 1189-1210.

Lounsbury, M., & Crumley, T. E. (2007). New Practice Creation: An Institutional Perspective on Innovation. *Organization Studies, 28*, 993-1012.

Maturana, H., & Varela, F. (1998). *The Tree of Knowledge: The Biological Roots of Human Understanding*. Boston, MA: Shambala.

Orlikowski, W. (2000). Using technology and constituting structure: A practice lens for studying technology in organizations. *Organization Science, 12*, 404–428.

Rheinfrank, J., & Evenson, S. (1996). Design Languages. In T. Winograd (Ed.), *Bringing design to software*. New York: Addison-Wesley.

Rheingold, H. (1994). *The Virtual Community: Homesteading on the Electronic Frontier*. Cambridge, MA: MIT Press.

Sack, W. (2000). Conversation Map: A Content-Based Usenet Newsgroup Browser. In *Proceedings of the 5th International Conference on Intelligent User Interfaces (IUI 2000)*, (pp. 233-240), New York: ACM Press.

Smith, A., M., & Fiore, T. A. (2001). Visualization Components for Persistent Conversations. In *Proceedings of the ACM SIGCHI Conference on Human Factors in Computing Systems* (CHI 2001), (pp. 136-143), New York: ACM Press.

Swan, J., Scarbrough, H., & Robertson, M. (2002). The construction of communities of practice in the management of innovation. *Management Learning, 33*, 476–96.

Turkle, S. (1995). *Life on the Screen: Identity in the Age of the Internet*. New York: Touchstone.

Viegas, B., F., & Donath, S., J. (1999). Chat Circles. In *Proceedings of the ACM SIGCHI Conference on Human Factors in Computing Systems* (CHI 99), (pp. 9-16), New York: ACM Press.

Willett, W., Heer, J., & Agrawala, M. (2007). Scented Widgets: Improving Navigation Cues with Embedded Visualizations. *IEEE Transactions on Visualization and Computer Graphics, 13*(6), 1129-1136.

Wellman, B., Salaff, J., Dimitrova, D., Garton, L., Gulia, M., & Haythornthwaite, C. (1996). Computer Networks as Social Networks: Collaborative Work, Telework, and Virtual Community. *Annual Review of Sociology, 22*, 213-238.

KEY TERMS

New Media: The tools and/or artifacts allowing users to engage in some sort of collaborative practice.

Social Practice: The collective wisdom (habits, rules of thumb and socially-defined modes of acting) through which a community negotiates meaning and articulates common ground.

Virtual Community: The virtual space in which a community's (social) practice is interactively manifested using computer-mediated tools and processes.

Section B
Communities of Practice

Chapter II
Conditions and Key Success Factors for the Management of Communities of Practice

Edurne Loyarte
VICOMTech Visual Communication Interaction Technologies Centre
San Sebastian, Spain

Olga Rivera
University of Deusto, San Sebastian, Spain

ABSTRACT

Communities of practice (CoPs) have been taken into account by both practitioners and academics during the last ten years. From a strategic point of view, CoPs have shown their importance for the management of organizational knowledge by offering repositories of knowledge, improved capacity of making knowledge actionable and operational (Brown & Duguid, 1998) and by facilitating maintenance, reproduction, and extension of knowledge (Brown and Durguid, 2001). CoPs are also reported to achieve value creation and competitive advantages (Davenport and Prusak, 1998), learning at work (Swan et alt., 2002) that promotes organizational competitiveness (Furlong and Johnson, 2003), innovation, even a radical type (Swan et alt., 2002), responsiveness, improved staff skills and reduced duplication (du Plessis, 2008). This impressive list of achievements is not for free; some authors have pointed out the limits of CoP's (Duguid, 2005; Roberts, 2006; Amin & Roberts, 2008) from diverse points of view, including diversity of working environments, size, spatial or relational proximity, but mainly emphasizing the specificity of CoPs as a social practice paradigm, as it was defined by Wenger (1999, 2000) credited as the "inventor" of the term "CoP" (Lave and Wenger, 1991). This chapter focuses on the consideration of CoPs as an organizational reality than can be managed (Thompson, 2005), the contradictions that the idea of managing them generates, and how these controversial points can be overcome in a sound and honest way. To do so, we review different cases of CoP's within organizations intended for the managerial team to achieve important organizational goals. Our analysis provides: (a) a reflection regarding the Key Success Factors in the process of integrating communities of practice, (b) insight to the structure of a model of cultivation, intended as a guideline for new experiences in this area, and (c) an informative account of this model's adaptation to the studied organizations.

IS THE IDEA OF MANAGING COP'S AN OXYMORON?

Communities of Practice (CoPs) are activity systems that include individuals who are united in action and in the meaning that action has for them and for the larger collective (Lave and Wenger, 1991). CoPs are not part of formal structures; they are informal entities that exist in the mind of each member. When people participate in problem-solving and share the knowledge necessary to solve problems, it is possible to speak about the generation of knowledge in CoPs (Wenger, 1998). Therefore, CoPs are groups whose members regularly engage in sharing and learning based on common interests, and can improve organizational performance (Lesser & Storck, 2001). CoPs can (and are more likely to) extend beyond the boundaries of the firm (Malone, 2002), and they are about content (about learning as a living experience of negotiating meaning) not about form. In this sense, they cannot be legislated into existence or defined by order. They can be recognized, supported, encouraged, and nurtured, but they are not reified, designable units (Lesser and Storck, 2001). All these arguments can lead managers to question if it's possible to consider CoP as a managerial initiative oriented to achieve organizational goals.

On the other hand some other authors, considering the epistemic components and theoretical background of CoP's have pointed out that CoP's may not always contribute to business settings, due to their self managed character (Kimble & Hildreth, 2004; Roberts, 2006). Others have shown that CoP's contribution to innovation is not always clear, while it only happens in some specific situations (Swan et al., 2002; Mutch, 2003), and even the negative impact that structure can exert over practice (Thompson, 2005) if the nature of the interrelations is not dressed in a sound way.

All this evidence makes the previous question even more complex: even if CoPs can be managed, it is not evident in which conditions or situation it should be the best option, or when the risks undertaken can exceed the potential gains.

In this chapter, the authors approach CoPs from a management perspective and practice. Although CoPs are organic and spontaneous, the purpose of the study is to analyse the CoPs promotion and cultivation from the organizational management point of view, therefore, as organizational management instrument. This framework can generate incoherencies between the situated and social learning theory and the consideration of a CoP's system as a management tool (CoP). For the purposes of advancing our understanding in this path, we have summarized the main contradictions between the epistemic component of CoPs (theoretical point of view) and its expected managerial use (management tool point of view) in the following questions:

- Should CoPs always be organic or could they be promoted by the organizations?
- Are CoPs designable units by the organizations?
- The cultivation of CoPs should be motivated by individuals or by organizations?
- How is it possible to achieve the sharing of knowledge? Is it necessary a tangible motivation or can it be intangible?

- Regarding knowledge management, should it be inside or outside the organizational culture?
- Should technology be a support or a purpose for the creation of CoPs?

Trying to find answers to those questions is the main purpose of this chapter that also will point out some apparent incoherence between the theory and practice related to CoPs. More specifically, key theoretical notions will be contrasted and linked to actual experiences based on a qualitative case study design, with main units of analysis being CoPs. The objective is achieved by analyzing the accomplishment of organisational results obtained in very different cases of promoted CoPs considering its epistemic components with a model based on the key dimensions created by R. McDermott (1999) and tested by the authors in previous research (Loyarte, 2006; Loyarte & Rivera, 2007). The reported research project involves analysing documented experiences of CoPs in more than 20 different kinds of organizations with a unique evaluation methodology developed for Loyarte's doctoral dissertation and inspired by the work of Mc Dermmott (McDermott, 2000). This methodology addresses the ten Critical Success Factors in building CoPs and the four challenges for building CoPs.

The chapter is structured as follows. The next section reviews the concept of CoP from a managerial point of view, which facilitates contrasting the theory of CoPs with actual experiences and clarifying what CoPs are and how they can be integrated in organizations. We then offer insights to avoiding the contradictory elements that emerge when we try to maintain the CoP's specificity as situated and social learning system, and also explore all its potential as an instrument to achieve organizational goals. Then, the next section analyzes cases of organizationally promoted CoP's, presenting the conditions of promotion and the results achieved, crossing these results with the previously identified paths. In the discussion

section we revisit our research questions providing answers based on our study and the analysis of its results. The chapter is wrapped up with conclusions and future work.

BACKGROUND

This section concentrates on reviewing, from a theoretical perspective, the concept of CoP and its organic nature. Although this review implies some important limitations of management-sponsored CoP, as the authors reveal in the first subsection, it also illuminates both the conditions for implementing CoP to achieve organizational goals and the kind of managerial intervention likely to have a positive effect.

CoP Within the Context of Social Learning Theory

The concept of Community of Practice (Lave & Wegner, 1991; Brown & Durguid, 1991; Wenger, 1998) is part of the social learning theory, which is based on the following premises:

- We are social beings – which is considered an essential aspect of learning
- Knowledge is a matter of competence in respect to certain valued practices, such as singing in tune, discovering scientific facts, fixing machines, writing poetry, being convivial, growing up, etc
- Knowing is a matter of participating in the achievement of these practices, engaging oneself actively in the world
- Meaning is what learning must ultimately produce

The main core of interest of this theory, which is based on the assumptions quoted above, rests on learning as social participation. Participation within this context does not refer to mere engagement, but rather to a process of greater reach that consists of actively participating in the practices of social communities and of building identities within them. As a result, the social learning theory developed here must integrate the necessary components in order to characterize social participation as a learning and knowing process. These components are listed below:

- **Meaning**, understood as a way of talking about our ability, both individually and collectively; of experiencing our lives and the world as something meaningful.
- **Practice**, understood as a way of talking about shared historical and social resources, frameworks, and perspectives that can sustain mutual engagement in action.
- **Community**, understood as a way of talking about social configurations in which the pursuit of enterprises is defined as valuable and participating in them is recognized as competence.
- **Identity**, understood as a way of talking about the change that learning effects on who we are and of how it creates personal histories within the context of communities.

These elements are deeply interconnected and define each other mutually, as shown in Figure 1.

CoP in Organizational Contexts

According to Davenport and Prusak (1998), communities of practice are a sign of the knowledge market. They are self-organized groups that share work practices, interests, or common objectives. They constitute a common body of experience and of joint problem solving. The community of practice is also defined by Lave and Wenger (1991) as an active system in which its participants share knowledge based on their daily tasks. They share the meaning of this knowledge in their life within the community. Therefore, it can be said that the participants of the community are united in the community's practice and in the meaning of said practice, both at the community level and at broader levels (Lave and Wenger, 1991:98).

One of the characteristics that define communities of practice is the fact that they emerge spontaneously among people who have similar interests or work activities (Lesser and Everest 2001; Lave and Wenger 1991; Wenger, 1998)[1]. Organizations are embracing various heterogeneous types of communities of practice that help

Figure 1. Inventory of social learning theory components (Adapted from Wenger, 1998)

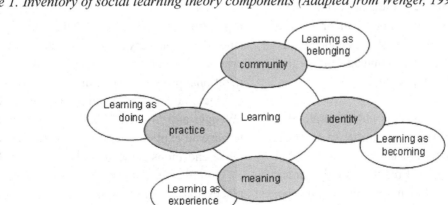

them to develop (Saint-Onge and Wallace, 2003). However, there are different kinds of groups which exhibit characteristics similar to CoPs (Thompsom, 2005; Bogenreider and Nooteboom, 2004; Lindkvist, 2005, Klein et al., 2005; Klein, 2008) and, in this sense, the term "CoP" has been recognized as somewhat problematic (Malone, 2002; Contu and Willmott, 2003; Thomson 2005; Handley, Sturdy Fincham and Clarke, 2006; Lindkvist, 2005; Roberts, 2006; Amin & Roberts, 2008). Moreover, some authors claim that in certain contexts, CoPs cannot be usefully identified (Engerstrom, 2001) or are may not be useful "per se" (Roberts, 2006).

In spite of the critiques, CoPs characteristics such as spontaneity and freedom that overcome organizational restrictions are precisely what allows authors to establish a relationship between communities of practice and the learning of knowledge flows, or even between communities of practice and innovation (Brown and Duguid, 2001; Orr, 1996)[2]. Wenger (1998) defines three important characteristics for communities of practice:

- **Mutual engagement:** Comes from the interaction of their members, since members are motivated to share their experiences as a result of said interaction
- **Negotiation of common initiatives:** This characteristic provides the community with a sense of coherence and a raison d'être
- **Shared repertoire:** Is the group of resources that members share: Stories, theories, etc. This repertoire is what shapes understandable information that is manageable for the community's components

The combination of these is what generates the theoretical value of the communities of practice to the organizational knowledge.

Since communities of practice are dynamic, interactive, and fluid, their management cannot be carried out with established control mechanisms.

In fact, Thompson (2005) demonstrated that when CoP's are heavily structured and controlled, they loose most of their potential. Instead each organization's management must understand that communities need an environment in which they can prosper, including features such as having time and resources at their disposal. The organization must promote participation, reduce barriers, give their members a voice in decision-making, and develop internal processes in order to manage the value created by communities (Wenger et al., 2002)[3].

Communities of practice contribute to promoting an environment in which knowledge can be created and shared in such a way that their members can carry out their work with the help of other people (Wagner, 2000)[4] and, even more importantly, knowledge can be used to improve efficiency, effectiveness, and innovation (Lesser and Everest, 2001:41)[5]. Brown and Duguid (1991) argue that these communities are an important space for local inventions, since they are constantly improving and adapting their behavior in order to face the formal limitations of organizations and canonical practices. Results of experiments carried out and important knowledge that organizations should bear in mind in their innovation management systems can emerge from communities of practice (Brown and Duguid, 1991).

Communities of practice are normally created in an informal manner to share experiences jointly. Contributions from members flow freely, which does not necessarily mean that this intangibility represents a failure in knowledge management, since this is the very reason why communities of practice develop creative ways of solving organizational problems, generating new business or product lines, and even managing new strategies (Wenger and Snyder, 2000). They do not tend to have an explicit mission either, but are able to make enormous achievements.

Communities of practice exist in many more places than each individual thinks. According to Wenger (1998), there are communities of practice everywhere, and every single person has undoubtedly been part of one at school, at home, when involved in a hobby, etc. Some are named and some aren't. In fact, there are many examples of communities of practice within organizations that are named differently, such as "learning communities" at Hewlett-Packard, "family groups" at Xerox Corporation, "thematic groups" at the World Bank, "peer groups" at British Petroleum, and "knowledge networks" at IBM. Regardless of their name, once they have been detected, it is obvious that all communities of practice have features in common (Gongla and Rizzuto, 2001).

Communities of practice constitute an opportunity to stimulate the process of socialization in organizations. One of the main reasons for the spontaneous action of cultivating a community of practice is the common interest of members (Orr, 1996; Wenger, 1998)[6]. In practice, it is people who build knowledge in a social manner, which helps members learn or share different points of view on technical or social problems and to exchange solutions - or even to create them (Orr, 1996[7]; Stewart, 2001[8]).

A community of practice has three important parts: An area where knowledge unfolds, the community (people), and the practice (group of ideas and points of view to be shared) (Wenger, McDermott, and Snyder, 2002). Communities of practice emerge from the moment in which people work together, and their identity is based on how their members structure and organize themselves. Through the engagement of the people belonging to the communities, these, as a group, are able to negotiate their identity and meaning within companies, and can eventually act as communication nodes in organizational learning. Communities, in turn, are the foothold for the identity of each component (Smeds and Alvesalo, 2003)). Each member develops their individual identity within the community, which contributes their personal meaning and interest in the development of their work and of the community. As a result, the negotiation of the identities of each member is an

important principle both at an individual level and at a community level (Wenger, 1998) and, therefore, learning can become a transformation of identity for each member in which the experience of learning per se is profound and difficult not to experience. As a result, the people who integrate the group find an important meaning in their work and individually (Schwen, 2003).

Within the context of communities of practice, learning is thought of as a path in which those who learn move from the group's periphery towards its core (while they contribute and learn, they become increasingly interested in the community and end up being active and important members of it), where, apart from sharing knowledge, members can also share beliefs and practices (Barab and Duffy, 2000)[9]. According to Barab and Duffy (2000), communities of practice have four characteristics:

- Shared knowledge, values, and beliefs
- Similar member histories
- Mutual interdependency
- Reproduction mechanisms

Barab (2001)[10], based on Wenger (1998), also includes the following characteristics:

- Common practices and initiatives
- Opportunities of interaction and participation
- Significant personal relationships
- Respect towards the diversity of perspectives and minority points of view

Therefore, considering the analysis carried out on the concept of the community of practice, it could be said that this concept goes beyond the organization as such, since it is based on the creation of an identity, a commitment for the group, and its members' continuous learning. This will end up creating value for the organization, which is the reason why it is so relevant to identify ways of promoting its use in firms and trying to move them to achieve organizational goals strategically defined.

Implementing and Operating CoPs

In this section authors tries to identify the factors that the theory of CoP's gives, in order to emphasize its importanceduring the process of cultivation of communities of practice, as well as the strategies that can be adopted for the integration of communities into organizations. Authors thinks that only the fundamentals provide a sound basis to do so, and that a honest use of CoPs requires coherence with its basis. Not considering the previous concepts, or using them opportunistly or only formally will lead to a failure.

Considerations for the Cultivation of Communities of Practice

The fact that communities of practice are created in a neutral manner does not mean that organizations should not influence their development (Wenger, 1998b). In fact, the existence of some communities of practice depends on the recognition that the organization awards them. A lot of communities, some more than others, require the attention of the organization for their development, even though no interference should be made in the community's management or organization per se.

Normally, the development of communities of practice depends fundamentally on internal leadership. Depending on the actual case, there are various types of leadership, such as:

- **Inspiring leadership:** Tries to lead to reflection and to gratify experts.
- **Everyday leadership:** Tries to organize the community's activities.
- **Interpersonal leadership:** Balances the community's social web.
- **Leadership based on limits:** Interrelates its own community with others.

- **Institutional leadership:** Tries to maintain uniting ties to other organizational instances, and to the hierarchy in particular.
- **Vanguard leadership:** Tries to promote original initiatives.

These types of leadership can emerge in a community either naturally or in a chosen manner, and can be concentrated in the community's main group or extended throughout the entire community. Regardless of these characteristics, however, leadership must be legitimate and intrinsic in the community. As a result, and in order to be effective, managers must work on communities of practice from the inside, rather than manipulating them from outside.

The creation of communities of practice within an organization includes the following aspects:

- **Legitimizing participation:** The introduction of the term "community of practice" into an organization's vocabulary can have a positive effect if the people who work in it are given the opportunity of commenting and sharing on how each of them contributes to the organization through participation in the communities.
- **Negotiating the strategic context:** Organizations must be capable of developing the way in which knowledge is linked to the organizational strategy and therefore help communities of practice articulate their own strategies of value for the company.
- **Becoming aware of the community's real practices:** Knowledge that is necessary for the organization is normally found within the organization itself, which is why promoting communities of practice that are able to identify and use the company's potential is an option worth pursuing.
- **Reciprocating the community's efforts (from the organization):** There are several elements within an organizational environ-

ment that have an influence on the promotion or inhibition of communities, including the interest of managers, compensation systems, work processes, corporate cultures, and organizational policies. These factors do not determine the participation of members in communities, but can make it easier or hinder it. As a result, directors should make sure that compensation systems in the company environment do not penalize work involved in developing communities.

- **Providing support:** Communities of practice are practically self-sufficient, even though they can benefit from organizational resources such as external experts, trips, facilities for meetings, and technological tools.

If there is a team of people selected for the creation of communities of practice, they would be in charge of the following tasks:

- Provide communities with advice and resources when they need them.
- Help communities adjust their agenda to the existing organizational strategies.
- Promote original initiatives in communities and community engagement.
- Make sure that the rights of each member arc upheld.
- Help communities associate with other communities.

This team could also help identify and eliminate the barriers that hinder the development of communities within a corporate structure or culture.

Summarizing, communities of practice do not require large institutional infrastructures, but their participants need time and space to collaborate. An external manager is not required, but internal leadership is. They are self-organized groups, but prosper when they learn how to adapt to the organizational environment. Therefore, the key

element is to help communities find resources and ways of communicating among themselves and with the organization, as well as to achieve a balance between communities and the organization that takes into account the fact that communities are not able to design others' learning or their own learning by themselves.

An important aspect to take into account in communities of practice is the fact that they do not exist as a formal structure, but rather inside the mind of each member - in members' relationships among themselves and with the organization per se (Liedtka, 1999). Another element to bear in mind is the fact that communities are as varied as the organizational situations behind them. As a result, people from communities of practice with different objectives and interests, as well as due to diverse situations (Wenger and Snyder, 2000).

Alignment of Interests Between the Organization & CoP Members

Communities of practice prosper when both the employees and the organization perceive benefits for each one of them. In order to achieve this, the interest of both parties must be aligned in order to generate joint value. According to a study by Van Winkelen and Ramsell (2003), the individual motivations of people who are members of communities of practice are:

- **Intellectual motivations:** Search of opportunities within the organization, exploration of various perspectives, improvement in professional position, generation of influences, comprehension, and ways of sharing diverse interests.
- **Emotional motivations:** Satisfaction of helping other people, recognition, increase in confidences, building new relationships, feeling of identification with groups.
- **Result-based motivations:** Financial recognition through improvement in performance.

Therefore, in order for the organization to get its employees to share their knowledge so that they cam improve their competitiveness and maintain existing communities, it should take the employees' interests into account[11]. The organization could then align its interests with those of people in the following manner (Lee, 2003):

- **Initial recognition:** By definition, communities of practice consist of people with similar interests, but the actual level of knowledge and experience can vary, depending on the people that form them. The organization can use a plan to effect formalized recognition by notifying members of communities of acknowledgments based on the contributions that they make to the organization. This recognition can initially consist of appreciation for people who sustain the community's base and its knowledge. If the organization abstains from this recognition, it is possible for contributors to the community's generation to end up feeling frustrated, since they could think that the work done is not useful for the community.
- **Subsequent recognitions and rewards:** Once communities have been consolidated, the organization must ensure that there are subsequent recognitions and rewards. Contributors of knowledge that is important for the community and the organization must be recognized for their contributions both within the community itself and within the organization.
- **Inclusion in action and revision plans:** Another important incentive can be acknowledgment on behalf of the organization by including the members of communities in action plans in order to have them share different points of view and knowledge, which can lead to the creation of new knowledge and its spreading, which, in turn, can lead to innovation.

- **Participation in feedback on the organization's actions:** Requesting an evaluation of the organization's actions from communities' means closing the loop that is necessary for maintaining communities in the long term by means of (necessary) recognition.

This way, both the organization and the members of communities perceive the benefits of the creation and maintenance of communities of practice, cushioning the drain of intellectual capital and creating an environment that allows people to share their knowledge in order to carry out tasks efficiently. This increase in efficiency, in turn, provides the organization with a significant advantage over other competitors.

Key Success Factors in the Cultivation of CoP

McDermott (2000) makes a valuable contribution regarding the main challenges in the cultivation and nourishing of communities of practice. He highlights 4 challenges, listed as follows:

- **The management challenge:** In order to show that communities of practice are truly important for business management, it is essential to make sure that they are formed around subjects that are important to the organization, so that the development of knowledge regarding these subjects will have an important impact on the company. If it's not the case, of course the CoP can continue existing, but will not be a priority for the organization and so, it would not receive organizational support. It is also necessary to take into account the fact that the success of a community of practice depends on the coordinator of it, as well as on its members. Therefore, and as far as the steward is concerned, it is necessary to make sure that the leader has the experience and prestige enough, as well as the social skills to motivate people and communicate with them. Regarding members, it is necessary to bear in mind that they themselves assume a commitment to participate in the community and that they must have enough time to do so. In addition, the community cannot go against the organizational culture in question, since the latter will always be stronger than the former. Because of this, it is preferable for the community to be created with a sense of respect for the organizational culture and, as a result, for it to deal with subjects that agree with the organizational values in question.

- **The community challenge:** The worst that can happen to a community is the loss of energy due to apathetic behavior on behalf of its members, leaving the coordinator with the entire responsibility for the community. This stage will always occur when it exist an organization goal but it does not match with any existing community goals. If it's not the case, it can be prevented by involving leaders from other networks, with forums that pursue the maintenance of contact among the members of the community. In fact, the members of the community's core are also its pillars; the people who contribute to the community living energetically.

- **The personal challenge:** One of the greatest values of CoP's is their space and artifacts for their members thinking and solving problems as a group. However, discussions, contributions, and sharing ideas, knowledge, and experience is not something that is revealed naturally, unless people are motivated

Figure 2. Key success factors in the cultivation of CoP (Adapted from McDermott, 1999b)

CRITICAL SUCCESS FACTORS IN BUILDING CoPs

Management Challenge

1. Focus on topics important to the business and community members.

2. Find a well-respected community member to coordinate the community.

3. Make sure people have time and encouragement to participate.

4. Build on the core values of the organization.

Community Challenge

5. Get key thought leaders involved.

6. Build personal relationships among community members.

7. Develop an active passionate core group.

8. Create forums for thinking together as well as systems for sharing information.

Technical Challenge

9. Make it easy to contribute and access the community's knowledge and practices.

Personal Challenge

10. Create real dialogue about cutting edge issues.

and engaged, and this last element is where the challenge resides.

- **The technical challenge:** Technology must be at the service of the community and strengthen its social part. It must help people to communicate and to get along with each other. Therefore, the community's technological development must be focused on people, i.e., on the social usefulness of the technology in question.

These four groups of challenges can be subdivided into ten factors that are critical for the success of communities of practice. Without them, communities are deemed to fail. These ten factors, which are grouped under the aforementioned challenges, are shown in Figure 2.

ANALYZING MANAGEMENT-PROMOTED CoP

In this section we will present an in depth analysis of the results of CoPs promoted and cultivated

from the management team of the firm. We will try to know if they have been able to overcome the possible contradictions and if they have done so accomplishing the key success factors identified above.

Case Study Methodology

According to McDermott (1999b) in his three dimensions cultivation model, and the concepts of practice and community (Wenger, 1998), the authors developed a model (see Figure 3) for the analysis of CoP's (Loyarte and Rivera 2007) that has been used for an in depth case analysis of management-promoted CoP's.

The analysis of compared experiences is based on this framework, through which the following information is analyzed in each experience:

- Company, location, year of implementation of communities of practice.
- Manner of creation of the communities of practice: Promoted or organic.

Figure 3. Analysis of the creation of CoPs within organizations (Adapted from Loyarte and Rivera, 2007)

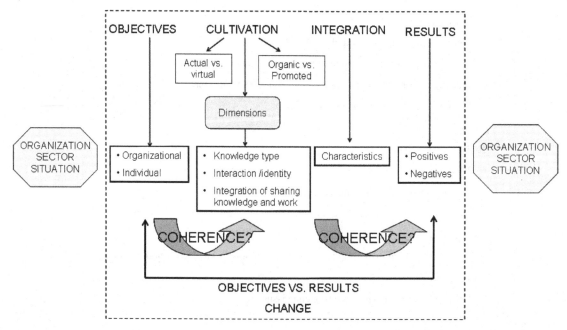

- Type of community of practice: Real or virtual.
- Primary Objective when creating the communities: Organizational, community, individual.
- Analysis of the cultivation of communities: According to McDermott (1999b), the result of experiences in organizations can be satisfactory only if the community of practice is the most suitable system to achieve the expected results. To do so, it's important to take into account the following issues:
- What is the type of knowledge that needs to be shared
- What is the type of link that unites the community's members and how strong it is
- What is the need for the new knowledge generated in the community to be transferred to the daily work of people in the organization

These questions, and their dichotomic answers, are shown in Figure 4, which constitutes the Three Dimensions Model of McDermott (2001). It is worth noticing that the closer our needs would be to the right, the CoP's will appear as being a more adequate learning and sharing system.

This model has been used to analyze the differences in the cultivation process of Communities of Practices followed by diverse organizations. The selection was made among specific published case studies that contain the required information to our research purposes.

Case Selection

Table 1 shows some of the companies that were studied, and some of their basic features, such as their respective profiles, the year of implementation of CoPs in them, and the main results derived from their experience. The authors are also integrating in this framework other documented experiences, such as (Thompson 2005) (called WorldSystem- largest global IT hardware and services organization), (Mutch 2003) (Pubs Managers), (du Plessis 2008) (SME's), (Wisker, Robinson et al. 2007) (Anglia Ruskin University), (Venters and Wood 2007) (British Council), (Sandrock and Tobin 2007) (AngloAmericanCorporation- Mining Company) and others. Therefore, the study is growing with the purpose of finding experiences of cultivation of CoPs when the organizations do not achieve their goals, as it happens in (Ferlie E 2005). It must be mentioned here that the selection of cases has not been an easy task, mainly because the authors have had to define for this

Figure 4. Three dimensions model (Adapted from McDermott, 1999b)

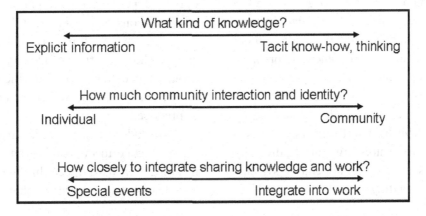

Table 1. Main features of the experiences analyzed

ORGANIZATION	SECTOR	COUNTRY	SIZE	CASE PUBLISHED BY
IBM Global Services	Telecomunication	USA	big	Gongla, P. & Rizutto. C. R. (2001)
World Bank	Bank	USA	big	
Andersen Consulting Education	Consultancy	USA	big	Graham, W. & Osgood, D. (1998)
Cap Gemini Ernest & Young	Consultancy	France	big	American productivity and quality center (2000)
DaimlerChrysler	Automotion	Germany	big	American productivity and quality center (2000)
Ford Motor Company	Automotion	USA	big	American productivity and quality center (2000)
Schumberger	Technological Services	USA	big	American productivity and quality center (2000)
Xerox Corporation	Technology and Services	USA	big	American productivity and quality center (2000)
Watson Wyatt	International consultancy	England	big	Hildreth, P. & Kimble, C. (2000)
International company	Distributor/Commercial company	England	small	Hildreth, P. & Kimble, C. (2000)
Defence Department	Civil Sevice	USA	big	Defense Department of USA (2004)
Medico	Bioscience	UK	big	Swan, Scarbrough, & Robertson (2002)
University of Indiana	Education	USA	big	Liedtka, J. (1999)
Open source software	open source software	All over the world	big	Mas, J. (2005)
Basque Company	Automotion	Basque Country	small	Calzada, I. (2004)

purpose which are the conditions that distinguish a CoP from just a group or a network. This is not an issue of being purists, but in order to advance in any field – and this one is no exception – concepts should be used with rigor. There is a certain respect that must be afforded to the term "community of practice," and the fact is that not every group is one, as some other authors have indicated (Roberts 2006)[12] (Lindkvist 2005)[13] and more recently (Amin and Roberts 2008)[14].

The three dimensions model established by McDermott (1999b) helps us to understand the diversity of CoP's that can emerge, and the diversity of mechanisms, artifacts and operating systems they can use, depending on the knowledge objec-tives they pursue and the contextual variables in which they operate. However, McDermott's model also gives the possibility of getting conscious that cultivating communities can be a failure option, depending on the chosen combination of dimensions. For instance, if the group shares explicit knowledge through e-mails and sporadi-cally without any type of identity regarding the group, it is better to consider the promotion of an informal network, rather than a community of practice.

To include an experience in our study of CoP's we have gone to the origins, and analyzed the meaning of each word according to Wenger (1998), establishing that the critical characteristics in a community are those that make it possible for the group to be called a community of practice in a strict manner. This entails the following:

- **Community:** Refers to members with a group identity that share experiences. Therefore, groups in which the motivation and identity of each member is exclusively individual and no common experiences are shared would be excluded.
- **Practice:** Is the uniting subject within the group. A subject that excites members so much that it leads them to share their experiences, problems, findings, etc. with the rest of their colleagues and to listen to, help, or discuss the experiences of other members. Therefore, the need for the transfer of experiences and of explicit and tacit knowledge can be perceived in this case. Tacit knowledge can be made explicit due to which not all communities oriented to share documents or reports (explicit knowledge) are excluded, as long as this functioning can be understood working under the terms of experience mentioned in this section. Perceiving the exchange of explicit knowledge in a community is easy, but perceiving the fact that tacit knowledge is being shared is not as easy, since this requires experiencing an encounter with the members of the community or examining the results at the level of knowledge of involved members (if it is perceived that they know more things with time).

Regarding the necessary dimensions, the dimension of group identity takes precedence, since it is the dimension that can guarantee the community's long-term continuity the most. If individual identity prevails, there are more risks of members abandoning the group, since any change or movement within the group can affect said people. However, with a group objective and identity, members will work jointly and for the group, which allows the community to follow its course.

The dimensions that are sufficient, however, in our work, have been established by the analysis of the objectives set by community cultivators. For example, it has been sufficient for being part of our sample of cases if the knowledge that is shared is directly related and linked to the work of the communities' members, even if only explicit knowledge is shared. In other contexts, the interaction of knowledge with work does not have to occur in a direct manner.

RESULTS AND DISCUSSION

The relevant features that can affect the configuration of communities of practice have been identified in each one of the cases studied and also the results obtained have been stated. This analysis is summarized in Table 2. It is now useful to discuss these results in relation to the questions formulated in the introductory section of this chapter and to each potential contradiction related to management-promoted CoP's.

The Creation of Communities: Organic or Promoted?

According to the background theory of communities of practice one of the requirements for these groups to be named as such is the fact that they must be born spontaneously or organically. Our research, however, shows that it's possible to promote the appearance of these groups to achieve organizational goals. In some of the cases studied, the way of promotion is an organizational culture in which staff is informed of the existence of this type of groups in order to encourage them to form communities within the organization (The World Bank, IBM); in others, CoP are born organically and the organization supports the initiative (Andersen Consulting Education); in others, CoP are implemented as a research project

Table 2. Comparative study of Communities of Practice

ORGANIZATION	CULTIVATION		DESIGN		KNOWLEDGE		INTERACTION & IDENTITY		KNOWLEDGE INTERACTION		OBJECTIVES	WERE THE OBJECTIVES ACHIEVED?
	PROM	ORG.	VIRT.	REAL	EXP.	TÁC.	INDIV.	COMUN.	EVENTS	WORK		
IBM Global Services		X		X	X	X	X	X		X	IBM's main objective when supporting CoPs is to relate knowledge management with the organizational strategy, where they create a value system in which people improve the organization by sharing knowledge.	YES
World Bank	X		X		X	X	X		X	X	The main objective is the effectiveness: access to information and knowledge (explicit and tacit) had to be easy and available when needed.	YES
Andersen Consulting Education		X		X	X		X			X	The main objective of the Programme is that CoPs are created in an organical ways since nobody better than themselves know which of the skills they need they develop.	YES
Cap Gemini Ernest & Young	X			X	X			X		X	The main objective is to increase its profit and effectiveness by increaseing individual and organizational competencies	YES
DaimlerChrysler	X	X		X		X	X			X	The company begins to establish knowledge management and CoPs in order to get people's tacit knowledge, since most of the staff are nearing their retiration.	YES
Ford Motor Company	X			X	X	X		X		X	The organization visualized a strategy to achieve low cost and value added worldwide excellence in the product. It was also visualized the strategy that would confer power to employees so that their colleagues would share their knowledge and it would be spread all over the organization.	YES
Schumberger		X		X		X	X			X	The organization is intensive in knowledge and this contributes a competitive advantage of the same through a better customer service. This is the key point that drives the company to emphasize the long-term importance of knowledge management and CoPs.	YES
Xerox Corporation		X		X		X		X		X	Knowledge is part of VICOMTech's strategy aand CoPs are created for the achievement of product innovation and the creation of practicals that improve the company's results. CoPs accelerate organizational learning and create competitive advantages.	YES
Watson Wyatt	X		X			X		X		X	International business organizations are undergoing staff loss and they face the challenge of managing their business internationally spread.	YES
International company	X		X		X	X		X		X	The main objective is to evaluate if the CoPs are valid for knowledge-sharing in spread environments (geographically separated) and allow its members to meet.	YES
Defence Department	X		X			X	X	X		X	To achive corporate knowledge remains within the organization even though experts retire, keeping basic organization compentences.	YES
Medico	X			X	X	X		X		X	The main objective is to evaluate if the CoPs are valid for radical innovation	NO
University of Indiana	X		X		X	X	X	X		X	The main objective of this investigation (creation of a virtual CoP) is the creation of a means of discussion for daily educational practices and the creation of an advanced community that allows the professional development of its members.	YES
Open source software		X	X			X		X		X	The main objective is the development of open source software	YES
Basque Company	X			X		X		X		X	Redesign of the organization with a big reaction capacity because of the unstable market conditions. People must be able to manage one own's knowledge in order to answer flexibly and soon.	NO

or as a pilot project in order to assess staff reaction (Indiana University); and in others, such as Cap Gemini Ernst & Young, CoP are created and their staff is forced to become a part of them. In this last case, both the spontaneity of creation of communities and the voluntary participation of their members comes into question, which may justify why they should probably be referred to by another name. However, the implementation of these community forms has been a success for the company, since it has achieved the objectives originally set. So is it really indispensable for the creation of communities to be spontaneous and led by members?

It is also true that any change today (especially in small and medium-sized enterprises) towards knowledge management or towards the creation of value-based on individual competencies entails important organization restructuring (as can be seen in the case of the Basque Country automotive company). Communities of practice can facilitate these goals as they are based on the transfer of knowledge in order to create value. So, even if CoPs are promoted, it's important to consider that achieving success requires respecting the identity basis, generating the truth between members and considering also the individual goals. This is in line with what Thompson (2005), based on a single case study, identified as the distinction between a Seeding and a Controlling Structure. In the case in which communities are formed due to an organizational initiative and attendance is mandatory, it would most likely evolve to some other knowledge mechanism, possibly more focused to transferring explicit knowledge, which can be interesting in order to save costs, mostly at the beginning, but does not yield the results that a community sharing tacit knowledge yields.

Can Communities of Practice be Structurally Designed?

Following along the lines of the previous argumentation, there is another controversy that is important to clarify. According to CoP's theoretical background, communities of practice are not units that can be designed – in this context design is understood as a systematic, planned, and reflexive colonization of time and space in the service of a task, while it may not only include the production of artifacts, but also the design of social processes such as organizations or education. Authors reiterate in any discussion on the design of learning—which cannot be designed because it belongs to the environment of experience and practice—that communities of practice have already existed for a long time and are not a new fashion in design or a type of pedagogical organization or device to be implemented. Communities are about content, about learning as a live experience of negotiating meaning, not about forms. Therefore, they can be recognized, encouraged, supported, and nourished, but not designed. Learning cannot be designed either, it can only be facilitated or thwarted.

The important and critical fact for our management-based perspective is that infrastructures, systems, resources, and connections can be chosen and reinforced in order to nourish communities of practice. As a matter of fact, the reflection on which type of community could be interesting at an organizational level through the dimensions studied in this research encourages organizations to create communities of practice, but not to design them. However, it is possible for an organization to understand the type of communication needed at an organizational level, the type of community that can make an impression on potential members, and the type of knowledge that must be shared in everyday work. With this information, the organization in question should have the ability to develop communities.

In short, the process of developing communities of practice is closer to agriculture (cultivation) than to architecture (design). Nevertheless, based on the experiences analyzed previously, it would seem that the role of organizations is to be sensitive to the importance of the communities of practice, thus identifying existing ones, extracting results from previous experience and fostering new ones, as needed. However, as mentioned earlier, the cornerstone of communities is people and their willingness to share knowledge. Therefore, the real organizational challenge is to strengthen, develop, cultivate, and support these organic groups and try to translate their energy and results to an organizational level. Moreover, although their creation and maintenance must be monitored, it must also be clear that the objective should not to design, implement, and analyze results, but rather to build on a day-to-day basis, even if it seems otherwise.

Interest in the Creation of Communities of Practice: Individual or Organizational?

Following our answers to the previous questions, another difference in how communities are created is where the idea originates from. According to theory, it could be said that communities are an individual (or group) initiative, but organizational initiatives were also documented in the experiences studied in our case analysis.

The initiative of implementing knowledge management programs can be at an organizational level and it may include the implementation of communities of practice (U.S. Department of Defense, for instance). If the initiative is taken at an individual level, at least there will be an important motivation at the beginning, even if members do not manage to sustain the community due to lack of organizational support (Andersen Consulting Education).

There are also companies that compensate participation in communities in order to motivate their staff (DaimlerChrysler). In this case, individual motivation could depend on the recognition and not on the interest in the practice or in the members of the community and, as a result, it may disappear when the recognition ceases to satisfy the compensation objectives of the staff. Furthermore,

it is possible that competition between personnel is being encouraged by detecting who contributes the most to the community, etc. This does not mean that members' motivation will assure by itself more sustainable CoP's just because the interest is in the practice or in the members, al least, emphasizing organizational purposes and goals. There could be members who leave the community, or the practice and customs could change along time, thus influencing the members as well. The fact of having an organizational support could help to overcome these necessaries and frequent changes in corporate evolution. Also, if a firm tries to achieve a broad scope of staff committed with the project, it should be considered that each individual shall be taken into account. The point is that it is not the same for motivations to be financial or to be intangible, and that there will be people who will not work without being compensated and others who will.

In our research, the experiences studied are coherent with McDermott's (2000) earlier analysis and conclusions. The long-term operation of a community requires an important commitment from the leader but it would never exist without the commitment from its members, since their contributions sustain the community. This commitment of each member to the community is part of the Community challenge, but our research also suggest that it should be useful to integrate as a community challenge getting the organization support to the CoP so that their members can obtain the resources (flexibility, financing, and infrastructure) necessary to continue its activities.

We don't under valuate the importance of community identity and trust that are also important and relevant issues related to this challenge. If members do not feel that they are part of the group and do not trust other members, it will be difficult for them to contribute to the transfer of knowledge.

We have also proved that the content and even process of knowledge sharing are very different if it's motivated by group reasons (Schlumberger) or by individual reasons (DaimlerChrysler), When motivations are exclusively individual, the participation in the community can be limited to what the community contributes to the member considered attending their own criteria; in the other case the motivation of each member will be aligned with the community, which will provide the group and the person with more integrity.

Is it Necessary a Tangible Motivation for Individuals or is the Most Powerful Motivation Intangible?

Nobody would deny the contribution of value that people achieve when they share their knowledge – which occurs when they are motivated and engaged-. However, the following questions arise: Why does a person share their knowledge? What leads them to do that? What motivations could they have to do so?

According to Davenport and Prusak (1998), there is a market of knowledge on which knowledge can be bought and sold. It doesn't have to be through financial transactions, since it is possible to give knowledge without receiving any compensation for it, but there must be some other motivation, such as trust between the giver and the receiver of knowledge, the practice of the community or interests, the engagement and group identity of people, etc.

Based on this idea, one of the premises for communities at the World Bank was that trust had to be built through group participation and that mutual recognition among professionals who valued contributions made in communities had to exist. This fact results in people feeling valuable, and encourages them to keep participating and sharing what they know. There was a similar environment at Andersen Consulting Education, where professionals perceived an important advantage in the transfer of knowledge.

Other cases showed that a lack of motivation can constitute a barrier in the implementation of communities, i.e. Medico or even the Basque Country automotive company, where the fear of losing a position of power (on behalf of certain people) in relation to others constituted an organizational problem to overcome in the implementation of communities. At Medico, this subject was considerably more prominent, since urologists did not want to participate in the implementation of new communities of practice when they saw their status, and their resulting organizational power in relation to other doctors, endangered.

Therefore, the individual challenge can be difficult to overcome if the organizational hierarchy in question is altered, since those who are bound to lose power or status will be reluctant to participate in the change. It is also important to consider what the motivations that could move people to share what they know are, and the leader of the community should be a key element in detecting said interests.

The most relevant contribution along these lines is the experiences resulting from communities of practice without organizational limits. These communities show not only that people share their knowledge for reasons that have nothing to do with financial ones, but also that intangible motivations are a key element for a community to work and work well. Regarding the 10 KSFs contributed by McDermott (2000), and explained earlier, it is worth mentioning that all of them are pretty much necessary for communities of practice to be successful and viable in the long run. Depending on the organization and environment in question, some KSFs will be fulfilled more than others, but our experience reveals that what companies' value in the success of the implementation of communities is always constituted by some of the KSFs established by McDermott (2000).

Knowledge Management: Within or Outside the Organizational Culture?

Within the organizational challenge, McDermott (2000) suggests focusing on knowledge due to its importance for both the organization and for people, but also suggests not imposing knowledge management within an organizational culture. In several of the analyzed experiences, companies developed a program of knowledge management including the implementation of communities in it. Other companies, on the other hand, decided to implement communities directly, without any previous knowledge management program. Neither one of the two systems can be considered wrong attending the results analyzed and their performance. Anyway, authors consider hat the process of cultivating CoPs is much easier to implement in communities that include a key practice for the company and therefore entail knowledge management implicitly, than trying to make people understand what knowledge management is without first implementing something tangible. The latter option makes people feel lost and start questioning what knowledge really is and if it can really be managed. As a result, it is easier for staff to perceive the benefits of knowledge transfer by experiencing it through a community, for instance, than by listening to the importance of knowledge management within the organization in informative sessions.

Should Technology be a Support or a Purpose for the Creation of CoPs?

In the cases studied in this research, some communities are completely dependent upon technology, either due to them being virtual communities or due to their reliance on an important technological platform (Indiana University, US Department of Defense, Watson Wyatt). In all cases, their creators felt that a key element in the development of platforms was for technology never to take precedence, but rather to be a support tool

that also guaranteed the community members' participation rather than their rejection due to the lack of technical knowledge or to the use of user-unfriendly technologies.

This is consistent with McDermott (2000), who states that technology must be at the service of the community, strengthening its social element. It is obvious that the important element in communities is people, not technology, and that if they do not perceive ease of using the technical support, and ability for building confidence and trust in an intuitive way (as Soto and alt, 2007 pointed out) they will reject it instead of using it, which can even lead to the community's existence being thrown into doubt.

In the experiences analyzed by this study, the design and creation of technological platforms implied the investment of many resources, including financial, technology expert personnel as well personnel in charge of promoting communities, while it built upon earlier analysis as to whether or not potential members would be willing to use the technology that was going to be developed in order to enable participation in the community. As a result, technological support can either be a facilitator or a terrible enemy, depending on how it is introduced into communities, which is why spending time on its design is well worth it. We also think that the recent work of Amin and Roberts (2008) can help managers to understand when the use of a technical support is more appropriate for the expected "knowing in action" objectives.

FUTURE WORK

Our research shows fairly the strengths of the CoP for achieving organizational goals, and also the real possibility of managing their process of creation and development, but also emphasizes the importance of people and their motivation in making CoP work. We have shown some potential signs of agreement between the management-promoted perspective and the emergent approach, and also some interesting reinforcement links between them. But also we are conscious that this approach can motivate some important contradictions, such as imposing formal structures upon existing CoPs, or treating as CoP structures which are not. This is why, in order to advance a future research on the topic of management-promoted CoP we would suggest a more detailed analysis of the specific dimensions of the cultivation process undertaken and comparisons with the dimensions followed by organic ones to assess differences in the development process and goal achievement.

It would also be extremely interesting to sum up the opinions of entrepreneurs regarding their vision on the strengths and weaknesses of the process of cultivating CoP in organizations and also the experience of community members receiving organizational support so as to compare the perceived pros and cons. Likewise, it would be a good idea to evaluate which is the present general situation in the industry regarding the existence of CoP in organizations, and the way they have been originated and developed.

Finally, the study of the alignment between individual and community interests is also an important issue, not only for our research focus, but also for CoP area in general. In fact, analyzing open-source software communities it is possible to note that they are effective communities, very often more effective than communities cultivated within organizations. This example can thus be extended to organizations themselves, in which it is obvious that it would be necessary to understand what CoP already exists and which kind of interest and goals are they serving.

CONCLUSION

Contributions

The main contribution of our study is demonstrating that CoP's can be promoted and led by man-

agement teams to achieve organizational goals, and this will not be an obstacle for their right development if they are honest with the means used for that purpose. To be honest means accept the four elements that constitute a CoP and working to develop them and not weaken them.

As we have seen, some of the measures that can weaken the development of the community, can have accelerate its emergence, so it's important to be conscious of the evolutionary process that the CoP will continue in case of success.

This study offers interesting insights for the implementation of communities of practice understood as a tool for knowledge management and for improving competitiveness in organizations.

The reflection made on the challenges of the creation of communities of practice clarifies possible uncertainties or incoherencies that could appear after reading the theory on these communities, as well as their applicability on a practical level. It also analyzes the various documented real experiences, which can contribute to better understand concepts such as design, cultivation of communities, promotion of communities, organic communities, etc.

Limitations of the Study

The most important limitation of this investigation projects are the following:

- All the cases of CoP studied are established within organizations, except for the free-software community experience. The important knowledge connection with clients, procurers, public bodies, universities and other actors of the innovation system and the role that CoP's can play on it, has been out of question.

- Most of the experiences were successful, no failure. This is the reason why these experiences allow the detection of Success Key Factors. Nevertheless, failure could occur during CoPs' cultivation process, even if the

Success Key Factors shown in this analysis were taken into account. Should there have been further failure cases, there could have been more details for those cases where CoPs are a valid knowledge management tool in companies.

- The sample is constituted by experiences documented and published by other authors, which of course prevent authors from having access to the information and knowledge needed to go deeper in their analysis. Authors hope that the variables analyzed could be considered for other researchers in future case studies to develop a more consistent research avenue.

General Interest

This chapter has been written having in mind a broad public, ranging from academics and researchers (MSc and PhD students) to professionals in industry, interested in the Knowledge Management field and the Communities of Practice from a pragmatic point of view, oriented to identify practices that had shown increased performance.

Authors have prioritized a managerial point of view, looking at case studies, and emphasizing results over firms in a challenging environment, considering its contribution on some key subjects such as innovation, knowledge management, learning, technology, and motivational approach, that are studied from this additional point of view.

Authors expect that academics and researchers will find the chapter useful in incorporating the Management approach to their advanced postgraduate and PhD materials on communities of practices. Industry professionals would obtain useful insight for re-considering management strategies, personnel relationship management and learning organizations.

REFERENCES

American productivity and quality center (2000). *Building and sustaining communities of practice*. Final Report. APQC, USA.

Amin, A., & Roberts, J. (2008). Knowing in action: Beyond communities of practice. *Research Policy, 37*(2), 353-369.

Barab, S. A., Mackinster, J. G., & Scheckler, R. (2003). Designing system dualities: Characterizing a Web-supported professional development community. *Information Society, 19*(3), 237-257.

Brown, J. S., & Durguid, P. (1991). Organizational Learning and communities of practice: Toward a unified view of working, learning and innovation. *Management Science*.

Brown, J. S., & Gray, E. S. (1995, November). The people are the company. *Fast Company Magazine*.

Calzada, I. (2004). Una forma organizativa para intervenir en las organizaciones: comunidad de prácticas (CoP). *MIK, S. Coop.*

Davenport, T. H., & Prusak, L. (1998). *Working knowledge: How organizations manage what they know*. Boston: Harvard Business School Press.

Defense Department of USA (2004). Information technology (IT) community of practice. *Defense & AT-L, 33*(5), 79-80.

du Plessis, M. (2008). The strategic drivers and objectives of communities of practice as vehicles for knowledge management in small and medium enterprises. *International Journal of Information Management, 28*(1), 61-67.

Engestrom, Y. (2001). Expansive learning at work: Toward an activity theory reconceptualization. *Journal od Eduaction and Work, 14*, 133-156.

Ferlie, E. F. L., Wood, M., & Hawkins, C. (2005). The nonspread of innovations: The mediating role of professionals. *Academy of Management Journal 48*(1), 117-134.

Finchman, R., & Clark, T. (2006). Within and beyond communities of practice: Making sense of learning through participation, identity and practice. *Journal of Management Studies, 43*(3), 641-53.

Gongla, P., & Rizutto, C. R. (2001). Evolving communities of practice: IBM Global Services experience. *IBM Systems Journal, 40*(4), 842-853.

Graham, W., & Osgood, D. (1998). A real-life community of practice. *Training & Development, 52*(5), 34-38.

Handley, K., Sturdy, A., Fincham, R., & Clark, T. (2006). Within and beyond communities of practice: making sense of learning through participation, identity and practice. *Journal of Management Studies, 43*(3), 641-53.

Hildreth, P., & Kimble, C. (2000). Communities of practice in the international distributed environment. *Journal of Knowledge Management, 4*(1), 27-38.

Iverson, J. O. (2003). *Knowing volunteers through communities of practice*. Arizona State University. Arizona, USA.

Kakadadse, N. K., Kakadadse, A., & Kouzmin, A. (2003). Reviewing the knowledge management literature: Towards a taxonomy. *Journal of Knowledge Management, 7*(4), 75-91.

Klein, J. H., Connell, N., & Meyer, E. (2005). Knowledge characteristics of communities of practice. *Knowledge Management Research and Practice, 3*, 106-114.

Klein, J. H. (2008). Some directions for research in Knowledge Sharing. *Knowledge Management Research and Practice, 6*, 41-46.

Lave, J., & Wenger, E. (1991). *Situated learning: Legitimate peripheral participation*. New York: Cambridge University Press.

Lee, J. (2003). Building successful communities of practice: CoPs are networks of activities. *Information Outlook.*

Lesser, E., & Everest, K. (2001). Using communities of practice to manage intellectual capital. *Ivey Business Journal, 65*(4), 37-42.

Liedtka, J. (1999). Linking competitive advantage with communities of practice. *Journal of Management Inquiry, 8*(1), 5-17.

Lindkvist, L. (2005). Knowledge communities and knowledge collectivities: A typology of knowledge work in groups. *Journal of Management Review, 42*(6), 1189-1210.

Loyarte, E., & Rivera, O. (2007). Communities of practice: A model for their cultivation. *Journal: Journal of Knowledge Management, 113*, 67-77.

Malone, D. (2002). Knowledge management: A model for organizational learning. *International Journal of Accounting Information Systems, 3*(2), 111-124.

Mas, J. (2005). *Software libre: técnicamente viable, económicamente sostenible y socialmente justo*. Zero Factory, S.L. Barcelona.

McDermott, R. (2000). Critical success factors in building communities of practice. *Knowledge Management Review, 3*(2), 5.

McDermott, R. (1999). Learning across teams: How to build communities of practice in team organizations. *Knowledge Management Review, 2*(2), 32.

McDermott, R. (1999b). Nurturing three dimensional communities of practice: How to get the most out of human networks. *Knowledge Management Review, 2*(5), 26.

Mutch, A. (2003). Communities of practice and habitus: A critique. *Organization Studies, 24*(3), 383-401.

Roberts, J. (2006). Limits of communities of practice. *Journal of Management Studies, 43*(3), 623-639.

Saint-Onge, H., & Wallace, D. (2003). *Leveraging communities of practice for strategic advance.* Butterworth & Heinemann, USA.

Sandrock, J., & Tobin, P. (2007). *Critical success factors for communities of practice in a global mining company.* Nr Reading, Academic Conferences Ltd.

Schewen, T. M. & Hara, N. (2003). Community of practice: A metaphor for online design? *Information Society, 19*(3), 257-271.

Smeds, R., & Alvesalo, J. (2003). Global business process development in a virtual community of practice. *Production Planning & Control, 14*(4), 361-372.

Soto, J. P., Vizcaino, A., Portillo-Rodriguez, J., & Piattini, M. (2007). Applying trust, reputation and intuition aspects to support virtual communities of practice. In *Knowledge-Based Intelligent Information and Engineering Systems*: Kes 2007 - Wirn 2007, Pt Ii, Proceedings, (pp. 353-360).

Swan, J. A., Scarbrough, H., & Robertson, M. (2002). The construction of communities of practice in the management of innovation. *Management Learning, 33*(4), 477-497.

Thompson, M. (2005). Structural and epistemic parameters in communities of practices. *Organizational Science, 16*(2), 151-164.

Urquhart, C., Yeoman, A., & Sharp, S. (2002). *NeLH communities of practice evaluation report.* University of Wales Aberystwyth, England.

Van Zolinger, S. L., Sreumer, J. N., & Stooker, M. (2001). Problems in knowledge management: A case study of a knowledge-intensive company.

International Journal of Training & Development, 5(3), 168-185.

Venters, W., & Wood, B. (2007). Degenerative structures that inhibit the emergence of communities of practice: A case study of knowledge management in the British Council. *Information Systems Journal, 17*(4), 349-368.

Wenger, E., McDermott, R., & Snyder, W. M. (2002). *Cultivating communities of practice.* Boston: Harvard Business School.

Wenger, E., & Snyder, W. M. (2000). Communities of practice: The organizational frontier. *Harvard Business Review, 78*(1), 139-146.

Wenger, E. (1998). *Communities of practice: Learning, meaning and identity.* Boston: Cambridge University Press.

Wenger, E. (1998b). Communities of practice: Learning as a social system. *Systems Thinker.*

Wisker, G., Robinson, G., et al. (2007). Postgraduate research success: Communities of practice involving cohorts, guardian supervisors and online communities. *Innovations in Education and Teaching International, 44*, 301-320.

KEY TERMS

Case Studies: A detailed intensive study of a unit, such as a corporation or a corporate division that stresses factors contributing to its success or failure.

Communities of Practice: An active system in which its participants share knowledge based on their daily tasks. They share the meaning of this knowledge in their life within the community. The participants of the community are united in the community's practice and in the meaning of said practice, both at the community level and at broader levels (Wenger, 1998).

Cultivation Model: A model of evaluation for communities of practice in the process of cultivation that makes it possible to estimate the probabilities of success for the proposal of creating communities at a specific moment and under a specific situation is included. The cultivation and integration of communities is a continuous process, due to which its evaluation must be performed periodically.

Knowledge Management: Managing the corporation's knowledge through a systematically and organizationally specified process for acquiring, organizing, sustaining, applying, sharing and renewing both the tacit and explicit knowledge of employees to enhance organizational performance and create value (Davenport, 1998).

ENDNOTES

[1]   Lesser and Everest 2001, quoted by Swan, Scarbrough, and Robertson, 2002.

[2]   Brown and Duguid, 2001; Orr, 1996, quoted by Swan, Scarbrough, and Robertson, 2002.

[3]   Wenger et al., 2002, quoted by Iverson and McPhee, 2002.

[4]   Wagner, 2000 quoted by Kakadadse, Kakadadse, and Kouzmin, 2003.

[5]   Lesser and Everest 2001:41, quoted by Swan, Scarbrough, and Robertson, 2002.

[6]   Orr, 1996, quoted by van Zolingen, Streumer, and M. Stooker, 2001.

[7]   Orr, 1996, quoted by van Zolingen, Streumer, and Stooker, 2001.

[8]   Stewart, 2001, quoted by Urquhart, Yerman, and Sharp, 2002.

[9]   Barab and Duffy, 2000, quoted by Barab; MaKinster and Scheckler, 2003.

[10] Barab, 2001, quoted by Barab; MaKinster and Scheckler, 2003.

[11] Heald, 2004.

[12] Roberts identifies also collectivities and constellations of practice

[13] This author differentiate collectivity-of-practice from Community of practice

[14] Those authors identified different varieties of knowing in action. The paper notes the differences - in organisation, spatial dynamics, innovation outcomes, and knowledge processes - between four modes: craft or task-based knowing; epistemic or high creativity knowing; professional knowing; and virtual knowing.

Chapter III
The Search for 'Hidden' Virtual Communities of Practice:
Some Preliminary Premises

Richard Ribeiro
University of York, UK

Chris Kimble
Euromed Marseille École de Management, France

ABSTRACT

This chapter examines the possibility of discovering a "hidden" (potential) Community of Practice (CoP) inside electronic networks, and then using this knowledge to nurture it into a fully functioning Virtual Community of Practice (VCoP). Starting from the standpoint of the need to manage knowledge and create innovation, the chapter discusses several issues related to this subject. It begins by examining Nonaka's SECI model and his notion of Knowledge Transfer; the authors follow this by an investigation of the links between Communities of Practice (CoPs) and Knowledge Management; the chapter concludes by examining the relation between Nonaka's Communities of Interaction and CoPs. Having established this the authors start their examination of the characteristics of "hidden" Communities of Practice. Following on from the previous discussion, they look at what is meant by "hidden" CoPs and what their value might be. They also look at the distinction between Distributed CoPs (DCoPs) and Virtual CoPs (VCoPs) and the issues raised when moving from 'hidden' CoPs to fully functioning VCoPs. The chapter concludes with some preliminary findings from a semi-structured interview conducted in the Higher Education Academy Psychology Network (UK). These findings are contrasted against the theory and some further proposals are made.

Jackson Grayson, chairman of the American Productivity & Quality Center, tells a story about a big-company CEO who, in a moment of contemplation, revealed a deep desire: "I wish we knew what we know," the CEO said. That wish is shared today by managers at dozens of large, decentralized companies. They fear the knowledge in their organizations is going to waste simply because hardly anyone knows it exists.'
Information Week, 20 October 1997

INTRODUCTION

It is important for institutions and companies to manage the knowledge they have. This knowledge represents not only the main asset an institution or company has, but it also can represent the future and survival in the time to come. As result, the majority of large companies include knowledge in their list of assets. This is not a new issue. For instance, Boersma and Stegwee have discussed this before (1996), but in our time that is more important than ever.

One tool that can help to reach this objective is represented by the social communities that reside within such organisations. These communities can create specialized knowledge that is vital for the 'host' institution. A special case of social communities, Communities of Practice (CoPs) (Brown & Duguid, 1991; Lave & Wenger, 1991; Wenger, 1998; Wenger et al., 2002) have been object of constant studies and analyses for several years. This interest can be explained by the fact that many see Communities of Practice as a powerful instrument for the management of knowledge and as source of innovation.

However, it is also necessary to take into account the advances in technology and communication present in today's world. The improvement in performance and the reduction in prices of personal computers, together with the spread of access to Internet in 1990s, resulted in an improvement in Computer-Mediated Communication (CMC). That enhancement has changed the nature of enterprises and institutions. As result, a new framework emerged, allowing social communities to grow and flourish across geographical boundaries – so-called virtual communities. With the creation of virtual communities came the possibility of easier 'transfer' of knowledge between people in different locations, even at an international level (Hiltz & Turoff, 1993; Sproull & Kiesler, 1992).

It is therefore important to examine the possibility of helping the growth of these communities, as this could open new possibilities for the management of the knowledge, which in turn could influence the success of an enterprise. For example, companies and institutions could create an environment suitable for innovation through the facilitation of contact between geographically separated groups with shared interests, thus, allowing the nurturing of Communities of Practice that could be of use to that organisation. These communities might be the 'seed' of an innovation that could lead to the development of new technologies, which in turn might lead to improvements in the company and institution or to the creation of new products and services. Similarly, research institutions might wish to discover potential groups and/or areas of collaboration and research as sometimes innovations are held back by a lack of communication or awareness, since the existence of similar groups inside the institution is unknown. The first step in this direction would be to discover the existence of 'hidden' communities that could, in time, represent the starting point of a fully functioning Community of Practice (CoP).

To accomplish this, it is necessary to analyse several related issues. First, we must be certain that 'hidden' communities can be located. Second, as we are considering distributed communities, we must also be sure that, what are often loosely termed Virtual Communities of Practice (VCoPs), can actually be considered to be CoPs. Finally, if the two previous conditions are met, we need to know if these 'hidden' communities can be developed to a level of fully functioning CoP. This chapter will discusses each of these steps and conclude with a small-scale study where the first premises under this approach are drawn.

CoPs, Knowledge Management and Knowledge Transfer

Before we discuss the subject of hidden CoPs in distributed networks, we will first discuss the reasons why those communities are important for organisations. In this section will consider the relationships between Knowledge Management (KM), Nonaka's work on Knowledge Transfer and Wenger's work on Communities of Practice. We will then use this as the background for a discussion on hidden CoPs and the roles they might play in an organisation.

Background

The traditional point to begin this discussion is the distinction between *tacit* and *explicit* knowledge. Currently, companies around the world are spending substantial effort and resources to manage their available (tacit and explicit) knowledge. *Explicit knowledge* refers to the knowledge that can be made available through a media (writing, audio, video, etc.) and it can be relatively easy to acquire, save and retrieve. That is the more commonly known type of knowledge. *Tacit knowledge*, on the other hand, refers to the knowledge that even if one wished to pass to another person, it would be very difficult to accomplish.

This distinction and its related issues have been the subject of several papers (Gourlay, 2002, 2003, 2004, 2006; Jorna, 1998; Nonaka, 1991, 1994; Nonaka & Takeuchi, 1995). For example, Gourlay (2002, 2004) points out that different authors disagree about the nature of tacit knowledge (e.g. does it exists only in individuals, in groups or in both?). Similar arguments exist concerning the

possibility of tacit knowledge being made explicit (Gourlay, 2002, 2003, 2006).

Notwithstanding the finer distinctions between tacit and explicit knowledge, much of the attention in this area has focussed on the need to exchange and reuse knowledge, so-called *knowledge transfer*. It is possible to find numerous models in publications dedicated to knowledge transfer. We will concentrate on the best known of these: Nonaka's *SECI model* (Nonaka, 1991, 1994; Nonaka & Takeuchi, 1995; Nonaka *et al.*, 1996).

This model has been widely discussed and has been viewed as the mainstay of Knowledge Management for many years. However, it is not without its detractors: Gourlay, for example, states that the model is not supported by empirical evidence, and that some of its phases are not coherent (Gourlay, 2003). Similarly, Jorna argues that the model lacks any background in learning theories, omits important philosophers, and does not have a methodology (Jorna, 1998). Others argue that the model needs to consider additional aspects related to the complex environment which is a workplace, for example taking in account the nature of tasks it performs (Becerra-Fernandez & Sabherwal, 2001).

However, for the purpose of this chapter, the SECI model offers a simple and straightforward model to discuss knowledge transfer. It is also particularly appropriate for this chapter as Nonaka also outlines the concept of *Communities of Interaction* and later links this notion of *Communities of Interaction* to that of *Communities of Practice*.

The SECI Model

Nonaka first presented the SECI model (*Figure 1*) in 1991 (Nonaka). The model first appeared in the early 1990s as a tool to explain Nonaka's ideas of how western companies could achieve the same levels of success as Japanese ones. In that period, Japanese companies were leading the global market; one of the reasons (according to

Figure 1. The SECI model [based on (Nonaka, 1994), (Nonaka et al., 1996) & (Nonaka & Takeuchi, 1995)]

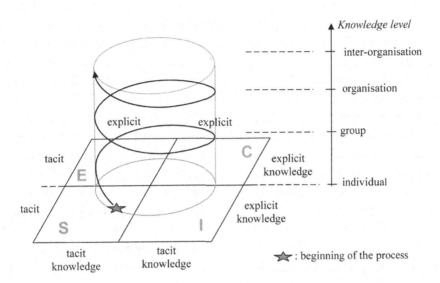

Nonaka) was the method the companies used to create and share knowledge.

The SECI model is based in the concept of apprenticeship. It explains how the tacit knowledge of an expert can be transferred to an apprentice through a process in four phases. Each phase represents a unique type of movement between tacit and explicit knowledge. Nonaka called the phases *modes of Knowledge Conversion* and the model, the *Spiral of Knowledge* (Nonaka, 1994) or *Knowledge Spiral* (Nonaka et al., 1996).

The four phases are:

- **(S)ocialisation.** Where the apprentice acquires the necessary skills (tacit knowledge) working with the expert(s). In this phase is said that the transfer occurs between tacit knowledge and tacit knowledge.

- **(E)xternalisation.** Where the person (former apprentice), after acquired the tacit knowledge, transfer it to a media or pass it on. In this phase is said that the transfer occurs between tacit knowledge and explicit knowledge.

- **(C)ombination.** Where the knowledge (now explicit) is combined with existing explicit knowledge. In this phase is said that the transfer occurs between explicit knowledge and explicit knowledge.

- **(I)nternalisation.** Where the knowledge after the previous interactions evolves to a richer and expanded tacit knowledge. In this phase is said that the transfer occurs between explicit knowledge and tacit knowledge.

The Spiral of Knowledge

Nonaka argues that knowledge transfer happens at several different levels within an enterprise. Looking at the *Figure 1* is possible also to see that the process moves upward in spiral. Nonaka called this *the Spiral of Knowledge* (Nonaka, 1991) or *Knowledge Spiral* (Nonaka et al., 1996).

The four processes are repeated in different levels. First, it occurs as described above at the individual level, moving to a group level, after the individual had shared the new ideas/concepts with a team or group. Later these ideas are divulged inside the company/institution, moving the knowledge to an organisational level. Finally, the knowledge might be divulged between organisations in different places, reaching the inter-organisational level.

Knowledge Transfer in a Distributed Environment

In 1994, Nonaka published a new study explaining in more details the SECI model (Nonaka, 1994). This time he related the model with the concepts of Organisational Knowledge Creation. That publication expanded several concepts of his first work. This time all the phases had a wider dimension, taking in consideration the interactivity of teams and groups within companies. That work helps us to situate better the SECI model in distributed environments; as here the possibility of non-collocated communities is explicitly discussed.

Later on Nonaka began to perceive the impact of Information Technology (IT) would have in future years to the concept of knowledge transfer, thus in 1995 he published another work discussing this issue (Nonaka & Takeuchi, 1995). In that work, he started considering the use of networks in the process of knowledge transfer. The authors discussed the impact of CMC in the process of creating new knowledge and consequently in the SECI model.

Further analysis came with another paper, published in 1996 (Nonaka et al.). This short paper gave, though, only a summary of the main aspects of the impact of IT in general and networks in particular to the SECI model and to the knowledge transfer, discussed in the previous work.

Seeing the progression of those publications, one can perceive clearly the evolution that the SECI model underwent. If in beginning the distributed scenario was subtly considered in the spiral of knowledge, after few years the expansion of CMC gave to Nonaka the certainty that electronic networks needed to be considered during the analysis of knowledge transfer in organisations.

Finally, in 1994, Nonaka defined an important concept in his work: *Communities of Interaction*. Although without outlining them precisely, he explained how important their existence is to accomplish successfully the knowledge transfer (Nonaka, 1994). What he did, however, was to trace a relation between *Communities of Interaction* and *Communities of Practice* (Nonaka, 1994) via the work of Brown and Duguid (1991). However, before explaining his arguments, it is necessary to review the concept of *Communities of Practice (CoPs)*.

Communities of Practice (CoPs)

While Nonaka's model presents an intuitively attractive model of knowledge transfer, many argue that it is flawed. Although the term knowledge transfer is widely used in knowledge management, one can argue that what happens is *learning*, as knowledge is not a object that can be simply passed on to another person. It is at this point that the notion Communities of Practice come into play (Kimble & Hildreth, 2002).

The idea of Communities of Practice was first introduced by Etienne Wenger and Jean Lave in 1991 when they published the book *Situated Learning: Legitimate Peripheral Participation* (Lave & Wenger, 1991). The book introduced the idea that learning is an informal social process, rather than a planned and individual one. In this model, the learning happens mainly through the social contact. The figure of apprentice moves from a situation of learning in peripheral position to full participation. The learning comes as consequence of social interaction and observation. The authors used a set of specific communities as case studies. Those communities were formed by persons that shared a common practical work (thus, sharing practices). The idea revealed a new realm in learning: social learning (constructivism) was used, in contrast to the behaviourism, in vogue during that period.

That first publication attracted considerable interest in different areas. It became clear that CoPs required a more detailed analysis. Consequently, several authors released publications discussing the subject (e.g. Brown & Duguid, 1991). Wenger then released an additional publication regarding CoPs, where he conducted a detailed analysis of them (Wenger, 1998). In 2002, as consequence of the increase interest in the topic, Wenger et al. released a third book, having a more practical and direct approach for CoPs (Wenger et al., 2002).

The Key Concepts of Communities of Practice

Since their first appearance in 1991, the concepts related to CoPs have changed. Kimble and Cox have analysed this issue in (Kimble, 2006) and (Cox, 2005) respectively. Cox summarised some of those concepts and their changes over time with a table (Cox, 2005). However, despite these alterations the main concepts remained practically the same. These concepts derive from the definition of CoPs:

Communities of Practice are groups of people who share a concern, a set of problems, or a passion about a topic, and who deepen their knowledge and expertise in this area by interacting on an ongoing basis. (Wenger et al., 2002)

This definition outlines the main characteristics that will be present in any CoP: the *domain*, the *community* and the *practice*. Wenger provides several slightly different definitions for these terms (Wenger, 1998, 2006; Wenger et al., 2002), but here they are taken to be:

- **Domain:** Responsible for creating a sense of common identity among the members. The shared domain produces a sensation of responsibility and participation in the community. It defines what the community is and is what attracts newcomers and allows them to identify themselves with it. It motivates participation, learning and gives meaning for member's actions.
- **Community:** Responsible for interaction and learning among the members. The community creates a strong social bond between its participants. It motivates the improvement of the shared knowledge through joint activities and discussions, creating mutual respect and trust.
- **Practice:** Represents the shared knowledge of the community. It is compounded by ideas, language, tools, frameworks and all tacit and explicit aspects of the knowledge that the community has.

The definition stands within a model with three principal dimensions of a community of Practice: *mutual engagement, joint enterprise*, and a *shared repertoire* of experiences (Wenger, 1998). The idea is based in the assumption that, as social beings, we always engage in enterprises with persons that share a passion, mutually learning and creating, as consequence, a common knowledge.

The Notion of Dualities in Communities of Practice

Wenger also saw a Community of Practice in terms of the interplay of four fundamental dualities or tensions that exist within them: *participation-*

reification, designed-emergent, identification-negotiability and *local-global*. Wenger views a duality as:

... a single conceptual unit that is formed by two inseparable and mutually constitutive elements whose inherent tensions and complementarity give the concept richness and dynamism (Wenger, 1998)

Although he describes four dualities, the participation-reification duality has been the focus of particular interest. According to Wenger, our experiences of meaning and our understanding of the world are formed primarily through two processes: participation and reification. Participation is how we learn through interaction with others, while reification is how we give our learning an independent existence.

In participation we recognise ourselves in each other, in reification we project ourselves onto the world (Wenger, 1998).

Both participation and reification are necessary for learning to take place. For Wenger participation represents:

... the social experience of living in the world in terms of membership in social communities and active involvement in social enterprises. [Participation] can involve all kinds of relations, conflictual as well as harmonious, intimate as well as political, competitive as well as cooperative. (Wenger, 1998)

BRINGING KNOWLEDGE MANAGEMENT, COMMUNITIES OF INTERACTION AND COMMUNITIES OF PRACTICE TOGETHER

It is this concept of the *participation-reification* duality that finally links the notion of Knowledge

Transfer in Knowledge Management to Learning in CoPs. While taking the risk of oversimplifying a more complex concept, it is possible to make a relation between the *duality of participation/reification*, of Wenger (1998) and *tacit/explicit knowledge* by Nonaka. Wenger uses the concept of *reification*

... very generally to refer to the process of giving form to our experience by producing objects that congeal this experience into 'thingness' (Wenger, 1998).

Reification is significant in that it is an attempt to encapsulate some of the meanings generated by the community: "... a certain understanding is given form" (Wenger, 1998). However, as Wenger also notes:

Reification as a constituent of meaning is always incomplete, ongoing, potentially enriching, and potentially misleading. (Wenger, 1998)

This link is explored in greater detail elsewhere by Kimble and Hildreth (2002, 2005). Similarly, in the beginning of this section, it was affirmed that Nonaka made use of an interesting concept in 1994: Communities of Interaction. It was also said that he traced a relation between Communities of Interaction and Communities of Practice. He did that through an analysis of Brown and Duguid (1991) work; he stated:

Although ideas are formed in the minds of individuals, interaction between individuals typically plays a critical role in developing these ideas. That is to say, "communities of interaction" contribute to the amplification and development of new knowledge. While these communities might span departmental or indeed organizational boundaries, the point to note is that they define a further dimension to organizational knowledge creation, which is associated with the extent of social interaction between individuals that share and develop knowledge. (Nonaka, 1994)

The significance of links between individuals that span boundaries, both within and outside the organization, has been highlighted by Brown and Duguid's (1991) revealing insight into the operation of "evolving communities of practice". These communities reflect the way in which people actually work as opposed to the formal job descriptions or task-related procedures that are specified by the organization. (...) The exchange and development of information within these evolving communities facilitate knowledge creation by linking the routine dimensions of day-to-day work to active learning and innovation. (Nonaka, 1994)

By contrast with conceptions of groups as bounded entities within an organization, evolving communities of practice are 'more fluid and interpenetrative than bounded, often crossing the restrictive boundaries of the organization to incorporate people from outside' (Brown and Duguid 1991, p. 49). Moreover, these communities can provide important contributions to visions for future development. Thus these communities represent a key dimension to socialization and its input to the overall knowledge creation process.(Nonaka, 1994)

Seeing together the three arguments, one can notice the similarity between *Communities of Interaction* and *Communities of Practice*. As Communities of Interaction amplify and develop new knowledge through social interaction, spanning boundaries, the same happens with Communities of Practice.

'HIDDEN' CoPs

Having established the link between CoPs and knowledge Management, and having established that Knowledge Management is of commercial

importance in today's world, we will now proceed to look at the topic of 'hidden' CoPs, and why these should be seen as an important contribution to the health of organisations. The search for 'hidden' CoPs raises some singular questions. For a start, the state of being 'hidden' is largely understudied in Communities of Practice. In addition, the search can have ethical implications, and finally, if a hidden CoP is to be found, this itself can raise a different set of issues.

What are 'Hidden' CoPs and Why Are They Important?

The type of Communities of Practice that is the focus for this chapter are not easy to find: they are communities that are in their early stages. Their members may not see themselves as 'members of a CoP' and the 'host' organisation may not be aware of the existence of it. To the company, and possibly even to the members, the community is 'hidden' from view.

The Concept of 'Hidden'

It is not our intention to look for illegal or illicit communities: the term 'hidden' is used here in a restricted sense to mean something potential, to-be-discovered, nascent, unseen, veiled, etc. It is perhaps easier to explain our concept of a 'hidden' CoP through an example.

Lundkvist (2004) provides an example of such community. He discusses a case study involving Cisco Systems and a group of users of the company's products. The study showed how Cisco Systems were able to use the knowledge generated by the experience of a group of well-informed users, even though the group itself was not part of Cisco and did not form with the intention of helping them.

Cisco Systems operates in networking market and is one the biggest companies supplying such equipment in the world. With the growth of Internet after 1990s, Cisco became one of the leaders of the sector. That expansion in business created new challenges for the company. They needed to expand support for customers and at the same time, reduce the administrative load caused by that expansion. Their solution was the automation of support, customer self-service and customer-to-customer support. Although this allowed the company to improve their existent equipment, it was at the cost of the loss of the feedback generated by the company's users.

In order to regain this lost feedback, the company wanted to gain access to the conversations the users had about their products, without crossing the limit of privacy. They needed to keep the interest of the users focused in a public and open channel of communication. Their salvation came in the shape of a group of technicians working in Swedish Universities.

This community of users had a strong interest in sharing their knowledge, but did not view themselves as a 'networking CoP' and even less a 'Cisco Systems CoP'. This was clearly stated:

One participant was very explicit about the problem: if social networks were identified and made known, corporate managers, by nature, would try to formalise and control them, a fact that would make everyday work harder. Consequently, the issue of CoPs was considered a highly delicate matter, one requiring a new managerial understanding. (Lundkvist, 2004)

The Value of 'Hidden' CoPs

'Hidden' communities can be everywhere. They can be inter or intra organisational communities and, as Lundkvist illustrates, in organisations, they can represent an invaluable force. They can be the seed of change or innovation that an organisation is looking for. They can aggregate members with different experiences, but with a shared passion, and these two factors can be nurtured more easily in a CoP than in a formal team.

Such communities can generate new ideas and services, as yet undreamt of by the company. They can become a group that can generate new ideas for improvements in existing sectors or departments. They can even evolve to spin-off companies, which in turn generate new products or services. Within educational institutions, as Universities or Colleges, they can lead to the creation of new areas for researches or courses. Such groups generally have the groundbreaking information that organisations sometimes miss. Moreover, because frequently they are disperse, that knowledge almost never produces results.

The principal issue with this type of community is that 'hidden communities' are very difficult to detect, even by their potential members. That is explained by the fact that being 'hidden' means that potential members are unaware of the existence of such communities. As it is, the community will be 'hidden' forever, or until a random situation happens to change that.

Another issue is that 'hidden' CoPs tend to be small when within organisations, so without the proper help or incentive they risk disappearance.

The Characteristics of 'Hidden' CoPs

'Hidden' groups can be people that work in the same company, but in different sectors. They even can be employees located in different cities or countries. Their principal characteristic is a shared passion for something common to all. Sometimes they know each other, and sometimes they know only very few of them. Sometimes they know that they share common interests and sometimes not.

The reasons a CoP is 'hidden' can be related to several specific situations, such as the political scenario inside the organisation, lack of awareness of others with similar concerns, or even conflict of interests between the community and the organisation. The literature lacks studies in this area. Even when referred to under a different term (e.g., potential), the literature about 'hidden' CoPs is scarce.

Wenger et al. discusses some aspects of them in (Wenger et al., 2002), when talking about the stages of the development of a CoP. They use the term *loose network* to express that type of community. The authors explain that they consider the beginning of the development of a Community of Practice through the existence of an *extant social network* (Wenger et al., 2002).

Another publication that examines the case of potential CoPs is (Cappe, 2008). She studies the cases of latent Communities of Practice in organisations, although here also the definition of a potential CoP is similar to that of Wenger et al (2002).

However, there are examples in the literature of the opposite situation: the 'disappearance' of CoPs (Patricia Gongla & Rizzuto, 2004). Using experiences with CoPs in IBM Global Services, the authors discuss the reasons and characteristics of Communities of Practice that 'disappear' from the organisational scene. They list the main paths followed by communities when disappearing, the reasons why the CoPs vanish and the steps required for avoiding or reducing that. The authors divided the disappearance cases in four patterns: *Drift into non-existence, Redefine themselves, Merge into other communities* and *Become organizational units* (Patricia Gongla & Rizzuto, 2004). They also discussed the reasons why the communities disappear: *Organizational change, knowledge domain change* and *community leadership change*.

Some Issues in the Study of 'Hidden' CoPs

When considering the possibility of discovering 'hidden' CoPs some novel issues are raised. There is always a risk that the community wants to be 'hidden' (as discussed before). For instance, it can be the case where a group of members

wishes to start a new company that can rival the host organisation. Another possibility is that the potential community do not want to be controlled by the organization, as discussed by Lundkvist in (2004). Nevertheless, it is important to highlight that sometimes the 'hidden' community do wishes to be revealed. It can be the case that the members only did not have the opportunity yet to develop further. It is this type of community that is the focus of our work.

Regarding the problems that can appear after finding the communities, Gongla and Rizutto (2004) give a good insight about some issues on this matter. Understanding why some communities disappear can prevent revealing ones that do not want to be exposed. It also gives awareness of the risks involved in disclosing them. Clearly, there is an ethical dimension that must be considered when searching for 'hidden' CoPs. It is possible to discover, for instance, communities that the host organisation can see as harmful. Another aspect is the use of technologies that cross the limit of personal privacy. The researcher needs to make careful choices on this part. It is important to consider that Communities of Practice are driven by passion, and any threat to its freedom can compromise this motivation.

CoPs and Virtual CoPs

As our goal is to work with virtual communities of Practice, we must clarify precisely what we mean by this term.

Distributed Communities of Practice (DCoPs) and Virtual Communities of Practice (VCoPs)

The term 'Distributed Communities of Practice (DCoPs)' can often be found in articles related to Communities of Practice and Internet. However, its exact meaning is not always clear. The term *distributed* refers to something divided or spread. Additionally, when used together with the term *community*, the word *distributed* has a geographical meaning. In that case, such community is not concentrated in a unique place, but rather is divided in one or more locations. Therefore, a good definition of DCoP could be:

Distributed Community of Practice (DCoP) is a CoP spread over a place, or without a precise delimitation of its space.

Similarly, it is easy to find publications with the term *Virtual Community (VC)*. It seems that Rheingold (1993) was the first to use it, but after that, it is possible to find many further definitions of this term, for example, by Roberts (1998) and Igbaria (1999). In Computer Science the term evolved from the idea of something that simulates the real equivalent (e.g. *virtual memory*), to the idea of something that is real, but only exist by means of computers and networks (e.g. *virtual world*). It can be seen that some elements are common to all definitions of Virtual Community. A general definition of *Virtual Community* based in the same common aspects might be:

Virtual Community (VC) is the type of social community that uses Computer-Mediated Communication (CMC) to maintain contact with its participants.

In the same way, with the expansion of *Computer-Mediated Communication (CMC)* and the Internet, the concept of *Distributed Communities of Practice (DCoPs)* had been reshaped to a point where it became almost natural to associate *Distributed* with *Virtual*. This can be seen in great part of the publications related to CoPs at the end of 1990s and beginning of 2000s. It is now commonplace to find references only to *Virtual Communities of Practice (VCoP)*; therefore, one definition that suits this approach can be:

Virtual Community of Practice (VCoP) is a non-collocated Community of Practice that uses

Computer-Mediated Communication (CMC) to maintain contact with its participants.

It is important to highlight that our use of the term *Computer-Mediated Communication (CMC)* is more adequate to our modern world. We include on this term all type of communication and interaction that occurs by mean of computers. That can include since the more typical use of internal networks, commonly found in organisations, until the Internet, where on this case it is possible to encompass the use of email, WWW, FTP or similar services.

Fully Functioning VCoPs

As indicated earlier, the main objective of this work is to look for ways to identify and nurture 'Hidden' Virtual Communities of Practice existing in electronic networks, in other words, to help them develop into potential *fully functioning Virtual Communities of Practice*. It is necessary, then, to clarify what is meant by this.

The term *fully functioning VCoP* is understood to refer to communities that attend all (but are not restricted to) the following components at the same time:

- **It is a Social Community.** This means that the community should be represented by a group of persons that participate in the same community and have active involvement in social enterprises. Participation in this sense is both personal and social, involves personal and shared feelings and is reciprocal. In addition, the members can recognize each other as belonging to the same group (Based on Wenger, 1998).
- **It is a Community of Practice (CoP).** This means that the community should follow the definition of Community of Practice stated previously. Moreover, this definition implies the existence of all the set of concepts defined in (Wenger, 1998).

- **It is a Distributed Community of Practice (DCoP).** This means that the community should follow the definition of Distributed Community of Practice stated before. The concept of *spread* can be understood as short as a few meters, or as far as thousands of kilometres.
- **It is a Virtual Community (VC).** This means that the community should follow the definition of Virtual Community stated above.

As consequence of the characteristics listed above, the community will be a (social) Community of Practice that is distributed, and communicates via CMC. It is essential to notice, however that the concept of fully functioning Virtual Community of Practice as described above corresponds to an ideal situation that can be reachable or not. Consequently, this chapter accepts variations on these definitions, as long as the core ideas are still valid.

Is it Possible to Change a 'Hidden' CoP into a Fully Functioning VCoP?

In addition to the issues listed above, new considerations should be taken in account when discussing how to change a 'hidden' CoP into a fully functioning one. Further development of a 'hidden' CoP is dependent on the 'discovery' of such communities.

First, it is crucial to determine the community's desires or intentions to 'evolve' and become a fully fledge community. Wenger always highlighted passion as the driving force that keeps the community together and strong (Wenger, 1998; Wenger et al., 2002). A real CoP cannot be created by force or by any artificial means. What is possible however, is to help the development of a CoP, as Wenger detailed in (Wenger et al., 2002). Although his advices in that publication is mainly related to collocated CoPs, the same can be applied to VCoPs.

Another step would be to establish the forms to be used in order to help the 'hidden' CoP to flourish. This step is very dependent on the community, as only through an analysis on a case-to-case basis is possible to determine the best plan of action to reach that goal. It is likely that some procedures could be used in some parts of the study (e.g., the initial interviews with the potential members), but the best method(s) will only be decided after a full analysis of the community's situation. Cappe (2008) and Wenger et al. (Wenger et al., 2002) offer some advices on this topic.

Yet another step is to determine for how long an intervention is necessary to keep the VCoP active. This is very much related to the specification of what it is expected to achieve with the community. As a product of human interaction, the communities usually do not follow strict rules or schedules, thus it is important to determine the limit of interference in the CoP that can be tolerated, under risk of undermining the community's self-interest.

Referring to our definition of a fully functioning VCoP, some aspects are not difficult to find or implement. In some cases, no intervention is necessary. Examples of that are the items 'Social Community' and 'Community of Practice (CoP)'. Although these two items are complex *per se*, they can be found with no much difficulty in a potential community that accepts to become a fully developed community of practice, or in a one that already has started establishing the connections to become a real CoP. The other two items are related mainly to the configuration and to the use of CMC in the contact among members.

Maybe the most difficult part in the process of changing a potential community is to sustain the existence of such new CoP. Wenger considers CoPs as having a lifecycle. In his work of 2002 he shows a graph with 'born', 'life' and 'death' of a CoP (Wenger et al., 2002). However, others think that CoP can have a different approach. Gongla and Rizzuto, for instance, proposed a different model to explain the existence of a CoP. They discuss an *evolution model* that '(...) *describes instead how communities transform themselves, becoming more capable at each stage, while at the same time maintaining a distinct, coherent identity throughout*' (P. Gongla & Rizzuto, 2001). That model sees CoP in a different way where it can grow and disappear in any phase of the model, becoming more mature with every step of its evolution.

SEARCHING FOR 'HIDDEN' VCOPS: A PRELIMINARY STUDY

The search for 'hidden' VCoPs will require knowledge on different aspects of the subject. Firstly, it is necessary to identify methods that can be used to recognize CoPs. Secondly, these methods need to be tested under a distributed (and possibly virtual) scenario. Finally, all the previous experience needs to be put together in such way that allows searching for 'hidden' VCoPs. Evidently, several subdivisions on these processes will be necessary, as the research advances.

As the first step in this direction, a small-scale study was set up. Its objective was to validate the parameters used to identify existent CoPs. The study has been implemented utilising the idea of reification as used in the concept of *participation-reification* duality (Wenger, 1998) where certain aspects of a CoP's activity are reified by its members as part of their participation in the CoP.

The Venue

The study was carried out in the *Higher Education Academy Psychology Network, UK*. The institution is one of 24 discipline-based centres within the Higher Education Academy in UK. The Psychology Network supports the teaching and learning of psychology across the UK. A core team, based at the University of York, works with staff, departments, professional bodies and overseas organisations to develop supportive networks and to improve the learning experience of psychology students in Higher Education.

The work environment is an open-plan area where all the employees have quick and easy access to each other. All the communication is made through face-to-face conversation or email. They can exchange electronic files via an Intranet and a file server. Regular meetings keep the group updated with objectives and future plans.

The Study

The approach to the research was broadly that of Action Research (Dick, 2003), consisting of two alternating cycles of purposeful action and critical reflection. The first component emphasizes on participation that builds shared understanding and shared commitment. Whereas the second one drives a better understanding of the wider process, allowing possible adaptation in future cycles (Dick, 2003). As the research is in its early stages, a first study has been drawn to confirm a method to detect the existence of Communities of Practice.

Wenger (1998) created a list of indicators that a CoP had been formed, which was used in this work as the basis for identifying the presence of a CoP; the list included:

1. Sustained mutual relationships – harmonious or conflictual
2. Shared ways of engaging in doing things together
3. The rapid flow of information and propagation of innovation
4. Absence of introductory preambles, as if conversations and interactions were merely the continuation of an ongoing process
5. Very quick setup of a problem to be discussed
6. Substantial overlap in participants' descriptions of who belongs

7. Knowing what others know, what they can do, and how they can contribute to an enterprise
8. Mutually defining identities
9. The ability to assess the appropriateness of actions and products
10. Specific tools, representations, and other artefacts
11. Local lore, shared stories, inside jokes, knowing laughter
12. Jargon and shortcuts to communication as well as the ease of producing new ones
13. Certain styles recognized as displaying membership
14. A shared discourse reflecting a certain perspective on the world

One of the authors (Richard Ribeiro) is an employee in the Psychology Network, which allowed us to gain an 'insider' understanding of the community. The research took a broadly qualitative approach using Wenger's list and semi-structured interviews as primary mechanisms to examine the subjective experience of participation in a VCoP. Each of the members participated in a semi-structured interview of approximately 30 minutes, which identified general information about the person and the role, and where 11 of 14 items where checked. Items 6, 8 and 14 had been excluded from the interview, as they were not applicable to the chosen environment. These exclusions should not affect the overall quality of the research outcomes as the list is not rigid, and different items are used to verify the same characteristic. The interview was applied to the other staff in the Psychology Network (7 people) and the results are briefly discussed below.

The Results

Most of the results described in this section come from the combination of the analysis of the answers and the inner understanding of the community. If any point of a topic was not completely confirmed or understood, it was scheduled for a later stage in the research. Even though the process of collecting data is still ongoing, it can be seen that the current results confirm the existence of a CoP in the work environment. The results show that the employee's behaviour is consistent with the majority of the indicators that show the existence of a CoP.

It can be seen that the group has a strong sense of identity and meaning. They share the view of the organisation's objective, and of the role of each one in the final goal of the organisation. Maybe one aspect that influenced this result is the community's size (only 8 persons, including the researcher) and the fact that they work in an open-plan space. However, the change in the workspace only happened two years ago; before that, the employees worked in separated rooms with an average of two persons per room. They work together and even with the fact that some of them work part time, it can be seen that this does not affect their relationships or their sense of community. In addition, although having different roles, the employees have a set of common activities and a shared way of operating.

Information is propagated rapidly within the community, maybe as consequence of the fact that they work in an open-plan space. However, this indicator can be confirmed by the fact that the use of communications by email is as frequent as the communication face-to-face. Innovation is another aspect that is rapidly spread. Again, maybe this can be explained by the same reasons as the previous item. Another fact that might explain this characteristic is the noticeable existence of a common concern to propagate any innovation that can help the community.

In general, conversations and interactions reflect the ongoing working process that the community has. Frequently, only small introductions or preambles are required. One factor that helps to explain this is the existence of weekly meetings, although the introduction of these is quite recent. Even before that innovation, though, the community could keep a reasonable update of the working situation. If there is a problem to be discussed, the community can rapidly set-up a meeting to solve it. Even when it was necessary to send files or documents related to the problem to be discussed, the existence of an electronic network helped to pass the information on. The community knows its members and its roles, allowing it to express who is responsible for what, and which knowledge that individuals have. The members showed in the interviews that they are capable of telling how each member can contributed in a shared enterprise.

As strongly connected and related group, the community was capable of demonstrating in the interviews that they could judge the appropriateness of actions and products related to their community. The sense of purpose is very clear, and in the cases where any doubt was present in a situation that required a decision of appropriateness, they knew who could provide an answer for the question. The community has a set of common tools, representations and artefacts, probably as consequence of the common goal and the nature of the work. The community's objective is clear and although with some specificity, it is well known among the members.

The members of the community share stories, experiences and local lore. They are able of recognise very subtle jokes that are related to some anecdotal experience they have had in common. Sometimes the jokes can only be understood by the members. Outsiders sometimes cannot grab the meaning on those jokes, even after explanations. They share a set of common jargon and shortcuts intended to facilitate and speed up the communication between them. For instance, the acronym *PLAT* can be used to refer to a conference (*Psychology Learning and Teaching* that runs every two years) or a journal published by the organisation. Sometimes when the term is used in a conversation, the members can recognise which *PLAT* the person is referring to.

In general, it is very noticeable that the community has the three main components needed in a CoP. The *domain* is always the same. They deal with all the aspects of the teaching and learning of Psychology in UK. Even though this concept embraces more nuances on it, the inner implications and relations are still present in the community. The *practice* is shared and always present in the everyday activities. They share ideas, language, tools, frameworks and the tacit knowledge that the organisation requires. The *community* is present through the existent bond among the members. They have joint activities and discussions that always improve the shared knowledge available to the community. They have a well-defined mutual respect and trust.

Regarding the indicators specified by Wenger, the study showed that the three dimensions of a Community of Practice were also present. The community of mutual engagement, a negotiated enterprise and a repertoire of negotiable resources collected over a period has been confirmed through the interviews and through the experience of one of the researchers as participant of the community.

CONCLUSION

Although the subject is not new, Virtual Communities of Practice are still full of potential. Several publications tried to discuss all that potential and how they can be useful within a managerial point of view. However, very little attention has been given to the Communities of Practice that are to be – the 'hidden' ones. They can represent a huge step in the direction of success of any organisation. The problem is how to discover them, and in addition, how to accomplish that in a modern world where the ubiquity of electronic networks has already created a new framework for social communities.

This chapter just scratched the surface of what can be a big area for future research. Combining concepts already well sedimented with brand new possibilities that Internet and an always-connected world can bring will be difficult. However, if successful, it will deliver a countless amount of benefits for future organisations.

More research will be carried out in the search for 'hidden' Virtual Communities of Practice. We know that our first study was just the first step to confirm and embrace different approaches within CoPs. However, additional study is already in plan to answer some of the underlined questions raised in this chapter. It is still necessary to clarify if Virtual Communities of Practice have similar behaviour to collocated ones, and if all the original concepts and models still apply for that case. The idea of 'hidden' CoPs is still new and understudied. In order to find fully developed VCoPs some case studies will be necessary. For last, the issue of revealing a 'hidden' CoP requires more study and analysis.

In order to achieve these goals it is necessary to conduct more studies in different CoPs and with different sizes, probably using different methods and techniques. Maybe an ethnographic study can be necessary to complement the understanding of the inside issues.

ACKNOWLEDGMENT

The authors are grateful to the Higher Education Academy Psychology Network for allowing its members to participate in the case study.

REFERENCES

Becerra-Fernandez, I., & Sabherwal, R. (2001). Organizational Knowledge Management: A Contingency Perspective. *Journal of Management Information Systems, 18*(1), 23-55.

Boersma, J. S. K. T., & Stegwee, R. A. (1996). Exploring the Issues in Knowledge Management. *Information Technology Management in Europe, Track of the 1996 Information Resources Management Association International Conference.*

Brown, J. S., & Duguid, P. (1991). Organizational Learning and Communities of Practice: Toward a Unified View of Working, Learning, and Innovation. *Knowledge and Communities, 2*(1), 40-57.

Cappe, E. (2008). *Conditions D'émergence Et De Développement Des Communautés De Pratique Pour Le Management Des Connaissances.* Unpublished PhD, Universite Pierre Mendes, Grenoble, France.

Cox, A. (2005). What Are Communities of Practice? A Comparative Review of Four Seminal Works. *Journal of Information Science, 31*(6), 527.

Dick, B. (2003, 4-5 may 2003). *What Can Action Researchers Learn from Grounded Theorists.* Paper presented at the Australia and New Zealand ALARPM/SCAIR Conference, Gold Coast, Australia.

Gongla, P., & Rizzuto, C. R. (2001). Evolving Communities of Practice: Ibm Global Services Experience. *IBM Systems Journal, 40*(4), 842-862.

Gongla, P., & Rizzuto, C. R. (2004). Where Did That Community Go? Communities of Practice That "Disappear". In P. Hildreth & C. Kimble (Eds.), *Knowledge Networks: Innovation through Communities of Practice* (pp. 295-307): Idea Group Publishing.

Gourlay, S. (2002, April). *Tacit Knowledge, Tacit Knowing or Behaving?* Paper presented at the Third European conference on organizational knowledge, learning and capabilities.

Gourlay, S. (2003). The Seci Model of Knowledge Creation: Some Empirical Shortcomings. *4th European Conference on Knowledge Management*, 377-385.

Gourlay, S. (2004). 'Tacit Knowledge': The Variety of Meanings in Empirical Research. *Fifth European Conference on Organizational Knowledge, Learning and Capabilities Innsbruck.*

Gourlay, S. (2006). Conceptualizing Knowledge Creation: A Critique of Nonaka's Theory. *Journal of Management Studies, 43*(7), 1415-1436.

Hiltz, S. R., & Turoff, M. (1993). *Network Nation: Human Communication Via Computer (Revised Edition)*: The MIT Press.

Igbaria, M. (1999). The Driving Forces in the Virtual Society. *Communications of the ACM, 42*(12), 64-70.

Jorna, R. (1998). Managing Knowledge, *Semiotic Review of Books* (9 ed., Vol. 9, pp. 5-8).

Kimble, C. (2006). *Communities of Practice: Never Knowingly Undersold.* Paper presented at the EC-TEL 2006 Workshops, Crete, Greece.

Kimble, C., & Hildreth, P. (2002). The Duality of Knowledge. *Information Research, 8*(1).

Kimble, C., & Hildreth, P. (2005). Dualities, Distributed Communities of Practice and Knowledge Management. *Journal of Knowledge Management, 9*(4), 102 - 113.

Lave, J., & Wenger, E. (1991). *Situated Learning: Legitimate Peripheral Participation*: Cambridge University Press.

Lundkvist, A. (2004). User Networks as Sources of Innovation. In P. Hildreth & C. Kimble (Eds.), *Knowledge Networks: Innovation through Communities of Practice* (pp. 96-105): Idea Group Publishing.

Nonaka, I. (1991). The Knowledge-Creating Company. *Harvard Business Review*(69), 96-104.

Nonaka, I. (1994). A Dynamic Theory of Organizational Knowledge Creation. *Organization Science, 5*(1).

Nonaka, I., & Takeuchi, H. (1995). *The Knowledge-Creating Company.* Oxford: Oxford University Press.

Nonaka, I., Umemoto, K., & Senoo, D. (1996). From Information Processing to Knowledge Creation: A Paradigm Shift in Business Management. *Technology in Society, 18*(2), 203-218.

Rheingold, H. (1993). *The Virtual Community: Homesteading on the Electronic Frontier.* Reading, MA: Addison-Wesley Pub. Co.

Roberts, T. L. (1998). *Are Newsgroups Virtual Communities?* Paper presented at the CHI 98, Los Angeles.

Sproull, L. S., & Kiesler, S. B. (1992). *Connections: New Ways of Working in the Networked Organization*: MIT Press.

Wenger, E. (1998). *Communities of Practice: Learning, Meaning, and Identity*: Cambridge.

Wenger, E. (2006). Communities of Practice - a Brief Introduction. Retrieved 10/11/2006

Wenger, E., McDermott, R., & Snyder, M. W. (2002). *Cultivating Communities of Practice - a Guide to Managing Knowledge*: Harvard Business School Press.

KEY TERMS

Communities of Practice (CoPs): Groups of people who share a concern, a set of problems, or a passion about a topic, and who deepen their knowledge and expertise in this area by interacting on an ongoing basis. (Wenger et al., 2002)

Distributed Communities (DC): Communities spread over a place, or without a precise delimitation of their space.

Distributed Communities of Practice (DCoPs): Communities of Practice spread over a place, or without a precise delimitation of their space.

Explicit Knowledge: Knowledge that can be made available through a media (writing, audio, video, etc.) and it can be relatively easy to acquire, save and retrieve.

"Hidden" Communities of Practice: Potential or unseen Communities of Practice.

Knowledge Transfer: Exchange and reuse of the available knowledge.

Social Community: Group of persons that participate in the same community and have active involvement in social enterprises. Participation in this sense is both personal and social, involves personal and shared feelings and is reciprocal. In addition, the members can recognize each other as belonging to the same group (Based on Wenger, 1998)

Tacit Knowledge: Knowledge that even if one wished to pass to another person, it would be very difficult to accomplish.

Virtual Communities (VC): Social communities that use Computer-Mediated Communication (CMC) to maintain contact with its participants.

Virtual Communities of Practice (VCoPs): Non-collocated Communities of Practice that use Computer-Mediated Communication (CMC) to maintain contact with their participants.

Chapter IV
The Generative Potential of Appreciative Inquiry for CoP:
The Virtual Enterprise's Emergent Knowledge Model

Kam Hou VAT
University of Macau, Macau

ABSTRACT

The chapter investigates an actionable framework of knowledge sharing, from the perspective of appreciative inquiry. This framework should accommodate the creation of appreciative processes that would encourage or better institutionalize knowledge sharing among people of interest in an organization. The idea is extensible to the building of communities in cyberspace so much facilitated in today's Internet and World Wide Web, and it is increasingly visible that such a model of knowledge sharing is quite promising for today's virtual enterprises. The premise in our exploration is that organizations were beginning to understand the power of unleashing knowledge among individuals. What they struggled with was how exactly to unleash that power, albeit that the very behavior of hoarding knowledge is what makes employees successful. The presence of an explicitly appreciative format rendered by the enterprise should allow many to say what is on their mind without being questioned, critiqued or put on the defense. And it could be done using the many electronic services of technology-enabled appreciative systems made available. However, the task of identifying what to watch in building a knowledge-sharing community online is not at all straightforward. For example, community can be examined by focusing on how users or participants work with and learn from the experience of community participation, or on the nature of collective imagination and feelings of identity as a tool for understanding belonging and attachment to particular virtual communities. Our investigation should provide a basis to think about the generative potential of some appreciative processes on a virtual community's knowledge activities. The design and refinement of technology as the conduit for extending and enhancing an organization's appreciative systems is an essential issue, but the role of the individuals as participants in a virtual community is as important. The emergent challenge is to de-marginalize the concept of appreciative sharing of knowledge among members of the organization, expositing on the effective meaning behind the organization's creation of the appreciative framework for knowledge work through which purposeful individual or organizational activities could be supported with the elaboration of suitable information technologies.

INTRODUCTION

Today, an organization's ability to learn is often considered as a process of leveraging the collective individual learning of the organization to attain a higher-level organization-wide goal. This is a continuous process of creating, acquiring, and transferring knowledge accompanied by a modification of behavior to reflect new knowledge and insight. We identify with Peter Senge (1990) that the organizations that will truly excel in the future will be the organizations that discover how to tap people's commitment and capacity to learn, and to produce a higher-level organizational asset. In the pages to follow, we write about the restoration of a basic human drive to share what we know, which is traceable to our hunter-gathers' organizational structure (Ehin, 2000) dating back to 10,000 BC, providing a powerful testimony of the value of knowledge sharing. We re-position that age-old knowledge practice at the intersection of the modernizing organization and the expanding electronic network, both of which could be considered as the habitat of our human social beings.

Realistically, organizations today cannot afford the high cost of replacing the knowledge of people they have trained and lost. Instead, to support knowledge sharing, organizations must change intelligently and constantly. Ongoing high-quality conversation (knowledge sharing) is a key to making that kind of change possible. Putting conversation to work means bringing the right people with the requisite knowledge together and motivating their online interaction solve real and immediate problems for the organization. To

reach that level of practical impact, there must be trust and commitment among the participants apart from software and online connectivity. For our organizations, that often means leading and fostering the kind of culture that mobilizes people to share what they know with their peers (co-workers) without a fear of being questioned, critiqued or put on the defense. In the specific context of our discussion, this culture of sharing which should be in the driver's seat for selecting and configuring the technology is developed from the idea of appreciative inquiry (AI) (Cooperrider & Whitney, 2005).

The word appreciation carries with it the recognition of the quality, significance, or magnitude of people and things, and a judgment or opinion, especially a favorable one, as well as an expression of gratitude according to The American Heritage Dictionary of the English Language, Fourth Edition. Therefore, appreciation is feeling validated for our opinion, our efforts, and the unique qualities we bring to bear on a situation. In appreciative inquiry, there is a deliberate action of selectivity and judgment The inquirer is choosing to look at some stimuli intently and in the process see them more fully. Interestingly, when changing the way we perceive a new situation, we have the power to keep clear of the deficit thinking that is inherent in an organization, though the way we are trained mostly makes it easy to focus on the negative and what is not working in a situation. Yet, it may seem simple and obvious that people who appreciate one another in the workplace will have a better working relationship than those who have an adversarial relationship. So, what then makes it so hard to create an appreciative environment for knowledge sharing? To this end, the discussion presented in the manuscript is organized around our deliberated exploration for a community-centered (communities of practice, CoP) (Wenger, McDermott, & Snyder, 2002; Wenger, 1998) approach of knowledge synthesis (Hemlin, Allwood, & Martin, 2004) in which developing a culture of knowledge sharing from the perspective of appreciative inquiry (AI) (Cooperrider, 1986), has the generative potential conducive to the fully functioning of knowledge networks (Figallo & Rhine, 2002) already running across many a virtual enterprise (Putnik & Cunha, 2005) operating over the Internet today.

THE BACKGROUND OF APPRECIATIVE INQUIRY

The contributions behind the work of appreciative inquiry (AI), is mainly attributed to David L. Cooperrider's (1986) doctoral research at Case Western Reserve University. The context of AI is about the co-evolutionary search for the best in people, their organizations, and the relevant world around them. In its broadest focus, it involves systematic discovery of what gives life to a living system when it is most alive, most effective, and most constructively capable in economic, ecological, and human terms. Principally, AI involves the art and practice of asking questions that strengthen a system's capacity to apprehend, anticipate, and heighten positive potential.

AI has been described in different ways since its publication: as a paradigm of conscious evolution geared for the realities of the new century (Hubbard, 1998); as a methodology that takes the idea of the social construction of reality to its positive extreme especially with its relational ways of knowing (Gergen, 1990); as the most important advance in action research in the last decade of the 20th century (Bushe, 1995); as offspring to Abraham Maslow's vision of a positive social

science (Chin, 1998; Curran, 1991); as a powerful second generation practice of organizational development (Watkins & Cooperrider, 1996); as model of a much needed participatory science (Harman, 1990); as a radically affirmative approach to change which completely lets go of problem solving mode of management (White, 1996), and as an approach to leadership and human development (Cooperrider & Whitney, 2005).

In essence, AI is an attempt to determine the organization's core values (or life giving forces). It seeks to generate a collective image of a future by exploring the best of what is in order to provide an impetus for imagining what might be (Cooperrider & Srivastva, 1987). Positively, Thatchenkery and Chowdhry (2007, p.33) says it well,

"To be appreciative, we must experience a situation, accept the situation, make sense of the situation (pros/cons), and do a bit of mental gymnastics to understand the situation, with an appreciative lens. Not only that, the appreciative lens that we put on the situation impacts our next experience as well."

Indeed, the interpretive scheme we bring to a situation significantly influences what we will find. Seeing the world is always an act of judgment. We can take an appreciative judgment or a critical or deficit oriented judgment. AI takes the former. Geoffrey Vickers (1965, 1968, 1972), a professional manager turned social scientist, was the first to talk about appreciation in a systematic way. Vickers' main contribution is that of appreciation and the appreciative process which constitutes a system. An appreciative system may be that of an individual, group, or an organization. In explaining appreciation, Vickers used systems thinking (Checkland & Casar, 1986), which provided basic concepts to describe the circular human processes of perceiving, judging, and acting. Specifically, Vickers focused on five key elements of appreciation, including respectively:

• The experience of day-to-day life as a flux of interacting events and ideas;

- Reality judgments about what goes in the present moment and a value judgment about what ought to be good or bad, both of which are historically influenced;
- An insistence on relationship maintaining (or norm seeking) as a richer concept of human action than the popular notion of goal seeking;
- A concept of action judgments stemming from both reality and value judgments; and
- Action, as a result of appreciation, contributing to the flux of events and ideas, as does the mental act of appreciation itself.

This leads to the notion that the cycle of judgments and actions is organized as a system. Simply put, as humans, we are in a state of flux. We judge the events we experience based on our individual history. We make meaning based on the interactions with other humans to enrich our lives. Our judgments, relationships, and values dictate how we act in subsequent events. By framing our perceptions and judgments on appreciation, we can change our behavior (Whitney & Trosten-Bloom, 2003). In the context of fostering online a knowledge culture among members of an organization, especially the various CoPs (Wenger, 1998), we can change the way we hoard knowledge to a philosophy of sharing knowledge (Lewis, Passmore, & Cantore, 2008; Orem, Binkert, & Clancy, 2007; Reed, 2007)). Indeed, the basic rationale of AI is to begin with a grounded observation of the best of what is, articulate what might be, ensure the consent of those in the system to what should be, and collectively experiment with what can be.

The Vision of Knowledge Networking

The last decade of the 20th century saw explosive growth in discussions about knowledge – knowledge work, knowledge management, knowledge-based organizations and the knowledge economy (Cortada & Woods, 2000). Against this backdrop, enterprises including educational institutes are challenged to do things more collaboratively in order to remain vital in an increasingly global environment of knowledge networking (Stalk, Evans, & Shulman, 1992). By knowledge networking, we mean there is a strong need to share knowledge in a way that makes it easier for individuals, teams, and enterprises to work together to effectively contribute to an organization's success.

This idea of knowledge sharing has well been exemplified in Rheingold's (1994) description of the WELL project (Whole Earth 'Lectronic Link), which is one of the first virtual communities, still going strong today. Rooted in the San Francisco Bay Area, the WELL (http://www.well.com) is an open-ended and self-governing community that started in 1985. Attracting people from a wide diversity of backgrounds, many of them professionals, it hosted computer conferences on a wide range of topics – education, arts, recreations, computers and entertainment. It went on to the Internet in 1992 where over two hundred separate conferences are hosted. Its introductory Web pages emphasize that it is not just another website or collection of web pages: "More than just another 'site' or 'home page' the WELL has a sense of place that is palpable". One spin-off of the WELL was the Global Business Network (GBN; http://www.gbn.com), created in 1986, that drew together planners and strategists from companies like ABB, AT&T, Volvo, BP and Bell South. This group used a mix of face to-face meetings and online conferences to develop scenarios of the future. Through GBN, company executives and leading thinkers in a variety of fields would openly share their knowledge and insights. This interplay of knowledge generated new thinking about the future. It also led to increased collaboration among GBN members. In fact, GBN represents an instance of the knowledge network, an interwoven system to support inter-organizational knowledge sharing over the Internet. Operationally, members of a knowledge network do not lose their legal identity; they retain their own culture and management structure and pursue their own strategies but they have to reduce their autonomy, share decision making, interconnect their organizational structure, jointly manage some activities or operations and open their company culture to outside influences.

Assuming this is the course that most organizations will follow, we must from a knowledge management (or rather knowledge sharing) perspective, perceive knowledge creation and transfer as taking place in the context of a network, rather than viewing it from a traditional organizational angle. Thereby, the term knowledge networking makes sense of itself, and making effective use of knowledge requires a network in which the knowledge and experiences of employees from various enterprises are embedded and made available. In this regard, knowledge barriers (Cherny, 1999; Davis & Brewer, 1997) can be overcome, and knowledge islands (as of individual organization), could be cross-linked to stimulate the evolution, dissemination and application of knowledge.

The Landscape of Communities of Practice

Interestingly, the WELL and the GBN could both be considered as an instance of the notion of a learning organization (Senge, 1990; Garvin, 1993; King, 1996; Levine, 2001; Garratt, 1987). Essentially, a learning organization could be considered as an organization, which focuses on developing and using its information and knowledge capabilities in order to create higher-value information and knowledge, to modify behaviors to reflect new knowledge and insights, and to improve bottom-line results. Practically, there are many possible instances of a learning organization that could be incorporated into our daily experiences. An obvious example to match our discussion above is the concept of communities of practice (CoP), which according to Wenger et al. (2002, p4), refers to groups of people who share a common concern, a set of problems, or

a passion about a topic, and who deepen their knowledge and expertise by interacting on an ongoing basis. As people in the community spend time together, they typically share information, insight, and advice. They help one another solve problems; they ponder common issues, explore ideas, and accumulate knowledge. Oftentimes, they become informally bound by the value that they find in learning together. This value is not merely instrumental for their work. Over time, they develop a unique perspective on their topic as well as a body of common knowledge, practices, and approaches. They also develop personal relationships, a common sense of identity, and established ways of interacting. Indeed, CoP is not a new idea (Wenger, 1998). They were our first knowledge-based social structures, back when we lived in caves and gathered around the fire to discuss strategies for cornering preys, the shape of arrowheads, or which roots were edible. They have captured our attention today because with the advent of the Internet, especially, the World Wide Web, we have come to realize that knowledge sharing, coupled with the possibilities of technological advances (especially, in the area of information and communications technologies, ICT) is the key to our sustainable development regardless of the temporal and spatial boundaries.

In this regard, the term virtual community, referring to many types of Internet-based social interaction today, has inspired many organizations to initiate their electronic transformation of various CoPs empowering their collective learning based not so much on delineated learning paths, but rather on experience sharing, the identification of best practices, and reciprocal support for tackling day-to-day problems in the workplace. Undeniably, in the emerging knowledge network, we are expected to continually improvise, and invent new methods to deal with unexpected difficulties and to solve immediate problems, and share these innovations or lessons learned with others through some effective channel such as the virtual CoP. Rheingold (1994), who appears to have coined the term "virtual community" in the first place, provides a definition that accords reasonably well with the context of being virtual:

... people in virtual communities do just about everything people do in real life (meet one another and exchange ideas and information), but we leave our bodies behind. We cannot kiss anybody and nobody can punch us in the nose, but a lot can happen within those boundaries (Rheingold, 1994, pp 57-58).

In the virtual communities of practice, relationship is typically defined not by proximity but by contents of individual interest – classes of objects, ideas, or events about which participants have differing level of both stored knowledge and stored values (Renninger, 2000). Participants' connections to the community are often cognitive and affective rather than simply spatial and temporal. Such a connection is also supported by affordances (Gibson, 1966) that invoke imagination about and identification with a site (an organization), such as autonomy, support and depth of content. Besides, the learning that is undertaken as participants work with a site has an opportunity for changed understanding of our self. Thereby, it is important to identify what a virtual CoP means for the organization's enculturation of knowledge sharing, what it offers, what it affords its participants, and what its boundaries are at the advent of the Internet that has undoubtedly created numerous possibilities for interaction that people did not have before (Cherny, 1999; Davis & Brewer, 1997; Herring, 1996).

Indeed, another reason to account for the development of virtual communities today is that organizations have come to realize that their competitive edge is mostly the intellectual capital of their employees (Stewart, 1997), and they need to be more intentional and systematic about managing knowledge through harnessing their human resources in order to stay ahead of the pack. Strategically, cultivating virtual CoPs

in specific areas is considered as a practical way to manage knowledge in terms of critical knowledge domains; organizations need to identify the people and the specific knowledge needed for their growth, and explore how they connect them into suitable virtual communities of practice so that together they could steward the necessary knowledge for the benefits of the organization.

Defining a Context for Virtual Enterprises

With the rapid advances in networking technologies since the eighties of the 20th Century, we have witnessed many an ongoing reshaping of intra- and inter-organizational processes and structures, which are described in the literature under different labels such as the networked organization (Miles & Snow, 1986), the intelligent enterprise (Quinn, 1990), the extended enterprise (Browne et al, 1995), the virtual enterprise (Byrne, et al.,1993; Drucker, 1990; Goldman, Nagel, & Preiss, 1995), and the virtual corporation (Davidow & Malone, 1992).

A review undertaken by Putnik and Cunha (2005) highlighted the existence of two concerns behind these labels: the first is the dynamic networking of enterprises; the second is the virtuality of the system as something not physically existing as such but made by software to appear to do so. In the case of the virtual enterprise, the National Industrial Information Infrastructure Protocols (NIIIP, 1996) reference architecture defines it as a temporary consortium or alliance of companies, which come together to exploit some fast changing market opportunity. Within the virtual enterprise, companies share costs, skills, and access to global markets with each participant contributing with its core competence. Camarinha-Matos et al. (1997) enhance this NIIIP definition by adding the cooperation based on ICT (information and communication technologies).

Nonetheless, the creation of a virtual enterprise requires an objective methodology, which must be instrumental to creating a productive and efficient organization model that enables individual enterprises to follow an iterative development sequence. This means being able to plan and prepare for a launch based on a new idea or lessons learned within a reasonable cycle time. In particular, this model should enable the organizations to launch and learn, and then incorporate those lessons and launch again. In this formulation, the methodology responsible for the electronic transformation from the bricks-and-mortar entity to its clicks-and-mortar counterpart in the virtual enterprise can be conceived as an approach to management (Harrington, 1991; Mowshowitz, 1997) that explicitly recognizes the conceptual distinction between functional requirements and the means for their realization in practice. It should also provide a framework for accommodating dynamic changes in both requirements and available services. In the specific context of our discussion, the methodology of virtual organizing, attributed to the work of Venkatraman and Henderson (1998), is found to be very promising in its support for the various appreciative processes among virtual communities of practice, distributed across different enterprises.

VIRTUAL ORGANIZING COMMUNITIES OF PRACTICE

The idea of virtual organizing, attributed to Venkatraman and Henderson (1998), can be considered as a method to operationalize a learning organization, dynamically assembling and disassembling nodes on a network of people or groups of people, to meet the demands of a particular business context. This term emerged in response to the concept of virtual organization, which appeared in the literature around the late twentieth century (Byrne, Brandt, & Port 1993; Cheng 1996; Davidow, & Malone 1992; Goldman, Nagel, & Preiss 1995; Hedberg, Dahlgren, Hansson, & Olve 1997).

There are two main assertions associated with virtual organizing. First, virtual organization should not be considered as a distinct structure such as a network organization in an extreme and far-reaching form (Jagers, Jansen, & Steenbakkers 1998), but virtuality is a strategic characteristic applicable to every organization. Second, information technology (IT) is a powerful enabler of the critical requirements for effective virtual organizing. In practice, virtual organizing helps emphasize the ongoing process nature of the organization, and it presents a framework of achieving virtuality in terms of three distinct yet interdependent vectors:

- Virtual encounter for organization-wide interactions
- Virtual sourcing for asset configuration
- Virtual expertise for knowledge leverage

The challenge of virtual organizing is to integrate the three hitherto separate vectors into an interoperable IT platform that supports and shapes the new organizational initiative, paying attention to the internal consistency across the three vectors.

Understanding the Three-Vector Framework

The first of the three vectors of virtual organizing deals with the new challenges and opportunities for interacting with the members of an organization. The second focuses on the organization's requirements to be virtually integrated in a network of interdependent (business) partners, so as to manage a dynamic portfolio of relationships to assemble and coordinate the necessary assets for delivering value for the organization. The third is concerned with the opportunities for leveraging diverse sources of expertise within and across organizational boundaries to become drivers of value creation and organizational effectiveness. All these three vectors are accomplished by the provision of suitable information system (IS) support, whose ongoing design represents the IS challenge of every organization in the Internet age.

Virtual Encounter

This idea of providing remote interaction with the organization is not new, but has indeed been redefined since the introduction of the Internet, and particularly, the World Wide Web. Many organizations feel compelled to assess how their products and services can be experienced virtually in the new medium of the Internet. The issue of customization is important. It requires a continuous information exchange with parties of interest, which in turn requires an organizational design that is fundamentally committed to operating in this direction. Practically, organizations need to change from an inside-out perspective to an outside-in perspective. This is often characterized by the emergence of electronic customer communities, with the capacity to influence the organization's directions with a distinct focus in a wider community. It is believed that as virtual organizing becomes more widespread, organizations must recognize communities as part of the value system and respond appropriately in their operational strategies.

Virtual Sourcing

This vector focuses on creating and deploying intellectual and intangible assets for the organization in the form of a continuous reconfiguration of critical capabilities assembled through different relationships in the business network. The mission is to set up a resource network, in which the organization is part of a vibrant, dynamic network of complementary capabilities. The strategic leadership challenge is to orchestrate an organization's position in a dynamic, fast-changing resource network where the organization can carefully analyze her relative dependence on other players in the resource coalition and ensure her unique capabilities.

Virtual Expertise

This vector focuses on the possibilities and mechanisms for leveraging expertise at different levels of the organization. In today's organizations, many tasks are being redefined and decomposed so that they can be done at different locations and time periods. However, the real challenge in maximizing work-unit expertise often rests not so much in designing the technological platform to support group work but in designing the organization structure and processes. The message is clear: though knowledge, alive in the human act of knowing, is often an accumulation of experience that is more a living process than a static body of information, it must be systematically nurtured and managed. In fact, many an organization is increasingly leveraging the expertise not only from the domain of a local organization but also from the extended network of broader professional community.

Adapting the Three-Vector Framework to Virtual CoP

What makes managing knowledge a challenge is that it is not an object that can be stored, owned, and moved around like a piece of equipment or a document. It resides in the skills, understanding, and relationships of its members as well as in the tools, documents, and processes that embody aspects of this knowledge. In response to such knowledge challenge in a learning organization, it is interesting to observe how the ideas of virtual organizing can be applied to nurturing the growth of various communities of practice (CoP) scattered throughout an organization.

Virtual Encountering the Various CoP

From a management perspective, it is important to identify what CoP's currently exist in the organization, and how, if they are not already online, to enable them to be online in order to provide more chances of virtual encounter of such communities, to the organizational members. For those communities already online, it is also important to design opportunities of interaction among different online communities, to activate their knowledge sharing. Since it is not a CoP's practice to reduce knowledge to an object, what counts as knowledge is often produced through a process of communal involvement, which includes all the controversies, debate and accommodations. This collective character of knowledge construction is best supported online with individuals given suitable IS support to participate and contribute their own ideas. An IS subsystem, operated through virtual encounter, must help achieve many of the primary tasks of a community of practice, such as establishing a common baseline of knowledge and standardizing what is well understood so that people in the community can focus their creative energies on the more advanced issues.

Virtual Sourcing the Various CoP

From the discussion built up in the first vector, it is not difficult to visualize the importance of identifying the specific expertise of each potential CoP in the organization, and if not yet available, planning for its acquisition through a purposeful expertise nurture in specific CoPs. In order to enable an organization to be part of a vibrant, dynamic network of complementary capabilities, in which the same organization could claim others' dependence and ensure her unique capabilities, an IS subsystem, operated through virtual sourcing, must help the organization understand precisely what knowledge will give it the competitive edge. The organization then needs to acquire this knowledge, keep it on the cutting edge, deploy

it, leverage it in operations, and steward it across the organization.

Virtual Expertizing the Various CoP

It is important to understand that not everything we know can be codified as documents and tools. Sharing tacit knowledge requires interaction and informal learning processes such as storytelling, conversation, coaching, and apprenticeship. The tacit aspects of knowledge often consist of embodied expertise – a deep understanding of complex, interdependent elements that enables dynamic responses to context-specific problems. This type of knowledge is very difficult to replicate. In order to leverage such knowledge, an IS subsystem, operated through virtual expertise, must help hooking people with related expertise into various networks of specialists, to facilitate stewarding such knowledge to the rest of the organization.

Conceiving Appreciative Processes for Virtual CoP

In order to facilitate the stewarding of knowledge through the various CoPs online in an organization, it is important to have a vision that orients the kind of knowledge an organization must acquire, and wins spontaneous commitment by the individuals and groups involved in knowledge creation (Dierkes, Marz, and Teele, 2001; Kim, 1993; Stopford, 2001). This knowledge vision should not only define what kind of knowledge the organization should create in what domains, but also help determine how an organization and its knowledge base will evolve in the long run (Leonard-Barton, 1995; Nonaka and Takeuchi, 1995).

The central requirement for organizational knowledge synthesis (or sharing) is to provide the organization with a strategic ability to acquire, create, exploit, and accumulate new knowledge continuously and repeatedly. To meet this requirement, we need an interpretation framework, which could facilitate the development of this strategic ability through the various virtual CoPs. It is believed that there are at least three major appreciative processes constituting the interpretation framework of a learning organization, including the personal process, the social process, and the organizational process.

What follows is our appreciation of these three important processes (Checkland & Holwell, 1998, pp.98-109; Checkland, & Casar, 1986) considered as indispensable in the daily operations of a learning organization. Of particular interest here is the idea of appreciative settings, which according to (Vickers, 1972 p.98), refer to the body of linked connotations of personal interest, discrimination and valuation which we bring to the exercise of judgment and which tacitly determine what we shall notice, how we shall discriminate situations from the general confusion of ongoing event, and how we shall regard them.

The Personal Process

Consider us as individuals, each conscious of the world outside our physical boundaries. This consciousness means that we can think about the world in different ways, relate these concepts to our experience of the world and so form judgments which can affect our intentions and, ultimately, our actions. This line of thought suggests a basic model for the active human agent in the world. In this model we are able to perceive parts of the world, attribute meanings to what we perceive, make judgments about our perceptions, form intentions to take particular actions, and carry out those actions. These change the perceived world, however slightly, so that the process begins again, becoming a cycle.

In fact, this simple model requires some elaborations. First, we always selectively perceive parts of the world, as a result of our interests and previous history. Secondly, the act of attributing meaning and making judgments implies the ex-

istence of standards against which comparisons can be made. Thirdly, the source of standards, for which there is normally no ultimate authority, can only be the previous history of the very process we are describing, and the standards will themselves often change over time as new experience accumulates. This is the process model for the active human agents in the world of individual learning, through their individual appreciative settings. This model has to allow for the visions and actions, which ultimately belong to an autonomous individual, even though there may be great pressure to conform to the perceptions, meaning attributions and judgments, which belong to the social environment, which, in our discussion, is the community of practice.

The Social Process

Although each human being retains at least the potential selectively to perceive and interpret the world in their own unique way, the norm for a social being is that our perceptions of the world, our meaning attributions and our judgments of it will all be strongly conditioned by our exchanges with others. The most obvious characteristic of group life is the never-ending dialogue, discussion, debate and discourse in which we all try to affect one another's perceptions, judgments, intentions and actions. This means that while the personal process model continues to apply to the individual, it is indeed carried out inter-subjectively in discourse among individuals often in an attempt to affect the thinking and actions of some other party. As a result of the social discourse that ensues, accommodations may be reached which lead to action being taken.

Consequently, this model of the social process which leads to purposeful or intentional action is one in which appreciative settings lead to particular features of situations as well as the situations themselves being noticed and judged in specific ways by standards built up from previous experience. Meanwhile, the standards by which judgments are made may well be changed through time as our personal and social history unfolds. There is no permanent social reality except at the broadest possible level, immune from the events and ideas, which, in the normal social process, continually change it.

The Organizational Process

Our personal appreciative settings may well be unique since we all have a unique experience of the world, but oftentimes these settings will overlap with those of people with whom we are closely associated or who have had similar experiences. Tellingly, appreciative settings may be attributed to a group of people, including members of a community, or the larger organization as a whole, even though we must remember that there will hardly be complete congruence between the individual and the group settings. It would also be naïve to assume that all members of an organization share the same settings, those that lead them unambiguously to collaborate together in pursuit of collective goals.

The reality is that though the idea of the attributed appreciative settings of an organization as a whole is a usable concept, the content of those settings, whatever attributions are made, will never be completely static. Changes both internal and external to the organization will change individual and group perceptions and judgments, leading to new accommodations related to evolving intentions and purposes. Subsequently, the organizational process will be one in which the data-rich world outside is perceived selectively by individuals and by groups of individuals. The selectivity will be the result of our predispositions to "select, amplify, reject, attenuate or distort" (Land, 1985, p.212) because of previous experience, and individuals will interact with the world not only as individuals but also through their simultaneous membership of multiple groups, some formally organized, some informal. Perceptions will be exchanged, shared,

challenged, and argued over, in a discourse, which will consist of the inter-subjective creation of selected data and meanings. Those meanings will create information and knowledge which will lead to accommodations being made, intentions being formed and purposeful action undertaken. Both the thinking and the action will change the perceived world, and may change the appreciative settings that filter our perceptions. This organizational process is a cyclic one and it is a process of continuous learning, and should be richer if more people take part in it. And it should fit into the context of the virtual enterprise scenario.

ESTABLISHING AN APPRECIATIVE MODEL FOR KNOWLEDGE SHARING

In order for knowledge sharing to be successful, it is convinced that the people involved must be excited about the process of sharing knowledge. For many people, the primary reason for knowledge sharing is not that they expect to be repaid in the form of other knowledge, but the conviction that their individual knowledge is worth knowing, and that sharing this knowledge with others will be beneficial to their reputation (Hoof et al., 2004, p.1). There is some psychological benefit to sharing knowledge as the sharer may be held in higher esteem by the receiver(s) of the knowledge and may gain status as a result. Thereby, an appreciative sharing of knowledge must be viewed as the non-threatening and accepting approach that makes people realize what they do can make a difference.

One common example is the communities of practice (CoP) (be it physical or virtual) discussed earlier. Many organizations today are comprised of a network of interconnected CoPs each dealing with specific aspects such as the uniqueness of a long-standing client, or technical inventions. Knowledge is created, shared, organized, revised, and passed on within and among these communities. In a deep sense, it is by these communities that knowledge is owned in practice. Yet, knowledge exists not just at the core of an organization, but on its peripheries as well (as part of the knowledge network). Communities of practice truly become organizational assets when their core and their boundaries are active in complementary ways, to generate an intentionally appreciative climate for organizational knowledge synthesis.

In this section, we examine an instance of the appreciative model for knowledge sharing, called Appreciative Sharing of Knowledge (ASK) attributed to Thatchenkery (2005). This model demonstrates how we can help our organizations learn to answer the questions: How do our companies and organizations process their experiences to learn from them, and how can they handle this responsibility better? It addresses the issue of implementation – how learning capability can be developed through changes in attitudes, behaviors, processes and structures.

Case Example: The ASK Approach of Knowledge Sharing

As in any organizational change effort, the basic rationale of the ASK approach is to begin with a grounded observation of the best of "what is", articulate "what might be", ensure the consent of those in the system to "what could be", and collectively experiment with "what will be". In practice, the application of ASK is largely facilitated if the climate of knowledge sharing and the technology that enables it, already exist in the organization. To discover the appreciative temperature of an organization, we can conduct interviews with people of interest. The focus will be on capturing what has worked so far in the organization and to extract the core processes supporting knowledge sharing. Throughout the story-telling shared by the interviewees, it is often not difficult to discover some emergent themes of interest, known as knowledge enablers (KEs). Such enablers are then validated through another

series of interviews and subsequent organizational analysis. As a result, we are able to build up a set of future-present scenarios of "what might be". Upon expanding and prioritizing the derived scenarios into more manageable and actionable options, we obtain a set of "what could be". Eventually, we end up with an action plan to realize "what will be".

Operationally, the ASK process comprises eight action steps:

1. Negotiating top management commitment and support;
2. Presenting the appreciative knowledge sharing paradigm;
3. Identifying organizational knowledge enablers;
4. Expanding the knowledge enablers through appreciative interviews;
5. Performing thematic analysis of the interview data to scrutinize the organization's knowledge infrastructure;
6. Constructing the future-present scenarios;
7. Validating the future-present scenarios with consensus of the knowledge stakeholders;
8. Creating and mandating an ASK implementation team.

These steps are mostly categorized under four stages, including: discovering "what is" (steps 1, 2, 3), creating "what might be" (steps 4, 5, 6), prioritizing "what could be" (step 7), and declaring "what will be" (step 8).

Discovering "What is"

There are three steps in this stage as mentioned above.

Negotiating Top Management Commitment and Support

Step 1, like all change management efforts, involves endorsement and support from top management. Ideally, the chief executive or someone at senior level is the champion or sponsor for the change efforts. To formalize the initiation of the project, the champion can send out a written communication (in the form of a memo) explaining the significance of the initiative, the approximate timeline, and the involvement expected of the staff. The people involved should include the ASK team members and the champion (sponsor) of the ASK initiative, preferably leader within the organization. The method of work involves meetings between ASK initiative team members and sponsor. The outcome should include the leadership endorsement and a written endorsement memo (e-mail) from sponsor to organization.

Presenting the Appreciative Knowledge Sharing Paradigm

Step 2, once the sponsor has initiated the ASK initiative, it is time to involve various stakeholders and the knowledge workers by grounding them in the context of the appreciative approach. Namely, it is crucial to invite the participants to take a hard look at the reality around them, but appreciatively. This does not mean ignoring or neglecting what is on people's mind. To be truly appreciative with our fellow employees, we need to empathize with them, acknowledge their feelings and respect his or her state of mind as genuine and as a source of understanding. Oftentimes, explaining the logic and philosophy of ASK through some formal presentation meetings would help in creating the right mindset and motivation to engage them in the project. The people involved should include the ASK initiative sponsor, the ASK team members, and the first round of participants (mostly numbered about 30 people). The method include meetings run by the ASK team members and the subsequent discussion sessions enabled by the sponsor. The outcome is letting the employees understand what ASK is.

Identifying the Knowledge Enablers

Step 3, the potential of ASK is often demonstrated through interviews (storytelling by the interviewees) in pairs among those who attended the presentation in Step 2. There are three tasks to accomplish subtly here: Firstly, the process works as an ice-breaker activity to get the ASK movement started. Secondly, the storytelling interviews help in identifying what are called knowledge enablers (KEs), the best of what is happening in the organization concerning knowledge sharing. Thirdly, members will later be given the opportunity to hear the content of the interviews as appreciative knowledge sharing episodes. Sharing and listening to a story creates the space for fellow organizational members to imagine what might be in their organization. We can get in the minds of individuals who collectively make up the organization. The storytellers share stories of knowledge events that are already working well in the organization, and this creates a framework to generate more ideas of what else could work well as well. The people involved in this step, include the ASK initiative sponsor, the ASK team members, and the first round of participants of ASK. The method involves meetings facilitated by the ASK team members, including a break-out session of pairs of two, in which each employee interviews a colleague using some ASK interview questions (Thatchenkery & Chowdhry, 2007, p.55), and a sharing session in which each employee reports to the larger group (meeting participants) the stories heard from their interview partners. As the stories are shared, the ASK team members capture main descriptors (be it on an electronic white board, or some other reporting tools), which generate the dozens of first cut of themes. With the help of the audience, the ASK team will analyze and narrow them down to a manageable set of key themes (or values) called knowledge enablers (KEs). The outcome of this step includes the fact that the employees have conducted their first round of ASK interviews, and the employees have begun identifying some KEs.

Creating "What might be"

There are also three steps in this stage as mentioned above.

Expanding the Knowledge Enablers Through Appreciative Interviews

Step 4, with the knowledge enablers identified in Step 3, the ASK team's next task is to explore the knowledge infrastructure factors (KIFs) that facilitate the existence and continuance of the KEs. Suppose the KEs include such elements as collegiality, teamwork, valuing autonomy, participation, and opportunity for personal growth. The ASK team need to explore those factors in the organization that sustain and nourish the same. This could be discovered through conducting appreciative interviews (Thatchenkery & Chowdhry, 2007, pp.57-59), involving one-on-one conversation with people who are preferably not those involved in Step 3 above. Two important aspects associated with each KE, are found to be critical in this exploration of KIFs: a) description of occasions/events where the interviewee experienced the knowledge enabler in its most alive manifestation; b) factors or conditions (personal, organizational, and/or environmental) that heighten, facilitate, or promote those knowledge enablers.

Performing Thematic Analysis of the Data Using KIFs

Step 5, once the KE factors have been identified and further explored, the next task for the ASK team is to enhance the operation of those factors within the organization. It is understood that in the knowledge sharing context, the KEs are considered as highly desirable that people desire to see more of them in practice in their work settings. Further, as long as the KEs have been relevantly identified, building on them is plausible by helping individuals imagine the ideal future as if it has already happened. Hence, it is important to analyze the interview data to get a sense of the KIFs. Understandably, knowledge infrastructure is the backbone of any knowledge enabler, without which KEs can hardly sustain themselves for long. KIFs are the pillars that support the knowledge architecture. Yet, they are not often externally visible to command appearance attention just as the hidden pillar support when looking at an architectural marvel. According to Thatchenkery (2005), the set of KIFs across enterprises remains interdependent including such factors as decision making, organizational practices and routines, incentives for knowledge sharing, leadership, and communication. However, for ease of analysis and interpretation, such KIFs are often treated as if they were independent. Thereby, the people involved in this step, include the ASK team members. The method requires the ASK team members to transcribe interviews notes and analyze them as a group, and organize the resulting data across different KIFs in the form of a matrix whose rows represent respective KIFs, and whose columns represent different KEs, and the cells in the matrix should contain examples of the KIFs that enhance the corresponding KEs. The outcome becomes the thematic analysis of knowledge enablers.

Constructing the Future-Present Scenarios

Step 6, a future-present scenario (FPS) bridges the best of "what is" with our image or anticipation of "what might be". Describing such a scenario requires a concrete depiction with rich details of a future desired state happening in the present reality. Imagine the future has come to the present. Sometimes called visualization exercise, the logic of constructing future-present scenarios is supported by research evidence in cognitive psychology (Oschner & Liebermann, 2001). Using FPS scenarios during the ASK process helps stakeholders in an organization think of the future as if it is already present and they therefore may get a better sense of what it feels to live that future. Putting FPS in words should heighten attention to visualized possibilities, because it represent potentials for knowledge sharing in the organization, making it more likely that such potentials will become reality, but it should mostly consist of what is possible rather than what is not. An FPS statement must be data-supported in the sense that the matrix of KIFs and KEs must be the launching pad. To realize such scenarios in a knowledge sharing organization, we need to link the scenarios with the KEs and KIFs to produce propositions related to each KIF that enhances the corresponding KE. The FPS scenarios are the key to making existing parts of the knowledge culture grow and thrive in the organization of tomorrow. One of the features that distinguishes ASK is that the methodology forces the future to be embedded in the meaningful aspects of the present involving the important elements of commitment, inspiration, and groundedness from the established CIG model (Lewin, 1951/1997; McGregor, 1960; Herzberg et al., 1959; Rogers, 1980/1995; Argyris, 1993) in the construction of the FPS. Without commitment, the new possibility will not materialize. Without inspiration, there is no driver that provides the energy for people to carry out the new possibility. Without groundedness, the FPS may not be realistic and plausible. If it is too far-fetched, looking too radical or beyond the capabilities of the organization, not many will have the energy to make it happen. Historically, individuals change when their desired change (inspiration) is synergistically combined with concrete baby-steps (groundedness), and a plan to stay on course (commitment). It is our experience that people's commitment to sustain any change would easily vanish if the change is too dramatic, or the expectations unrealistic. Thereby, the people involved in this step include ASK team members and employees of the organization. The method is for the people involved to pull from interview data to create future-present scenario statements. The outcome is the set of FPS statements produced.

Prioritizing "What Could Be"

There is only one step in this stage according to Thatchenkery (2005).

Validating the FPS Statements Consensually
Step 7, after the future-present scenario statements have been written, it is important to double check if the propositions derived could accommodate such criteria as: Is the statement really challenging or merely a re-statement of something already in practice? Is it specific, concrete, and tangible, as opposed to something very general and abstract? Does it inspire you as the participant? Does it stay grounded and connected to the knowledge enabler and the knowledge infrastructure factor under consideration? Next, it is important to invite different groups to visit one another and comment on the statements of those groups, and come up with a revised set of propositions. Once this has been done, the next task is to ask every one in the audience (group) to valence the propositions with a suitable scale of measure, using such guiding questions as:

- How much of an ideal is it? (5 → very much, 4, 3, 2, and 1 → not much)
- How much of it may already be present? (5 → a lot, 4, 3, 2, and 1 → not much) and
- How soon do you want this to happen? (immediately, within six months, within two years).

After performing the evaluation and tabulating the scores, we should have all the propositions prioritized through a set of criteria that are important to the organization. Thereby, the people involved in this stage include the ASK initiative sponsor, all ASK participants, and the ASK team members. The method is simply the ASK team members presenting FPSs, and received upgrades and validation. Then the ASK team ranks the propositions based on the three criteria mentioned. The outcome includes the upgraded and validated FPSs and the organization has ranked the future-present scenarios.

Declaring "What Will Be"

There is only one step in this stage, but it is the most important step in the ASK process.

Creating and Mandating an Implementation Team

It is relatively easy to come up with exciting possibilities, but implementing them is often where the hard work really begins. It is suggested by Thatchenkery (2005) that to avoid such traps, ensuring that the propositions in the high priority list are indeed those for which a true desire for implementation exists, the ASK team may work with the client organizational unit in setting up the implementation team and do periodic follow-ups on how the process is working. Such an implementation team is then charged with prioritizing and implementing the highest priority possibility propositions and making them a reality. A change contract between the ASK team and the unit concerned (owner of change), that includes an implementation phase, would be perfect in this context. Thereby, the people involved in this stage include the ASK initiative sponsor, all the ASK participants, and the ASK team members. The method is to enable the implementation owners to design and present an action plan for successful implementation. The outcome is to see the highest ranked FPS have an action plan and an owner for each FPS task.

FUTURE TRENDS TO MEET KNOWLEDGE CHALLENGE

In 1969, Peter Drucker emphasized that knowledge had become the crucial resource of the economy. He claims the credit for coining the notion of 'knowledge work', which he contrasted with more traditional forms of work such as service work and manual work. Today, the term 'knowledge work' tends to refer to specific occupations which are "characterized by an emphasis on theoretical knowledge, creativity and use of analytical and social skills" (Frenkel et al., 1995, p.773). Knowledge work, interpreted this way, encompasses both what is traditionally referred to as professional work, such as accountancy, scientific and legal work, and more contemporary types of work, such as consultancy, software development, advertising and public relations. Understandably, these types of knowledge work are not susceptible to be easily imitated because there is a significant application of both tacit and explicit knowledge (Nonaka, 1994). Those engaged in these types of work are often individuals with high levels of education and specialist skills, who demand autonomy over their work processes to get the job done; namely, to demonstrate their ability to apply those skills to identify and solve problems. What is significant about these types of knowledge workers is that they own the organization's primary means of production – that is, knowledge. Nowadays, the management of knowledge workers assumes greater importance for sustaining productivity than the management of machines, technologies, or work processes. Like musicians, Drucker (1988) sees such employees exploring outlets for their creative abilities, seeking interesting challenges, enjoying the stimulation of working with other specialists. This, he argues, poses new management challenges in knowledge-based organizations (such as the virtual enterprise): developing rewards, recognition and career opportunities; giving an organization of specialists a common vision; devising a management structure for coordinating tasks and task teams; and ensuring the supply and skills of top management people. In the following discussion, we summarize a community approach to managing knowledge work, based on our earlier context established for the communities of practice, situated on appreciative inquiry.

Community Approach to Managing Knowledge Work

Earlier in the manuscript, we have associated the context of communities of practice (CoP) (Wenger, 1998) to that of a learning organization (Senge, 1990), and the connotation of a virtual community (Rheingold, 1994). In this regard, there is an active role CoPs can play in enabling the organization to learn from the experience of its members. Traditional organizational (hierarchical) structures are designed to control activities and often discourage the easy sharing of knowledge and learning. Communities, nonetheless, help to foster relationships based on mutual trust (social capital) which are the unspoken and often unrecognized channels through which knowledge is shared. In fact, CoPs have profound implications for the management of knowledge work. They highlight the limits of management control in that CoPs are voluntary entities, depending entirely on the interest and commitment of their members. They cannot be designed or imposed in a top-down manner. Knowledge does not circulate through them in any officially prescribed form of rules, procedures and targets. Rather knowledge is disseminated through stories, jokes and anecdotes which enlighten or just lighten a shared experience.

Perceiving the Importance of Story-Telling

Interestingly, among CoPs, story-telling has become a more important way of communicating knowledge than codifying it using specific ICT systems. There are several reasons provided by Brown and Duguid (1991): Firstly, stories present information in an interesting way with a beginning, a body, and an end, as well as people behaving goodly or badly. Secondly, stories present information in a way people can empathize with

– recounting a situation which each of us might face, so it has greater perceived relevance. Thirdly, stories personalize the information – instead of talking about situations in the abstract, we hear about the doings of individuals whom we might know or have heard of. Fourthly, stories bring people together, emphasizing a shared social identity and interests – we share knowledge rather than transfer it. More, stories express values – they often contain a moral about certain kinds of behavior leading to either positive or negative outcomes. In this way, stories link information with interest, values and relevance, giving us a sense of the context in which experience has been developed and helping us to grasp the tacit nature of some of the knowledge being communicated.

Understanding the Nature of Community Knowing

Perceptively, the importance of story-telling also provides a further insight into the limits of technology for managing knowledge. Often, the design of ICT systems is based on a cognitive model of seeing knowledge as a "thing" (Malhortra, 2000) which is possessed by individuals, whereas the community approach sees it as the product of social interaction and learning among members of the same. By being a member of a community, individuals are able to develop their practice (work or hobby), sharing experience and ideas with others involved in the same pursuit. In light of this, the essence of meeting the challenge of managing knowledge work comes down to a few key points about the nature of knowing (Nonaka and Takeuchi, 1995; O'Leary, 1998; Wenger, 1998; Wenger et al., 2002):

Knowledge Lives in the Human Act of Knowing

In many instances of our daily living, our knowledge can hardly be reduced to an object that can be packaged for storage and retrieval. Our knowledge is often an accumulation of experience

—a kind of residue of our actions, thinking, and conversations—that remains a dynamic part of our ongoing experience. This type of knowledge is much more a living process than a static body of information.

Knowledge is Tacit as Well as Explicit

Not everything we know can be codified as documents or tools. Sharing tacit knowledge requires interaction and informal learning processes such as conversation, coaching, and apprenticeship. The tacit aspects of knowledge often consist of embodied expertise – a deep understanding of complex, interdependent elements that enables dynamic responses to context-specific problems. This type of knowledge is very difficult to replicate. This is not to say that it is not useful to document such knowledge in whatever manner serves the needs of practitioners. But, even explicit knowledge is dependent on tacit knowledge to be applied.

Knowledge is Dynamic, Social as Well as Individual

It is important to accept that though our experience of knowing is individual, knowledge is not. Much of what we know derives from centuries of understanding and practice developed by long-standing communities. Appreciating the collective nature of knowledge is especially important in an age when almost every field changes too much, too fast for individuals to master. Today's complex problems solving requires multiple perspectives. We need others to complement and develop our own expertise. In fact, our collective knowledge of any field is changing at an accelerating rate. What was true yesterday must be adapted to accommodate new factors, new data, new inventions, and new problems.

Nurturing Communities of Practice Online

Literally, the term virtual community is not hard to understand, yet it is slippery to define owing to its multi-disciplinary nature. In order to develop communities online – a complex practical activity, we need a disciplinary definition to guide our practice. According to Jenny Preece (2000, p.10), a virtual community consists of four important elements: the people, who interact socially as they strive to satisfy their own needs, or perform special roles, such as leading or moderating; a shared purpose, such as an interest, need, information exchange, or service that provides a reason for the community; policies, in the form of tacit assumptions, rituals, protocols, rules, and laws that guide people's interactions; and computer systems, to support and mediate social interaction and facilitate a sense of togetherness. Indeed, this definition is sufficiently general to apply to a range of different communities, including physical communities that have become networked and those that are embedded in Web sites (Lazar & Preece, 1998). Undeniably, the idea of virtual community has somehow become a blanket term to describe any collection of people who communicate online, as exemplified by the networked communities (Cohill & Kavanaugh, 1997), also known as the community networks (Schuler, 1996) to which citizens can link through the Internet to discuss typical community issues. For better or worse, we shape and are shaped by the communities to which we belong. As more people gain Internet access, people are increasingly empowered to organize themselves across local, national, and international boundaries. A call to action, a warning message, a cheer of encouragement, and the inspiring words of a leader can be distributed to members at lightning speed and at almost no cost, with just the click of a few keys. Yet, developing successful virtual CoPs is not trivial. Successful virtual CoPs satisfy their members' needs and contribute to the well-being of society in specific areas or expertises. The role of a community developer is to work with community members to plan and guide the community's social evolution. Putting basic policies in place helps members know how to behave, what to expect from each other, and provides a framework for social growth. As the community develops and forms its own character, its social policies and structure also evolve. Sociability is concerned with planning and developing social policies which are understandable and acceptable to members, to support the community's purpose. The software that supports the continuous evolution of a community must be dynamically designed and adapted to its growth. More importantly, the software must be designed with good usability so that people can interact and perform their tasks intuitively and easily. Software with good usability supports rapid learning and high skill retention. Understanding a community's needs is essential for developing virtual communities of practice with good sociability and usability: the former focuses on social interaction, and the latter focuses on human-computer interaction. Developers and users have the responsibility to plan, guide, and mold communities to support the people in them. Like contemporary town planners and architects, we can profoundly shape the virtual CoP's landscape in support of knowledge work, paying particular attention to the issues of usability and sociability therewith to support the activities of knowledge sharing.

Re-Positioning the Purpose of ICT Systems

The move to virtualization has been developing rapidly over the last decade, and has attracted a lot of attention in the development of different ICT systems to support virtual communities. Yet, what makes managing knowledge work among CoPs online a challenge is that today many an organization has come to the realization that unless knowledge is owned by people to whom it matters,

it will not be developed, used, and kept up to date optimally. Knowledge is not a thing that can be managed at a distance like in an inventory. It is part of the shared practice of communities that need it, create it, use it, debate it, distribute it, adapt it, and transform it. As the property of a community, knowledge is not static; it involves interactions, conversations, actions, and inventions. Thereby, networking knowledge in a virtual community is not primarily a technological challenge, but one of community development. Addressing the kind of dynamic knowing that makes a difference in practice requires the participation of people who are fully engaged in the process of creating, refining, communicating, and using knowledge. The thrust to develop, organize, and communicate knowledge must come from those who will use it. What matters is not how much knowledge can be captured, but how documenting can support people's abilities to know and to learn when the community itself becomes the living repository of people's knowledge. ICT systems work best when they are used to connect communities, not just to capture or transfer knowledge (Allen, 1993). Because much knowledge is embedded in particular communities or context, developing a shared understanding and a degree of trust is often the most critical step towards knowledge sharing. ICT systems can complement but not replace the importance of social networks in this aspect (Ehn, 1989; DiSessa & Minstrell, 1998). Indeed, ICT systems can support the development of new communities through problem-solving interactions that allow individuals to appreciate the different perspectives which others bring to their work. Specifically, ICT systems can sustain the development of communities by allowing them to develop and exchange shared cultural objects of interest, such as texts, stories, and images, which help to reinforce the meaning and purpose of the communities (Bodker, 1991). From a community-building perspective (Bajjaly, 1999; Cohill & Kavanaugh, 1997), the design of ICT systems must be based on understanding such concerns as: communities must be viewed as supporting networks of personal relationships in which people can collaboratively construct understanding that enable the exchange of resources and the development of a common framework for analysis of these resources. CoPs often consider resources as a collection of ideas or interactions that are accessible to community members and can be incorporated into their practice. Besides, members of the community are expected to jointly analyze resources and develop a common set of criteria for evaluating those resources. It is important to consider how different strategies of ICT implementation can progressively involve individual members by helping them become resources for other community members.

CONCLUSION

Undoubtedly, organizations today need to coordinate in joint action – more precisely, collaborate – to achieve tasks larger than any single organization could accomplish alone. That is the motivation behind the knowledge network. Through the acculturation of appreciative processes in knowledge sharing, organizations are transformed as they interact, define new problems, and take on new challenges. The primary question for any learning organization is how we can learn from one another so as to increase our knowledge together. The answer lies in the recognition that an organization is a distributed system of knowledge, in which knowledge is embedded within particular contexts and communities (Tsoukas, 1996); hence, the cultivation of different knowledge-building communities of practice (CoPs) (Scardamalia & Bereiter, 1994), where individuals are committed to sharing information for the purpose of building understanding (knowledge) in all the participants, becomes an important concern.

Indeed, the development of virtual communities for knowledge networking is a complex, and multi-faceted endeavor. If our goal is to help solve the puzzle of how to nurture such communities, there are quite a number of issues to be examined according to Hoadley and Pea (2002, p. 345-351): defining learning communities, examining existing practice, identifying potential changes to improve practice, finding ways that technology might effect these changes, designing and building the technology, cultivating a community of use, understanding the consequences of the technology, and evaluating the community with respect to the original goal. The investigation of these issues constitutes an important context to understand the intricacies behind the building of virtual communities of practice for the purpose of knowledge building and learning.

In practice, each of the eight types of inquiry above draws on a different research paradigm, demonstrating the multi-disciplinary challenge of supporting such communities. We need to emphasize the holistic nature of these issues. Oftentimes, the issues of technology seem to have marginalized the other issues in the discussion of virtualizing communities of practice in support of knowledge sharing.

In closing our discussion, it is essential to articulate the promise of appreciative inquiry (AI) (Reed, 2007) for knowledge sharing (or knowledge networking) among virtual CoPs expected to be distributed around any of today's virtual enterprise. In the broadest sense, the major theme of knowledge networking in and among virtual communities could be understood from the perspective of effectively applying information and communications technologies (ICT) to improve the lives of people (organizational members) in different locales (organizations), in terms of getting knowledge to those of a community who need it in the right time. Of much concern here is an effort to theorize the social dimensions of ICT-based knowledge sharing. In the words of David Hakken (2002, p.362), we have to ask:

...what kinds of theorizations make sense in analyzing what happens when a concerted effort

is made to introduce a technology supportive of knowledge sharing in a 'holistic' way – that is, to try to anticipate and address the social context/consequences of the interventions."

In simpler terms, we can describe AI as an exciting philosophy for change. The major assumption of AI is that in every organization something works and change can be managed through the identification of what works, and the analysis of how to do more of what works. A key characteristic of AI is that it is a generative process. That means it is a moving target, and is created and constantly re-created by the people who use it. While the virtualization of a community is based upon technology, its success rests with its people – organizers, information and knowledge providers, sponsors, users, volunteers – who support the virtual community in a variety of ways. Therefore, when attempting to design technology in support of such learning communities, it is important to remember "what is working around here?" in the community (or organization). The tangible result of the inquiry process should be a series of vision statements that describe where the organization wants to be, based on the high moments of where they have been. Because the statements are grounded in real experience and history, it is convinced that people in the community (or organization) know how to repeat their success. In retrospect, think about a time when you shared something that you knew that enabled you or your company to do something better or achieve success. What happened? Share your story. Such activities include not only information capture and transmission, but also the establishment of social relationships in which people can collaboratively construct understanding. It is this energy that distinguishes AI's generative potential that presumably has no end because it is a living process.

REFERENCES

Allen, C. (1993). Reciprocal evolution as a strategy for integrating basic research, design, and studies of work practices. In D. Shuler and A. Namioka (Eds.), *Participatory design* (pp. 239-253). Hillsdate, NJ: Lawrence Erlbaum Assoicates.

Argyris, C. (1993). *Knowledge for action: A guide to overcoming barriers to organizational change.* San Francisco: Jossey-Bass.

Bajjaly, S. T. (1999). *The community networking handbook.* Chicago and London: American Library Association.

Bodker, S. (1991). *Through the interface: A human activity approach to user interface design.* Hillsdale, NJ: Lawrence Erlbaum.

Brown, J., & Duguid, P. (1991). Organizational learning and communities-of-practice: Towards a unified view of working, learning and innovation. *Organization Science, 2,* 40-57.

Browne, J., Sacket, P. J., & Wortmann, J. C. (1995). Future manufacturing systems – Towards the extended enterprise. *Computers in Industry, 25,* 235-254.

Bushe, G. R. (1995). Advances in appreciative inquiry as an organization development intervention. *Organization Development Journal, 13*(3), 14-22.

Byrne, J. A., Brandt, R., & Port, O. (1993). The virtual corporation. *BusinessWeek,* February 8, (pp. 36-41).

Camarinha-Matos, L. M., Afsarmanesh, H., Garita, C., & Lima, C. (1997). Towards an architecture for virtual enterprises. *Journal of Intelligent Manufacturing, 9*(2), 189-199.

Checkland, P. B., & Casar, A. (1986). Vicker's concept of an appreciative system: A systematic account. *Journal of Applied Systems Analysis, 3,* 3-17.

Checkland, P., & Holwell, S. (1998). *Information, systems and information systems: making sense of the field.* New York: John Wiley & Sons Ltd.

Cheng, W. (1996*). The virtual enterprise: Beyond time, place and form.* Economic Bulletin, Singapore International Chamber of Commerce, 5-7 February.

Cherny, L. (1999). *Conversation and community: Chat in a virtual world.* Stanford, CA: CSLI Publications.

Chin, A. (1998). Future visions. *Journal of Organization and Change Management.*

Cohill, A. M., & Kavanaugh, A. L. (1997). *Community networks: Lessons from Blacksberg, Virginia.* Norwood, MA: Artech House.

Cooperrider, D. (1986). *Appreciative inquiry: Toward a methodology fo understanding and enhancing organizational innovation.* Unpublished doctoral dissertation. Case Western Reserve University, Cleveland, Ohio.

Cooperrider, D. L., & Srivastva, S. (1987). Appreciative inquiry in organizational life. In W. Pasmore & R. Woodman (Eds.), *Research in organization change and development, 1,* 129-169. Greenwich, CT: JAI Press.

Cooperrider, D. L., & Whitney, D. (2005). *Appreciative inquiry: A positive revolution in change.* San Francisco: Berrett-Koehler.

Cortada, J. W., & Woods, J. A. (2000). *The knowledge management yearbook 2000-2001.* Butterworth-Heinemann.

Curran, M. (1991). Appreciative inquiry: A third wave approach to organization development. *Vision/Action*, December, (pp. 12-14).

Davidow, W. H., & Malone, M. S. (1992). *The virtual corporation–Structuring and revitalizing the corporation for the 21st century.* New York: HarperCollins.

Davis, B. H., & Brewer, J. (1997). *Electronic discourse: Linguistic individuals in virtual space.* Albany: State University of New York Press.

Dierkes, M., Marz, L., & Teele, C. (2001). Technological visions, technological development, and organizational learning. In M. Dierkes, A.B. Antal, et al. (Eds.), *Handbook of Organizational Learning and Knowledge* (pp. 282-304). Oxford University Press.

DiSessa, A. A., & Minstrell, J. (1998). Cultivating conceptual change with benchmark lessons. In J. G. Greeno & S. Goldman (Eds.), *Thinking practices* (pp.155-187). Mahwah, NJ: Lawrence Erlbaum.

Drucker, P. F. (1988). *The coming of the new organization* (pp. 53-65). Harvard Business Review, Summer.

Drucker, P. F. (1990). *The emerging theory of manufacturing.* Harvard Business Review (May/June), (pp. 94-102).

Ehin, C. (2000). *Unleashing intellectual capital.* Boston, MA: Butterworth-Heinemann.

Ehn, P. (1989). *Work-oriented design of computer artifacts.* Stockholm: Arbetslivscentrum.

Figallo, C., & Rhine, N. (2002). *Building the knowledge management network.* New York: John Wiley & Sons.

Frenkel, S., Korczynski, M., donoghue, L., & Shire, K. (1995). Re-constituting work: Trends towards knowledge work and info-normative control. *Work, Employment and Society, 9*(4), 773-796.

Garratt, B. (1987). *The learning organization: And the need for directors who think.* Aldershot, Hampshire, England: Ashgate.

Garvin, D. A. (1993). Building a learning organization. *Harvard Business Review, 71*(4), 78-91.

Gergen, K. J. (1990). Affect and organization in postmodern society. In S. Srivastva, D.L. Cooperrider, & Associates (Eds.), *Appreciative management and leadership: The power of positive thought and action in organizations* (1st ed., pp. 289-322). San Francisco: Jossey-Bass Inc.

Gibson, J. J. (1966). *The senses considered as perceptual systems*. Boston: Houghton Mifflin.

Goldman, S., Nagel, R., & Preiss, K. (1995). A*gile competitors and virtual organizations: Strategies for enriching the customer*. New York: van Nostrand Reinhold.

Hakken, D. (2002). Building our knowledge of virtual community: Some responses. In K. A. Renninger & W. Shumar (Eds), *Building virtual communities: Learning and change in Cyberspace* (pp. 355-367). Cambridge, UK: Cambridge University Press.

Harman, W. W. (1990). Shifting context for executive behavior: Signs of change and re-evaluation. In S. Srivastva, D. L. Cooperrider, & Associates (Eds.), *Appreciative management and leadership: The power of positive thought and action in organizations* (1st ed., pp. 37-54). San Francisco: Jossey-Bass Inc.

Harrington, J. (1991). *Organizational Structure and Information Technology*. Hertfordshire, U.K.: Prentice-Hall International.

Hedberg, B., Dahlgren, G., Hansson, J., & Olve, N. (1997). *Virtual organizations and beyond: Discover imaginary systems*. John Wiley & Sons Ltd.

Hemlin, S., Allwood, C. M., & Martin, B. R. (2004). *Creative Knowledge Environments: The influences on creativity in research and innovation*. Northampton, MA, USA: Edward Elgar.

Herring, S. (1996). Posting in a different voice: Gender and ethics in computer-mediated communication. In C. Ess (Ed.), *Philosophical approaches to computer-meidated communication* (pp. 115-145). Albany: SUNY Press.

Herzberg, F., Mausner, B., & Snyderman, B. B. (1959). *The motivation to work*. New York: John Wiley & Sons.

Hoadley, C., & Pea, R. D. (2002). Finding the ties that bind: Tools in support of a knowledge-building community. In K. A. Renninger & W. Shumar (Eds), *Building virtual communities: Learning and change in Cyberspace* (pp. 321-354). Cambridge, UK: Cambridge University Press.

Hoof, B. van den, Ridder, J. de & Aukema, E. (2004). *The eagerness to share: Knowledge sharing, ICT and social capital*. Working Paper, Amsterdam School of Communication Research, University of Amsterdam, The Netherlands.

Hubbard, B. M. (1998*). Conscious evolution: Awakening the power of our social potential*. Novato, CA: New World Library.

Jagers, H., Jansen, W., & Steenbakkers, W. (1998, April 27-28). Characteristics of virtual organizations. In P. Sieber and J. Griese (Eds.), *Organizational Virtualness*, Proceedings of the VoNet-Workshop, Simowa Verlag, Bern.

Kim, D. (1993). The link between individual and organizational learning. *Sloan Management Review*, (Fall), (pp. 37-50).

King, W. R. (1996). IS and the learning organization. *Information Systems Management, 13*(3): 78-80.

Land, F. (1985). Is an information theory enough? *The Computer Journal, 28*(3), 211-215.

Lazar, J., & Preece, J. (1998). *Classification schema for online communities*. Paper presented at the 1998 Association for Information Systems, Americas Conference.

Leonard-Barton, D. (1995). *Wellsprings of knowledge: Building and sustaining the sources of innovation*. Boston: Harvard Business School Press.

Levine, L. (2001). Integrating knowledge and processes in a learning organization. *Information Systems Management*, (Winter), (pp. 21-32).

Lewin, K. (1951/1997*). Field theory in social science*. Wahsington, DC: American Psychological Association.

Lewis, S., Passmore, J., & Cantore, S. (2008). *Appreciative inquiry for change management: Using AI to facilitate organizational development*. London: Kogan Page.

Linn, M. C. (2000). Designing the knowledge integration environment: The partnership inquiry process. *International Journal of Science Education*, *22* (8), 781-796.

Malhotra, Y. (2000). Knowledge management and new organization forms: A framework for business model innovation. In Y. Malhotra (Ed.), *Knowledge management and virtual organizations* (pp. 2-19). Hershey, PA: IGI Global Publishing.

McGregor, D. (1960). *The human side of enterprise*. New York: McGraw Hill.

Miles, R. E., & Snow, C. C. (1986). Organizations: New concepts for new forms. *California Management Review, 28*, 62-73.

Mollison, B. (1990) *Permaculture: A practical guide for a sustainable future*. Washington, DC: Island Press.

Mowshowitz, A. (1997). Virtual organization. *Comm. ACM, 40*(9), 30-37.

NIIIP. (1996). *The NIIIP reference architecture*. National Industrial Information Infrastructure Protocols. Retrieved from: http://www.niiip.org.

Nonaka, I. (1994). A dynamic theory of organizational knowledge creation. *Organization Science, 5* (1), 14-37.

Nonaka, I., & Takeuchi, H. (1995). *The Knowledge creating company: How Japanese companies create the dynamics of innovation*. Oxford University Press.

O'Leary, D. E. (1998). Enterprise knowledge management. *IEEE Computer, 31*(3), 54-61.

Ochsner, K. N., & Lieberman, M. D. (2001). The emergence of social cognitive neuroscience. *American Pyschologist, 56*(9), 717-734.

Orem, S. L., Binkert, J., & Clancy A. L. (2007). *Appreciative coaching: A positive process for change*. San Francisco: Jossey-Bass.

Preece, J. (2000). *Online communities: Designing usability, supporting sociability*. Chichester: John Wiley & Sons, Ltd.

Putnik, G. D., & Cunha, M. M. (Eds.) (2005). *Virtual enterprise integration: Technological and organizational perspectives*. Hershey, PA: IGI Global Publishing.

Quinn, J. B. (1990). *The intelligent enterprise*. New York: The Free Press.

Reed, J. (2007). *Appreciative inquiry: Research for change*. London: Sage Publications.

Renninger, K. A. (2000). Individual interest and its implications for understanding intrinsic motivation. In C. Sansone & J. M. Harackiewicz (Eds*.), Intrinsic and extrinsic motivation: The search for optimal motivation and performance* (pp. 373-404). New York: Academic.

Rheingold, H. (1994). *The virtual community*. Available at http://www.rheingold.com/vc/book/ [Last access on December 31, 2004].

Rogers, C. (1980/1995*). A way of being*. Boston: Houghton Mifflin.

Scardamalia, M., & Bereiter, C. (1994). Computer support for knowledge-building communities. *Journal of the Learning Sciences, 3*(3), 265-283.

Schuler, D. (1996). *New community networks: Wired for change*. Reading, MA: ACM Press and Addison-Wesley.

Senge, P. (1990*). The fifth discipline: The art and practice of the learning organization*. London: Currency Doubleday.

Stalk, Jr., G., Evans, E., & Shulman, L. E. (1992). *Competing on capabilities: The new rules of corporate strategy*. Harvard Business Review, March-April.

Stewart, T. A. (1997). *Intellectual capital: The new wealth of organizations*. New York: Doubleday.

Stopford, J. M. (2001). Organizational learning as guided responses to market signals. In M. Dierkes, A.B. Antal, et al. (Eds.), *Handbook of Organizational Learning and Knowledge* (pp. 264-281). Oxford University Press.

Thatchenkery, T. (2005). *Appreciative sharing of knowledge: Leveraging knowledge management for strategic change*. Chagrin Falls, OH: Taos Institute Publishing.

Thatchenkery, T., & Chowdhry, D. (2007). *Appreciative inquiry and knowledge management*. Northampton, MA: Edward Elgar.

The Complete Oxford English Dictionary. (1971). Oxford: Oxford University Press.

Tsoukas, H. (1996). The firm as a distributed knowledge system: A social constructionist approach. *Strategic Management Journal, 17*(Winter Special Issue), 11-25.

Venkatraman, N., & Henderson, J. C. (1998). Real strategies for virtual organizing. *Sloan Management Review, 40*(1), 33-48.

Vickers, G. (1972). Communication and appreciation. In Adams et al (Eds.), *Policymaking, Communication and Social Learning: Essays of Sir Geoffrey Vickers*. New Brunswick, NJ: Transaction Books.

Vickers, G. (1965). *The art of judgment*. New York: Basic Books.

Vickers, G. (1968). *Value systems and social process*. New York: Basic Books.

Watkins, J. M., & Cooperrider, D. L. (1996). Organization inquiry model for global social change organizations. *Organization Development Journal, 14*(4), 97-112.

Wenger, E. (1998). *Communities of practice: Learning, meaning, and identity*. Cambridge University Press.

Wenger, E., McDermott, R., & Snyder, W. M. (2002). *Cultivating communities of practice: A Guide to managing knowledge*. Harvard Business School Press.

White, T. W. (1996). Working in interesting times. *Vital Speeches of the Day, LXII*(15), 472-474.

Whitney, D., & Trosten-Bloom, A. (2003). *The power of appreciative inquiry: A practical guide to positive change*. San Francisco: Berrett-Koehler Publishers, Inc.

KEY TERMS

Appreciative Inquiry (AI): Appreciative Inquiry is about the co-evolutionary search for the best in people, their organizations, and the relevant world around them. In its broadest focus, it involves systematic discovery of what gives "life" to a living system when it is most alive, most effective, and most constructively capable in economic, ecological, and human terms.

Appreciative Knowledge Environment (AKE): A work, research or learning environment to incorporate the philosophy of appreciative inquiry in support of a cultural practice of knowledge sharing among organizational members.

Appreciative Processes: These are processes to leverage the collective individual learning of an organization such as a group of people, to produce a higher-level organization-wide intellectual asset. This is supposed to be a continuous process of creating, acquiring, and transferring knowledge accompanied by a possible modification of behavior to reflect new knowledge and insight, and to produce a higher-level intellectual content.

Appreciative Settings: A body of linked connotations of personal or collective interest, discrimination and valuation which we bring to the exercise of judgment and which tacitly determine what we shall notice, how we shall discriminate situations of concern from the general confusion of ongoing event, and how we shall regard them.

Appreciative Sharing of Knowledge (ASK): An organizational approach to enable knowledge work or sharing that is based on the tenets of Appreciative Inquiry.

Community of Practice (CoP): These are people who come together around common interests and expertise. They create, share, and apply knowledge within and across the boundaries of teams, business units, and even entire organizations – providing a concrete path toward creating a true knowledge organization.

Virtual Organizing: A method to operationlize the context of appreciative inquiry, with the technology-enabled capability to assemble and disassemble nodes on a network of people or groups of people in an organization, to meet the demands of a particular business context. In virtual organizing, virtuality is a strategic characteristic applicable to every organization.

Chapter V
The Role of Participatory Design in Constructing the Virtual Knowledge Commons

Natalie Pang
Monash University, Australia

ABSTRACT

The main goal of this chapter is to demonstrate how purposeful participatory design can be used to construct a virtual knowledge commons that both serves and is defined by communities. Other than the proposition that participatory design is a technique to guide participation within a community, the chapter also explores how this technique can be used to nurture and sustain a shared knowledge commons in the virtual environment. To this end, the conditions and consequences of the virtual environment are discussed, illustrating how with participation, the virtual commons is possibly sustainable. The chapter also raises the role of cultural institutions and examines a number of contemporary examples, resulting in a preliminary spectrum of participation by which practices of participation in the virtual knowledge commons by cultural institutions can be mapped. More research and fieldwork needs to be done to refine this model and generate exemplary practices for policy development and best practices in cultural institutions.

INTRODUCTION

Historically, the commons refer to resources that are made freely available for all in society to build relationships and cultural democracy. The origins of the commons are most usually traced back to the 18th century, when shared pieces and plots of land were held and governed in common by communities of farmers. The sharing of land in common were popular (Fox, 1981), until a series of policies from the governments converted these lands into commercial or private properties and warranted payments from farmers to use these lands (Williamson, 1987). Such privatisation and market appropriations became known as enclosures.

Almost as intriguing as the issue of enclosures to the availability of the commons is the proposition of the commons being a tragedy (Hardin, 1968). A debate made popular by Hardin (1968), the idea of the commons being a disaster was deliberated based on assumptions that individuals will seek first their self-interests, that a pool of resources shared and used in common will result in overuse, and the problem of free-riding will also lead to unfair distributions of resources.

There are key factors which are relevant to sustainability issues of knowledge resources in the virtual environment. Unlike the case of the historical commons which was argued by Hardin (1968) to be a 'tragedy', conditions in the virtual environment has resulted in key structural changes. As a consequence, people are now able to participate easily in the creation and distribution of resources, and increase in such participation may not necessarily lead to overuse. Such participation can exist in various forms. As a concluding discussion, the paper aims to identify a spectrum by which different forms of participation can be utilized by cultural institutions in the virtual knowledge commons. This is done through raising contemporary examples from cultural institutions.

BACKGROUND

Understanding the historical origins of the commons is instrumental to elucidate concepts relating to the virtual knowledge commons. The knowledge commons in today's context refer to the availability of knowledge resources to be shared by communities of people, either free or at nominal charges. The knowledge commons therefore exists in physical forms (such as library or museum collections) or virtually.

Before defining what is meant by the virtual knowledge commons, it is necessary to justify the importance of the topic. There is a certain critical threshold that has been brought about by changes in the virtual environment. By the 'virtual environment' here the chapter is referring to the advent of personal computing and communication technologies, with knowledge resources in the forms of text, video, audio, and images being widely created and distributed amongst people via the World Wide Web. Social networking sites, commonly associated with Web 2.0 have also increased the intensity and velocity of such transactions of knowledge resources between people. These resources are impossible to access without the Internet, which is made up of computing devices, mobile devices such as mobile phones, handheld computers, personal digital assistants, and cables that connect these devices to one another.

Resources and the Issue of Scarcity

The tragedy of the commons as proposed by Hardin (1968) argued for the issue of resource destruction due to self-interests' seeking and free-riding individuals. Because of these individuals, resources in a commons generally deplete in quantity and quality over time. This is most commonly seen in environmental issues such as global warming, climate changes, and the depletion of the ozone layer. These assumptions, however, are challenged in the context of knowledge resources in the virtual environment.

With faster computing, development of media technologies and infrastructure, copies of knowledge resources can be duplicated and distributed relatively easily. Unlike physical resources, the appropriation of a resource in the virtual environment does not significantly reduce the availability of the same resource for others. In other words, the prevalence of digital copies radically negates the issue of resource scarcity. In addition, recent evidence has also shown how the quality of resources in the virtual environment has changed in relation to its use. Wikipedia is an online encyclopaedia on the Internet that allows anyone to edit its pages. When it began, sceptics were doubtful of its ability to provide quality resources on its pages. Wilkinson and Huberman (2007), however, showed evidence that the number of edits in a Wikipedia page correlated positively to the perceived quality of knowledge contained in the page. Such findings highlight that the increase of participation as witnessed in the creation and shaping of knowledge resources point out significant opportunities for the sustainability of the knowledge commons in the virtual environment.

Changes in Human Interactions

Another key factor contributing to the sustainability of the knowledge commons lies with the collective processes transforming the interactions between people. Resources in the knowledge commons are shared—not just in their use or distribution, but potentially in their creation. A page in Wikipedia is created and edited by different people. A video may have other related video responses and distributed by people in different ways, which adds to the culminated versions of an original video. A collection of rare books in a library may be put together by an institution; but the signification of the collection requires a community of people who collectively construct the meanings behind the collection.

Because of such actions which ultimately involve at least one other person at some point, when one examines human actions involved in the knowledge commons he is also addressing how people participate in the creation of value of a resource. In other words, the creation, use, and distribution of resources, even though they may be intangibles, require the collective participation and action of communities.

Traditional collective action theory as originally conceptualised by Olson (1965) states a number of conditions for collective action. Specifically, for collective action to occur, Olson (1965) argued that there must be a conscious pursuit of common goals, communicated to every person in the group. This supports Olson (1965)'s argument that small groups are better than large groups for successful collective action. The argument however, can be contested with contemporary evidence. Bimber, Flanagin and Stohl (2005) have done significant work towards arguing for the reconceptualisation of collective action theory based on evidence from the contemporary media environment.

Indymedia, a large network of citizen journalists and writers makes use of a vast network of people widely distributed across the globe to contribute to alternative press coverage of important events happening around the world. Heavy use of communication technologies can be found in Indymedia, while its success challenges Olson (1965)'s collective action theory that small groups are better. Other examples, such as the sharing of bookmarks via applications like Del.ici.ous, facilitate contributions to a shared goal of making meanings and knowledge around bookmarks on the Internet (Bimber, Flanagin, and Stohl, 2005). Users who tag their bookmarks may often be unconscious that they are contributing important knowledge about the bookmarks. Such actions confront the notion that collective action needs to be a conscious pursuit of shared goals.

Bimber, Flanagin, and Stohl (2005) suggest that collective action theory should therefore be re-examined, while maintaining that this does not mean that the theory is irrelevant. Instead, it should be recognised that new forms of collective action has emerged especially in the virtual environment, and collective action theory needs to take such actions into account. There are also significant implications for the knowledge commons. With a large network of people who may also be unconsciously contributing to the quality and quantity of resources in the knowledge commons, there are both opportunities and threats. On one hand there is potentially a rich amount of resources to be found, but conversely it may also not be clear that these resources belong to the commons to be shared openly. This scenario is often clear, with resources that have been openly shared but privately appropriated through actions such as plagiarisms.

THE VIRTUAL KNOWLEDGE COMMONS

Knowledge resources, as discussed earlier, exist in physical and virtual forms. Resources in the context of the virtual knowledge commons refer to digital forms of resources – text or other rich media objects such as images and videos. These resources exist on computers and handheld devices and are distributed through the Internet. In other words, they are created, used, and distributed by large networks of people in the virtual environment. This discussion attempts to discuss the criteria that can be used to identify resources in the virtual knowledge commons.

Linguistic Meanings

Closely associated with the notion of the knowledge commons is the term 'public domain', which is defined by Macquarie Dictionary as:

1. the status of a writing in which no copyright subsists2. the status of an invention which has not been patented or where the patent has expired.

Although it is recognised that there are overlaps between resources in the public and commons domains, a distinction is asserted here that the knowledge commons belongs to a domain that is not state-owned. This was also differentiated by the ancient Romans, in their definitions of *res communes*: 'rights to be included in benefits streams as a member of a well-defined group' (Runge and Defrancesco, 2006, p. 1714) and *res*

publicae: referring to the state, or the commonwealth (Haakonssen, 1995).

Macquarie Dictionary asserted that the use of the word 'commons' in the context of knowledge resources in current times is in the context of the Internet, 'where material is freely available'. In other words, the term knowledge commons always implies the inclusion of resources residing in the virtual environment. As it will be discussed later, this, however, is not without challenges.

Distinction from the Market

Benkler (2003, p 6) refers to the commons as 'institutional spaces where human agents can act free of the particular constraints required for markets'. Benkler identified property rights as the 'most important constraints under-girding markets'. Bollier (2003, p. 10) discussed the commons in relation to the market as follows:

The commons' is a useful term for contemporary political discourse because it provides a new lexicon for re-situating market activity in a social and political context. It helps us identify resources that should not be alienated for market use, but should remain non-propertized and 'owned' (in a civic or democratic sense) by everyone. Our culture has no serious vocabulary for contextualising 'the free market' in a social framework; it assumes that it is a universal, a historical force of nature. The commons helps rectify this conceptual problem by offering a rich, countervailing template to the market paradigm, one that can speak about the economic and legal aspects of a commons as intelligibly as its social and personal aspects.

The commons is largely, but not entirely, distinct from the market. Many knowledge objects in the commons such as folktales or sites on the Internet are created initially as non-proprietary knowledge, for free sharing by all. Subsequently, however, they may become – at least in part – proprietary resources when they are used as the basis for product development. Conversely, other items in the commons may have been initially created as proprietary knowledge, but become part of the commons when they pass out of personal or corporate ownership. Examples are copyrighted works or patented inventions that enter the commons after statutory periods of intellectual property protection have elapsed.

Clearly the status of a knowledge resource in terms of ownership and the market is an important consideration in characterising a commons, but it seems too simplistic to define the commons just in terms of market and non-market status, even though it is only within the scope of the virtual environment.

Access and Use

Access and use are also a potent ways of explicating the knowledge commons. The common law of England came about because at various stages rulers attempted to systematise the law by finding out what everyone believed they and others were entitled to and why. Thus a field might be owned by a landlord, but by custom and usage the public had right of way to cross that land.

Some of the greatest cultural institutions and collections of today started out as private property. The Bibliotheque de France began as the monarch's personal library. The Guggenheim and numerous other museums in both the old and new worlds began as private collections which over time became accessible to all. Resources that were previously held as private collections, once they are made accessible in the virtual environment, they become part of the landscape of the knowledge commons.

Benkler's Design Typology of the Knowledge Commons

Benkler (2003) argued that commons can be divided into four types based on two parameters. The first parameter identified by Benkler (2003,

p 6) 'is whether they are open to anyone or only to a defined group'. Thus:

- **Commons type 1:** If a commons is open to anyone, Benkler calls it an open commons. Examples are the ocean, air, water, and highway systems.
- **Commons type 2:** If a commons is open only to a defined group he calls it a limited access commons. An example is a private golf course.

Benkler's second parameter Benkler (2003, p 7) is 'whether a commons system is regulated or unregulated'. Thus:

- **Commons type 3:** A commons without rules is an unregulated commons. Example: unexplored outer space.
- **Commons type 4:** A commons ordered by rules is a regulated commons. Examples: Wikipedia or a library.

Using this typology, commons type 1 or 2 must be paired with types 3 or 4 in order to describe the design of a particular knowledge commons. An example of how Benkler's typology can be used to characterise a case of the knowledge commons is the Cooperation Commons (http://www.cooperationcommons.com/) founded by Howard Rheingold (Rheingold, 2002). This initiative belongs to Types 2 and 4, in that it is a limited access commons governed by rules. In the Cooperation Commons resources are shared by all who care to visit the site, yet in order to contribute to this commons one must be a member. Many research groups take on this form as well, where there is a limited membership but unlimited access to the resources created within the community. As the Cooperation Commons site stated:

You do not need a login to view the documents, the blog, or any section of this site. You do need a login to add an entry to the summary documents or to blog. If you are interested in summarizing or blogging, or in being a member of our Google Group discussion, contact ...

The Community is Essential in the Virtual Commons

De Angelis (2006) stated that 'there is no commons without community within which the modalities of access to common resources are negotiated'. In other words, the knowledge commons cannot exist without the community – as it is inevitably bounded by the very community that produces and uses it, even in the most open commons.

The participation of individuals and communities is therefore instrumental in shaping common resources, and the potential scope for such participation is in turn shaped by these resources. This process is an example of what the social theorist Anthony Giddens called 'structuration' (from the French for 'structuring') and is demonstrated in the development of both the physical and knowledge commons. Structuration theory is therefore used as a key perspective to address the topic of participatory design in the virtual knowledge commons.

Spaces in the commons facilitate certain activities, and these activities in turn influence how spaces are developed in the future. Likewise technologies enable certain capabilities, and those capabilities play a part in the shaping of future technologies. The notion of participatory design in the commons can thus be viewed as an interplay of the modalities in structuration theory. Cultural patterns and trends are (re)interpreted and expressed in the (re)allocation of resources, which in turn (re)establish the normative patterns that become the framework and target of the next (re)design initiative. This community process continuously both establishes and changes the social culture – the 'rules' about what can be done and how it can be done at any point in time or space.

STRUCTURATION THEORY AS A KEY PERSPECTIVE

The point being made here is that there is inseparability between concepts of commons and community, which goes beyond their linked etymology. No object or resource is intrinsically a commons. Even air, sea or outer space can be 'enclosed' or converted into private property.

The Ubiquity of Rules

The commons is ultimately and fundamentally a knowledge phenomenon: a commons exists either because a community believes it exists, and there are rules – however broad – that govern its existence. Lose this community of knowledge or belief and you lose the commons. Create or strengthen such a community and you can create, develop or defend a commons.

On this note, Levine (2002) argued that there is no such thing as a rule-free commons. He identified as a key shortcoming in Hardin's (1968) account of the 'tragedy' that Hardin assumed a commons that was uncontrollable and unorganized, open to abuse by any greedy individual or group.

Authorisation and Allocation in the Commons

It is proposed that there are two types of knowledge commons. A common exists because 'common knowledge' of a community recognises its existence, and some level of rules – however informal and fragmentary – is implied by this recognition. The rules may be as minimal as an understanding of what falls within or outside the physical or virtual boundary of the commons.

Giddens calls such rules 'resources', and sees a distinction between 'authoritative' and 'allocative' resources (Giddens, 1984). The first type of the knowledge commons maps on to Gidden's concept of an authoritative resource. An authoritative resource consists in the community consensus that a particular social patterning (otherwise called a social institution) can and should exist – in other words the basic or enabling rule(s). Giddens' 'allocative' resources map on to the second type of knowledge commons. An allocative resource consists in the rules that social institutions follow in order to share finite goods among people. It should be noted that in bringing up the term 'resources' it is the second type – 'allocative' resources that is discussed. This refers to the content of the commons rather than the rules governing the commons, but Giddens' special use of the term as rules has great explanatory power and is important to be introduced.

All types of virtual communities create and use the knowledge commons to some degree; although the form of such resources might differ. For example, a business community might create understandings of how hierarchical relationships work in an organisation, terms of references, and so on (authoritative resources) – even though they may not share the actual content (allocative resources) produced from such shared understandings. On the other hand, some communities such as those based on similar interests share both authoritative and allocative resources of the knowledge commons.

Structuration Theory and Participatory Design

Elucidating the fundamental principle of structuration theory contributes to understanding the recursive relationship between actions and social structures. In structuration theory, social structures constraint or empower the actions of human agents – and at the same time, are shaped by actions. In other words, the relationship between action and structure is a fundamental component of social theory (Giddens, 1979). Therefore, no study of communities can exist without the study of action - a part of production and reproduc-

tion in communities which ultimately make up culture. Action is therefore an inevitable part of communities and upheld in structure, and at the same time are reflections of the very same binding structures.

Participatory design functions primarily as an approach to design actions from stakeholders. Borrowing insights from structuration theory, the study of participatory design therefore involve the study of actions and how they may shape the social structures that constrains or empower them.

The application of participatory design in various contexts has been widely covered in the literature of human computer interaction (HCI) and information systems. One of the key principles advocated in participatory design is that it involves the collective participation of all stakeholders (Schuler and Namioka, 1993) and aims to include stakeholders in institutional activities, working with, rather than for 'end users'.

In HCI literature, participatory design goes beyond designing around the interface – viewing stakeholders as participants and shifting responsibilities, such as prototyping, to the users instead of only the designers (Gulliksen et al, 2003). The developments in PD have much to thank the Scandinavian efforts in their advocacy for extensive user involvement in design (Gulliksen et al., 2003). Schuler and Namioka (1993) also noted that the motivation in the majority of the early PD projects in Scandinavia was an agenda of empowering workers when technologies were introduced in the workplace. This empowerment and transposition of power and responsibilities is a significant aspect of the design process that is central to a community.

These principles are investigated for their enactment in virtual knowledge commons. Designing participation in this context would therefore imply designing stakeholder involvement in creating, sharing and using resources in the knowledge commons. Such participation has been made easier and more diverse with contemporary technologies.

PARTICIPATORY DESIGN

Participatory design is seen as central to the realisation of the knowledge commons because it is based upon the active participation of communities involved in collective action.

The relevance of participatory design is largely thanks to digital technologies in the current environment that actively seeks to foster social networks and collaborative innovation between people. As such, the potential for participation through continuous design can be much more inclusive. Perhaps as importantly, categories of knowledge not held by experts – 'grass roots' knowledge, in Giddens' terms tacit or practical rather than discursive (Giddens 1984, p.5, 22) – can be brought strongly into play. The challenge in design is to have an encompassing approach where both techno-centric and user-centric approaches are included; and where all contexts or realities as perceived by actors can be accommodated: in Giddens' formulation trustworthy ontologies (1984, p. 375) or in Bell's formulation the realities of the social world, the natural world, and the technical world (Bell 1996). Moreover the approach must harness the potentialities of more rapid and intensive cycles of reflexivity (Giddens 1984, p.5) resulting from the engagement of more actors and their viewpoints, while guarding against the potentially disruptive effects of heightened reflexivity on society (the kind of danger that autocratic regimes typically warn against when a transition to democracy is proposed).

Heightened consciousness and sensibility of all three of Bell's inter-connected realities are necessary for sustainability of communities and society. Recalling the interplay of action and structure mediated by reflexivity that is the essence of structuration it becomes clear that the theory presents an appropriate framework to account for not only the intentional outcomes but also the unintended consequences and non-explicit conditions of participative design (Giddens 1984, p5).

Bell (1996) proposes that the change of perspective from objective to subjective—from all things as objects to all things as 'a web of consciousness' (p.149)—is a fundamental shift in social awareness and sensibility.

Addressing design through the lens of structuration theory highlights the recursive nature of design – the impacts of technology on people are perhaps as significant as the impacts of people on technology. Kuhn and Muller (1993) argued for participatory design as an effective strategy to avoid the devaluation of human work with the introduction of technologies, and the harnessing of workplace democracy to improve design.

In relation to shared knowledge resources, design becomes a key attribute in the production and use of resources in the knowledge commons by communities, which are sometimes facilitated by institutions in the virtual environment. Its emergence within the realm of institutions is observable particularly where 'new media' and community memory are being brought into creative conjunction. These institutions may be cultural institutions such as libraries, museums, and national archives; political institutions such as governments and statutory boards, and so on. For the purpose of this discussion, the focus is on cultural institutions.

To illustrate these points, two contemporary examples are brought up, focused on how participatory design is implemented as an action within communities, its structural conditions and consequences, and how various forms of virtual knowledge commons are created and/or sustained. The resultant interplay of design is reflected as a continuous dialogue between communities and the knowledge commons – which not only leads to a more dynamic shaping of the virtual commons, but an insight to the rapid generation and regeneration of community cultures in the virtual environment.

StoryCorps and Hurricane Katrina

In August 2005, one of the costliest and strongest hurricanes ever recorded in history struck the northern-central coast of the United States, with Louisiana and Mississippi being the worst-hit states. The disaster left many detrimental effects: economical, environmental, political, and often-forgotten, social and psychological damages. A survey done soon after the disaster found alarming figures amongst survivors: the percentage of serious mental illnesses had doubled, the percentage of people diagnosed with mild to moderate mental illness had increased by 10%, and records of stress, depression, and nightmares increased (Karkosi, 2006).

StoryCorps, a national oral history project purposed to help 'instruct and inspire Americans to record one another's stories in sound' (Library of Congress, 2003), is a joint effort of the Library of Congress and a non-profit company, Sound Portraits Productions. In response to Hurricane Katrina, StoryCorps has facilitated the creation of numerous stories shared by survivors, rescuers, and other Americans which contributed to the level of support and cohesion in the aftermaths of the disaster. Using vehicles equipped with video and audio facilities, StoryCorps travelled to key places and allowed anyone with a story to record their recollections and the meanings they have made of the disaster. For example, accounts of how separated family members found each other, stories from rescue workers, volunteers, and doctors all contributed to the collection.

Instead of relying on reported stories from mainstream media journalists, the project had enabled the collection of resources directly from the communities affected by the disaster. Such stories are preserved as archives in the American Folklife Centre at the Library of Congress, contributing to the overall richness of its collections. At the same time, these stories are also freely available online, augmenting themselves as a virtual knowledge commons.

StoryCorps' approach to elicit participation from the American communities, especially those who were the most affected by the disaster made heavy use of communication technologies and the Internet. By going to where these communities were, they were also instrumental in getting people participate together in the recording of stories; fostering social bonds between people in the process. This was attested to by Karkosi (2006), who reported a decrease in suicidal tendencies amongst survivors mainly due to increased feelings of bonding and belonging to families, communities, and churches. In addition, the action also brought together a rich collection of oral stories that were representative of the experiences shared by residents and rescue workers who survived the disaster. The capture of these memories, in a recursive sense, is important in shaping the culture of the communities who share these stories.

Museum Victoria (MV) and the Women on Farms Gathering (WoFG) Collection

The Women on Farms Gathering (WoFG) is a forum that brought together a community of women from rural backgrounds (women who are farmers or connected in other ways with farming), for the purpose of building better understandings of their own lives and experiences, and convey these understandings to the wider (mostly urbanised) Australian population.

In 1990, the very first gathering of WoFG in Warragul saw participants bring together memorable objects reflective of their identities as rural women living and working on farms in Victoria. Intricately associated with these objects were stories that highlighted meanings and contexts shared by the community of rural women. Thereafter, the forum became an annual event through which the women could make meaningful sense of their collective identity. The event was referred to fondly by members of the community as 'The Gathering'.

Yet the conception of items collected as a heritage and significant collection was not realised until the gathering in 2001, when, items from past gatherings were brought together to contribute to a series of history boards displayed at the Beechworth Gathering in 2001. There were also other issues relating to the resources (objects and stories accumulated over the years), such as potential damages to the resources, given that they were dispersed and stored under different conditions in a number of private residences. Some items and information about stories and objects in the collection had already been lost, with little hope of recovering them. What was also obvious to many in the community was the inconsistent level of responsibility and care for the collection, and divergent interpretations on the meaning of adequate responsibility and care. As a result, a group of representatives collectively called the 'Heritage Group' were appointed from within the community with the task of approaching Museum Victoria (MV) for advice on protecting and sustaining the collection.

In 2003, representatives of the Women on Farms Gathering Heritage Group and Museum Victoria signed an agreement to work together in making visible a story that has long been ignored: the vital and creative role of Victorian women in sustaining their rural industries and communities. Over 260 participants signed a three-metre long scroll as witnesses to this special occasion. With the involvement of the Museum, and growing awareness of the group in realising the significance of the collection, the collection now includes a number of symbolic objects and stories such as: two large banners, videos, photographs, oral histories, memorial plaque, and a range of memorabilia (t-shirts, mugs, bags), uniforms and symbolic icons such as a cow pat and irrigation shovel, magic wand, cheque, Mallee stone, Mallee root, peaked cap, computer motherboard, a jar of Mallee soil and seeds, farm work boot,

horseshoe, spring, ceramic hands and an open lock and key.

One of the ways by which participation was engaged from the community was through the construction of a digital version of the WoFG collection. By this action, the facilitation of dialogue was amplified and made apparent in the community – as women in the community other than those already in the Heritage Group were able to contribute to the collection and communicate with others and the museum even more. At the same time, the community and MV were also able to add a substantial number of stories and meanings to the collection. Images of physical artefacts were also taken and included in the online collection, making up a significant portion of the resources that are shared both within the community and others outside the community.

The development of the digital collection was also aligned with a participatory style. Tasks and needs of the community were discussed iteratively over the period of the case study alongside members of the community and curators, using prototypes (whenever possible) to stimulate such discussions and thoughts. Feedback was solicited at laboratory sessions, focus groups, and via email. Over the course of the case study, functional requirements and feedback for design iterations were also gathered by the researcher through reflective laboratory sessions with the community and the museum.

It may very well be that the same requirements and outcomes could have been generated by other approaches, but the process was seen as empowering, rather than not. This was demonstrated by the Heritage Group who were initially apprehensive about the community taking ownership of managing the digital resources and learning the administrative functionalities of the portal for themselves.

Having the digital collection deeply grounded in the cultural context of the community and the museum ensured a sense of continuing engagement and control, rather than a 'hand-over' or alienation of significant objects and the accompanying heritage to 'experts'. By the end of the case study, the digital collection has become integrated into the annual gatherings of the community, acting as a mobile exhibition for the gatherings and becoming part of the total communicative interactions that are instrumental in constructing and reconstructing the identity of the community.

Although the participatory approach adopted in the design and development of the portal required a significant amount of time and iterations, its impacts were felt deeply. For example, the website housing the digital collection empowered the community to contribute and reflect on the meanings of resources in the collection and overcome barriers that previously prevented some women in the community to participate. New experiences are created for these women. The increase in community involvement can be attested to in the way meanings are constructed around resources, and the increased participation over time. Not only did such outcomes contribute to the richness of each resource in the collection (i.e. the knowledge commons for the WoFG community), they were also instrumental in strengthening the identity and culture of practices emergent in the community.

A SPECTRUM OF PARTICIPATORY DESIGN

There is an increasing amount of research being conducted on how cultural institutions are engaging the participation of their communities in the virtual knowledge commons (Middleton and Lee, 2007). Middleton and Lee's work documented current practices showing such illustrations of participation. The 'Steve' project in America, for example, draws together American art museums to take 'a folksonomic approach to their online collections. They allow patrons to supplement the specialized terminology of the museum professionals (curators and registrars) in order to represent the general public viewpoint (Middleton and Lee, 2007, p. 8). The State Library of Victoria in Australia has also launched a website titled 'Inside a dog' for young people, enabling them to 'read and write reviews, meet the library's online author-in-residence, listen to podcasts and talk about books on the forum (Middleton and Lee, 2007, p. 15).

Based on such work and the earlier examples discussed, a spectrum of participatory design is proposed in Figure 1.

At the left end of the spectrum, cultural institutions (designers) can be seen participating in the world(s) of their communities (users) through outreach activities, for example mobile libraries bringing services to their local communities. On this end of the spectrum, it should also be recognised that there are significant activities which may not include a cultural institution. This has important considerations for resource properties and collective processes emergent in those communities. Indymedia for example, has often been faced with challenges arising from issues of control, and governance as a community network of citizen journalists without formal institutional participation. It should not be misunderstood that this implies a lack of structure – as discussed

Figure 1. Spectrum of participation by design

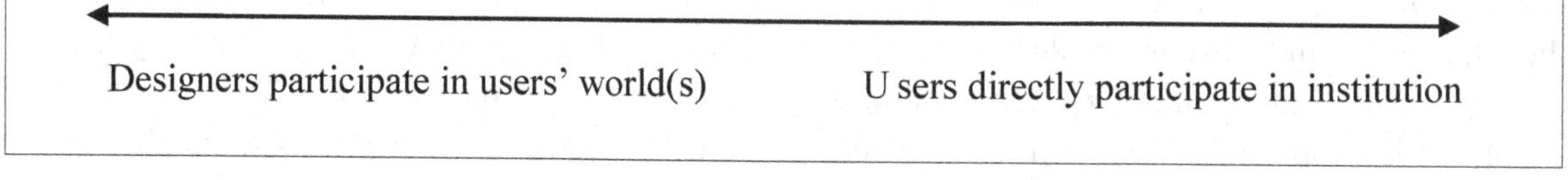

Designers participate in users' world(s)   U sers directly participate in institution

earlier, all actions are also seen to give birth to structures, and there is an intimate interplay between the two. This is especially significant for the virtual knowledge commons, given the ease of self-publishing and participatory technologies prevalent in the media environment.

On the other end of the spectrum, local communities often participate in the design of the activities of cultural institutions, for example, the involvement of communities in bringing together a collection in the case of StoryCorps. Quite often, libraries elicit participation from the communities they serve in the form of periodical feedback, surveys and interviews; and the dialogue generated is significant in the planning and design of services and resources for the coming years. Hybrids or mixtures of the two forms of participation can be placed along the spectrum, recognising the extent to which there has been user or designer inputs.

It should also be noted that participation can occur in different, hybrid forms, for example both by engaging communities in design activities and at the same time immersing themselves in the world(s) of communities through collaborative partnerships.

Perhaps one of the greatest implications of the virtual environment for participatory design is the erosion of the physical spaces where participation takes place. Giddens (1990) reinforced this view when addressing modernity. In pre-modern societies, space was the area in which one moved, and time was the experience one had while moving. In modern societies, however, space is no longer confined by the boundaries in which one moves. Virtual space and time allows the imagination of space, even if one has never been there. This is manifested keenly by the virtual environment, where virtual spaces are prevalent through wireless and wired technologies, and devices link people and the spaces in which they interact.

A significant point here is the recognition that different forms of the knowledge commons exists, especially in the virtual environment. Future

work investigating these different forms and their relationships needs to be done. Further fieldwork documenting best practices from cultural institutions in the ways they engage participation from their communities are also needed, to refine the model and for the enhancement of policy guidelines.

FUTURE TRENDS

Although resources in the virtual environment such as information pages on the World Wide Web has often been said to be a commons, it is also important to draw lessons from the historical origins of the commons in the 19th century. Even though in the case of the knowledge commons which is largely intangible in its form, there are threats from potential enclosures that could challenge the sustainability and accessibility of the knowledge commons. As pointed out in the earlier discussion, there are various forms of the knowledge commons in relation to the level of institutional involvement – and this insight is also important to consider in thinking about potential enclosures or private appropriations of the knowledge commons. One example is the appropriation of resources whose copyrights have already expired and turning these resources into commercial products. Cultural institutions and governments needs to re-examine their roles in the virtual environment, and more work needs to be done in drawing the implications for these institutions, especially with regards to the sustainability and accessibility of the knowledge commons.

Another immediate implication of such trends is the legal and political frameworks governing the use and distribution of such resources. Current copyright frameworks are currently contested for their applicability to resources in the virtual environment; and open content licenses such as the Creative Commons are suggested to be more suitable for the knowledge commons. Undoubtedly there will be more developments in this arena as both developed and developing countries explore the relevance of alternative licensing frameworks for the governance of information resources on the World Wide Web.

On this note, another trend is foreseen; which involves an increase of dialogue between developed and developing nations. As they explore new ways of governing resources in the virtual environment with one another they begin to identify common grounds and share knowledge with one another. Again, such shared knowledge contributes substantially to the first type of the knowledge resources ('authoritative' resources) and provides the grounds for further 'allocative' resources to be created and shared. The process of participating in such sharing of knowledge also provides a bridge to narrow the digital divide between developing and developed countries.

CONCLUSION

The chapter has discussed the relevance of participatory design in the virtual environment, and in enhancing the sustainability of the virtual knowledge commons. In this context, perspectives from structuration theory are essential as important insights to the concept of rules and resources in the virtual knowledge commons. Based on the discussions of two cases of cultural institutions utilising participatory design to construct and enhance virtual knowledge commons with their communities, a spectrum of participatory design is proposed. Not all knowledge commons resources see the involvement of institutions and it is proposed that this spectrum is useful to help study the relationships between communities and their cultural or public institutions.

REFERENCES

Anderson, B. (1991). *Imagined communities* (Second ed.). New York: Verso.

Bell, D. (1996). *The cultural contradictions of capitalism.* New York: Harper Collins Publishers.

Benkler, Y. (2003). The political economy of commons. *UPGRADE: European Journal for the Informatics Professional, 4*(3), 6-9.

Bimber, B., Flanagin, A. J., & Stohl, C. (2005). Reconceptualizing collective action in the contemporary media environment. *Communication Theory, 15*(4), 365-388.

Bollier, D. (2003). The rediscovery of the Commons. *Upgrade, 4*(3), 10-12.

De Angelis, M. (2006). *On the "tragedy of the commons" (that is, the tragedy of commons without communities).* Retrieved 4 December, 2006, from http://www.commoner.org.uk/blog/?p=79

Division of Health Promotion, World Health Organisation. (1998). Health promotion glossary [Data file]. Available from World Health Organisation Web site, http://www.who.int/hpr/NPH/docs/hp_glossary_en.pdf

Fox, H. S. A. (1981). Approaches to the adoption of the midland system. In T. Rowley (Ed.), *The origins of open field agriculture.* London: Croom Helm.

Giddens, A. (1979). Central problems in social theory: Action, structure and contradiction in social analysis. Berkeley: University of California Press.

Giddens, A. (1984). *The constitution of society: outline of the theory of structuration.* Berkeley: University of California Press.

Giddens, A. (1990). *The consequences of modernity*. Stanford, Calif.: Stanford University Press.

Gulliksen, J., Göransson, B., Boivie, I., Blomkvist, S., Persson, J., & Cajander, A. (2003). Key principles for user-centred systems design. *Behaviour & Information Technology, 22*(6), 397-409.

Haakonssen, K. (1995). *Republicanism: A companion to contemporary political philosophy*. Cambridge: Blackwell.

Hardin, G. (1968). The tragedy of the commons. *Science, 62*, 1243-1248.

Karkosi, K. (2006). *Hurricane Katrina changed people in uncommon and unknown ways*. Retrieved 16 January 2007, 2007, from http://www.associatedcontent.com/article/59042/hurricane_katrina_changed_people_in.html?page=2

Kuhn, S., & Muller, M. J. (Eds.). (1993). *Participatory design: Special issue of the communications of the ACM* (Vol. 36): Associated Computing Machinery.

Levine, P. (2002). Symposium: Democracy in the electronic era. *The Good Society, 11*(3), 3-9.

Library of Congress. (2003). *American Folklife Center at the Library of Congress to House the Storycorps Archive*. Retrieved 18 April, 2006, from http://www.loc.gov/today/pr/2003/03-168.html

Middleton, M., & Lee, J. (2007). *Cultural institutions and Web 2.0*. Eveleigh, New South Wales: Smart Internet Technology CRC.

Olson, M. (1965). *The logic of collective action*. Cambridge: Harvard University Press.

Rheingold, H. (2002). *Smart mobs:The next social revolution*. Cambridge: Perseus Books Group.

Runge, C. F., & DeFrancesco, E. (2006). Exclusion, inclusion, and enclosure: Historical commons and modern intellectual property. *World development, 34*(10), 1713-1727.

Schuler, D., & Namioka, A. (Eds.) (1993). *Participatory design: Principles and practices*. Hillsdale, New Jersey: Lawrence Erlbaum Associates.

Wilkinson, D. M., & Huberman, B. A. (2007, 20 February 2007). *Assessing the value of cooperation in Wikipedia*. Retrieved 12 February, 2007, from http://www.hpl.hp.com/research/idl/papers/wikipedia/wikipedia.pdf

Williamson, T. (1987). Common land. In J. Eatwell, M. Milgate & P. Newman (Eds.), *The new Palgrave: A dictionary of economies* (Vol. 1). London: MacMillan.

KEY TERMS

Allocative Resources: 'Material resources involved in the generation of power, including the natural environment and physical artefacts; allocative resources derive from human dominion over nature' (Giddens, 1984, p. 373). Resources on the World Wide Web are examples of allocative resources.

Authoritative Resources: 'Non-material resources involved in the generation of power, deriving from the capability of harnessing the activities of human beings; authoritative resources result from the domination of some actors over others' (Giddens, 1984, p. 373).

Commons: Historically land used in common by people of a community especially for pasture. In today's context, different manifestations of the commons can be observed. The knowledge commons is one example.

Community: A term used by many individuals and organisations, but in the context of the thesis this is used in its widest sense. Communities are groups of people who share common interests, culture, values, spaces, and practices; and are 'arranged in social structures according to relationships which the community has developed over a period of time' (Division of Health Promotion, 1998, p. 5). They display 'some awareness of their identity as a group, and share common needs and a commitment to meeting them' (Division of Health Promotion, 1998, p. 5). They are bounded together by affective accounts, or by the 'style in which they are imagined' (Anderson, 1991, p. 6).

Knowledge Commons: A concept that evolved out of the original concept of the commons. Lately, the term 'knowledge commons' has become applied to cultural institutions and the creation of intellectual property. Libraries may now refer to themselves as sites of shared and available resources and places where collaborative work happens. Public institutional spaces which support the creation, use, and storage of public knowledge, which are free from market constraints, and equally accessible to all in the local community. Public knowledge can exist in the forms of (but is not limited to) resources, services, physical facilities, and digital networks.

Participatory Design: Situated within user-centric design, this approach to design is characterised by the iterative participation of stakeholders in different stages of a project, policy, or service. This is argued to support the potentialities of reflexivity and rationalisation, accounting for not only the intentional outcomes but also the unintended consequences of actions. By its ability to capture this process with much intensity and velocity, this approach is argued to be a sensible guiding principle for building up the knowledge commons, and managing potential conflicts by cultural institutions. There are various examples of participatory design in different disciplines, forms, and cultures.

Structuration: Adapted from a French word, the term structuration is used by Giddens in the development of a social theory addressing the classic structure / actor dualism. Inherent in the word is the ongoing interplay between action and structure, through which culture is produced and reproduced. The cultural context is continuously generated and re-generated through the interplay of action and structure (the 'duality of structure'). Social structure both supports and constrains the endeavours of individuals, communities, and societies. (Giddens, 1984, p. 1-40.) In essence, structuration theory holds that 'man actively shapes the world he lives in at the same time as it shapes him' (Giddens, 1982, p. 21).'The structuring of social relations across time and space, in virtue of the duality of structure' (Giddens, 1984, p. 377).

Chapter VI
The 'Social Experience Factory' and the Fabrics of Collaboration in Virtual Communities of Practice

Demosthenes Akoumianakis
Technological Education Institution of Crete, Greece

ABSTRACT

This chapter proposes and discusses the "social" experience factory (SEF). The SEF provides a general model and architecture supporting information-based product assembly by cross-organization communities of practice using interactive toolkits and practice-specific technologies. In terms of engineering ground, the SEF builds on two prevalent research tracks, namely experience-based and reuse-oriented proposals for the management of virtual assets and automated software assembly as conceived and facilitated by recent advances on software factories. Our account of the SEF focuses on functions facilitating electronic squads (i.e., cross-organization virtual community management) and workflows (i.e., practice management) which collectively define the scope of collaboration using the SEF. Further technical details on operational aspects of the SEF as deployed in the tourism sector to facilitate vacation package assembly are presented in Chapter XXI in this volume.

INTRODUCTION

Over the years, increasingly mature ICT infrastructures and novel software platforms and tools either general purpose or domain-specific, have established new grounds for augmenting human intellect across a variety of application domains and engineering disciplines. Amongst the primary beneficiaries are enterprises which face new opportunities for innovation, through novel means of production and customer-relationship management models. This is particularly evident in information-based industries whose products are non-material (intangible) and knowledge is central to gaining competitive advantage. In such domains, new product development is progressively dependent upon the capability to manage virtual (knowledge-based) assets through inter- or intra-organizational virtual partnerships.

In this chapter our objective is to describe a technical framework for appropriating the benefits of virtual networking to assemble new information-based products and services from shared virtual assets. We refer to this framework as the 'social' experience factory (SEF) to highlight three characteristic properties. Firstly, the 'social' qualification is derived from the SEF's orientation to provide support for the articulation of shared practices devised to establish a social protocol of cooperation between (otherwise autonomous) members of communities of practice. We are interested in communities of practice formed by representative knowledge workers engaged in virtual partnerships whose mission is to build and support a 'collective' information-based product. In this context, product assembly is conceived of as a *social practice* framed in designated workflows as much as in *social interaction*—considered as informal exchanges—concerning expression of opinion, commenting, reflecting upon and critiquing aspects of the product being developed – expressed electronically through dedicated tools.

Secondly, the primitive knowledge-based assets of the SEF are in the form of codified *experience* stored and manipulated in shared and reusable repositories (or data stores). These experiences include software product specifications (typically encoded as XML product families), visual domain-specific vocabularies for visualizing the product and its evolution, as well as reusable components for executing statements of the visual vocabulary.

Thirdly, the production process is highly automated, implying a *factory* setup whereby final products are assembled as instances of a corresponding product line/family. To this ef-

fect dedicated software plug-ins are needed to undertake the required transformation of an abstract model into a concrete offering matching the requirements and expectations of the intended customer base.

In the remaining of the chapter we provide insights to the theoretical roots and rationale of the SEF as well as its functional and structural underpinnings as established in the context of recent research and development work. We also review on-going efforts to provide supporting software tools for enacting a variety of software engineering processes within a deployed SEF, thus establishing an effective operational model for collaboration in cross-organization communities of practice.

THEORETICAL LINKS AND STATE OF PRACTICE

The SEF in its basic form constitutes a reference model for a mature virtual enterprise in which new product development is the collaborative outcome of virtual partnerships operating as communities of practice. The qualification 'mature' to the virtual enterprise is used to designate the SEF's commitment towards continuous improvement of engineering practices to achieve high quality through mass customization and adaptations. In terms of theoretical ground, the SEF links with recent works on virtual organizations and cross-organization communities of practice. As for its engineering base, the SEF builds upon recent developments on software product assembly and in particular the notion of software factories so as to attain the goal of mass customization through adaptation. In the following we provide a brief review of relevant recent works in these research fields emphasizing how the SEF expands some of the prevalent conceptions.

Virtual Partnerships and Cross-Organization Communities of Practice

In a recent article Ripeanu et al. (2008) define virtual organizations as '... flexible networks of independent, globally distributed entities (individuals or institutions) that share knowledge and resources and work toward a common goal...'. Typically, the set of shared resources may range from computing power and storage to elements as diverse as data sets, analysis tools, and instruments. There are various connotations and operational models for virtual organizations (for a review see Travica, 2005), including the virtual corporation (Davidow and Malone, 1992), the virtual alliance (Strader et al., 1998), virtual teams (Lipnack and Stamps, 1997; Powell et al., 2004), as well as a variety of studies reflecting upon alternative structures, behaviours and capability for innovation (Jarvenpaa et al., 1998; Vartiainen et al., 2001; Lethbridge et al., 2001; Dustdar & Gall, 2003).

Moreover, recent works indicate both the promises and the challenges confronting enterprises seeking to attain inter-organizational virtual networking in a variety of industries. Representative examples include software development (Scacchi et al., 2006), business travel management (Sigala, 2007; Cardoso and Lange, 2007; Stockdale and Borovicka, 2006), the ship construction industry (Kern and Kersten, 2007), global inter-firm product development (Jin and Hong, 2007), the automobile industry (Schultz and Pucher, 2003; Wenger et al. 2002), etc. The common theme in all these efforts is the intention to appropriate the benefits of novel organizational and technical infrastructures to integrate virtual resources so as to fabricate the required degree and intensity of collaborative practice. To this effect, a variety of methods have emerged with some being explicitly focused on and targeted to capitalizing upon new technologies for knowledge creation during new product development. In a recent study, Hoegl and

Schulze (2005) provide convincing evidence of the value of 14 such methods as experienced by 94 new product development projects. The authors admit that a criterion for selecting and studying candidate methods was that they should be well known and widely used (p. 264). As a result, some recent developments such as software factories (Greenfield and Short, 2004), community-based innovation (Fuller et al., 2006) and user toolkits for innovation (von Hippel, 2001; von Hippel and Katz, 2002; Franke and Piller, 2004) were not explicitly addressed.

Our current effort links with virtual organizations established to promote multi-sector collaborations and end user involvement for new product development. A multi-sector collaboration is a partnership formed by representatives of at least two sectors (non-profit, private, and public organizations and community members) to solve problems that impact the whole virtual enterprise. In cases that collaborations are sought for to facilitate new product development, end users' involvement is known to provide a source for incremental innovation (von Hippel, 1988). Recently, the literature on the management of innovation has proposed concepts such as toolkits for user innovation and design (Thomke and von Hippel, 2002; von Hippel, 2001), user design (Dahan and Hauser, 2002) and community-based innovation (Fuller et al., 2006), providing convincing evidence of the value resulting from setting up and maintaining inter-organizational partnerships as virtual communities involving end users, engaging in the practice of new product development. The idea is that creative users manipulate a domain-specific toolkit to devise virtual prototypes of new products which can then be appropriated by the manufacturing partners. This type of set-up is characterized by sense of community amongst the members which is maintained by the members' improved capacity to exercise control and influence the development of a product with high anticipated added value. In turn, this added value motivates both the end users' contributions as well as the member's commitment of resources towards realizing a common goal.

For the purposes of the SEF, the notion of a user toolkit (von Hippel, 2001) is generalized to the concept of practice-specific toolkit, used by members of a virtual community for engaging in the practice the community is about. This makes explicit the link between the SEF and the concept of virtual communities of practice (Wenger, 1998; Wenger and Snyder, 2000) and in particular the type fostering cross-organization partnerships formed as cross-sector coalitions to attain a specific mission. Cross-organization virtual communities of practice, although less studied and understood, do exist in engineering domains such as open source software development (Scacchi et al., 2006) and scientific practice communities (Foster and Kesselman, 1998). Despite this, the vast majority of empirical works report virtual communities of practice setup and operated in single organizations either public or private (Juriado and Gustafsson, 2007). The more demanding problem of community formation across organizational boundaries – either through inter-organizational partnerships or external communities of practices – is seldom addressed (Dewhurst and Cegarra Navarro, 2004). The complexity of this challenge in terms of organizational and technological set up is explored in a recent study by Kern and Kersten (2007) where the authors investigate technologies for Internet-based inter-organizational product development and identify the problems involved in designing the partnership interaction.

Genres of Supporting Tools

General-Purpose Community Management Tools

The tools supporting cross-organization virtual communities of practice fall into different genres, with the vast majority aimed to fostering the social construction of knowledge (Erickson and Kellogg,

2001). Examples include virtual prototyping suites (Franke & Piller, 2004), tools for idea exploration (Erickson et al., 1999), tools for organizational memory management (Ackerman, 1998; Ackerman and Palen, 1996; Hackbarth and Grover, 1999), collaboratories (Olson and Olson, 2000), Grids (Foster and Kesselman, 1998), as well as tools for information sharing such as electronic mailing lists, or listservs, MOOs, Blogs, Wikis, etc. Typically, tools such as the above almost exclusively focus on managing what organisations know (Davenport and Prusak 2000), rather than what organizations should know (Lueg, 2003). Although the latter is widely acknowledged as a potential source of innovation and a drive for improvement, managing what an organization needs to (but does not yet) know remains a challenge and turns out to be a difficult undertaking. Market research indicates that companies do invest on monitoring on-line discussions aiming to find out what is being said about a company and its products using tools such as eWatch, CyberAlert and IntelliSeek. Moreover, there is also evidence indicating that companies are often not prepared to deal with potential criticism expressed in these forums (Lueg, 2001; MacInnes, 2006). Whatever the case, however, the key question is how such findings are translated into new knowledge and experience.

Another common characteristic of the vast majority of tools, which limits their uptake in the context of cross-organization virtual communities of practice, relates to the type, range and scope of the practice elements supported. Establishing a common ground on what constitutes practice in a virtual community of practice is far from trivial. In general, practices emerge from accumulated wisdom or rules of thumb. Shared practices represent the collective wisdom or repertoire of resources accepted and used widely by practitioners of a domain of discourse towards a goal (Wenger, 1998). In their recent analysis of information infrastructures for distributed collective practices, Turner et al. (2006) offer two alternative interpretations of what may be accounted as practice. The first frames distributed collective practicing in the context of the social interactions taking place between members of a virtual team or a community of practice. The authors' conclusion is that this view on practicing suggests that '… designing infrastructures for supporting on-going collective practices lies in better understanding the dynamics of interacting at a distance – not in the sense of being physically distant as opposed to being co-located in close proximity, but distance in the sense of being emotionally challenged by the position taken by another and requiring breathing room in order to be able to continue to perform independently in a capable manner (p. 105)…'. Nevertheless, this is not the only valid view upon practicing. An alternative is to frame collective practices in shared processes, the artifacts and the tools used for manipulating the artifacts. Turner et al. (2006) acknowledge this view upon practicing and declare that it is more challenging but also less studied in the literature. Indeed our reading of the relevant literature reveals that very few of the efforts reported claim convincingly that the systems studied provide a 'place' for engaging in the practice the community is about.

In the case of the SEF, such an encompassing interpretation of practice is more relevant as it allows distinguishing between organization-specific practices and community-oriented (or social) practices. The former type includes 'local' practices employed and used by an organization to plan and execute own business activities. These practices are grounded on the organization's context of work and may be embedded in dedicated technological tools (i.e., enterprise databases, intranet) and local procedures. The second type, namely community-oriented (or social) practices represent the accepted medium (i.e., processes, tools and artifacts) through which different organizations joining the virtual partnership engage in the practice the community is about. This type of practicing is shared and constitutes the 'social'

protocol for participating in the virtual space of the community of practice. de Souza and Preece (2004) refer to these practices collectively as sociability implying the means through which members participate and contribute in the virtual community.

Software Factories as Practice-Specific Toolkits

In contrast to community management which is served by a variety of tools, practice-specific toolkits are rare and less studied. For information-based products, an emerging virtuality which holds the potential to catalyze the development of powerful domain-specific practice toolkits is the notion of a software factory (Cusumano, 1989; Fernstrom et al., 1992; Aaen et al., 1997). In the software engineering literature, software factories are known for quite some time now and there have been various proposals. We are primarily interested in proposals which address the factory support environment (i.e., the computerized support components of a software factory), rather than its institutional character, as well as proposals for factory setups supporting communicating and enacting software engineering activities. In this context, the literature describes various proposals with the most prominent focusing on software assembly lines (Greenfield and Short, 2004) and software process improvement (Basili, et al., 1993).

Software assembly lines concentrate of establishing patterns, frameworks and models and integrating them into software schemas and domain-specific design languages so as to build software form components. Generally speaking, a software factory of this type is installed to extend an organization's development environment, adding guidance-related tools and resources. For example, a software factory might include design patterns, reusable code and solution templates that make it easier to start a new application. Furthermore, it might provide wizards and design guidance throughout the entire development cycle. The basic premise of a software factory is that architects customize the various code recipes that are available with a software factory and then they can redeploy the customized software factory to development teams. This gives architects a practical mechanism for distributing their own guidance to developers.

In contrast, Basili introduced the notion of the experience factory as a pathway towards software process improvement relying heavily upon reuse and deployment of previous codified experiences (Basili, et al., 1993). The experience factory denotes an institutional setup intended to support development teams to appropriate the benefits of empirical evidence and previous project experience. Even for small organizations, large amounts of information can be built up over the years comprising expertise, project data, lessons learned, quality models, etc. For such information to be usable, it needs to be modelled, structured, generalized, and stored in a reusable form in order to allow the effective retrieval of relevant artefacts (Cubranic et al., 2004). A continuous build-up of knowledge requires a suitable organizational structure and appropriate tools. Basili introduced the notion of the experience factory (Basili, 1993) as an institutional concept comprising three distinct components, namely the software development organization, the experience organization and a support organization separate from the other two components. The task of the support organization is to carefully package, document and certify (where applicable) software artefacts. In the original formulation of the experience factory, Basili did not prescribe a particular role for technology or the type of tools needed to support the operation of an experience factory. However, in subsequent publications several examples of codified and packaged experiences have been described as well as the ingredients of the underlying technological set-up (Basili et al., 2001; Seaman et al., 2003).

THE SEF AND THE MANAGEMENT OF COLLECTIVE PRACTICES

In light of the above, the present work aims to contribute to the debate regarding the engineering ground and the type of tools needed to facilitate cross-organization virtual communities and management of collaborative community practices in information-based industries. A key theme in this context is what constitutes 'practice' in a cross-organization virtual community of practice and how such practices can be technologically mediated, shared and capitalized upon to foster new high quality information-based products and services. Our understanding of the efforts reported in the relevant literature is that they characterize virtual communities of practice through constructs which represent valid connotations for online communities of interest or action, rather than virtual communities of practice. The underlying difference is that in virtual communities of practice, the elements of 'practice' are embodied as much (if not more) into shared processes, tools and artifacts, as into social interaction and information sharing. Consequently, interpersonal interaction in the form of feedback, among the members is necessary but not sufficient. Feed-through becomes equally important (if not more critical) and amounts to shared responsibility and exercising influence on the work of peers. In this view, the systems needed to form, maintain and sustain the virtual community of practice should provide a 'place' for engaging in the practice the community is about.

In our recent work, we are experimenting with a model for knowledge and experience management, which is motivated by Basili's experience factory (Basili, 1993), although it fosters an alternative perspective with regards to both the building components (constituents) and the activities being undertaken. We refer to this model as the 'social' experience factory (SEF) and it aims to address a number of specific objectives briefly summarised below.

The SEF's Objectives and the Products Assembled within its Scope

The SEF seeks to provide the basic model for appropriating the benefits of virtual networking in information-based industries whose products are non-material (intangible) and knowledge is central to gaining competitive advantage. To this effect, it aims to setup and operate a 'virtual' software factory tuned to managing and reusing shared assets, tools and domain-specific software components. This requires an orientation towards implementing assembly lines rather than programming-intensive production lines. Consequently, our primary objective is to describe a domain-independent archetype of a virtual organisation in which domain-specific elements and practices are realised by dedicated tools (such as domain-specific design languages, model building components, visual manifestation of artefacts and sound XML-based protocols) to assemble information-based products.

Products assembled within the scope of the SEF have designated characteristics. First of all, they are intangible, information-based artefacts i.e., the end user does not actually experience the end product at the time of purchase, while purchasing behaviour is determined by the information available. Secondly, they are user- or circumstance-driven in the sense that the rationale for building the product is either induced by customers or found in purely circumstantial factors such as foreseen or unforeseen events taking place in the wider social environment of the virtual enterprise – hence the need for adaptation and mass customization for such products to meet varying requirements and preferences. Thirdly, they are fabricated (or assembled) in a moderated fashion by virtual teams using a flexible assembly line (i.e., practice-specific toolkit) and a product family specification. Fourthly, such products have a 'local' character (i.e., they are regionally bound and can be assembled and offered by locals), and

short life cycles. Finally, these products cannot be effectively and efficiently developed by anyone member of the virtual partnership alone. Instead, they require collective contribution which makes them orthogonal to other products and services offered by members of the virtual partnership. Consequently, assembling and packaging such services (on-demand) amounts to articulating distributed collective practices so as to yield added-value for all parties concerned including the end user. As these products are the result of collaboration between members in a virtual partnership, they are owned by the coalition for as long as the product / service is offered. To realize these objectives the SEF is organized in distinct and separate constituents, which can be considered from a functional and structural view. We will review first the functional archetype of the SEF and in a subsequent section we will discuss the structural view which relates to the SEF's assembly line.

The SEF's Functional View: Constituents and Archetype

The functional archetype of the SEF, which is depicted in Figure 1, shares common ground with Basili's Experience Factory, although it is distinctively different in terms of organization and processes. As shown, it is structured around two distinct and separate constituents, namely the squad organization and the experience organization. The rationale for this separation of functions is to be found in the type, range and scope of tasks allocated to each constituent. Specifically, the SEF implements an activity-specific work environment referred to as 'squad organisation' and a separate knowledge construction and experience compilation organization referred to as the 'experience organization'. Parallels are to be drawn between the software development organization and the experience organization in the original formulation of the experience factory and our notions of squad and experience organizations respectively.

Figure 1. Archetype of the 'social' experience factory

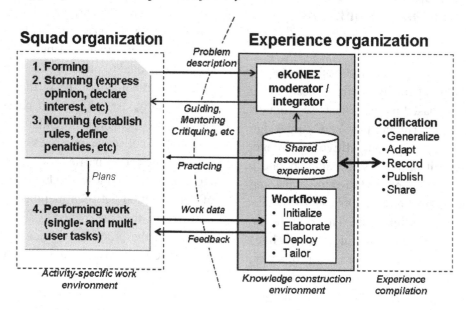

However, the processes being executed by the two constituents are different from those in Basili's experience factory.

The squad organization encapsulates the distinct lifecycle stages followed by collaborating teams / virtual partnerships as they attain joint goals. On the other hand, the experience organisation encapsulates two sub-components the knowledge construction environment and the experience codification. A virtual partnership or squad is formed across the two constituents and comprises members from different sectors of the industry and at least one moderator from the experience organization. The virtual and cross-organization nature of such partnerships necessitates that community practices are encapsulated into computer-mediated tools and workflows to allow incremental and collaborative construction of artefacts. Thus, a normative objective of the SEF is to provide the grounds for a platform enabling rich collaborative interactions between members of virtual groups.

The Squad Organization and Lifecycle

Squads are cross-neighborhood coalitions (virtual teams) tasked to attain common goals by aggregating and negotiating primitive resources (i.e., neighbourhood assets). Neighbourhoods are virtual communities with topical/thematic interest, a collective memory and cultural vocabulary. For instance, neighbourhoods in the tourism sector include transport, accommodation, cultural heritage communities, etc. Each neighbourhood sets up own rules of engagement which determine participation and acceptable social behaviour within the neighbourhood. As these neighbourhoods exist virtually, rules are embedded into processes covering registration and access rights, acceptance of new members, rules for acceptable behaviour, security, privacy, freedom of speech/act and moderation.

Squads are formed to carry out a designated mission, thus they are mission-specific. The mission may vary depending on the domain of application (i.e., tourism, learning or construction). The SEF is functionally organised in such a way so as to support the social interactions taking place between collaborating group members. In this context, social interactions imply exchanges taking place between group members and being dependent on the group's lifecycle stage and level of stability. Such exchanges differ as the group progresses from formation, to storming (i.e., getting to know each other), norming (i.e., resolving conflicts and reaching agreement) and performing towards the common goal (Tuckman, 1965). The second reason for the 'social' qualification (of the SEF) is that the above distinct stages in the group's lifecycle are explicitly supported (by dedicated tools) and characterize the design of the SEF. In other words, the SEF assumes that group work entails attainment of distinct goals during the forming, storming, norming and performing stages. Throughout these stages, an experience function / organization compiles experiences by monitoring, analyzing and consolidating persistent outcomes of a group's collaborative exchanges. In the following we provide a detailed account of the squad organization function of the SEF as currently supported in the eKoNEΣ pilot in the area of tourism.

Once formed, squads follow distinct stages to reach their ultimate target (see Figure 1). Initial formation is determined by the mission's requirements (or primitive services required) and the assets of neighbourhood members as declared during electronic registration to neighbourhoods. Each squad comprises one moderator and several participants joining forces to address a problem (i.e., develop a vacation package). The moderator designates the type of input required and establishes a pace of working. In due time, a squad may change in form and structure depending on contextual and circumstantial factors (i.e., a member may be temporarily unavailable or unwilling to commit further resources). This means that at any time, a member can opt out from a squad only through an explicit request for withdrawal.

Nevertheless, dynamic formation seldom ensures stabilization and effective performance. Instead, empirical evidence suggests that group stabilization is strongly correlated with the group's ability to effectively move from the initial forming and storming stages into norming and performing. In other words, the group's level of stabilization increases as the group progressively moves from forming (i.e., trying out activities, expression of opinions), to storming (i.e., resolving conflicts) and into norming (i.e., enfolding group coherence, setting group objectives) and performing (i.e., carrying out activities towards the group's mission). The SEF provides explicit tools for moderators to manage squads as they move from formation to performance. These tools are transparent to squad members and utilize data posted / exchanged through the SEF's shared collaborative message board.

The Experience Organization

The experience management organization of the SEF is broadly defined in terms of three sub-constituents namely a distinct role (i.e., moderators), a collection of domain-specific workflows and the persistent experience data store. As indicated in Figure 1 these constitute components of the knowledge construction environment which mediates and interacts both with the squad operational settings (i.e., activity-specific work environment) and the experience compilation component. The important issue to be highlighted is that in contrast to the squad organisation, which is flexible and independent of organisational model, the experience organization assumes a centralized institutional setting with designated roles and functions.

At the core of the SEF's experience management organization is a domain-specific ontology, which serves as the main knowledge and experience-modelling repository. In the context of our current work, we are using Protégé (http://protege. stanford.edu/) to build the ontology for the pilot application domains where the SEF is deployed. The design philosophy of the ontology is as follows. Member organizations are registered in neighbourhoods. Each neighbourhood maintains its own social policies and rules of engagement. Neighbourhoods are specialized into sub-classes depicting structure of the neighbourhood and custom member offerings. Shared resources deposited by members are of two types namely `primitiveServices` and `packages`. A `primitiveService` is a neighbourhood specific activity (i.e., accommodation). `Packages` are built by assembling instances of `primitiveServices` and are negotiated by squads. They represent resources, which do not pre-exist but rather are compiled by members to facilitate an articulated demand. However, the process of assembling them and negotiating their details is distinct and totally different than conventional practices. Specifically, an instance of `Package` is derived from the archetype of a package family, in a similar fashion as a product inherits properties of a product line. Thus assembling a package involves incremental tailoring of properties of a family of packages. Each package is owned by the squad contributing to the package. Moreover, all deliberations made by squad members leading to the package are persistent and can be traced.

The moderating role is responsible for (a) organizing, leading, mentoring and facilitating the group's virtual activities (b) extracting information from, updating and mining the shared experience data store and (c) codifying successful practices and experience by generalizing, adapting, recording, publishing and sharing artefacts. The moderator is mandatory and there can be no squad without at least one moderator. This role involves active engagement in a range of social interactions and knowledge-based tasks. Social interaction entails monitoring, guiding, facilitating, mentoring and critiquing squads as they move from formation to performing. On the other hand, the knowledge-based tasks involve manipulation of the 'soft' components of the experience orga-

nization (i.e., visual models, templates, evidence, etc). Accordingly, the moderator's work may be seen as a complex undertaking with a dual responsibility. The first responsibility is acting as a competence centre or an experience broker mediating between the virtual assets of the community of practice and the active squads. In this capacity the moderator offers advice on problem solving strategy, tools, and best practices, based on existing experiences. The second responsibility of the moderator is acting as a silent critic to mine the data generated by a squad as it works to accomplish its set targets and to codify these data in the form of persistent new knowledge. These responsibilities are further detailed in the next section where operational details of the SEF are described.

The second important constituent in the experience organization is the domain-specific component in the knowledge construction environment, which designates the distinct workflow stages (i.e., initiation, elaboration, deployment and tailoring) characterising the fidelity of the artefacts produced (see Figure 1). The initiation workflow is the responsibility of the moderator and aims to define the squad's mission. The mission is typically a product specification derived from a corresponding product family. Each product family includes mandatory fields to be defined in the initiation workflow (i.e., assignment of a name, indication of resources required such as type of neighbourhood resources and duration). In effect, this task amounts to creating a new instance under the abstract product family. This instance will incrementally be transformed to a concrete offering. Once the instance of the product family is defined a corresponding squad is initially formed as a coalition of all members offering the resources required by the product.

The elaboration workflow requires a stable squad. A squad is stable if for every neighbourhood resource declared in the initiation phase there is at least one, ideally more, committed members. During elaboration, and prior to expressing commitment or withdrawal, squad members seek to populate the designated product with all possible or alternative offerings. Their contributions may range from requests for clarifications to designation of specific parameters of the product, such as pricing of services, discount policies, temporal constraints of a service and other product-specific details. These exchanges are persistent and result in updates in the product's model or the introduction of pending issues requiring agreement. In case of conflicts between the squad members or unresolved issues, the moderator launches a virtual meeting in the form of a synchronous session. This is an innovative component of the current version of the software as it supports typical groupware functions (i.e., object sharing, floor control) as well as role-based access to and various collaborative practices over the shared objects. Notably, throughout such exchanges the object of collaboration (i.e., a graphical version of the product) remains fully synchronized, using a powerful object replication model. At the end of the elaboration phase, a new product has been populated including a variety of possible options to be selected by end users.

In the deployment stage the product has been agreed and becomes an active resource through the portal available for review and refinement. This entails selection and authoring of one or more template layouts so as to facilitate the product's multi-platform presentation (e.g., desktop using Java or HTML, PDA or a cellular phone). In case an existing template layout does not suffice, then a new one can be created and stored as a reusable component in the experience data store. A dedicated software component undertakes to provide the container for deployed products and to allow exploration by users. Moreover, through an asynchronous notification mechanism, all end users who have registered their interest in the product are informed and prompted to consider making a personalized reservation.

Personalization / tailoring is the stage where end users (i.e., prospective customers) are exposed to the product and adapt it so as to reflect own preferences. Product adaptation entails making choices from the variety of alternatives encapsulated in the deployed product, thus specifying a customised instance within a product family. For instance, users may select a particular feature from the range supported. Since the product is fully populated, end users can access it through a variety of devices including desktop computers, mobile devices or other network attachable terminals using the suitable templates. It is also worth mentioning that during tailoring users can engage in a variety of social interactions commonly found in on-line communities. For instance, prospective buyers of a product are presented with the feedback provided by persons who have already bought a similar product in the past. Also during tailoring, customers are presented with information on patterns of tailoring which have emerged. Finally, customers are also encouraged to provide ratings and write reviews for services offered and products obtained.

The SEF's Structural View: The Assembly Line

Having described the primitive constituents of the SEF, we now turn to some operational details and in particular the issue of assembling products initiated, elaborated and deployed using the SEF. Our aim is to provide a general description of an assembly line which makes use of concepts such as domain-specific design languages and software factories to automatically compile an information-based product. Such an assembly line has been fully implemented for building vacation packages in the context of the eKoNEΣ project (see Chapter XXI for further details). We will not repeat such details here. Instead, we will try to sketch the engineering ground supporting the SEF's operation.

A structural view for the workflow component in the SEF's experience organization is depicted in Figure 2 highlighting the four workflows which

Figure 2. Overview of the assembly line

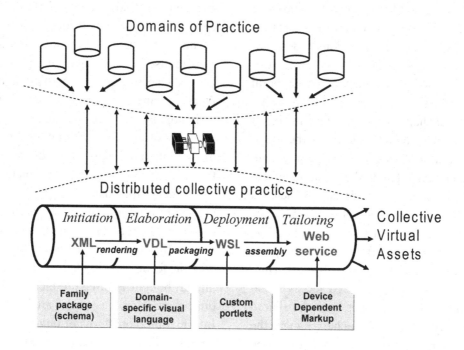

collectively establish the process through which virtual assets are manipulated as distributed collective practice as well as the basic technologies involved. These technologies are embedded into an interoperable software suite which provides the operational context of the SEF. It is worth noticing that this assembly line is located within the experience organization of the SEF to convey that it is transparent to the members of the community of practice. In other words, the community of practice through dedicated tools feeds these workflows without the members' knowing of the involved stages.

Attempting to further characterize the ingredients of such an assembly line we can derive the software schema specification which is needed to facilitate interoperability across workflows and enactment of distributed collective practices. This is shown in Figure 3 which bundles the key ele-

ments identified in Figure 2 into a concise software schema specification. As shown, the assembly line intertwines with two logical constituents annotated as the preparation and deployment. The preparation constituent is responsible for determining process-related aspects involved in the assembly of a particular type of artefact. On the other hand, the deployment constituent delivers the results of the assembly line to the wider environment of the community. For the purposes of the present work, we will assume that this amounts to deploying assembled artefacts in a portlet context of a community portal.

The assembly line operates on a domain-specific product line specification which characterizes products assembled within the scope of the assembly line. This model is populated by different types of tools devised to facilitate squad collaboration and workflow management

Figure 3. Components of the assembly line

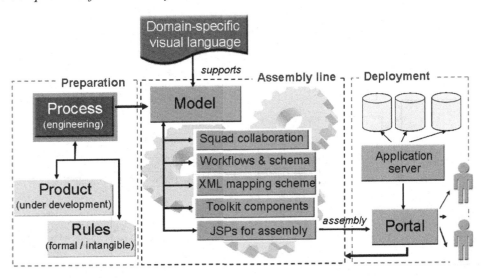

so as to derive an instance of a product under a product line specification (or a product family). These tools include general purpose collaboration software (i.e., collaborative message boards, virtual meeting tools, synchronous communication, etc) and practice-specific toolkits supporting the designated distributed collective practice. The practice-specific toolkit provides the community medium through which electronic squads contribute to the development of new products and services within the scope of the assembly line. As the basic user roles in an electronic squad are two, namely the moderator and the squad member, the practice-specific toolkit encapsulates both these roles and offers appropriate functionality in each case.

The key idea behind the above conceptual foundation is that the product is assembled in its entirety from XML. This is illustrated in Figure 4 which describes a relevant extract of a vacation package family and the corresponding XML segments. Both these constitute elements of pre-packaged experience codified in the SEF prior to the initiation of a squad. For purposes of simplicity we have intentionally omitted details

of the package family description which are not needed for the present discussion. As shown, the package is considered as a hierarchical structure comprising activities taking place within a day. Such containment hierarchies can be extended to depict alternative application domains. Activities represent instances of neighbourhood services and can be interrelated. Currently, four activity operators can be used to designate activity relationships, namely *overlap* for activities belonging to different neighbourhoods and having partial temporal execution, *sequence* for serial activities following one after the other, *parallel* for activities belonging to different neighbourhoods and having exactly the same duration and start/end points, *containment* for activities belonging to the same neighbourhood and having partial temporal overlap.

The result of such an assembly line is a concrete product manifested as a collective outcome available for review and manipulation. For our vacation package example, this signals an automatic update of a custom container which undertakes to assemble the components of the new package automatically and publish it either as device-

Figure 4. Class model of a package family

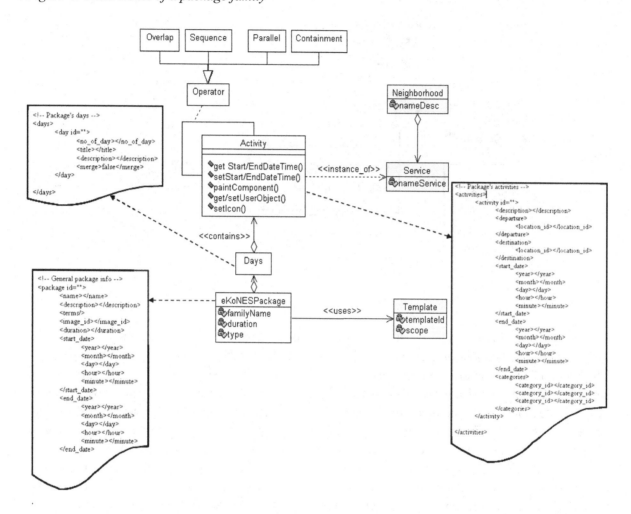

dependent mark-up or in any other form deemed suitable. In all cases, the assembled package includes clear indication of the tailoring that the user can undertake to reflect a customer's detailed requirements and preferences.

DISCUSSION: SEF AND THE DESIGN OF TOOLS FOR vCoP

The SEF promotes a knowledge management model which is built around one generic and one domain-specific component. The generic component is the squad organization, comprising distinct stages in the lifecycle of social groups,

while the experience organization is by intention domain-specific. Nevertheless, there are elements and components of the experience organization which may easily be reused, extended and applied to other domains. One issue deliberately not addressed in our discussion so far relates to the technological foundations and engineering base of the SEF. Although our current perspective and thinking on this is documented elsewhere (see Akoumianakis et al., 2007; Akoumianakis et al., 2008; Chapter XXI in this volume), we chose not to make explicit link with the concept of the SEF, as it may be supported through different means and tools. Therefore, in this section, our intention is to provide a critical discussion of the implications raised by the SEF on software tools for virtual communities of practice. Expressed in a different way, our aim is to highlight the SEF's requirements as related to software platforms for managing distributed collective practices (Turner et al., 2006)

Over the years a wide range of technologies have emerged to facilitate collaborative tasks and social interactions in community settings. Bos et al. (2007) provide a classification highlighting tools for ontology engineering (Cragin and Shankar, 2006), scientific data repositories and collaboratories (Chin and Lansing, 2004), organizational memories (Ackerman and Halverson, 2004), digital libraries (van House, 2003), community networks (Schuler, 1996; Kavanaugh et al., 2005), recommendation systems (Reichling et al., 2007), etc. Despite the plethora of tools very few efforts have studied the integration of such tools in unified architectures (or information infrastructures) for managing distributed collective practices (Turner et al., 2006). This is not surprising as such a task is both complex and demanding, while several research issues need resolution before a consolidated information infrastructure for distributed collective practices can be conceived. Our work offers insight to this as the SEF constitutes one approach to building technologies for practice. Specifically, we consider that software platforms for communities of practice, such as the SEF, require two separate but interoperable software components, one devoted to community management (i.e., discovering, building and maintaining community) and one devoted to the management of the practice the community is about. From these two, it is the practice management component which is of interest to the current discussion, as it is less studied and understood. To gain some insight, it is perhaps useful to briefly consider what practice is and how off-line practice is influenced and intertwined with on-line practice in different application domains.

On-Line vs. Off-Line Practices

Although it is far from straight forward to define the term 'practice', we will adopt the view that practices represent the collective wisdom, rules of thumb and common ground (i.e., processes, tools and artefacts) characterizing a community, whether professional such as accounting, medicine, landscape engineering, etc., or otherwise. In our account of the term, we also consider that in cross-organizational virtual communities of practice, practice is manifested as on-line or off-line practice, with the two frequently being strongly intertwined. On-line practices are computer-mediated and subsume technology for their enactment, processing and transmission elements of practice. The literature offers a variety of empirical evidence regarding the type of on-line practices prevailing across different application domains such as free and open source software projects (Scacchi, 2005; Scacchi et al., 2006), new product development (von Hippel and Katz, 2002, Franke and Shah, 2001, Franke and Piller, 2004), the automobile and airspace industries (Schultz et al. 2003; Wenger et al. 2002), etc.

In some of these examples practice is solely bound and bundled in the social interactions taking place between the members of the community. It is this social interaction which influences and determines intertwining on-line and off-line practice. In such cases, on-line practice is manifested through the design of tools for engaging in social interactions. Nevertheless, there are application domains, in which practice may be framed in the process, tools and artefacts being produced as well as in social interactions. The implication is that tools for social interaction do not suffice, but instead, practice-specific toolkits are needed for the members of the community to engage in the designated practice. These more involved situations require special components (such as domain-specific visual languages, workflow engines, assembly lines, virtual prototyping toolkits, custom groupware, 'socially' designed user interfaces, community data mining) for manifesting practices, as well as models for codifying knowledge and experience. We use the term new virtuality (Winograd, 1996) to designate the new context offered by these tools for manifesting on-line practice. Thus, new virtualities result in variations in practice codification, enactment and processing, and frequently in totally new (and innovative) practices. Framing practice in this way has implications on the communityware infrastructure. Specifically, mere support for social interaction does not suffice, while the design of the communityware is much more demanding and sensitive to a range of issues. Some of them are elaborated below.

Community Workflows vs. Workflow Engines

Typically, practice domains such as architecture, engineering and software design, are distinctly characterized by workflows, visual languages, domain-specific vocabularies and social semiotics. Even within the same domain of practice some of these tools may evolve and change. For instance, in software design object-orientation brought about a totally different design language (methodology, guidelines, visual languages, etc) than the more traditional structured systems analysis. In tourism, Semantic-Web technologies have begun to change both the traditional workflows and models of cooperation and work; for example dynamic package technologies (Cardoso and Lange, 2007) have changed the way in which tourist packages are compiled, marketed and traded. Similarly, scientific digital libraries have totally altered the practice of preparing, submitting, processing and publishing scientific works. In all these cases, the difference is brought about from the digital medium and the new virtuality being established by software mediating the institution of the underlying practices. Moreover, in all these cases, the computer-mediated environment encapsulates

different workflows, practice vocabularies and artefacts. We can therefore conclude that *'infrastructures for cultivated virtual communities of practice should be designed so as to support designated workflows encapsulating the community's shared wisdom of practice'*.

Such workflows should prescribe how the community reaches collective outcomes and how distributed collective practices are instituted. In other words, they should depict stages in an evolutionary continuum of joint activities resulting in a collective outcome. For instance, Figure 5 depicts possible workflows through which a vacation package is assembled from a vacation package family. As shown, each stage involves several actions on behalf of the vacation package development team (squad), with some of them being manifested through on-line practices (agreed and shared by all) and others being off-line (local, individualistic or custom) practice. The collective outcome, namely an assembled vacation package, is constituted by the entirety of on-line and off-line practices, which means that the team accomplishes its mission only if the vacation package is deployed and tailored so as to become a concrete offering available to potential customers. This example emphasizes two key points:

- Supporting community workflows amounts to designing to facilitate an effective intertwining between on-line and off-line practices, and
- The social role of practitioners who are embedded in an institution of on-line (shared and agreed) and off-line (relatively autonomous) practices.

Distributed Collective Practice Toolkits vs. Groupware

The next relevant issue relates to the practice vocabulary articulated in community workflows and how this vocabulary is structured, manifested and

Figure 5. Stages in a vacation package assembly

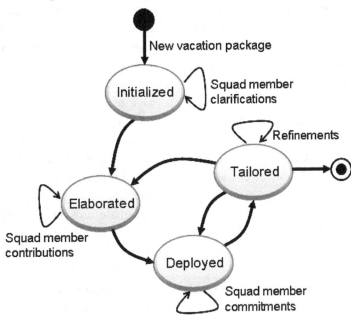

processed so as to support distributed collective practices. Traditionally, groupware technologies have emphasized the technical aspects of asynchronous and synchronous collaboration focusing on casual interaction systems such as *instant messengers* (Nardi et al., 2000) where participants carry out communications-oriented tasks, *virtual worlds*, including MUDs, chat rooms, on-line games (Bartle, 2004) where people meet other inhabitants of the virtual world, participate in joint activities and manipulate visual artefacts that comprise the virtual world, *media spaces* (Mackay, 1999) where physical offices and public spaces are linked through networks of audio and video, thus allowing members to easily see who is around and what they are doing. More recent efforts make use of screen sharing technology (Kimberly et al., 2006) to address the limited support for activity and artefact awareness of conventional groupware systems.

One major issue which stands out very promptly in all these efforts, and which is vital for collaboration in communities of practice, relates to the type, range and scope of the artefacts of collaboration, as these constitute elements of the practice-oriented vocabulary. The vast majority of existing works concentrate on conventional artefacts such as documents, communication transcripts and media (i.e. video, audio, images), assuming implicitly that practice is bundled to the social interactions taking place between community members. However, as already pointed out, this is only one view of what practice is about. The alternative view is to frame practice as an institution of processes, tools and artefacts. This view, though less popular in the literature, is the most challenging and useful in the context of communities of practice.

The SEF, as presented so far, supports the latter view. Specifically, it is claimed that designing collaborative practices entails (a) defining the core elements of a suitable practice-specific design language, typically codified as graphical models or notations, integrity constraints, guidelines, and operations on models, and (b) devising mechanisms for computer-mediated collaborative manipulation and execution of valid statements (or artefacts) of this language. Collectively, the design language and its execution environment constitute the *toolkit* for managing distributed collective practices. As enactment and reconstruction of collaborative practice is the sole objective of such a toolkit issues such sharing, mutual awareness (conceived of as comprising social awareness, action awareness, workspace awareness and situation awareness), coordinative tasks, asynchronous and synchronous session management, etc., should lie at the core of its design.

Social Community Mining vs. Data Management

Social community mining refers to the process of exploiting the community's knowledge, discovering patterns, codifying reusable experiences and improving practice in a community of practice. There are two issues of particular interest in the context of our current work. The first is extracting patterns and codifying reusable experience. The second relates to applying data mining to discover social networks and 'hidden' or emergent communities. To some extent the two issues are interrelated in the sense that identification of a 'hidden' or emergent community will inevitably result in the consolidation of new patterns and work experiences. However, for the purposes of this discussion, we will address them separately since they constitute subject matters of distinct research communities.

Identifying 'hidden' communities reveals periodic or permanent clusters or cliques formed dynamically as a result of exchanges between members of a social network. For instance, consider the scenario where a community of practice is formed by representatives of a regional tourism industry to assemble vacation packages comprising accommodation, transportation, food and beverage, etc. In such a situation two types of cliques may occur. The first may be a repeatedly recurring clustering between members from dif-

ferent neighbourhoods. For instance, elderly may be consistently choosing bed & breakfast accommodation, public transportation, and two meals from food and beverage while business travelers may favor luxury hotel accommodation, private transportation and no food and beverage. Being able to discover such tendencies (i.e., 'hidden' communities designated or implied by choice of neighbourhood members) or recurring patterns in purchasing behaviours is useful for targeting marketing strategies and building profile-based vacation packages. The second type of clique may designate cross-neighbourhood coalitions (i.e., specific members of a neighborhood that tend to be associated with specific members of another neighborhood). For instance taverns near by a historical site may be more popular than taverns farther away. In this case, the clique amounts to a community within the community with possible negative implications. Indeed, there may be effects such as community desegregation (i.e., establishment of new neighbourhoods), which in turn, may damage the community's stability, coherence and members' trust.

The second relevant application of social mining is for extracting patterns and codifying them as reusable experience. This is a knowledge management and experience building activity aiming to increase the competencies and the capacity for differentiation of a virtual organization. In the context of virtual communities of practice in tourism, such experience building is critical for sustaining an acceptable level of stability between the community members. Moreover, it turns out that it is the presence or absence and periodic refinement and endorsement of community participation policies and rules, which determine both structural and behavioural aspects of the community. To build, maintain and assure endorsement of such rules requires experience and access to community's memoir of interactions. A typical example is the negotiation between customers and providers of a vacation package. Frequently, providers of the same type of service, such as accommodation, in a vacation package including accommodation, transport and visit to local cultural heritage, develop antagonistic behaviours manifested as discounts or last minute offers. Such behaviours may damage the community's stability leading to providers opting out, internal clustering of members, etc. To avoid such negative implications, the community should impose rules of participation and acceptable behaviour. These rules may govern registration and access, acceptance of new members, rules of acceptable behaviour, security, privacy and freedom of speech/act. Moreover, they should be extracted by intelligently manipulating persistent data reflecting each member's behaviour, and negotiated and agreed upon before coming to effect. It turns out, therefore, that moderating such communities is not only about managing access to shared collaborative resources but more importantly a knowledge-based and experience-building task.

SUMMARY AND CONCLUSION

In this chapter, an attempt was made to describe the notion of a social experience factory and how it is substantiated in the context of virtual communities of practice. Our treatment was rather general and abstract. However, the reader may find further details of the SEF and how it was deployed in a pilot application in the tourism sector in Chapter XXI in this volume. The SEF, as presented here, provides a conceptual model and an engineering method for tightly coupling social activities performed in the course of team formation, storming, norming and performing with collaborative workflows such as initiation, elaboration, deployment and tailoring of information-based products.

The SEF has now been used in the area of tourism, which is the main pilot application in which the concept is being validated, but also in other engineering domains through small-scale case studies. These case studies serve a two-fold purpose in the context of the present work. Firstly, they contribute to the verification of the basic operational model of the SEF as described in Figure 1, both in terms of squad lifecycle stages and package development workflows. Secondly, they unfold commonalities which can be generalized across application domains, abstracted to form reusable components and codified to become shared experience through the SEF.

The main contributions of the SEF to the literature on virtual communities of practice can be summarized as follows. First of all, the SEF provides a frame of reference and a guide for building software tools to support knowledge-based virtual communities of practice in their efforts to construct information-based products by assembling components and reusing experience. As such, it is not only concerned with computer-mediated communication, but instead, it seeks to provide a place for engaging in the practice the community is about. Secondly, the SEF emphasizes the social aspects of collaborative practicing, in the sense that it links explicitly practice-related outcomes to evolutionary stages of a virtual team's lifecycle. In other words, the outcome of a virtual team is intertwined with the team's level of stability. Thus, a mission is complete only when the team engages in certain performative practices of a designated workflow. Thirdly, the SEF adopts a model-based approach to establish the fabrics for collaboration. This approach integrates several technological tools to allow role-based access to shared artefacts, adaptable interactive manifestation of domain-specific objects and model editing. Finally, the SEF implements a factory-oriented model for assembling resources into new packages. Such packages are information-based services assembled from components rather than constructed from scratch. Moreover, they represent added value both for the end users (prospective customers) and the coalition members (participating organizations), since no single member of the latter could offer the package cost effectively.

REFERENCES

Aaen, I., Bøtcher, P., & Mathiassen, L. (1997). Software factories. *Proceedings of the 20th Information Systems Research Seminar in Scandinavia*, Oslo. Retrieved May 13 from http://www.cin.ufpe.br/~in953/lectures/papers/Software_Factories_17.pdf

Ackerman, M. S. (1998). Augmenting organizational memory: A field study of Answer Garden. *ACM Transactions on Information Systems*, *16*(3), 203-24.

Ackerman, M. S., & Palen, L. (1996). The Zephyr help instance: Promoting ongoing activity in a CSCW system. *ACM Conference on Human Factors in Computing Systems (ACM CHI '96)*, (pp. 268-275). New York: ACM Press.

Ackerman, M. S., & Halverson, C. (2004). Organizational memory as objects, processes, and trajectories: An examination of organizational memory in use. *Computer Supported Cooperative Work*, *13*, 155-189.

Akoumianakis, D., Vidakis N., Vellis G., Milolidakis G., & Kotsalis D. (2008). Interaction scenarios in the 'social' experience factory: Assembling collaborative artefacts through component reuse and social interaction. In D. Cunliffe (Ed.), *IASTED-HCI'2008 Human Computer Interaction*, (pp. 611-068), Anaheim: Acta Press.

Akoumianakis, D., Vidakis, N., Vellis, G., Milolidakis G., & Kotsalis, D. (2007). Experience-based social and collaborative performance in an electronic village of local interest: The eKoNEΣ framework. In J. Cardoso, J. Cordeiro, & J Filipe (Eds.), *ICEIS'2007 - 9th International Conference on Enterprise Information Systems, Volume HCI* (pp. 117-122), Funchal, Madeira, Portugal: INSTICC.

Basili, V. R. (1993). The Experience Factory and its relationship to other improvement paradigms.

In I. Somerville, & M. Paul, (Eds.), *4th European Software Engineering Conference (ESEC), Lecture Notes in Computer Science 717*, (pp. 68-83), London: Springer-Verlag.

Basili, V. R., Lindvall, M., & Costa, P. (2001). Implementing the Experience Factory Concepts as a Set of Experience Bases. *International Conference on Software Engineering and Knowledge Engineering (SEKE '01) – Conference Proceedings*, Buenos Aires, Argentina. Retrieved May 13 from http://www.cs.umd.edu/~basili/publications/proceedings/P90.pdf

Bos, N., Zimmerman, A., Olson, J., Yew, J., Yerkie, J., & Dahl, E. (2007). From shared databases to communities of practice: A taxonomy of collaboratories. *Journal of Computer-Mediated Communication*, *2*(2), article 16. Retrieved May 13 from http://jcmc.indiana.edu/vol12/issue2/bos.html

Bartle, R. (2004): *Designing virtual worlds*. New Riders.

Cardoso, J., & Lange, C. (2007). A framework for assessing strategies and technologies for dynamic packaging applications in e-tourism. *Information Technology & Tourism*, *9*, 27-44.

Chin, G., Jr., & Lansing, C. S. (2004). Capturing and supporting contexts for scientific data sharing via the biological sciences collaboratory. *Proceedings of ACM CSCW Conference*, (pp. 409-418), New York: ACM Press.

Cragin, M., & Shankar, K. (2006). Scientific data collections and distributed collective practice. *Computer Supported Cooperative Work*, *15*(2-3), 185-204.

Cubranic, D., Murphy, C. G., Singer, J., & Booth, S. K. (2004). Learning from project history: A case study for software development. *ACM Conference on Computer Supported Cooperative Work (CSCW '04)*, (pp. 82-91), New York: ACM Press.

Cusumano, F. M. (1989). The software factory: A historical interpretation. *IEEE Software, 6*(2), 23-30.

Dahan, E., & Hauser, J. (2002). The virtual customer. *Journal of Product Innovation Management, 19*(5), 332-353.

Davenport, T., & Prusak, L. (1998). *Working knowledge: How organizations manage what they know.* Boston: Harvard Business School Press (paperback version published in 2000).

Davidow, W. H., & Malone, M. S. (1992). *The virtual corporation: Structuring and revitalizing the corporation for the 21st century.* New York: Harper Collins.

Dewhurst, F. W., & Cegarra Navarro, J. G. (2004). External communities of practice and relational capital. *The Learning Organization: The International Journal of Knowledge and Organizational Learning Management, 11*(4/5), 322-31.

Dustdar S., & Gall, H. (2003). Pervasive software services for dynamic virtual organizations. In Camarinha-Matos, L., & Afsarmanesh, H. (Eds.), *PRO-VE'03 – Processes and Foundations for Virtual Organizations, IFIP TC5/WG5.5 Fourth Working Conference on Virtual Enterprises* (pp. 201-208). Kluwer Academic Publishers.

de Souza, C., & Preece, J. (2004). A framework for analyzing and understanding on-line communities. *Interacting with Computers, 16*, 579-610.

Erickson, T., & Kellogg, W. (2001). Knowledge communities: Online environments for supporting knowledge management and its social context. In Ackerman, M., Volkmar, P., & Wulf, V. (Eds.) *Beyond knowledge management: Sharing expertise* (pp. 299-325). Cambridge, MA: MIT Press.

Erickson, T., Smith, D. N., Kellogg, W. A., Laff, M. R., Richards, J. T., & Bradner, E. (1999). Socially translucent systems: Social proxies, persistent conversation, and the design of Babble. In *ACM Conference on Human Factors in Computing Systems* (pp. 72-79). New York: ACM Press.

Fernstrom, C., Narfelt, H. K., & Ohlsson, L. (1992). Software factory principles, architecture and experiments, *IEEE Software, 9*(2) pp. 36-44.

Foster, I., & Kesselman, C. (1998). *The Grid: Blueprint for a new computing infrastructure,* San Francisco: Morgan Kaufmann Publishers Inc.

Franke, N., & Piller, F. (2004). Value creation by toolkits for user innovation and design: The case of the watch market. *The Journal of Product innovation management, 21*, 401-415.

Franke, N., & Shah, S. (2001). How communities support innovative activities: An exploration of assistance and sharing among innovative users of sporting equipment. *Sloan Working Paper #4164.*

Fuller, J., Bartl, M., Ernst, H., & Muhlbacher, H. (2006). Community based innovation: How to integrate members of virtual communities into new product development, *Electronic Commerce Research, 6*, 57-73.

Greenfield, J., & Short, K. (2004). *Software Factories - Assembling Applications with Patterns, Frameworks, Models & Tools.* New York: John Wiley & Sons.

Hackbarth, G., & Grover, V. (1999). The knowledge repository: Organization memory information systems. *Information Systems Management, 16*(3), 21-30.

Hoegl, M., & Schulze, A. (2005). How to support knowledge creation in new product development: An investigation of knowledge management methods. *European Management Journal, 23*(3), 263-273.

Jin, Y., & Hong, P. (2007). Coordinating global inter-firm product development. *Journal of Enterprise Information Management, 20*(5), 544-561.

Jarvenpaa, S. L., & Leidner, D. E. (1998). Communication and trust in global virtual teams. *Journal of Computer-Mediated Communication, 3*(4), 1-38.

Juriado, R., & Gustafsson, N. (2007). Emergent communities of practice in temporary inter-organisational partnerships. *The Learning Organization: The International Journal of Knowledge and Organizational Learning Management, 14*(1), 50-61.

Kern, E-M., & Kersten, W. (2007). Framework for Internet-supported inter-organizational product development collaboration. *Journal of Enterprise Information Management, 20*(5), 562-577.

Kimberly, T., Greenberg, S., & Gutwin, C. (2006). Providing artifact awareness to a distributed group through screen sharing, In *Proceedings of the ACM CSCW'06 conference* (pp. 99-108), New York: ACM Press.

Lethbridge, N. (2001). An I-based taxonomy of virtual organizations and the implications for effective management. *Informing Science, 4*(1), 17-24.

Lipnack, J., & Stamps, J. (1997). *Virtual teams: Reaching across space, time, and organizations with technology.* New York: Wiley & Sons Ltd.

Lueg, C. (2001). Information dissemination in virtual communities as challenge to real world companies. In *Towards the E-Society: E-Commerce, E-Business and E-Government, 74,* 261-270.

Lueg, C. (2003). Knowledge sharing in online communities and its relevance to knowledge management in the e-business era. *International Journal of Electronic Business, 1*(2), 140-151.

MacInnes, I. (2006). Property rights, legal issues, and business models in virtual world communities. *Electronic Commerce Research, 6*(1), 39-56.

Mackay, W. (1999). Media spaces: Environments for informal multimedia interaction. In

Beaudouin-Lafon (Editor), *Computer supported cooperative work* (pp. 55-82). New York: John Wiley & Sons Ltd.

Nardi, B., Whittaker, S., & Bradner, E. (2000). Interaction and outeraction: Instant messaging in action. In *Proceedings of the ACM CSCW Conference* (pp. 79-88). New York: ACM Press.

Olson, G., & Olson, J. (2000). Distance matters. *Human-Computer Interaction, 15*(2-3), 139-178.

Powell, A., Piccoli, G., & Ives, B. (2004). Virtual teams: A review of current literature and directions for future research. *The DATA BASE for Advances in Information Systems, 35*(1), 6-36.

Ripeanu, M., Singh, P. M., & Vazhkudai, S. S. (2008). Virtual organizations. *IEEE Internet Computing, 12*(2), 10-12.

Reichling, T., Veith, M., & Wulf, V. (2007). Expert recommender: Designing for a network organization, *Computer Supported Cooperative Work, 16*(4-5), 431-465.

Scacchi, W. (2005). Socio-technical interaction networks in free/open source software development processes. In Silvia T. Acuna & Natalia Juristo (Eds), *Software process modelling* (pp. 1-27). New York: Spinger.

Scacchi, W., Feller, J., Fitzgerald, B., Hissam, S., & Lakhani, K. (2006). Understanding free/open source software development processes. *Software Process – Improvement and Practice, 11*(2), 95-105.

Schultz, F., & Pucher, H. F. (2003). www.deck - Wissensmanagement bei Volkswagen. *Industrie Management, 19*(3), 64-66.

Seaman, B. C., Mendonca, G. M., Basili, R. V., & Kim, Y-M. (2003). User interface evaluation and empirically-based evolution of a prototype experience management tool. *IEEE Transactions on Software Engineering, 29*(9), 838-850.

Sigala, M. (2007). Investigating the Internet's impact on interfirm relations: Evidence from the business travel management distribution chain. *Journal of Enterprise Information Management, 20*(3), 335-355.

Schuler, D. (1996). *New community networks: Wired for change.* New York: ACM Press.

Kavanaugh, A., Carroll, J. M., Rosson, M. B., Zin, T. T., & Reese, D. D. (2005). Community networks: Where offline communities meet online. *Journal of Computer-Mediated Communication, 10*(4), article 3. Retrieved May 13 from http://jcmc.indiana.edu/vol10/issue4/kavanaugh.html

Stockdale, R., Borovicka, M. (2006). Developing an online business community: A travel industry case study. In *Proceedings of the 39th Hawaii International Conference on System Sciences* (pp. 134-143). IEEE Press.

Strader, T. J., Lin, F. R., & Shaw, M. J. (1998). Information infrastructure for electronic virtual organization management. *Decision Support Systems, 23*(1), 75-94.

Thomke, S., & von Hippel, E. (2002). Customers as innovators: A new way to create value. *Harvard Business Review, 80*(2), 74-81.

Travica, B. (2005). Virtual organization and electronic commerce. *The DATABASE for Advances in Information Systems, 36*(3), 45-68.

Tuckman, B. (1965). Developmental sequence in small groups. *Psychological Bulletin, 63*, 384-389. Retrieved May 13 from http://dennislearningcenter.osu.edu/references/GROUP%20DEV%20ARTICLE.doc

Turner, W., Bowker, G., Gasser, L., & Zacklad, M. (2006). Information infrastructures for distributed collective practices. *Computer Supported Cooperative Work, 15*(2-3), 93-110.

Vartiainen M. (2001). The functionality of virtual organizations. In Suomi (Ed.) *Proceedings of*

Workshop on t-world (pp. 273-292).Helsinki.

van House, A., N. (2003). Digital libraries and collaborative knowledge construction. In Ann Peterson Bishop, Nancy A. Van House, & Barbara P. Buttenfield (Eds), *Digital library use: Social practice in design and evaluation* (pp. 271-296). Cambridge, MA: MIT Press.

von Hippel, E. (1988). *The sources of innovation.* New York: Oxford University Press.

von Hippel, E. (2001). Perspective: User toolkits for innovation. *The Journal of product innovation management, 18*(4), 247.

von Hippel, E., Katz, R. (2002). Shifting innovation to users via toolkits. *Management Science, 48*(7), 821-833.

Wenger, E. (1998). *Communities of practice: Learning, meaning, & identity.* Cambridge: Cambridge University Press.

Wenger, E., McDermott, R., & Snyder, W. (2002). *Cultivating communities of practice: A guide to managing knowledge.* Boston: Harvard Business School Press.

Wenger, E., & Snyder, W. M. (2000). Communities of Practice: The organizational frontier. *Harvard Business Review, 78*(1), 139-145.

Winograd, T. (Ed.) (1996). *Bringing design to software.* New York: Addison Wesley.

KEY TERMS

Codified Practice: Elements of a practice embedded in processes, tools and artifacts.

Distributed Collective Practice: Activities executed by electronic squads and relating to the enactment of virtual practices leading to the achievement of a collaborative mission / task.

Electronic Squad: A moderated cross-organization / neighborhood coalition (virtual community of practice) tasked to attain a common mission by aggregating and negotiating primitive resources (i.e., neighborhood assets).

Social Experience Factory: A software engineering setup aimed to provide the computer-mediated environment for managing moderated electronic squads in their engagement in distributed collective practices .

Section C
Social Media and Tools

Chapter VII
Social TV:
Building Virtual Communities to Enhance the Digital Interactive Television Viewing Experience

Evangelia Mantzari
Athens University of Economics and Business, Greece

George Lekakos
University of the Aegean, Greece

Adam Vrechopoulos
Athens University of Economics and Business, Greece

ABSTRACT

Until recently, television viewing was perceived as a passive experience that aimed in satisfying a person's or a group's need for entertainment, information and, in some cases, education. However, the development of Interactive Digital Television (iDTV) and the significant change of society's expectations due to the appearance of the World Wide Web brought new dynamics on the medium. To that end, nowadays, iDTV adopts a more social role (Social TV) in order to satisfy the individuals' request for active participation, communication and (virtual) community formulation. This chapter aims at describing the characteristics of Social TV, while providing information about its systems and business applications. Similarly, the present study attempts to explain if and how Social TV can become a new setting for virtual communities and what are the potential implications for its viewers.

INTRODUCTION

Until recently, television was basically regarded as a mass medium which the viewer used for entertainment, information and education, watching it solely or within a group of others (family or friends). Watching TV has almost always been described as a passive experience (Cunningham, 2003). Its impact was related to its content, to the time spent watching or to whether the viewer was watching attentively or while performing other tasks. Television has been considered as the most preferable mass medium, granting to its major players—like broadcasters, technology providers, content creators, TV personas—a great power of social influence.

The above situation changed radically with the introduction of the Internet in everyday lives, providing an alternative medium for entertainment, education, information gathering, shopping, but also communication without time or space limitations. Society started to become increasingly organized around interactive communication technologies (Mason and Hacker, 2003), as it was becoming more technologically literate, the cost of personal computers and Internet connections was decreasing, and the opportunities of a global community were becoming more evident. Thus, the challenge for television to include communicative features became more eminent (Rainie, 2006).

Nowadays, television is incorporating the necessary technology that enhances audio and video quality, enriches TV content, provides more data components and improves the broadcasting rates. Also, it focuses on becoming a medium that supports active viewing, intrigues the viewers' participation and engagement and, even, allows each one to communicate with others through its services. That brings us to the new reality of interactive digital television (iDTV).

iDTV has all the inherent qualities of the traditional mass medium, but it also possesses some capabilities of the Internet: specifically, the level of iDTV's interactivity is limited—but not determined—by what the technology allows; its service offerings can be personalized independently of time and space limitations; and it can be used for electronically induced communication, consumption and even community formulation (Vorderer, 2000).

However, one should also keep in mind the conditions of television use, considering the distance of the viewer from the screen, the use of a simple remote control in most cases (instead of a keyboard), its massive, differentiated audience and, more importantly, the reasons why a person watches television (e.g., to relax, to be informed or entertained or even, to have a 'companion').

Overall, the critical change in Media was that the interest for innovation with the use of interactive services in TV shifted from the business producers to users (Pesce, 2005). This change has been slowly observed from early models of technology and content based around individual use of media to one that integrates the existing collective use of media and the social practices, which surround media products and technologies in everyday use (Stewart, 2004). This phenomenon is also due to the attraction of user-generated content, i.e. the ability of almost anyone to produce and distribute content (Spannerworks, 2006), while expressing preferences, opinions and needs. The current reality proves that people cherish the opportunity to communicate with others, expose aspects of their lives in public and even participate in virtual communities. Accordingly, each viewer becomes more demanding regarding the capabilities of his/her television set and expects to use TV as a platform similar to the Web. For that reason, Interactive Digital Television is gradually engaging a more active social role (Social TV) and evolves in such a way as to satisfy the modern consumer trends, while incorporating technological innovations and respecting the audience's behavioral characteristics.

Under this spectrum, the aim of this chapter is to review the current developments and future trends related to the social character of Interactive Digital Television, while examining its potential for the individual as a viewer, content generator and communicator. Our starting point is that Social TV has the ability to become a platform for virtual communities, where people's participation will enhance their overall viewing experience. Along these lines, we attempt to set the research agenda by discussing some straightforward future research directions. Finally, we try to provide some insight on how the evolution of TV viewing might affect the current business practices.

INTERACTIVE DIGITAL TELEVISION

In order to discover the potential of Social TV, it is necessary to understand the definition and general characteristics of Interactive Digital Television. iDTV is one significant example of technology that evolved from a traditional mass medium to one that can address the modern consumer demands of personalization and direct communication and offer to the viewers compelling new experiences. Viewers are able now to actively engage with the TV by selecting information from teletext-style services, by enjoying enhanced TV shows, and/or by participating in live interactive TV games (e.g. Broadbandbananas, 2005).

However, in order for TV to be interactive it presupposes its digitization. So, "Digital TV encodes the television picture as a series of binary numbers, and then uses computer processing to compress it so it is transmitted in a fraction of the bandwidth, or capacity, taken by the equivalent analogue TV signal" (The Parliamentary Office of Science and Technology, UK).

Digital TV signal can be transmitted to the viewers via three different channels:

- **Terrestrial (DVB-T)** signal is transmitted via air and it requires aerial for receiving the signal

- **Handheld (DVB-H)** signal is a superset of DVB-T with additional features to meet the specific requirements of handheld, battery-powered receivers (e.g., for Mobile TV)
- **Satellite (DVB-S)** signal is also transmitted via air and it requires a satellite receiver (a dish)
- **Cable (DVB-C)** signal is distributed via fixed cable and receiving cable signal requires a specific cable receiver box.

In order to use interactive services, users also need a return channel. The need for return channel and type of channel depends on the service used. Examples of the return channels are mobile phone (SMS/MMS) and Internet connection via dial-up or adsl connection. Cable connection is two-way connection already by its nature and therefore it is able to provide a built-in return channel for the user. IPTV (Internet protocol TV) is also an emerging distribution model for TV content. IPTV utilizes Internet connection for both distributing the content and for return channel purposes.

Since interactions between television viewers are tightly interwoven with the structure of the program they are watching, it is important to identify the qualities of television content that contribute positively to sociability. Certain qualities in TV shows encourage sociability more than others. In particular, shows with bursty rhythms or redundant content provide plenty of pauses and opportunities for interaction. People-centred content provides audiences with many "conversational props" (Lull, 1990). Poor quality movies are also often mentioned as a good way to foster social interaction. The kinds of TV programs genres that are preferably developed for interactive applications include Animation, Sports Events, Documentaries, Action-Adventure, and Reality Television (Oehlberg et al., 2006).

Accordingly, some types of interactive programming have been applied more extensively[1]. These are:

- **Enhanced content:** Enhanced TV content is the optimal way to deliver additional content that gives viewers more from the programs they've come to watch.
- **Synchronized:** Interactive elements can be synchronized to a show or commercial's video content. Interactive elements can be made available to viewers during pre-set segments of the show or commercial.
- **Voting & poling:** Voting and polling applications allow audiences to participate and influence the outcome of live broadcasts. When viewers cast their votes, they receive immediate confirmation and polling results. This guarantees live audiences to advertisers by minimizing the time shifting and ad skipping that occurs with recorded programs. Additionally, voting and polling applications give advertisers an additional sponsorship opportunity.
- **Play along / kids' educational programming:** Children's shows naturally lend themselves to interactivity, as kids sing, dance and clap along. With interactive programming, they can also participate through their remote control. Play-along elements enhance a child's learning experience, help build curiosity and expand their imagination.
- **Games:** Interactive games can be added to program guides and menus to keep viewers engaged during programming – or games can be offered as stand-alone content, accessible through the program guide. Game options range from puzzles and word challenges to card games and pinball. Viewers can play against each other, or earn points for contests. Games provide incremental revenue opportunities for programmers and operators.
- **News and information:** Interactive news and information services engage viewers by providing real-time access to in-depth information on the topics that interest them, including electronic programming guides, stock tickers, news and public affairs resources.
- **Sports:** Sports programming provides a wide range of opportunities for interactivity. With the click of a button, viewers can watch multiple sporting events in mosaic format, select camera angles, access instant replays, select their audio tracks and get player bios and statistics.
- **Electronic program guides (EPGs):** Interactive EPGs enable subscribers to access the content they want, when they want it.

Besides the development of new types of programming, the characteristics of iDTV also brought along the development of new formats for e-commerce in television (t-commerce). In detail, t-commerce applications take television shopping to a new level, providing the platform from simple impulse purchases to large-scale shopping channels, where viewers can make purchases using their remote controls. The simplicity of t-commerce drives sales, because consumers no longer need to make telephone or Web orders, which takes them away from the TV and distracts them with competing devices.

Accordingly, a significant effect has occurred for the production and distribution of TV advertisements, with the introduction of interactivity. So, interactive advertising is no longer a concept only usable on the Internet, but it becomes applicable on television as well (Cauberghe and De Pelsmacker, 2006). One of the significant potentials of iDTV advertising is the ability accurately to target messages towards specific market cross sections or even individuals—or rather to each individual set-top box—with personalized messages based on their customer profiles (Jensen, 2005). Also, advertising formats like the "long-form commercials" allow consumers to browse products and access information that interests them at their own pace, overcoming the 30-seconds limit. Moreover, the format of "interactive branded entertainment" assists advertisers to present show-specific products and services, offering coupons and special promotions, and allows viewers to order samples, search more information about suppliers, products and brands and request brochures – with a simple click of their remote control.

SOCIAL TELEVISION

Although some types of iDTV programs offer to the viewers the opportunity to interact with other individuals, their majority had focused on the viewers' interaction with the TV material or the content provider. But, the transformation of society's media expectations made explicit the request for interaction between individuals or groups of people, and Social TV came as an answer to this request.

Social Television is regarded as an evolution of iDTV and it is generally considered as a technology that supports communication and interaction in the context of watching television, or related to TV content. It also includes the study of television-related social behavior. Specifically, one could define Social TV as 'communication and social interactions—remote or co-located—in a TV-watching content, or related to a TV experience; and technology that supports these communications and interactions' (Geerts et al., 2007).

The aims of Social TV Systems are: (a) to enable viewers at different locations to communicate with one another, (b) to allow direct (and indirect) sociability, (c) to support the emotional sphere of sociability, (d) to train viewers on generating their own content and distributing it to similar others, and (e) to support the formulation of virtual communities (Iatrino and Modeo, 2007).

As a concept, social television is not linked to a specific architecture such as cable, IPTV, peer-to-peer delivery, or internet television. Nor is it necessarily limited to a traditional television screen, but it could also be presented on a computer or handheld device such as a cell phone.

Of course, one can suggest that Social TV attempts to combine the dynamics of different "principal technology domains" in the current multimedia landscape organized in a vertical manner (Hesselman et al., 2008), in order to provide an intriguing experience to the viewers.

Social TV Systems

Since Social Television is currently an active area of research and development, most existing social television systems are still on a conceptual stage, or exist as lab prototypes, beta or pilot versions. Social TV applications are primarily based on the ways users wish to incorporate them into everyday life (Orbist, 2007) and on the fact that personalization allows users to browse programs more efficiently according to their taste, while building social networks. For instance, they can integrate voice communication, text chat, presence and context awareness, TV recommendations, ratings or video-conferencing with the TV set.

The guidelines for designing Social TV systems have not yet become rigid or formal, although many researchers have contributed on the issue. However, there are some general recommendations that are widely accepted. For example, Schibelsky et al. (2007) suggest that in order to offer a usable interface, it is important that:

- **The content must be perceivable:** Consisting of look-and-feel guidelines (fonts, colours, symbols), as well as TV assistive services provision
- **Interface components in the content must be operable:** Following guidelines to provide accessible navigation and interaction mechanisms.
- **Content and controls must be understandable:** Concerning readability and use of user's language.
- **Content must be robust enough to work with current and future user agents:**

Receiver's requirements being compatible with assistive technologies.

On the other hand, when designing for Social TV, one should consider the fact that group viewing (in the same room or not) must be facilitated. Under this spectrum, Oehlberg, Duchenaut et al. (2007) provide some guidelines. Specifically, they envision Social TV as a communication module that: "would allow viewers to establish connections with as many of their remote friends as they wish (probably using a mechanism similar to Chuah's (2002) "buddy surfing"), opening up a shared audio channel between these locations (using, for instance, voice-over-IP). Participants would communicate with each other simply by talking into a microphone that could be placed in the room or, alternatively, on a small headset worn by each viewer. The main value of the technology, however, would be in the software available in each Social TV system. By processing each participant's utterances and transmitting the appropriate mix of social audio content to all viewers, Social TV would act as a "clearing house" facilitating distributed television viewing".

So, according to their research, this software would be valuable if designed to:

- Support the proper timing of social interaction during group television viewing
- Minimize disruptions in the television program's flow
- Isolate exchanges that are beneficial to the group from side conversations and non-sequitur
- Allow viewers to move in and out of the audience smoothly
- Avoid drawing viewers' attention away from the television screen

Further design guidelines keep on appearing continuously since the development of Social TV systems (as a new trend of iDTV) is growing in importance and interest, both to the academic and business community, describing in detail the necessary conditions for the systems' acceptance and use by the people (e.g. Ahonen et al. 2006, Lee et al. 2008). However, this chapter's attempt is to provide insight on the big issues concerning Social TV's development, especially regarding the facilitation of communication among viewers and the formulation of virtual communities.

A review of existing Social TV applications has revealed the following issues as important for understanding the design of Social TV systems and applications:

- **Communication channel.** How a communication channel among viewers can be established? For example, several systems use several text (instant-messaging), audio (using microphones and speakers to allow discussions during watching a program) or video (live camera recordings) features exclusively or combined.
- **Interaction elements.** How viewers can feel the presence of others: using avatars, emoticons or electronic hand gestures of agreement/disagreement, approval/rejection?
- **Co-viewing experience.** How viewers can have the experience of co-viewing in an asynchronous manner: with annotations on the TV content with others' comments or with audio recordings of other viewers (usually buddies) laugh tracks and voices?
- **Content selection.** How viewers can find TV material in accordance to their taste: with suggestions by other viewers with similar sociodemographic or consumption characteristics, with selections made by individuals that are considered friends (buddy list) or with the introduction of an EPG feature that categorizes the TV content based on past viewing behavior?

- **Interaction devices.** How a viewer can interact with the system: using the remote control only or with a keyboard e.t.c.?
- **Accessibility features.** How a viewer can be supported by the system in case of a physical or mental disability?
- **Safety and privacy.** How the system can provide to the viewer the necessary sense of safety and privacy?
- **Sociability.** How a viewer can formulate virtual communities and share user-generated content?

Indicative examples are the Amigo TV (Bouwen, Vanderlinden and Staneker, 2005), SocialTV (Oehlberg, 2006), ChaTV (Fink et al., 2006), ConnecTV (Boertjes, 2007), Living@ Room (Ghittino, Iatrino, Modeo and Ricchiuti, 2006) and Second Life (Spannerworks, 2006) systems that enabled viewers to understand when their friends are watching at the same time and interact with them with the use of avatars (see Figure 1). In those systems attention has been

paid to create the circumstances for interaction in real-time, while designing a virtual world that could augment the experience of communication and sharing.

Generally, much effort has been dedicated on how people can 'feel' the presence of others while interacting with their TV. In June 2001, TV Cabo became one of the first operators in the world to launch a digital interactive TV service. The service was the world's first interactive cable TV service featuring Digital Video Recording (DVR) in an integrated cable set-top box with return path, powered by Microsoft TV Advanced. The TV Cabo Interactiva was divided in two major areas: the Walled Garden (see figure 2) and the Channel's interactive applications. The TV Cabo Interactiva's Walled Garden, or Portal TV, provided the users with services such as the Electronic Programming Guide, e-mail, TV-Shopping, TV Banking and games, amongst many other applications. As far as the channels' interactive applications are concerned, TV Cabo offered interactive application in 39 channels, out of which seven channels

Figure 1. Amigo TV's example of voice chatting over football, with personal avatars (Coppens et al., 2004)

Figure 2. TV Cabo Interactiva Walled Garden Home Page (Quico, 2003)

Figure 3. CollaboraTV's Virtual Audience & Interest Profile (Harrison and Amento, 2007)

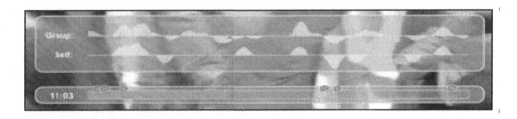

already had transmitted interactive/ enhanced television programs (Quico, 2003).

Nowadays, more systems are designed, like CollaboraTV (Harrison and Amento, 2007) which supports asynchronous annotation of shows (see Figure 3), currently limited to text. These comments can be generated at any point while watching a show. All future viewers can see these comments at the equivalent time they were created, and can leave their own. Users can also generate temporally linked interest points in order to indicate a positive or negative response to a show's content. In CollaboraTV, the virtual audience simulates the effect of a movie theatre, where avatars are seated and shown as silhouettes against the show.

Also, some known systems that are based on supporting communication among viewers are the AOLTV, where viewers can watch television using their existing broadcast signals and choose from a variety of popular AOL features including e-mail, instant messaging, chat and a built-in programming guide, and the Motorola's Social TV that merges television and instant messaging to let communities form by snarking and sniping about the latest episode of a specific program.

Accordingly, other systems, like the 2BeOn (Abreu, Almeida and Branco, 2001), focused on enabling people to be in live contact during a TV show or created ad hoc communities based on real-time ambient audio for further interaction (Fink et al., 2006).

One of the first systems, focusing on that direction, was Chuah's (2002) "reality instant messenger", which provided both "buddy surfing" (an awareness that friends are watching the same television program) and an IM-based communication channel between viewers.

Furthermore, one should mention the Tribler distribution system (see Figure 3), that gives people access to all television stations around the world by exploiting the Peer-to-Peer Networks on digital TV (Wang, Pouwelse, Fokker and Reinders, 2006), as well as Goromi-TV (Goro Otsubo, 2007) that tries to help people overcome the issue of overwhelming video choices, by enabling the user to navigate video data freely. With this system, the user can select either extracted keywords or a TV program simply by clicking, and then the system will immediately update the TV program listing and keywords.

Another approach has been to transform television into an inhabited virtual world. In Benford et al, (1998), audience members control avatars in a 3D space and can interact with the performers of the show they are watching. The

Figure 4. Screenshot of Tribler System [showing content](Fokker et al., 2007)

Figure 5. Screen shots of a 3-person Reflexion session (Agamanolis, 2006)

focus is on breaking down the barriers between audience members and performers, as opposed to facilitating group interaction while watching television. Reflexion (Cullinan and Agamanolis, 2002) is another example of social application: it is a video communication system that acts like a "magic mirror". User can see a reflection of herself together with the reflections of other people in remote locations (see Figure 5).

SOCIAL TV AND VIRTUAL COMMUNITIES

Interaction and communication among virtual community members take place through a technological interface. This means that the primary relationship is not between the sender and the receiver of information, but rather with the technology-mediated environment (Hoffman & Novak 1996). Our view follows the idea that 'iDTV applications can act as virtual community builders' (Quico, 2003), since the major characteristics outlined for virtual communities (Rheingold, 2001) can be found in Social TV applications: each interactive television application can enable people to communicate with others, in a text-based or audiovisual way, relatively uncoupled from face-to-face social life in geographic communities, bringing together people who do not necessarily know each other before meeting online.

However, for Social TV to be able to support the formulation of virtual communities, some necessary conditions should be respected. In particular, Jones (1997, p. 6) suggested that: 'A class of computer-mediated group communication that takes place within a specified communication structure is labeled a virtual community when the following four conditions are met: (1) a minimum level of interactivity, (2) a variety of communicators, (3) a minimum level of sustained membership, and (4) a virtual common-public-space where a significant number of computer-mediated group communications occur'.

Adding to the previous argument, one can declare that Social TV can act as a platform for Virtual Communities because:

- It possesses the necessary applications to support minimum interactivity
- TV viewers can present vast differences in their sociodemographic profiles, due to the extensive adoption of the medium
- The design of the Systems for Social TV ensure a minimum level of membership sustainability, either by their participation rules or/and the viewers' intense interest in the subject
- It provides the technology-mediated public-common environment where a significant number of group communications is able to occur

Virtual communities are formed around all possible topics and shared characteristics (Hagel and Armstrong, 1997) and describe virtual spaces where people with common interests can interact. In the case of virtual communities established within Social TV, their formulation is usually based upon the viewers' interest in a TV program (a show, a game or a TV series) or related to the notion that those watching the same TV content also share some common characteristics. Then, viewers expect to find like-mindedness among other members and connect to them in order to reach better information (e.g. find out details of a TV hero), receive more credible suggestions (Price and Feick, 1984; Herr et al., 1991) and express themselves in public (Giddens, 1991).

ISSUES, CONTROVERSIES, CHALLENGES

Following the research on the development of Social TV, a number of critical issues are revealed. In designing for and understanding Social TV, one could argue that the claim from usability studies about 'making it simple and easy' for the individual user must be elaborated and confronted with the communicative and social complexity of the living room, the aesthetical demands of text production and the development of resources for participating in public and cultural spheres of communication (Rasmussen, 2005).

In particular, there are several issues corresponding to the usability of Social TV systems in the living room, since current TV sets still face limitations in relation to their input (e.g. remote control, keyboards, cameras, microphones) and output devices (e.g. speakers) (Ghittino, Iatrino, Modeo and Ricchiuti, 2006). Despite the difficulties, several studies have shown that people express different usability preferences mainly based on their previous experiences. For example, Americans are keener on placing their laptop close to the TV set and using it in the living room, while Europeans regard the PC as a tool for work and place it on a different room, excluding it as a facilitator for interaction. Another example concerns the use of the remote control (Haque, 2008, Roberto et al., 2008, Lee et al., 2008), where it is reported that youngsters usually find it easy to use for text-messaging (using it just like their cell-phone), but if the iDTV application is too complex, then they may prefer a keyboard (Jakob Nielsen's Alertbox, 1997). On the same note, elders often require a different design for their remote controls that facilitates their navigation to the different interactive services. Overall, findings concerning usability have not yet offered exclusive specifications for the design of Social TV applications, since they lie heavily on the complexity and variety of interactive services (Baca and Holtzman, 2008, Goldin, Rochat, & Anderson,

2008). There are only indications relating specific kinds of services to specific usability rules.

On the other hand, the media environment includes a complex set of broadcasters, content providers, public authorities and telecommunication companies. It differentiates substantially according to the economic and technological standards of a country, to the business practices and investment margins, as well as to the size, the level of technological literacy, the cultural and behavioural characteristics of the public. So, it is extremely difficult to set a common ground for the development of Social TV applications and confront the obstacles presented by the major players of the market.

In addition, there is a critical issue concerning the choice of adapting television to individual viewers or to a group of viewers. The debate on sole or group viewing is inexhaustible, because it depends mainly on the researcher's standpoint. Indicatively, McQuail (1998) supports the fact that media use can be as sociable or as solitary as a person wants it to be, while Masthoff (2004) suggests that is essential for iDTV to adapt to a group of viewers, since television viewing is largely a family or social activity (Kasari and Nurmi, 1992). Although much research effort has been spent to group viewing in the context of family viewing, there is much evidence that group viewing could refer to quite heterogeneous groups, and age, gender, intelligence and personality influence what types of TV programs people enjoy (Kotler et al., 2001; Livingstone and Bovill, 1999). So, television might once have championed as the "electronic heart", which would bring families together (Tichi, 1991), but, nowadays, people are increasingly watching TV without their families, with studies suggesting at least half of viewers usually watching alone (Putnam, 2000).

Compounding this problem is the volume of content catering to different interests and demographics on TV today. The number of channels available to the average household and the sheer quantity of content make it less likely for people to watch the same shows. TV viewers are more and more confronted with a myriad of information sources due to the higher number of digital channels and the availability of on-line data. In such scenario, television is losing its role as a promoter of social ties, since the users, when absorbed by this overload of information, may relegate their interpersonal relationships.

However, this problem does not seem to be directly related to the surplus of information, but mainly to the absence of a common referential usually associated with the establishment of a conversation between peers. The lack of this common referential is connected to the information on demand paradigm: in such segmented information offer, the probability of seeing what the other person saw is permanently decreasing (Wolton, 1997).

This problem becomes even greater when thinking about the viewers' possibility to download a TV program to their set-top box or Digital Video Recorder (DVR). The emergence of the DVR is changing the way people watch television. First and foremost, there is an increasing amount of time-shifted television viewing, that is, television watched asynchronously outside the scheduled program time slots (Jensen, 2005). Digital Video Recorders are not only impacting the time families spend together, but also the ability for friends, co-workers and extended family to discuss shows — the so called "water-cooler effect" (Putnam, 2000). This fact can raise some worries, when considering television's role of a medium that creates instances of discussion among individuals.

Nevertheless, this issue can be seen from another point of view, where the segmentation of information, namely in the television arena, may promote a deeper relationship between members of micro communities that share the same interests and, thus, consume the same type of information (Abreu, Almeida and Branco, 2006). Then, the members of these micro communities are expected to better accept commercial practices that are closer to the ones applied to the Web.

The previous suggestion brings to light the need of developing new business models for the Media market. These models must be designed, in order to foresee the involvement of the additional players in the market, like telecommunication companies that provide the transmission channels, virtual companies that may wish to sell their products, production companies that might attempt to override the distributors, and, more importantly, those individuals that can and wish to generate their own content and share it with the public.

Especially to what promotion is concerned, there are serious challenges to address. Initially, interactive advertising is affected by the iDTV services of fast-forwarding or skipping the ads, while some DVRs also offer the selection of recording shows without ads. To continue, the number of available channels and programs makes zapping an uncontrollable action, while the effectiveness of common ads is losing its strength when compared to the opinion of an individual the viewer appreciates. Also, the application of personalized ads according to a viewer's content preferences and personal characteristics can present serious challenges, because of the concerns about personal data, privacy and exploitation (Macklin, 2002).

Finally, the most critical issue - and the one Social TV is expected to address - is the modern viewers' preferences, influences and expectations. Nowadays, the need for every person to be able to create his/her own content is gradually emerging as a way to find, interact and actually connect with others that might appreciate the same things (Foster et al., 2002). Thus, Social TV systems should consider the viewers' desire to create and share content, prevent the difficulties of involving viewers as producers and provide adequate training and methods (Rasmussen & Christensen, 2006). Also, they must facilitate

viewers in finding and communicating with other people that share similar interests, while developing the necessary features that will serve as facilitators of technology-mediated -but still interpersonal- communication (Sherry and Kozinets, 2000). Furthermore, they should establish a common ground for the formulation of virtual communities (small-group or network based) that will be open to every viewer, irrespectively of his/her sociodemographic characteristics and personal abilities.

CONCLUSION AND FUTURE TRENDS

Based on the fast development of Social TV, consumers - users will be given the choice not only to decide when and how they want to watch a TV program distributed by a mediator, but also to access content generated by other independent viewers and even to interact by introducing their own material. Those interactive features that allow user-to-user communication may provide some interesting solution to the issue of advertising by exploiting word-of-mouth practices, and have a positive effect on how users perceive the "sincerity" of television as a medium by exploiting the dynamics of virtual communities (Thorson and Roggers, 2006).

More importantly, the establishment of TV virtual communities suggests that users could express their preferences both implicitly and explicitly, and allow social networking to happen both on real-time and post- time. One idea regarding the introduction of virtual communities in Social TV is the development of an application that imitates webblogs, because they are based on textual formats (i.e. posts), they can facilitate synchronous and asynchronous communication and be sustained irrespectively of the community's size or the viewers' participative dedication (Mantzari et al., 2007). Actually, there is evidence that blogs create communities of similar interests quickly and efficiently (Jayasinghe, 2006), exactly as some Social TV systems (like Telebuddies) have tried to do (Luyten et al., 2006).

Also, interactivity in Social TV can enable marketers to capitalize on the concept of community to help customers derive value from a company's products and means of promotion (Dibb et al., 2006). For this case, an important recommendation would be to apply the promotional methods of e-commerce, designing campaigns that will attract the members of the virtual communities and affect them indirectly. This can happen by engaging the leaders of the community - whose positive opinion has a significant value- or perhaps by presenting special offers for the members, based on the community's central focus and specifications. Accordingly, personalized advertising might change in form and goal, addressing first the interests of a relevant community (mass-customization) and at a second level the individual viewers. Although it may seem farfetched, business strategies may also be affected by the indication of the individuals pattern of participation in the virtual community, suggesting that different tactics could interest leaders or simple participants (e.g. in their segmentation as customers). From another point, one should expect that if the dependency on virtual iTV communities prove to be great, then media providers might select to implicate participants in the production of relevant (to the community's focus) programs for iDTV, just like it is currently done through the Web. However, future research in interactive shopping, information processing and communication environments (i.e. Web, mobile, iDTV, etc.) should investigate the issue of personalization and mass customization under the perspective of *who is going to control this process.* For example, while in the traditional shopping environment (i.e. one-to-many) the retailer is the one who controls the key manipulated variables (e.g. colors, product display techniques, layout, etc.) of the store towards influencing the behavior of customers, online (i.e. in an interactive environ-

ment) this control, technology enabled, could be provided to customers (e.g. "personalize your web site" options available today in many commercial Web sites). This paradigm shift provides ample opportunities for designing and executing empirical research designs (mainly lab or field experiments) towards testing research hypotheses that could be well derived and formulated through reviewing the established conventional knowledge (Marketing, Information Systems) as well as packed-up with the recent knowledge available in the emerging iDTV landscape.

If the trend of user-generated content gains further importance, then Media providers might have to re-think their offerings in order to provide more opportunities for people generating their own material and sharing it with others. So, the idea of TV channels broadcasting user-generated content might become a practice. In conclusion, it is expected that future systems and applications will be further developed, so as to enhance the participation of viewers in Social TV virtual communities in text, audio or video mode.

Looking beyond the year 2012, it is believed that two key drivers will define long-term TV industry disruption: (a) open content access, (b) highly involved media consumers. The new potential of Social TV creates both opportunities and risks for its major players – broadcasters, content producers, marketers, and end-users. Along these lines, vast research opportunities emerge in this fast evolving channel. Some of them are thoroughly discussed in the present research study.

Additionally, the vast adoption of the Web and the success of e-commerce have sophisticated consumers by offering access to detailed information regardless of their economic, geographical or social boundaries, and have influenced the business practices in emphasizing on the individual's bargaining power, on the gathering of as much precise and complete information as possible and on the recognition of consumers' ability and desire to communicate extensively with others and even create virtual communities of common interest. Similarly, the emergence of the multichannel retailing phenomenon implies that consumers are increasingly adopting alternative channels to conduct shopping, enjoy themselves, search for information, communicate, etc. To that end, Social TV could potentially serve for some viewers as an "one-stop-shop" vehicle through which they (i.e. users/viewers/consumers) could conduct their various activities through one single channel. Besides, the high potential of Social TV is also indicated by the high penetration of TV sets, familiarity with the medium, friendly device and interface compared to PCs and mobile phones, etc.

Following Anthony Giddens' (1991) line of thinking, we start from the standpoint that people in late modernity wants to, and needs to tell their own stories, create their own experiences in order to gain an identity and a sense of belonging. So, Social Television can become a vehicle for bringing people to a satisfactory level of their current needs' fulfilment, because it incorporates the abilities to serve as a medium of self-expression, communication, and involvement with community. Thus, Social TV should not be examined only as a "mechanical combination of technical components" that allows communication, but as a technology designed to satisfy the social impetus (Kim and Sawhney, 2002).

Under this spectrum, it is logical to assume that more sophisticated systems and applications will appear promoting the social status of the medium and attracting those who wish to maximize their chances for self-expression, communication, knowledge and entertainment, without parting from their couch.

REFERENCES

Abreu, J., Almeida, P., & Branco, V. (2001). 2Be on – Interactive television supporting interpersonal communication. In *Proceedings of the 6th Eurographics workshop on Multimedia.*

Agamanolis, S. (2006). At the intersection of broadband and broadcasting: How ITV technologies can support human connectedness. In *Proceedings of the 4th Euro iTV Conference* (pp. 17-22). Athens, Greece.

Ahonen, A., Turkki, L., Saarijärvi, M., Lahti, M., & Virtanen, T. (2006). Guidelines for designing easy-to-use interactive television services: Experiences from the ArviD Programme. In *Proceedings of the 4th Euro iTV Conference* (pp. 225-233). Athens, Greece.

Baca, M., & Holtzman, H. (2008). Television meets Facebook: Social networks through consumer electronics. In *Adjunct Proceedings of the 6th Euro iTV Conference* (pp. 35-36). Salzburg, Austria.

Benford, S., Greenhalgh, C., Brown, C., Walker, G., Regan, T., Rea, P., Morphett, J., & Wyver, J. (1998). Experiments in inhabited TV. In *Proceedings of CHI' 98* (pp. 289-290). New York: ACM.

Boertjes, E. (2007). ConnecTV: Share the experience. In *Proceedings of the 5th Euro iTV Conference* (pp. 139-140). Amsterdam.

Bouwen, J., Vanderlinden, K., & Staneker, T. (2005). Communication meets entertainment: Community television. *Alcatel Telecommunications Review*, 1st Quarter.

Broadbananas (2005). http://www.broadbandbananas.com

Cauberghe, V., & De Pelsmacker, P. (2006). Belgian advertisers' perceptions of interactive digital TV as a marketing communication tool. In *Proceedings of the 4th Euro iTV Conference* (pp. 371-381). Athens, Greece.

Chuah, M. (2002). Reality instant messenger. In *Proceedings of the 2nd Workshop on Personalization in Future TV (TV02)*. Malaga, Spain.

Coppens, T., Trappeniers, L., & Godon, M. (2004). AmigoTV: Towards a social TV experience. *In Proceedings of the 2ⁿᵈ Euro iTV Conference,* Aalborg, Denmark.

Cullinan, C., & Agamanolis, S. (2002). Reflexion: A responsive virtual mirror. *Conference Companion, UIST 2002 Symposium on User Interface Software and Technology.*

Dibb, S., Simkin, L., Pride, W. M., & Ferrell, O. C. (2006). *Marketing – Concepts and strategies.* 5th Ed. New York: Houghton Mifflin.

Fokker, J., Brinke, M., Ridder, H., Westendorp, P., & Pouwelse, J. (2007). A demonstration of Tribler: Peer-to-peer television. In *Adjunct Proceedings of the 5th Euro iTV Conference* (pp. 185-186), Amsterdam.

Foster, R., Daymon, C., & Tewungwa, S. (2002). Future reflections: Four scenarios for television in 2012. *Condensed Report for the Future Reflections Conference* led by Bournemouth Media School.

Fink, M. (2006). Social and interactive television: Applications based on real-time ambient – audio identification. In *Proceedings of the 4ᵗʰ Euro iTV Conference* (pp. 138-146). Athens, Greece.

Gawlinksi, M. (2003). *Interactive television production.* Oxford: Focal Press.

Geerts, D., Harboe, G., & Massey N. (2007). *Overview of social TV workshop, 5ᵗʰ Euro ITV Conference,* Amsterdam.

Ghittino A., Iatrino A., Modeo S., & Ricchiuti F. (2006). Living@room: A support for direct sociability through interactive TV. In *Adjunct Proceedings of the 5th Euro iTV Conference* (pp. 131-132). Amsterdam.

Giddens, A. (1991). *Modernitet og selvidentitet,* Kobenhavn Hans Reitzels Forlag. As transferred by Rasmussen, T.A. and Christensen, L.H. (2006), from user generated content and community communication for television. In *Proceedings of the 4ᵗʰ Euro iTV Conference* (pp. 27-31). Athens, Greece.

Goldin, R., Rochat, A., & Anderson, G. (2008). Pluralizing the screen: Converging gesture, environment & interface. In *Adjunct Proceedings of the 6ᵗʰ Euro iTV Conference* (pp. 138-141). Salzburg, Austria.

Goro Otsubo (2007). Goromi-TV browsing for thousands of videos at will. In *Adjunct Proceedings of the 5ᵗʰ Euro iTV Conference* (pp. 187-188). Amsterdam.

Hagel III, J., & Armstrong, A.G. (1997). *Net gain: Expanding markets through virtual communities.* Boston: Harvard Business School Press.

Haque, R. S. (2008). Social TV: Lean-in versus lean-out. In *Adjunct Proceedings of the 6ᵗʰ Euro iTV Conference* (pp. 142-143). Salzburg, Austria.

Harrison, C., & Amento, B. (2007). CollaboraTV – Making TV social again. In *Adjunct Proceedings of the 5ᵗʰ Euro iTV Conference* (pp. 137-138). Amsterdam.

Herr, P. M., Kardes, F. R., & Kim, J. (1991). Effects of word-of-mouth and product-attribute information on persuasion: An accesibility-diagnosticity perspective. *Journal of Consumer Research, 17*(March), (pp. 454-462).

Hesselman, C., Derks, W., Broekens, J., Eertink, H., Gülbahar, M., & Poortinga, R. (2008). An open service infrastructure for enhancing interactive TV experiences. In *Adjunct Proceedings of the 6ᵗʰ Euro iTV Conference* (pp. 23-24). Salzburg, Austria.

Hoffman, D. L., & Novak, Th. P. (1996). Marketing in hypermedia computer-mediated environments: Conceptual foundations. *Journal of Marketing, 60*(July), 50-68.

Iatrino, A., Modeo, S., & CSP - ICT Innovation (2007). Living@room: A support for direct sociability through interactive TV. In *Adjunct Proceedings of the 5th Euro iTV Conference* (pp.131-132). Amsterdam.

Iatrino, A., & Modeo, S. (2006). Text editing in digital terrestrial television: A comparison of three interfaces. In *Proceedings of the 4th Euro iTV Conference* (pp. 198-204). Athens, Greece.

Jakob Nielsen's Alertbox (1997). *WebTV Usability Review*. Retrieved May 13 (2008) from http://www.useit.com/alertbox/9702a.html

Jayasinghe, N. (May 2006), *Spannerworks White Paper*. Retrieved from http://www.spanerworks.com

Jensen, J. F. (2005). Interactive television: New genres, new format, new content. In *Proceedings of the Second Australasian Conference on Interactive Entertainment* (pp. 89-96). Sydney, Australia.

Jones, Q. (1997). Virtual communities, virtual settlements & cyberarcheology: A theoretical outline. *Journal of Computer-Mediated Communication*, (3). Available at http://www.ascusc.org/jcmc

Kim, P., & Sawhney, H. (2002). A machine-like new medium - Theoretical examination of interactive TV. *Media, Culture and Society, 24*, 217-233.

Lee, H., et al. (2008). Balancing simplicity and functionality in designing user-interface for an interactive TV. In *Adjunct Proceedings of the 6th Euro iTV Conference* (pp. 277-278). Salzburg, Austria.

Livingstone, S., & Bovill, M., (1999). Young people, new media. *Summary report of the research project: Children, Young People and the Changing Media Environment*. As accessed on http://www.lse.ac.uk/Depts/Media/people/slivingstone/young people report.pdf

Lull, J. (1990). *Inside family viewing: Ethnographic research on television's audiences.* London: Routledge.

Luyten, K., Thys, K., Huypens, S., & Coninx, K. (2006). Telebuddies: Social stitching with interactive television. *CHI 2006*, Montreal Canada. Available at: http://research.edm.uhasselt.be/kris/research/projects/telebuddies/

Macklin, B. (2002). What every marketer needs to know about iTV. *eMarketer*, http://www.broadbandbananas.com/wem.pdf

Mantzari, E., & Vrechopoulos, A., (2007), "My Social Tube": User fenerated content and communication on interactive digital television. In *Adjunct Proceedings of the 5th European Interactive TV Conference*, (pp. 241-246). Amsterdam.

McQuail, D. (1998). *Mass communication theory: An introduction.* London: Sage Publications.

Masthoff, J. (2004). Group modelling: Selecting a sequence of television items to suit a group of viewers. *User Modelling and User-Adopted Interaction, 14*, 37-85. Netherlands: Kluwer Academic Publishers.

Oehlberg, L., Ducheneaut, N., Thornton, J. D., Moore, R. J., & Nickell, E. (2006). Social TV: Designing for distributed, sociable television biewing. In *Proceedings of the 4th Euro iTV Conference* (pp. 251-259). Athens, Greece.

Orbist, M. (2007). My Home: Let users design their own social TV. In *Adjunct Proceedings of the 5th European Conference of Interactive Television* (pp. 133-134). Amsterdam.

Pesce, M. (2005). The human use of human networks. Presented at *Designing the Future*, ISOC Australia.

Price, L. L., & Feick, L. F. (1984). The role of interpersonal sources and external search: An informational perspective. In Th.C. Kinnear, (Ed.), *Advances in Consumer Research, 11,* 250-255. Provo, UT: Association for Consumer Research.

Putnam, R. D. (2000). *Bowling alone.* New York: Simon & Schuster.

Quico, C. (2003), Are communication services the killer applications for Interactive TV? Or "I left my wife because I am in love with the TV set". In *Proceedings of the 1st European Conference on Interactive TV,* (pp. 99-107). Brighton, UK.

Rainie, L. (2006), Life online: Teens and technology and the world to come. In *Proceedings of the Annual Conference of Public Library Association.*

Rasmussen, T. A. (2005), The sociability of interactive television. In J.F. Jensen (Ed.), *User-centred ITV systems, Programmes and Applications, Proceedings of the 3rd Euro iTV Conference,* Aalborg, Denmark.

Rasmussen, T. A., & Christensen, L. H. (2006). User generated content and community communication for television. In *Proceedings of the 4th Euro iTV Conference* (pp. 27-31). Athens, Greece.

Rheingold, H. (2001), Mobile virtual communities. *The Feature,* July 2001, Tapscott. Available at: http://www.thefeature.com/index.jsp? url=article.jsp?/page id=12070

Roberto, M., Fer, A., & Botelho, C. (2008). iTVProject: An authoring tool for MHP based on a Web environment. In *Adjunct Proceedings of the 6th Euro iTV Conference* (pp. 214-216). Salzburg, Austria.

Sherry, J. F., & Kozinets, R. V. (2000). Qualitative inquiry in marketing and consumer research. In

D. Iacobucci (Ed.), *Kellogg on marketing* (pp. 165-194). New York: John Wiley & Sons.

Schibelsky, L., Piccolo, G., Menckie Melo, A., & Calani Baranauskas, M. C. (2007). A convergent proposal for accessible interactive TV applications development. In *Adjunct Proceedings of the 5th European Conference of Interactive Television* (pp. 259-264). Amsterdam.

Spannerworks (2006). *What is social media?, an e-book.* Available at: http://www.spannerworks.com/ebooks

Stewart, J. (2004). Interactive television at home: Television meets the Internet. *The Future of TV,* v.4.2, March (Published in Cathy Toscan - Jens Jensen eds. 1999, Aalborg University Press).

Tichi, C. (1991). *Electronic hearth: Creating an american television culture.* New York: Oxford University Press.

Thorson, K. S., & Rodgers, S. (2006). Relationships between blogs as eWOM and interactivity, perceived interactivity and parasocial interaction. *Journal of Interactive Advertising, 6*(2), 39-50. Spring Eds. Published at: http://jad.org/vol6/no2/thorson

Vorderer, P. (2000). Interactive entertainment and beyond. In D. Zillman & P. Vorderer (Eds.), *Media entertainment: The psychology of its appeal.* Mahwah, NJ: Lawrence Earlbaum.

Wang, J., Pouwelse, J., Fokker, J., & Reinders, M. J. T. (2006). Personalization of a peer-to-peer television system. In *Proceedings of the 4th Euro iTV Conference* (pp. 147-155). Athens, Greece.

Wolton, D. (1997). *Penser la communication.* Paris: Flammarion.

KEY TERMS

Digital Television encodes the television picture as a series of binary numbers, and then uses computer processing to compress it so it is transmitted in a fraction of the bandwidth, or capacity, taken by the equivalent analogue TV signal. [The Parliamentary Office of Science and Technology, UK]

Interactive Television is a medium providing "greater selection of programming on hundreds of channels, ... more control over and customization of television content, ... on-demand delivery of specific programs or movie, ... real-time interaction between people in different households via game playing and communication". [Kim, P., & Sawhney, H. (2002). A Machine-Like New Medium - Theoretical Examination of Interactive TV, *Media, Culture and Society*, vol. 24, (pp. 217-233)]

Social Television is defined as "communication and social interactions – remote or co-located – in a TV-watching content, or related to a TV experience; and technology that supports these communications and interactions" [Geerts, D., Harboe, G., & Massey N. (2007). *Overview of Social TV Workshop*, *5th Euro iTV Conference*, Amsterdam, Netherlands]

A **Virtual Community** is defined as "a class of computer-mediated group communication that takes place within a specified communication structure is labeled a virtual community when the following four conditions are met: (1) a minimum level of interactivity, (2) a variety of communicators, (3) a minimum level of sustained membership, and (4) a virtual common-public-space where a significant number of computer-mediated group communications occur" [Jones, Q. (1997). Virtual Communities, Virtual Settlements & Cyberarcheology: a Theoretical Outline. *Journal of Computer-Mediated Communication* (3). Available at: http://www.ascusc.org/jcmc]

"**Virtual Communities** are organized among affinities, shared interests, bringing together people who did not necessarily know each other before meeting online – enabling many-to-many communication". [Rheingold, H. (2001), Mobile Virtual Communities, *The Feature*, Tapscott, July 2001 Available at: http://www.thefeature.com/index.jsp?url=article.jsp?page id=12070]

ENDNOTE

[1]   www.Ensequence.com

Chapter VIII
Evaluating the Effectiveness of Social Visualization Within Virtual Communities

Diana Schimke
University of Regensburg, Germany

Heidrun Stoeger
University of Regensburg, Germany

Albert Ziegler
Ulm University, Germany

ABSTRACT

Participation and system usage is crucial for virtual communities to develop and sustain. However, many communities report very low participation rates of members. Finding and studying strategies for fostering participation in virtual communities is therefore a growing field of research and different approaches for strengthening participation in virtual communities exist – among them social visualization. While many tools for visualizing social interactions have been developed, not much empirical evidence about their actual effectiveness exists. To find out more about the effectiveness of social visualization on the participation rate (number of logins, forum posts, personal messages, and chat posts) the authors conducted an empirical study within CyberMentor – a virtual community for high school girls interested in science and technology. In their sample of N=231 girls the authors did not find a significant difference between the number of logins in the phases before and after the introduction of the visualization tool. The number of forum post, chat posts and personal messages however increased significantly after the incorporation of the visualization tool. Long-term effects were found for one-to-many communication technologies (forum, chat), but not for personal messages (one-to-one).

INTRODUCTION

In this chapter we present results of an empirical study about visualizing usage behaviour of community members within CyberMentor – a virtual community for girls who are interested in science, technology, engineering, and mathematics (STEM). We conducted a timeline study and divided the ten months duration of our study (September 2006 till June 2007) in four phases: starting phase (month 1 and 2), consolidation phase (month 3), short-term effect phase (month 4 and 5), and long-term effect phase (month 6 through 10). The visualization tool (CyberCircle) we developed was incorporated into the platform after the consolidation phase. To find out if social visualization has an effect on the users' participation behaviour we compared community members participation rates (number of logins, forum posts, personal messages, and chat posts) of the consolidation phase with average participation rates of the short- and the long-term phase.

We will start with some background information about virtual communities in general, the technology acceptance model which serves as our theoretical background, and social visualization. The chapter focuses on virtual communities or online communities in general rather than on virtual communities of practice. The virtual community described in this chapter offers great opportunities for formal and informal learning though, which will be discussed later. Since virtual communities and virtual communities of practice are extensively covered in other chapters, we will not go into detail concerning this topic. As background of our own work we chose the technology acceptance model which will be described before defining and showing examples of social visualization. An overview of evaluation approaches of visualization techniques within communities shows that only little evidence of the effects of social visualization within virtual communities exists (e.g. concerning the participation rate). Next, we describe the aim of our research and the hypotheses concerning the effects of social visualization on participation. In the method section we will present the virtual community (CyberMentor) that we used as a research tool for our study. We also describe the community platform, and the social visualization tool (CyberCircle) we developed. After a description of the subjects, research design, and measurement variables, we present the results of our study and discuss them. We conclude our chapter by naming some limitations of our study and making suggestions for future research and practice.

BACKGROUND

Virtual Communities

In the research literature a wide variety of definitions on virtual communities exists, which range from technical to people-centred. Lazar and Preece (2002) define virtual communities as "a set of users who communicate using computer-mediated communication and have common interests, shared goals, and shared resources" (p. 128). Preece (2000) identifies key elements of virtual communities: (1) people, who interact as they strive to satisfy their own needs, (2) shared purpose, such as a common interest or need that provides a reason for the community, (3) policies, that guide peoples interaction, and (4) computer systems, to support social interaction and facilitate a sense of togetherness. Virtual communities encourage research of different disciplines (e.g. computer science, psychology, sociology, anthropology, etc.) and one finds various methods for studying and answering research questions about virtual communities. One important research field deals with investigating usage behaviour of community members. Reasons for joining an online community are examined (e.g. Ridings & Gefen, 2004) as well as reasons for lurking (reading but not posting) (Katz, 1998; Nonnecke & Preece, 2001; Preece, Nonnecke, & Andrews,

2004). A growing body of research examines strategies and mechanisms to foster participation and contribution in virtual communities based on theories from social psychology (e.g. Cheshire, 2007; Cheshire & Antin, 2008; Harper et al., 2007; Ling et al., 2005; Rafaeli, Raban, & Ravid, 2007; Rashid et al., 2006). Harper et al. (2007) for example conducted field experiments involving members of an online movie recommendation community (MovieLens) and studied effects of personalized invitation messages designed to encourage users to visit or contribute to the forum. They found that personalized invitations led to an increase in participation (reading and posting). Cheshire & Antin (2008) examined the effects of various feedback mechanisms on repeated contributions. The types of feedback they examined were "Gratitude" for providing a contribution, a "Historical Reminder" on one's entire contribution record, and the "Relative Ranking" on one's contributions compared to others (p. 712). The authors report significant impacts of all three feedback mechanisms on repeated contributions of users. Techniques of visualizing social interaction within the community platform offer another approach for strengthening participation in virtual communities. Our research focuses on that approach. Before we give a short overview over some main ideas and findings in the field of social visualization, we describe the technology acceptance model (TAM) (Davis, 1989, 1993; Davis, Bagozzi, & Warshaw, 1989) and its successor TAM2 (Venkatesh & Davis, 2000) on which our assumptions concerning social visualizations are based on.

Technology Acceptance Model

Besides other models of technology acceptance (for an overview see Venkatesh, Morris, Davis, & Davis, 2003), the technology acceptance model TAM (Davis, 1989, 1993; Davis et al., 1989) and its successor TAM2 (Venkatesh & Davis, 2000) are influential models to explain and predict system usage behaviour. The technology acceptance model (TAM) is theoretically based on the Theory of Reasoned Action (TRA) by Fishbein and Ajzen (1975). According to the TRA behaviour is directly influenced by the intention to perform a behaviour. The intention in turn is influenced by the attitude towards the behaviour and the subjective norm concerning the behaviour. Attitude stands for "an individual's positive or negative feelings (evaluative affect) about performing the target behaviour" (Fishbein & Ajzen, 1975, p. 216). Subjective norm is defined as a "person's perception that most people who are important to him think he should or should not perform the behaviour in question" (Fishbein & Ajzen, 1975, p. 302). The theory states that people perform the anticipated behaviour if they a) judge the behaviour as positive and b) believe that important others do so too. The TAM, proposed by Davis (1989) adapts the TRA to the field of Information Systems. Two new constructs, perceived usefulness and perceived ease of use are introduced in the TAM. Perceived usefulness is "the degree to which a person believes that using a particular system would enhance his or her job performance" (Davis, 1989, p. 320); perceived ease of use is "the degree to which a person believes that using a particular system would be free of effort" (Davis, 1989, p. 320). In the TAM those two constructs are seen as determinants of an individual's attitude towards using an application.

The subjective norm component is not included in the first version of TAM. However, research conducted on the influence of subjective norms on intention led to mixed results. While some researchers found significant effects of subjective norm on behavioural intentions (Cheung, Lee, & Chen, 2002; Igbaria, Zinatelli, Cragg, & Cavaye, 1997; Riemenschneider, Harrison, & Mykytyn, 2003; Taylor & Todd, 1995), others found no significant effects (Lau, Yen, & Chau, 2001; Mathieson, 1991; Roberts & Henderson, 2000). Although Davis, Bagozzi, & Warshaw (1989) also found no significant effect of subjective norm on intentions they highlighted the need for more research to find out more about "the conditions and mechanism governing the impact of social influences on usage behaviour" (1989, p. 999). In a further study Venkatesh & Davis (2000) hypothesized that subjective norm would influence perceived usefulness and usage intention if system use is mandatory. They found that subjective norm indeed exerts a significant direct effect on usage intentions for mandatory systems. Further on, subjective norm influenced usage behaviour via perceived usefulness (Venkatesh & Davis, 2000). Venkathesh & Davis (2000) summarized their new findings in a follow-up model called TAM2 including subjective norm into the model.

With the aim of examining the convergence or divergence of published research results Schepers & Wetzels (2007) conducted a quantitative meta-analysis with 63 studies in which TAM/TAM2 had been assessed empirically. Besides confirming the original TAM relationships (significance of perceived usefulness and perceived ease of use towards attitude and behavioural intention to use) via correlation analysis and structural equation modelling, the authors examined the influence of subjective norm. Correlations between subjective norm and behavioural intention were tested in 22 studies. They found that in most studies (19), subjective norm is directly and significantly related to users' intention to use a system. According to the research reviewed, one possibility to strengthen the subjective norm component and thereby the system usage is to make the social group salient to the users. Important here seem to be perceptions of group distinction (e.g. Henri Tajfel & Turner, 1986) which lead to higher commitment towards the own group, as well as an increased ambition to strengthen in-group identity through participation. Although Michinov, Michinov & Toczek-Capelle mention that in computer based environments "nonverbal and paralinguistic cues may prevent the development of a sense of belonging among group members who are geographically distant from one another" (2004, p. 28), they concede that

the social identity theory (H. Tajfel, 1978) contradicts this assumption by providing an alternative perspective. In their view identification with an online group becomes possible when the salience of the group is enhanced. This enhancement of salience of a group could be achieved by social visualization techniques. Visualizing additional information – for example usage behaviour of community members – makes the platform a less anonymous place. Utz (1999) conducted a study about MUDs (Multi-User Dungeons) and found out that users with a higher identifiability showed a higher orientation towards collectivist norms than users who were less identifiable. Therefore we assume that visualizing social interactions (and thereby making community members more identifiable) has a positive influence on the subjective norm and thus on the usage behaviour. Before presenting our aim of research we define social visualisation, show some examples and discuss first findings concerning social visualization and its influence on participation rates.

Social Visualization

Erickson (2003) defines social visualization as 'a visual (or sonic or other perceptual) representation of information from which the presence, activities, and other characteristics of members of a social collectivity may be inferred, and, by extension, can provide the basis for making inferences about the activities and characteristics of the group as a whole' (p. 846). In the literature one can find different operationalizations of social visualization within virtual communities (e.g. Bouras, Igglesis, Kapoulas, & Tsiatsos, 2005; Bradner, Kellogg, & Erickson, 1998, 1999; Erickson, Halverson, Kellogg, Laff, & Wolf, 2002; Erickson & Kellogg, 2000; Erickson & Laff, 2001; Erickson et al., 1999; Lee, Girgensohn, & Zhang, 2004; Perry & Donath, 2004; Sun, 2004; Sun & Vassileva, 2006; Vassileva & Sun, 2007; Xiong & Donath, 1999). They all visualize "hidden" information about users and usage behaviour. Erickson et al. (2002)

believe 'that such systems – by supporting mutual awareness and accountability – will make it easier for people to carry on coherent discussions; to observe and imitate others' actions; to engage in peer pressure; to create, notice, and conform to social conventions; and to engage in other forms of collective interaction' (p. 40). They developed a communication tool called Babble (Bradner et al., 1998, 1999; Erickson, 2003; Erickson et al., 2002; Erickson & Kellogg, 2000; Erickson & Laff, 2001; Erickson et al., 1999) which allows synchronous and asynchronous multi-channel text chat. The Babble system provides a social proxy, "a minimalist visualization of people and their activities" (Erickson et al., 2002, p. 40) called Cookie, which visualizes cues about the presence, number and ways of participation in the online environment. Participants are represented as coloured dots within the Cookie. The distance of the person's dot to the circle's centre indicates how recently that person had either "spoken" (typed a command) or "listened" (scrolled or clicked on the interface). A second social proxy within the Babble system, the Timeline, represents each user as a row. When logged on to Babble, users leave a line, and when "speaking" in the chat, they leave a vertical mark to the line. That way other users can see when people were online and when they were involved in conversations. For this social visualization no detailed evaluation but rather user experiences are reported and summarized as "in general, users report that the social proxy is engaging and informative" (Erickson et al., 2002, p. 41).

Another early visualization approach, the PeopleGarden, was developed by Xiong and Donath (1999). The PeopleGarden is a message board community that visualizes users' posting histories. Each user is represented as a flower. The height of the flower shows the length of membership. The number and colour of the flowers' petals indicate the number of messages sent and how recent they are. Also for this approach no empirical evaluation was conducted; instead

the authors summarized the users' informal feedback and conclude that users prefer realistic encodings.

Lee et al. (2004) developed two social browsers (People and eTree) for two different community Web sites - CHIplace and Portkey. CHIplace (see also Girgensohn & Lee, 2002) was developed for the ACM CHI 2002 conference to extend interactions among people. The Portkey Web community was developed for summer interns at IBM TJ Watson Research Center to enable them to exchange with others and develop social networks. The CHIplace People browser provides a community map of the site members' different roles. Each user is represented as a dot and grouped with others who are having similar roles. Related clusters of member dots are closer together than unrelated ones. The own user dot appears in red and one can easily see the own position within the community. By clicking on a dot one can open the person's profile page. For the eTree visualization within the Portkey community Lee et al. (2004) used an ecosystem metaphor consisting of the different parts of a tree.

Forums are represented as branches; threads are mapped in form of leaves. The colour of the leaves indicates the age of the posts. The community members are represented as coloured circles placed around the tree. The circle's colouring tells the user's role (intern or IBM authors) and its distance from the tree shows how active the user participates. The Portkey eTree was introduced shortly before the end of the interns' stay and the authors could only collect informal feedback about the metaphor. They reported that many people found the visualization attractive and that they liked the ability to view the growth and evolution of the discussions.

A main concern that came up was privacy. For the CHIplace People browser, usage data was collected and reported. The announcement of the People browser caused an overall usage spike. However, the percentage of sessions in which the People browser was used decreased from 35 percent in the announcement week to about six percent after eleven weeks. Lee et al. (2004) concluded that user feedback and comments provided strong support of the value of the two browsers and suggested "further studies to examine how such techniques can alter people's participation and behaviour in Web communities" (p. 75).

A more recent version of a visualization tool was developed by Sun and Vassileva (2006). They developed a paper sharing online community called Comtella. Within this community each user is represented as a star. The size of it indicates the users' participation level (number of shared links to papers). Based on the activity level each user is assigned to one of four levels, restricting the "best" 10% to the top level, 36% to the second level and 27% to the two lowest levels. The authors evaluated their visualization tool within an online class of students (N = 35) over a period of three months and reported increases in participation after their social visualization tool was incorporated into the platform after 6 weeks usage. However the methodology is not described exactly and no statistical test is mentioned. In a further study of Vassileva and Sun (2007), students (N = 32) were divided in two groups showing the visualization to each group half of the time (about 5 weeks to each group). However, as one group was more active independent of working or not working with the tool, the authors' initial hypothesis that the visualization would motivate the subjects to participate more actively could not be confirmed.

AIM OF RESEARCH

Social visualization tools that display hidden information about members' interactions have been developed and deployed within several virtual communities. While many researchers hope to increase participation and interaction of community members with the help of social visualization, not much empirical evidence ex-

ists. Only few evaluation results are reported in the literature and too many shortcomings exist to suppose that social visualization leads to an increase in participation. In our research we want to evaluate the effectiveness of social visualization on the participation rate of virtual community members. As most studies concerning participation in virtual communities study short-time effects, we will differentiate between short-term effects and long-term effects. We also distinguish between various participation criterions like (1) the number of logins into the platform, (2) the number of posts to the discussion forum, (3) the number of personal messages sent to other community members, and (4) the number of chat messages.

Based on findings by (1) Hartwick and Barki (1994) that system usage drops significantly after about three months due to subsiding subjective norm as well as by (2) Agarwal and Prasad (1997) who reported that mandating system use can increase initial system utilization, we assume that participation declines after the starting phase (see H1). We further assume that visualizing social interactions has an impact on community member's subjective norm and thus leads to increased system usage, like predicted by the technology acceptance model TAM2 (Venkatesh & Davis, 2000). We therefore expect that after the introduction of the social visualization tool CyberCircle the participation rate of community members increases within a short-term phase (see H2a) as well as for a long-term phase (see H2b). To test our assumptions we propose the following hypotheses:

H1: *Participation in virtual communities decreases significantly after the starting phase.*

H2a: *The incorporation of the CyberCircle increases the short-term participation rate of community members.*

H2b: *The incorporation of the CyberCircle increases the long-term participation rate of community members.*

The three hypotheses will be tested for four different participation criterions: (1) the number of logins into the platform (visits), (2) the number of posts to the discussion forum, (3) the number of personal messages sent to other community members, and (4) the number of chat messages.

Conducting a study aiming to test those hypotheses requires an appropriate virtual community plus platform. Using an existing virtual community does not usually allow such kind of research since log files are not available. Further on, many communities are based on one communication technology (e.g. discussion forum, mailing list, etc.) instead of the different kinds of technologies we are interested in, such as discussion forum, personal messages, and chat room. In order to conduct this study we first needed to create an appropriate virtual community and to build a platform. The community, its platform, and the social visualization tool we tested within this community will be described in the method section below.

METHOD

In the following the community itself, its platform and the visualization tool called CyberCircle will be described, followed by a description of subjects and the study design.

CyberMentor: Virtual Community for Girls Interested in STEM

Building a sustainable virtual community from scratch is a challenging task. You need a good purpose and the idea of the community has to be attractive to potential members. Doing research in the field of gender and science (Stoeger, 2007;

Stoeger, Ziegler, & David, 2004; Ziegler & Stoeger, 2004, 2008) and knowing about the female shortage of skilled labour in science, technology, engineering, and mathematics (STEM) in Germany (Statistisches-Bundesamt, 2006) we decided to build a virtual community to foster girls' interest and participation rate in STEM. Mawasha, Lam, Vesalo, Leitch, and Rice (2001) identified strategies to foster interest in science and technology among girls. These strategies involve (1) increasing girls' knowledge about STEM, (2) providing information about career opportunities in STEM, and (3) allocating role models, contact persons, and mentors. Based on these requirements and further empirical evidence about gender, girls and STEM (for more information refer to Deaux & Lafrance, 1998; Eccles-Parsons, 1984; Eccles, 1994; Packard, 2003; Packard & Hudging, 2002) we developed the virtual community CyberMentor. One important aspect of our community is "mentoring" between girls (mentees) who are interested in science and female mentors who are vocationally engaged in STEM. Over the course of ten months mentors and mentees communicate via e-mail in one-to-one relationships. This approach provides the girls with female role models and increases their knowledge about the field of STEM and possible careers in various STEM domains. By offering this virtual community, formal and informal learning about science topics takes place. On the one hand, participants learn from their mentors, on the other hand, they also learn from and together with other female students. As same-age role models are as important as older role models (Breakwell & Beardsell, 1992) the participating girls are encouraged to engage in team work projects (Schimke & Stoeger, 2007) and to communicate with each other via our community platform.

The Community Platform

"Just as traditional communities require a vehicle for participation, virtual communities require a system that supports the exchange of electronic information among members" (Moore & Serva, 2007, p. 154). The community platform we developed serves as a virtual meeting place for the community members. It is accessible for community members only. Each applicant's identity is verified (mentees need signatures from legal guardians; mentors need to name two contact persons for enabling the program administrator to recheck identities) before login information is provided. Within this platform, each participant can introduce herself by filling out a personal profile and uploading a picture. Each personal page includes a wall for posting comments. For group communication we incorporated an open source discussion forum (http://www.phpbb.com/) as well as an open source chat room (http://www.phpfreechat.net/). The personal message system – like the whole community platform - is based on common Web technologies (PHP, HTML, CSS, JavaScript, and Ajax) and was developed by us. One important function of the platform is its tracking capacity, which allows us to store information about logins, number of posts to the discussion forum, number of chat messages and the number of personal messages in a MySQL database.

The platform was developed, tested and adjusted in a first CyberMentor season from September 2005 till June 2006.

CyberCircle: Visualizing Social Interaction

The CyberCircle is a social visualization tool that provides information about the users' participation rates. It assigns each community member to one of the following categories: Beginner, Amateur, Professional, V.I.P., Top-CyberMentee. The assignment to either category or "status" is based on different criterions: (1) number of community logins, (2) number of posts to the discussion forum, (3) number of personal messages, and (4) number of chat posts. For each category each person gets points according to her activity level; the sum of all points assigns a person to one of the five categories. However, the assignment is not fixed. It involves the factor "time" and calculates the current status based on an algorithm which values more recent activities stronger than older ones. Unlike Sun and Vassileva (2006) we did not apportion the levels; instead every member could be in the top or any other level. The users' status is displayed on the first page within the community platform as well as on the CyberCircle site. Within the CyberCircle view users can click on the different levels (Beginner, Amateur, etc.) to see all members assigned to these levels. To get an idea of the average usage level of all users, the mean group level is also displayed. Figure 1 shows and explains the visualisation tool.

SUBJECTS AND STUDY DESIGN

The study was carried out within the CyberMentor platform which is accessible to registered members only. During the time the study was conducted (September 2006 – June 2007) the CyberMentor community had 231 female student members and as many female mentor members. The mentors however were not included in this study and will not be mentioned in the following anymore. The 231 student members – the subjects of this study – were all middle and high school students visiting grades six through thirteen. The mean age was M = 15.19 (SD = 1.97). Since CyberMentor is about science, technology, engineering, and mathematics (STEM), the participating girls were all interested in those topics. For being accepted into the CyberMentor program interested girls had to apply and state reasons for participation. After applying online, they had to print out the e-mail with their application data, sign it (under aged girls also needed a signature from legal guardians) and send it or fax it back to the program administrators. By signing the application they agreed to take part in our research study.

Figure 1. Visualization tool CyberCircle

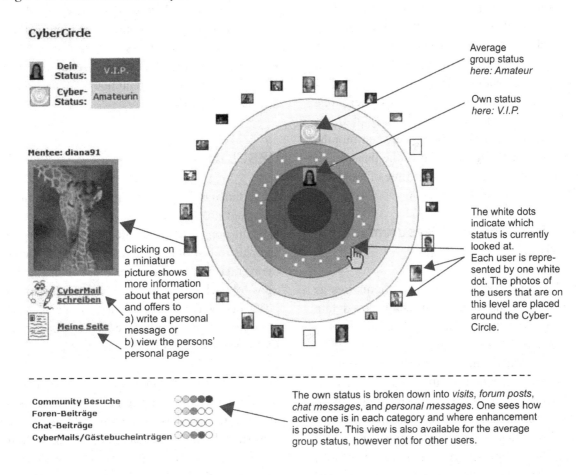

Figure 2. Phases of our ten months study and point of time of inclusion of the CyberCircle

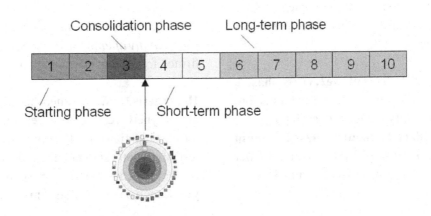

To answer our research questions we conducted a timeline study and divided the ten months duration of the study (September 2006 till June 2007) in four phases: the starting phase (month 1 and 2), the consolidation phase (month 3), the short-term effect phase (month 4 and 5), and the long-term effect phase (month 6 through 10). The CyberCircle was incorporated into the community platform after the consolidation phase (between months three and four). Figure 2 shows the phases and lengths of phases as well as the time of inclusion of the social visualization tool CyberCircle.

Data Selection and Measurement Variables

For this study we did not use questionnaires as measurement instruments, instead we used data stored in a database and gathered through log file analysis. Based on the technology acceptance model TAM2 (Venkatesh & Davis, 2000) we assumed that the incorporation of a visualization tool would lead to greater system usage. To be able to measure and compare system usage rates in different phases, we stored the timestamps and number of (1) logins into the community platform, (2) posts to the discussion forum, (3) personal messages, and (4) chat messages for each subject in a MySQL database.

Due to different lengths of the phases (starting phase: 2 months, consolidation phase: 1 month, short-term phase: 2 months, and long-term phase: 5 months), we calculated mean values of the mentioned variables for each phase for each subject. Doing this we had the following sixteen variables for each subject:

- **visits phase1, visits phase2, visits phase3, visits phase4:** Mean number of logins into the community platform in each phase.
- **forum phase1, forum phase2, forum phase3, forum phase4:** Mean number of posts to the discussion forum in each phase.

- **messages phase1, messages phase2, messages phase3, messages phase4:** Mean number of personal messages sent to other community members in each phase.
- **chat phase1, chat phase2, chat phase3, chat phase4:** Mean number chat messages in each phase.

RESULTS

Since our data showed no normal distribution, we could not use the t-test. For this reason we used the nonparametric Wilcoxon test for paired samples to test our hypotheses. Figure 3 shows the average participation rates and standard deviations for each criterion (visits, discussion forum posts, personal messages, chat messages) for the four phases (starting phase, consolidation phase, short-term phase, and long-term phase).

Hypothesis 1: For hypothesis 1 we wanted to test if participation in virtual communities decreases after the starting phase (two months duration). We compared the mean participation rates for the four participation criterions (number of visits, forum posts, personal messages, and chat messages) of the starting phase (first bar in each diagram in figure 3) to the consolidation phase (second bar). We found a decline for the number of visits ($Z = -10.52, p < .001$), the number of discussion forum posts ($Z = -4.76, p < .001$), the number of personal messages ($Z = -7.34, p < .001$), and the number of chat posts ($Z = -5.26, p < .001$). Hypothesis 1 *"Participation in virtual communities decreases significantly after the starting phase"* can be confirmed for all four participation criterions.

Hypothesis 2a: We assumed that the incorporation of the CyberCircle tool would enable an increase in the participation rate of community members. To test this hypothesis we compared the participation rates of the consolidation phase (no *CyberCircle* yet; second bar in the diagrams in figure 3) to the

Figure 3. Means and standard deviations of activity levels of interest in the four phases

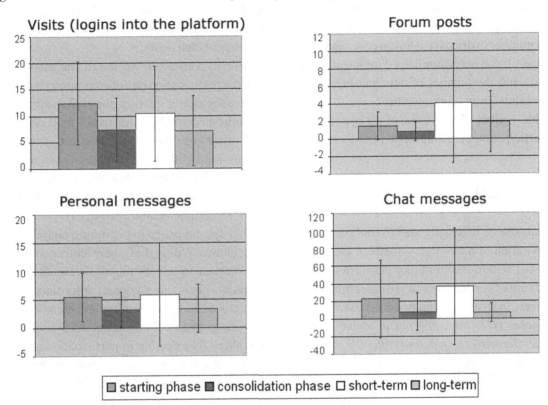

short-term phase (this is the phase right after the *CyberCircle* was incorporated into the platform; third bar in each diagram) using the *Wilcoxon* test for paired samples. Concerning the number of visits to the platform, no significant increase could be found ($Z = 1.15$, $p > .10$) between the consolidation and the short-term phase. For the discussion forum ($Z = 6.19$, $p < .001$), the number of personal messages ($Z = 2.24$, $p < .05$), and chat messages ($Z = 5.29$, $p < .001$) we found significant increases in the short term phase. Hypothesis 2a *"The incorporation of the CyberCircle increases the short-term participation rate of community members"* can therefore be confirmed for the number of discussion forum posts, the number of personal messages and the number of chat posts. It can not be confirmed for the logins into the platform (visits) however.

Hypothesis 2b: For hypothesis 2b we wanted to test if the incorporation of the CyberCircle increases the participation rate of community members in the long run. We compared the mean participation rates before the *CyberCircle* was incorporated into the platform (consolidation phase; second bar in each diagram in figure 3) with the participation rates of the long-term phase (forth bar in each diagram), which covers months six through ten. We did not find a significant increase in the number of visits, instead we found a significant decrease ($Z = -3.24$, $p < .01$). The participation rate within the discussion forum however was significantly higher in the long-term phase compared to the consolidation phase ($Z = 2.44$, $p < .01$) as well as the participation rate in the chat room ($Z = 1.96$, $p < .05$). No significant increase was found for the number of personal messages. Instead we found a significant decrease ($Z = -3.24$, *p* < .01). Hypothesis 2b *"The incorporation of the CyberCircle increases the long-term participation rate of community members"* can be confirmed for the number of discussion forum posts and chat messages. It can not be confirmed for the number of visits and the number of personal messages sent to other community members.

Table 1 gives an overview of all hypotheses and participation criterions tested in this study.

DISCUSSION

The purpose of this study was to find out if the incorporation of a tool that visualizes social interactions within a community platform affects the amount of system usage of virtual community members. To answer this question we tested three hypotheses (***H1**: Participation in virtual communities decreases significantly after the starting phase,* ***H2a**: The incorporation of the CyberCircle increases the short-term participation rate of community members,* ***H2b**: The incorporation of the CyberCircle increases the long-term participation rate of community members*) and analyzed the

four participation criterions (1) number of visits to the platform, (2) number of discussion forum posts, (3) number of personal messages, and (4) number of chat posts.

For hypothesis 1 we tested the assumption that the participation rate of community members decreases after a starting phase (2 months). The hypothesis could be confirmed for all participation criterions (visits to the platform, number of discussion forum posts, number of personal messages, and number of chat posts). These results are in line with findings of Hartwick and Barki (1994) and Agarwal and Prasad (1997) who report higher system usage in beginning phases versus later phases. Within the CyberMentor community the decrease in activity makes also sense because mentor's names and contact information were announced in the beginning and members were curious to find out more about other community members. The decline in participation after two months was therefore not surprising. As participation is crucial for virtual communities to survive we needed to find strategies for fostering members' participation. On the basis of the TAM we assumed that this could be done by the incorporation of a

Table 1. Overview hypotheses and results

Hypotheses	Tested for participation criterion	Hypothesis confirmed?
H1: Participation in virtual communities decreases significantly after the starting phase.	Visits	yes
	Discussion forum posts	yes
	Personal messages	yes
	Chat posts	yes
H2a: The incorporation of the *CyberCircle* increases the short-term participation rate of community members.	Visits	no
	Discussion forum posts	yes
	Personal messages	yes
	Chat posts	yes
H2b: The incorporation of the *CyberCircle* increases the long-term participation rate of community members.	Visits	no
	Discussion forum posts	yes
	Personal messages	no
	Chat posts	yes

social visualization tool. For this reason we built a visualization tool and introduced it to the community after a three months period. To test its effectiveness we compared mean participation rates of the phases before and after the incorporation. We found no increase in the number of visits to the platform – neither for the short-term, nor for the long-term phase.

However, we found significant increases of the actual amount of interaction within the virtual community platform, concerning posts written in the discussion forum and messages posted within the chat room for both, the short and long term, phases. A possible explanation for the increases in these two participation criterions might be that people who were reading others posts without contributing before (such community member are usually defined as lurkers; for more information about lurkers and lurking refer to Nonnecke & Preece, 2000) got motivated and actively engaged in discussions after the incorporation of the *CyberCircle*. Preece, Nonnekce, and Andrews (2004) studied reasons for lurking and conveyed strategies to get lurkers (more) involved. These strategies involve clearly stating that interaction is wanted and honouring activity with a high(er) status within the virtual community. Both those strategies are fulfilled by the *CyberCircle*: its incorporation clearly states that interaction is wanted and if getting involved more users reach a higher status.

Interestingly, an increase in participation for personal messages could only be confirmed for the short-term phase (H2a), not for the long-term phase (H2b). A reason for this result might be that users feel more pressure to interact within public spaces where their presence is witnessed by more than one other person – which applies to the discussion forum and chat room. This would fit the idea that the subjective norm does have an influence on usage intention – especially when there is a higher visibility in the community that might lead to pressure, like in mandatory systems. Another explanation could be through social fa-

cilitation, which states that the presence of others serves as a source of arousal (Zajonc, 1965) which might influence participation. Contributions to a discussion forum or a chat room have a greater audience than one-to-one communication via personal messages. Therefore social facilitation might have a greater effect. This might explain why we found long-term effects among one-to-many communication technologies but not among one-to-one communication technologies. However, more research is needed to confirm this assumption.

LIMITATIONS AND DIRECTIONS FOR FUTURE RESEARCH

Some important factors need to be considered regarding our study. First, we did not have a control group, which means that we cannot completely disqualify the assumption that the results are based on effects other than the incorporation of the visualization tool. Since only few research results about the effectiveness of visualization tools exist so far, it was important for us to conduct a study evaluating the *CyberCircle* systematically. Based on experiences of our pilot study (September 2005 till June 2006) and from literature review (e.g. Preece, 2000; Whittaker, 1996) we knew, that a critical mass of users is needed in order to initiate a sustainable interactive discourse. Splitting all members in two halves and creating two separate communities with the same conditions would probably not have worked in our case due to too few members. Having enough members and the opportunity to set up two comparable communities of which one uses social visualization while the other one does not would be an interesting investigation for the future.

Another shortcoming of our study is that we used the technology acceptance model only as an explanation. We did not actually measure the components of the model such as subjective norm or perceived usefulness. For future research it would be important to test the components of the model and see if and how strongly subjective norm is influenced by social visualization. With our approach we tried to build a community that fits accepted definitions of a virtual community and that allows us to conduct our research and collect the data we needed. However, more research in different virtual communities and with different target groups needs to be done to find out if our results can be generalized.

There is also a shortcoming concerning the design of our social visualization tool as it is only applicable for relatively small virtual communities with three hundred community members or less. For virtual communities with more members it might get too crowded and unclear. For this reason different design options should be tested in future research. We see, there is a wide range of factors that needs to be considered and many more questions have to be answered before a clear statement about the impact of social visualization tools within virtual communities can be made. Concerning our future research we plan to answer some of the questions mentioned above.

CONCLUSION

First studies on virtual communities were reported in the early nineties. Back then, the research mainly focused on the question if virtual communities are "real" communities and what consequences arise through participation in virtual communities. Some critics worried that the involvement in virtual communities would cause the disengagement from "real" communities (e.g. Kraut et al., 1998). In the mean time, research has provided evidence that virtual communities can indeed be "real" communities (e.g. Baym, 1995; Utz, 1999) and many people today use virtual communities as a new way of "meeting" and staying in contact with each other, while still being engaged in face-

to-face interactive groups. Utz (2008) supposes that fundamental principles underlying virtual communities are similar to those underlying face-to-face groups. However, she names some aspects in which virtual communities differ, such as (1) an easier connection of people from all over the world, (2) the facilitation of large-scale collaboration, and (3) access to information that would not be available otherwise.

Based on these findings research nowadays focuses mainly on topics like the emergence and persistence of virtual communities, the content exchanged within virtual communities, or the potential of virtual communities for learning. Researchers agree that virtual communities depend on its members and their interaction, thus one important field of study deals with participation in virtual communities. This is also the domain we are interested in. For our study presented in this chapter we conducted an empirical study based on theories from social psychology and computer science and found interesting hints how to increase participation in a virtual community. After the incorporation of a visualization tool displaying community members' usage behaviour, the number of forum posts, chat posts and personal messages increased significantly. While the results of our study give answers to some first questions concerning the effectiveness of visualization in virtual communities, many questions remain open and need to be answered. For example: "Does visualization encourage participation in all virtual communities?", "Does it affect all users in the same way?" or, "What happens if people want to stay anonymous in the virtual community – do they get discouraged by a visualization tool?". There is more research needed in this young field of study. Cooperation of researchers with different backgrounds and from different disciplines is surely needed to further advance this field of research.

REFERENCES

Agarwal, R., & Prasad, J. (1997). The role of innovation characteristics and perceived voluntariness in the acceptance of information technologies. *Decision Science, 28*(3), 557-582.

Baym, N. K. (1995). The emergence of community in computer-mediated communication. In S. Jones (Ed.), *CyberSociety* (pp. 138-163). Newbury Park, CA: Sage.

Bouras, C., Igglesis, V., Kapoulas, V., & Tsiatsos, T. (2005). A Web-based virtual community. *International Journal of Web Based Communities, 1*(2), 127-139.

Bradner, E., Kellogg, W. A., & Erickson, T. (1998). Babble: Supporting conversation in the workplace. *SIGGROUP Bull., 19*(3), 8-10.

Bradner, E., Kellogg, W. A., & Erickson, T. (1999). *The adoption and use of 'BABBLE': A field study of chat in the workplace.* Paper presented at the Sixth conference on European Conference on Computer Supported Cooperative Work, Copenhagen, Denmark.

Breakwell, G. M., & Beardsell, S. (1992). Gender, parental and peer influences upon science attitudes and activities. *Public Understanding of Science, 1*, 183-197.

Cheshire, C. (2007). Selective incentives and generalized information exchange. *Social Psychology Quarterly, 70*(1), 82-100.

Cheshire, C., & Antin, J. (2008). The social psychological effects of feedback on the production of Internet information pools. *Journal of Computer-Mediated Communication, 13*(3), 705-727.

Cheung, C. M. K., Lee, M. K. O., & Chen, Z. (2002). *Using the Internet as a learning medium: An exploration of gender difference in the adoption of FaBWeb.* Paper presented at the 35th Hawaii International Conference on System Science.

Davis, F. D. (1989). Perceived usefulness, perceived ease of use and user acceptance of information technology. *MIS Quarterly, 13*(3), 319-340.

Davis, F. D. (1993). User acceptance of information technology: system characteristics, user perceptions and behavioral impacts. *International Journal of Man-Machine Studies, 38*(3), 475-487.

Davis, F. D., Bagozzi, R. P., & Warshaw, P. R. (1989). User acceptance of computer technology: A comparison of two theoretical models. *Management Science, 35*(8), 982-1003.

Deaux, K., & Lafrance, M. (1998). Gender. In D. T. Gilbert, S. T. Fiske & G. Lindzey (Eds.), *Handbook of social psychology* (Vol. 4, pp. 788-827). New York: Random House.

Eccles-Parsons, J. (1984). Sex differences in mathematics participation. In M. W. Steinkamp & M. L. Maehr (Eds.), *Advances in motivation and achievement: Women in science* (Vol. 93-137). Greenwich, CT: JAI Press.

Eccles, J. S. (1994). Understanding woman's educational and occupational choices: Applying the Eccles et al. model of achievement-related choices. *Psychology of Women Quarterly, 18*(4), 585-609.

Erickson, T. (2003). *Designing visualizations of social activity: Six claims.* Paper presented at the CHI '03 Human factors in computing systems, Ft. Lauderdale, Florida, USA.

Erickson, T., Halverson, C., Kellogg, W. A., Laff, M., & Wolf, T. (2002). Social translucence: Designing social infrastructures that make collective activity visible. *Commun. ACM, 45*(4), 40-44.

Erickson, T., & Kellogg, W. A. (2000). Social translucence: An approach to designing systems that support social processes. *ACM Trans. Comput.-Hum. Interact., 7*(1), 59-83.

Erickson, T., & Laff, M. R. (2001). *The design of the 'Babble' timeline: a social proxy for visualizing group activity over time*. Paper presented at the CHI '01 Human factors in computing systems, Seattle, Washington.

Erickson, T., Smith, D. N., Kellogg, W. A., Laff, M., Richards, J. T., & Bradner, E. (1999). *Socially translucent systems: Social proxies, persistent conversation, and the design of "babble"*. Paper presented at the SIGCHI conference on Human factors in computing systems: the CHI is the limit, Pittsburgh, Pennsylvania, United States.

Fishbein, M., & Ajzen, I. (1975). *Belief, attitude, intention, and behavior: An introduction to theory and research*. Reading, MA: Addison-Wesley.

Girgensohn, A., & Lee, A. (2002). Making Web sites be places for social interactions. In *Proceedings of ACM 2002 Conference of Computer Supported Cooperative Work* (pp. 136-145): ACM Press.

Harper, M. F., Frankowski, D., Drenner, S., Yuqing, R., Yuqing, Kiesler, S., Terveen, L., et al. (2007). Talk amongst yourselves: inviting users to participate in online conversations. In *12th international conference on Intelligent user interfaces* (pp. 62-71). Honolulu, Hawaii, USA: ACM.

Hartwick, J., & Barki, H. (1994). Explaining the role of user participation in information system use. *Management Science, 40*(4), 440-465.

Igbaria, M., Zinatelli, N., Cragg, P., & Cavaye, A. L. M. (1997). Personal computing acceptance factors in small firms: A structural equation model. *MIS Quarterly, 21*(3), 279-305.

Katz, J. (1998). *Luring the lurkers* [Electronic Version]. Retrieved 09.04.2008, from http://slashdot.org/features/98/12/28/1745252.shtml

Kraut, R., Patterson, M., Lundmark, V., Kiesler, S., Mukophadhyay, T., & Scherlis, W. (1998). Internet paradox. A social technology that reduces social involvement and psychological well-being? *American Psychologist, 53*(9), 1017-1021.

Lau, A., Yen, Y., & Chau, P. Y. K. (2001). Adoption of on-line trading in the Hong Kong financial market. *Journal of Electronic Commerce Research, 2*(2), 58-65.

Lazar, J., & Preece, J. (2002). Social considerations in online communities: Usability, sociability, and success factors. In H. van Oostendorp (Ed.), *Cognition in the digital world* (pp. 127-152). Mahwah: NJ: Lawrence Erlbaum Associates Inc. Publishers.

Lee, A., Girgensohn, A., & Zhang, J. (2004). Browsers to support awareness and social interaction. *IEEE Computer Graphics and Applications, 24*(5), 66-75.

Ling, K., Beenen, G., Ludfort, P., Wang, X., Chang, K., Li, X., et al. (2005). Using social psychology to motivate contributions to online communities. *Journal of Computer-Mediated Communication, 10*(4), article 10.

Mathieson, K. (1991). Predicting user intentions: comparing the technology acceptance model with the theory of planned behavior. *Information Systems Research, 2*(3), 173-191.

Mawasha, P. R., Lam, P. C., Vesalo, J., Leitch, R., & Rice, S. (2001). Girls entering technology, science, math and research training (GET SMART): A model for preparing girls in science and engineering disciplines. *Journal of Women and Minorities in Science and Engineering, 7*(1), 49-57.

Michinov, N., Michinov, E., & Toczek-Capelle, M.-C. (2004). Social identity, group processes, and performance in synchronous computer-mediated communication. *Group Dynamics, 8*(1), 27-39.

Moore, T. D., & Serva, M. A. (2007). *Understanding member motivation for contributing to different types of virtual communities: A proposed framework*. Paper presented at the ACM SIGMIS CPR conference on Computer personnel doctoral consortium and research conference: The global information technology workforce, St. Louis, Missouri, USA.

Nonnecke, B., & Preece, J. (2000). *Lurker demographics: Counting the silent. Proceedings of CHI 2000. 73-80. The Hague, Netherlands: ACM.* Paper presented at the CHI, The Hague, Neatherlands.

Nonnecke, B., & Preece, J. (2001). *Why lurkers lurk.* Paper presented at the Americas Conference on Information Systems, Boston, MA.

Packard, B. W.-L. (2003). Web-based mentoring: Challenging traditional models to increase women's access. *Mentoring & Tutoring, 11*(1), 53-65.

Packard, B. W.-L., & Hudging, J. A. (2002). Expanding college women's perceptions of physicists' lives and work through interactions with a physics careers Web site. *Journal of College Science Teaching, 32*(3), 164-170.

Perry, E., & Donath, J. (2004). *Anthropomorphic visualization: A new approach for depicting participants in online spaces.* Paper presented at the CHI '04 Human factors in computing systems, Vienna, Austria.

Preece, J. (2000). *Online communities: Designing usability and supporting socialbilty.* John Wiley & Sons, Inc.

Preece, J., Nonnecke, B., & Andrews, D. (2004). The top five reasons for lurking: Improving community experience for everyone. *Computers in Human Behavior, 20*(1), 201-223.

Rafaeli, S., Raban, D., & Ravid, G. (2007). How social motivation enhances economic activity and incentives in the Google answers knowledge sharing market. *International Journal of Knowledge and Learning, 3*(1), 1-11.

Rashid, A. M., Ling, K., Tassone, R. D., Resnick, P., Kraut, R., & Riedl, J. (2006). *Motivating participation by displaying the value of contribution.*

Paper presented at the Conference on Human Factors in computing systems, Montréal, Québec, Canada.

Ridings, C. M., & Gefen, D. (2004). Virtual community attraction: Why people hang out online. *Journal of Computer-Mediated Communication, 10*(1), Arcticle 4.

Riemenschneider, C. K., Harrison, D. A., & Mykytyn, P. P. J. (2003). Understanding it adoption decisions in small business: integrating current theories. *Information & Managemeint, 40*(4), 269-285.

Roberts, P., & Henderson, R. (2000). Information technology acceptance in a sample of government employees: A test of the technology acceptance model. *Interacting with Computers, 12*(5), 427-443.

Schepers, J., & Wetzels, M. (2007). A meta-analysis of the technology acceptance model: Investigating subjective norm and moderation effects. *Information & Managemeint, 44*(1), 90-103.

Schimke, D., & Stoeger, H. (2007). Web-basierte Teilnahme an SchülerInnenwettbewerben als Möglichkeit der Förderung begabter Mädchen im mathematisch-naturwissenschaftlichen Bereich [Web based Competitions for Students as a Way to Promote Talented Girls in the Field of Natural Sciences]. *Journal für Begabtenförderung, 2007*(1), 21-28.

Statistisches-Bundesamt. (2006). Im Blickpunkt: Frauen in Deutschland 2006 [In the Spotlight Women in Germany 2006] [Electronic Version]. Retrieved 30.12.2007, from https://www-ec.destatis.de/csp/shop/sfg/vollanzeige.csp?ID=1018095

Stoeger, H. (2007). Berufskarrieren begabter Frauen [Careers of talented Women]. In K. A. Heller & A. Ziegler (Eds.), *Begabt sein in Deutschland [Being Gifted in Germany]* (pp. 265-293). Berlin: LIT.

Stoeger, H., Ziegler, A., & David, H. (2004). What is a specialist? Effects of the male concept of a successful academic person on the performance in a thinking task. *Psychology Science, 46*(4), 514-530.

Sun, L. (2004). *Motivational visualization in peer-to-peer systems.* CS Dept, University of Saskatchewan.

Sun, L., & Vassileva, J. (2006). *Social visualization encouraging participation in online communities.* Paper presented at the CRIWG 2006, Medina del Campo, Spain.

Tajfel, H. (1978). *Differentiation between social groups: Studies in the social psychology of intergroup relations.* London: Academic Press.

Tajfel, H., & Turner, J. C. (1986). The social identity theory of intergroup behavior. In S. Worchel & W. G. Austin (Eds.), *Psychology of Intergroup Relations* (pp. 7-24). Chicago: Nelson Hall.

Taylor, S., & Todd, P. A. (1995). Understanding information technology usage: A test of competing models. *Information Systems Research, 6*(2), 144-176.

Utz, S. (1999). *Soziale Identifikation mit virtuellen Gemeinschaften - Bedingungen und Konsequenzen. [Social identification with virtual communities - causes and consequences].* Lengerich: Pabst.

Utz, S. (2008). Social identification with virtual communities. In E. Konijn, S. Utz & S. Barnes (Eds.), *Mediated interpersonal communication.* New York: Routledge Taylor & Francis Group.

Vassileva, J., & Sun, L. (2007). *An improved design and a case study of a social visualization encouraging participation in online communities.* Paper presented at the CRIWG 2007, Bariloche, Argentina.

Venkatesh, V., & Davis, F. D. (2000). A theoretical extension of the technology acceptance model: Four Longitudinal Field Studies. *Management Science, 46*(2), 186-204.

Venkatesh, V., Morris, M. G., Davis, G. B., & Davis, F. D. (2003). User acceptance of information technology: Toward a unified view. *MIS Quarterly, 27*(3), 425-478.

Whittaker, S. (1996). *Talking to strangers: An evaluation of the factors affecting electronic collaboration.* Paper presented at the ACM conference on Computer supported cooperative work, Boston, Massachusetts, United States.

Xiong, R., & Donath, J. (1999). *PeopleGarden: Creating data portraits for users.* Paper presented at the 12th annual ACM symposium on User interface software and technology, Asheville, North Carolina, United States.

Zajonc, R. B. (1965). Social facilitation. *Science, 149*(3681), 269-274.

Ziegler, A., & Stoeger, H. (2004). Evaluation of an attributional retraining to reduce gender differences in chemistry instruction. *High Ability Studies, 15*(1), 63-81.

Ziegler, A., & Stoeger, H. (2008). Effect of role models from films on short-term ratings of intent, interest, and self-assessment of ability by high school youth: A study of gender-stereotyped academic subjects. *Psychological Reports*, in press.

KEY TERMS

E-Mentoring: Mentoring that is mainly based on computer-mediated communication like e-mail, chat, or bulletin boards.

Mentee: A less experienced person who is mentored by a more experienced and usually older person. A common synonym for mentee is protégé.

Mentor: The term was derived from Homer's epic tale The Odysseus. In the tale, Mentor, a friend of Odysseus, served as a friend and council to Odysseus's son Telemachus, while Odysseus was in the Trojan War. Today a mentor is usually an older and more experienced person who guides, instructs, and encourages a less experienced person.

Mentoring: Mentoring aims at promoting less experienced persons. One can differ between informal and formal mentoring. Informal mentoring usually develops randomly – for example between a faculty member and a student. In formal mentoring programs the mentor-mentee-tandems are usually arranged and temporal.

Social Visualization: Erickson (2003) defines social visualization as "a visual (or sonic or other perceptual) representation of information from which the presence, activities, and other characteristics of members of a social collectivity may be inferred, and, by extension, can provide the basis for making inferences about the activities and characteristics of the group as a whole" (p. 846).

STEM: Abbreviation for Science, Technology, Engineering, and Mathematics.

Technology Acceptance Model (TAM): A theoretical model by Davis (1989, 1993), based on the Theory of Reasoned Action (TRA) (Fishbein and Ajzen, 1975), that explains and predicts usage behaviour of information systems.

Virtual Community: A simple but appropriate definition of a virtual community (synonym: online commuity) is from Lazar and Preece (2002) who define virtual communities as "a set of users who communicate using computer-mediated communication and have common interests, shared goals, and shared resources" (p. 128).

Visualization tool: A tool that visualizes usage behaviour of community members or relationships between members of a virtual community.

Chapter IX
GRIDS in Community Settings

Ioannis Barbounakis
Technological Educational Institute of Crete, Greece

Michalis Zervakis
Technical University of Crete, Greece

ABSTRACT

The authors have been running the second decade since the time that pioneers in Grid started to work on a technology which seemed similar to its predecessors but in reality it was envisioned totally divergent from them. Many years later, the grid technology has gone through various development stages yielding common solution mechanisms for similar categories of problems across interdisciplinary fields. Several new concepts like the Virtual Organization and Semantic Grid have been perfected bringing closer the day when the scientific communities will collaborate as if all their members were at the same location, working with the same laboratory equipment and running the same algorithms. Many production-scale standard-based middlewares have been developed to an excellent degree and have already started to produce significant scalability gains, which in the past, were considered unthinkable.

INTRODUCTION

Grid computing means different things to different individuals. However, in the view of grid computing as an analogy to power grids (see Figure 1), computing becomes pervasive and individual users through their applications gain access to computing resources (processors, storage, data, applications, and so on) according to their needs irrespective their location as well as the underlying technologies, hardware, operating system, and so on (Fukui, et al., 2005).

Though this vision of grid computing can capture one's imagination and may indeed someday become a reality, there are many technical, business, political, and social issues that need to be addressed. If we consider this vision as an ultimate goal, there are many smaller steps that need to be taken to achieve it. Therefore, grid computing can be seen as a journey along a path of integrating various technologies and solutions that move us closer to the final goal. Its key values are in the underlying distributed computing infrastructure technologies that are evolving in support of cross-organizational application and resource sharing and virtualization across technologies, platforms, and organizations.

This kind of virtualization is only achievable through the use of open standards. Open standards help ensure that applications can transparently take advantage of whatever appropriate resources can be made available to them. An environment that provides the ability to share and transparently access resources across a distributed and heterogeneous environment not only requires the technology to virtualize certain resources, but also technologies and standards in the areas of scheduling, security, accounting, systems management, and so on.

The first implementations of grid computing have tended to be internal to a particular company or organization. However, cross-organizational grids are also being implemented and will be an important part of computing and business optimization in the near future. As Internet connect speed increases though, the difference between having two PCs in the same office, the same building, the same city or the same country shrinks. By developing sophisticated middleware which makes sure that widely distributed resources are used effectively, Grid computing gives the user the impression of shrinking the distances further still. In addition, as the middleware gets more sophisticated, it can deal with the inevitable differences between the types of computers that are being used in a highly distributed system, which are harder to control than within one organization. Globus (http://www.globus.org/) is such a popular middleware package today, and it is essentially a software toolkit for making Grids. With such middleware, the aim is to couple a wide variety of machines together effectively, including supercomputers, storage systems, data sources and special classes of devices such as scientific instruments and visualization devices.

Grid computing involves an evolving set of open standards for Web services and interfaces that make services, or computing resources, available over the Internet. Very often grid technologies are used on homogeneous clusters, and they can add value on those clusters by assisting, for example, with scheduling or provisioning of

Figure 1. Grid computing vision

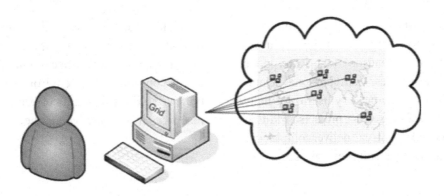

the resources in the cluster. The term grid, and its related technologies, applies across this entire spectrum. One definition of Grid computing, by Ian Foster (2002), one of the pioneers who helped coin the term, distinguishes it from other forms of computing such as distributed computing, metacomputing, cluster computing and peer-to-peer computing. The definition is that a Grid must satisfy three criteria:

- No central administrative control of the computers involved (that eliminates clusters and farms, and also local Grid computing)
- Use of general-purpose protocols
- High quality of service (that eliminates peer-to-peer and means that Grids should not rely on cycle scavenging from individual processors, but rather on load balancing between different independent large resources, such as clusters and local Grids)

During the last years, however, as computational science has matured, an increasing number of scientific communities rely upon third-party software (including both open source community science projects and commercial applications) rather than developing codes from scratch. Lowering the barrier of entry for access to high performance computing (HPC) codes and data collections proves to be a technical and sociological challenge because resources and services are complex and distributed, HPC environments change frequently and more importantly, users often lack the specialized expertise to deal with the complex HPC environments.

Web browser-based portal user interfaces provide access to a large variety of resources, services, applications, and tools for private, public, and commercial entities. Computational science portals have proven to be very useful for many large-scale application science projects. Additionally, Grid-enabled portals can deliver complex grid solutions to users wherever they have access to a web browser running on the Internet without the need to download or install specialized software or worry about setting up networks, firewalls, and port policies. Hence, Grid-enabled portals have been proven to be effective mechanisms for exposing computing resources and distributed systems to general user communities without forcing them to deal with the complexities of the underlying systems. Science portals now exist for a broad range of science collaborations, including efforts in astronomy (US National Virtual Observatory, http://www.us-vo.org), physics (Fusion Grid, http://www.fusiongrid.org), Particle Physics Data Grid (http://www.ppdg.net), Cactus (http://www.cactuscode.org/), the Biomedical Informatics Research Network (http://www.nbirn.net), nanotechnology (http://www.nanohub.org), geophysics (http://www.geongrid.org), climate and weather (http://www.earthsystemgrid.org/, Plale et al., 2006), and NASA QuakeSim (http://gf7.ucs.indiana.edu:8080/gridsphere/gridsphere).

This chapter reviews the evolution of grid technologies in comparison with both relevant concurrent and predecessor technologies. It also describes extensively the grid underlying concepts, the features they integrated during their development phase and the standards that followed trying to solve interoperability issues. Following the presentation of computational and data grids, we briefly elaborate the concept of the semantic grid where the importance of the knowledge layer when building grids for scientific communities is distinguished. In the last section, an attempt is made to address the turn taken by worldwide research initiatives, mainly during the last five years, towards bringing all these grid scalability benefits to the various scientific user communities in a transparent way. Special emphasis is given on the community user environments, which are built around Grid portals offering services and resources in a collective manner.

GRIDS VS. DISTRIBUTED, PEER-TO-PEER AND CLUSTER COMPUTING

The first grid systems were very simple. They consisted of just a few machines, all of the same hardware architecture and same operating system and they were connected on a local network. This kind of grid uses homogeneous systems so there are fewer considerations and may be used just for experimenting with grid software. The machines are usually in one department of an organization, and their use as a grid may not require any special policies or security concerns. Because the machines have the same architecture and operating system, choosing application software for these machines is usually simple. Some people would call this a "cluster" implementation rather than a "grid."

The next progression was the collection of heterogeneous machines. In this setup, more types of resources are available. The grid system is likely to include some scheduling components. File sharing may still be accomplished using networked file systems. Machines participating in the grid may include ones from multiple departments but within the same organization. Such a grid is known as an "Intragrid."

As the grid keeps expanding to many departments, policies may be required for how the grid should be used. For example, there may be policies for what kinds of work is allowed on the grid and at what times. There may be a prioritization by department or by kinds of applications that should have access to grid resources. Also, security becomes more important as more organizations are involved. Sensitive data in one department may need to be protected from access by jobs running for other departments. Dedicated grid machines may be added to increase the quality of service for grid computing, rather than depending entirely on scavenged resources. This grid may grow geo-

Figure 2. Example Intergrid of increased complexity

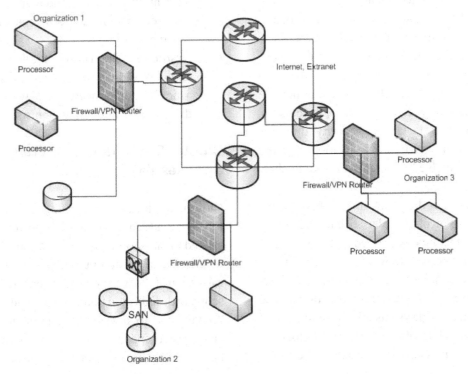

graphically in an organization that has facilities in different cities. Dedicated communications' connections may be used among these facilities and the grid. In some cases, VPN tunnelling or other technologies may be used over the Internet to connect the different parts of the organization. Security increases in importance once the bounds of any given facility are traversed. The grid may grow to be hierarchically organized to reduce the contention implied by central control and the increasing scalability.

Over time, as illustrated in Figure 2, a grid may grow to cross organization boundaries, and may be used to collaborate on projects of common interest. This is known as an "Intergrid." The highest levels of security are usually required in this configuration to prevent possible attacks and spying. The Intergrid offers the prospect for trading or brokering resources over a much wider audience. Resources may be purchased as a utility from trusted suppliers.

Distributed Computing Systems

The major distributed technologies including CORBA, J2EE, and DCOM are well suited for distributed computing applications; however, these do not provide a suitable platform for sharing of resources among the members of the virtual organization. Some of the notable drawbacks include resource discovery across virtual participants, collaborative and declarative security, dynamic construction of a virtual organization, and the scale factor involved in potential resource-sharing environments.

Another major drawback in distributed computing systems involves the lack of interoperability among these technology protocols. However, even with these perceived drawbacks, some of these distributed technologies have attracted considerable Grid Computing research attention toward the construction of grid systems, the most notable of which is Java JINI. This system, JINI, is focused on a platform-independent infrastructure to de-

liver services and mobile code in order to enable easier interaction with clients through service discovery, negotiation, and leasing.

Peer-to-Peer Computing Systems

Peer-to-peer (P2P) computing is a relatively new computing discipline in the realm of distributed computing. Both P2P and distributed computing are focused on resource sharing, and are now widely utilized throughout the world by home, commercial, and scientific markets. Some of the major P2P systems are SETI@home and file sharing system environments (e.g., Vuze, Morpheus, and Gnutella). Grid Computing and P2P computing differ on the following notable points:

* **Target communities:** Grid communities can be small with regard to number of users, yet will yield a greater applications focus with a higher level of security requirements and application integrity. On the other hand, the P2P systems define collaboration among a larger number of individuals and/or organizations, with a limited set of security requirements and a less complex resource-sharing topology.
* **Resources:** The grid systems deal with more complex, more powerful, more diverse, and a highly interconnected set of resources than that of the P2P environments.

Cluster Computing and Web Services (WS)

Clusters are local to the domain and constructed to solve inadequate computing power. They are related to the pooling of computational resources to provide more computing power by parallel execution of the workload. Clusters are limited in scope with dedicated functionality and local to the domain, and are not suitable for resource sharing among participants from different domains. The nodes in a cluster are centrally controlled and the cluster manager is aware of the state of the node. This forms only a subset of the grid principle of more widely available, intra/interdomain, communication, and resource sharing.

Web services have become an important component of cluster computing and distributed applications over the Internet (Humphrey, 2004) as they provide standard infrastructure for data exchange between different distributed applications. On the other hand, grids provide an infrastructure for aggregation of high-end resources for solving large-scale problems in science, engineering, and commerce. The World Wide Web is not yet in itself a grid; its open, general-purpose protocols support access to distributed resources but not the coordinated use of those resources to deliver negotiated qualities of service (Foster, 2002). So, whereas the World Wide Web is mainly focused on communication, grid computing enables resource sharing and collaborative resource interplay toward common business goals. While most Web services involve static processing and moveable data, many grid computing mechanisms involve static data (on large databases) and moveable processing.

However, there are similarities as well as dependencies. First, similar to the case of the World Wide Web, grid computing keeps complexity hidden—multiple users experience a single, unified experience. Second, Web services are utilized to support grid computing mechanisms. In the future, Web services are expected to play a key constituent role in the standardized definition of grid computing since they have emerged as a standards-based approach for accessing network applications. The recent trend is to implement grid services as web services that conform to a set of conventions that provide for controlled, fault-resilient, and secure management of services (http://www.cs.mu.oz.au/~raj/GridInfoware/grid-faq.html, Fox, et al., 2003).

GRID TYPES AND INFRASTRUCTURE

The information infrastructure behind grid environment should support a virtualized view of the computing and data resources, should be autonomic (driven by policies) in order to meet application goals for quality of service, and should be compatible with the standards being developed in the technical community (Bourbonnais et al., 2004).

Computational Grids and Information Infrastructure

For a large-scale, distributed grid to be successful, the grid infrastructure should make application development easy. Ideally, all the resources used in computing—processors, storage, databases, applications—should be virtualized in such a way that the application developers, administrators, and users are shielded from the details and dynamics of how the necessary services are provided. Specifically, a requestor of grid services should not be affected by the number of data and computing resources, their locations, their failures, and their specific hardware and software configurations.

The grid infrastructure should transparently provision the right data and computing resources for each application. Moreover, application programmers should be able to specify end-to-end goals for the quality of the provisioning. Those goals, often referred to as quality of service (QoS) goals, may include goals for the system availability, response time, throughput, number of concurrent users supported, currency or accuracy of the data, and so on. The grid infrastructure needs to support the definition of policies that set QoS goals and define the conditions under which they must be met.

Thus, the information infrastructure should consist of a set of services that individually and collectively support a set of transparencies. By this way, the underlying resources are virtualized, simplifying application development. A set of policies governs the functioning of these services. A set of services for the information infrastructure for the grid is illustrated in Figure 3. While no system provides all of these capabilities today, prototypes and even commercial versions of some services do exist. Standards activities in Global Grid Forum (GGF) will ensure that as more of the pieces are created, they can be put together to form the information infrastructure of the future grid.

The information infrastructure provides applications, such as those shown at the top of Figure 3, with transparent access to heterogeneous, dispersed information sources, like those that appear at the bottom of the figure. To add an information source explicitly, it is first registered via the Registration Services. This step provides information pertaining to that source to the Meta-data Services, which know about all available sources and how they ought to be represented within a unified view to the consuming applications. Discovery Services can be used to automatically identify possible information sources and to help knit them into a unified view by depositing the required meta-data into the Meta-data Repository (not shown) using Meta-data Services. A Discovery Service might use a Registration Service to enter sources it has found in the Meta-data Repository.

Arguably the most essential of the services shown are Data Services. Data Services handle requests for information from applications or

Figure 3. Services for an information infrastructure for the grid

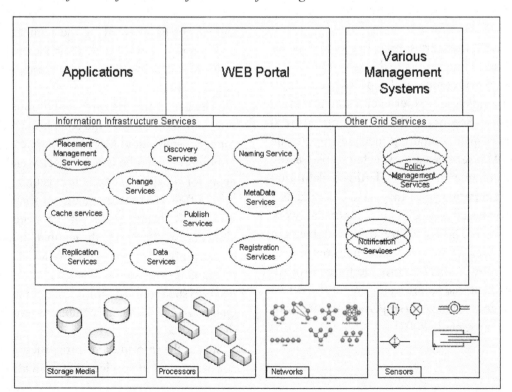

from other services. A particular Data Service may represent one specific information source, for example, a file (myword.doc) or a relational database (a single DB2 instance). However, it could also be implemented by middleware that encapsulates and translates among several data sources. Distributed file systems, gateways, mediators, and federated systems are examples of such middleware. In this case the Data Service represents the collection of information accessible by the middleware that implements it. By using the other services of the information infrastructure, it is possible to build a very sophisticated Data Service that can handle complex queries, locate relevant information sources for a query, and ensure that QoS goals are met.

Depending on the access patterns and locality of the consuming applications, a Placement Management Service can improve response time or availability by creating caches or replicas. In effect, a Placement Management Service automatically distributes copies of the data to optimize performance. The Placement Management Service provides intelligence to determine what data to copy to meet the QoS goals. It relies upon Replication or Cache Services to actually do the work, creating the data copies, registering their existence with a Meta-data Service, and then populating the copies. Of course, Replication and Cache Services can also be used independent of the Placement Management Service. For example, an administrator might use a Replication Service to ensure the availability of certain data for a disaster recovery scenario. Change-Publish Services can detect changes in data and deliver them to a consumer, providing the ability to "publish" changes. A Replication Service might use a Change-Publish Service to know when to propagate and apply changes for a replica, or an application might subscribe to changes in data it particularly cares about.

Finally, these services provided by the information infrastructure can use other grid services as indicated on the right-hand side of Figure 3. For example, the overall grid architecture provides a Notification Service, which could be used to inform an autonomic Meta-data Service of relevant changes in the state, meta-data, or location of information sources. Another important grid service is the Policy Management Service, which is used by most of the information infrastructure services to discover what QoS goals they must sustain.

The information infrastructure supports virtualization with the above provided services through the notion of transparencies. There are a number of different kinds of transparency that will have to be provided before a complete information infrastructure is realized for usage under the grid. Each transparency masks from the user some type of difference or implementation detail of the underlying data sources.

The most fundamental type of transparency for the grid is location transparency. Location transparency shields the user from awareness of where data are stored. Without location transparency, users must make requests directly of a particular data source. Location transparency is usually implemented via some middleware (often called a mediator or broker) that is responsible for interpreting each information request and directing it to the right location. True location transparency is not really possible without heterogeneity transparency. This transparency protects the user from the details of how data are stored and accessed by the actual source systems, including the language or programming interface supported by the data source, how the data are physically stored, whether the data are partitioned, or the networking protocols used. The user should see a single uniform interface, complete with a single set of error codes.

However, even with location and heterogeneity transparency, users typically need to know the name of the data they need. Replication transparency extends the concept further: one name can now be used to access any of several copies, depending on which is available or more cost-effective. Name transparency is a generalization of these transparencies that suits the dynamic, large-scale, grid environment. With name transparency, a user does not have to know the name of the data, only the logical characteristics or QoS properties. The alternative solution of hard-coding the tables or documents in the query or application would mean that every source entry, exit, or failure would result in rewriting the query or recompiling the application. With name transparency, the sources can be migrated, cached, or replicated without changing the applications because the application does not specify the data sources explicitly. As part of the data access request, applications can specify QoS goals such as proximity, staleness, and cost, and suitable replicas are chosen automatically.

If grids are successful in the long term, they will evolve to span organizational boundaries, and will involve multiple autonomous data and computational resources. As far as possible, applications should be spared from separately negotiating for access to individual sources, whether in terms of access authorization or in terms of resource usage costs. Ownership and costing transparencies address these needs.

If such an infrastructure is to autonomously meet QoS goals, two other transparencies are needed. Parallelism transparency gives applications processing data on a grid the benefits of parallel execution over grid nodes without explicit coding. The application should only have to specify the dependencies among the tasks it needs to execute and the policies that will affect scheduling, such as priority of the job or response time required. A workflow coordination service should automatically orchestrate this workflow in a parallel fashion, taking care of data movement, node failures, and so forth, to meet the response time goals. In cases where the processing consists of traditional data management tasks like online transaction processing or online analytical processing (OLTP or OLAP), the system should automatically expand (or shrink) by adding (or removing) nodes in response to workload fluctuations to meet QoS goals such as transaction throughput and response time. Finally, applications should be able to maintain distributed data in a unified fashion, as if the data were stored in one central place (distribution transparency). This maintenance involves several tasks, such as ensuring consistency and data integrity, auditing access, taking backups, and so on.

"Policy" has been a general concept, used not only by the information infrastructure but by many other grid services. Here, a policy is a prioritized set of QoS goals for making decisions that guides the operational behaviour of a system. For the information infrastructure, QoS goals have to do with the availability and latency of data, with query performance, replication throughput, and so on. QoS goals have criteria that must be met and conditions that constrain the goal. A service level agreement (SLA) is a formal contract (both monetary and legal) that is struck between provider and consumer. This contract specifies minimum expectations (or obligations), known as terms and conditions, that the provider must meet. It usually includes penalties or refunds if the terms and conditions are not met. Although the process for arriving at the terms and conditions, that is, the negotiation among selected parties, as well as the process for compliance monitoring, are both important aspects of an SLA, they are not different for the information infrastructure than for other grid systems.

In summary, an autonomic grid should be driven by policies and SLAs. It would require the collaboration of multiple grid services, some part of the core information infrastructure, others part of the general grid environment. Cooperation in this autonomic environment would have a number of benefits for our information infrastructure, including:

- More elastic data repositories, that is, database clusters that can grow and shrink automatically in response to demand

- Improved access to data through caching or replication, automatically determined based on access patterns, locality of consumers relative to providers, and locality of data relative to the processing of the data
- More transparent access to heterogeneous, dispersed data sources (because automatic data caching hides the distribution and heterogeneity)

Autonomic management is essential to maintaining the transparencies needed for this information infrastructure. A more powerful Meta-data Service will be needed to provide mappings between sources and the unified schema; Caching, Replication, and Placement Management Services may be needed to meet policy goals, as well as a Workload Management Service to monitor compliance and then call the appropriate service—or that could be built into the Data Service or the Placement Management Service. The Placement Management Service is concerned with the location and movement of data within the information infrastructure, to deliver a QoS that meets the policies of an SLA. Placement management functions address the need for improved response time by reducing network costs in remote geographies, say, or by precomputing queries into an equivalent data set. They also support high availability (by allowing the use of an equivalent table when a primary source is unavailable) and increased scalability (by, say, offloading a server before it gets saturated and distributing its data to a pool of perhaps less expensive servers). Work-load characteristics, system and user policies, available hardware and software resources, and security considerations determine the type of placement:

- Caching (on-demand transient copy)
- Replication (synchronized long-lived copy)
- Extracting and transforming (on demand copy, typically long-lived, possibly with transformations)

- Federation (access in place, no copy), or
- Archiving (move to long-term storage)

The difference between a cache and a replica is subtle and needs some explanation. The creation of a cache is primarily an optimization decision; a cache is a transient copy by nature, and applications should never be aware of or depend on the existence of a cache beyond their QoS requirements. The creation of a replica is primarily availability.

A complete realization of such an information infrastructure vision will require enhancements to the technology in order to (1) make individual technologies more dynamic and autonomic, (2) incorporate a general policy mechanism that will be used by all technologies to understand QoS goals and guide their actions towards meeting those goals, and (3) fit all technologies into a standards-compliant services architecture. Other enhancements are needed to individual services (for example, to expand the types of caching available). The net result will be that applications can access the data from diverse and distributed data sources as if from a single virtual data store.

Data Grids

Data Grids address not only computational and but also data intensive applications that combine very large datasets and a wide geographical distribution of users and resources. In addition to computing resource scheduling, Data Grids address the problems of storage and data management, network-intensive data transfers and data access optimization, while maintaining high reliability and availability of the data.

The European Data Grid project started with the goal to develop a computational and data-intensive grid to provide all scientists participating in research projects with the best possible access to data and resources, irrespective of geographical. All the Data Grid concepts presented here come after the current literature, but the work is strongly influenced by experiences gained with data management in the context of the EU Data Grid project (http://cern.ch/grid-data-management/). In particular, data management in the EU Data Grid project was focused primarily on file-based data management.

In most of the existing architectures, the data management services are restricted to the handling of files. However, for many VOs, files represent only an intermediate level of data granularity. In principle, Data Grids need to be able to handle data elements – from single bits to complex collections and even virtual data, which must be generated upon request. All kinds of data need to be identifiable through some mechanism – a logical name or an Identifier – that in turn can be used to locate and access the data. The following is a nondefinitive list of the kinds of data that are dealt with in Data Grids.

- **Files:** For many of the VOs the only access method to data is file-based I/O, data is kept only in files and there is no need for other kind of data granularity. This simplifies data management in some respect because the semantics of files are well understood. For example, depending on the QoS requirements on file access, the files can be secured through one of the many known mechanisms (Unix permissions, Access Control Lists (ACLs), etc.). Files can be maintained through directory services like the Globus Replica Catalog (http://www.globus.org/toolkit/), which maps the Logical File Name (LFN) to their physical instances.

- **File collections:** Some VOs want to have the possibility of assigning logical names to file collections that are recognized by the Grid. Semantically there are two different kinds of file collections: *confined* collections of files in which all files making up the collection are always kept together and are effectively treated as one – just like a *tar* or *zip* archive – and *free* collections that are composed of

files as well as other collections not necessarily available on the same resource – they are effectively a bag of logical file and collection identifiers. Confined collections assure the user that all the data are always accessible at a single data source while free collections provide a higher flexibility to freely add and remove items from the collection, but don't guarantee that all members are accessible or even valid at all times. Keeping free collections consistent with the actual files requires additional services.

- **Relational databases:** The semantics of data stored in a Relational Database Management System (RDBMS) are also extremely well understood. The data identified by a Grid Data Handler may correspond to a database, a table, a view or even to a single row in a table of the RDBMS.

- **XML databases and semistructured data:** Data with loosely defined or irregular structure is best represented using the semistructured data model. It is essentially a dynamically typed data model that allows a 'schema-less' description format in which the data is less constrained than in relational databases. The XML format is the standard in which the semistructured data model is represented.

- **Data objects:** This is the most generic form of a single data instance. The structure of an object is completely arbitrary, so the Grid needs to provide services to describe and access specific objects since the semantics may vary from object type to object type. VOs may choose different technologies to access their objects – ranging from proprietary techniques to open standards like SOAP/XML.

- **Virtual data:** The concept of virtualized data is very attractive to VOs that have large sets of secondary data that are derived from primary data using a well-defined set of procedures and parameters. If the secondary data are more expensive to store than to regenerate, they can be virtualized, that is, only created upon request. Additional services are required to manage virtual data.

- **Data sets:** Data sets differ from free file collections only in that they can contain any kind of data from the list above in addition to files. Such data sets are useful for archiving, logging and debugging purposes. Again, the necessary services that track the content of data sets and keep them consistent need to be provided.

In all existing Data Grids, data management is one of the cornerstones of the architecture. The data management services need to be very flexible in order to accommodate the peculiarities and diverse requirements on QoS of the VOs and their peculiarities with respect to different kinds of data and data access. In the vision of a Data Grid, the data management services maintain, discover, store, validate, transfer and instantiate the data for the user's applications transparently. Because of the multitude of different kinds of data, it is essential that the data can be described and validated in the Data Grid framework. Both Grid Data Handlers (GDH) and Grid Data References (GDR) are the core concepts of data management. In addition, there is need for the following data management functionalities in Data Grids:

- **Registration of data:** The first obvious functionality is to register new or existing data on the Grid. The data will be correlated to a GDH; first instances will have to be described through their GDR, and the corresponding mappings need to be registered in the Data Registry.
- **Materialization of virtual data:** This functionality of the data management services will materialize virtual data according to a set of materialization instructions. These instructions include references to the ex-

ecutables and any input datasets required, as well as to any additional job parameters. All information pertaining to the materialization of virtual data is stored in a catalog. After materialization, physical copies of the data exist and the corresponding catalogs need to be updated and a GDR assigned.

- **GDH assignment and validation:** The uniqueness of the GDH can only be assured by the data management services themselves. The VOs may have their own GDH generation and validation schemes but in order to be certain, those schemes should be pluggable and complementary to the generic GDH validation scheme of the Data Grid. In order to scale well, the GDH validation and generation functionality should not be assured by a central service.
- **Data location based on GDH or metadata:** The Data Registry is the service that provides the mapping functionality between GDH and GDR. It should be a distributed service that enables the location of local data even if the other Grid sites are unreachable. In the case of the location of data based on metadata, there will be higher-level services, probably databases and not just registries that can execute complex queries to find data. It is also necessary to be able to do the reverse mapping from GDR to GDH.
- **Pre- and post-processing before and after data transfer:** In addition to data validation, there might be necessary pre- and post-processing steps to be executed before and after data transfer, respectively. For example, the data might need to be extracted, transformed into a format that can be transmitted, stripped of confidential data, and so on, before transfer. After transfer, there may be additional steps necessary to store the data in the correct format in its designated store.
- **Replica management:** The replication process including processing, transfer, reg-

istration and validation should appear as a single atomic operation to the user. In order to assure correct execution of all steps, a replica manager (RM) service is necessary that orchestrates and logs each step and can take corrective action in the case of failures. It also needs to query the destination data store to determine whether the application or user initiating the replication has the required access rights to the resource, and whether enough storage space is available. All replication requests should be addressed to the RM service.

- **Replica selection:** The job scheduler will need to know about all replicas of a given GDH in order to make a qualified choice as to where to schedule jobs, or whether replication or materialization of data needs to be initiated. The replica selection functionality of the data management services can select the optimal replica for this purpose.

- **Subscription to data:** Automatic replication may be initiated by a simple subscription mechanism. This is very useful in VOs in which there is a single data source but many analysts all around the world. Data appearing at the data source adhering to certain criteria can be automatically replicated to remote sites.

Semantic Grid

In recent years, there has been an increased emphasis on collaboration between large scientific teams, an increased use of advanced information processing techniques, and an increased need to share results and observations between participants who are not physically co-located. When taken together, these trends mean that researchers are increasingly relying on computer and communication technologies as an intrinsic part of their everyday research activity. At present, the key communication technologies are predominantly e-mail and the Web. Whereas, these two technologies have shown a glimpse of what is possible, the e-Scientist needs a much richer, more flexible and more transparent in use next generation of technology.

The computing infrastructure for e-Science of tomorrow is commonly referred to as Grid (either Computational or Data) and this is, therefore, the term adopted here. While this aspect is certainly an important enabling technology for future e-Science, it is only a part of a much larger concept that also includes information handling and support for knowledge processing within the e-Scientific process. This enhanced concept of the e-Science infrastructure is adopted here under the name "Semantic Grid" (Roure, Jennings & Shadbolt, 2003). Similarly to the Semantic Web, the Semantic Grid is characterized as an open system in which users, software components and computational resources come and go on a continual basis. Under these usage scenarios, there should be a high degree of automation that would enable flexible collaborations and computation on a global scale. Moreover, the semantic grid environment should allow personalization per each individual participant and should offer seamless interactions with both software components and other relevant users.

Based on this view of e-Science infrastructure as a set of services that are provided by particular individuals or institutions for consumption by others, a service-oriented view of the Grid is a matter of course. Given that view of e-Science, it has become common approach to characterize the computing infrastructure as consisting of three conceptual layers:

- **Data/computation:** This layer deals with the way that computational resources are allocated, scheduled and executed and the way in which data is exchanged between the various processing resources. It is characterized by its ability to deal with large volumes of data, through fast networks and diverse resources. This layer builds on the physical

'Grid fabric', that is, the underlying network and computer infrastructure, which may also interconnect scientific equipment. Here data is understood as uninterpreted bits and bytes.

- **Information:** This layer deals with the way that information is represented, stored, accessed, shared and maintained. Here information is understood as data equipped with meaning. For example, the characterization of an integer as representing the temperature of a reaction process, the recognition that a string is the name of an individual.

- **Knowledge:** This layer is concerned with the way that knowledge is acquired, used, retrieved, published, and maintained to assist e-Scientists to achieve their particular goals and objectives. Here knowledge is understood as information applied to achieve a goal, solve a problem or enact a decision. For example, the recognition by a plant operator, that in the current context a reaction temperature demands shutdown of the process.

There are a number of observations and remarks that need to be made about this layered structure. Firstly, all Grids that have or will be built have some element of all three layers in them. The degree to which the various layers are important and utilized in a given application will be domain dependent – thus, in some cases, the processing of huge volumes of data will be the dominant concern, while in others the knowledge services that are available will be the overriding issue. Secondly, this layering is a conceptual view of the system that is useful in the analysis and design phases of development. However, the strict layering may not be carried forward to the implementation for reasons of efficiency. Thirdly, the service-oriented view applies at all the layers. Thus, there are services, producers, consumers, and contracts at the computational layer, at the information layer, and at the knowledge layer (see Figure 4). Although this view is widely accepted, to date most research and development work in this area has concentrated on the data/computation layer and on the information layer.

While there are still many open research problems concerned with managing massively distributed computations in an efficient manner and in accessing and sharing information from heterogeneous sources, it is strongly believed that the full potential of Grid computing can only be realized among the various scientific communities by fully exploiting the functionality and capabilities provided by knowledge layer services. This is because it is at this layer that the

Figure 4. Three-layered architecture viewed as services

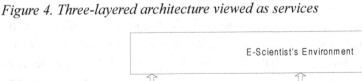
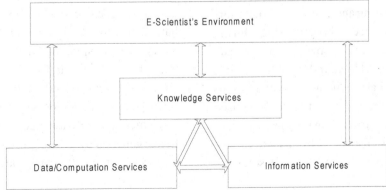

reasoning necessary for seamlessly automating a significant range of the actions and interactions takes place.

BUILDING A GRID: OPEN SOURCE GRID MIDDLEWARE AND TOOLKITS

During all these years, grid technologies have been boosted due to development of various Open Source software projects. Although, there have been developed many middleware products to build and run Grids, ranging from open source software to commercial products, there are interoperability problems between various among them. Examples of open source toolkits include the gLite distribution developed in the context of the EGEE project (http://glite.web.cern.ch/glite/) and the Globus Toolkit which is probably the most popular and one of the most actively researched upon middleware products. To provide an illustrative account of the state of the art offerings of such products, we will briefly review the Globus Toolkit and reflect upon its current practice and experience. The reader may obtain a more elaborate insight from the available documentation and the toolkit's manuals.

Globus Toolkit

It is already known, that the first Grid efforts resulted when computer scientists got involved in either building or integrating a diverse range of high-end computing applications for real users in other areas of science and engineering. During these efforts, the same problems kept showing up over and over again. The founders of the Globus Alliance realized that producing general solutions to these kinds of problems that could be reused from application to application was a worthwhile goal. The Globus Toolkit (http://www.globus.org/toolkit/) began as a collection of solutions to these problems.

The Globus Toolkit, therefore, constitutes an outcome of the Grid community's efforts to solve real problems that are encountered by real application projects. It contains components that have proven useful in addressing the challenging problems that come up when implementing Grid applications and systems. The components have been generalized so that they become useful within a wide variety of applications.

The Globus Toolkit doesn't provide a complete solution for Grid projects. The components in the Globus Toolkit (along with components from other sources) have to be organized and fitted together ("integrated") according to a plan that fits the requirements of the rest of the project. Each product will likely have its own unique customized user interface that the end users interact with, making use of standardized components for deeper system functionality.

To summarize, the Globus Toolkit does not provide a "turnkey" solution for any project or product. It provides standard building blocks and tools for use by application developers and system integrators. In what follows, we review the main challenges addressed by the Globus Toolkit and how they are facilitated by building blocks and tools proven useful in other projects.

Heterogeneity

A major theme that comes up over and over in distributed collaboration activities is *heterogeneity*. However, it is not practical to enforce homogeneity in such scenarios. Instead, mechanisms have to be provided that make it easier to develop applications despite the unavoidable heterogeneity. Versions 1.0 through 4.0 of the Globus Toolkit have largely focused on simplifying heterogeneity for application developers by providing tools that implement standard interfaces for interacting with heterogeneous system components. These tools largely fit into the "resource layer" of the OGSA architectural model (see Figure 5) and those below it. Tools for addressing specialized issues that come up in different classes of applications, such as data replication, metadata management, and authorization are going to be included in future versions of the Globus Toolkit in the form of "collective layer" services (Figure 5).

Standards

The Globus Toolkit has been designed and implemented to capitalize on and encourage use of existing standards from communities such as IETF, W3C, OASIS and GGF. The tools in the Globus Toolkit use these standards rather than creating new mechanisms that do the same things in different ways. Some examples of standard mechanisms used in the Globus Toolkit are:

- SSL/TLS v1 (from OpenSSL) (IETF)
- LDAP v3 (from OpenLDAP) (IETF)
- X.509 Proxy Certificates (IETF)
- SOAP (W3C)
- HTTP (W3C)
- GridFTP v1.0 (GGF)
- OGSI v1.0 (GGF)

The Globus Toolkit also includes reference implementations of several new and proposed standards in these organizations, providing the community with code that they can use to try out the standards and provide feedback on their usefulness. Examples include WSRF (GGF, OASIS), DAI (GGF), WS-Agreement, WSDL 2.0 (W3C), WSDM, SAML (OASIS), and XACML (OASIS).

Figure 5. OGSA architecture

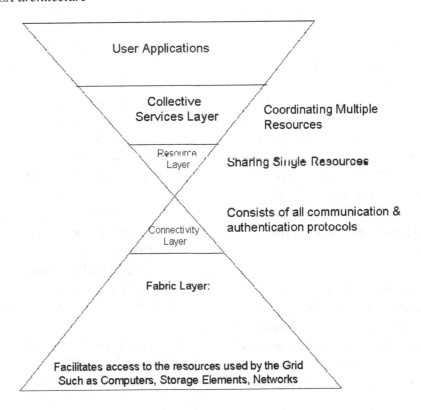

Tools and Components of Globus Toolkit

The Globus Toolkit is not a turnkey solution for a specific problem. Instead, it is a collection of solutions to sub-problems that have proven useful in real projects. Specific applications will find different combinations of Globus Toolkit components more useful than others. To this end, an informal and non-exhaustive review of the basic components is provided.

Two important software development kits (SDK) of particular interest to software developers building new Grid software services within the OGSA framework, are the Web Services Core (WS-Core) Implementation used to develop and run OGSA-compliant Grid Services (available in Java and C/C++) and the Grid Security Infrastructure (GSI) Implementation, used to secure communication (e.g., between services and clients).

Developers are also offered a variety of basic grid services which provide uniform interfaces to the most typical types of system elements and they currently include both OGSA and non-OGSA implementations. The services support Computing / Processing Power (GRAM), Data Management (GridFTP, DAI, RLS), Monitoring/Discovery (MDS), Authorization/Security (CAS), while in development are services for Telecontrol (NTCP/GTCP), Metadata (MCS) and Virtual Data (Chimera, Pegasus). All of the services and tools above include C/C++ libraries and Java classes for building Grid-aware applications and tools.

Practice and Experience with the Globus Toolkit

The Globus Toolkit has surprisingly little direct value to end users of distributed collaborative projects or products. Very few of the components in the Toolkit include user interface elements that would be immediately useful to scientists, engineers, or other application users. One most certainly cannot get useful results simply by directing scientists, engineers, or marketing specialists to the Globus Toolkit and telling them to do something useful with it! On the other hand, the Globus Toolkit can be extremely useful to application developers and system integrators. In order to make good use of the Toolkit, one must have a specific application or system in mind, preferably one that involves shared use of physical or logical resources from several administrative domains. Having the right expertise on hand (system design and architecture, software development, user interface design, and of course familiarity with end user requirements) is essential. The most ambitious projects and products (those that the Globus Toolkit is aimed at) require sophisticated project planning and strong, experienced leadership to achieve success. Practice and experience shows that the most fundamental grid components that are found in the Globus Toolkit, are:

- **Security** describes a number of useful software tools for meeting the security requirements in Grid systems.
- **Monitoring and discovery** describes software components that can provide monitoring and discovery features in Grid systems.
- **Computation** describes software tools that can be used to manage computational tasks in Grid applications.
- **Data** describes software tools that can be used to manage data and datasets in data-intensive applications.
- **Collaboration** describes software for facilitating and encouraging collaboration in distributed projects.
- **Packaging and distribution** describes tools for helping to create integrated software distributions for use in Grid projects.

These components are readily available to grid developers and have all been used with the Globus Toolkit in real projects to accomplish ambitious goals. Consequently, it is highly recommended that application developers and system builders consider reusing them in new efforts rather than ignoring them:

CURRENT AND EMERGING TRENDS

An increasing number of national and international efforts are devoted to appropriating the benefits of grid technologies and infrastructure to support visionary concepts and to facilitate long-term scientific research. In this section, an attempt is made to briefly review two such trends, namely the impact of grids on virtual organizations and the deployment of grids to foster research in social and natural science communities.

Grids as Enablers for Virtual Organizations

One of the significant operational concepts in Grid Computing is the notion of the virtual organization. This involves the dynamic computation-oriented task of defining groupings of individuals, such as multiple groups or organizations. Although this is perhaps simple to understand, in theory, it remains complex across several dimensions. The complexities involved in this dynamic assembly revolve around identifying and bringing in those humans that initially defined the conditions in order to instantiate the grid. For instance, automated consideration of the rules, the policies, and the specific conditions affecting operations in the grid are, hence, the generating force for processing and sharing the information with those individuals in any virtual organization of a grid.

The simplest way of thinking about this advanced Grid Computing concept is captured in the term virtual organizations. This type of computation-oriented grouping serves as the basis for identifying and managing the grid computer groups, associated with any particular grid community of

end users. A virtual organization is conceived of as a dynamic set of individuals and/or institutions defined around a set of resource-sharing rules and conditions. All these virtual organizations share some commonality among them, including common concerns and requirements, but may vary in size, scope, duration, sociology, and structure. The members of any virtual organization negotiate on resource sharing based on the rules and conditions defined in order to share the resources from the thereby automatically constructed resource pool. Assigning users, resources, and organizations from different domains across multiple worldwide geographic territories to a virtual organization is one of the fundamental technical challenges in Grid Computing. This complexity includes the definitions of the resource discovery mechanism, resource sharing methods, rules and conditions by which this can be achieved, security federation and/or delegation, and access controls among the participants of the virtual organization. This challenge is both complex and complicated across several dimensions.

Let us explore two examples of virtual organizations in order to better understand their common characteristics. The first example concerns the case in which thousands of physicists from different laboratories around the world join together to create, design, and analyze the products of a major detector at CERN, the European high energy physics laboratory. This group forms a "data grid" with intensive computing, storage, and network services resource sharing, in order to analyze petabytes of data created by the detector at CERN. This is one example of a virtual organization. Another example may be found in a company doing financial modeling for a customer based on the data collected from various data sources, both internal and external to the company. This specific virtual organization customer may need a financial forecasting capability and advisory capability on their investment portfolio, which is based on actual historic and current real-time financial market data. This financial institution customer can then be responsive by forming a dynamic virtual organization within the enterprise for achieving more benefit from advanced and massive forms of computational power (i.e., application service provider) and for data (i.e., data access and integration provider). This dynamic, financially oriented, virtual organization can now reduce undesirable customer wait time, while increasing reliability on forecasting by using real-time data and financial modeling techniques. This is another example of a virtual organization.

With a close observation of the above-mentioned virtual organizations, we can infer that the number and type of participants, the resources being shared, duration, scale, and the interaction pattern between the participants all vary from one type of virtual organization to another. Nevertheless, we can also infer that there exist common characteristics among competing and sometimes distrustful participants that contributed to their virtual organization formation. They may include some of the following items for consideration:

- **Common concerns and requirements on resource sharing**. A virtual organization is a well-defined collection of individuals and/or institutions that share a common set of concerns and requirements among them. For example, a virtual organization created to provide financial forecast modeling share the same concerns on security, data usage, computing requirements, resource usage, and interaction pattern.
- **Conditional, time-bound, and rules-driven resource sharing**. Resource sharing is conditional and each resource owner has full control on making the availability of the resource to the sharable resource pool. These conditions are defined based on mutually understandable policies and access control requirements (authentication and authorization). The number of resources involved in

the sharing may dynamically vary over time based on the policies defined.

- **Dynamic collection of individuals and/or institutions**. Over a period of time a virtual organization should allow individuals and/or groups into and out of the collection; provided they all share the same concerns and requirements on resource sharing.
- **Sharing relationship among participants is peer-to-peer in nature**. The sharing relation among the participants in a virtual organization is peer-to-peer, which emphasizes that the resource provider can become a consumer to another resource. This introduces a number of security challenges including mutual authentication, federation, and delegation of credentials among participants.
- **Resource sharing based on an open and well-defined set of interaction and access rules**. Open definition and access information must exist for each sharable resource for better interoperability among the participants.

Grids for Scientific Communities

Many projects and/or initiatives have been funded during the last years in an attempt to make available the technological advances of grids (computational/data) and their benefits to broader scientific communities. One of these projects, namely "The National Centre for e-Social Science (NCeSS) is funded by the Economic and Social Research Council (ESRC) to investigate how innovative and powerful computer based infrastructure and tools developed over the past five years under the UK e-Science program can benefit the social science research community (http://www.ncess.ac.uk).

The project research has been divided in areas such as the User Environment, Services & Resources and Continuous Improvement Strategies through e-Science. The user environment is the front-end to the services offered by the grid infrastructure. It should be as efficient and friendly through customization as possible. There are three basic elements that a user environment should have in order to succeed in its goal. First, the social science community should be provided the whole bunch of the applications through a portal. This way, not only research tools such as simulation models, flexible powerful geographical information systems but also collaboration tools such as wikis, forums and video conferences should become available. Second, the various applications should be extended so that they allow simultaneous access to multiple datasets for powerful cross-dataset interrogation. Last, there should be tools related to workflows that would automate and speed up repeatable processes that form part of many social scientists' research work.

Regarding the services and resources area, the emphasis is given in the refinement of various applications that were first developed under the NCeSS Research Node program in order to make them more generic, thus helping more social scientists reap the benefits of their use. Examples include decision-making tools in the areas of health and land-use policy as well as tools to assist in the annotation of research resources. Apart from these services, there is also the potential to gain fascinating new insights through the combination of inconsistent datasets in terms of geographical coverage and age ranges. This will allow the social scientists who usually interrogate individual datasets by first downloading them on their workstations to work more flexibly with a number of datasets.

In social scientists' communities, some data are highly sensitive because whilst it is anonymous, there is a risk of revealing the owner's identities. Nowadays, in order to comply with data privacy laws, there are a number of secure rooms know as "Safe Settings" where only trusted scientists have access. The work, in this area, aims at extending this concept over the Internet, based on

Grid technologies without sacrificing the privacy and anonymity obligations. Moreover, there is an ongoing review of all social science related datasets in order to define the most appropriate ones in terms of yielding powerful new insights when combined.

Although, the goal of this project is to yield a number of useful services and resources as well as to create the infrastructure that will host them, the real improvement of Social Science through e-Science will come only when a strategy has been formulated and enacted. Only when, more and more social scientists conceive their future becoming more fruitful and productive through e-Science communities, only then this and similar projects will have achieved their original goals.

Apart from the NCeSS supported project aiming at making available the technological advances of grids (computational/data) and their benefits to the social science communities, there are numerous other projects across the world with similar goals targeting various scientific communities. One of them is the Telescience project (Peltier, et al., 2003) which provides a complete, end-to-end, single sign-on solution enabling remote and collaborative biomedical image analysis for structure-function correlation studies. The objective of this project is to increase the throughput of data acquisition and processing, and to ultimately improve the accuracy of the final data product, addressing an imminent need for domain scientists: the amount of data that is possible to collect from instruments is out-pacing the traditional methods used to compute, analyze and collaborate upon that data. The service-based architecture, that enables this project, provides a fabric for seamless interoperability among user interfaces (web portals and applications) and externally addressable Grid resources (instruments and computers). What Telescience has finally achieved, is to provide a Grid-based architecture to combine the use of Telemicroscopy with tools for parallel distributed computation, distributed data management, access to federated digital libraries of multi-scale, cell-structure data and interactive integrated visualization tools to provide an end-to-end solution for high-throughput microscopy.

The D-Grid-Integration project (http://www.d-grid.de/) has undertaken the mission to bring the vision of e-Science in Germany to reality, through the creation of a robust, flexible and sustainable Grid infrastructure, which would consist of network, computing and storage components as well as of Grid services and middleware layers. Such an infrastructure can be built by concentrating the current ongoing Grid activities in Germany. The D-Grid integration project will create a general purpose Grid infrastructure by combining existing activities in an international context and by supporting and coordinating the community projects of the D-Grid initiative. This Grid infrastructure will be used by the scientific community and later by the industry to establish new Grid-based methods. One of the primary D-Grid objectives is to establish and support user specific "community projects" to extend the number of Grid end-users. This Grid foundation infrastructure is the basic requirement for a sustainable development of Grid and e-Science methods in Germany. The synergetic and coherent usage of the infrastructure by many different scientific communities will be initiated. By the generalization, standardization and homogenization of results from communities, new methods for the daily scientific work will be moved to mainstream, and later be used by small and medium size enterprises too. A gain in efficiency is expected by the seamless integration of existing services, resources and infrastructures of one or more user communities. As most of the Grid activities in Germany did not yet address all aspects of a general e-Science architecture, the vision of a general Grid and e-Science infrastructure can be reached by an interactive approach. Therefore the obvious success of other projects (like the Cyber-Infrastructure in US, the e-Science program in UK or the DutchGrid in Netherlands) will be

taken into account as well as the needs and developments of the D-Grid communities.

The primary goal of the Earth System Grid (http://www.earthsystemgrid.org/) is to enable worldwide climate research community access to climate simulation results distributed across supercomputers with large-scale data and analysis servers located at numerous national labs and research centers in the U.S.A. It features user registration, authorization groups, file download, browse collection of usage and discovery-level metadata, free-text search, access to data on archival systems, "virtual data services" that provide flexible spatiotemporal subsetting from aggregated collections of files, user management, and metrics reporting. The project is funded by the U.S. Department of Energy and its primary point of entry is the portal at the address http://www.earthsystemgrid.org/.

Back in mid-September 2003, the National Science Foundation (NSF) formally announced funding for the 5-year Linked Environments for Atmospheric Discovery (LEAD) project with the University of Oklahoma (OU) serving as the lead institution LEAD initiative. LEAD (Plale et al., 2006) makes meteorological data, forecast models, and analysis and visualization tools available to anyone who wants to interactively explore the weather as it evolves. The LEAD Portal brings together all the necessary resources at one convenient access point, supported by high-performance computing systems. With LEAD, meteorologists, researchers, educators, and students are no longer passive bystanders or limited to static data or pre-generated images, but rather they are active participants who can acquire and process their own data. The LEAD portal effort allows users to manage data-driven, high performance weather simulations. These simulations can also be event-triggered, as data mining analysis on the data stream may indicate severe weather events. Detected events trigger simulation workflows on the Grid that are delivered to end users through the Web portal.

LEAD software enhances the experimental process by automating many of the time consuming and complicated tasks associated with meteorological science. The "workflow" tool links data management, assimilation, forecasting, and verification applications into a single experiment. The experiment's output also includes detailed descriptions of the product, also called "metadata."

FUTURE CHALLENGES

Despite the rise of interest in grid computing there are important challenges still pending and driving research and development efforts worldwide. One such multi-faceted challenge standing out very promptly is concerned with the plethora of security issues involved in managing the heterogeneous nature of resources of a Grid Computing environment. Indeed, as Grid computing moves from research/academic laboratories to commercial organizations, security remains one of the fundamental barriers to adoption of Grid computing in a wider commercial context. It is not always obvious however exactly what security concerns are most significant. Some of the issues raised can be related to restrictions on intellectual property, while others relate to specific constraints imposed by organizational structures. In other instances, some commercial institutions relate issues of security to trust and competence. Simply speaking, current middleware solutions should address local security integration, secure identity mapping, secure access/authentication, secure federation, and trust management.

Any other security requirements are often centered on the topics of data integrity, confidentiality, and information privacy. The Grid Computing data exchange must be protected using secure communication channels, including SSL/TLS and oftentimes in combination with secure message exchange mechanisms such as WS-Security. The most notable security infrastructure used for securing grid is the Grid Security Infrastructure (GSI). In most cases, GSI provides capabilities for single sign-on, heterogeneous platform integration and secure resource access/authentication.

These mechanisms help to enable very strong platform identity (so that impersonating a compute node would become infeasible), strong guarantees of software identity (so that good programs and middleware cannot be substituted for rogues), and strong separation of virtual machines (so that jobs could run in an entirely isolated virtual environment, without significant loss of performance). These capabilities are now becoming widely available in commodity hardware: they potentially allow grid jobs submitted at a distance to be protected even from the administrator of the node undertaking the work. This theme, then, will elicit detailed technical requirements from the application areas, relate them to the emerging technologies for improved trust, and set an agenda for the next generation of grid security development, in order to meet these challenges.

It is also necessary to consider security implications at various lifecycle phases of a resource – such as when it is provisioned, when it is operational and finally when it is decommissioned. Each of these phases may provide a different set of security requirements. The following include some of the threats and risks based on the unique characteristics of cross-organizational grid environments:

- **Access control attacks:** Defines risks with unauthorized entities and authorized entities bypassing or defeating access control policy.
- **Defeating Grid auditing and accounting systems:** Includes threats to the integrity of auditing and accounting systems unique to an enterprise Grid environment. This may include false event injection, overflow, event modification, and a variety of other common attacks against auditing systems.

- **Denial of Service (DoS):** Describes an attack on service or resource availability. As a Grid is often expected to provide a better availability compared to a non-Grid environment, the various DoS threats must be considered as part of a risk assessment.

- **Malicious code/"malware":** This describes any code that attempts to gain unauthorized access to the Grid environment, to subsequently elevate its privileges, hide its existence, disguise itself as a valid component, or propagate itself in clear violation of the security policy of the enterprise Grid.

- **Object reuse:** This describes how sensitive data may become available to an unauthorized user, and used in a context other than one for which it was generated. In the grid context, this is a risk if a Grid component is not properly decommissioned.

- **Masquerading attacks:** Describes a class of attacks where a valid Grid component may be fooled into communicating or working with another entity masquerading as valid Grid component. Such an attack could permit the disclosure or modification of information, the execution of unauthorized transactions, etc.

- **Sniffing/snooping:** Involves watching packets as they travel over the network. An enterprise Grid potentially introduces additional network traffic between applications/services, the Grid Management Entity and grid components that should be protected. Failure to address this threat may result in other types of attacks including data manipulation and replay attacks.

During the last years, much effort has been invested into authenticating access to particular Grid resources, culminating in the launch of the International Grid Trust Federation (IGTF). The work of IGTF and its three regional Policy Management Authorities (PMA) – which include the European, Asia/Pacific and Americas PMA – has

as its goal to ensure that Grid users can obtain a single electronic identity (generally an X.509 certificate) and use this on any Grid infrastructure which is part of a Certificate Authority (CA) affiliated with IGTF.

At the same time, Grid Authorization seems to be much less mature. Although authorization for individual users is performed at institution level (such as a University or an organization) – as only the institution can verify the credentials of a user connecting from that location – the authorization mechanism however somehow then has to be propagated to the VO (as VO includes participation from various institutions). Identifying how such a "collective" authorization mechanism can be enforced is therefore an important prerequisite to allowing users involved in a VO to effectively collaborate. To achieve this, it is necessary to aggregate security policies/assertions that exist at an institution level with specific policies that must be supported within the VO as a whole. This leads, therefore, to particular requirements on the type of underlying infrastructure that should be used to combine local/institution-level policy with global application-related VO policy (Rama & Hilton, 2006). More specifically, the VO policy must be at least as restrictive as a policy of an individual institution involved in the VO.

Provision of security within a VO has often been based on user roles. The type of data an individual has access to therefore changes as the role changes. Each role is also assigned one or more tasks, and associated with these tasks can be access to data sources. A key theme in such work is determining how permissions on the underlying data sources (object-level permissions) can be mapped onto particular roles that exist in the system. Shibboleth (http://shibboleth.internet2.edu), a project of Internet2/MACE (http://middleware.internet2.edu/MACE), is developing architectures and policy structures to support inter-institutional sharing of Web resources subject to access controls. Shibboleth makes use of the concept of Federations to specify a set of parties who have agreed to a common set of policies. Therefore the bi-lateral agreements between parties are eliminated. Community Authorization Service (CAS) (http://www.globus.org/toolkit/docs/4.0/security/cas/) is built on the Globus Toolkit Grid Security Infrastructure (GSI) and allows resource providers to specify access control policies to blocks of resources to a community as a whole, and the community uses the CAS server to perform fine-grained access control to the resources by its members. The Virtual Organization Management (VOM) Portal is a project to enable security management through a Portal interface. It is intended for members wishing to join a VO to first of all register with the VO using their X.509 certificate. A VO manager will then approve (or not) the user and assign them a role within the VO. Once this registration is complete, the user's role information is forwarded to the resource manager responsible for allowing access to resources within the system they control. The user can then access the requested resource to the limit of the authority level they have been allocated. Grid Enabled web eNvironment for site Independent User job Submission (GENIUS) (Barbera et al., 2003) is another example of a Portal for supporting secure access to Grid resources. It makes use of EngineFrame on the portal server to provide an HTML interface and it uses client programs and tools to access the electronic services.

CONCLUSION

At present, most production-scale Grids are still restricted to the academic/research community. However, with the merger between the Global Grid Forum and the Enterprise Grid Alliance, there has been created a significant interest in also deploying Grids within multi-national companies. An example of that is the SIMDAT (http://www.simdat.org/about_simdat.html) project where distributed virtual product development enables improved product quality and faster time to

market while reducing costs and risks. The SIM-DAT project takes industrial product and process development forward by introducing advanced Grid technology in the automotive, aerospace, pharmaceutical and meteorological verticals. The results of SIMDAT will facilitate the transition of other industrial areas to Grid technologies. It is, however, a complex task: data and processes have to be shared and integrated among departments and locations of a company, between different disciplines or across all partners that participate in a product development effort. At the same time, information that is confidential to a party must be protected. Grid technology promises to reduce this complexity substantially.

In a similar vein, a number of "production" scale Grid systems (Gagliardi, 2006) have recently been announced. One example includes the European EGEE project (Laure, 2006) which brings together more than 120 organizations to produce a reliable and scalable computing resource available to the European and global research community. As of May 2008, the project supports 250 sites in 48 countries and more than 68,000 CPUs available to some 8,000 users 24 hours a day, 7 days a week. The EGEE project is primarily aimed at supporting science and engineering applications ranging from biomedicine to fusion sciences, which generally have large computation and data requirements.

It stands to argue therefore that grids constitute a critical technology fostering large-scale, cross-organizational communities in science and engineering as well as in industrial settings. Available experience indicates that in every domain that this technology has been applied, it has offered new ways of collaboration, not previously possible, and it has driven the science at a faster pace.

The challenges are many but it seems the commitment exists to advance further the current middleware products thus bringing them closer and closer to every scientific domain as well as to the industry. The time has come when the computation and the knowledge will be utilized as the information is utilized today.

REFERENCES

Barbera, R., Falzone, A., & Rodolico A. (2003). *The GENIUS Grid Portal, Computing in High Energy and Nuclear Physics.* La Jolla, California.

Bourbonnais, S., Gogate, V. M., Haas, L. M., Horman, R. W., Malaika, S., Narang, I., & Raman, V. (2004). Towards an information infrastructure for the grid. *IBM Systems Journal, 43*(4), Grid Computing.

Foster, I. (2002). *What is the Grid? A three point checklist.* Argonne National Laboratory and University of Chicago.

Fox, G., Pierce, M., Gannon, D., & Thomas, M. (2003). *Overview of Grid computing environments.* GFD-I.9. The Global Grid Forum.

Fukui, K., Jacob, B., Brown, M., & Trivedi, N. (2005). Introduction to Grid computing. *IBM Redbooks.*

Gagliardi, F. (2006). *Production Grids: General overview.* Production Grid Session at Global Grid Forum 2006, Athens, Greece.

Humphrey, M. (2004). *Grid computing using .NET and WSRF.NET.* Tutorial at GGF11, Honolulu.

Laure, E. (2006). *EGEE – A large scale production Grid infrastructure.* Production Grid Session at Global Grid Forum 2006, Athens, Greece.

Peltier, S., et al. (2003). The Telescience Portal for Advanced Tomography Applications. *Journal of Parallel and Distributed Applications, Special Edition on computational Grids, 63*(5), 539-550.

Plale, B. D., Gannon, J., Brotzge, K., Droegemeier, J., Kurose, D., McLaughlin, R., Wilhelmson, S., Graves, M., Ramamurthy, R. D., Clark, S., Yalda, D. A., Reed, E., Joseph, V., & Chandrasekar (2006). CASA and LEAD: Adaptive cyberinfrastructure for real-time multiscale weather forecasting. *IEEE Computer (special issue on System-Level Science), 39*(11), 56-63. Retrieved May 10, 2008, from http://doi.ieeecomputersociety.org/10.1109/MC.2006.375

Rama, O., & Hilton, J. (2006). Securing the virtual organization – Part 1: Requirements from Grid computing, *Network Security, 4,* 7-10.

Roure, D., Jennings, N., & Shadbolt, N. (2003). The Semantic Grid: A future e-science infrastructure. In F. Berman, A. J. G. Hey, & G. Fox, (Eds.), *Grid computing: Making the global infrastructure a Reality* (pp. 437-470). John Wiley & Sons.

KEY TERMS

Grid Computing: Grid computing, or simply grid, is the generic term given to techniques and technologies designed to make pools of distributed computer resources available on-demand. Grid computing was originally conceived by research scientists as a way of combining computers across a network to form a distributed supercomputer to tackle complex computations. In the commercial world, grid aims to maximize the utilization of an organization's computing resources by making them shareable across applications (sometimes called virtualization) and, potentially, provide computing on demand to third parties as a utility service.

Globus Toolkit: Open source toolkit for building computing grids developed and provided by the Globus Alliance.

Virtual Organization: A dynamic set of individuals and/or institutions defined around a set of resource-sharing rules and conditions. Its members share some commonality among them, including common concerns and requirements, but may vary in size, scope, duration, sociology, and structure.

OGSA, (Open Grid Services Architecture):
The industry standard for grid computing. "Open" refers to both the standards-development process and the standards themselves. OGSA is "service-oriented" because it delivers functionality among loosely-coupled interacting services that are aligned with industry-accepted Web service standards. "Architecture" defines the components, their organizations and interactions, and the overall design philosophy.

Chapter X
Socializing in an Online Gaming Community:
Social Interaction in World of Warcraft

Vivian Hsueh Hua Chen
Nanyang Technological University, Singapore

Henry Been Lirn Duh
National University of Singapore, Singapore

ABSTRACT

Massive Multiplayer Online Games (MMOG) allows a large number of players to cooperate, compete and interact meaningfully in the online environment. Gamers are able to form social network with fellow gamers and create a unique virtual community. Although research has discussed the importance of social interaction in MMOG, it fails to articulate how social interaction takes place in the game. The current chapter aims to depict how gamers interact and socialize with each other in a popular MMOG, World of Warcraft. Through virtual ethnography, specific interaction patterns and communication behaviors within the community are discussed. It is concluded that the types of social interaction taken place in the gaming world is influenced by the temporal and spatial factors of the game as well as the game mechanisms.

INTRODUCTION

Digital games play an increasingly central role in the life of many adolescents and adults. Massive Multiplayer Online Games (MMOG) is a game genre that allows gamers to be immersed in a three dimension dynamic world. It has attracted many to try out – approximately 56% of American college students have played online games before (Pew Internet Project, 2003). Studies have argued that social interaction and relationship building are the key reasons why MMOG gain its popularity

(Griffiths, Davies & Chappell, 2003). Jakobsson & Taylor (2003) contend "social networks form a powerful component of the game play and the gaming experience, one that must be seriously considered to understand the nature of massively multiplayer online games" (p.81). Similarly, Ducnheneaut & Moore, (2004a) noted how

gamers need to do much more than mindlessly accumulate XP: they also need to increase their social capital within the game's society...they need not only learn the game commands, but they must also become socialized into the game community. To be recognized as a good player [one needs] to learn the lingo, perform [his/her] role well when grouped with others, and more generally demonstrate that [he/she is] an interesting person to play with (p. 2)

Also, in an online survey, it was found that 39.4% of male respondents (n = 2971) and 53.3% of female respondents felt their MMOG friends were comparable or better than their real-life friends (Yee, 2006b).

The assumption of the importance of sociability in sustaining the interest of gamers has resulted in the development of MMOG designed to encourage social interactions. Game developers are trying to make MMOG more sociable by implementing game activities that promote social interaction within the game (Ducheneaut, Moore & Nickell, 2004). Yee (2006a) noted how "most MMOG are designed such that users must often collaborate to achieve goals within the environment" (p. 4) and "[m]ost forms of advancement in MMOG require increasing cooperation or dependency on other users, oftentimes mutually beneficial". Often, the game design places players in "high stress crisis" scenarios which are also "trust-building scenarios" thus potentially facilitating relationship formations (Yee, 2006a, p. 16). In a study of the popular MMORPG, Star Wars Galaxies, Ducheneaut & Moore (2004b) showed how game designers of Star Wars Galax-

ies developed game features and game quests that "promote interactions among the players... [as] these encounters are essential to the success of ...virtual worlds" (p.1). Social interaction is also found as a key factor that makes gamers become engaged in the game and play the game continuously (Chen, Duh & Phuah, 2006).

Designers of MMOGS thus place great emphasis on sociability, and implement features to encourage social interactions and collaboration among gamers (Duchenaut et al, 2004). However, past studies did not provide clear explanation of exactly what social interaction is within the game. They also fail to address how in-game factors affect social interaction. This chapter narrates social interaction within the game World of Warcraft (Wow). It also provides explanation of what and how different factors affecting social interaction.

BACKGROUND

Previous research on social interactions in MMORPGs attempted to use various different measures to study social interactions. Quantitatively, social interactions in MMORPGs have been studied by several authors in various manners. Ducheneaut & Moore (2004b) provided quantitative data on the social interactions of Star Wars Galaxies players by collecting data on "who is interacting with whom"; "in what way (gesture or chat)"; where (starport or cantina), at what date and time, and what the content of the interaction was (text chat or "social" command). It was found that the ten most popular social gestures were: Smile, cheer, clap, wave wink, grin, nod, bow, thank, greet (p. 4). They also found that on average, "a player goes into the cantina, makes about one gesture towards another player, exchanges four sentences with him or her, and receives one gesture in return" (p. 4). Ducheneaut & Moore (2004b) noted some shortcomings in the way they have analyzed social interaction. For example, data collected was purely from publicly observable behavior in the general chat and does not analyze private messages players send to one another and within their player groups and guilds. Moreover, part of the social interaction measured originated from spammers who use a macro to constantly repeat a message (spam the chat) to achieve some aims (level up a profession or sell game resources). Hence, figures are sometimes misleading. This has led to a pre-occupation by the authors to differentiate 'genuine social interaction' from senseless spamming in later studies where they computed a signal to noise ratio measuring the extent of spamming versus unique conversations in Star Wars Galaxies (Ducheneaut et al, 2004).

Besides direct measures, several studies indirectly quantify the importance of social interaction in gaming through survey questionnaires that ask respondents how important is it for them to socialize while in MMOG. For example, Griffiths, Davies & Chappell (2003) conducted secondary data analysis of two fan sites of the popular MMOG, Everquest and found that social interaction make up 41% of the favorite aspects of the game compared to 4% for killing players or mobs. They attributed the figures to the importance of the social element in MMOG. In another example, an online survey of 30,000 MMOG players revealed that platonic and romantic relationships occur frequently in MMOG environments indicating the prevalence of meaningful social interaction in gaming (Yee, 2006a).

Qualitatively, social interactions in MMOG have been studied through virtual ethnographies with the researchers becoming active participants in the game. One such study by Jakobsson & Taylor (2003) found that social networks within the game Everquest bear a striking similarity to the classic mafia stereotype in a TV show 'The Sopranos'. Players rely on the social networks they have built to provide in-game support that will help them overcome quest objectives. Often, such networks are found in guilds and are maintained through a system of trust and reputation just like the mafia. A gamer's reputation is used to gain access to a guild, and to maintain one's status within a guild thereby forming the implicit social hierarchy of a guild with members of high repute holding important positions such as 'guild leader' and 'guild officer'. In another ethnographic study, Steinkuehler (2004) analyzes the language used by gamers during the game and the way Lineage gamers relate to the larger Lineage community.

Existing literature cannot adequately articulate 'social interaction' in games. Some studies suffer from the limitation of the research tools used. For example, Ducheneaut & Moore (2004b) collected data purely from publicly observable behavior in the general chat and do not analyze private messages players send to one another and within their player groups and guilds. This chapter therefore suggests that an interpretive approach utilizing symbolic interactionism as a guiding theory would serve the needs of researchers better by providing a more encompassing, dynamic and flexible way of viewing social interactions in MMOG. It articulates what is meant by 'social interaction' in the game World of Warcraft (Wow). This will help shed light on whether socialization in Wow promotes game play and how to develop games to promote socialization. This chapter uses Herbert Blumer's symbolic interactionism theory as a guiding conceptual approach to study social interaction in Wow. The methodology adopted is virtual ethnography with the researchers as active participants of the game. The discussion will be presented in a series of narratives with theoretical notes from Blumer's symbolic interactionism theory.

IMPORTANT FACTORS FOR STUDYING SOCIAL INTERACTION IN WoW

In WoW, players interact with one another through their in-game avatar. Each player has a front stage self (their avatar) and a backstage self (the player sitting in front of the computer). The game environment presents a stage for players to literally play out their symbolic selves (Goffman, 2004). In Northshire (the newcomer's zone of WoW), players (level 1-10) often engage in an exaggerated play of their symbolic selves by telling unsolicited and unbelievable tales of themselves such as "I SOLOED ONYXIA". Onyxia is an end-game monster that commonly requires 40 level 60 players to take down. More often, players love to brag about their high level alternate characters in other servers e.g., 'Blizzard sucks. I'll be back on my 70 main (my level 70 character, that I most commonly play) once Dragonmaw (another world server) is up'. Bragging gives players a sense of power, the sense of identity is so important some players feel the need to justify why they are so low level. In the example given, the player blames his current level 1 state on the server failure where his main character is. He chooses to define his weak level 1 self in relation to his powerful level 70 self in another server.

Under the veil of anonymity in the online context, there is no way for players to check on others' backstage persona. With this common understanding, players are free to brag as they please. Authenticity becomes a problem that researchers have to deal with in the meaningful discussion of virtual relationships as 'trust' is a major factor of relational building (Ducheneaut & Moore, 2004b; Jakobsson & Taylor, 2003).

Besides inauthenticity, the online context is also fragmentary, anonymous and fluid with little capacity for encouraging relational commitment (Ducheneaut & Moore, 2004c). Some researchers have found the authenticity and fluidity of social interactions within MMOG problematic. For example, the use of macros to spam messages selling items has been labeled as a form of social 'noise' by Ducheneaut et al. (2004) and has led to the differentiation of genuine interaction from inauthentic (macro-programmed) interaction. In a study of how gamers switch between their main avatars and secondary avatars, Ducheneaut &

Moore (2004c) noted that MMORPGs 'fragment an individual's online life into several disconnected digital identities' (p. 3). They observed that

Because of the 'alt switching' practice…on occasion, players who have previously met will meet again under alternate identities that they don't know about. They will therefore have to rebuild their relationship from scratch. This potentially weakens the social fabric of the game (p. 3).

Ducheneaut et al (2006) have also interpreted that guilds are sparse networks because of high guild churn rates. They argue that many players are not playing the game as a social game. It is our view that high guild churn rates are characteristic of the fluidity and fragmentary nature of online social relationships. Therefore, the presence of high guild churn rates and low grouping rates may not mean that MMOG are not social. Rather, it points towards a qualitatively 'different kind of social factor' (Ducheneaut et al., 2006, p. 413) which is at the same time, characteristic of computer-mediated communications in general. Moreover, in the game world social interactions may be similar to real life social interactions in some ways. However, it is also qualitatively different due to the online context in which it takes place. Therefore, this chapter suggests that an interpretive approach utilizing symbolic interactionism as a guiding theory would serve the needs of researchers better.

Symbolic Interactionism and WoW

MMOG are essentially role-playing games. The game encourages players to try out different self-concepts and players can define their self-concepts in a number of ways through: race, gender, player class, avatar appearance…etc. Symbolic interactionism studies how individuals create symbolic meanings through their interactions (Blumer, 2004). An individual's self-conception is therefore reconstructed with each interaction with another. Individuals invest symbolic meanings into these interactions to make them socially real. That means actors use language to communicate in the process of meaning-making. Like social structures, language is symbolic, dynamic and subjected to constant re-interpretation. Language can be verbal or non-verbal, informal or formal (Denzin, 1974).

Social structures are formed when many social actors experience and understand joint actions similarly thus developing 'collectivities' of joint actions such as marriage, trading transactions or church services (Blumer 2004, p. 322). Additionally, Blumer (2004) noted that social structures are dynamic 'it is just not true that the full expanse of life in a human society… is but an expression of pre-established forms of joint action. New situations are constantly arising within the scope of life that are problematic and for which existing rules are inadequate' (p. 323) and therefore, social interaction is a dynamic process with actors constantly making symbolic meaning out of their interactions. Thus, by extension, social structures can also evolve with changes in social interactions.

To understand the dynamics of social interaction and in-game joint actions, three factors need to be considered: temporality, spatiality and community factors.

Temporality: Historical Context

Based on Blumer's (2004) framework, it is important to understand joint actions in the context they occur and consider the meanings of those joint actions based in conjunction with previous joint actions. He claims, 'any instance of joint action, whether newly formed or long established, has necessarily arisen out of a background of previous actions of the particular participants' (p. 324). Therefore, social interaction occurs within a historical context where participants always bring to the formation of new joint action 'the sets of

meanings, and the schemes of interpretation that they already possess. Thus, the new form of joint action always emerges out of and is connected within a context of previous joint action' (p.324). Without an understanding of gamers' previous joint action, it is difficult to interpret their new joint action. To consider this factor in the study of Wow, one must seek to understand a gamer's previous gaming experiences, the contextual change of gaming world (server) in Wow and the progression of gamers' in-game avatar.

Spatiality: Interactional Arena

Besides the historical context, we also propose that in-game spatiality is important in the study of social interactions in MMORPGs. As Ducheneaut *et al* (2004) have argued in a study of Star Wars Galaxies, game designers tried to create spaces of social activity such as 'cantinas' where players are encouraged to engage in social interactions. They likened such spaces of social activity to Oldenburg's notion of the third place. However, it was found that instead of using the 'third places' for social interactions, some players were using informal gathering points such as spawn points for social interactions. Also players were using cantinas as quick 'drive-throughs' (p.7) to accomplish their instrumental needs and altogether bypassing the chance to interact with other players. Therefore, the authors questioned the effectiveness of such in-game 'third places'. From a symbolic interactionist approach viewpoint, an interactional setting does affect the way social interaction develops. In the presence of two or more actors, 'interactional settings' are transformed into 'interactional arenas' where meaningful symbolic exchange can take place (Denzin, 1974, p.270). Therefore, we propose the use of interactional arena as the approach to study how in-game spatiality can influence social interactions. Such a definition is more encompassing given that players sometimes do not utilize social spaces in the manner which game designers intended.

Adopting such an approach may give insights into the sort of social spaces gamers desire rather than focusing on the in-game spaces game designers have hard-wired for social engineering.

Community: Level of Social Aggregation

Additionally, we propose that researchers should be conscious of the different levels of social aggregation while examining social interactions in MMORPGs. As defined by Kolo & Baur (2004) in a study of Ultima Online, the different levels of social aggregation in MMOG are (para. 16): 'the social micro-level' of individual players (for example, the specific motivation to play or the strategy used) on one hand and that of the related characters on the other (for example, the skills or the possessions); 'the meso-level' of social formations among players (for example, player clubs, offline events) or among characters (for example, guilds); 'the social macro-level', spanned by the community of all *Ultima Online* players or all the 'citizens' of Britannia'.

From Blumer's (2004) theory, we suggest that social interaction in MMORPGs is a dynamic process of meaning-making occurring within a historical context and examinable through the analysis of in-game language and in-game joint actions of players. The following section illustrates how social interaction is like and how proposed factors influence the way social interaction takes place in Wow.

SOCIAL INTERACTION IN WORLD OF WARCRAFT (WOW)

The analysis of social interaction in game is presented in first person narrative of one of the researchers' character Tip and recorded in-game dialogue.

The fifty-ninth hour since server started. I'm Tip, a female Paladin. I'm a fighter-healer, an upholder of the Holy Light and a defender of the Alliance. Clothed in my new identity, I clicked the "Enter Realm" button, expecting to save the world. An impressive video set to a stirring soundtrack and spanning the majestic city of Stormwind starts.

With the alliance battle cry still ringing in my ears I was more than amused to find myself standing in the midst of a different kind of battle… More than 10 players of different classes were running around the fields of Northshire slaughtering young wolves. Slashing daggers, arcane missiles and all manner of weapons of mass destruction rained, fast and furious on the poor wolves. There was plenty of competition to kill wolves. Everyone was trying to get the first hit to 'tag their kill'. Welcome to Northshire the n00b (newbie) starting zone for Humans in WoW. Without anyone noticing, I have quietly made my entrance in Anetheron, a new player versus player (PvP) server of WoW.

Generally, there are three types of servers in WoW: the Player versus Environment Server (a.k.a the safe and friendly gameworlds where players can't murder each other), the Role-Playing server (a.k.a the gameworlds where you mainly role-play as a citizen of Azeroth) and lastly, the player versus player server (a.k.a the most bloodthirsty of all servers where players kill one another with legalized abandon). The choice of a PvP server for this chapter is deliberate as it offers the potential for the study of the most confrontational social interaction of all three types of servers. Officially, player versus player killings are couched in the stuff of mythic legends with the heroic Alliance and the fearless Horde engaged in a never-ending battle. More often however, in-game fights resemble petty muggings with powerful players from each side guilty of bullying weaker players. The practice of repeatedly killing another player is called *camping*.

The Influence of Level of Aggregation (Community)

In WoW, part of the observable social interactions takes place in a nondescript scrolling text box on the bottom left of the screen:

Joined Channel: [1. General - Elwynn Forest]
Joined Channel: [2. Trade - Elwynn Forest]
Joined Channel: [3. LocalDefense - Elwynn Forest]
Joined Channel: [4. LookingForGroup - Elwynn Forest]

By default, players join the four chat channels listed above. By Kolo & Baur's (2004) definition of levels of social aggregations, all of the above are macro-social channels. Each channel serves a need, most of which are instrumental. LookingForGroup and Trade are self-explanatory. LocalDefense is a channel peculiarly important to PvP servers and most utilized in areas where both Horde and Alliance players are free to *gank* (player-kill) each other. Certain locales in WoW such as *Stranglethorn Vale* (STV) are notorious for *gank parties* where players indulge in murderous hunts for members of the opposing faction. The LocalDefense channel is used to summon aid when one is *camped* (repeatedly killed) by members of the opposing faction. Often a friendly warning to members of the same faction will read like this:

"Three undeads by Nessie's. lvl 48 priest and 2 rogues. Rogues are skull to me."
(Three horde players are skulking around Nessingway's camp. There's a level 48 priest with two rogues who are both ten levels higher than me.)

If someone is willing to help, a typical reply may read:

"Omw! I love ganking horde."
(On my way to assist. I love to kill horde.)

Besides the general channel, players can choose to speak to others in their proximity using the /say command. It appears in a box above the avatar's head. Anyone nearby can see what one types. All the other types of conversations appear at the left bottom of individual players' screen (see Figure 1). In the following exchange Carthelm, Cheatsheat and Tip are engaged in a conversation with one another. At the same time other players in the general channel, Channel 1 (General Chat) are planning a naked lowbie raid (raiding a city is akin to attacking the city) through the horde city of Ogrimmar. Apparently, a group of taurens (a horde race often derogatorily called bulls for their bull-like appearance) raided SW (Stormwind City) on the world server Garona:

Carthelm: where to
Tip: how old is this server?
Cheatsheat: new
Carthelm: the kobold one
Xyuna: any guilds recruiting
Areth: we should start a noobie raid! lol
Chainz: i was thinking that .... get 50 naked humans runnin through Ogrimm
Areth: but only lvls 1-6
Nightmarez: this server just added today?
Chainz: horde had a "running of the bulls" in SW on Garona... good laughs there
Areth: so who is up for raid? we can only have lvls 1-6.
Kuroneko: a day and a half ago
Chainz: naked taurens... bout 75 of 'em
Seczy: raid... lol

In this case, the /say channel is a micro-social channel. Besides the /say channel there is also a group channel where only people in a 5 man group can see the conversation and a private whisper channel where players can speak to one another privately. Figure 1 shows an ongoing conversation within a 5 man group (in blue) when they are fighting together in an instance. The purple text is a private conversation between 2 players only (whisper).

At the meso level, there is a guild channel where guildies can speak to one another (green in Figure 1) and a raid channel where people in a group larger than 5 people can talk to each other with. Therefore, an individual player can simultaneously observe and hold conversations at multiple levels with multiple gamers.

It is through all the different chat channels gamers 'talk' to each other and build a unique gaming community. Socializing and cooperating in this virtual community with fellow gamers are often integral aspects of the game play in MMORPGs. It also encourages gamers to join guilds where gamers can cooperate in many other ways. Guild is probably the most important social group a gamer belongs to in WoW.

Guilds are formalized long-term player associations and social networks that are integral to the game play of most MMORPGS (Jakobson & Taylor, 2003; Ducheneaut et al., 2006). Within the

virtual WOW community, guilds provide gamers with membership to exclusive distribution lists, bulletin boards and group chat channels in the game, and members' characters will have the guild's name tagged under their avatars' names. Guilds encourage players to play more frequently and the guild's chat channels provide support. In a typical guild, members have access to shared resources, knowledge, and game partners. In one of the field notes done by one of the researcher, it is recorded:

...playing in a good guild can make a difference in the level of enjoyment and commitment to the game. In a good guild, you want to keep up and level up with the rest of the people. You want to run instances with your guild because they are good, so chances of you dying is much lesser. Incidences, where people misbehave and do crazy stuff like swear and slap others are less likely to happen, and that makes game play more enjoyable.

Figure 1. The chat channels at the bottom left

However, conversations in guild can be less instrumental and more personal. In another conversation occurred in the guild chat, it's rather amusing.

Norrisaurus: hey everyone
Spastor: hey man how are you
Norrisaurus: depressed, my girlfriend has a hideous haircut
Spastor: lol
Tarshay: lol
Norrisaurus: im very tempted to break up with her
Tarshay: im a hair dresser
Spastor: have you told her?
Zukfarom: oh man
Norrisaurus: I told her it doesn't look nice
Zukfarom: just because she has a bad haircut?
Sayia: slack
Norrisaurus: but my mom had to spoil it by saying she looked nice.
Zukfarom: then that's your problem buddy
Norrisaurus: I know its weak
Norrisaurus: but like seriously. She looks bad.
Tarshay: lol
Spastor: well all u could do was tell her your opinion. It'll grow out man
Norrisaurus: then she'll cute it back to the same haircut
Spastor: buy her a nice hat then get hurt when she doesn't wear it

This type of conversation is unlikely to happen in the general, trade, local defense, party or raid chat. Based on the topics and the relationship a gamer has with others in each of the channel, conversations can have different focus and depth.

Also, the language WoW players use is clearly not standardized English. Turkle (as cited in Steinkuehler, 2004, p. 4) describes the linguistic practice of online gamers as 'closed world of references, cross-references and code". The study of language use in MMOs and its relations to social structures and social identity of gamers has been attempted by Steinkuehler (2004), who conducted a discourse analysis of the players' speech in the MMOG Lineage to illustrate how language can convey social information on a player's in-game identification within the larger Lineage community. Similarly, we find that language used by players in WoW is a valuable social artifact that allows researchers to understand the evolution of social interaction in WoW.

The language used by players in WoW is appropriated from the larger community of geek speakers and other MMOGs. Informal dictionaries in the form of WoW guides are easily obtainable for newbs (newbies) trying to socialize with the more experienced WoW players (Glossary, n.d.; WoW specific slang, n.d.). Language is constantly evolving. An illuminative moment when this can be seen happened on Tip's 11th day in Anetheron in an area known as Westfall. Westfall is home to an instance called Deadmines. Instances are 'dungeons' with quests that often requires a full party of five to adventure in. To complete the quests given, players must form a balanced team (often, comprising of a healer, a tank to distract monsters from the healers/mages and a damage causing class such as a mage to cut the monsters down). Instances range from the low level ones e.g. Deadmines (level 17- low 20s) to the high level ones e.g. Dire Maul (level 60s) In Westfall, Alliance players often spam the general channel looking for groups to do Deadmines quests. In this incident, a player Ernie was looking for a healer for Deadmines (DM) in the General chat channel. However DM also stands for Dire Maul which is a level 60 instance. The resulting confusion which followed clearly illuminates how language is constantly evolving in WoW.

Ernie: Looking for healer DM
Fletcher: looking for party for DM
Emendil: Aren't u a bit low for Dire Maul?

(Emendil mistook Deadmines (DM) for Dire Maul (DM))

Twinie: not that again
Hurl: are you a jerk?
Deity: First time alliance maybe?
Himor: need a healer for VC

(Himor, also forming a party for Deadmines substitutes DM for VC which stands for Van Cleef a monster that is found in Deadmines. The use of VC in place of DM clarifies the confusion.)

Emendil: lol calm down ppl... just kidding :D
Deity: DM =Deadmines as well as Dire Maul, commonsense usually leads to what the person is talking about
Ernie: looking for healers VC

(Similarly, Ernie follows Himor's example, switching to "VC" to clarify the confusion.)

Adrasatus: call deadmines VC

(Adrasatus, in a bid to clarify the confusion, tells others to call deadmines "VC")

Romuluss: arent u a little stupid to be playing this game?
Ernie: every1 knows DM is VC.

(the illuminative moment happens when Ernie voices the assumption that seasoned WoW alliance players all know DM is VC).

The confusion in this case is compounded because Deadmines is an instance that is usually available to the Alliance players only. Experienced WoW players who do not play Alliance races often do not know of Deadmines. In this example, Emendil is either a n00b (newbie) poorly versed in WoW lingo or, as Deity proposed, a first time alliance player since he/she knows that DM stands for Dire Maul, a high level instance which is avail-

able to both Horde and Alliance players. Emendil, on seeing the breach in his conduct tries to repair his 'face' (Goffman, 2004) by passing off the mistake as a joke 'laugh out loud (lol) calm down ppl (people)... just kidding'. The consequences to such a breach in conduct is public castigation 'aren't u a little stupid to be playing this game?' as well as changes in the way the community now defines Deadmines. Instead of DM, Himor starts to refer to Deadmines by the abbreviations 'VC'. Ernie (the initial perpetuator of the confusion) too adopts the term 'VC', followed by Adrasatus who calls on the community to use the abbreviations 'VC' for deadmines instead.

Language is therefore the by-product of how actors make sense of each others' actions. A common understanding that unites the community is reached when all actors agree upon a shared understanding i.e. that from hence, 'VC' should be used to refer to Deadmines. Social interaction is therefore a study of how social actors interact to create shared understandings. The shared understandings are dynamic and evolve according to the context of the action. In this example, the interactional setting is Westfall.

The Influence of Interactional Arenas (Spatiality)

As Denzin (1974) has noted interactional settings are transformed into interactional arenas in the presence of two or more actors. DM symbolically refers to Deadmines in Westfall because actors within the interactional arena of Westfall share a common understanding that "every1 knows DM is VC". Social interaction and its empirically observable unit "language" are therefore situated in the context of the interaction. In this case, the defining factor is the location or what we termed as the "interactional arena". Therefore, we propose that researchers take note of interactional arenas when studying social interactions as its form, conduct and function may be influenced by the nature of the interactional arena.

From our ethnographic journeys into WoW, we found qualitative differences in the kind of social interactions occurring in different regions within WoW. The most obvious are found by comparing and contrasting contested areas (areas where player-killing is allowed) with city areas (non-player-killing). Ducheneaut *et al* (2004) have suggested that the 'neutrality' of Cantinas (the closest WoW equivalent is a city) have favored the formation of instrumental actions over other interactions. Similarly, we observed that the murderous atmosphere of Stranglethorn Vale (notorious for its popularity with gank parties) sometimes creates a sense of social solidarity amongst players. Often, players watch each other's back and serve as 'surveillance' patrols. Suspicious gank

parties are noted and their levels and classes are reported in the General Chat. Players with time on their hands, of a high enough level or simply harboring bloodthirsty thoughts will voluntarily help out players who are camped or bullied by the other faction. In safe areas like Stormwind City, social interactions are strikingly instrumental with players often congregating just to do some fast trading or group formation. Social interactions in city areas are also often more "spectatorial" in nature. Players gather in cities to check out other players' epic mounts, epic gears, or simply goof around by dancing naked etc.

One such incident is humorously illustrated in Figure 2, where two players were captured parading their epic mounts in Stormwind. Besides

Figure 2. Players showing off their epic mounts and mounts

interactional arenas and levels of social aggregation, we also observed that changes in historical
context may influence the form and type of social
interactions observed.

The Influence of Historical Context (Temporality)

Historical context is a larger concept which includes a player's previous experience with WoW,
the maturity of the server and also a player's level
at which the behavior is encountered.

A player's previous experience is not equated
to one's in-game level. More experienced players
are judged by their skills with the game. They
are likely to know their role in the team, and
they are familiar with strategies needed to cope
with troublesome monsters (mobs) in instances.
Helping others gives them a sense of power or
what we would like to term as 'self-reinforcing
encounters' where one's self-conception is given
an ego boost. Sometimes experienced players
help so much, their frontstage roles become too
overwhelming to keep up. This happened to one
of my guild mates, documented in one of our
field notes:

*When I (Tip) first joined my current guild, Chrisha-
kimi is around the same mid-20s level range as I
was. He was already an officer of the guild, an experienced player and an offline-friend of the guild
master. The guildies often refer to Chrishakimi as
Uncle Chrish (as a form of cheeky endearment
and respect) or Chrishy for short. Chrish is the
carebear of the guild. He gives free green and
sometimes even blue items to guildies and he's
the twenty-four hours, all-instance tank for almost all of the guild runs. It got to the point when
Chrish helped so often that he stopped leveling at
one stage altogether. Tanks and priests are two
highly sought after classes in WoW. Every party
needs a tank to hold the monsters at bay while
the rest of the team members perform their roles.
It is not uncommon to logging in to find Chrish*

*(a level 30+ warrior) helping the guildies tank
Deadmines which is an instance that is too low
level for Chrish. When a high level player runs
guildies through a low level instance it is known
as power-levelling. At first I thought nothing much
of Chrish's helpfulness. However, I soon realized
it was a running thorn among some of the officers
of the guild.*

On the 53th day since server started, Tip was
promoted to Officer Level within the guild and
gained access to the Guild officer chat which is
restricted to leaders of the guild. Usually, officer
chat is used to chat about non-consequential subjects or subjects that we don't want all guildies to
know (i.e. gossips) but sometimes things get pretty
serious when experienced players start discussing
the direction of the guild and the dkp (dragon
killing point) system. In the guild chat:

*Some officers were unhappy with the way Chrish
was power leveling the newbs. The concern was
level 60 newbs, who are power-levelled and
unskilled in their roles will be disastrous for
end-game instances like Molten Core. Apparently
guildies often cite the lack of a tank at the late
hour we play in and rope Chrish in to help out in
lower level instances like Razorfen Deep (RFD)
and VC. Chrish is also very willing to help as ours
is a growing-guild and since we have restricted it
to Singaporean players, retaining guidies has also
been one of our top priorities. Helping guildies is
one way to retain their loyalty to the guild. The
subject was brushed off but revisited again and
again in the subsequent weeks.*

The breaking point came when two of the more
experienced officers, a tank (Chloeris) and a priest
(Priestdave) reached the highest level while the
rest of the guilds were still strangling in the 40s.
The level disparity was exacerbated as Chloeris
and Priestdave started parading their loot in the
guild chat. The seeds of discords were sowed on
Day 76th on the officer chat channel.

Chrishakimi: Some guildies have been asking why we aren't helping.

Tip: they did?

Chloeries: I dont help at all for the past week ; D

Tip: the st (Sunken Temple) thing is not that Chrish can't tank, is that we don't have priests. (in a reference to an earlier squabble when Chloeries and Priestdave back out on a promise to go to Sunken Temple with some of us. We couldn't find a pick up priest.)

Chloeries: eh Chrish, this point i have to disagree

Chrishakimi: Duh I am the one taking the brunt... will realli be happy if Chlowee or Dave could help them in juz one instance a dae.

Tip: actually we need priests...

Chloeries: i mean u need 60s to run instances for u? then when we were leveling which lvl 60 help us?

Tip: hey.. chrish doesn't mean that

Chrishakimi: Not not only the ST thingy... but for eg.. the 30 and 40 lvls... i explain to them i wan them to gather their own peeps for better team work

Tip: actually the running through is not a matter of levelling or powerlevelling I really learn a lot when u run me through like how to macro etc.

Chloeries: i never had a level 60 tank for me in ST... Like i said i tank ST when i was lvl 51 ... and not prot spec

Chrishakimi: is not tat... i told U liao.. with or without Chlowee help I will go soon.. is the other lower level peeps.

Chloeries: i never play warrior before so i got by all the instances by learning.

Tip: no lah... just when dave and u running me through mara (mauraudon, an instance) that time i really learnt a lot of tricks... or else always aggro.

Chrishakimi: i juz hope to see dave and chlowee help the guilides more.. not juz showing off your loot.. once a while is ok to bait them to go instance... but not all the time.

Chrishakimi: and dave knowing that we need healers shld be volunteering to help us more.

Tip: speaking of healers should i turn holy now?

Chrishakimi: half the time no guilides even bother to ask them coz we dun do it any more.. sighz..

Tip: yeah... a bit sad like that...

Chloeries: yeah sad for me too since i had to do everything myself without help from guild when i hit lvl 50.

(Chrish logs off)

Here, Chrish's carebear role has become a burden for him. Every time Chrish logs in, guildies were literally demanding him to run some instance for them. On the other hand, guildies often do not approach Chlowee for similar help. Both are warrior-tanks. How the guildies interact with Chlowee and Chrish depends on the way they perceived their roles historically. Guildies often look to Chlowee for advice since he's a more experienced player than Chrish and had played practically every single class in WoW. For instance runs however, Chrish's the man to seek because as Chlowee acknowledges, he had refused to help guildies for the past week (and from my observation even before that). Players' previous experiences therefore influence how they make social demands on others. Besides interpersonal experiences based on previous experiences, a player's experience with WoW is also exhibited in his/her conduct and communicated to others. Skilled players are usually deferred to. Social interaction is therefore grounded in a tangled historical web of inter-personal and intra-personal past experiences.

A player's level at which a social interaction is encountered also influences the type of social interaction one experiences. The most straightforward is example of this is looting behavior. In lower level instances players often use a group loot system. In higher level instances when the loot drops become too precious, players often adopt a form of looting system known as master-loot which requires the players to trust the raid leader (see appendix 3 for detailed explanation). Also higher-level players often encounter low-level beggars. Higher level player also get a certain amount of deference and grudging respect from others.

Player level is a relative concept, the differences in social interaction is due to the level differential of two actors. However, absence of level differential can also influence the outcome of social decisions. Often times, when encountering solitary horde around my level in Stranglethorn Vale, We'll proceed to check on their PvP rank. A low PvP rank e.g. such as a Grunt probably means this player does not gank much and it is safer to keep the peace. For that one moment of pause when one is regarding the Other, a quick

decision has to be made either to /wave (signifying peace) or attack (signifying hostility). However on encountering a player between five to ten levels above me, I usually flee for my life, without a single glance at the Other. Therefore, player level is a type of non-verbal communication that either intentionally or unintentionally causes some form of a social reaction when one actor encounters another. Player level is a chronological concept because as a server grows older (matures), there are more high level players (in absolute terms), the presence of a level 70 player simply does not carry its social weight compared to the past when there were less high level players.

Therefore, we also propose that server maturity influences the form and evolution of social interactions in WoW. In the first days of a

Figure 3. The competition for mobs in Moonbrook

new server, there is a preoccupation with power watching and power display of all forms. People are competing to be the first to reach the highest level, the first to get a mount, the first to get an epic mount etc. In particular, people were using the /who command to look at who's the highest level player on the server. A hunter, Kugoo became quite legendary for being the first level 40 within the first the few days of Anetheron's launch. In the general chats, people were asking for the highest level player and rumours were flying around about "Kugoo" being played by 3 people in shifts all round the clock. One of my guildies also openly declared that he must be "one of the first level 60s" in this server.

Besides levels, players were also competing for scarce resources. In particular, players were competing to kill monsters. Figure 3 shows a scene in Moonbrook in the early days of the server, where a whole camp of players was literally fighting over monsters to kill.

The resultant effect is more collaboration even though players did not need extra help. Collaboration in this case happened because the mobs were too few and parties questing together would have lessened the demands on mobs. One in-game example which requires players to kill a messenger who does not spawn very frequently resulted in collaboration:

Sixth day since server started.

Daninja: ^&%"! man there r too many ppl here in westfall
(*swears* man there are too many people here in westfall)

*Laila: pst remadin for messenger invites... don't be a **** like bluesheep and tag him by yourself while there's 5 people waiting.*
(please send a private whisper to Remadin to get invited to the group for the quest to kill messenger. Don't be a f*** like bluesheep and kill messenger by yourself when five other people also need messenger for the quest)

In sum, interactional arena, level of social aggregation, and historical context are the three factors that influence social interaction in Wow. Historical context influences gamers' desire to keep on playing in a given sever, a given guild, and interact with certain (type of) players. The depth and breath of social interaction change as the game server matures (temporal factor). There are qualitative differences in the kind of social interactions occurring in different regions within Wow (interactional arena/ spatial factors). Level of social aggregation usually influences the topic and nature of the conversation.

FUTURE TRENDS

Another part of our research projects (Chen & Duh, 2007) has developed a typology of various forms of social interaction. It also addresses how the three aforementioned factors influence specific forms of social interaction in WoW. The proposed framework in Chen and Duh (2007), with analysis in the current chapter, aims to inform future research in social interaction in MMOG. The framework is still in its developmental stage and it needs further validation.

There are several research issues that can help improve the proposed framework. There are qualitative differences in the kind of social interaction occurring in different regions within Wow, but we cannot assert that interactional arenas influence the forms of social interaction that occur. Future research can look into the differences in the forms of social interaction within each interactional arena. We observe that social interaction change as server matures, but we cannot pinpoint when and how each form of social interaction changes as servers mature. Future research can look into this issue. Further research can also look at how the change of the game features changes the dynamic of social interaction.

CONCLUSION

This chapter offers readers a slightly different perspective to complement the data driven and micro-sociological analyses that already exist in the literature. It illustrates in-game social interaction and explains the different factors that influence social interaction within Wow to fill in gaps in current literature. Spatiality (interactional arena), temporality (historical context) and community (level of social aggregation) are the three main factors influencing how social interaction takes place in Wow. Spatiality and temporality heavily influence how social interaction takes place in Wow. Quantitative research may obtain different outcomes depending on where and when researchers start their research. Therefore, studies of social interaction should take into account historical context and interactional arena.

REFERENCES

Blizzard (n.d.). Glossary. Retrieved 2 July 2006, from http://www.worldofwarcraft.com/info/basics/glossary.html

Blumer, H. (2004). Society in action. In S.E.Cahill. (Ed.). *Inside social life: Readings in sociological psychology and microsociology* (4ᵗʰ ed., pp.320-324). Los Angeles: Roxbury Publishing Company.

Chen, H., & Duh, H.B.L. (2007). Understanding Social Interaction in World of Warcraft. In *Proceedings of the International Conference on Advances in Computer Entertainment Technology, 203,* 21-24.

Chen, V.H.H., Duh, H.B.L., Phuah, P.S.K., & Lam, D.Z.Y. (2006). Enjoyment or Engagement? Role of Social Interaction in Playing Massively Multiplayer Online Role-playing Games (MMORPGS). *Lecture Notes in Computer Science, 4161,* 262-267.

Denzin, N. K. (1974). The methodological implication of symbolic interactionism for the study of deviance. *The British Journal of Sociology, 25*(3), 269-282.

Ducheneaut, N., & Moore, R. J. (2004a, April). *Gaining more than experience points: Learning social behavior in multiplayer computer games.* Position paper for the CHI2004 workshop on Social Learning Through Gaming, Vienna, Austria.

Ducheneaut, N., & Moore, R.J. (2004b). The social side of gaming: a study of interaction patterns in a massively multiplayer online game. In *Proceedings of the 2004 ACM conference on Computer Supported Cooperative Work,* 360-369.

Ducheneaut, N., & Moore, R. J. (2004c, November). *Let me get my alt: digital identiti(es) in multiplayer games.* Position paper for the CSCW2004 Workshop on Representation of Digital Identities, Chicago, IL.

Ducheneaut, N., Moore, R.J., & Nickell, E. (2004). Designing for sociability in massively multiplayer games: an examination of the 'third places' of SWG.' In J.H. Smith and M. Sicart (Eds.), *Proceedings of the Other Players conference.* Copenhagen: IT University of Copenhagen.

Ducheneaut, N., Yee, N., Nickell, E., & Moore, R.J. (2006). Alone Together? Exploring the Social Dynamics of Massively Multiplayer Games. In *Proceedings of the SIGCHI Conference on Human Factors in Computing Systems,* 407-416.

Goffman, E. (2004). The presentation of self. In S.E. Cahill. (Ed.), *Inside social life: Readings in sociological psychology and microsociology* (pp.108-116). Los Angeles, California: Roxbury Publishing Company.

Griffiths, M. D., Davies, M. N. O., & Chappell, D. (2003). Breaking the stereotype: The case of online gaming. *CyberPsychology and Behavior, 6,* 81–91.

Jakobsson, M., & Taylor, T.L. (2003). The Sopranos meets EverQuest. Social networking in massively multiplayer online games. In *Proceedings of Digital Arts and Culture Conference,* 81-90.

Kazzak does Stormwind (n.d.). Retrieved 2 July 2006, from http://video.google.com/videoplay?docid=-982380251124231965

Kolo, C., & Baur, T. (2004). Living a virtual life: social dynamics of online gaming. *Game Studies: International Journal of Computer Game Research, 4* (1). [online journal], viewed 15 July 2005, http://www.gamestudies.org/0401/kolo/.

Ogaming.com (n.d.). WoW specific slang. Retrieved 2 July 2006, from http://wow.ogaming.com/data/1679~WoWSpecifcSlang.php

Pew Internet Project. (2003). Let the games begin: Game technology and entertainment among college students. Available: http://www.pewinternet.org/pdfs/PIP_College_Gaming_Reporta.pdf [2008, Jan 1]

Steinkuehler, C. A. (2004). A Discourse analysis of MMOG talk. In J. H. Smith & M. Sicart (Eds.), In *Proceedings of the Other Players Conference,* Copenhagen: IT University of Copenhagen.

Yee, N. (2006a). The Psychology of MMORPGs: Emotional Investment, Motivations, Relationship Formation, and Problematic Usage. In R. Schroeder & A. Axelsson (Eds.), *Avatars at Work and Play: Collaboration and Interaction in Shared Virtual Environments* (pp. 187-207). London: Springer-Verlag.

Yee, N. (2006b). The Demographics, Motivations and Derived Experiences of Users of Massively-Multiuser Online Graphical Environments. *PRESENCE: Teleoperators and Virtual Environments, 15,* 309-329.

KEY TERMS

In-Game Social Interaction: Socializing and communication behaviors occur in online-gaming environment

In-Game Spatiality: It refers to locations where meaningful symbolic exchange can take place.

In-Game Temporality: It refers to historical context of virtual games. It is a larger concept which includes a player's previous experience with WoW, the maturity of the server and also a player's level at which the behavior is encountered

Level of Community: It refers to the size and scope of the social network.

Chapter XI
Social Semantic Web and Semantic Web Services

Stelios Sfakianakis
ICS-FORTH, Greece

ABSTRACT

In this chapter the authors aim to portray the social aspects of the World Wide Web and the current and emerging trends in "Social Web". The Social Web (or Web 2.0) is the term that is used frequently to characterize Web sites that feature user provided content as their primary data source and leverage the creation of online communities based on shared interests or other socially driven criteria. The need for adding more meaning and semantics to these social Web sites has been identified and to this end the Semantic Web initiative is described and its methodologies, standards, and architecture are examined in the context of the "Semantic Social Web". Finally the embellishment of Web Services with semantic annotations and semantic discovery functionality is described and the relevant technologies are explored.

INTRODUCTION

The World Wide Web (WWW or, simply, the "Web") has been used extensively as a huge network of interconnected islands of data where documents are linked, searched for, and shared, forming a massive, albeit not always well organized, digital library. Sharing of digital content has always been the major requirement for the Web since its inception and will continue to be one of

its most important features in the years to come. Nevertheless, what we experience nowadays is the endeavor for extending this sharing to cover also additional artifacts beyond plain documents, like data, information, and knowledge. The power of the hyperlinks, connecting different, possibly disparate entities, can also be exploited in order to connect information sources and people: not just "dumb" machine readable data but dynamic content like user profiles and ultimately people themselves for building virtual communities. The vision is that the current web of computers and documents will be broadened to the web of people. A "People Web" is the one where users are the nodes of the graph, the edges being their relationships and interactions in space and time, thus constructing new virtual societies (see Figure 1).

This new environment is leveraged by the introduction of an array of technologies collectively identified as Semantic Web (Berners-Lee, Hendler, & Lassila, 2001). The Semantic Web builds upon the existing Web and provides the necessary substrate for giving "meaning" and "Semantics" to Web resources and Web interactions. The benefits will be many in a number of application domains and while the challenges, technological and other, are numerous, the momentum is strong and the Semantic Web slowly but steadily enters in a number of diverse domains like health and life sciences.

Furthermore the Semantic Web promises a great potential for supporting the construction and smooth operation of Web communities of people. In this chapter we study its fusion with social software and software for machine to machine communication over the Web for supporting this vision.

BACKGROUND

Since its launching in 1990, the Web has grown exponentially both in terms of size and in terms of use and utility to people and organizations. The inherent simplicity of hypertext and its feature limited, in comparison to previous hyper linking systems, one-way, inexpensive links (Universal Resource Identifiers – URIs) but also the employment of the Internet as its networking substrate led to its wide adoption and success.

In spite of its success and popularity the early version of the Web lacked in many respects, ranging from user accessibility and user interface design to the ability to repurpose and remix existing Web-based data in not pre-established ways. Although the hyper linking facility allowed the interconnection of different documents on the

Figure 1. A social graph

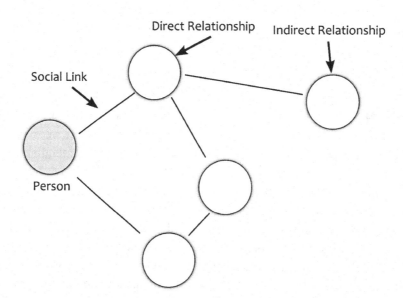

Web, the "traditional" Web suffers from fragmentation in the sense that the huge graph lacks any organization and discipline. This "anarchy" in the Web has also been its driving force for the success it has enjoyed so far but created the need for having special machinery, e.g. search engines like Google, to deal with the efficient indexing and discovery of the available information. Despite the fact that the search engine technology has made important steps in indexing and searching massive amounts of data on the Web, there's still the issue that keyword based searching is limited on its potential and usually finding "what the user wants" proves to be a tedious task. Another major limitation of this environment is that the people are not part of the equation. Users are expected to be the actors triggering the Web interactions but they are not allowed to participate and be involved enough in these interactions:

- Content delivered is not personalized. What the user gets back is usually not inline with her interests or other preferences and there's no feedback link going from the user back to the system she interacts with so as to guide future interactions.
- Contextual information is not taken into consideration. The people as complex systems do not act in an easily predetermined way and the context of their actions is usually ignored or not taken advantage of. This context information ranges from the user's profile, which is also dynamic in nature, to the specific objective she/he is trying to achieve at a specific point in time.
- Content is passive and static, stored and maintained in back end databases, which the users do not have the ability to enrich or customize to their own needs
- Communication and collaboration of the users to build Web communities are not supported enough. Discussion forums were the sole way to build such communities but

with no means to support intelligent integration of the different forums or to enhance the user collaboration experience.

These and other requirements are the ones that the Social Web tries to tackle. Social Web does not represent a shift or radical change in technology per se but rather a shift on the perception of the human–machine interaction by placing the users in the centre of the system and in control of these interactions. But from the other end of the spectrum there is also a clear need for making the Web itself more intelligent to support these machine facilitated social interactions. The Semantic Web could provide for such an enabling technology and recently the convergence of the Social and the Semantic Web and the experimentation of the two working in complementary ways have gained a lot of attention and research interest.

SOCIAL WEB OR WEB 2.0

The situation described in the previous section led to the emergence of a new breed of Web applications and sites that were collectively identified as "Web 2.0" by Tim O'Reilly (2005) and whose major design principle is to *"harness network effects to get better the more people use them".* The value of "Web 2.0" sites and applications therefore comes to a large extent by the number of users participating and actively communicating and sharing through them so the term *"Social Web"* is actually a synonym. The social nature of this Web is evident when the collaboration of people and their active contribution is considered. The very essence of such sites is the building and maintenance of Web based *virtual communities* of people that produce and maintain *collective knowledge.* Examples of such community oriented and social networking sites include:

- Blogs, i.e. Web sites managed by individuals that provide news or opinions on certain subjects (typically personal online diaries), where typically other people are able to leave comments. In addition to comments, the hyperlinking facility of the Web has been extensively used to provide "trackbacks" (i.e. reverse hyperlinks that identify who is talking about me) and recommended blogs ("blogrolls"). Therefore blogging has been emerged as a method for anyone to publish content on the Web and building online communities of people that communicate, share, and integrate.

- "Social bookmarking" sites (e.g. http://del.icio.us/) where users can store and share their bookmarks with the additional possibility to provide metadata through the means of tags, i.e. terms that denote concepts, meaning, intent, etc. These sites provide for user maintained and collaborative indexing of the Web content in a way that it may be more efficient to search there for something than in general purpose Web search engines.
- "Wikis" (e.g. http://en.Wikipedia.org), which are collaboratively built Web sites where the users, through custom made and user friendly interfaces, are able to create, share, enhance, and manage the content.
- Content sharing sites, e.g. YouTube (http://www.youtube.com/) for videos or Flickr (http://www.flickr.com/) for photographs, where the users upload their multimedia content and share it online with other users.
- Social networking sites, such as Facebook (http://www.facebook.com/) and MySpace, for online communities of people who share interests and activities or who are interested in exploring the interests and activities of others.
- Classified advertisement sites, e.g. Craigslist (http://www.craigslist.org), which offer advertisements for jobs, resumes, services, etc. grouped in categories.

If we take only "Wikis" as an example we can see that these Web sites have been used in a multitude of ways:

- As online encyclopedias, e.g. Wikipedia
- As free dictionaries, e.g. Wiktionary (http://en.wiktionary.org)
- As free libraries of educational books, e.g. Wikibooks (http://en.Wikibooks.org)
- As software development repositories and issue tracking systems, e.g. Trac (http://trac.edgewall.org/)
- As open forums to promote research interests, like OpenNetWare (http://openwetware.org/) for biology and biological engineering
- As open educational centers to support learning activities, e.g. Wikiversity (http://en.Wikiversity.org/)
- As social event calendars, like Upcoming (http://upcoming.yahoo.com/)

The single distinctive feature of Wikis and a central trait of the social Web sites is the *user generated content* and its "open" editing: anyone can edit an existing Wiki article or create a new one for a particular topic if it doesn't exist already. The users therefore are responsible for adding content and maintaining the information that is available from these sites. Of course such an approach can raise a lot of concerns about the validity of the content, the lack of authority, etc.[1] and there have been cases in the past where such skepticism was proven true, such as the Seigenthaler incident[2]. Nevertheless this open model has worked quite well in practice and in general so that at the time of this writing Wikipedia is considered by many a serious competitor to the Encyclopedia Britannica. The reason for this can be explained as another instantiation of the "wisdom of crowds" phenomenon (Surowiecki, 2004): the participation of many people, possibly with different background, habits, way of thinking, and so on, in a decision making process usually yields better results than when the individual opinions are considered separately from one another.

The contribution of user content and the sharing of the uploaded information are the main forces for the formation of *online communities* of people. In Figure 2 an example of this community creation process is shown for the Del.icio.us online bookmarking site. Online bookmarking sites like this provide the means for storing and organizing bookmarks of Web sites on the Web instead of the users' desktop browsers. By storing their bookmarks in a central area the users are additionally enabled to create their online social networks by registering other users as members of their network so that they can be notified about the bookmarking activity of these users. These networks therefore connect users with their friends, family, coworkers, or even totally strangers when they unexpectedly meet each other on the

Internet and discover they have similar interests. Facilitated by these network links the users can subsequently observe each other's online behavior and even proactively send interesting Web sites addresses to their peers, easier and quicker than using email or instant messaging.

What the previous examples show is that in the Social Web users are in the limelight: they are the primary actors in the data sharing process through their contributions and online behavior. They are usually indulged by the low cost entry and participation in these Web sites, and, to a lesser extent, by the visual appeal the Web 2.0 sites offer to the viewer. The modern Web sites are actually Rich Internet Applications (RIA), where the majority of the business and control logic resides on the client (i.e. the Web browser), leveraged by technologies like AJaX[3] and Comet[4] which provide more responsive user interfaces.

Figure 2. Del.icio.us networks of users

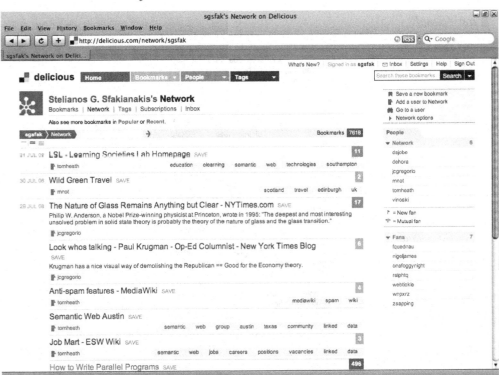

The Social Web offers a meeting point for people to collaborate and share information in an open environment. The openness is a distinctive characteristic of Web 2.0 and it's supported by Open Data APIs like content syndication via RSS/Atom[5] and lightweight Web services interfaces like Open Search[6] . These technologies enable the view of Web sites as Web applications and their synthesis ("mashup") in more complex applications. An example of such combination of existing Web sites and their data to create new/aggregated content is Housing-Maps (http://www.housingmaps.com/) where houses to rent or buy are located through Craiglists and projected over geographic maps drawn from Google Maps (http://maps.google.com) so that a user can easily locate the information he wants in an interactive and visual way. A more general and reusable way to combine and "mix" content from different Web sites is offered by Yahoo! Pipes[7] which can be thought of a simple but effective way to build "workflows" and "dataflows" on the Web.

The above discussion shows that collaboration between people but also between Web sites/applications supports the notion of "collective intelligence" to the Social Web. An instance of this intelligence built collectively is the creation of "folksonomies" for categorization of resources. A quite popular way of classifying content in Web 2.0 Web sites is through "tagging". A tag is a keyword which acts like a subject or category. The user is allowed to attach whatever keywords she wants to identifiable content such as links in the case of social bookmarking, or videos and photographs in the case of digital content sharing. The important thing is that tags can be shared, used in searches, or recommended based on the choices of other users for the same content.

The new term "folksonomy", as a fusion of the words "folks" and "taxonomy", has been suggested to describe this method of classifying content through tags that are collaboratively gen-

Figure 3. A tag "cloud"

erated and shared. Of course these "poor man's" classification schemes are informal in nature, could contain duplication in meaning, or be simply erroneous but again they are contributed by the users and the more people contributing the more robust and stable these "folksonomies" become. A self adapting and auto regulating method is usually followed through the use of tag clouds (Figure 3). In simple terms a tag cloud is a visual representation of a user's tags where each tag is weighted based on the user preferences and how many times he has used the tag. Through such an approach "good" tags are likely to prevail assuming that the user participation is high.

Collaboration, sharing, "mashing", annotating and "tagging" content are roughly the distinctive features of Web 2.0 and although in most of the cases the approach is not formal or the solutions are suboptimal the user participation and their socialization needs have driven the evolution of Web of documents to the Web of People (Ramakrishnan & Tomkins, 2007).

SEMANTIC WEB

To the other end of the spectrum, with roots in Artificial Intelligence research, the Semantic Web emanated as an extension to the current version of the Web that aims to enhance it by the promotion of higher level sharing and integration of data and information. According to Berners-Lee et al. (2001):

The Semantic Web is not a separate Web but an extension of the current one, in which information is given well-defined meaning, better enabling computers and people to work in cooperation.

The Semantic Web aims to support the representation and exchange of information in a meaningful way so as to make possible the automated processing of descriptions on the Web. The objective is to enrich the unstructured information in the current Web with machine processable descriptions of the Semantics in order to make

its navigation and exploration by software agents as easy as it's for the human users today, or even easier. In this context Semantic Web promotes a shift from the current "syntactic" world to the future "Semantic" world of services, applications, and people and aims to make the machine to machine communication feasible so that not only data but also information and finally knowledge are shared.

The Semantic Web Technology Infrastructure

In technological terms the Semantic Web architecture consists of an array of technologies that can roughly be visualized in a layered design layout as depicted in Figure 4. The basic infrastructure in the bottom layers in this stack of technologies is the exactly the same to the syntactic Web: Uniform Resource Identifiers (URIs) used for identification of Web resources, universal encoding schemes for characters, i.e. Unicode, and XML and its related technologies (e.g. XML Namespaces) as a ubiquitous data serialization format. Some of the upper layers like Proof and Trust are missing or are work in progress. Here we will concentrate on the middle layers where the core infrastructure technologies of the Semantic Web reside: RDF, RDF Schema/OWL, and SPARQL.

The *Resource Description Framework* (RDF) is a syntax neutral data model that enables the description of Web resources in a simple way (Lassila, Swick, et al., 1999). At the core of RDF there is a model for representing and describing *resources* through named *properties* (also known as *predicates*) and their values. The resources can be anything that can be identified with a URI. Although in the initial specification of RDF resources were limited to Web documents and Web sites, it is possible and quite frequent in practice to describe, by the means of RDF and the various URI schemes, real world entities like people, or more abstract things like relationships and concepts. The use of URIs and especially

Figure 4. The Semantic Web stack of technologies

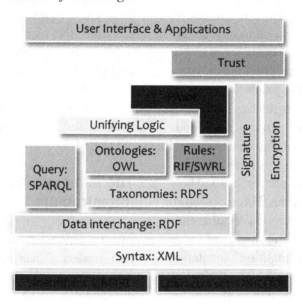

the HTTP based ones for identifying persons or other physical entities may seem strange at first but this is in compliance with the architecture of the World Wide Web (Berners-Lee et al., n.d.) which strongly suggests the use of URIs for identifying anything that can be of importance irrespective of how abstract or tangible it may be.

The properties serve both to represent attributes of resources and to represent relationships between resources. They are also identified though URIs to make them unique. The combination of resources and the properties that connect them builds the simple RDF data model. In this data model the primary informational building block is the "triple" which denotes the subject – property - object expressions (Figure 5). The subject denotes the resource, and the predicate denotes traits or aspects of the resource and expresses a relationship between the subject and the object. Since an object of a triple can be the subject of another one, a set of RDF triples forms a *directed graph* where the RDF resources, both subjects and objects, are the nodes of the graph and the predicates are the labeled arcs. As an example, in

Figure 6 there's a simple RDF graph. The graph shown in the figure describes an entity identified through the URI "http://ssfak.org/stelios/", apparently denoting a person, which has a "name" property with the value "Stelios Sfakianakis", a property denoting the homepage of an organization a person works for relating it to the resource "http://www.ics.forth.gr/cmi-hta/", and a "maker" property that connects it (backwards, as an object) to the resource identified as "http://ssfak.org".

RDF as an abstract model is independent of any specific serialization syntax. The normative representation syntax for RDF graphs is XML but more lightweight formats, such as Turtle (Beckett & Berners-Lee, 2008), exist.

The simplicity and flexibility of RDF is evident but in certain cases its generality must be formally confined so that software entities are able to correctly exchange the encoded information. For example, stating that an animal is the creator of a Web page does not make sense in the real world but RDF does not forbid anyone for making such a claim. Ontologies (Uschold & Gruninger, 1996) provide such a tool to specify what can be

Figure 5. RDF Data Model

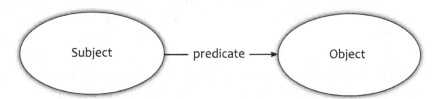

Figure 6. Abstract representation of RDF triples

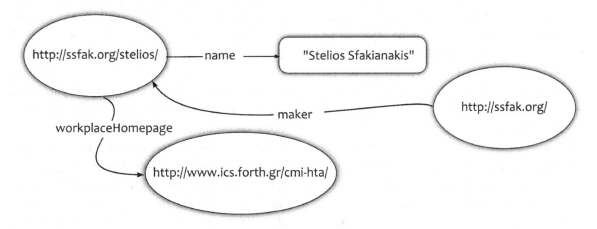

expressed in the context of an application domain or in a real world scenario, what is the underlying meaning, and how the information presented can be further processed to generate more information. Moreover ontologies and their less powerful relatives like taxonomies and thesaurus provide the means for achieving a common interpretation of a domain and a shared understanding of the concepts and relationships involved. In the Semantic Web there are two main technologies for providing such rigor: RDF Schema and OWL (Brickley & Guha, 2004; Dean, Schreiber, et al., 2004). RDF Schema provides the means for defining classes, class hierarchies, properties, property hierarchies, and property restrictions. Its expressive power is basically limited to the representation of concepts, their relations, and taxonomies of concepts. On the other hand the

Web Ontology Language (OWL) was introduced to address the need for more expressiveness and extends the RDF Schema by providing three variants: OWL-Lite, OWL-DL, and OWL-Full. Without delving into details, the different species of OWL provide different degrees of expressiveness and are able to define existential restrictions, cardinality constraints in properties, property types like inverse, transitive, and symmetric, and a lot more. The added features of OWL allow the ontologies built in conformance to it to be formally treated and the data represented are amenable to "reasoning" and inference, i.e. they can be processed according to formal logic rules to deduce new information. All these happen on the basis of the Web infrastructure: RDF resources and their URI references are used, the open world assumption is followed, since partial information on the Web is a quite frequent phenomenon, and the ontologies themselves can be freely intermixed and meshed since hyperlinks are employed everywhere.

Since RDF is the common interchange and representation model of information, the Semantic Web transforms the hyperlinked syntactic World Wide Web to a huge database or a Global Giant Graph, as Tim Berners-Lee put it. The standard query language for this huge database is SPARQL (Prudhommeaux & Seaborne, 2008), which is similar to SQL. In addition to the query language the SPARQL standard defines an application protocol for the submission of queries to RDF sources and the retrieval of results. With the query language and the access protocol defined, the SPARQL specifies a Web friendly interface to RDF information, whether this is actually stored as RDF triples or not. It is therefore feasible to make SPARQL queries to relational or other databases through an appropriate wrapper or transformation process that translates, either online or in some preprocessing step, the internal data to an RDF compliant format. As a result these Semantic Web technologies enable the connection of data between different and heterogeneous data sources, effectively allowing data in one data source to be linked to data in another data source. (Bizer, Heath, Idehen, & Berners-Lee, 2008)

SOCIAL SEMANTIC WEB

In recent years the cross pollination of Semantic Web technologies and Social Networking has emerged as an interesting roadmap. The Semantic Web technology can significantly enrich and expedite the Social Web in order to establish the *Semantic Social Web* (*Greaves, 2007;* Gruber, 2007*)*. In the Semantics-enabled social Web content can be easily connected, integrated, navigated, and queried so that the benefits of today's Social Web can be greatly enhanced and augmented beyond the limited user experience offered by

social networking sites alone or the restricted keyword based search and matching.

What does the Semantic Web offer to the Social Web? First and foremost, the Semantic Web technologies can be used to provide rigor and structure to the content of the user contributions in a form that enables more powerful computation. Currently social Web applications are more focused on the distribution and the management of content and the social interactions around it rather than the provision of Semantically rich descriptions of the data. Although there are popular, "low end" technologies like "microformats" and tagging/"folksonomies" to cater for the annotation and the description of data, these seem to be ad hoc and unstructured efforts in comparison to the formal Web ontologies and metadata descriptions. On the other hand, as already described, the Semantic Web promotes the global distribution and integration of resources in a single, giant, interoperable graph. So, additionally, the standards and infrastructure of the Semantic Web can enable data sharing and computation *across* independent, heterogeneous social Web applications.

Furthermore, the Semantic Web can enhance the Social Web with additional intelligence as Jemima Kiss (2008) wrote:

If Web 2.0 could be summarized as interaction, Web 3.0 must be about recommendation and personalization.

An example of such added value is the case of Semantic Wikis (e.g. Schaert, 2006; Völkel, M., Krötzsch, M., Vrandecic, D., Haller, H., & Studer, R., 2006). The Semantic Wikis support the annotation with Semantics descriptions the links and the content they provide and take advantage of these annotations for providing more intelligent search and navigation. The annotation is usually done by some extended version of the Wiki editing syntax so that every link to another page or any important attribute of the current page is annotated with a property identifier. For example in a Semantic Wiki's page about the Europe the amount of its population, which is a number, can be wrapped with the appropriate metadata that denote that this number represents the population. Such metadata annotation makes structured search easy, e.g. for queries like what is the population of Europe, or which continents have population above a certain amount. Additionally it facilitates the users in providing more active content in the pages by incorporating "online queries" in the Wiki pages, in the sense that the page's content can be dynamically generated by the results of these queries on the metadata annotations. Although the details may vary from one implementation to another, there's usually an underlying model based on RDF and OWL to support these Wikis and the content can be exported in a Semantic Web compliant format. DBPedia is an interesting example of a truly Semantic Web Wiki which offers the content of Wikipedia in a machine-readable and searchable format (Auer et. al., 2007).

In another application area, Semantic Web technologies can facilitate the browsing experience of people and the searching capabilities of the Web search engines. Unlike traditional search engines, which "crawl" the Web gathering Web pages information, Semantic Web search engines index RDF data stored on the Web and provide an interface to search through the crawled data. Because of the inherent Semantics of RDF and the other Semantic Web technologies, the search and information retrieval capabilities of these search engines are potentially much more powerful than those of current search engines. Examples of such early Semantic Search Engines include the Semantic Web Search Engine (SWSE, http://www.swse.org/), Swoogle (http://swoogle.umbc.edu/), and Zitgist Search (http://www.zitgist.com/). These and other Semantic Web search engines explore and index the documents of the Semantic Web and its ontologies by the means of user friendly interfaces that hide the details and complexities of the technology.

Blogs, which are one of the most prominent examples of the Social Web, can also be enhanced with Semantics. Augmenting a blog with content and structural metadata is usually called Semantic Blogging (Cayzer, 2004; Bojars, Breslin, & Moller, 2006). Putting Semantics in a blog's contents means that the topic of the content is described in a machine processable way. On the other hand describing the structure of the blog Semantically entails the description of the entities that compose it: the posts, the comments, the users, etc. To this end there are a number of efforts to make the Semantic Web more social by building new ontologies to support people in their social interactions and provide Semantics to the Social Web. Two of such ontologies, SIOC and FOAF, are of particular importance in the context of Semantic Blogging and are described below.

SIOC

Existing online community sites usually provide rich information for specific interest groups but they are isolated from one another, which makes difficult the linking and merging of complementary information among different sites. The Semantically-Interlinked Online Communities (SIOC) project aims to link online community sites using Semantic Web technologies. It defines methods to describe the information that communities have about their structure and contents, and to find related information and new connections between content items and other community objects. SIOC again is based around the use of *machine-readable information* provided by these sites.

The main entities of SIOP are shown in Figure 7 and it's easy to see the role and the function of the main concepts. The entity Site refers to the location of an online community or set of communities, which hosts one or many blogs. A Forum can be thought of a discussion area on which posts are made. In a Forum a number of posts are contained where a Post represents an article or a

Figure 7. The main classes and relationships of SIOC

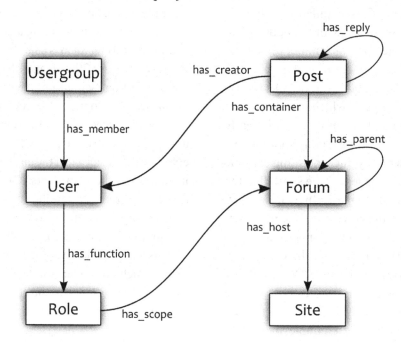

message send by a user to the forum. Posts can be connected as people reply to previous posts and these connections can cross site boundaries since the identifiers of posts (as well as any Semantic Web resource) are universal and unique.

From the figure above it can be said that SIOP defines a common schema for the different blog sites and discussion forums. This of course needs not be their internal schema but a common, shared, and standard representation of their information model. Adopting SIOP therefore is a major step in achieving the integration of social content in Web 2.0.

FOAF

The Friend-Of-A-Friend (FOAF) project focuses on expressing mostly personal information and relationships in a machine-readable form. A central entity in the FOAF vocabulary and the one most frequently used is the Person (Figure 8). According to FOAF a Person may have names, e-mails, interests, publications, etc. It can also be connected to other resources like the Web site of the organization he/she works for (foaf:work-placeHomepage property), a personal blog site (foaf:weblog), the Website of his/her school (foaf:schoolHomepage), or to other people that he/she knows (foaf:knows). A lot of personal information can be therefore represented and parts of the real world's social graph can be inferred by following the foaf:knows relationship.

Of particular importance to the Social Web is the support the FOAF vocabulary offers to link the physical persons (foaf:Person) to the accounts they hold in a number of social Web sites (e.g. Flickr, Facebook) through the foaf:holdsAccount

Figure 8. The main classes and relationships of FOAF

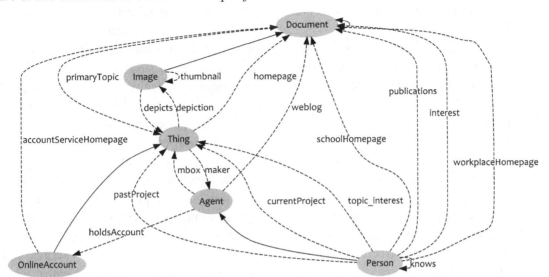

property. It is therefore possible through a single FOAF document that could be indexed in a Semantic Search engine to join all these different accounts and the information each of them exposes. Integration of different social content and behavior can be achieved and the resulting graph of information is searchable in an unambiguous and machine interpretable way.

Semantic Web Services

Application integration requires an agreed infrastructure to be in place for the exchange of information over the network. Over the last couple of decades there have been several attempts for defining such an infrastructure, such as Sun/RPC, CORBA, Microsoft's DCOM, Java RMI, and others. Currently Web Services are the favorite and most popular technology for building distributed systems over the Internet. As a middleware technology Web Services represent a new generation that tries to mitigate the problems of legacy integration technologies such as CORBA by adopting a more Web friendly substrate. Such a different approach seems to be needed in order to support business-to-business integration over the Internet

where crossing organization borders has implications on the security, interoperability, scalability, maintenance, flexibility, and other aspects of application integration. In order to achieve these goals the Service Oriented Architecture (SOA) has been proposed. Informally speaking, in such architecture (Web) Services are network accessible entities that offer a number of functionalities to their callers. The SOA environment should be highly dynamic as suggested by a number of real world phenomena, like network instability, changing real world requirements and settings, etc. The need for "late binding" of services and clients is important and Figure 9, depicting the main entities of SOA and their interactions, shows that a middle service repository or registry is introduced. This repository stores "offers" of functionality as these are published by service providers, and subsequently performs matching with the corresponding "requests". After some matching has been performed the corresponding parties (services and their clients) are free to communicate and exchange data.

On the technology side Web Services put more emphasis on the following:

- Transport over widely accepted Web and Internet protocols like HTTP/HTTPS and SMTP
- XML message payloads to provide the extensibility, introspection, and interoperability required in building complex multi party systems
- Platform and programming language independence

The Web itself is built around these very directions: open protocols, text based (markup, e.g. HTML) message and document content, and abstraction over implementation details. In essence the underlying infrastructure is roughly based on the following technologies:

- SOAP messaging format, which is based on XML, to provide a wrapper format and protocol for data interchange between Web services
- Web Service Description Language (WSDL) documents to describe the services' functionality and data exchange

On top of these a number of standard technologies have been specified for handling discovery (UDDI), security (WS-Security), trust (WS-Trust), composition (WSBPEL, WSCL), etc. Nevertheless for this discussion the WSDL standard is the most pertinent specification because it specifies in a machine readable format the structure of the XML messages exchanged.

Integration of computation and functionality is an additional field where Semantic Web shows a great potential of use because the Web Services, at their present incarnation, provide syntactic interoperability only. The WSDL service descriptions are restricted to the syntactic aspects of service interaction: how the service can be invoked, which operations may be called, what are the number and the type of the parameters each operation needs, etc. However, what the service does and in what order its operations have to be called in order to achieve certain functionalities is usually described only in natural language either in the comments of a WSDL description or in UDDI entries or other documentation. *Semantic Web Services* (McIlraith, Cao Son, & Zeng, 2001) is an "umbrella" definition to include the annota-

Figure 9. Web service architecture

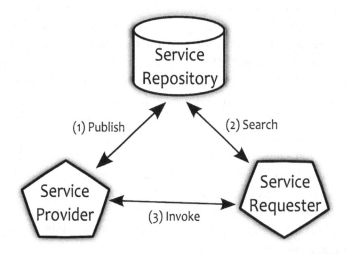

tion of existing Web services with Semantics and their publication, discovery, and composition.

The vision again is to make feasible the machine to machine communication by providing machine interpretable descriptions of the services. Such descriptions will make possible the automatic discovery, composition, and invocation of services. Because of this a lot of efforts in metadata descriptions are centered on the Semantic Web and its technologies, namely RDF and OWL. In the area of the Semantic Web Services the following technologies and standards are relevant to the Semantic description of Web services:

- **UDDI (Universal Description, Discovery and Integration)** allows the discovery of potential business partners on the basis of the services they provide. Each business description in UDDI consists of a businessEntity element that describes a business by name, a key value, categorization, services offered (businessServices) and contact information for the business. Each businessService element contains descriptive information such as names and descriptions, and also classification information describing the purpose of the relevant Web service. Using UDDI, a Web service provider registers its advertisements along with keywords for categorization. A Web services user retrieves advertisements out of the registry based on keyword search. So far, the UDDI search mechanism relied on predefined categorization through keywords, but more recently specifications to use OWL in UDDI are emerging as a uniform way to express business taxonomies.

- **Semantic Annotations for WSDL and XML Schema** (SAWDL; Kopecký et. al., 2007) is a means to add Semantics inline to WSDL. It is actually a set of extensions to WSDL 2.0 but can also be used for WSDL 1.1. With these extensions the service provider can attach references to Semantic concepts for the functionality of an operation or the type/meaning of a parameter and additional information for the transformation (mapping) of the XML data either to ("lift") or from ("lower") the corresponding Semantic terms. The Semantic domain model used is external to these annotations and could be expressed in OWL or other ontology language of choice.

- **OWL-S** (formerly DAML-S) builds on top of OWL and allows for the description of a Web service in terms of a Profile, which tells "what the service does/provides", a Process Model, which tells "how the service works", and a Grounding, which tells "how to access the service" (Martin et al., 2004). The service profile describes what is accomplished by the service, any limitations on service applicability and quality of service, and requirements that the service requester must satisfy in order to use the service successfully. The process model gives details about the Semantic content of requests, the conditions under which particular outcomes will occur, and, where necessary, the step by step processes leading to those outcomes. In the process model a service can be described as an atomic process that can be executed in a single step or a composite process that, similar to a workflow, can be decomposed in other processes based on control structures like 'if-then-else' and 'repeat-while'. Finally, Grounding descriptions supply information about the communication protocol and other transport information (such as port numbers) and the message formats and serialization methods used in contacting the service. The only currently specified grounding mechanism is based on WSDL 1.1 and will be extended to WSDL 2.0 as soon as it's finalized.

- **The Semantic Web Services Framework (SWSF)**, initiated by the Semantic Web Services Initiative (SWSI, 2004), includes the

Semantic Web Services Language (SWSL) and the Semantic Web Services Ontology (SWSO). SWSL is a logic-based language for specifying formal characterizations of Web service concepts and descriptions of individual services. SWSO is an ontology of service concepts defined using SWSL and incorporates a formal characterization ("axiomatization") of these concepts in first-order logic.

- **WSMO (Web Services Modeling Ontology)** defines the modeling elements for describing several aspects of Semantic Web services (Feier et al., 2005). These elements are Ontologies, which provide the formal Semantics to the information used by all other elements, Goals which specify objectives that a client might have when consulting a Web service, Web services that represent the functional and behavioral aspects which must be Semantically described in order to allow semi-automated use, and Mediators that are used as connectors and they provide interoperability facilities among the other elements. It also defines the Web Service Modelling Language (WSML) which formalizes WSMO and aims to provide a rule-based language for the Semantic Web.

- **BioMOBY** (http://www.biomoby.org/) is a Web Service interoperability initiative in the field of bioinformatics aiming to facilitate the integration of Web-based bioinformatics resources. Currently there are two approaches to achieve such integration: The first approach, based on the Web Services paradigm, is referred to as "MOBY Services" (MOBY-S), while the second one is called "Semantic MOBY" (S-MOBY) and is based on concepts from the Semantic Web. MOBY-S uses a set of simple, end-user-extensible ontologies as its framework to describe data Semantics, data structure, and classes of bioinformatics services. These ontologies are shared through a Web Service

registry system, MOBY Central, which uses the ontologies to Semantically bind incoming service requests to service providers capable of executing them. S-MOBY on the other hand employs RDF and OWL and the document oriented infrastructure of the WWW (the GET/POST methods of HTTP) for publishing and retrieving information from its discovery servers.

As shown above this is an area of active research. So far SAWDL enjoys the approval of W3C being one of its recommendations but of course is lacking when compared with WSMO and OWL-S. Nevertheless SAWSDL can be combined with these most prominent technologies and it remains to be seen whether such approaches are adequate or something more powerful should be introduced.

CONCLUSION

The social aspects of the Web show an uprising evolution and all the indications imply that this trend will continue. The current Web 2.0 sites are quite successful in attracting people share their data and interests, and build online communities, but the next step will be to enrich them with more Semantics in the lines of the Semantic Web to provide a unifying platform for people and machines to use and collaborate. The need for Semantics (Breslin & Decker, 2007) is evident for enhancing the social networking sites with advanced filtering and recommendation services and also to provide data portability and integration between different sites and networks. This is an active area where the Semantic Web technologies can greatly help.

There have been a lot of discussions about what will be the "killer application" of the Semantic Web, which means some breakthrough in the domain that will show beyond any doubt the full potential of the Semantic Web. Nevertheless we think that Semantic Web technologies are used slowly and without much "noise" in a lot of different areas and as "extension to the existing Web" are not clearly visible but are certainly catching on. There is a common view nowadays that the Semantic Web will not supersede the Syntactic Web in any way but they will happily coexist in a symbiotic manner: the Web of documents will be enriched by the Web of data and information.

In terms of the core infrastructure what we see as emerging trend is the use of simple REST Web services (Fielding & Taylor, 2002) that present a small entry barrier and a transition from the SOAP and WSDL Web Services technologies backed by big commercial corporations like IBM and Microsoft to more flexible and agile architectures. These architectures are more bound to the existing Web and also are more Semantic Web friendly since they share common basic infrastructure and interaction protocols (e.g. Web protocols like HTTP used as application protocol and not for transport, full support for URI to access network resources and Semantic concepts, etc.). The whole history of the Web clearly shows that successful distributed systems of this scale are built on open access, open protocols, and open source methodologies combined with collaborative behavior by the people (developers, users) involved.

Research questions and issues for further investigation abound in this Semantic new world. First of all the issue of trust and security and how this is incorporated in the Semantic Web machinery should be tackled on. For example currently a user can claim anything in his FOAF document, or a malicious application can publish RDF information that contains false statements. The notion of identity and validation of the identity is important and there is ongoing work in this area, e.g. the incorporation of user certificates or Web based authentication mechanisms like OpenId[8]. Semantic Web has also increased demands for supporting indexing and reasoning over the managed content. The scalability concerns are real when we think about a Semantic Web search engine of the size of Google. Finally the adoption of these technologies by the users needs work to be done in the presentation layers as well. Easy to use, friendly, and functional user interfaces are necessary for making the transition to the Semantic Web more painless and transparent for the users.

REFERENCES

Auer, S., Bizer, C., Kobilarov, G, Lehmann, J., Cyganiak, R., & Ives, Z. (2007). DBpedia: A nucleus for a Web of open data. *The 6th International Semantic Web Conference (ISWC 2007).*

Ayers, D. (2007). Evolving the link. *IEEE Internet Computing, 11*(3), 94-96.

Beckett, D., & Berners-Lee, T. (2008). Turtle - Terse RDF triple language. *W3C Team Submission*. Latest version available at http://www.w3.org/TeamSubmission/turtle/

Berners-Lee, T., Hendler, J., & Lassila, O. (2001). The Semantic Web. *Scientific American, 284*(5), 28-37

Berners-Lee, T., Bray, T., Connolly, D., Cotton, P., Fielding, R., Jeckle, M., et al. (2004). *Architecture of the World Wide Web, Volume One.* W3C, Retrieved 15 June 2008, from http://www.w3.org/TR/webarch/

Bizer, C., Heath, T., Idehen, K., & Berners-Lee, T. (2008). Linked data on the Web (ldow2008). In *WWW '08: Proceeding of the 17th International Conference on World Wide Web* (pp. 1265-1266). New York: ACM.

Bojars, U., Breslin, J., & Moller, K. (2006). Using Semantics to enhance the blogging experience. In *Proceedings of 3rd European Semantic Web Conference*, ESWC 2006, (pp. 679-696).

Breslin, J., & Decker, S. (2007). The future of social networks on the Internet: The need for Semantics. *IEEE Internet Computing,* (pp. 86-90).

Breslin, J., Harth, A., Bojars, U., & Decker, S. (2005). Towards Semantically-interlinked online communities. In *Proceedings of the 2nd European Semantic Web Conference* (ESWC05), Heraklion, Greece, LNCS, 3532, 500-514.

Brickley, D., & Guha, R. (2004). *RDF Vocabulary description language 1.0: RDF schema*. W3C Recommendation 10 February 2004. World Wide Web Consortium.

Cayzer, S. (2004). Semantic blogging and decentralized knowledge management. *Communications of the ACM, 47*(12), 47-52.

Dean, M., Schreiber, G., et al. (2004). *OWL Web ontology language reference*. W3C Recommendation, 10.

Decker, S (2006). The social Semantic desktop: Next generation collaboration infrastructure. *Information Services & Use, 26*(2), 139-144.

Feier, C., Roman, D., Polleres, A., Domingue, J., Stollberg, M., & Fensel, D. (2005). Towards intelligent Web services: The Web service modeling ontology (WSMO). *International Conference on Intelligent Computing (ICIC)*.

Fielding, R. T., & Taylor, R. N. (2002). Principled design of the modern Web architecture. *ACM Transactions on Internet Technology (TOIT), 2*(2), 115-150

Greaves, Mark (2007). Semantic Web 2.0. *IEEE Intelligent Systems, 22(2), 94-96*

Gruber, T. (2007). *Collective knowledge systems: Where the social Web meets the Semantic Web*. To appear in Journal of Web Semantics, 2007; http://tomgruber.org/writing/CollectiveKnowledgeSystems.htm

Kiss, J. (2008). Web 3.0 is all about rank and recommendation. *The Guardian*, February 4 2008, Retrieved 15 May 2008, from http://www.guardian.co.uk/media/2008/feb/04/web20?gusrc=rss&feed=media

Kopecký, J., Vitvar, T., Bournez, C., & Farrell, J. (2007). SAWSDL: Semantic annotations for WSDL and XML schema. *IEEE Internet Computing*, (pp. 60-67).

Lassila, O., Swick, R., et al. (1999). Resource description framework (RDF) model and syntax specification. *W3C Recommendation, 22*, 2004-03.

Martin, D., Paolucci, M., McIlraith, S., Burstein, M., McDermott, D., McGuinness, D., et al. (2004). Bringing Semantics to Web Services: The OWL-S Approach. In *Proceedings of the First International Workshop on Semantic Web Services and Web Process Composition (SWSWPC 2004)*, (pp. 6-9).

McIlraith, Sheila A., Cao Son, Tran, & Zeng, Honglei (2001). Semantic Web Services. *IEEE Intelligent Systems, 16*(2), 46-53

Moller, K., Bojars, U., & Breslin, J. (2006). Using Semantics to enhance the blogging experience. In I3rd *European Semantic Web Conference (ESWC2006), LNCS, 4011*, 679-696.

O'Reilly, T. (2005). *What is Web 2.0: Design patterns and business models for the next generation of software*. Retrieved 15 May 2008, from http://www.oreillynet.com/pub/a/oreilly/tim/news/2005/09/30/what-is-web-20.html

Prudhommeaux, E., & Seaborne, A. (2008). *SPARQL query language for RDF. W3C Recommendation 15 January 2008*. Available from http://www.w3.org/TR/rdf-sparql-query/

Ramakrishnan, R., & Tomkins, A. (2007). Toward a peopleweb. *Computer, 40*(8), 63-72.

Schaert, S. (2006). IkeWiki: A Semantic Wiki for collaborative knowledge management. In *Proceedings of the 15th IEEE International Workshops on Enabling Technologies: Infrastructure for Collaborative Enterprises*, (pp. 388-396).

Surowiecki, J. (2005). *The wisdom of crowds.* Anchor. Paperback.

SWSI (2004). *Semantic Web services initiative* (SWSI). Retrieved 15 May 2008, from http://www. swsi.org/

Uschold, M., & Gruninger, M. (1996). Ontologies: Principles, methods and applications. *Knowledge Engineering Review, 11*(2).

Völkel, M., Krötzsch, M., Vrandecic, D., Haller, H., & Studer, R. (2006). Semantic Wikipedia. *Proceedings of the 15th international conference on World Wide Web*, (pp. 585-594).

KEY TERMS

Semantic Web (SW): The creator of the World Wide Web Tim Berners-Lee defines the SW as "a web of data that can be processed directly or indirectly by machines". A similar definition coming from the World Wide Web Consortium (W3C) describes the Semantic Web as "a Web that includes documents, or portions of documents, describing explicit relationships between things and containing Semantic information intended for automated processing by our machines."

Social Web/Web 2.0: The way people socialize and interact with each other through the World Wide Web. This term is also used to denote a large number of Web sites that are devoted to people and their social interactions through the creation of online communities of users that share digital content and information, discuss, or enable communication in any possible, Web-facilitated way.

Web Service (WS): A Web Service is defined by the World Wide Web Consortium (W3C) as "a software system designed to support interoperable machine-to-machine interaction over a network". Since this definition is quite general the term "Web Service" commonly refers to systems that communicate using XML messages that comply with the SOAP messaging format. In such systems, there is often machine-readable description of the operations offered by the service written in the Web Services Description Language (WSDL).

ENDNOTES

[1]   Despite the irony in itself as a fact, an extensive survey of this criticism can be found in the Wikipedia at http://en.WikipedSia. org/Wiki/Criticism_of_Wikipedia

[2]   http://en.Wikipedia.org/Wiki/Seigenthaler_incident

[3]   http://en.Wikipedia.org/Wiki/Ajax_(programming)

[4]   http://en.Wikipedia.org/Wiki/Comet_(programming)

[5]   http://en.Wikipedia.org/Wiki/Web_syndication

[6]   http://www.opensearch.org

[7]   http://pipes.yahoo.com

[8]   http://openid.net/

Section D
Practice Toolkits and Design Perspectives

Chapter XII
Virtual Community Practice Toolkits Using 3D Imaging Technologies

George Triantafyllidis
Technological Education Institution of Crete, Greece

Nikolaos Grammalidis
Centre for Research and Technology Hellas, Greece

Dimitiros Tzovaras
Centre for Research and Technology Hellas, Greece

ABSTRACT

Extending visual communications to the third dimension (3D) has been a dream over decades. The ultimate goal of the viewing experience is to create the illusion of a real environment in its absence. However limitations of visual quality and user acceptance prevented the development of relevant mass markets so far. Recent achievements in research and development triggered an increasing interest in 3D visual technologies. From technological point of view, this includes improvements over the whole 3D technology chain, including image acquisition, 3D representation, compression, transmission, signal processing, interactive rendering and 3D display. In the center of all these different areas, the visualization of 3D information stands as the major aspiration to be satisfied, since 3D enriches the interaction experience. This enhanced user experience that 3D imaging offers compared to 2D, is the main reason behind the rapid increase of the virtual communities using and managing 3D data: Archaeological site 3D reproductions, virtual museums (in the field of cultural heritage); 3D plays, special effects (in the field of entertainment); virtual classes (in the field of learning) are only some examples of the potentialities of 3D data. It's clear that 3D imaging technologies provide a new and powerful mechanism for collaborative practicing. In this context, this chapter focuses on the utilization of 3D imaging technology and computer graphics, in various virtual communities in the domains of education, cultural heritage, protection, commerce, and entertainment.

INTRODUCTION

"Virtual community" reflects the social, political and economic impact of information and communications technology, changing the architecture of interaction (Hummel, 2002). In the last decade, utilization of three-dimensional (3D) information in virtual communities has become more widespread since 3D enriches the interaction experience and due to the rapid advances in computer graphics, capturing technology, image-based rendering methods and VLSI systems.

3D digital technology is a diverse group of various technologies and products, and many related issues need attention. Apart from technical problems, there are also issues like price, produceability, demand, applications, market segments, sizes, market penetration schedules, etc. However, applications that require 3D imaging first emerged over a century ago. The general public has been excited about 3D stereophotographs since the 19th century, 3D movies in the 1950's, holography in the 1960's, and 3D computer graphics and virtual reality in collaborative practicing today. The 3D-image systems provide both physiological and psychological depth cues required by the human visual system to perceive 3D objects and thus offer a more "real" experience compared to 2D-image systems.

According to Hammann (Hammann, 2000) a virtual community is characterized by:

1. A clearly defined group of people
2. The interaction between the members
3. The bonding among the members
4. The common place - the electronic medium that facilitates interaction.

To this target, the new 3D imaging technologies provide a powerful mechanism for practicing in virtual communities, enhancing the experience of people gathering and communicating in an online "space". Archaeological site 3D reproductions, virtual museums (in the field of cultural heritage); 3D plays, special effects (in the field of entertainment); virtual classes (in the field of learning) are only some examples which prove the idea that 3D imaging technology can facilitate community based collaboration: User communities can utilize 3D to build novel designs from scratch or tailor existing pre-defined/default designs.

In this chapter, we first present the basic principles for the 3D imaging and some general applications of 3D technologies. Then, we focus on the utilization of the 3D imaging technology and its components in virtual communities in the domains of education, cultural heritage, protection, commerce and theater, by presenting specific projects, in which the authors participated or currently participate. We also try to forecast the near future in virtual communities. The final section summarizes and concludes the paper.

THREE-DIMENSIONAL IMAGING TECHNOLOGIES

A picture that appears to have height, width and depth is three-dimensional (3D) in contrast to two-dimensional (2D) image which has no depth (Franklin, 2008). 3D imaging consists of a long chain of acquiring, compressing, transmitting and visualizing 3D images. Real scenes can be captured and encoded into 3D data, which are sent over the network and decoded on user's terminal, to be animated (see Figure 1).

Hundreds of different principles, ideas and products for 3D imaging have been presented especially during the last decade. Two main categories can be identified in 3D imaging solutions according to user's display: 3D computer graphics, which trick eyes into thinking that the flat 2D screen extends depth and systems that employ 3D displays which provide full 3D experience.

Figure 1.3D imaging chain (Adapted from 3DTV - Potential applications, 2006)

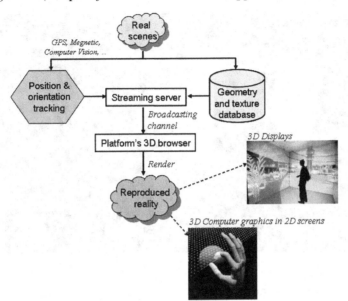

Three-Dimensional Computer Graphics

Applications using 3D information first emerged in the field of computer graphics in 2D screens, in order to create a realistic visual content from the available 3D models. 3D computer graphics (in contrast to 2D computer graphics) are graphics that use a 3D representation of geometric data that is stored in the computer for the purposes of performing calculations and rendering 2D images (Wikipedia-3D computer graphics, 2008). 3D modeling is the process of developing a mathematical, wireframe representation of any 3D object via specialized software (Wikipedia-3D modeling, 2008). The product is called a 3D model. It can be displayed as a 2D image through a process called 3D rendering.

No matter how large or rich the virtual 3D world is, a computer can depict that world only by displaying pixels on a 2D screen. The goal here is how to make what we see on the screen to look realistic and as close as possible to what we see in the real world. There are some factors

needed to satisfy certain rules, for an object to seem real. Among the most important of these are shape, surface texture, lighting, perspective, depth of field and anti-aliasing. An example of 3D computer graphics is given in Figure 2.

Three-Dimensional Displays

A 3D display is any display device capable of conveying three-dimensional images to the viewer. Our eyes capture 2D images on the retina and the human mind perceives distance or depth by using the many available depth cues. Human depth cues of disparity, motion parallax, ocular accommodation and other cues are essential for image recognition. Accommodation and vergence are linked with one another at a muscular reflex level. Conflicting cues are one of the leading causes for discomfort and fatigue when viewing 3D displays (3DTV- Display Techniques: A Survey, 2005).

There are many types of 3D displays: stereoscopic 3D displays show a different image to each eye; autostereoscopic 3D displays do this without

Figure 2. 3D computer graphics

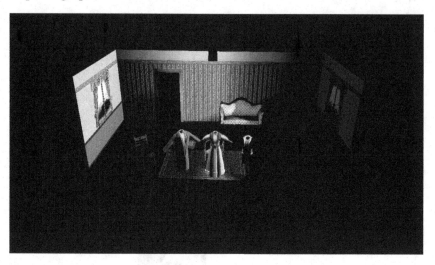

the need for any special glasses or other head gear; holographic 3D displays reproduce a light field which is identical to that which emanated from the original scene. There are also head mount displays (HMD) which use stereo images and may cause eye-strain, nausea, or headaches. In addition there are volumetric displays, where some physical mechanism is used to display points of light within a volume. Such displays use voxels instead of pixels. Volumetric displays include multiplanar displays, which have multiple display planes stacked up; and rotating panel displays, where a rotating panel sweeps out a volume (3DTV- Display Techniques: A Survey, 2005). Only time will show which one 3D display will prevail in the future.

General 3D Imaging Applications

3D imaging is applicable to an enormous range of things, since it is both useful and entertaining. The application of 3D has been thought in nearly any field of science, techniques, and arts. The three-dimensional representation of data is very much related to the human experience: The main sensor of a human being is its visual system, which is developed as a 3D-system. Nobody can really think in two dimensions. According to this, it is

an essential fact, that in all sciences the models of the described objects are three- dimensional (3DTV - Potential applications, 2006). Therefore, 3D imaging is a huge effort since modern imaging methods are invented.

In this respect, 3D has many applications in the field of education, training and simulation such as medical education (e.g. virtual surgery), diagnosis and therapy, lip reading teaching tools in education of hard of hearing people, flight simulation and training of pilots, 3D simulation of industrial products before production, traffic training for new drivers, etc.

Recently, a large number of applications of 3D graphics and Virtual Reality in the field of cultural heritage have been developed. The broad term "heritage" refers to the study of human activity not only through the recovery of remains, as is the case with archaeology, but also through tradition, art & cultural evidences, narratives, etc. Virtual heritage applications use the immersive and interactive qualities of 3D graphics to give students or museum visitors access to 3D reconstructions of historical sites that would normally be inaccessible, due to location or fragile condition. They also provide the possibility of visiting places that no longer exist at all, or of viewing

Figure 3. (a) stereoscopic glasses (HMD), (b) autostereoscopic 3D displays (Adapted from 3DTV- Display Techniques: A Survey, 2005)

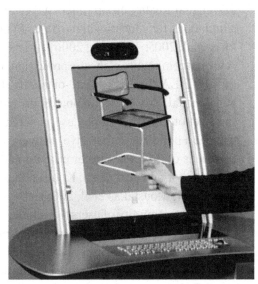

how the places would have appeared at different times in history.

Three-dimensional tools are also extensively used in a variety of engineering applications. Computer aided drawing (CAD) packages provide 3D visualization of 3D geometric models that may be easily modified. Computer aided engineering tools provide visualization and verification of mechanical, acoustic, thermal and geometric models that would be otherwise impossible to achieve.

Another useful and large application area for 3D systems is the virtual shopping using 3D imaging techniques. Reconstructing virtual shopping objects much closer to real objects, by the application of 3D imaging techniques enhances the experience of e-shopping. A consumer would wish to see and explore a product before buying, perhaps by manipulating and looking around the object, determining the colour, size, form, and producing a "3D feel" for the object.

Finally, one of the main applications of 3D is entertainment. There have been different approaches for 3D-television and 3D-cinema. 3D gaming is

also a big market for 3D viewing technologies, since 3D gives the users freedom to wander into the 3D environment (within certain limits), observe and interact with different objects.

3D IMAGING FOR VIRTUAL COMMUNITY PRACTICING

A virtual community refers to a group of people that primarily interact via communication media rather than face to face, for social, professional, educational or other purposes. 3D imaging technologies can be applied to nearly any virtual community, since 3D information enhances this interaction experience. In this context, eight showcases of 3D imaging practicing in virtual communities are presented in this section. These virtual communities employ 3D computer graphics for the needs of communication and interaction. 3D displays may be also used to provide full 3D experience:

- A virtual community of students (VR-LAB) for conducting real experiments through a 3D Virtual Reality environment as well as simulations for educational purposes (Tsakiris et al, 2005; Tzovaras, 2006).

- A virtual community of theatre professionals (VR@THEATRE) using state-of-the-art 3D and Virtual Reality technologies providing a set of tools that can be used to create specific applications that give answers to the needs of different theater professionals (Papadogiorgaki et al, 2004; Koutsonanaos et al, 2004; Moustakas et al, 2005).

- A virtual community of users (e.g. students or visitors) who employ a system providing 3D virtual tour of cultural heritage sites on a GIS system (e.g. Google Earth™) (Zabulis, 2008; Bastanlar, 2008).

- A virtual community of people working on fire prevention using a forest fire 3D simulation on a GIS system (e.g. Google Earth™) (Kose et al, 2008).

- A virtual community of students and museums visitors using a system providing interactive 3D simulation of ancient technology works (Moustakas et al, 2007; Nikolakis et al, 2004).

- A virtual community of visitors studying 3D virtual museum tours (Tzovaras, 2006).

- A virtual community of e-shoppers using an on-line intelligent platform providing a smart configuration of 3D products (Tzovaras, 2006).

All these showcases come from projects in which the authors of this chapter have participated. In the following, the aforementioned projects are briefly presented to justify the important role of 3D imaging technologies and computer graphics in the practice of virtual communities.

High-School Virtual Communities for Science Experiments

VRLab (http://avrlab.iti.gr/HTML/Projects/recent/VRLAB.htm) provides a multi-user remote experiment system that utilizes video, interactive VR, and graphical representations in order to provide an immersive learning experience. The system is completely web-based and is aimed in creating a virtual community of high school students.

Throughout the educational curriculum, students are called to master various topics on physics, chemistry, informatics etc. that require a practical understanding of certain processes. This practical training is often feasible through the use of experiments that cover such topics. However, not all institutions have the means to provide the equipment, maintenance or the expertise required to carry out such experiments in-house. Reasons for this include financial restrictions, small student audiences, safety regulations or remote location of such educational institutions.

VRLab provide users (teachers or students at different educational levels) with a system accessible via the Internet, to conduct experiments, which are located in a remote laboratory with safety and no financial or time restrictions. In the same time the students are able to observe the real experiment through a camera, as well as a 3D representation of the experiment progress in real time. The same 3D representation can be used in an offline mode in order to perform a simulation of the experiment according to the applicable physical laws. The system is able to support specific virtual reality devices, such as a head-mounted display, if available, in order to immerse the user into the experiment or the simulation so as to offer new and more natural ways of interaction with the experiment.

To achieve these goals, three sub-systems were designed, namely the system's server, which consists of a PC for each experimental setup to be supported, the client system, which includes a user interface based on 3-D graphics and virtual reality technologies and the Web portal, which provides community members with additional information and functionalities and an integration platform for the entire project

The central server consists of three experimental stations, each one containing:

- A PC with specialised software, which is required for the performance of a specific experiment and the collection of measurements,
- A digital camera for visual inspection mounted on a mechanism that allows camera control from the PC,
- An online data logger using appropriate sensors, which is needed to record measurements from the experiment and store them in the server PC,
- A specialized control board necessary for controlling the experimental setup
- An experimental setup with standard laboratory equipment.

The three experimental stations are connected to a local network and communicate with a central server, which acts as the Internet gateway of the server station, handling requests from the users connected to the system (Figure 4). The Web portal, which will be implemented within this project, will be installed in the same central server. The remote user can use a web-based client application developed as a set of Java applets, in order to access the server station. From his workstation, he is able to select an experimental setup to work with, to watch real-time video during the performance of the experiment and to control remotely the camera. The user interface also contains a 3D VR visualization of the experiment progress, which helps the user understand the experiment better and allows him to set-up the parameters of the experimental setup and sensors, as well as to control the flow of the experiment and the measurement collection, by activating certain "hotspots". This 3D visualisation can also be used offline in order to provide experiment simulations. Additionally, virtual reality equipment, such as a Head Mounted Display are also supported and used, if available, in order to immerse the user

Figure 4. VRLab system architecture

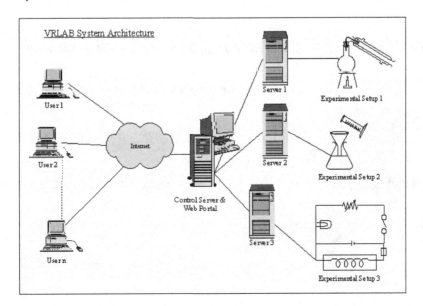

into this virtual experiment environment, aiming at providing the user with a more "vivid" display of the experiment progress.

Further, the system is able to receive measurement values from the experiment in nearly real time and to display them in corresponding graphs through the same web-based interface. The overall procedure can be observed simultaneously by all users connected to the system, however each time instant only one user has the permission to control the experimental setup. Nevertheless, the control of the experiment may be passed from one user to the other, according to the time-scheduling of the experiment's performance, which is controlled by the Web portal. In addition to that, a user chat option is available, for exchange of information, comments, questions and guidelines. The Graphical User Interface (GUI) is illustrated in Figure 5a. The experiments and simulations have been selected from heterogeneous fields (physics, personal computers) covering the areas such as Gas laws, study of the magnetic field of a coil and digital design simulation (see Figure 5b).

Virtual Theater Community Practices

VR@THEATER (http://avrlab.iti.gr/HTML/ Projects/current/VRTHEATER.htm) focuses on

the strengthening sense of community between theatre professionals by using virtual reality technologies to significantly simplify the users work and collaboration. VR@THEATER has been designed as a set of seven core modules which will be used by five basic applications each serving the needs of a specific theatre professional (scenographer, costume designer, director or producer, choreographer and actor). The presentation of this information will be performed using either off-the-shelf VR tools or conventional computer displays. In addition, the simulations created using this tool can be stored as images, videos or VRML scenes, thus providing a means of communication between different theatre professionals. Furthermore, final results can be communicated via the Internet, to serve as interactive public community advertisements for people wishing to attend the specific theatrical performance. Special emphasis has been given in the design and implementation of the user interface of each application, which has to be as friendly as possible, to be practical for scenographers, directors and other professionals of the field, who may not be familiar with computer use. For this reason, an intelligent agent user interface is used, serving as a "virtual" guide of the user, in all VR@THEATER applications.

Figure 5. VRLab User Interface (top), b) VRLab Digital Design Simulation (bottom)

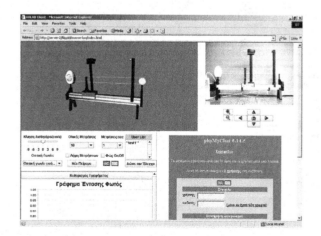
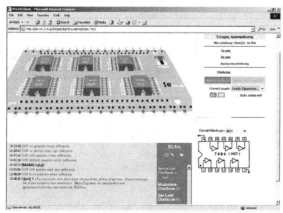

More specifically, the set of modules comprising the VR@THEATER authoring and simulation environment are:

- A scenery and lighting module, which supports (a) the definition of the virtual model of a real theater stage and (b) the creation and modification of scenic objects and lights in a "virtual" representation of the real stage.
- An avatar creation/customisation module, which supports the creation or customisation of avatars (virtual characters) that correspond to the real actors of the play. The avatars to be created or modified will be fully compliant with the recently developed H-anim standard, which allows the definition of body parts and application of body animation sequences, to create animations using these avatars.
- A body motion capture module is used to capture body motion of actors or dancers. For this reason, specific motion tracking hardware will be used (e.g. the Ascension MotionStar Tracker).
- A costume design/customisation module that applies state-of-the-art techniques for the creation and modelling of e-garments from scratch or by digitisation of real garments. The latter is achieved by using a 3D scanner booth that allows real garments/costumes to be accurately digitised. The process requires minimal manual specialised labour as it is on 3D scanning and not manual 3D modelling. Costumes are fitted on mannequins and placed in the garment booth. Subsequently the mannequin is scanned form a number of different angles which allow advanced software modules to extract information about the garment form, texture and colour. Basic requirements for this tool are that the resulting e-garments should be able to be customized, modified, fit on avatars and to produce realistic animations.

- A script design module, that is responsible for the definition, editing, and storage of the script of the act, i.e. avatar animations, sound effects, light effects.
- A simulation module that supports the visualization of the information provided by all other VR@THEATER modules (scenery, avatars "wearing" costumes, animations). For the animation of avatars wearing costumes, collision detection techniques is used, based on a fast bounding-box hierarchies algorithm, which will also consider self-collision effects. In addition, the presentations generated using the authoring and simulation platform will be exported to common image formats, AVI and VRML files so that they can be easily integrated in an Internet portal.
- An intelligent agent user interface module will provide to the resulting applications an "intelligent agent" interface, which is an "intelligent" avatar that is able to guide the user, present the features of the system, answer to his questions, etc.

The general architecture of the VR@THEATER system is illustrated in Figure 7.

To support this architecture the following special-purpose applications were designed and implemented:

- A scenographer application that allows scenographers and stage designers to create, modify and visualize scenery in a specific theater stage (see Figure 7a).
- A costume designer application that allows a costume designer to fit, observe and animate a costume on an avatar of an actor (see Figure 7b).
- A director application that allows a director or producer to create dynamic animations by a) importing scenery developed by the scenographer application, b) importing

Figure 6. VR@THEATER system general architecture

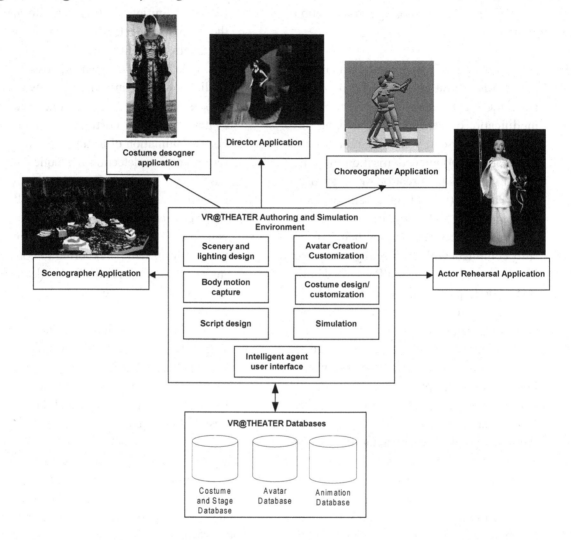

avatars "wearing" costumes in this scene, c) defining a script (avatar animation, light and sound effects) and d) visualizing these animations, using full 3-D graphics (see Figure 7c).

- A choreographer application that allows a choreographer to enter and edit the desired choreography movements with a user-friendly user interface as well as to include animation sequences (or parts of them) from the animation database, that have been previously recorded using motion capture techniques (see Figure 7d).

- An actor rehearsal application that allows an actor to rehearse parts of his/her role, by recording his body movements and voice and producing a 3-D visualization his performance within a virtual scene environment (see Figure 7e).

Virtual Communities in Cultural Heritage

A recent trend in museums and exhibitions of Ancient Greek Technology is the use of advanced 3D imaging and virtual reality technologies for

Figure 7. (a) scenographer application, (b) costume designer application, (c) director application, (d) choreographer application, (e) actor rehearsal application

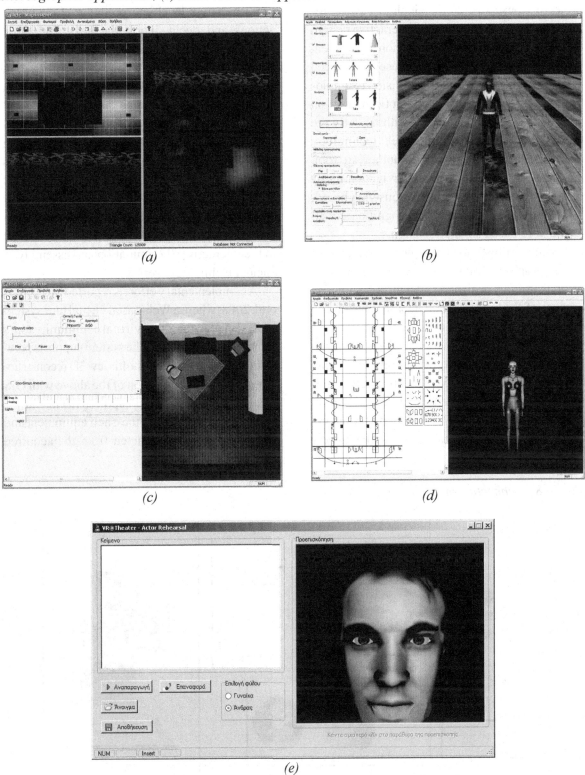

building virtual communities and improving the educational potential of their exhibitions. This project (Moustakas, 2007; Nikolakis, 2004) focuses on the development of an interactive system for the presentation and simulation of Ancient Greek Technology works with the use of advanced virtual reality and 3D computer vision technologies. The system consists of the haptic interaction module, gesture recognition algorithms, software agents simulating ancient Greek technology mechanisms and the scenario-authoring tool. The features of the system are navigation in 3D scenes, user interaction using mouse/keyboard, VR haptic devices and gesture recognition as well as the Web based simulation engine.

Figure 8 illustrates the general architecture of the proposed framework. A simulation scenario is initially designed using the available 3D content of the multimedia database. During the interaction with the user the core simulation unit takes as input the user's actions and the scenario. Moreover, there are two types of software agents implemented in the context of the proposed framework, namely the geometry and the simulation agents (Moustakas, 2007). The geometry agents apply constrains to the movement of the objects

so as to enable the use of the ancient technology works in a natural way. The simulation agents perform a high level interpretation of the user's actions and decide upon the next simulation steps. They enable or disable specific actions and control the assembling of components in order to construct a mechanism. The core simulation unit triggers each of the agents during each step of the interactive simulation. In parallel, the collision detector checks for possible collision during each simulation step and whenever collision is detected the haptic rendering engine provides the appropriate force feedback to the user that is displayed using either the Phantom or the Cyber-Grasp haptic device. All these procedures result in the interactive 3D simulation and assembly of ancient technology works.

A complementary effort is reported in (Zabulis et al, 2008) where a Web-based virtual tour system is presented to facilitate virtual community tours to archaeological sites. The system supports powerful techniques such as multiview 3D reconstruction, as well as, integration of the above with GIS technologies. The scene is captured from multiple viewpoints utilizing off-the-shelf equipment and its 3D structure is extracted from the acquired

Figure 8. Architecture of the proposed framework

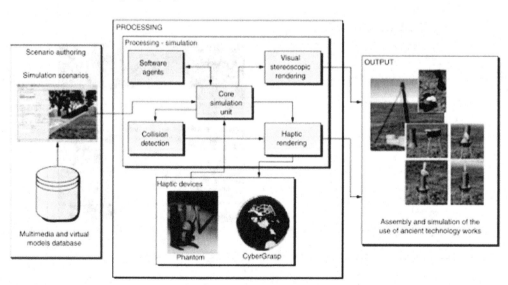

images based on stereoscopic techniques. Color information is added to the generated 3D model of the scene and the result is converted to a common 3D scene modeling format. The 3D models and interactive virtual tour tools such as 360° viewing are integrated with GIS technologies in which the excavation site plans can be added as detailed raster overlays. In short, the steps are:

1. Acquisition of multiple images (preferably of high resolution) or video-recording and subsequent selection of key frames.
2. Computation of internal camera calibration parameters.
3. Estimation of lens distortion and image rectification.
4. Extrinsic calibration of the acquired images, based on robust feature extraction, tracking and camera motion estimation techniques,
5. Multi-view stereo reconstruction of the scene using the acquired images and intrinsic and extrinsic calibration parameters.
6. Conversion of the reconstruction output to textured VRML format, which includes triangulation of points into a mesh, combination of textures from different images
7. Generation of KML/KMZ file from VRML format.
8. Display of the reconstructed portion of the archeological site which the excavation site plans as detailed raster overlays, on the Google Earth™ system (Google Earth, 2008) or other GIS tools that support KML/KMZ format.

As is the case for most multiview stereo reconstruction techniques, the accuracy of the final results greatly depends on the quality of both camera calibration and motion estimation (Steps 2 to 4). To efficiently tackle the problem of fully-automatic motion estimation, the proposed approach employs state-of-the-art techniques. Custom modifications were made to these techniques to improve accuracy of the calibration

results, namely, robust feature point detection and matching using SIFT and bundle adjustment.

For the scene reconstruction, the conventional space-sweeping approach is slightly modified to employ a sweeping spherical, instead of planar, back-projection surface. Result is a more accurate and memory-conserving technique. Moreover, this extension facilitates the acceleration of the methods, based on a coarse-to-fine depth map computation.

This approach offers to the user the ability to reconstruct a scene from a few snapshots acquired with an off-the-shelf camera, preferably of high resolution. This way, a few snapshots suffice for the reconstruction and the image acquisition process becomes much simpler than capturing the scene with a video camera or with a multicamera apparatus.

The reconstructed VRML models are integrated with GIS technologies within a web-based virtual tour system, after converting them to the XML-based Collada 3D file format and then referencing to them in Keyhole Markup Language (KML), a format supported by the Google Earth™ GIS platform (Bastanlar, 2008). Thus the reconstructed 3D models and their virtual walkthrough applications can easily become a part of a large GIS.

Reconstructed part of the archaeological site is placed at its exact location on the terrain. Sample Google Earth™ views for Knossos (Greece) archaeological site are given in Figure 9. If the resolution of Google Earth™ at that location is not satisfying, excavation site plan can be used as detailed raster overlay, draped over the terrain. Then the reconstructed 3D model is seen on the site plan.

Virtual Community Practices in Environmental Protection

The increase in the number of forest fires in the last few years has forced governments to take precautions. Besides prevention, early interven-

Figure 9. Viewing models in Google Earth™ - Overall view of the site together with the reconstructed wall (top); Close view of the 3D model of the reconstructed section (bottom-left); Real photograph taken from archaeological site (bottom-right)

tion is also very important in fire fighting. If the fire-fighters know where the fire will be in some time, it would be easier for them to stop the fire. Therefore a big need for simulating the fire behaviour exists. This system comprises a virtual community for forest fire prevention and supports decision makers during large-scale fire incidents, by introducing the 3D simulation of the fire behaviour and propagation in time. The propagation of fire can be visualized in any 3D-GIS environment that accepts KMZ as a file format (Kose et al, 2008). Besides, the system supports the visualization of a large number of output data from the simulations, according to the user needs. This facilitates fire planning. 3D visualization at

3D screens is also supported. Therefore, a better understanding of the terrain can be obtained.

In this approach, FireLib library (FireLib, 2008) is employed. Using the functions defined in this library and some extensions of these functions, the algorithm can calculate the propagation of the fire in 2D. FireLib uses the algorithms defined in BEHAVE fire model. BEHAVE (Andrews, 1986) was developed by the U.S. Department of Agriculture Forest Service in mid 80's and consists a very popular tool for predicting forest fire propagation. The simulator can calculate the propagation of the fire on a landscape with varying conditions. Fire-Lib divides the area of interest into cells. Each of the cells can have its respective fuel type, aspect, slope, etc. However, these parameters for each cell are assumed to be constant with respect to time. When a cell is ignited, the calculation of the ignition times for its neighbouring cells is performed. The propagation of fire from one cell to another depends on the ignitability of the cell, which is done only once per cell. This calculation yields an ignition time instant as well as an estimated flame length. However as the time increases and fire propagates further, some of the parameters in some cells may change (e.g. wind, moisture, fuel type). This issue is not taken into account in FireLib model. To cope with this problem, the dynamically changing parameter values are taken into account within a recursive computation of the ignition times.

An important aspect of the system is the visualization of the calculated propagation data on a 3D-GIS environment. The fire propagation software in the literature yield a 2D view (mostly a top view) of the fire-site which may not provide

a clear view of the situation to the persons responsible for the deployment of fire-fighting forces. Our aim is to visualize this raw propagation data on a more user-friendly 3D-GIS environment. For this purpose Google Earth™ (Google Earth, 2008) is used in the proposed system. The main reason of choosing Google Earth™ is because it is public available and widely used by experts and non-experts. Also it allows the creation of impressive 3D animations of the fire propagation, in addition to the static view. Moreover, due to its layered design, it provides the developer and the user enhanced flexibility to visualize various types of additional information on the map. For instance, the timeline of the propagation can be colour-coded and displayed. Positions of the deployed equipment, observation posts, fire-fighting units etc. can also be visualized on the map. An example view of a grey-scale coded propagation visualization can be seen in Figure 10.

Figure 10. Ignition times using grey-scale coding: which will be burnt first and which areas later

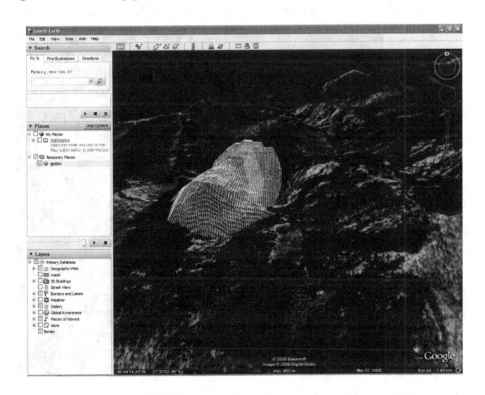

Another layer is the flame length layer. Especially in the animations of fire propagation, the flame length layer yields visually interesting results. The model provides an estimate of the flame length at each cell and time instant, so realistic flame length animations can be created (Figure 11). Another possible layer can be the roads, rivers, and fountains etc, which also play a crucial role to finalize the fire-fighting plan. All these layers are independent from each other; therefore the user can visualize all of them at once or chose the one he/she wants. Using these functionalities of the proposed approach, fire-fighters can more easily plan their movements and actions to confront the fire.

Google Earth™ gives the availability of tilting and panning the view, thus allowing user interaction and enhancing the 3D feeling of the visualization. By this way a more realistic visualization of the topographical information of the terrain can achieved. The user can view the fire area from any angle and a more efficient fire deployment can be achieved.

Recently, a Web interface has been developed to allow users to specify all necessary parameters related to the fire modelling procedure (e.g. number and dimension of cells, geographic coordinates of the ignition point, etc.), as well as the desired type of visualization (ignition time, dynamic animation of flame length, etc). By pressing a specific button, the fire simulation can be executed in the server and the resulting KML file is provided to the user, which can be visualized on Google Earth™ or stored for future reference.

Virtual Cultural Tours (Poleis)

The project POLEIS-Virtual Cultural Tours (Tzovaras, 2006) led to the development of an integrated information system, which supports

Figure 11. Animation showing the flame length with respect to time

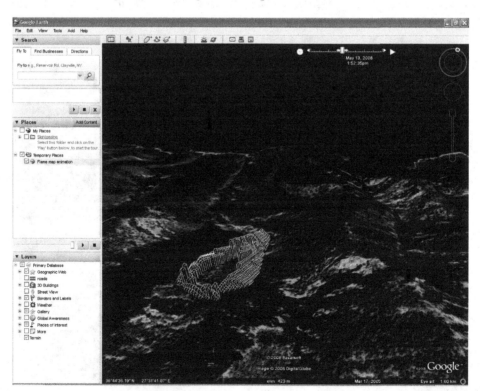

the efficient collection, storage, organization, administration and representation of cultural elements. These cultural elements refer to various topics of Greek productive and cultural activity, as for example a museum's exhibits. The POLEIS platform supports the creation of virtual communities and especially virtual museums. The users can connect to the virtual museum and move within the three-dimensional simulated space of the museum, observing exhibits, as they would do at a real museum. The users can observe avatars of other users that are visiting the museum, talk to them exchanging opinions and ideas, create their personal collections of favorite exhibits, exchange items from their personal collections etc.

The platform supports virtual guides who undertake the user's tour through the museum's halls and its exhibits. The virtual guides are programmed and have extra capabilities of text-to-speech synthesis. So, every guide can move trough the museum and talk to the users attending him. The platform also includes a special system administration unit with extended capabilities for efficiently managing, extending, maintaining and modifying the virtual museums. The users logging on to the system are provided with an integrated interface. This interface includes the virtual museum room, the visitors' chat, and a special area in which information is displayed about the various exhibits the user selects (see Figure 12). The users, while navigating inside the virtual museum, can examine the exhibits using the desired view angle and detail, as depicted at the image on the right. The users can also create their own personal collection of exhibits. Furthermore, they can exchange exhibits from their personal collections with the other users.

Commerce-Oriented Communities and User Toolkits

Electronic commerce is a part of electronic business and stands for all commercial activities taking place between market participants. Online shops realize some these activities for the business to business (b2b) and business to consumer (b2c) market. Although on-line shops have become very popular lately, there are still some sectors of industry, such as clothing and furniture, where the on-line shop concept has not penetrated the market yet. The main reason for that is the diversity of the specific sectors, the mentality of the market players and the lack of user-friendly environments, where the customer could actually "see" the products. Therefore an online shop, designed for the above sectors, has to be very flexible, user friendly and should support more sophisticated IT-technologies for e-business.

Figure 12. Virtual museum tour

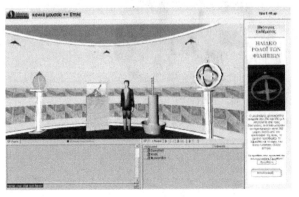

This work (Tzovaras, 2006) offers a user-friendlier e-commerce solution, by adopting additional technologies such as a configuration utility supported by an intelligent help desk system and 3D visualisation in a virtual reality environment (see Figure 13). Thus the overall objective of the project is to build an electronic commerce system with virtual reality product representation, on-line configuration of product variants, an Internet on-line help desk, and corresponding integrated security and privacy mechanisms. The main objective is to enable the suitable representation of products including all practicable variants in electronic commerce systems to achieve the most realistic possible visualisation. User friendliness, simplified access to the service, trust in security and privacy of the service, high quality of information managed and represented, and the use of international standards are also key objectives.

The user interaction with the virtual reality environment includes addition / removal of 3D object parts, selection of textures, semantic search mechanisms, selection of different viewpoints for watching the configuration, storing the 3D

Figure 13. 3D assembly tool(top) and 3D visualization for furniture (bottom)

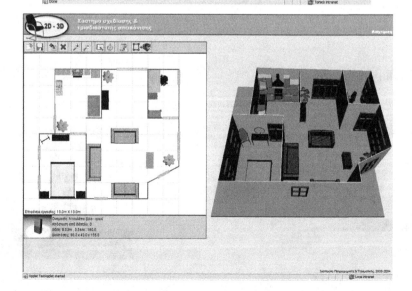

configuration process and playback of the 3D configuration process.

THE FUTURE IN VIRTUAL COMMUNITIES: FULL 3D TELE-PRESENCE

Tele-presence means, being present at a distant event, while being at some other place or time. The goal of a 3D tele-presence system is to provide the feeling of 3D presence. Full 3D tele-presence such as those featured in science fiction films (Star Wars, Star Trek etc.) have been a long-held dream for many. As 3D imaging technology matures it becomes more feasible for achieving this full 3D tele-presence capability, which is expected to change, among other things, the way that virtual communities are constructed, used and experienced.

At present there are various prototypical implementations of full 3D tele-presence applications for museums, medicine, education, entertainment and access to remote/hazardous environments. In general, 3D tele-presence systems can be viewed as generally composed of three parts (3DTV – Potential applications, 2006): a capture system to record and represent the information from the remote site; a network transmission system; and rendering and display technologies to make the local user feel as if he is somehow present in the remote scene. It is of critical importance for the system design that tele-presence systems apply the notion of "real-time", in terms of observing events happening in a distant geographical location. Furthermore, telepresence must allow communication and interaction with other people sharing the same perceptual space. Thus, real-time constraints are imposed on all parts of the system, and to date, in all available systems there exists a tradeoff between speed, quality, and cost. For the sensor system, collecting and processing more data requires greater computation time, but generally yields more accurate representations

of the scene. For the network, more accurate representations tend to be larger and thus more costly to transmit. The speed and quality of arriving data limits how compelling the sense of being present in the remote location can be. At the same time, large amounts of processing and transmitting capacity may nowadays be accessed, but still at significant cost. The goal of producing a system to create the illusion of "being there", faces significant challenges.

CONCLUSION

Interest in 3D has never been greater. The amount of research and development on 3D imaging systems is getting bigger (Starks, 1996). The use of 3D graphics is expected to become increasingly important in the near future due to the great advances in 3D graphics hardware and other related technologies. From technological point of view, this includes improvements over the whole 3D imaging chain, including image acquisition, 3D representation, compression, transmission, signal processing, and interactive rendering and 3D display.

The applications that require 3D information have first aroused in the field of computer graphics in order to create a realistic visual content from the available 3D models. Then the requirement for the utilization of 3D information has further diffused into the animation films, video games and stereoscopic displays. During the last years, the applications using and managing 3D data are quickly increasing due to the enhanced user experience that 3D offers compared to 2D imaging.

In this context, the employment of 3D imaging technologies in the practice of a virtual community appears to be very important, since 3D information can enrich the virtual interaction experience within the members of a virtual community, linking people with common interests, professional occupations, or sharing habits. This 3D imaging practicing allows humans to interface and interact with computer-generated environments in a way that mimics real life and engages all the senses.

During the last years the virtual communities practicing 3D data are quickly increasing: archaeological site reproductions, virtual museums (in the field of Cultural Heritage); games, animations of plays, (in the field of entertainment); enhanced user navigation and e-commerce, are only some examples of the potentialities of such data. In the near future, full 3D tele-presence will be possible and will result in the creation of real-like virtual communities.

ACKNOWLEDGMENT

This work was supported by the FP6 IST Network of Excellence: "3DTV-Integrated Three-Dimensional Television - Capture, Transmission, and Display" (contract FP6-511568). The authors should like to thank all their partners of the projects presented in this chapter and especially X. Zabulis.

REFERENCES

3DTV Network of Excellence. (2005). *Display techniques: A survey*. Retrieved from http://www.3dtv-research.net/

3DTV Network of Excellence. (2006). *Technical report on 3DTV potential applications*. Retrieved from http://www.3dtv-research.net/

Andrews, P. L. (1986). *Behave: Fire behavior prediction and fuel modeling system - BURN* Subsystem Part 1. USDA Forest Service General Technical Report INT-194.

Bastanlar, Y., Grammalidis, N., Zabulis, X., Yilmaz, E., Yardimci, Y., & Triantafyllidis, G. (2008). 3D reconstruction for a cultural heritage virtual tour system. In *Proceedings of the International Society for Photogrammetry and Remote Sensing*, ISPRS 2008, Beijing, China.

FireLib. (2008). *FireLib software implementation*. Retrieved May 10, 2008, from http://www.fire.org/n=content&task=category&sectionid=2&id=11\&Itemid=29

Franklin, C. (2008). *How 3-D graphics work*. Retrieved May 10, 2008, from http://computer.howstuffworks.com/3dgraphics.htm

Google Earth software. (2008). Retrieved May 10, 2008, from http://earth.google.com/

Hammann, R. B. (2000) Computernetze als verbindendes Element von Gemeinschaftsnetzen. In U. Thidecke, (Ed.), *Virtuelle Gruppen: Charakteristika und Problemdimensionen*, (pp. 221-243). Wiesbaden.

HHI Fraunhofer. (2008). *Free2C autostereoscopic display*. Retrieved May 10, 2008, from http://www.hhi.fraunhofer.de/en/departments/im/products-services/interaction-modules/free2c.html

Hummel, J., & Lechner, U. (2002). Social profiles of virtual communities. In *Proceedings of the 35th Hawaii International Conference on System Sciences*.

Kose, K., Grammalidis, N. Yilmaz, E. E., & Cetin, E. E. (2008). 3D wildfire simulation system. In *Proceedings of the International Society for Photogrammetry and Remote Sensing, ISPRS 2008*, Beijing, China.

Koutsonanos, D., Moustakas, K., Tzovaras, D., & Strintzis, M.G. (2004). Interactive cloth editing and simulation in virtual reality applications for theater professionals. In *5th International Symposium on Virtual Reality, Archaeology and Cultural Heritage* (Eurographics), Brussels.

Moustakas, K., Koutsonanos, D., Tzovaras, D., & Strintzis, M.G. (2005). Enhancing costume designer creativity utilizing haptic interaction in cloth editing applications. In *HCI International Conference*, Las Vegas USA.

Moustakas, K., Tzovaras, D., & Nikolakis, G. (2007). Simulating the use of ancient technology works using advanced virtual reality technologies. *International Journal of Architectural Computing, Special Issue on Cultural Heritage, 02*(05), 255-282.

Nikolakis, G., Moustakas, K., Tzovaras, D., & Harissis, T. (2004). Interactive simulation of ancient technology works. In *5th International Symposium on Virtual Reality, Archaeology and Cultural Heritage* (Eurographics).

Papadogiorgaki, M., Grammalidis, N., Sarris, N., & Strintzis, M.G. (2004). Synthesis of virtual reality animations from SWML using MPEG-4 body animation parameters. In *Workshop on the Representation and Processing of Sign Languages, 4th International Conference on Language Resources and Evaluation LREC 2004,* Lisbon, Portugal.

Starks, M., (1996). *3D for the 21st century-The Tsukuba Expo & beyond.* Retrieved May 10, 2008, from www.3dmagic.com/pdf/21ST-CEN.PDF

Tsakiris, A., Filippidis, I., Grammalidis, N., Tzovaras D., & Strintzis, M. G. (2005). VRLAB: Remote experiment laboratories using virtual reality technologies: The VRLab Project. In *Proceedings of the ICTAMI-International Conference on Theory and Applications in Mathematics and Informatics*, Alba Lulia, Romania.

Tzovaras, D. (2006). *INCOVIS: An intelligent configurable electronic shop platform based on 3D Visualisation.* Retrieved May 10, 2008, from http://avrlab.iti.gr/HTML/Projects/recent/INCOVIS.htm

Tzovaras, D. (2006). *POLEIS: Virtual cultural visits.* Retrieved May 10, 2008, from http://avrlab.iti.gr/HTML/Projects/recent/POLEIS.htm

Tzovaras, D. (2006). *VRLAB: Experimental remote control laboratories using virtual reality technologies.* Retrieved May 10, 2008, from http://avrlab.iti.gr/HTML/Projects/recent/VRLAB.htm

Wikipedia. (2008). *3D computer graphics.* Retrieved May 10, 2008, from http://en.wikipedia.org/wiki/3D_computer_graphics

Wikipedia. (2008). *3D modelling.* Retrieved May 10, 2008, from http://en.wikipedia.org/wiki/3D_modeling

Zabulis, X., Grammalidis, N., Bastanlar, Y., Yilmaz, Y., Cetin, Y.Y. (2008). *3D scene reconstruction based on robust camera motion estimation.* 3DTV-CON2008, Istanbul, Turkey.

KEY TERMS

3D Computer Graphics: Graphics that use a 3D representation of geometric data that is stored in the computer for the purposes of performing calculations and rendering 2D images.

3D Display: It is any display device capable of conveying three-dimensional images to the viewer.

3D Imaging: A picture that appears to have height, width and depth is three-dimensional (3D) in contrast to two-dimensional (2D) image which has no depth

3D Modeling: It is the process of developing a mathematical, wireframe representation of any 3D object via specialized software

3D Vision: It is concerned with the theory for building artificial systems that obtain information from 3D images

Human Visual System: Human's eyes capture 2D images on the retina and the human mind perceives distance or depth by using the many available depth cues. Human depth cues of disparity, motion parallax, ocular accommodation and other cues are essential for image recognition

Telepresence: It is the experience of being fully present at a live real world location remote from one's own physical location

Toolkit: It is a set of basic programming units for building applications

Virtual Communities: A community of people sharing common interests, ideas, and feelings over the Internet or other collaborative networks

Chapter XIII
Using Activity Theory to Assess the Effectiveness of an Online Learning Community:
A Case Study in Remote Collaboration Using a 3D Virtual Environment

Theodor G. Wyeld
Flinders University, Norway

Ekaterina Prasolova-Førland
Norwegian University of Science and Technology, Norway

ABSTRACT

Remote, collaborative work practices are increasingly common in a globalised society. Simulating these environments in a pedagogical setting allows students to engage in cross-cultural exchanges encountered in the profession. However, identifying the pedagogical benefits of students collaborating remotely on a single project presents numerous challenges. Activity Theory (AT) provides a means for monitoring and making sense of their activities as individuals and as a collective. AT assists in researching the personal and social construction of students' intersubjective cognitive representations of their own learning activities. Moreover, AT makes the socially constructed cultural scripts captured in their cross-cultural exchanges analysable. Students' reflection on these scripts and their roles in them helps them better understand the heterogeneity of the cultures encountered. In this chapter Engestrom's (1999) simple AT triangular relationship of activity, action and operation is used to analyze and provide insights into how students cooperate with each other across different cultures in a 3D collaborative virtual environment.

INTRODUCTION

As part of an ongoing study in online learning communities by the authors, a series of remote collaboration pedagogical exercises have been conducted since 2000. They involve ITC, multimedia, and design computing students from three different universities on different continents and in different timezones collaborating on a single project using the online 3D Active Worlds environment, in conjunction with social software such as MSN, Skype and Blogs. This chapter uses the latest iteration of these remote collaboration exercises as its case study for the establishment of a consolidated methodological framework for these types of exercises using Activity Theory (AT). AT provides a methodological framework that situates the individual's contribution within a collective. In this manner it is possible to identify the pedagogical benefits from the exercise at the level of the individual's goals and activities leading to goal attainment, and the individual historically situated within the collective goals and its associated activities.

AT is based on the idea that culturally defined tools, or artifacts, mediate all activities. These tools and artifacts are historically situated within the activities in which they are used. For learning environments, social interaction and the way activity is organized can only be understood from its historical context: learners complete multiple cycles in attaining their goals and those of the collective; create an identity within the learning community; and, trade their cultural capital in the relationship between their actions and socioeconomic structures. However, much of the analyzable data is derived from heuristic methods, thus being open to interpretation. AT helps concretize this otherwise subjective information by providing a structure for its interpretation. It does this by incorporating Leont'ev's (1978, 1981) three-level schema: activity, action and operation; corresponding with: motive, goal and instrumental conditions, and the transformations between these levels. In so doing, the meaning-making object of their endeavors is taken from the surrounding activities they engage in, in their learning practices.

The AT framework outlined here is used to analyse, guide and influence the construction and conducting of the remote collaboration exercises. It may be useful to others interested in formalizing their own remote 3D collaboration exercises who wish to extract the pedagogical value of these exercises and guide their formation. The AT framework is particularly pertinent to students using online technologies in collaborative exercises, as it assists in the research of personal and social construction of intersubjective cognitive representations in education. Indeed, there is a pressing need for long-term development of thoughtfulness and personal and social identity in an increasingly globalised society. AT makes socially constructed cultural scripts analysable (Hedegaard 1986, 1987, 1990; Bruner, 1986; Wittgenstein, 1953). Graduating students need the cultural tools (Bruner, 1986; Cole, 1990; Wertsch, 1990) to enable them to manage the heterogeneity of the cultures they will encounter in a global work environment.

THEORETICAL LINKS AND MOTIVATION

Activity Theory

Cultural-historical theory of activity, or Activity Theory for short, is based on the work by Vygotski (1978), Leont'ev (1981) and later Engestrom (1987). The fundamental unit of analysis is human activity. Activity Theory is based on the idea that culturally defined tools, or artefacts, mediate all activity. Individuals and groups can be seen as situated within the context of larger communities mediated by rules of participation and division of labour. Artifacts are continuously modified and shaped to meet evolving needs. We can use work activity as a basic unit for analyzing cooperative working situations (Kuutti, 1994; Bedny & Meister, 1997). Activity Theory can help us understand the way work activities are cooperatively realized in order to better understand learning communities. Marx (1968) is referred to in AT to demonstrate how, within the concept of activity, social change cannot be reduced to individual self-change but is a society-wide process.

AT is a method for understanding learning focused on the cognitive capabilities and needs of the learner. The emphasis is on the social nature of learning and learning as participation in a cultural practice. All activities are part of what Engestrom (1999) calls an 'expansive learning cycle'. In this context, learning development can be defined as a continuous motion through successive forms of participation, connecting the past, the present and the future (Wenger, 1999). Other elements in the model are cultural tools (artifacts), teachers and collaborative user groups. These serve as a checklist for the design of learning environments. The implications for the design of learning environments are:

- Social interaction and conversation plays a fundamental place in learning
- The way activity is organized can only be understood from its historical context

This means learning designers should pay attention to the interaction between the multiple cycles of the learner. The cycles include the development of cultural practice, the development of people within a practice and development of ways of participating within the cultural practice. An example can be a student's movement through different forms of participation in a project group: from novice to expert and leader.

Learning Communities

Communities of practice situated within workplace environments is a central component of Activity Theory. In a pedagogical context, communities of practice can be thought of as sharing a history of learning, or a learning community. Each activity is situated within a learning cycle. Learners move through activities, progressing from partial to full participation (Gifford & Enyedy, 1999; Wenger, 1999). Continuous negotiation of meaning is the core of social learning and involves two processes: participation, reification and reflection, forming a shared repertoire. The repertoire of a community includes routines, tools, words, ways of doing things, stories, actions, and concepts, that the community has produced or adopted in the course of its existence, and which have become part of its practice. Participation is the complex process that combines doing, talking, thinking, feeling, and belonging. It involves the individual's whole person including body, mind, emotion, and social relations. Reification is the process of giving form to one's experience by producing objects that congeal this experience into 'thingness' (Wenger, 1999). The collection of shared artefacts can be used by individuals in the community for further activities and to support their movement through the learning cycle as well as self-reflection and construction of meaning.

Identity within learning communities is defined by Wenger (1999) as negotiated experience, community membership, learning cycle and nexus of multi-memberships. A learning community can strengthen the identity of participation by incorporating its members' past into its history and opening new cycles. As identity is connected to the activities in the learning cycle, it can be expressed by the artifacts that comprise the outcome of the activities. In this way, the past experiences and history of community members are reified within the shared repertoire as documents, and plans of action. Multiple memberships, involve the reconciliation of boundaries and creation of bridges across a landscape of practice. In some cases, the boundaries are reified with explicit markers of membership, for example, titles and degrees. They connect and coordinate different practices and communities. Participation and reification can create continuities across boundaries. For example, an artifact, or product of reification, can be present in different communities. At the same time, people can participate in different communities. In this scenario, learning should be primarily addressed in terms of identities and modes of belonging and only secondary in terms of skills and information. From this perspective, experiences involving new forms of membership, multi-membership and ownership of meaning are at least as important as the curriculum itself. Social relations and interests thus play an important role in the development of a learning community.

Within communities, members join in interactions, forming groups. Members of groups go through different cycles of participation and build up a history of their own. We can consider a group as a subgroup of the larger community. The result of activities performed by the subgroups of a community is an artefact – a reification of experience. A group goes through a number of phases during its development: belonging, control and interdependence (Schutz, 1958), thus moving through common learning and participation cycles. In order to perform activities and proceed through the phases successfully, negotiate the roles and division of labor, it is crucial to provide effective group communication. Communication structures in the group are also important as indicators of the group's power structure (Cartwright & Zander, 1968). The distribution of resources and control over them provide a clue of the patterns of relationships within the group.

METHODOLOGY AND STUDY DESIGN

Prior behavioral and social science studies have tended to focus on the division of labor, separating socioeconomic structures from individual behavior and agency. This makes the socioeconomic structures appear stable and self-sufficient – the actions of the individual not impacting on these structures. But this does not help us understand the deep relationship between human action and these structures. The focus of AT, on the other hand, is on the relationship between human action and socioeconomic structures. Human activity takes multifarious, mobile and rich forms (Engstrom, 1999). AT attempts to develop a theory of a self-organizing system of interacting subjects or participants. The difficulties are that the research methods rely on both vague and concrete data. AT addresses the apparent anomaly between vague and concrete data by identifying 'situated action' as an important part of its research agenda (Suchman, 1987). The notion of situated action is used to overcome the dualism of imposed structure and individual experience. Whereas prior methods focused on actions that highlight goal attainment and problem solving per se, AT reveals much of the socio-cultural and motivational basis of the forming of goals and problem identification (Engestrom, 1999). It incorporates Leont'ev's (1978, 1981) three-level schema: activity, action and operation; corresponding with: motive, goal and instrumental conditions, and the transformations between these levels.

AT identifies discursive communication as an inherent aspect of all object-oriented activities. It unifies labour actions and social intercourse, generating a shared object action. Hence, objects (which can be words, physical objects, virtual objects, images, symbols and so on) take their meanings from the activities that surround them. Activity, action and operation can thus be seen as a simple triangular relationship (see Figure 1). In the remaining of this chapter, we discuss how this model was used to frame and analyze how students cooperate with each other across different cultures using a 3D collaborative virtual environment (3DCVE) and various types of social software.

Figure 1. Engestrom's (1999) simple triangular relationship linking actions and outcomes

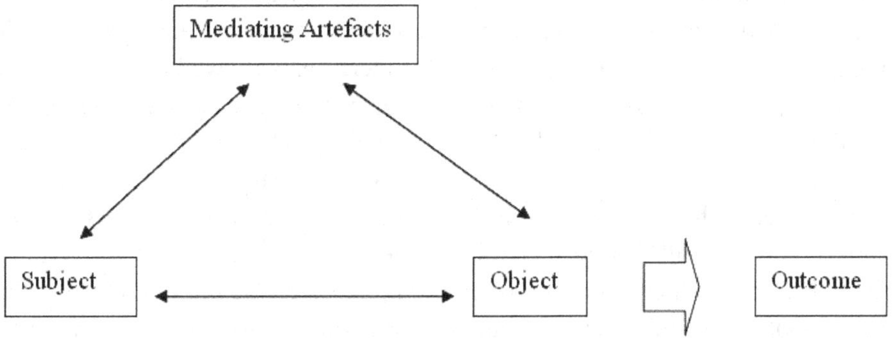

A Virtual Tower of Babel

The virtual construction of a *Tower of Babel* by remote collaboration in a 3D virtual environment was formed as an exercise to address the need for graduating ITC students to work in increasingly internationalized cross-cultural environments. The *Tower of Babel* story was chosen as a historically and culturally distant text to bring into sharp contrast differences with contemporary culture and within its own story – the confusion arising from the diversity of languages interfering with communicating a common goal. Using a suite of tools, central to which was the 3D collaborative virtual environment ActiveWorlds, students worked in teams collaborating across time zones on a single project complimenting each other's skills and learning about new ways to work and learn in a global environment. This fostered deeper understandings of alternative meanings to everyday occurrences and work practices. The project involved students from *The University of Queensland* (Australia); *the National Yunlin University of Science and Technology* (Taiwan); and, *the Norwegian University of Science and Technology* (Norway). It built on previous exercises conducted by the authors (see Wyeld et al, 2006).

The introduction of cultural interaction to the curriculum in the form of a remote collaboration exercise was made adaptable and flexible so that it reflected and respected the various local conventions of the learners involved. This was conducted in a playful atmosphere where students were actively encouraged to experiment with the tools given and cultures encountered within and across teams. This is a known approach to effective learning (Hubbard, 1980; Bourdieu & Wacquant, 1992; Dewey, 1957). This followed a process of acculturation to a new knowledge community (Leidner & Jarvenpaa, 1995), resulting in participants reinforcing and expanding their ability to comprehend new challenges, risks and opportunities. Trust was a crucial mitigating factor in cooperation between remote team partners and hence, overall feelings of control and satisfaction of the students within the exercise (Clear and Kassabova, 2005; Jarvenpaa & Leidner, 1998; Seifert, 2004; Marks et al, 2001).

A key factor in groupwork motivation for the students was addressing the need for explicit and implicit 'meaning' in the project – how it related to the wider world of the students' experiences. Recognizing their own cross-cultural understandings tended to occur after the exercise had been completed and they were reflecting on it. It was then that the 'click' of recognition of alternate cultural understandings occurred (in Kuhn's (1996) terms of a paradigmatic shift in understanding) that led to transformative outcomes and more culturally aware ITC professionals. The reflective reports the students prepared following completion of the exercise were central in this shift in cultural awareness.

Groups were formed with members from each institution, thus representing all 3 cultural views. Each group included a team leader who organised various forms of contact, including email, chat, videoconferencing and meetings in AWs. Explicit tasks were allocated to Australian, Norwegian and Taiwanese team leaders by the teachers. Norwegian team members were allocated the task of choosing 20 different building blocks to use in the final tower design. Taiwanese team members were required to assist in the scripting of specific functions for the building blocks such as hyperlinks, teleports, textures, animations, and so on. Australian team members were required to direct the building of towers using the allocated blocks and their scripts.

All other decisions were the domain of the individual groups to negotiate amongst themselves. Teachers only intervened if irreconcilable difficulties arose – these were rare. Construction of the tower involved the manipulation of the blocks, managed through the simple 3D AWs interface. It allowed students to move, copy, and change the type of blocks and add simple scripts. These blocks were then stacked on top of each other to create a tower. Restrictions to the tower construction included the use of only twenty different types of blocks and a maximum height that represented the limit of the AWs application (see Figure 2). Various social software applications were used (videoconferencing, email, blogs and chat). Videoconferencing was essential as an initial 'ice-breaker' to get members of a team to start collaborating with their other, remote members. It was here that many interesting cultural exchanges took place (see Figure 3).

Email and Blogs were used to exchange images and textual explanations. The exchange of images and serendipitous meetings in the AWs environment itself proved instrumental in overcoming some of the confusion due to text-only communication (see Figure 4).

In the final performance, towers were constructed from scratch in a one hour time limit per

Figure 2. Typical construction space in Active Worlds browser showing chat field below

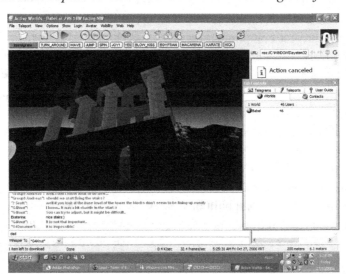

Figure 3. Active Worlds browser use in conjunction with MSN videoconferencing

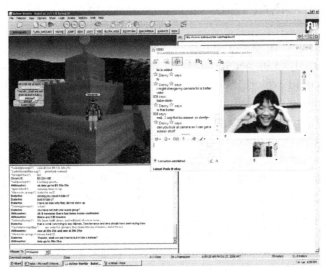

Figure 4. Blogs were set up by the students for sharing their ideas as images

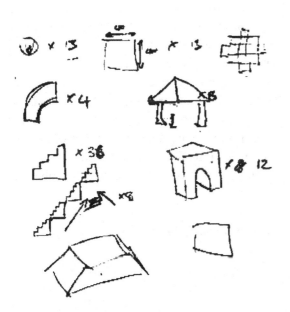 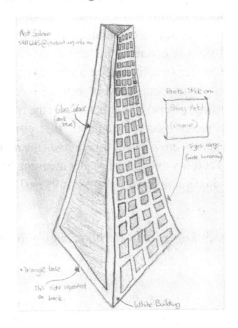

group (3 groups constructed at the same time, hence total time for all groups was 3 hours). A number of practice constructions preceded the final construction. Towers constructed during the practice sessions were critiqued by group members and designs were continuously being modified until considered appropriate within the constraints given. On completion of the project, students were required to prepare reflective essays on their cross-cultural experiences in the teamwork exercise.

ACTIVITY THEORY AS MODEL FOR INVESTIGATION AND ANALYSIS

AT was used as a framework for both organizing the exercise and to analyze its pedagogical outcomes. With AT, we could explore the notion of the mediation of the students' activities with the given tools and communities to isolate an individual student's actions from the collective. In this way we could transcend the apparent oppositions between activity and process, activity and action, and activity and communication. Engestrom's (1999) simple triangulation of an individual's activity system (see Figure 1) can be expanded to formulate a structure for the more complex group activity system (see Figure 5).

As a collective system, the subject in this case is not the individual per se but the group that the individual identifies with, the subgroup of the larger collaborative community in general. The object is what connects the individual's actions to the collective activity. The projected outcome consists of important new objectified meanings and lasting patterns of interaction. It is the "projection from the object to the outcome that, no matter how vaguely envisioned, functions as the motive of this activity and gives broader meaning to the individual's actions" (Engestrom, 1999, p31). The rules are largely tacit conventions of exchange, and the division of labor consists of multiple layers of fragmented and compartmentalized tasks within the project structure.

This model was used to move from the analysis of individual actions to their broader context within the group collective and back again. Actions involve failures, disruptions and innovations normally difficult to explain at the level of the actions themselves. At the broader level however, the contradictions that give rise to these failures, disruptions and innovations can be illuminated. The model highlights the interrelationships between subject community and communicative relations as an integral aspect of the activity system as a whole. In turn, these systems interacted with other activity systems (go-betweens, internal, one-to-one and so on).

From this model, we saw that, over time, externalization (of an individual's internalized creativity contributing to the group as a whole) tended to dominate. On the other hand, internalization of the collectives' rules was requisite for socializing and training students to become competent members of the joint activity. From here, discrete individual innovations could feed externalized creativity. But this was not without its disruptions and contradictions by other members

Figure 5. Engestrom's (1999) triangulation model for a group activity system

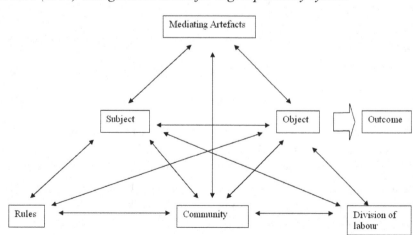

of the group. When this happened, it was the critical self-reflection on these external forces which is where the search for solutions occurred. Only when these were resolved could a new model for the activity be fully externalized and thus realized or implemented. Once stable and accepted by the group, the individual returned to their internalized innovative thinking and the cycle repeated. It was in these cycles that learning and development occurred.

Engestrom (1999) tells us that such activity systems represent the collective voices of a group; that, expansive cycling of learning and developing, identifying problems and solving them, is a constant reorchestration of these voices – the different viewpoints and approaches of the various participants. Its historicity is contained in identifying the past cycles – precedents which informed current or future understandings. Hence, these collective, historically situated voices, can be seen as complementary competencies within an activity system. Based on this model we were able to move from identifying the role of the individual and the individual as a member of a subgroup to the collective whole – the explication of the components and internal relations of the collective activity system revealing patterns of interaction.

Patterns of Interaction

The Babel project represents a social setting, circumstantially framed by the Babel story and its collaborative reconstruction in a 3DCVE. It involved three different universities on different continents across different time zones. These are institutions that cooperate with adult students, and specific external bodies (academic and commercial). Hence, several simultaneous social worlds or frames are operating:

- The project required participants from the 3 different institutions to cooperatively construct an imaginary Babel tower

- The teaching staff from the 3 different institutions cooperated with each other towards a common pedagogical goal
- An essential aspect of the whole enterprise was mutual collaboration between all teaching staff and students, and students and students

This mutual collaboration can be interpreted as the merging of two activity systems: pedagogy and cross-cultural understanding (the pedagogical motive). They had a common object: training ITC students in cross-cultural understanding. Interactions between collaborating students took place in a university setting, home, and other, with the guidance of the teaching staff. Space and facilities were provided for the activities, time was set aside for assistance, a program was developed and the students were expected to follow it. From the students' point of view, their role was dictated by circumstances. They could not choose who their peers were and the time they could construct their interactions – due to time zones and other scheduled university responsibilities. Hence, some common objects were a problem for both the students and teachers alike. These manifest themselves as conflicts, difficulties or technical flaws. In such cases, the teacher had to intervene. Hence, the co-construction of common objects was not always seen by all students. The students could see the teachers as outside their activity system interfering with their interactions. Yet, students' interactions took place in a social situation created by the teachers. Hence, any withdrawal from the interactive situation by the teachers did not necessarily eliminate their influence through the mediation of the social setting.

The students' interactions can be mapped as a collective Endeavour constituted by the two activity systems of pedagogy and cross-cultural understanding. The co-construction of a common outcome was the result of the merging of institutional knowledge and student knowledge which evolved through the realization and implementation of the project (see Figure 6). Various groupware applications were used to facilitate the collaboration (AWs, videoconferencing, email, blogs and chat). These are the mediating artifacts of their cultural exchange activities (see Figure 7). These artifacts of mediation provided a conduit for cultural evolution within the system. The specifics of which depended on the institutional contexts. We were working with our students within their activity and the history of the activity itself. This involved a 'within-context' and 'between-context of the interactions as constitutive of the activity itself' approach. In so doing, we were able to link theory with practice. At the individual level, we can see the role of one of the mediating artefacts, email, as a microcosm of the greater exchange (see Figure 8). The subject was the need to communicate information, represented as both goal and motive. The object was the need for a response to the request for information, which is also represented as both goal and motive. The outcome of this exchange was a shift in understanding.

Engestrom's (1999) activity system as a model for investigation and analysis proved useful in terms of isolating the individual's actions from the collective yet retaining the context of those actions as a part of a whole. Contradictions in the system manifest as disruptions, interference and innovation. As a mapping exercise, it was possible to see the students' patterns of interaction as part of a collective voice. The impact of this collective voice, while always present, was most recognisable on reflection – an important feature of the pedagogical benefits of such exercises is getting students to reflect on their own understandings and recognise the shift to new understandings an the role of the tools employed to do this.

DISCUSSION

Following the AT model we are able to identify the constitutive elements of the individual's ac-

tions within their subgroup actions within the whole collective. A central feature of the Babel project was the playful nature of the interactions. As ostensibly a socialising activity, play was an integral part of the pedagogical motive for getting students to engage in the task (Dewey, 1957; Schon, 1983). The exercise was couched as an opportunity to meet and play with fellow students from other institutions its seriousness was in the pedagogical goal of inculcating cross-cultural understandings. This was background in favour of semi-structured tasks in a game-like environment (the 3D AWs interface). This was also manifest by the sorts of activity structures that emerged from the exercise. The nature of the interchange was predicated on the role of the students' (actors') prior knowledge and history of the text used. Within the process of revealing their prior knowledge and history they were able to establish constructive identities within their subgroup and the collective as a whole. This can be understood as part of Engestrom's (1999) expansive learning cycle – the role of tacit and explicit knowledge, witnessed as a shift from abstract to concrete understandings.

The Structure of Activity

AT tells us that activities dictate what a person does and the environments they find themselves in. In activity, actors take into account the laws and rules of the collective. When we listen to the actors' stories we begin to understand the meanings they attach to their activities. Using AT to analyse what students said and did, we got a better idea how new meanings emerged through their group activities. We had many opportunities to do this throughout the project (online, emails, unstructured interviews and reflective essays).

We found two basic processes were operating continuously. The internalisation and externalisation of their activities. The internalisation of their activities was related to the reproduction of their prior cultural understanding of the tasks at

Figure 6. Using Engestrom's triangulation to map the common outcome of the merging of two activity systems (pedagogy and its motive: cross-cultural understanding) from two different knowledge bases: institutional and the students'

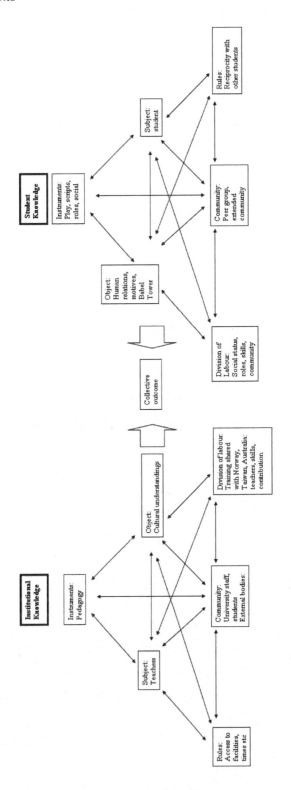

Figure 7. Array of mediating artifacts and their forms of communication used in the students' cultural exchange activities

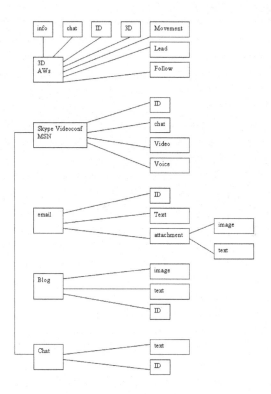

Figure 8. The role of email as a mediating artifact in the exchange of information resulting in a shift in understanding

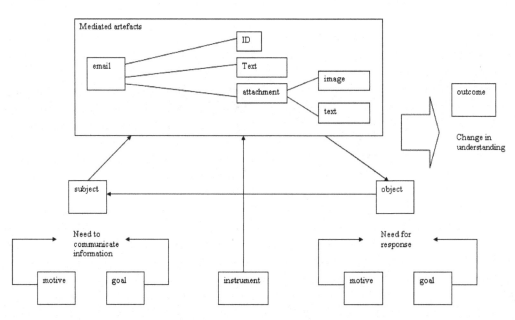

hand, and externalisation was the creation of new artefacts making possible new transformations in understanding (Engestrom et al, 1999). Individuals acted in collective practices, not reducible to sums of individual action, but more like a string of goal-directed acts.

From this, the structure of their activities began to emerge. We can think of the difference between activity and action as the difference between the project and the individual's role within the project. The gross activity was the project, while the actions of the individual may have been peripheral to the outcome (Leont'ev, 1981). It was the purposeful change of natural and social reality that was being acted out in the specific form of a societal existence or activity (Engestrom et al, 1999). The goals of the activity manifest itself as visualisations of an end product of a collective creative effort (a virtual tower of Babel). Transformations in understanding occurred when the individual saw the nature of their purposeful activity in light of its social and historical context – when they reflected on their activity. Thus, activity determined the individual's social being, and collective social laws were revealed through their activities. Hence, transformations in understanding occurred when they recognised the essence of their prior understandings and altered them.

We can define the structure of their activity as including needs, motives, goals, actions, operations, and the means to solve a problem. This involved perception, imagination, memory, thinking, feelings, and will. The products of their activities helped concretise their perception and thinking. It was in this concretisation, in the product or artefact of their creativity, that solutions and methods for solutions to sensory or cognitive problems were found.

Each type of activity had definite needs, motives, tasks, and goals. A morphological model of their structural interrelationships could be developed from the particular context of the activity. The individual or collective 'ideal' manifestation of the activity was the object or

artefact created, revealed through group dialogue on values, perceptions, beliefs, likes, dislikes and so on (Davydov, 1999).

The Role of Play

Play was an integral part of their social interaction. It allowed for a subjective reflection on the reality of the task at hand. As such, creative activity gave new meanings to their actions and objects (Engestrom et al, 1999). It provided for risk-free interaction between members of the local and extended groups. Learning communities benefited from play as a pedagogical motive in that rules, activities and outcomes were easily recognisable by all. The serious component of play was the subsequent revelation of new meaning and transformative outcomes on reflection.

Their motive for play was not conscious, although the rules may have been explicit. Students were able to master new ideas and engaged in more advanced actions than are normally possible through their play. Play raised the demand on the students, bringing them into Vygosky's (1978, p86) zone of proximal development, defined as

the distance between the actual developmental level as determined by independent problem solving and the level of potential development as determined through problem solving under adult guidance or in collaboration with more capable peers.

New knowledge, skills, and actions appeared through their play activity. Play changed the situation and through this change new content emerged. In play, students moved from unconscious motives to conscious motives. Role play helped students become conscious of their own role in an activity and master new forms of play, with rules. In planning for play, decisions were formulated verbally, in drawings, diagrams and other models. Such models helped students with self-esteem, awareness of their own role in the collective, and encouraged reflective thought (Davydov, 1990).

However, motives did not always correspond to goals in play. Some players simply adjusted themselves to the circumstances they found themselves in rather than connect with others around them and made the necessary shifts in understanding. In this case, the student concerned felt the context went beyond their zone of proximal development (more than they wanted to engage in). This was displayed in the way they tended to wait for other students in their group to take the initiative.

In play, students reflected their own life experiences and took independent initiatives. They 'played up' to each other and made use of the challenges they were confronted with. They brought each other into the zone of proximal development. The play drew on the students' pre-existing interests and motives, and first-hand experiences connected with the task at hand. Such organised play contributed to the development of qualitatively new understandings and meaning structures in the students' psyche and activity which continued after the exercise was completed (Engestrom et al, 1999, p232) (see Figure 9).

We found play was intrinsically motivating because it was internally rewarding. Socially situated play was a social activity that expressed relations between peers. Through the guidance and collaboration with their peers, cooperating students raised their actions to a more advanced level initiating new processes of development, through which new knowledge, skills, and actions appeared (Vygotsky, 1978).

The Role of Text

We found individual acts were abstracted out of whole social acts (Mead, 1938). For example, serendipitous meetings in the 3D AWs environment led to individual feelings of contribution to a whole, particularly if prior collective misunderstandings were resolved through the individual's actions. Hence, the study of small groups and their internal effectiveness was useful revealing the local, idiosyncratic, contingent, nature of action, interaction and knowledge. It uncovered local patterns of activity and cultural specificity of thought, speech and discourse (such as the misunderstandings of specific words used in different contexts). To make a connection to the greater structure of the collective within which they fell, we recognized that the localized activities, by their very nature, drew on historical contexts common to the collective as a whole. For example, different conversational 'tones' were

Figure 9. Mapping 'play' as an activity system

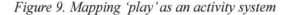

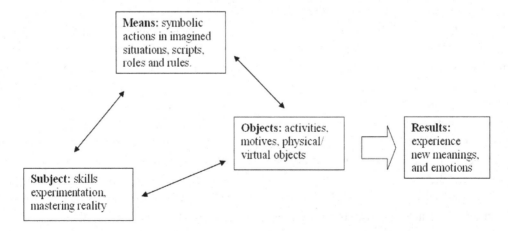

attributed to different cultural expectations of acceptable individual behavior in a local context not always understood by the other's culture. The overall network provided for the movement of these novel cultural artifacts which were re-combined in new ways. This resulted in individuals solving problems using general means created by other team members applied in new contexts (Latour, 1994).

Within the intersubjectivity of knowledge and concepts represented in their discursive practices, meaning was essentially collective. As such, an individual's questions and judgements were initially framed by their own cultural state of knowledge – understanding the meanings of words in their cultural contexts. For example, the use of the word 'fit' in the Australian context had different meanings in other cultural contexts. In Australia these included: 'physically fit' (going to the gym), 'a good fit' (the way a nut fits a bolt) and 'fit for the job' (suitably competent), among others. While these were often understood also by the other cultures present, the specific exchange

context in which they were uttered did cause some inter-cultural confusion. Hence, meaning had to be embedded in the typified action sequence to be understood – going to the gym, screwing a nut onto a bolt, or being assessed for job suitability. This is where the text-rich chat interface, used extensively for communicative purposes, did not always support the sorts of tacit understandings more common in face-to-face communication (see Figure 10). It follows that, students acquired and handled knowledge in ways that were partly culturally universal, partly spontaneous, and partly internalized notions of a self culture. Students had trans-cultural experiences and others that were products of enculturation to a local or shared culture also.

Vygotsky's (1981) heuristic framework was used to research these multifarious forms of intercultural discourses and shared conventions. This was useful in making sense of the sociocultural processes involved, situated within specific sociocultural contexts identified by Bruner (1986). Even within local contexts, the intersubjectivity

Figure 10. Typical online chat interfaces used extensively for real-time communication between remote team members

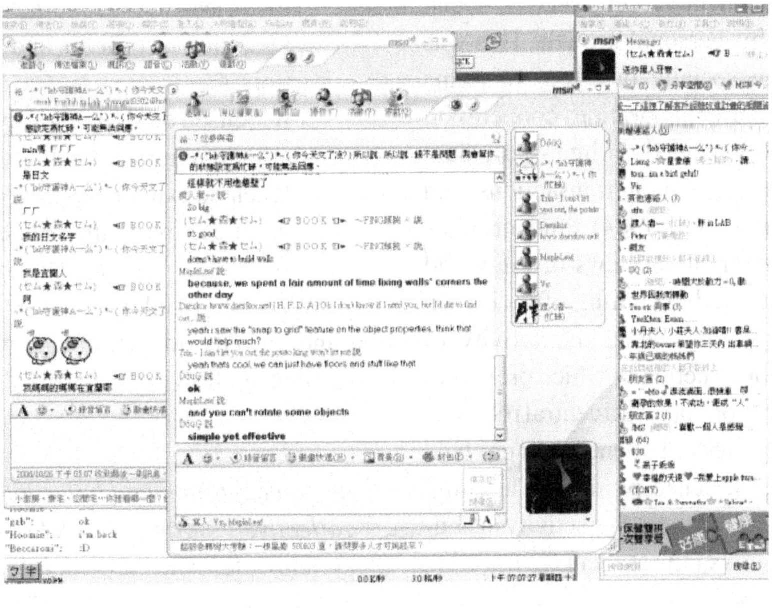

of understandings could be seen. For example, teachers and learners were not equal in their understandings of all situations. They learned from each other. The teacher-learner dynamic, in hypothetical and critical thinking activities, was a discursive activity in which the teacher's job was to try to provide the students with worthwhile socio-semiotic activities. Under the Vygotskian framework, it was the intertextuality of exchange where the focus on the production of new personal meanings was achieved. Constructing the exercises within the text provided (the Babel storyline) was one way of allowing students to subjectively collectively reinterpret both the text and their textual communications about the text (Davydov, 1988).

Not only were new collective meanings fostered and enriched by this but, students' self-identity development was influenced by the refraction and reconstruction in these socioculturally mediated joint interactions. Students did not create new, meaningful images of the world from scratch, rather they built on pre-existing ones, and these shaped how their activities proceeded. Their prior understandings of the Babel story fed their natural inquisitiveness and need to debate the issues raised as a raison d'etre for communicating with their remote partners.

Students drew on their constructive social relationships for this personal growth. This was both selective and socially oriented. In terms of the pedagogics of collaboration, cooperation as a learning task depended on inter-individual interaction involving explicit transactions and negotiations (Amonashvili, 1984). Students were confronted with alternative views of the world which led to better understanding of their own beliefs. Students introduced to the activity of shared meaning construction in which pre-existing sociocultural canons played a central role, was used as a didactic model to challenge their pre-held cultural perspectives. Hence, productive learning was essentially a multi-perspective activity including the belief systems of the students in question

and the historically constructed representations of the given sociocultural content – the virtual construction of a tower of Babel and what this meant to them specifically and generally.

To concretize this concept, the historically culturally distant Babel story was useful. Students contemporaneously re-contextualized the text and defended it publicly (in a playful format). As such, their prior didactic understandings were challenged. The outcome was the establishment of a new personalized mode of communicating their new intercultural knowledge of the world to each other and better understanding their own beliefs.

Engestrom's Expansive Learning Cycle

Analysis of work, within and between teams, involved detailed insights to the discursive processes, practical actions, and mediated artifacts employed in a step-by-step production of innovative solutions or ideas (Argyris and Schon, 1978). Using AT, we found this approach was well suited to analysis of innovative learning in work practice for three main reasons:

- It was contextual and thus inclusive of historical and local practices, their objects, mediated artifacts, and social organization
- It focused on the creativity potential of their cognitive understandings
- It helped explain qualitative changes in their practices over time (Engestrom, 1999)

We recognized the two main types of knowledge activity in their team work as tacit and explicit. Following Lektorsky (1984, p380-381) we saw:

human cognition and behaviour as embedded in collectively organised, artefact-mediated activity systems. Activities are social practices oriented at objects. An entity becomes an object of activity when it meets a human need. The subject constructs the object, singles out those properties that prove to be essential for developing social practice, using mediated artifacts that function as forms of expression of cognitive norms, standards, and object-hypotheses existing outside the given individual. In this constructed, need-related capacity, the object gains motivating force that gives shape and direction to activity. The object determines the horizon of possible actions.

From this we found, the object of their activity was not the goal itself. Actions proceeded from their goals. They had beginnings and ends. However, their activity systems evolved from historically situated social cycles making their beginnings and ends difficult to determine. Hence, goals could not be used to explain their actions as they emerged concurrently and could only be explicated on reflection (in their reflective essays and interviews).

Their goals emerged from their team action through their internal representations externalized by their speech, gesture, writing, and physical means. The artifacts of their creative activities were used to identify objects that they built with (such as the elements of the tower itself), but they were also used as a symbol of cooperation (how high, large or resolved was theirs compared to

others?). This was recognized on reflection. The goal of the building element was not a symbol of status. However, in the activity of a struggle for recognition in the wider community, the elements were often appropriated as a symbol of their status within the greater activity.

It was in reflecting that they moved from abstract to concrete conceptions of their own activities. Engestrom's (1999) expansive learning describes this process. An object first takes form as an abstract concept. This can be traced through its historical formulation. This is concretized in an expanding learning cycle from the simple to the complex idea and finally transformed into a concrete object and new form of practice in its production. The expansive cycle begins with the questioning of existing practices, and evolves into a collective movement or instituted practice (Latour, 1987). Such epistemic or learning actions facilitate the move from the abstract to the concrete. They form an expansive cycle of epistemic actions involving: questioning, analyzing, modeling, experimenting, implementation, reflecting, and consolidating (Engestrom, 1999) (see Figure 11).

The process of their expansive learning as a team can thus be understood as construction and resolution of successively evolving tensions or contradictions in the complexity of the activity system they were engaged in. It included the

Figure 11. Engestrom's (1999) expansive learning cycle

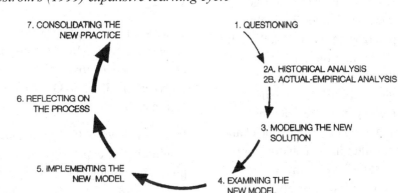

object of their endeavor, the mediating artifacts that brought it to fruition, and the reflective perspectives of the various participants. The various large scale expansive cycles involved also smaller cycles.

CONCLUSION

According to Vygotsky (1981, p161), "the analysis of reality on the basis of a concept emerges much earlier than analysis of the concept itself." We observed this where participants engaged in successful goal-directed activities yet experienced difficulty in communicating the strategies and concepts that underpinned their actions. In their reflective essays and recorded chats, they were required to explicate what they were doing and communicate this to others. This need to reflect upon their activities and communicate it to others was one of the major educational benefits of the system in place, promoting deep learning and self-reflective development in cross-cultural understandings and self understanding.

By incorporating AT as a framework to guide the formation of the remote collaboration exercises and their subsequent analysis, two goals were met: pedagogical justification for inclusion of remote collaboration exercises in the curriculum and a method for its framing. Although not as widely adopted as a method for pedagogical direction or analysis as Guba and Lincoln's (1981; 1998) constructivist method—AT is more familiar to workplace analyses—AT provides a rigorous methodology and clear guidelines for qualitative understanding of pedagogical activities. With the specific task of ascertaining the effectiveness of shifts in cross-cultural understandings—a valuable attribute for graduating ITC students—we found AT instrumental in its revelations. The simple triangular mapping of subject, object and mediating artifacts resulted in definable outcomes. This was consistent at the level of the individual, group and collective alike. It was a useful resource for better understanding learning communities in general.

REFERENCES

Amonashvili, S. A. (1984). Development of the cognitive initiative of students in the first grades of elementary education. *Voprosy Psychologii, 5,* 36-41 (in Russian).

Argyris, C., & Schon, D. A. (1978). *Organisational learning: A theory of action perspective.* Reading: Addison-Wesley.

Bedny, G., & Meister, D. (1997). *The Russian Theory Of Activity Current Applications To Design.* London: Lawrence Erlbaum Assoc.

Bourdieu, P., & Wacquant, L. J. D. (1992). *An invitation to reflexive sociology.* University of Chicago Press.

Bruner, J. (1986). *Actual minds, possible worlds.* Cambridge, MA: Harvard University Press.

Cartwright, D., & Zander, A. (1968). *Group dynamics: Research and theory.* New York: Harpercollins College Division.

Clear, T., & Kassabova, D. (2005). Motivational patterns in virtual team collaboration. In A. Young, & D. Tolhurst (Eds.), *Proceedings of Australasian Computing Education Conference 2005,* Newcastle, Australia, conferences in *Research and Practice in Information Technology,* Vol. 42.

Cole, M. (1990). Cultural Psychology: A once and future discipline? In J. J. Berman, (Ed.), *Cross-cultural perspectives, Nebraska Symposium on Motivation, 37,* 279-335. Lincoln: University f Nebraska Press.

Davydov, V. V. (1988). Problems of developmental teaching: The experience of theoretical and empirical psychological research. *Soviet Education, Part I: 30*(8), 15-97; Part II: 30(), 3-38; Part III: 30(10), 3-77.

Davydov, V. V. (1990). *Types of generalisation in instruction: Logical and psychological problems in the structuring of school curricula.* Reston: National Council of Teachers of Mathematics.

Dewey, J. (1957). E*xperience and education.* New York: MacMillan.

Engstrom, Y. (1987). *Learning by expanding: An activity-theoretical approach to developmental research.* Orienta-Konsultit, Helsinki.

Engstrom, Y., Miettinen, R., & Punamaki, R-L. (1999). *Perspectives on activity theory.* Cambridge University Press, UK.

Gifford, B. R., & Enyedy, N. D. (1999, December 12-15). Activity centered design: Towards a theoretical framework for CSCL. *In proceedings of Computer Supported Collaborative Learning,* (pp. 189-196). Palo Alto, CA. Lawrence Erlbaum Associates.

Guba, E. (1981). Criteria for assessing the trustworthiness of naturalistic inquiries. *Education Communication and Technology Journal, 29*(2).

Guba, E., & Lincoln, Y. (1998). Competing paradigms in qualitative research. In N. Denzin & Y. Lincoln (Eds.), *The landscape of qualitative research.* California: Sage Publications.

Hedegaard, M. (1986). Instruction of evolution as a school project and the development of pupils' theoretical thinking. In M. Hildebrand-Nilshon & G. Ruckreim, (Eds.), *Workshop contributions to selected aspects of applied research. Proceedings of the 1ˢᵗ International Congress on Activity Theory* (Vol. 3). Berlin: System Druck.

Hedegaard, M. (1987). Methodology in evaluative research on teaching and learning. In F. J. van Zuuren, F. J. Wertz, & B. Mook (Eds.), *Advances in qualitative psychology: Themes and variations* (pp. 53-78). Lisse, Swets & Zeitlinger.

Hedegaard, M. (1990). The zone of proximal development as basis for instruction. In L. Moll (Ed.), *Vygotsky and education: Instructional implications and applications of sociohistorical psychology* (pp. 349-371). Cambridge: Cambridge University Press.

Jarvenpaa, S., & Leidner, D. (1998). Communication and trust in global virtual teams. *Journal of Computer Mediated Communication, 3.*

Kuhn, T. S. (1996). *The structure of scientific revolutions.* Chicago and London: University of Chicago Press.

Kuutti, K. (1994). *Information systems, cooperative work and active subjects: The activity-theoretical perspective.* Doctoral thesis. (Research papers Series A 23, Department of Information Processing Science, University of Oulu, Finland).

Latour, B. (1987). *Science in action: How to follow scientists and engineers through society.* Cambridge, MA: Harvard University Press.

Latour, B. (1994). *We have never been modern.* Harvest Wheatsheaf, Hertfordshire.

Leidner, D., & Jarvenpaa, S. (1995). The use of information technology to enhance management school education: A theoretical view. *MIS Quarterly*, Sept.

Lektorsky, V. A. (1984). *Subject, object, cognition.* Moscow: Progress.

Leont'ev, A. N. (1978). *Activity, consciousness, and personality.* Engelwood Cliffs, NJ: Prentice-Progress.

Leont'ev, A. N. (1981). *Problems of the development of the mind.* Moscow: Progress.

Marx, K., & Engels, F. (1968). *The German ideology.* Moscow: Progress.

Marks, M., Mathieu, J., & Zaccaro, S. (2001). A temporally based framework and taxonomy of team processes. *Academy of Management Review, 26*, 356-376.

Mead, G. H. (1938). *The philosophy of act.* Chicago: University of Chicago Press.

Schon, D. A. (1983). *The reflective practitioner.* New York :Basic Books, Inc.

Schutz, W. (1958). *Firo: A three-dimensional theory of interpersonal behavior.* New York: Holt, Rinehart, and Winston.

Seifert, T. (2004). Understanding student motivation. *Educational Research, 46*, 137-149.

Suchman, L. A. (1987). *Plans and situated actions: The problem of human-machine communication.* Cambridge: Cambridge University Press, .

Vygosky, L. S. (1978). *Mind in society.* Cambridge, MA: Harvard University Press.

Vygotsky, L. S. (1981). The genesis of higher mental functions.I J. V. Wertsch (Ed.), *The concept of activity in Soviet psychology,* (pp. 144-188), Armonk: M.E. Sharpe.

Wenger, E. (1999). *Communities of practice: Learning, meaning and identity.* Cambridge University Press.

Wertsch, J. V. (1990). *Voices of the mind.* Cambridge, MA: Harvard University Press.

Wittgenstein, L. (1953). *Philosophical investigations.* London: Basil Blackwell.

Wyeld, T. G., Prasolova-Førland, E., & Chang, T-W. (2006, July 5-7). Virtually collaborating across cultures: A case study of an online theatrical performance in a 3DCVE spanning three continents. In *Proceedings of the International Conference on Advanced Learning Technologies,* Kerkrade, Netherlands: IEEE CS Press.

KEY TERMS

Activity Theory: A theory based on the notion that all activities are mediated by the tools or artifacts used in work practices, and that these tools or artifacts are specific to particular cultures and the culture of that work practice.

Artifact: An artifact, in the context of AT, is a tool, object or concept used to mediate an activity. It may be a physical object, textual or visual rule or protocol, or tacit understanding.

Cross-Cultural: Each workplace activity generates its own cultural understandings within its specific cultural context. Workers or learners invest capital in adopting, adapting, exchanging and sharing these cultural understandings over time.

Learning Community: A learning community is a community that progresses through cycles of learning together. Albeit at different rates, collectively the community shares a common learning trajectory.

Object-Oriented Activities: Activities that involve the shared manipulation of artifacts.

Shared Repertoire: A term used to describe the shared, negotiated meanings at the core of learning in a social context.

Chapter XIV
Interaction, Imagination and Community Building at the Math Forum

Wesley Shumar
Drexel University, USA

ABSTRACT

This chapter draws upon contemporary social theory to make an argument about the ways that teachers create personalized communities of practice at The Math Forum, an online educational resource center. The discussion of social networks and personalized community is brought into dialogue with sociologically oriented strands of math education research to suggest that the collaborative community building work that Math Forum teachers do online allows them to not only form a learning community but allows them to overcoming tensions around mathematical identity formation which are important for advancing one's thinking as a math teacher. The chapter discusses some of the interview data conducted with math forum teachers and the importance of that information for the future of teacher professional development and the way an online community can support teacher learning.

INTRODUCTION

This chapter focuses on research among teachers using The Math Forum, http://mathforum.org/. Over the last ten years data has been collected on teachers using The Math Forum through, focus groups, observation of classroom and laboratory usage of the site, and in-depth interviews with teachers about their usage of technology in general and The Math Forum specifically[1]. The research has focused on the efforts to understand the ways teachers have used and continue to use The Math Forum Site.

Further, the research into teacher usage of the site has identified ways in which teachers creatively imagine themselves and others to: support their own intellectual development, establish "communities of practice" to which they can contribute, negotiate different worldviews between their local school communities and members of the online community, and look at effective ways to find and share resources, and get help and support that they need while dealing with the contextual impediments they face.

The chapter is organized around a set of different theoretical ideas. First it looks at the ideas put forth by Barry Wellman (2001) and his colleagues (Quan-Haase & Wellman, forthcoming; Wellman, Quan-Haase, Boase & Chen, 2002) that new informational technologies are allowing people to reorganize their social lives in new ways and have greater control over crafting "personalized communities" that can be spatial distributed but still very much part of a person's everyday world. Wellman's ideas are brought into dialogue with the work of Paul Cobb and his colleagues (Cobb & Hodge, 2003; Cobb & McClain, 2003) as well as those of James Greeno and James Gee who have all been working on the notion of negotiation of identity as part of the classroom learning process. Finally the chapter draws on the community of practice literature to suggest that the personalization of community and the identity transformations take part in groups that are organized around education practices and specifically those of teaching. It is suggested that interactive digital libraries like The Math Forum create unique opportunities to support the boundary crossing and identity work that can not only be successful for student learners but can support teachers in their movement from novice to expert, from peripheral community member to leader.

The chapter moves from a theoretical discussion about the contemporary social context of developed nations to a discussion of the potential of interactive digital libraries like The Math Forum in this social context. The chapter then moves to the research at The Math Forum, which demonstrates that there are profound interactional possibilities for education brought about by the new informa-

tion technologies that can add dimensions the classroom does not allow. Finally the discussion returns to the issue of virtual community and the affordances created by the new generation of "interactive digital libraries" that are being created for teachers and students and offers a bit of hope to the more dystopic views of information technology and rise of performativity (Ball, 2000; Lyotard, 1984).

INDIVIDUALIZED COMMUNITIES

Barry Wellman is a sociologist and a network theorist who argues that the new information infrastructure that has created the Internet, mobile telephony and other wireless communications has changed the nature of how social groups are organized. In general he has argued that groups are in decline and personalized networks are taking their place.

Part of the argument that Wellman is making is about the changing nature of communities due to information technology. Communities are less bound by space and time and are now increasingly "flexible" with boundaries that can be stretched by many different forms of communication technologies that allow for "at a distance" synchronous or asynchronous communication (Wellman, 2001; Shumar & Renninger, 2002). These more flexible communities can involve combinations of virtual and face-to-face interaction. They can also come together for a variety of reasons from those that are local political entities to groups bound together by common interests.

Another part of the argument Wellman is making is about the "personalized networking" that is at the core of the new more flexible forms of community. One example of this process that we could point to is the way telephony is changing due to the introduction of new technology and how those changes are emblematic of changes in the nuclear family.

In the twentieth century, the telephone has played a big part in the social landscape and the way people are able to interact. It has certainly changed the way families, businesses and other groups communicate with each other (Fischer, 1992). By the mid-twentieth century one stable pattern of middle class family interaction was the family phone. A family would have one phone number and often one phone attached to that number. In this way the telephone was part of the infrastructure that helped to define the nuclear family. The telephone number was part of what defined the boundary of that family. Different parts of the extended family would have their own numbers and usually be located in different dwellings.

By the late twentieth century we see this pattern changing even before the widespread use of cell phones with many nuclear households having two, three and even more "lines" some being dedicated to individuals and some being dedicated to equipment like faxes and computers. Finally with the widespread adoption of the cell phone, we now see the individual, and their related individual phone number, becoming a separate node in a much more diffuse pattern of family networking. The cell phone and the personal phone number is becoming, for the individual, the way they manage their relationship with a number of primary social groups as well as with other information services. And what we see in this process, as Wellman suggests, is the rise of a personalized network and the decline of the more traditional bounded group, "the family". It is important to point out, as Fischer (1992, p. 16-20) does when talking about the history of the telephone, that it is not the technology that causes these changes, but rather the way these new technologies get socially constructed and for forms of sociability that grow out of those constructions.

Wellman's notion of the rise of "personalized networking" is related to other ideas in social theory such as the notion of the risk society and reflexive modernization (Beck, 1992; Beck, Gid-dens & Lash, 1994) the idea of liquid modernity (Bauman, 2000) as well as current thinking about individualization and globalization (Appadurai, 1996; Beck & Beck-Gernsheim, 2002; Castells, 1996; Held & McGrew, 2003; Sassen, 1998, 2000). Several distinct "risks" come together in this literature. First is the risks produced by modern society. Society is capable of putting people at great risk through industrial pollution, weapons of mass destruction, bio-engineering, etc. Further, we have a much greater ability to calculate and assess risks, both those that are produced by the modern industrial society, as well as those produced by nature. Finally the conditions in contemporary society have tended to atomize the individual and limit the ability of people to form social groups. Without strong social groups the risks people face must be faced alone without the support of collective entities to lobby the powerful for resources that might help mitigate difficult circumstance. So then much of this literature is a lamentation of the loss of collective social power. The risk society also is one where there is an increasing ideological turn to neo liberal economic ideas and social Darwinist notions of the individual in competition for survival. Today there are many collective problems shared by members of particular social groups, but unlike the trade union movement of the 19th and first half of the 20th centuries, these problems are not experienced collectively. They are private problems where individuals feel they must come up with private solutions (Bauman 2000:58). The solutions individuals explore exist within a reified universe where knowledge is disconnected from the social context of its production. The individual feels that the solution to life's work problems is really just a matter of picking the right set of information products. And so the commodification and marketization of the knowledge products play right into this more private world where there is no collective social action only things that seem to have a magical power of their own.

Without needing to negate the above critique of contemporary society, there are many other consequences of the information revolution that might be to the advantage of individuals and allow for new kinds of social groups. Linking Wellman's work and the data that has come from research we have done at The Math Forum to these theories is important because, while it is true that much of the current condition is problematic, there is a need to see social change more dialectically and to see that there are contradictions. The Math Forum research points to potential upsides of the current state of technological development and use. This chapter began with Wellman's analysis of the opportunities afforded to the individual to shape a community to her/his own set of personal needs. Burrows and Nettleton (2002) in a recent article demonstrate how individuals who are facing serious health risks can leverage the Internet and form communities for support and information. This is important because in the past, for many rarer illnesses, an individual might not be able to meet enough people who share their problems. But the Internet allows a space/time compression (Harvey 1999) that makes communities at a distance practical and useful. Further, what Burrows and Nettleton describe is an online Community of Practice. New individuals can come to the community and get introduced to people who have already been in this community for some time. Older members will share information and socialize the new members into the community itself. As new members become more seasoned members of the group they will have a lot more information to share with the next generation of newcomers.

It is this more positive side of the information society and reflexive modernization that is seen at educational sites like The Math Forum. Further I would like to suggest that the Internet not only can bring people together who are at a distance, but its most profound potential for learning is the potential to create a context where learners can creatively overcome their own resistances to

learning as they re-imagine themselves and the community of practice to which they belong and rethink their identities as learners and knowledgeable community members (Wenger, 1998; Anderson, 1991). These new "utopian" possibilities brought about by the information revolution are extremely important given the kinds of risks that are created by contemporary society. People will need to be able to expand their knowledge base and creatively redefine the groups they work with in order to struggle with some of the problems brought about by the "risk society". This work also offers a potential important corrective to those who have been thinking about the disciplinary technologies of performativity (Ball, 2000; Roberts, 1998; Lyotard, 1984). This idea is something we will return to in the conclusion.

In order to make the above argument I will spend a little time talking about Paul Cobb's work on the social context of learning. While much of Cobb's work focuses on students, I am going to apply these ideas to the teachers that have been studied at The Math Forum. Cobb's thinking about identity work fits very well with the patterns of interaction we see at The Math Forum and I would argue that digital libraries like The Math Forum have unique potential for allowing individuals to do the identity work necessary for learning. These ideas also have profound implications for thinking about social groups, culture and the individual.

Drawing on Gee (2002) and Boaler and Greeno (2000) among others Cobb and his colleagues' work with students has shown that the normative identities promoted by schools are often in conflict with the core identities of students and it is the work of what he calls the personal identity to struggle between the normative and the core identities (Cobb & Hodge, 2003). In this way student work in class is a process of social construction and one with a good deal of conflict. I would argue that this process described by Cobb and his colleagues is useful not only for classroom students but for all types of learners. And it is a very nice model for thinking about some of the cognitive processes that might go on in an individual when they face a learning situation. It nicely describes the psychology of resistance so much explored in the sociology of education literature.

Similarly Cobb and McClain (2003) argue that teachers are constrained by institutions and their structural context and we have to see the problems with teacher learning as one of overcoming these structural constraints. While these structural constraints are not always directly about teacher learning, they often involve some of the same issues. In our interviews with teachers working with The Math Forum, many teachers talked about how onerous teacher professional development was. Many teachers engaged in classic forms of school resistance when dealing with their own professional development. And there were of course good reasons for this, the programs were often district driven and had little to do with the teacher's perceived needs. Teachers will often work around these official efforts to improve their skills and come up with their own creative solutions to learning needs. Many times in our research we saw teachers use the resources and groups at The Math Forum as means of informal professional development. In doing this they generated personal networks of colleagues that become communities that they learned with.

Cobb's work demonstrates that central to the process of learning for teachers (as well as students) is a process of boundary crossing and identity work where one has to safely imagine oneself as a valuable member of a community of practice in order to collaboratively construct knowledge with other. In this way the individual's knowledge will grow rather than being channeled into a struggle to maintain an identity in the face of an uncaring system. Wenger (1998) in his work has suggested that identity work is also a central part of a community of practice. Communities of practice negotiate meaning in the process of training and share of knowledge and in the process of producing new knowledge. That process

of meaning production involves identity at both the individual and collective levels.

To close this section of the chapter the work of Wellman and Cobb and their colleagues is consistent with developments in the area of cognitive anthropology (Strauss and Quinn, 1997; D'Andrade, 1995; Shore, 1996). The anthropological work and its thinking about the relationship between individuals and culture is valuable for this discussion and something we will return to in the analysis portion of the chapterr. In general this work suggests that cultures are not internally homogeneous entities with clear simple boundaries. But rather they are overlapping sets of habitual ways of thinking and acting that reside in the heads of the individuals who participate in these worlds. The potential of interactive digital libraries then is to help people create new forms of community and culture that will allow them to enhance their own learning as they better negotiate traditional structural impediments to individual development.

MATH FORUM TEACHERS

Below are four brief stories about how teachers have used the Math Forum site. These stories, three about individual teachers, and one about a group of teacher in a larger Math Forum project will give a glimpse into some of ways The Math Forum is being used by teachers for their own personal development. It should be said at the outset that what makes The Math Forum interesting is that it was an early digital library starting before the beginning of the Web. It has grown to be a huge resource with millions of pages in the library, very busy well-known interactive services (i.e., Problem of the Week services, Ask Dr. Math), and many discussion groups that are hosted on the site. It is a very rich interactive space.

Further, the vision of The Math Forum has been one that has been very successful for fostering communities of practice. When talking with the director of The Math Forum he pointed out that the community results from people doing things together. People want the ability to do purposeful meaningful activities that they perceive as needed. They don't come together to form community for communities sake, but because these technologies help meet a need that might be otherwise difficult to meet. It is important to note that The Math Forum is an organization that has focused on the creative use of new technologies in order to help people work together on the math they want to do. Because of that focus on human activity they have avoided some of the fetishism of the technology and the ideas of virtual community that some other groups have fallen into. For The Math Forum, activities that people need to do leads to community and not the other way around. Below are some samples of the creative ways that some teachers used both the resources and the community of practice they found at the Math Forum.

One teacher we spoke with used The Math Forum to enhance his network of colleagues and then shared that network with his local faculty. He was a new high school math teacher with less than two years of teaching experience. He had recently graduated from a prestigious university and had a very strong background in math. He used The Math Forum site for math resources and, like all the teachers we talked to, thought the collection of resources on the site was tremendous. But what this young recent graduate lacked was an extended network of colleagues with whom he could discuss pedagogical and curricular activities. His math faculty was a very active group that had regular discussions about issues they were facing and at the time that we talked to our informant they happened to be very involved in a pedagogic discussion about how to teach certain concepts to kids, make it real for them, and keep their attention. Of course our young teacher had little to contribute to this discussion and felt less useful to the group. He hit on the idea of taking the issues in the discussion and sharing them

online with teachers in one of the discussion groups hosted on The Math Forum site. He then took ideas from that conversation and brought them back to his faculty. His faculty, who were in general older, was very impressed both with the new ideas as well as with his technological skills and expanded network of colleagues.

This story is a nice example of the kinds of re-imagination of one's "personal community" as well as a re-imagination of the self that is made possible by the Internet and rich interactive digital libraries such as The Math Forum. This teacher, while he had little personal experience teaching, could draw on a large number of people who had much more experience. And the people in The Math Forum discussion were interested in his faculty's issues because they were pedagogical issues that many people shared. Further, the culture of "generalized reciprocity" (Kollack, 1999) on the Internet is such that many contributors to discussion forums believe that contributing value to the discussion will ultimately be in their own enlightened self interest (Putnam, 2000). That is to say that they too will benefit from the ideas shared by the community. The last point I would like to make here is that The Math Forum creates a discussion space where, like the local café, people can talk about issues that concern them and get to some detail about teaching and learning, where the profession development in their schools might be a good bit more instrumental.

Many of the teachers we have spoken to, especially the elementary and middle school teachers but even some of the high school teachers, felt particularly nervous about their math abilities. Math is a field that is very logical and hierarchically organized in terms of its concepts so it is easy to feel inadequate. Further, there is a folk mythology that surrounds math in many math departments that says you are either good at math or you are not. Learning math is often seen as an issue of basic ability and not good teaching. Consequently, because of that mythology many math teachers have not been taught well themselves. For these teachers The Math Forum site is a safe place to get math resources and to ask questions from people who are not in one's immediate network. For example, another teacher we talked to had taught algebra in her high school and thought of herself as an algebra teacher. She was assigned a geometry class one year and was very nervous about teaching geometry because she felt she was not as strong in that area of math. She also did feel safe sharing her feelings of inadequacy with her local faculty, after all these were the people who were evaluating her performance. So she turned to The Math Forum and both began to look for resources but also people who she could ask for help when there were things that she was unsure of. This scaffold that The Math Forum provided allowed her to increase her knowledge, be more confident about her geometry skills and in a sense to be mentored as she was developing a new area in her teaching.

Of course in principle, there is no reason why her school should not have a mentoring program and help her in that was as well. But often the structural constraints of local institutions are such that they are not that interested or knowledgeable about mentoring and helping teachers develop in ways that the teacher needs. They are often very good however at summative evaluation and assessments of weaknesses. This is a fact that drives both students and teachers underground not wanting to have their inadequacies publicly acknowledged. Once an individual gets stigmatized as "not good at math" or "not good at geometry" it is very difficult to overcome that stigma (Goffman, 1963). Here is where a different kind of community, one that offers more anonymity but also one that offers a more apprenticeship model of learning can be a great advantage for the learner. There are much fewer risks of stigma and hence the identity shifts discussed by Cobb that need to be negotiated become much easier.

This second story illustrates an important facet of The Math Forum culture (Renninger and Shumar 2004). The Math Forum understands that

schools are often not good contexts for learning. Schools are the site of what Cobb calls normative identities. They are the site of bureaucratic expectation of correct performances. And further this situation has just gotten worse. And this is perhaps because schools are more bureaucratic and too imbalanced toward reification (Wenger 1998). The discourse around school reform has brought with it a language of outcomes and accountability. In that context it becomes very difficult for teachers to discuss their weaknesses and pursue a genuine path of professional development.

Schlager and Fusco (2004) point out that while there is a lot of talk about communities of practice in schools, there are few examples of such communities. In a related way, Lave (1997) talks about how in schools there is the dominant discourse of "acquisition" and how that discourse fails to focus on the importance of an integrated practice. She reports on a study that shows that even when learning specific math techniques from teacher's instruction the children fail to integrate this learning. Lave's point is that the problems that the students do need to be integrated into the community and that only community problems as ones that people learn and hold on to.

The Math Forum is set up specifically to be the opposite of this kind of bureaucratic assessment. The Math Forum focuses on process of learning by fostering a genuine mathematic discourse that is integrated as much as possible into people's lives and the everyday activities they engage in. Mathematical thinking is encouraged and individuals are provided with the necessary scaffolds to grow their knowledge (Renninger and Shumar 2002).

A third teacher we talked with was a long-term substitute teacher in an elementary school. He worked in an area where there was little demand to hire new teachers and so there was little hope of a permanent job without relocation. In his school he had become sort of the informal technical person and had found a niche for himself supporting other teachers' technical needs. This teacher found The Math Forum useful in several ways. The resources and services on The Math Forum site were something that he could point students, parents and other teachers too in order to help develop their math understanding. His knowledge of The Math Forum site made him a kind of local mentor for the whole community. At the same time he found a community of long-term substitute teachers he could talk with online. This group became one that shared the experience of being a more marginalized school community member as well as discussed strategies for achieving more permanent employment. In this example the teacher both found a community online that shared his circumstances, but he also increased in local value and found a place in his existing school community by being the local technical expert with the resources to help the whole community out.

The final example in this section is a group of teachers who came together to work on a Math Forum project called Bridging Research and Practice (BRAP). The BRAP project was one where seven middle school teachers came together to work with Math Forum staff to link current research in math education to their practice. The final result of the project was a videopaper about the group's exploration of research and practice (http://mathforum.org/brap). The BRAP group met face-to-face several times over the three years of the project. But much of their work was done remotely using instant message meeting sessions and through email. There are many things that came out of that project[2] but the one thing I would like to talk about here is the group's reflection on their different expertise. Initially when the group met there was a sense that some members were better in math than others and they seemed to be the natural leaders of the group. But as they continued to work together they discovered many new things about their own practice. They found that sometimes the strong in math were not as strong in pedagogy and that those with less ability in math had things to teach those who were strong.

They also learned that some of their colleagues were very good with technology and others were not. They learned a whole host of other things about people's time to put into projects, which was more and less organized. They also learned that they all needed help with research and writing and depended upon Math Forum staff for support in these areas.

In a very real way this group became a very interesting learning community where all of the members got a great deal out of the group's interaction. They became for each other a group of colleagues who were very important to their own intellectual development and the experience was much more powerful than most local faculty development. While this group met face-to-face, they were very much a virtual community. The level of closeness they achieved was only possible with the virtual communication tools and the scaffolding organized through The Math Forum. The BRAP group illustrated one of the important features of the way many people use advanced communication technologies. They used these tools and the virtual site of The Math Forum as a way to increase the frequency and depth of their interactions. This allowed them to work more closely and get more from working with each other.

DISCUSSION

Each of the above examples from research on teachers at The Math Forum was chosen to illustrate some of the patterns of interaction that have been seen in the research. These patterns have profound implications for the potential of interactive digital libraries like The Math Forum to support teacher and student learning. Each case involved ways in which individuals "imagine the other", make realizations about the potential for new kinds of group boundaries and ways to cross group boundaries, and how they can negotiate their identity in this process. The identity negotiation process is critical for learning in that the learner must come to think about her/himself and their place in the learning community differently[3]. Further this work illustrates some of the ways that the new definition of culture coming out of cognitive anthropology is very valuable for understand the new relationship of individual to group made possible by the Internet.

In each of the individual case examples discussed above, there is some way in which the individual finds their local community problematic and they see the need to go outside of that group. In it often because the individual perceives themselves or the group to be inadequate, so in our first example the teacher felt he did not have the teaching experience to bring to the faculty meetings, the second teacher felt her skills were not up to par and it was not safe to share that, and the third teacher was marginalized by his long term substitute status. At a deeper level one could say that in each of the examples the individuals were part of a reified bureaucracy where they were unable to engage in an authentic practice that would enable their own learning and that of their students. And in each of these cases the individual uses the communities and resources available at The Math Forum to not only expand redefine their own communities of practice but also to transform their identities with new assets that allow them to be new members of their face-to face communities.

In the BRAP example we see a slightly different variation on this process. Here we have not focused on the limitation of their home communities that has brought these teachers together, but rather on the kinds of "at a distance" collaborative workgroups that can get established and then again on the identity transformation process is that is possible when one has the power to define the groups one is a member of and shape the way they interact with these groups.

If we can return for moment to the work of Wenger, Gee, Cobb, and their colleagues discussed in the beginning of the paper we can now understand why interactive digital libraries like The Math Forum can be so powerful. Critical to the learning process in this model is getting around the normative identities that as shaped by the institutions individuals find themselves in. Often these normative expectations do not fit with individual's core identities and so the result is stigma, feelings of inadequacy, fear, hiding, and forms of resistance. An option that often doesn't exist for individuals in their institutional context is look outside their home institution to transform their identity[4].

In order to understand the boundary-crossing potentials of The Math Forum, work in cognitive anthropology (Lave, 1993, 1997; Shore, 1996; Holland, D., Lachicotte, W. Jr., Skinner, D., & Cain, C., 1998; Strauss & Quinn, 1997) and symbolic anthropology (Barth, 1981; Cohen, 1985) can be used to talk about the ways communities are symbolically constructed and the ways actors use these symbolic boundaries to define inside and outside. These ideas are critical in understanding teacher interaction on the Math Forum site where there are multiple ways inside and outside operate. There is both inside and outside The Math Forum and specific groups and areas of the site but there is also inside and outside each individual's professional worlds.

In earlier work at the Math Forum (Shumar & Renninger, 2002; Renninger & Shumar, 2004) we have talked about the way social anthropologists like Fredrik Barth and Anthony Cohen have pointed out that the symbolic boundary that defines a specific group is often very fluid and something that tends to be used politically. Very often the administration of a school will refer to "the faculty" as a homogeneous group, but the faculty themselves often see more subtle divisions between themselves. These boundaries tend to be used by individuals and groups to do the social work they feel needs to be done. And so a greater ability to play with boundaries make them more flexible gives individuals more opportunities to move within an institutional context. In the specific examples we have seen here The Math Forum has allowed for a greater personalization of the pedagogic interaction and allowed for ways that traditional hierarchical relations between say between younger faculty and older faculty or faculty and administrator to be transformed into a more egalitarian interaction. This is perhaps one of the more utopian possibilities that Bernstein (1996) discusses in his work or what Lifton (1993) has referred to as "protean possibilities".

Further, the Math Forum allows for multiple channels of parallel interaction, (e.g. IM, email, synchronous and asynchronous discussion groups, archived interactions) which can be used by the faculty member or student to complicate interaction in important ways. Teachers seek information and ideas as they grow out of interest and this greatly enhance the potential motivation for learning. At the same time, the lack of "bandwidth" on the Internet gives individuals at the Math Forum a level of anonymity that allows them to escape from some forms of power relationships. Individuals can re-position (Harré and Van Langenhove, 1991) themselves in relation to authority figures making it possible to escape some of the negative implications of hierarchical authority relationships in learning situations (Shumar & Renninger, 2002).

These creative potentials are also about the way that groups and cultures can be transformed in the process. Contemporary cognitive anthropology has suggested that our traditional understandings of culture are false and that we need new ways to understand what culture is and how it works. In the past when we used culture we tended to see it as an internally homogenous set of norms, values, beliefs, practices and etc. And so the culture of school X would be seen in this way. But culture is not a uniform set of ideas that exists in the ether, rather it is a set of habitual practices and the mental ideas associated with those practices that tend to cluster in groups of individuals (Strauss & Quinn, 1997, p. 7). That means that culture is both inside individuals' heads and outside in the

world. It also means that cultures are overlapping and can be contested. And so potentially the culture of resistance held by a group of teachers in a school is at odds with the culture of professional development promoted by the institution. Knowing that culture and community are both mental and physical sites of contestation allows us to see why new communication technologies can be so powerful for the individual.

While there continues to be a lot of discussion of virtual community in the literature, the Math Forum is one of the most unique educational sites for online community development. The teacher projects and groups that have developed at The Math Forum have demonstrated that individuals can shape their own communities and develop a sense of attachment to each other. Further that attachment existed in a context where the products of their work had high social value. With their emphasis on creative learning through personal interaction, the Math Forum staff encourages teachers not to reify the goals of their activity but to focus on the activity itself.

Through their online activities at The Math Forum teachers are able to not only transform themselves as they creatively change the social context in which they are learning but also change the cultures that they are part of. They are able to confront the weaknesses in their own training or teaching style, seek help from others, become empowered and contribute to this community. These changes are then ones that help teachers confront their students' needs as well. The empowerment of teachers that has been documented on The Math Forum site has important implications for student learning as well.

CONCLUSION

The theoretical implications of the research at The Math Forum for thinking about the present state of reflexive modernization are also important. They will only be briefly discussed here but deserve a much wider treatment in the future. As discussed in the first part of the chapter, much of the literature around the "risk society", "liquid modernity" or "performativity" focus on the dystopic potential of the new ways society is organized and the new technologies for disciplinary control of human subjects. Lyotard (1984) suggests in The Postmodern Condition that knowledge will be commodified and reduced to forms that can be transferred from point to point effectively through computer networks and used to produce profit. Traditional liberal ideas about teaching and learning will be lost in the new world of accountability. All that will matter are the instrumental gains that can be made through the movement of knowledge products (Lyotard 1984, Roberts 1998). Ball (2003) suggests that in this process the identities of teachers will be transformed as they will be disciplined into being workers who are accountable for the improved scoring of their students on standardized performance measure, rather than mentors and thinkers who support the development of a student's potential. In sort education will stop being educative (Dewey, 1938).

Certainly we are beginning to see these instrumental forces operate in educational institutions worldwide. We are also seeing them in legislation like the No Child Left Behind Act in the United States. Ironically, while these forces are affecting the practices of teachers and students in brick and mortar schools, they Internet and online educational communities like The Math Forum are in a place to resist these practices and provide opportunities for people to think learn and grow in ways that are becoming harder in face-to-face locations.

Contrary to the Lyotardian vision of computers and the Internet as sounding the final death knell and being the replacement technology for the traditional teacher, I would argue the Internet has created the potential for an interesting site of resistance to some of the forces of performativity and allows for a kind of thinking and learning that is more difficult now in many face-to-face school sites. As Mark Poster (2001) suggests in 'What's the Matter with the Internet?' the Internet by its organization tends to make communication and the sharing of information free and easy. In this way the Internet tends to run against the issues of the culture of consumption, profit making and instrumentality. It has a much greater potential for democratic community building and the enhancing of sharing of thoughts and ideas across distances. But as Fischer (1992) points out, these potentials of technologies are tied up with the histories of use, development and control so any future is possible. It will be up to people and organizations to both individual and collectively craft communities of practice where the practices that teachers and students engage in are connected directly to their collective work and where participation is the central way that learning takes place in these online communities.

REFERENCES

Appadurai, A. (1996). *Modernity at large: Cultural dimensions of globalization*. Minneapolis, MN: University of Minnesota Press.

Ball, S. J. (2000). Performativities and fabrications in the education economy: Towards the performative society. *Australian Educational Researcher, 27*(2), 119-129.

Ball, S. J. (2003). *Class strategies and the education market: The middle classes and social advantage*. London, New York: Routledge Falmer.

Barth, F. (1981). *Process and form in social life*. Boston: Routledge & Kegan Paul.

Bauman, Z. (2000). *Liquid modernity*. Cambridge: Polity Press, Malden, MA: Blackwell.

Beck, U. (1992). *Risk society: Towards a new modernity*. (Translated by Mark Ritter). London, Newbury Park: Sage Publications.

Beck, U., & Beck-Gernsheim, E. (2002). *Individualization: Institutionalized individualism and its social and political consequences.* London: Thousand Oaks: SAGE.

Beck, U., Giddens, A., & Lash, S. (1994). *Reflexive modernization: Politics, tradition and aesthetics in the modern social order.* Stanford: Stanford University Press.

Bernstein, B. (1996). *Pedagogy, symbolic control, and identity: Theory, research, critique.* London, Bristol, PA: Taylor & Francis.

Boaler, J., & Greeno, J. G. (2000). *Identity, agency, and knowing in mathematical worlds.* In J. Boaler (Ed.), *Multiple perspectives on mathematics teaching and learning* (pp. 171-200). Stamford, CT: Ablex.

Bourdieu, P. (1977). *Outline of a theory of practice.* Richard Nice, Trans. New York, NY: Cambridge University Press.

Bourdieu, P. (1980). *The logic of practice.* Stanford, CA: Stanford University Press.

Castells, M. (1996). *The rise of the network society.* Cambridge, MA: Blackwell Publishers.

Cohen, A. (1985). *The symbolic construction of community.* London: Tavistock Publications.

Cobb, P. & Hodge, L. L. (2003 April 23). *Students' construction of identities as doers of mathematics in the context of statistical data analysis.* Talk presented as part of the session Identity, Equity and Mathematical Learning in the Context of Statistical Data. Chicago, IL. American Educational Research Association.

Cobb, P., & McClain, K. (2003, April 24). *Situating teachers instructional practices in the institutional setting of the school and school district.* Talk presented as part of the session, Supporting and Sustaining the Learning of Professional Teaching Communities in the Institutional Setting of the School and School District. Chicago, IL. American Educational Research Association.

D'Andrade, R. (1995). *The development of cognitive anthropology.* Cambridge: Cambridge University Press.

Dewey, J. (1938). *Experience and education.* New York: The Macmillan Company.

Fischer, C. S. (1992). *America calling: A social history of the telephone to 1940.* Berkeley: University of California Press.

Gee, J. P. (2002). Literacies, identities, and discourses. In M. J. Schleppegrell & M. C. Colombi (Eds.) *Developing advanced literacy in first and second languages: Meaning with power.* Mahwah, NJ: Lawrence Erlbaum Associates.

Goffman, E. (1963). *Stigma: Notes on the management of spoiled identity.* Englewood Cliffs, NJ: Prentice-Hall.

Harré, R., & Van Langenhove, L. (1991). Varieties of positioning. *Journal for the Theory of Social Behavior, 21*(4), 393-407.

Held, D., & McGrew, A. (2003). *The global transformations reader: An introduction to the globalization debate.* Cambridge: Polity Press in association with Blackwell Pub.; Malden, MA: Distributed in the USA by Blackwell Pub.

Holland, D., Lachicotte, W. Jr., Skinner, D., & Cain, C. (1998). *Identity and agency in cultural worlds.* Cambridge, MA: Harvard University Press.

Lave, J. (1993). The practice of learning. In S. Chaiklin & J. Lave (Eds.), *Understanding practice: Perspectives on activity and context.* New York: Cambridge University Press.

Lave, J. (1997). The culture of acquisition and the practice of understanding. In D. Kirschner & J. A. Whitson (Eds.), *Situated cognition: Social, semiotic and psychological perspectives.* Mahwah, NJ: Lawrence Erlbaum Associates, Inc.

Lave, J., & Wenger, E. (1991). *Situated learning: Legitimate peripheral participation.* New York: Cambridge University Press.

Lifton, R. J. (1993). *The protean self: Human resilience in an age of fragmentation.* New York: Basic Books.

Lyotard, J-F. (1984). *The postmodern condition: A report on knowledge.* Minneapolis: University of Minnesota Press.

Quan-Haase, A., & Wellman, B. (forthcoming). How does the Internet affect social capital? In M. Huysman, & V. Wulf, (Eds.), *IT and social capital.*

Putnam, R. D. (2000). *Bowling alone: The collapse and revival of American community.* New York: Simon and Schuster.

Renninger, K. A., & Shumar, W. (2002). Community building with and for teachers: *The Math Forum* as a resource for teacher professional development. In K. A. Renninger & W. Shumar (Eds.), *Building virtual communities: Learning and change in cyberspace.* New York: Cambridge University Press.

Renninger, K. A., & Shumar, W. (2004). The centrality of culture and community to participant learning at and with The Math Forum. In S. Barab, J. Grey, & R. Kling, (Eds.), *Designing Virtual Communities.* New York: Cambridge University Press.

Roberts, P. (1998). Rereading Lyotard: Knowledge, commodification and higher education. *Electronic Journal of Sociology* 3(3) Special issue, April 1998, http://www.sociology.org/content/vol003.003/roberts.html

Sassen, S. (1998). *Globalization and its discontents: Essays on the new mobility of people and money.* New York: New Press.

Sassen, S. (2000). Spatialities and temporalities of the global: elements for a theorization. *Public Culture,12*(1), 215-232.

Schlager, M. S., & Fusco, J. (2004). Teacher professional development, technology, and communities of practice: Are we putting the cart before the horse? In S. A. Barab, R. Kling, & J. H. Gray (Eds.), *Designing for virtual communities in the service of learning* (pp. 120-153). New York: Cambridge University Press.

Shore, B. (1996). *Culture in mind: Cognition, culture and the problem of meaning.* New York: Oxford University Press.

Shumar, W., & Renninger, K. A. (2002). On community building. In K. A. Renninger & W. Shumar (Eds.), *Building virtual communities: Learning and change in cyberspace.* New York: Cambridge University Press.

Shumar, W., & Sarmiento, J. (2008). Communities of Practice at the Math Forum: Supporting teachers as professionals. In P. Hildreth, & C. Kimble, (Eds.), *Communities of practice: Creating learning environments for educators,* (pp. 223-239). Hershey, PA: IGI Global Publishing.

Strauss, C. & Quinn, N. (1997). *A cognitive theory of cultural meaning.* New York: Cambridge University Press.

Wellman, B. (2001). Physical place and CyberPlace: The rise of personalized networking. *International Journal of Urban and Regional Research, 25.*

Wellman, B., Quan-Haase, A., Boase, J., & Chen, W. (2002). *Examining the Internet in everyday life.* Keynote address given by B. Wellman to the Euricom Conference on e-democracy. Nijmegen, Netherlands, October, 2002.

Wenger, E. (1998). *Communities of practice: Learning, meaning, and identity.* Cambridge, UK: Cambridge University Press.

ENDNOTES

[1] Data was collected during the first three years of The Math Forum's funding with NSF (grant number) and then through subsequent projects, BRAP (grant #) and the ESCOT project (Grant #).

[2] For a more detailed discussion of the BRAP project see Renninger, K. A. & Shumar, W. (2004).

[3] See Renninger and Shumar (2002) for another discussion of these issues.

[4] I've often thought about the status differences between faculty in higher education and faculty in k-12 education (at least in the US context). And it is interesting to note that higher education faculty do look to these external networks of colleagues for verification of their expertise much more. An educational anthropologist credentials may reside more with other educational anthropologists with whom the individual works with than with the anthropological colleagues at the home university. In this way negotiating identity in higher education allows for a lot more of the community boundary crossings that I am talking about than k-12 education offers at least so far.

Chapter XV
Designing
Practice–Oriented Interactive
Vocabularies for
Workflow–Based Virtual CoP

Demosthenes Akoumianakis
Technological Education Institution of Crete, Greece

Giannis Milolidakis
Technological Education Institution of Crete, Greece

George Vellis
Technological Education Institution of Crete, Greece

Dimitrios Kotsalis
Technological Education Institution of Crete, Greece

ABSTRACT

This chapter concentrates on the development of practice-specific toolkits for managing on-line practices in the context of virtual communities of practice. The authors describe two case studies in different application domains each presenting alternative but complementary insights to the design of computer-mediated practice vocabularies. The first case study describes how established practices in music performance are encapsulated in a suitably augmented music toolkit so as to facilitate the learning objectives of virtual teams engaged in music master classes. The second case study is slightly different in orientation as it seeks to establish a toolkit for engaging in new coordinative practices in the course of building information-based products such as vacation packages for tourists. This time the virtual team is a cross-organization virtual community of practice with members streamlining their efforts by internalizing and performing in accordance with the new practice. Collectively, the case studies provide insight to building novel practice-specific toolkits to either encapsulate existing or support novel practices.

INTRODUCTION

Several chapters in this book have addressed, explicitly or implicitly, the issue of what constitute the 'practice' elements in virtual communities of practice. As a result, a variety of research questions are raised which are seldom addressed in the relevant literature on virtual communities of practice. In this chapter, we will argue that community management is distinct and different from practicing. Moreover, our intention is to support the view that although community management fosters social tights, it is practicing in community settings that may lead to improved capacity, deepening of professional knowledge and innovation.

In general, defining practice is not trivial as there are alternative views and perspectives (i.e., sociology, organization and management science, philosophy) to frame the term. However, independently of theoretical standpoint there are some issues that seem to be common concerns for practice-oriented researchers. Firstly, practice is conceived of as activities or sets of activities. Such activities have to be meaningful for the people or the practice being analyzed. Thus, their object of reference, its symbolic manifestation and relational properties must be clearly defined and labeled so as to make sense. Secondly, activities embedded in or subsumed by practice are built on knowledge, skills or competences of those performing the activities or of the community in which the activities are performed. In turn, knowledge may be expressed through communication acts or codified into routines, procedures or patterns through which the world is made sense of. Thirdly, practices involve human agents who may share, obey and adhere to a designated practice without necessarily enacting it in the same manner. As a consequence practice articulation may vary according to cultural background, folklore knowledge and experience.

In this chapter we are concerned with the design of on-line collaborative practices for workflow-based communities of practice. The emphasis on workflow highlights intertwined activities and staged accomplishment of an engineering goal. Moreover, our objective is not to advance the theoretical thinking behind practice in general, how it is instituted and what effects it may have. Instead, we will concentrate on designing vocabularies for enacting either established or new practices. Specifically, we are equally interested on two issues, namely how practices are technologically mediated (i.e., enacted using dedicated software tools), as well as how new practices may arise and become institutionalized within a virtual community of practice. A related issue, briefly commented but not exhausted in the present context, is that of the interrelationship between on-line and off-line practices in virtual organizations.

The approach followed is to briefly review existing literature on collaborative practices to solicit requirements for designing practice-specific toolkits and then to present two case studies which provide a context for reflecting upon these requirements. It is worth clarifying from the start that although the two case studies are different in orientation and perspective, they share common engineering grounds with respect to how practice-specific toolkits are designed. Specifically, the case studies present alternative pathways towards expanding the design language of modern graphical toolkits to facilitate new types of interaction components and techniques for visualizing coordinative practice and collective artifacts. The experience gained from these case studies will then be consolidated into a few guidelines useful for developers of interactive practice-oriented toolkits.

UNDERSTANDING PRACTICE IN VIRTUAL COMMUNITIES

Practice is not easy to define formally as there is no unified theory of practice (see Schatzki et al. 2001). Nevertheless, there is a diverse and growing literature that has taken practice seriously from theoretical and philosophical standpoints (Lave and Wenger, 1991; Orlikowski, 2002; Jarzabkowski, 2005; Schmidt, 2000). Particularly useful with regard to the aims of the present work is the effort by some practice scholars to draw on activity theory (Engeström 1999) in order to conceptualize practice in terms of characteristic properties. Specifically, the activity theoretic view considers practice as subsuming activity. For example, Jarzabkowski in a series of published works (Jarzabkowski, 2003; Jarzabkowski, 2004; Jarzabkowski, 2005) makes a distinction between activity and practice defining activity as constituted by the actions of and interactions between actors as they perform their daily duties and roles, while practice is used to refer to activity patterns across actors, which provides order and meaning to a set of otherwise banal activities. Another characteristic of practice is that it is performative in the sense that it is accomplished by skilled actors who rely on both codified knowledge and experience to understand and assess how practices can be applied, altered or tailored in order to attain specific goals. In turn, the performative nature of practice affords variation in its enactment (Schmidt et al., 2007). Such variation may be attributed to institutional or technological factors. An illustrative example of how technology affects and in fact may change television practices is provided in Ducheneaut et

al. (2008), where the authors describe distributed, shared television viewing practices in the context of their SocialTV project and offer several guidelines for designing for sociability.

In light of the above and given the focus of this work on on-line collaborative practices in virtual communities of practice, we will adopt the normative perspective that practice represents the collective wisdom (habits, rules of thumb and socially-defined modes of acting) through which a community, be it professional with a shared interest on a topic such as accounting, medicine, landscape engineering, etc., or otherwise articulates common ground (i.e., processes, tools and artifacts). Practice may be manifested either as on-line or off-line praxis, with the two frequently being intertwined. On-line practices represent the information commons prevailing in networks of practice (Brown and Duguid, 2001; Duguid, 2005), especially when the members are not co-located, thus not interacting directly with one another because of geographical or organizational distance. Furthermore, on-line as indeed off-line practices do not arise from the conscious orchestration of individual actions, but more often, from 'social agents who constantly modify their habitual individual responses as they interact with each other, in order to sustain 'a shared practice' (Barnes 2001, p. 23–24). Consequently, practices are learnt from others and, although individually administered, this learning occurs through an ongoing sensitivity to what other practitioners are doing (Barnes 2001, p. 26). In other words, through practices disclosed in and transmitted through some form or language, people are revealed as social peers. It stands to argue, therefore, that practices should act, on the one hand, as mediators between potentially different views of an artifact, and on the other hand, they should express the relational possibility of such artifacts. This raises their cognitive demands and makes on-line practice design complex and cumbersome.

Traditionally, information technology served as a medium through which members of the network of practice transmit, communicate, store and circulate information regarding their professional practice (Wasko & Faraj, 2005; Vaast 2004). More recently, new virtualities (Winograd 1996) such as the WWW, internet technologies and virtual communities, have established a totally new context or culture for enacting, processing and transmitting practices, thus making new ground and leading to innovation and creative performance. Specifically, in virtual communities of practice, the new culture of a practice resulting from the community's virtual nature, typically results in a distinction between 'local' practices and community or 'coordinative' practices (Schmidt, 2000; Detienne, 2006). Local practices are undertaken by individual members as part of carrying out daily work or private activities. Coordinative practices concern activities and objects of work with impact on the community. In most of the cases, coordinative practices are more complex institutions, acting as catalysts for distributed collective performance and requiring both design for usability and sociability (Preece, 2000).

The literature offers a variety of empirical evidence regarding the type of on-line practices prevailing across different application domains. Examples include free and open source software projects (Gasser & Ripoche, 2003; Scacchi, 2005; Scacchi et al., 2006), new product development (von Hippel and Katz, 2002, Franke and Shah, 2001, Franke and Piller, 2004), the automobile and airspace industries (Schultz et al., 2003; Wenger et al., 2002), etc. Moreover, it turns out that there are several genres of software tools designed to support different aspects of on-line (generative) practices, including tools for information sharing (i.e., electronic mailing lists, or listservs, MOOs, Wikis, Blogs and RSS), tools for memory management (Ackerman, 1998; Ackerman and Palen, 1996), collaboratories (Olson and Olson, 2000), and tools for idea exploration (Erickson et al., 1999). Although their effectiveness as amplifiers of community management and social interaction is beyond doubt, their use as media for engaging

in a designated virtual community practice is not as obvious or immediately evident.

DESIGNING TOOLKITS FOR COORDINATIVE PRACTICES

In computer-mediated cooperative work, which is the primary issue of concern in this chapter, the design of coordinate practices is conceived as entailing two distinct aspects. The first concerns the practice vocabulary per se and the extent to which it is affected (i.e., expanded and/or extended) by technology. The second relates to how established common practices are articulated by and transmitted amongst practitioners. In their account of information infrastructures for distributed collective practices, Turner and colleagues (Turner et al., 2006) propose two complementary interpretations of what on-line practice may be considered to be. One interpretation frames practices in the context of the interpersonal interactions taking place amongst members of a virtual team. Another interpretation conceives practice as relative to the context of work and specifically, the processes, tools and artifacts used by virtual teams to accomplish cooperative tasks. In a similar vein, Gasser and Ripoche in their analysis of free and open source software development consider distributed collective practice as comprising of several elements, including activities, information objects, sociotechnical infrastructures, common problems and common methods and processes (Gasser & Ripoche, 2003).

In this view, one prominent question which stands out very promptly when designing for coordinate practices is what information infrastructure is appropriate and how to build such information infrastructures (Turner et al., 2006). Although this question has been raised and partially addressed in the relevant literature (see for example the special issue of the journal Computer Supported Cooperative work, 2006), our understanding of the issues involved is slightly different in terms of orientation and normative perspective. Specifically, we consider of primary importance two interrelated aspects. The first addresses the coordinative practice vocabulary and its interactive manifestation through visual (although this need not be always the case, see for example Ducheneaut et al., 2008) symbols. As the second aspect, we recognize mutual awareness and the extent to which the practice vocabulary is designed so as to afford awareness. We make this explicit link between awareness and the practice vocabulary because it is widely acknowledged that awareness involves two selective processes – displaying and monitoring – which are complementary aspects of coordinative practices (Schmidt, 2000). Awareness is only meaningful if it refers to a person's awareness of something (Detienne, 2006). Depending on the type of referent, Carroll et al. (2003) distinguish several awareness mechanisms such as social awareness (i.e., who is around), action awareness (i.e., what is happening) and situation awareness. The first two of these types are of particular relevance to the current work as they offer useful insight to the design of coordinate practice.

Visualizing Practices Through Domain-Specific Visual Vocabularies

In general, design vocabularies consist of primitive elements, which can be assembled into meaningful collaborative artifacts of various types. One category of artifacts specifies the properties of the result of individual contributions, e.g., product models, standards, drawings, visual encodings, style sheets, etc. Another category of assembled artifacts may detail interdependencies of tasks or objects in a cooperative work setting, e.g., organizational charts, classification schemes, taxonomies, groupware tools, etc. Yet another category may comprise artifacts that specify a protocol of interaction in the light of task interdependencies in a cooperative work setting, e.g., production processes and workflows, schedules,

office procedures, bug report forms.

Recently, domain specific languages (DSLs) have emerged as a promising approach to encapsulating practice-oriented knowledge and facilitating its generative articulation in order to derive new artifacts within the scope of the design language. Examples of DSLs include modern graphical toolkits for building user interfaces, the SQL database definition and manipulation language, the XML document transformation language, etc. In general, DSLs are developed for specific application domains that tend to be rather narrow. Their prime benefit is that they allow practicing (such as designing) to take place on a higher level of abstraction by separating between the language's constructs and the computational manifestation of these constructs. The language constructs reflect a relevant subset of an underlying ontological domain (i.e., engineering practice), while their notation is tailored to the principles and perspectives used by domain experts to express their work. The computational manifestation of a design language defines the framework for executing the language's notational statements. DSLs are typically, but not always, supported by visual languages for a number of reasons. Firstly, domain experts often prefer graphical rather than textual descriptions as the former are easier to learn, comprehend and apply, thus their users gain in productivity. Additionally, high level constructs and complex relations between them are usually better captured by visual (i.e., iconic, graphical) representations, using connections in two or three dimensional layouts.

DSLs would be ideal tools for building practice-specific vocabularies, if only their development was made simple and straight forward. It turns out that this is not the case. Building DSLs is design-intensive and requires substantial and frequently advanced programming skills. One reason contributing to the problem is the limited interaction elements supported by modern graphical toolkits, which constrain the types of visual models / artifacts built, as well as their affordance for collaborative praxis by communities of practice.

Mutual Awareness and Coordinative Practices

Although awareness is a widely studied concept in psychology, it poses several challenges in the context of computer-supported cooperative work. Early accounts of the issue by Gutwin and Greenberg (1995) consider this challenge to result from a trade-off between being well informed about other's activities, while being distracted by the information. In a similar vein, Hudson and Smith (1996) recognize the dual trade-off between privacy and awareness, and between awareness and disturbance. Subsequent studies provide a more detailed and informative review of the concept of awareness in the context of computer-supportive cooperative work and qualify the concept in terms of social awareness, action awareness, workspace awareness and situation awareness (Schmidt, 2002). In terms of translating awareness to relevant design issues, Carroll and colleagues provided recently a non-exhaustive list (Carroll et al., 2006). Specifically, they argue that awareness entails the following:

- Collaborators' assurance that their partners are 'there' in some sense
- Knowledge of what tools and resources collaborating partners can access
- Indication of what relevant information collaborators can provide, and what they expect, as well as their attitudes and goals.
- The moment-to-moment focus of attention and action of the partners engaged in the collaborative work
- An understanding of each partner's view of the shared plan, the work actually accomplished as well as how it may evolve over time.

Mutual awareness refers to the situation where (i) community members engaged in the practice the community is about become (somehow) aware of what co-practitioners are doing or not doing and accordingly adjust their own line of action, and (ii) conversely, practitioners make their actions 'publicly visible', that is, available and accessible, so that colleagues, can adjust their activities as appropriate (Schmidt, 2000). In light of this, it stands to argue that mutual awareness involves skilful praxis, thus it cannot be attained by simply assuring collaborating partners 'being there'. Instead, it requires an explicit effort to make sense of what is being done. Making sense of what others are doing necessitates that the practitioner invokes his or her knowledge of the common practice, that is, the setting, the process and the tools, as well as the explicit or implicit norms governing acceptable conduct in the designated domain of practice. In doing so, practitioners may be influenced by circumstantial factors, state indicators or events happening around them or in the collaborative information space. Similarly, when practitioners decide to expose their current activity to others, they do so selectively by modulating their activities in such a way that others will notice what is to be noticed. The above assume the establishment of some sort of coordinative practices, which impact both the workflows as well as properties of the underlying design vocabulary.

A Meta-Model for Building Interactive Practice Vocabularies

In light of the above, we can now exemplify the basic elements of practice which need to be supported by a practice-specific toolkit. This is shown in Figure 1 which is illustrative rather than exhaustive. The logic behind the model is as follows. Practice in general encapsulates the collective wisdom of a community of a practice. This wisdom is continuously refined and elaborated through empirical evidence, the advancement of

Figure 1. A meta-model for understanding online practice

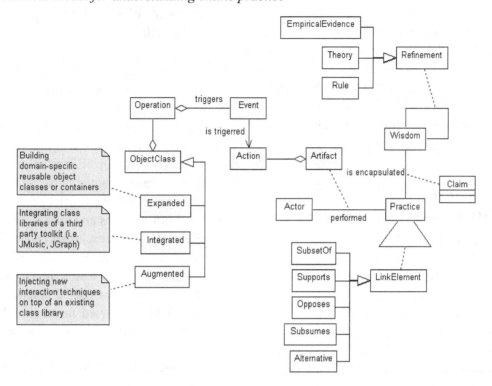

theory or by setting rules of thumb derived from experience and/or situated action. Moreover, practices may be intertwined with other practices in a variety of ways, thus establishing institutions of practices. Such intertwining may be through a practice being subset of / supporting / opposing / subsuming or otherwise related to another practice. Collectively, all the above establish the ontological context of a practice domain. At a more concrete level, practices are enacted by actors through performing activities on artifacts. This level allows an operational account of practice as computer-mediated action manifested by operations afforded by interaction objects. In turn, interaction objects are either conventional graphical widgets supported by modern toolkits or custom interaction elements developed (on-top of toolkits) by augmenting, expanding or integrating interaction platforms.

It is worth making a few additional qualifying remarks about the above conceptual model. First

of all the model does not claim to be generative and inclusive of all aspects constituting practice. Rather, it is proposed as a reference for designing interactive practice vocabularies as valid combinations or manipulation of (primitive and composite) interaction components. Secondly, the model although expressed using a static class diagram, does not aim to suggest that practice is static. On the contrary, it makes an effort to convey that practice is both social and evolving, just as are human knowledge and wisdom upon which it is based. Finally, although not explicitly stated, the model is intended as a unified space of on-line / computer mediated and off-line practices. It is assumed that practice may be manifested either as on-line or off-line or a combination between on-line and off-line practices. The recursive relationship linking practice with itself serves this goal. Thus, for instance an on-line practice may subsume an off-line practice and off-line practices may be subsets of on-line practices. Finally, the model adheres to the notion of variation in the enactment of a practice by separating between practice and artifact and allowing multiple alternative artifacts to be associated with the same practice. Indeed, in subsequent sections we will refer to situations where collaborators co-engage in the same practice, which however, is encapsulated into and manifested through different visual models each prompting for different actions.

CASE STUDIES ON PRACTICE-SPECIFIC TOOLKITS AND VOCABULARIES

In recent research and development work, we have attempted to investigate different practice domains and design practice-specific vocabularies to (a) encapsulate widely accepted practices and improve their enactment, processing and transmission (Akoumianakis et al., 2008a), or to (b) introduce new practices and support them by dedicated tools and computer-mediated environments (Akoumianakis, et al., 2008b). In this section we will briefly report our experience in two radically different case studies. The first case study considers collaborative music performance and aims to reveal how the design of on-line practices is intertwined and influences off-line practice of the collaborators. The second case study concentrates on devising new practices for building vacation packages as distributed collective practice by cross-organizational virtual communities of practice. Despite their differences in orientation and problem formulation, the two case studies share common ground. This is the engineering approach followed to build the respective practice toolkits. Specifically, our efforts in this direction are targeted to improving the capabilities of user interface development toolkits so as to allow new types of interaction objects with novel look and feel.

Intertwining On-Line and Off-Line Practice in Music Learning Communities

This section reports on work carried out in the context of the DIAMOUSES project which is elaborated in Chapter XIX in this volume. Our task was to design a toolkit allowing members of a learning community to engage in music learning practices. DIAMOUSES virtual communities of practice are distributed music squads jointly attaining a common goal such as music rehearsals, live performances and master classes. Goal achievement is almost exclusively dependent upon the collaborative contributions of all partners. Specifically, a music lesson in DIAMOUSES is conducted as a co-engaged practice between geographically dispersed members of a learning community comprising one moderator and several students. The learning objective amounts to collaborative performance of music theory exercises which is materialized as an institution of intertwined on-line and off-line practices. On-line practices are constituted by activities performed on shared and/or replicated objects in a private or public context and in a coordinated manner. Off-line practices involve the performance of the exercises by individual members, as well as the feedback / feed through expressed by the partners.

A prototype of a practice-specific toolkit has been built to facilitate collaborative music performance during music lessons. The prototype supports both personal/synchronous tasks carried out by members during music performance and community-oriented/asynchronous tasks carried out prior to or after music performance. As these tasks are distinct, different component tools have been designed to support them. Community-oriented / asynchronous tasks are hosted by a suitably customized version of the LifeRay Content Management System. Access to the contents is role-based. Teachers and students are two roles relevant to conducting music lessons.

They are entitled to download application suites which allow them to take part in music lessons. Access to these tools pre-supposes successful registration using an electronic registration system developed on top of the basic Liferay registration mechanism. A dedicated portlet has also been developed as a container for music lessons. It is open for registered participants and acts as a reference point, hosting shared objects and sonic artifacts relevant to the lesson.

To take part in a music lesson, members of the learning community download a dedicated application which serves as the practice-oriented toolkit. An instance of this application is depicted in Figure 2. As shown, the design of the user interface groups in distinct containers interaction objects intended to convey private and public interaction spaces. The user's private information space supports several tasks. One is visual access with members in remote sites through a camera. Another task is the control of various aspects of the remote user's performance such as the volume

of the signal received from a remote site, by using the sliders at the bottom-centre. Users can also manipulate shared contents (bottom right tabpane) made available by the teacher through the lesson's room portlet in the portal. Finally, members of the learning community can engage in live discussions with others by setting a suitable notification policy. It turns out that these are the dominant elements of the private tasks during the music lesson.

In terms of public tasks, they are focused on the manipulation of the music score occupying the central part of the user interface (see Figure 2). This is a 'shared' object, uploaded from the corresponding CMS room. It is a custom extension of the JMusic API and acts as the referent object for all coordinative practices. In synchronous sessions (of remote music lessons) the object is replicated across the connected clients and remains synchronized at all times. Access to this object by dispersed members is coordinated by a floor manager. Once the floor is requested and

Figure 2. The practice-toolkit for synchronous music lessons

occupied by a user, a range of on-line practices are afforded, as coordinative actions on shared objects. The on-line practice vocabulary was designed to facilitate activities on shared objects. For purposes of illustration we describe below some of these shared objects and how they afford prevalent music performance practices.

Metronome

The metronome is needed in order to keep a common tempo among performers in the context of a music lesson. Our domain analysis revealed that this metronome should have a visual manifestation and support basic functions such as those depicted in Figure 3. Since music is communicated either as digital audio signals or as MIDI messages, the metronome supports such selection (Figure 3a). All collaborators should have the same settings with respect to the tempo and rhythm of the music performed. Changes to the settings of the metronome (see Figure 3b) are done in a coordinated manner following access permission. Once these settings are changed all collaborators obtain the new settings (Figure 3c). Finally, it is worth mentioning that in contrast with other shared objects, the metronome is extremely sensitive to time offsets. As a result, the beat of the metronome is not activated locally but transmitted through a streaming server to all clients.

Floor Manager

On-line practices subsuming activities in the public information space are coordinated by a simple floor manager undertaking permission assignments. Typical floor management functions such as request / release floor are implemented through explicit function activation controls (see Figure 4).

Musical Score

The basic element of coordinative practices is the shared music score which is replicated across all registered clients. Figure 5 presents an example music score built using the JMusic API. To facilitate the required functionality we have implemented a number of extensions on the basic JMusic API to allow a more encompassing manipulation of this object.

Manipulate Score

Users in possession of the floor control can manipulate elements of the shared replicated musical score using the toolbar above the shared object. Thus, they can delete / add notes, add rest, change of tempo, clear music score (i.e., delete all notes), etc. Some of these tasks, such as manipulation of duration and tone of a note and turning note to a rest can also be carried out by direct manipulation of a note. For instance, selecting and dragging a

Figure 3. The DIAMOUSES metronome

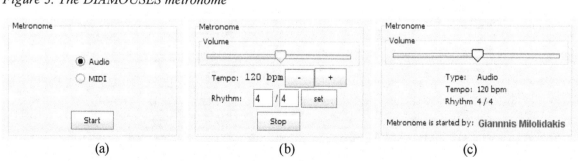

(a)   (b)   (c)

Figure 4. Floor manager's activation and states

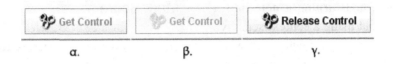

Figure 5. Alternative views of the music score

Figure 6. Pop-up menu for manipulating score elements

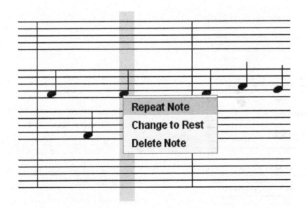

note in a horizontal dimension changes its duration, while dragging it in the vertical dimension changes its pitch. Tasks such as deletion of note, repetition of a note and turning a note into a rest can be carried out using a context sensitive pop-up menu (see Figure 6). Such tasks when performed enact a synchronization mechanism which broadcasts the changes and updates the shared object across all clients. In addition to the above, we have also implemented coordinative on-line practices which affect off-line practices of users. These are briefly reviewed below.

Annotate Score

Annotation is a common practice in document-based collaboration. The user can select a specific part of the music score and add an annotation (see Figure 7). The annotation container is a custom

dialog which allows the user to assign a persistent comment or instruction to the chosen object.

Mark Score

Another popular practice is to mark / unmark parts of the music score to express aggregate music expressions (i.e., cords, phrases, parts, etc). Figure 8 illustrates this practice as performed in the current version of the system.

Distributed Collective Practice in Information-Based Product Development

Assembly of information-based products by cross-organization virtual communities of practice is another domain in which we have experimented

Figure 7. Enacting annotations

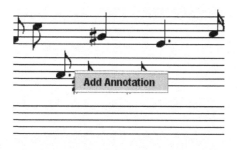

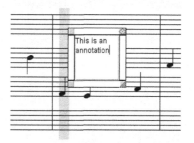

Figure 8. Pop-up menu in state of marking

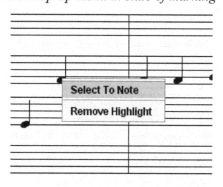

with practice-specific vocabularies. The case study reported here relates to assembling vacation packages and was carried out in the context of the eKoNES project which is further detailed in Chapter XXI in this volume. Information-based products have the characteristic that purchasing behavior is catalyzed by the information surrounding the product rather than the customers' actual experience or test of the product in advance. For instance tourists in the majority of cases are not able to experience a vacation package in advance. Instead, they rely on information services, which determine purchasing patterns. eKoNEΣ concentrates on advancing on-line practices for assembling vacation packages through distributed collective practices (Turner et al., 2006).

A skeleton of this practice in the form of partitioned narrative is presented in Table 1 which summarizes the activities of three distinct constituents, namely the customers' context, the community context and the practitioners' context during the development of a vacation package. We have intentionally oversimplified some of these activities to depict a logical sequence of steps without necessarily striving for the maximum of analytical insight. Indeed some of the activities such as 'raise/respond to issues', 'update model/parameters', etc., are demanding in terms of technological set-up (i.e. need for synchronous groupware, persistent exchanges, mining social interactions, etc) but this is further developed in Chapter XXI.

Distributed Collective Practices for Vacation Package Assembly

Before presenting the details of the toolkit designed to facilitate the designated practice, we will first attempt to extract the context for the distributed collective practices implied. Distributed collective practice as defined by Turner and colleagues (Turner et al., 2006) refers to 'collective activity mediated through geographical and conceptual distances, time, collective resources, and heterogeneous perspectives or experiences' (p. 97).

Referring to the assembly of vacation packages, and given the practice described in Table 1,

Table 1. Partitioned narrative

The customers' context	The community context	The practitioners' context
1: Customer request for service	2: Create package	
	3: Announce new package	
	4: Invite participation	5: Confirm / reject invitation
		6: Contribute to package
	7: Update model	
	8: Raise issue	9: Respond to issues raised
	10: Request offer / bit	
		11: Update parameters
		12: Request clarification
	13: Clarification of issues	
	14: Consolidate issues	
	15: Publish package	
16: Tailor package / request changes		

an attempt at qualifying the notion of a collective object is to consider the stakeholders involved. In our reference example the stakeholders include members of a community of practice, namely representatives of tourism service providers who register their offerings in shared pool and devote resources so as to contribute to a collective objective (i.e., new vacation packages), and consumers whose participation is motivated by individual goals and requirements.

Consequently, in such a setting, collective objects represent contributions by both these groups which in some way generate interest for, shape the characteristics of, articulate demand for and define the scope and limits of a new vacation package. This new artifact may have commonalities with other artifacts (i.e., it need not necessarily be an innovation); nevertheless it results from a conscious effort to appropriate the benefits of an earlier innovation. In practice, this requires a certain amount of reuse and manipulation of codified experience.

As for distributed activity, the literature offers two connotations. One refers to the technologically mediated interactions contrasting distributed activities to co-located activities or face-to-face interactions (Hinds and Keisler, 2002), while the other uses the term 'distributed' to underline the distribution of cognition as an alternative paradigm to traditional cognitive science (Hutchins, 1991; Norman, 1991). Considering the community of practice implied in our vacation package example, clearly the latter offers an appropriate ground for framing the issue. Specifically, distinct service providers (i.e., accommodation providers, cultural sites, museums, etc) with established own processes join forces under a shared practice to contribute their own offerings towards attaining the collective goal (i.e., a vacation package).

Finally, in terms of practice, Table 1 implies two separate types, namely coordinative and local practices. Local practices represent efforts by collaborating organizations to plan and execute their own business activities. These practices are

grounded on the organization's context of work and may be embedded in dedicated technological tools (i.e., enterprise databases, intranet) and local procedures. For instance, making a reservation for a hotel room is totally different – in terms of process followed, tools used and the codified outcomes – from making a reservation for a table in a restaurant. Coordinative practices are shared and constitute a 'social' protocol for participating in the virtual community of practice. They are primarily related to the community's sociability (de Souza and Preece, 2004) and how members participate and contribute. To embed such practices into tools requires dedicated software and interoperable components to bridge across individual perspectives into a collaborative repository or community collective.

Designing the Vacation Package Assembly Vocabulary

We devised a design language to provide a visual notation for assembling 'local' vacation packages as distributed collective practice of a virtual group. In this context, local vacation packages are conceived of as comprising primitive services offered by different organizations. As a service of a certain type may be offered by different candidates, they may be considered as a sub-community or neighborhood. Ultimate choice of service offering is to be determined by customers so as to suit their own preferences and constraints. In terms of its core elements, our vacation package practice vocabulary is required to provide for representing graphically not only the ultimate package but also variations suit to different users. Analysis of the constituents of a package reveals three key elements that need to be interactively manifested, namely (a) the package as a container object, (b) the basic composition units of a package, i.e., days and the individual activities scheduled within a day, and finally (c) spatial semantics and temporal constraints (i.e., containment, overlap, etc) between individual activities.

Elastic buttons provide an abstraction for representing neighborhood offerings. The physical properties of an elastic button are different from those of a conventional button. However, the underlying dialog model is minimally changed. The main feature of an elastic button is that it can be resized in two directions. Figure 9 depicts some representative examples of elastic buttons. As shown, their visual appearance is different from a conventional two-state button. Specifically, their color designates neighborhood while they can host labels and icons to designate some of their features.

The rationale for such components results from the need to be able to manipulate a suitable interaction object class whose physical properties can be augmented to derive the required semantic meaning. For instance, it would be possible to visualize activities as instances of the panel widget, hence affording a label, color and size assignment, etc. Nevertheless, as panels are typically single-state widgets, the derived activity object would inherit this feature—thus, not being clickable, selectable, etc—unless the basic dialog model for panels is extended.

The alternative adopted in the present work is to consider activity objects as customized buttons (with a label, color and size manipulation) thus inheriting the two-state dialogue model of an abstract button. Moreover, as these 'buttons' would represent neighborhood offerings additional semantic notions should be allowed. For

Figure 9. Examples of elastic buttons

(a) Activities within a day

(b) Activity spanning across two days

Figure 10. Alternative activity panels

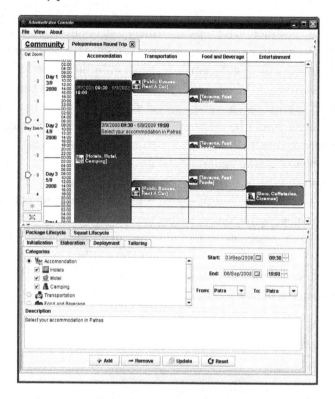

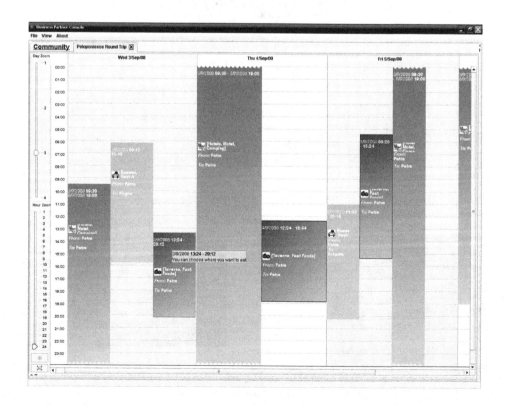

example, distinct types of neighborhood offerings could be separated by allowing manipulation of a suitable physical property (i.e., color) of the object of activity. Similarly, as activities have duration, this semantic notion can be derived by allowing for size manipulation of the object. As for the nested icons, these are used as a complementary means for designating neighborhood type for an activity.

Tailorable activity panels can be used to provide visual representations of a package. In general, an activity panel provides an interactive manifestation of a package and organizes neighborhood offerings (i.e., elastic buttons) in a particular layout. We have constructed two concrete examples of alternative layouts to represent role-specific views of a vacation package. One layout (top instance in Figure 10) provides the moderator's view of the vacation package concentrating on neighborhoods and their relative organization. In this layout, activities scheduled for a particular day constitute horizontal cross-sections in the panel layout. On the other hand, the squad members' layout (bottom instance in Figure 10) depicts the vacation package as a sequence of days laid out horizontally. This time,

activities scheduled for a designated day are presented through vertical cross sections of the panel layout, thus emphasizing the institution of a day as a set of interrelated activities of variable type and duration. Whereas this latter layout is the only option for squad members, the moderator may choose layout view interchangeably depending on the situation and the task at hand. One difference worth noticing is the representation of activities spanning across several days. In the moderator's view these are represented by a single / continuous elastic button, whereas in the squad members view they are populated as a series of elastic buttons with slight modification of appearance to convey continuity of the offering across several days.

As these packages are the result of collective contributions and negotiation of details there was an explicit need to support mutual awareness during collaborative praxis on shared objects. This required various enhancements whose detailed description is beyond the scope of this chapter. However, to illustrate the concept, Figure 11 presents examples of collaborative practices which can take place in a synchronous session while Table 2 provides details of the scenario depicted.

Table 2. Collaborative patterns in a synchronous session

Practice	Referent	Interaction sequence	Effect on target objects
Change activity start point; end point remains constant	'Blue' activity button in accommodation column	1. Pick top-border of button 2. Move to desired start point maintaining interim feedback through color 3. Add 'accept/reject' buttons in the direction of the change	1. Resize the target button maintaining interim feedback 2. Add 'accept/reject' buttons in the direction of the change
Change activity end point; start point remains constant	Lower button in the 'food & beverage' column	1. Pick bottom-border of button 2. Move to desired start point maintaining interim feedback through color 3. Add 'accept/reject' buttons in the direction of the change	1. Resize the target button maintaining interim feedback 2. Add 'accept/reject' buttons in the direction of the change
Move entire activity	Lower button in the 'transportation' column	1. Pick button 2. Move to desired start point	1. Replace button to target position maintaining interim feedback 2. Add 'accept/reject' buttons in direction of replacement

Figure 11. Collaboration patterns in synchronous sessions

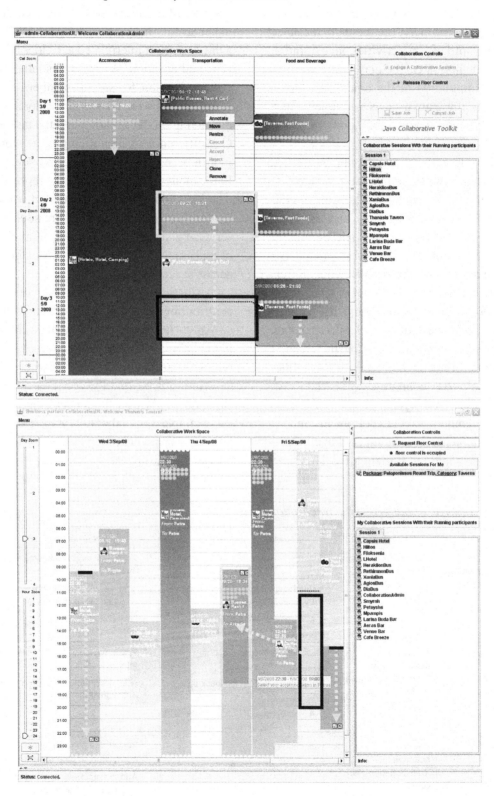

The examples assume that the moderator (upper screen) is the holder of the floor, thus the initiator of the collaborative tasks. Floor status is also described in the floor control dialogue which outlines for each view the next available action (release – request) for manipulating the floor in each case. The lower screen depicts the effects of the initiator's actions as propagated to a collaborating partner's user interface. For purposes of illustration, we have annotated the screens so as to describe start / end conditions for the collaborative interactions. Thus, the red rectangles indicate start conditions, while the yellow arrows depict end conditions for each interaction object class.

IMPLICATIONS FOR TOOLKIT DESIGNERS

Throughout this chapter we have referred to virtual community of practice-specific toolkits as interactive software vocabularies (or components) serving the function of providing a virtual place for engaging in the practice the community is about. This should be distinguished from community management environments or community support systems such as Internet Relay Chat, MUDS, Wikis, Blogs and other similar technologies, which are used to facilitate establishment and maintenance of community, sharing information, engaging in social interaction with peers, etc. Practice-specific toolkits serve a totally different role and should be designed accordingly. Our recent experience with the systems and the case studies reported earlier reveals several useful guidelines for designers of practice-specific toolkits for virtual communities of practice. We have grouped them under four relevant topics which are briefly discussed below.

Scope of Design

Practice-specific toolkits should be conceived as a 'protocol' for engaging in the practice the community is about. Consequently, they should be minimally designed with an explicit focus on encapsulating elements of practice rather than servicing general community support functions (i.e., social interaction through chat or community forums). In case social interaction is needed as a supportive element of practice, then it should be embedded and tailored to the context in which practice is experienced. For instance, in our case study on music master classes components such as chat, speech-based interaction through microphones and maintenance of visual contact through an IP camera were considered as supportive elements of practice and were bundled into the music performance toolkit as additional media for expressing opinion and coordinating actions in synchronous collaborative sessions. This need not be the case in other domains of practice, as for instance in the case of assembling vacation packages. It can then be concluded that the scope of designing a practice-specific toolkit should be primarily focused on the practice itself and use media which are best suited for transmitting this practice.

Designing a Tailorable Virtual Asset

Since the practice toolkit is intended for registered and authorized users, it should be made available to every member of the community irrespective of geographic location, physical proximity or the member's local computing context. This requires a certain degree of tailorability on the part of the toolkit and a mechanism for obtaining access to the toolkit. In terms of access, the toolkit could be made available as downloadable software once a member is successfully registered to the community and obtains the rights of a particular role. In the case studies reviewed in this chapter, we implemented a separate community registration system in top of the community portal. In both cases, the registration system was designed so as to support role-based access to virtual community assets. Thus, the toolkit is treated as a virtual asset, similar to the community's forum and message board, with the difference that it is made available to members who successfully obtain rights of a designated role. As for tailoring the toolkit, this implies adapting to the locale of the various registered community members.

Designing the Workflow

A critical design issue when building practice-specific toolkits is the workflows embedded in the practices articulated. In this context our case studies reveal two alternative options which may influence design decisions. The first, which is representative of our music master class example, promotes the view that the toolkit should encapsulate existing and established practice. The second alternative, representing the case of assembling vacation packages, postulates the design of the toolkit as new practice. Figure 12 illustrates this schematically, differentiating between virtual community of practice as facilitator and as an enabler of change. The implication this may have on the design of the practice-toolkit is that in cases where the toolkit is an enabler of new practice, it will have to harmonize institutionalized 'local' practices of the members, which need not be compatible. Our experience with collaborative assembly of information-based products reveals in such cases, software factories (Greenfield & Short, 2004) or the Social Experience Factory presented in Chapter VI in this volume, may be used to establish the common information space or infrastructure for distributed collective practicing.

Domain-Specificity

Although not explicitly stated thus far, at least from the two case studies presented, it becomes evident that irrespective of the toolkit's scope (i.e., encapsulation of practice or enabler of new practice), it needs to be domain-specific. In other words, it cannot be a general purpose tool such as a word processor supporting document management practices or a community forum supporting asynchronous dialogue practices. This is not to say that such tools are not needed or suitable as

Figure 12. Alternatives for designing the practice-specific toolkits

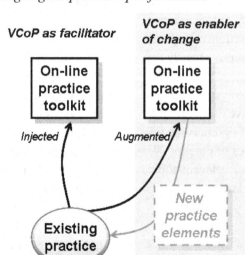

supporting systems, but simply that practice-specific toolkits should reflect the domain they are intended to serve. The literature on tools for virtual communities on practice tends to dismiss this issue, as it focuses almost exclusively on community management rather than community practicing. Nevertheless, in other scientific fields, such as management science, knowledge management and electronic commerce, the role of toolkits as drivers for innovation appears very promptly. For instance, Fuller and colleagues (Fuller et al., 2006) in their recent account of community-based innovation conclude that:

... the novelty of these approaches is that community members are not only asked about their opinions, wants and needs. They are invited to contribute their creativity and problem solving skills by generating and evaluating new product ideas, elaborating a detailed product concept, evaluating or challenging it, discussing and improving optional solution details, selecting or individualizing the preferred virtual prototype, testing and experiencing the new product features by running simulations, getting information about the new product or just consuming it...(p. 59).

In this area of inquiry, the domain-specificity of the practice toolkit is facilitated through support for virtual prototype manipulation, simulation and custom communication tools. These toolkits typically do not extend beyond encapsulating proven practice (see also previous section), thus serving primarily as alternative media for market research rather than as new practice enablers. Indeed, in none of the works reviewed in this area could we find convincing evidence that the toolkit changed or established novel engineering practices.

Designing User Interaction

In contrast with recent works in which the practice-specific toolkit is manifested through visual prototyping and simulation tools, in our

case studies the practice-specific interaction vocabulary emerged through metaphor articulation. Specifically, we used metaphors (i.e., music score and two dimensional schedules) to devise visual notations and custom interaction objects which are best suited for the intended practice domain. This effort is in the province of Human Computer Interaction (HCI) which provides a main thrust for our past and on-going work. Moreover, recent experience is almost explicitly related to the specialized tracks of user interface software technologies with loose extensions to groupware systems. In this section, we do not intend to provide a detailed and exhaustive account of possible implications of building practice-specific toolkits on the wider field of HCI. Instead, we will comment on how practice-specific vocabularies can be compiled by extending the prominent design language supported by modern graphical user interface development toolkits. To this effect, we are developing a complete engineering method referred to as platform administration in order to facilitate novel interactive vocabularies built by augmenting, expanding, integrating and abstracting user interface development toolkit-level components (Akoumianakis et al., 2008b).

Platform administration is a process carried out by tool developers and aims to assist them when deciding what is to be augmented, expanded, developed from scratch and/or integrated to provide the suitable interaction vocabulary. It also addresses issues such as choice of native toolkit components and application programming interface extensions to facilitate toolkit interoperability, object synchronization and run-time adaptive behaviors which may critically determine the implementation approach and the capabilities of the visual design language. Our recent experience from a range of design cases can be summarized into a few guidelines useful to developers of such visual design libraries using standard or cutting edge graphical toolkits.

Firstly, toolkit augmentation is appropriate and effective when the target is the introduction of new interaction techniques or modification of visual attributes of existing widgets. Toolkit augmentation was the technique employed to introduce new capabilities in JMusic for the music master class case study, as well as to build the elastic buttons in the vacation package assembly case study. This technique is not appropriate for building radically new types of widgets or novel container type objects. Prior to deciding what is to be augmented, developers should pay attention to the affordances of native widgets as implemented in a toolkit (i.e., parameters, layout managers, implemented dialog, etc) so as to gain insight to the constraints imposed, and accordingly decide on which widgets are to be augmented and how. Furthermore, augmentation should be spread out (or delegated) to as many as required native widgets to maximize compliance with the toolkit's underlying philosophy. The alternative, which binds the augmented functionality to a single or a small number of widgets, has proved to be problematic and non-effective. Finally, when toolkit augmentation is used, it is likely that the revisions in the target toolkit will cover components and toolkit elements relatively deep in the toolkit hierarchy.

Toolkit expansion is appropriate when new types of container objects are required. It was the technique used to build the activity panels in our vacation package assembly case study. Important design decisions influencing toolkit expansion include the choice of native container to be manipulated and corresponding layout managers. In serious expansions it is more than likely that the development of new layout managers is imperative. It may also be desirable / appropriate for toolkit expansion to utilize previously implemented augmented components, as shown in the examples presented in this chapter. This raises the complexity and demands careful and disciplined programming. Finally, it is worth noticing that expansion a strategy which introduces changes relatively high in the toolkit hierarchy.

Toolkit integration is a multi-faceted strategy and can be more complex than augmentation and expansion. There are two alternative perspectives to consider and plan for integration. The first is to integrate a third-party library which is compliant to the chosen toolkit and make provisions for synchronization of concurrent views. This was the case of integrating the JMusic library in our Swing-based music performance toolkit. The second, more demanding view is to raise the compliance requirement and to allow concurrent execution of alternative run-time libraries and environments (i.e., Swing and C++ toolkits). This turns out to require special developments and dedicated architectural models to alleviate mismatches in the programming models of the designated toolkits and their implemented libraries. As this was not used in either of our case studies is not further elaborated.

Finally, in our two case studies toolkit abstraction was used to support mutual awareness and shared and replicated interaction object synchronization across clients in a synchronous collaborative session. The abstraction entailed mechanisms for broadcasting changes in the replicated objects' states and local view updates. This is more clearly illustrated in the vacation package assembly case study were local views of the vacation package, although different in visual detail and layout, remain fully synchronized to assure common reflections upon the shared display by the registered participants.

CONCLUSION

This chapter presented recent experiences on the development of practice-oriented interactive toolkits as media for engaging (either encapsulating or improving) the practice a community is about. Two recently conducted case studies were presented covering radically different application domains (i.e., music performance and assembly of vacation packages) and corresponding practices. In both cases, a dedicated practice-specific interactive toolkit was developed to facilitate different goals. Specifically, in the music performance case, the toolkit was designed so as to encapsulate existing and proven practice and to intertwine on-line with off-line practices. In the vacation package assembly case, the toolkit was devised to establish a new practice for cross-organization virtual communities of practice. Our conclusions from these experiences are two fold. Firstly, practice-specific toolkits for virtual communities of practice need to be designed with an explicit focus on the elements of practice involved, rather than the functions of community management (i.e., discovering, establishing and maintaining community) which should be the sole responsibility of the community support system. Secondly, practice-specific interactive toolkits could be developed either as facilitators of existing practices or enablers of new and innovative practices. In both cases, they can be extremely useful and powerful means for expressing opinion, sharing information, building consensus and collaborative practicing.

REFERENCES

Ackerman, M. S. (1998). Augmenting organizational memory: A field study of answer garden. *ACM Transactions on Information Systems, 16*(3), 203-24.

Ackerman, M. S., & Palen, L. (1996). The Zephyr Help Instance: Promoting ongoing activity in a CSCW system. *ACM Conference on Human Factors in Computing Systems (ACM CHI '96)*, (pp. 268 – 275). New York: ACM Press.

Akoumianakis, D., Vellis G., Milolidakis I., Kotsalis D., & Alexandraki, C. (2008a). Distributed collective practices in collaborative music performance. *In Proceedings of 3rd ACM International Conference on Digital Interactive Media in Entertainment and Arts (DIMEA 2008)*, (pp. 368-375), New York: ACM Press.

Akoumianakis, D., Vidakis N., Vellis G., Milolidakis G., & Kotsalis D. (2008b). Interaction scenarios in the 'social' experience factory: Assembling collaborative artefacts through component re-use and social interaction. In D. Cunliffe (Ed.), *IASTED-HCI'2008 Human Computer Interaction*, (pp. 611-068). Anaheim: Acta Press.

Barnes, B. (2001). Practices as collective action. In T. R. Schatzki, K. Knorr-Cetina, and E. von Savigny (Eds.), *The practice turn in contemporary theory*, (pp. 17-28). London: Routledge.

Brown, J. S., & Duguid, P. (2000). *The social life of information*. Boston: Harvard Business School Press.

Carroll, J. M., Rosson, M. B., Convertino, G., & Ganoe, H. C. (2006). Awareness and teamwork in computer-supported collaborations. *Interacting with Computers, 18*, 21-46.

Carroll, J. M., Neale, D. C., Isenbour, P. L., Rosson, M. B., & McCrickard, D. S. (2003). Notification and awareness: Synchronizing task-oriented collaborative activity. *International Journal of Human–Computer Studies, 58*, 605-632.

Detienne, F. (2006). Collaborative design: Managing task interdependencies and multiple perspectives, *Interacting with Computers, 18*, 1-20.

Ducheneaut, N., Moore, R.J., Oehlberg, L., Thornton, J.D., & Nickell, E. (2008). SocialTV: Designing for distributed, social television viewing. *International Journal of Human-Computer Interaction, 24*(2).

Duguid, P. (2005). The art of knowing: Social and tacit dimensions of knowledge and the limits of the community of practice. *The Information Society, 21*, 109-18.

Engeström, Y. (1999). Activity theory and individual and social transformation. In Y. Engeström,

R. Miettinen & R. L. Punamäki (Eds), *Perspectives on activity theory* (pp. 19-38). Cambridge, MA: Cambridge University Press.

Erickson, T., Smith, D. N., Kellogg, W. A., Laff, M. R., Richards, J. T., & Bradner, E. (1999). Socially translucent systems: Social proxies, persistent conversation, and the design of Babble. In *ACM Conference on Human Factors in Computing Systems* (pp. 72-79). New York: ACM Press.

Fuller, J., Bartl, M., Ernst, H., & Muhlbacher, H. (2006). Community based innovation: How to integrate members of virtual communities into new product development. *Electronic Commerce Research, 6*, 57–73.

Gasser, L., & Ripoche, G. (2003, December 3-4). Distributed collective practices and free/open source software problem management: Perspectives and methods. *2003 Conference on Cooperation, Innovation & Technologie (CITE'03)* (Université de Technologie de Troyes, France).

Greenfield, J., & Short, K. (2004). *Software factories - Assembling applications with patterns, frameworks, models & tools.* New York: John Wiley & Sons.

Gutwin, C., Greenberg, S., & Roseman, M. (1996). Workspace Awareness in real-time distributed groupware: Framework, widgets, and evaluation. In A. Sasse, R. J. Cunningham, & R. Winder (Eds.), *People and computers XI,* (pp. 281-298). Berlin: Springer-Verlag.

Hudson, E. S., & Smith, E. I. (1996). Techniques for addressing fundamental privacy and disruption tradeoffs in awareness support systems. In *Proceedings of the 1996 ACM conference on Computer Supported Cooperative Work,* (pp. 248-257). New York: ACM Press.

Jarzabkowski, P. (2003). Strategic practices: An activity theory perspective on continuity and change. *Journal of Management Studies, 40*(1), 23-56.

Jarzabkowski, P. (2004). Strategy as practice: Recursiveness, adaptation, and practices-in-use. *Organization Studies, 25*(4), 529–560.

Jarzabkowski, P. (2005). *Strategy as practice: An activity-based approach.* London: Sage.

Lave, J., & Wegner, E. (1991). *Situated learning – Legitimate peripheral participation.* Cambridge, MA: Cambridge University Press.

Olson, G., & Olson, J. (2000). Distance matters. *Human-Computer Interaction, 15*(2-3), 139-178.

Orlikowski, J. W. (2002). Knowing in practice: Enacting a collective capability in distributed organizing. *Organization Science, 13*(3), 249-273.

Preece, J. (2000). *Online communities: Designing usability, supporting sociability.* Chichester, England: John Wiley & Sons.

Scacchi, W. (2005). Socio-technical interaction networks in free/open source software development processes. In S. T. Acuna & N. Juristo (Eds.), *Software process modelling* (pp. 1-27). New York: Spinger.

Scacchi, W., Feller, J., Fitzgerald, B., Hissam, S., & Lakhani, K. (2006). Understanding free/open source software development processes. *Software Process – Improvement and Practice, 11*(2), 95-105.

Schatzki, T. R., Knorr-Cetina, K., & von Savigny E. (2001). *The practice turn in contemporary theory.* London: Routledge.

Schmidt, K. (2000, September 19-22). Distributed collective practices: A CSCW perspective'. *Invited Talk, Conference on Distributed Collective Practices,* Paris, France 2000.

Schmidt, K. (2002). The problem with 'awareness'. *Computer Supported Cooperative Work, 11*, 285-298.

Schmidt, K., Wagner, I., & Tolar, M. (2007). Permutations of cooperative work practices: A study of two oncology clinics. In T. Gross, et al. (Eds.), *GROUP 2007: Proceedings of the International Conference on Supporting Group Work,* (pp. 1-10). New York: ACM Press.

Schultz, F., & Pucher, H. F. (2003). www.deck - Wissensmanagement bei Volkswagen. *Industrie Management, 19*(3), 64-66.

Turner, W., Bowker, G., Gasser, L., & Zacklad, M. (2006). Information infrastructures for distributed collective practices. *Computer Supported Cooperative Work, 15*(2-3), 93-110.

Vaast, E. (2004). O brother, where are thou? From communities to networks of practice through intranet use. *Management Communication Quarterly, 18*(1), 5-44.

von Hippel, E., Katz, R. (2002). Shifting innovation to users via toolkits. *Management Science, 48*(7), 821-833.

Wasko, Molly M., & Faraj, S. (2005) Why should I share? Examining social capital and knowledge contribution in electronic networks of practice. *Management Information Systems Quarterly, 29*(1), 35–57.

Wenger, E., McDermott, R., & Snyder, W. (2002). *Cultivating communities of practice: A guide to managing knowledge.* Boston: Harvard Business School Press.

Winograd, T. (ed.) (1996) *Bringing design to software.* New York: Addison Wesley.

KEY TERMS

Coordinative Practices: Practices aimed to convey social and activity awareness within a shared information space .

Domain-Specific Practice Vocabulary: Objects (primitive or composite) used to synthesize elements of a virtual practice.

Practice-Oriented Toolkit: A software suite allowing members of a virtual community of practice to engage in the practice the community is about.

Visual Language: A social protocol with a suitable interactive manifestation for manipulating objects of a domain-specific practice vocabulary .

Virtual Practice: A practice encoded, enacted and transmitted using a dedicated practice-oriented toolkit.

Chapter XVI
Developing User Interfaces for Community–Oriented Workflow Information Systems

Josefina Guerrero García
Université catholique de Louvain, Louvain School of Management (LSM), Belgium

Jean Vanderdonckt
Université catholique de Louvain, Louvain School of Management (LSM), Belgium

Juan Manuel González Calleros
Université catholique de Louvain, Louvain School of Management (LSM), Belgium

ABSTRACT

Technology to support groups is rapidly growing in use. In recent years, the Web has become a privileged platform for implementing community-oriented workflows, giving rise to a new generation of workflow information systems. Specifically, the Web provides ubiquitous access to information, supports explicit distribution of business process across workers, workplaces, and computing platforms. These processes could be all supported by platform-independent user interfaces. This chapter presents a model-driven engineering method that provides designers with methodological guidance on how to systematically derive user interfaces of workflow information systems from a series of models. For this purpose, the workflow is recursively decomposed into processes which are in turn decomposed into tasks. Each task gives rise to a task model whose structure, ordering, and connection with the domain model allows the automated generation of corresponding user interfaces in a transformational approach. The various models involved in the method can be edited in a workflow editor based on Petri nets and simulated interactively.

INTRODUCTION

There are a variety of definitions on virtual communities with all of them having in common the participation of people working and sharing information or knowledge in a shared space toward the accomplishment of a goal. Virtual communities are formed around different disciplines such as sociology, anthropology, medicine, computer science, management science, distance learning, bring together people sharing a common interest, concern or desire. Sometimes such virtual settings may impose a shared community-wide workflow, but this need not be always the case. In this chapter we will be concerned with virtual communities in which members share a common practice (i.e., learning, business process) which is to be interactively manifested to dispersed community members using different tools and computational devices. In such cases, one important aspect to consider is the design of the user interfaces (UIs) of the system that will be used by the community to foster collaboration. Ideally, such a design should be greed from the specificities of platforms, access terminals and local workflow bindings. To this effect, it is important to generate user interface software for community-oriented workflows in a manner which platform independent, customizable and extensible.

In this chapter we introduce the FlowiXML methodology for developing the various UIs of a community-oriented workflow information system (WIS). Traditionally, workflow information systems are designed to be used by different types of users to accomplish a variety of tasks and in different situations; usually include communications and coordination between people and actions of several persons on shared objects and in shared workplaces including the Internet. For several years now, people have been using online virtual spaces to communicate and carry out work-oriented tasks. Prior to the World Wide Web, BBS, or electronic bulletin boards and email loops connected folks across time and space. With the advent of the Web several issues such as ubiquitous access to information, distribution of processes, and platform-independence emerged as first-class design issues.

Workflow information systems are a specified way of working to accomplish a task in a collaborative setting, just as it is the case of a community of practice. Consequently, creating a community workflow involves a level of design above the institutionalized workflows supported by individual members of the community of practice. Our method can be exploited to facilitate user interfaces to shared community-wide workflows within the context of a cross-organizational virtual alliance, thus establishing a shared practice which is interactively manifested through dedicated interaction components.

FlowiXML method generates UIs following a model-driven engineering (MDE) approach that is user-centric, based on the requirements and processes of the community. The methodology seeks to: 1) integrate human and machines based activities, in particular those involving interaction with IT applications and tools, 2) identify how tasks are structured, who perform them, what their relative order is, how they are offered or assigned, and how tasks are being tracked.

In the remaining of the chapter, we provide a background research in understanding the variety of approaches to build workflow information systems, and then we describe a workflow framework and the FlowiXML methodology for building UIs that can be used as well for developing community-oriented workflow information systems. Following this, a case study and a tool supporting the method are presented. The chapter is wrapped up by summarizing our work, deriving conclusions and addressing future trends and challenges.

BACKGROUND

In recent years, there has been a vast interest in how groups of people work together, and in how collaboration and cooperation might be supported. Virtual communities are formed and exploited by a variety of social and professional groups interacting via the Internet. Howard Rheingold (2000) mentions that virtual communities form *"when people carry on public discussions long enough, with sufficient human feeling, to form webs of personal relationships"*. A virtual Community is a network of individuals who share a domain of interest about which they communicate online. The participants share resources (for example experiences, problems and solutions, tools, methodologies) and the environment (space).

At the same time there have also been significant advances in information technology (IT) to support group work, normally with the use of an information system (IS). IS provide a technology enabler allowing corporations to gain competitive advantage, by reducing costs, automating processes, timely exchange of information, reducing production time and time-to-market or just simply to keep in business (Kitta, 2007). The users of a IS interact with it through its user interface, which is the aggregate of means by which people (the users) interact with a particular machine, device, computer program or other complex tool (the system).

Recently, the Web had become a privileged platform for implementing workflow systems. The Workflow Management Coalition (1999) defines workflow as "the automation of a business process, in whole or part, during which documents, information or tasks are passed from one participant to another for action, according to a set of procedural rules" (p.8). However, there is surprisingly little work emphasizing community-oriented workflows and the way in which such workflows are interactively manifested to community members. Typically, researchers have devoted their efforts to studying and developing tools for community

management (i.e., Blogs, Wikis, forums) which come with a pre-packaged workflow. For instance, the workflow through which a user can contribute to a thread in an on-line discussion is fixed and cannot be easily changed. Moreover, the user interface is tightly coupled to this workflow and cannot be modified, tailored or ported to a different execution context. These, however, are shortcomings which may impede participation to the social encounters of the virtual community, especially for novice users or users acquainted with a different way of working.

Designing community-oriented workflows entails several challenges and requires attention to a variety of issues. A non-exhaustive list includes number of participants, productivity, errors in accessing community information or in interaction and variation of enactment. It also brings to the surface social and coordinative considerations such as task, activity and user awareness, synchronization, etc. All these may potentially influence the design of the user interface to a community-workflow. Consequently, a method such as FlowiXML could be exploited to facilitate the design of UIs to shared community-wide workflows of a cross-organizational alliance so as to allow member to engage in a shared practice irrespective of how business is carried out locally by individual members.

Model-Based User Interface Development for Workflows

Model-based user interface design is intended to assist in designing UIs with a more formal computer supported methodology; model-based is concerned with the development of models. A model can be defined as an international and simplified representation of a real-world thing. Model primitives (i.e., model building blocks) are gathered in meta-models i.e., models describing other model's concepts and relationships. Model-based interfaces have recognized advantages in terms of methodology, reusability, and consistency. A fundamental requirement for a model-based to be operational consists in its relying on a specification language, with which the various models involved in the process could be obtained. Nowadays, eXtensible Mark-up Languages (XML) represent an attractive way to define a concrete syntax from the model Semantics. UsiXML is a XML-compliant mark-up language; it consists of a User Interface Description Language (UIDL) that is a declarative language capturing the essence of what a UI is or should be independently of physical characteristics. It describes at a high level of abstraction the constituting elements of the UI of an application: widgets, controls, containers, modalities, interaction techniques, etc.

Due to the importance of workflow nowadays, several workflow notation descriptions have been proposed to design and specify it, among them:

- **Statechart diagrams.** A Statechart diagram is a graph that represents a state machine describing the response, of an object of a certain class, to the receipt of outside stimuli.
- **Petri nets,** as a modeling language, graphically depict the structure of a distributed system as a directed bipartite graph with annotations. Petri Nets are a technique for modeling and analyzing processes.
- **Business Process Model Notation (BPMN)** is a standardized graphical notation for drawing business processes in a workflow. BPMN will provide a simple means of communicating process information to other business users, process implementers, customers, and suppliers.

Also, there are some workflow languages that represent complex scenarios and can describe the logical presentation. They capture their structure, dynamics and states. Workflow languages are tools that can be used to model a workflow and to execute it, for instance:

- **Yet Another Workflow Language (YAWL)** is a language based on Petri nets. A workflow specification in YAWL is a set of processes definitions that form a hierarchy. Tasks are either atomic task or composed ones. The lower level in the hierarchy refers to a process definition. Atomic tasks form the leaves of the graph structure. Each process definition consists of tasks and conditions which can be interpreted as places. Each process definition has one unique input condition and one unique output condition (van der Aalst, 2005).
- **Exchangeable Routing Language (XRL)** is a language that uses eXtensible Markup Language (XML) for the representation of process definitions and Petri nets for its Semantics. Since XRL is instance-based, workflow definitions can be changed on the fly and sent across organizational boundaries (Verbeek, 2002).

To manage the workflow, many academic and industrial research projects have been developed. The capabilities of these products are being enhanced in significant ways. Some of them are:

- The **Progression model** (Stavness, 2004) has incorporated some of the managing concepts of workflow to increase the flexibility in IS. It makes explicitly the steps and transactions as user undertakes when using an IS. As the user progresses towards accomplishing a task or goal, the progression model infrastructure records each step and the state of the transaction and workflow.
- **Microsoft Windows Workflow Foundation (WWF)** (Kitta, 2007) is an extensible framework for developing workflow solutions on the Windows platform. It provides a single, unified model to create end-to-end solutions that span categories of applications, including human workflow and system workflow.

- **Business Process Visual ARCHITEC (BP-VA)** (Visual Paradigm, 2007) is a visual modeling tool that provides the most extensive support for BPMN.
- **WebSphere® MQ Workflow** (IBM, 2005) supports long-running business process workflows as they interact with systems and people. Automates and tracks business processes in accordance with business design. Provides integration processes with rich support for human interactions.

Due to the great number of workflow products a group of researchers have identified a group of workflow patterns that provide the basis for an in-depth comparison of a number of commercially available workflow systems.

- **Control-flow patterns** identify useful routings construct as sequence, parallel split, synchronization, exclusive choice, etc. From a data perspective, there are a series of characteristics that occur repeatedly in different workflow modeling paradigms (van der Aalst, ter Hofstede, Kiepuszewski & Barros, 2003).
- **Workflow data patterns** aim to capture the various ways in which data is represented and utilized in workflows (Russell, ter Hofstede, Edmond, & van der Aalst, 2004).
- **Workflow resource patterns** correspond to the manner in which tasks are allocated to resources, i.e. an entity that is capable of doing work; the focus of these patterns is on human resources (Russell, van der Aalst, ter Hofstede, & Edmond, 2005).

Workflows and Tasks

Tasks are a fundamental aspect in workflow, a common definition for a task is "an activity performed to reach a certain goal" (van Welie, van der Veer, & Eliëns, 1998); task models play an important role because they indicate the logi-cal activities that an application should support to reach user's goals. In the literature, there are several definitions for task models. Task modeling is "the activity of transforming raw task and user related data or envisioning ideas into structured pieces of task knowledge" (van Welie, van der Veer, & Koster, 2000). While the purpose of task analysis is to understand what tasks should be supported and what are their related attributes, the aim of task modeling is to identify more precisely the relationships among such tasks. Task models are explicit representations of user tasks that can help support certain rigorous forms of task analysis.

In the literature there are different approaches to task models with similarities, (task decomposition, task flow, and graphical representations to show the information of the model) although each task model is designed for a certain purpose. Most of the models have a tool to support the modeling of tasks. For instance, Concur Task Trees (CTT) was developed by Paternò (1999) on five concepts: tasks, objects, actions, operators and roles. CTT constructors, termed as operators, are used to link sibling tasks, on the same level of decomposition. It is also important to note that CTT holds a formal definition for its temporal operators. CTT provides with means to describe cooperative tasks. Tasks are further decomposed up to the level of basic tasks defined as tasks that could not be further decomposed. Actions and objects are specified for each basic task. Objects could be perceivable objects or application objects. Application objects are mapped onto perceivable objects in order to be presented to the user.

An interesting feature of CTT is the specification of both input actions and output actions that are associated to an object. The last modification brought to CTT is the integration of the concept of platform in the method in order to support multi-platform UI development. A task can be associated with one or several previously defined platform descriptions for which it is applicable. Views on the task model are obtained by filtering a task model depending on one or several platform. CTT uses a tool, CTTE, for building the task model that is used to specify tasks, roles and objects as well as the a task hierarchy with temporal operators.

CONCEPTUAL MODELLING OF WORKFLOW

As indicate above, workflow is the automation of business process, so we need to know the elements that are involved in business process. We propose an ontology called FlowiXML (see Figure 1), where a workflow model is composed of:

- **Process model:** Its goal is to describe the business processes. A process consists of a number of tasks and a set of relationships among them. The definition of a process indicates which tasks must be performed and in what order. The work list allows workflow manager to view and manage the tasks that are assigned to resources.

- **Task model:** Its goal is to describe how the organization works. Task models describe end users' view of interactive tasks while interacting with the system. A task model represents a decomposition of tasks into sub-tasks linked with task relationships. A task model is a quadruple TM (T, H, R, δ) where

  o T is a nonnegative finite set of tasks $\{t_1, t_2, t_3 \cdots t_n\}$

  ➢ $\forall\ t_i \in T: t_i = (taskname_i, category_i, iteration_i, optional_i)$ where $taskname_i$ is a label, $category_i \in \{manual, interactive, system, mechanic, abstract, cooperative, collaborative, competitive, coopetitive\}$, $iteration_i \in \{2, ..., n\}$, $optional_i \in \{0,1\}$

  o H is the hierarchy resulting from the task decomposition: H is a tree i.e. an acyclic simply connected graph: ($\forall\ t_i$,

$t_j \in T : t_i$ dec t_j) $\land$ ($\exists\ (t_1, ..., t_m)$ m$\geq$3$\dagger$ $\forall p \in \{1,..,m\text{-}1\}: t_p$ dec t_{p+1}, $t_1 = t_m$). Let us define t_0 as the root task: $t_0 \in T: \exists\ t_i \in T: t_i$ dec t_0

  o R is a finite set of temporal operators: R= {enabling, disabling, suspend/resume, order independence, concurrency with information passing, independent concurrency, enabling with information passing, cooperation, inclusive choice, deterministic choice, undeterministic choice, disabling with information passing}

  o δ is a simple transition function between siblings $\delta : T \times R \rightarrow T: t_i \times r \rightarrow t_j$

  ➢ $\forall\ t_i \in T \dagger \exists!\ t_{i1}, \dots t_{in} \in T: t_i$ dec t_{i1} , ..., t_i dec t_{in} ; $\exists!\ r_1, \dots r_{n\text{-}1} \in R \dagger t_{i1}\ r_1\ t_{i2}\ r_2\ t_{i3} \dots r_{n\text{-}1}\ t_{in}$

- **Organizational model:** Its goal is to describe the organizational environment. The key elements of an organization are its resources, structure, tasks, politics, culture, etc. An organizational unit is a formal group of resources working together with one or more shared goals or objectives; three types of resources can be found: human resources (i.e. a user stereotype), material resources (e.g., hardware, network, machines), and immaterial resources (e.g., software, operating system). The job concept allows assembling tasks under a same umbrella in a way that is independent of individual resources in the workflow. In this way, several individuals could play a particular job, and jobs could be interchanged dynamically. To organize tasks and resources we use an agenda, it is a list of activities to be taken up. It includes one or more agenda items to carry out.

More details about the attributes and methods of this workflow model could be found in (Guerrero, Vanderdonckt, & Gonzalez, 2008). Figure 1 only represents the UML class diagram without any attributes or methods.

Of a particular interest from a resource perspective is the manner in which tasks are advertised to specific resources for execution. For this purpose, workflow resource patterns (Russell, van der Aalst, ter Hofstede, & Edmond, 2005) have been considered and introduced in a mapping model.

The rationale for identifying these patterns was the need to master the many ways according which work can be distributed. The patterns are grouped into seven categories: creation patterns, push patterns, pull patterns, detour patterns, autostart patterns, visibility patterns, and multiple resource patterns. The researchers have developed a Web site (http://www. workflowpatterns. com/patterns/resource/) that contains descriptions and examples of theses patterns, along with sup-

porting papers and evaluations of how workflow products support the patterns.

Three modeling levels have been proposed: workflow, process and task. Therefore, it is necessary to clearly specify when and where each model starts and finishes. Since a task is defined as an operation executed while four dimensions remain constant (i.e., time, space, resources, information), any variation of any of these four dimensions, taken alone or combined, thus generate a potential identification of a new task in the task modeling activity. In Table 1 we propose a set of parameters to identify a workflow, a process or a task.

Once the identification criteria have been established, from our conceptual model it is possible to:

- Identify processes and tasks; thereby specify *how we will do the work?*
- Identify organizational units to know *where*

Figure 1. Partial view of the workflow model

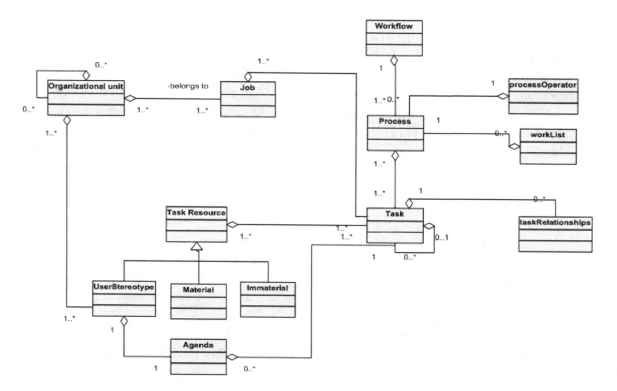

Table 1. Identification criteria

	Time	Space (location)	Resource	Type
Workflow	Series of time periods	Different locations; same organization	Same or different groups of resources	-
Process	Series of time periods	Different locations	Within groups, group as a whole, or among groups	Primary (production), secondary (support), or tertiary (managerial)
Task	Same time period	Same location	One or two types of resources	User, interactive, system, abstract, or machine task

we will do it?

- Identify jobs and resources available, and the way to assign tasks to them, so we establish *who will do it?*

Considering that resources are not alone, that are part of an organization, software engineering must guide the development of applications to support working groups, in order to cover some aspects such as collaboration, communication, coordination, information sharing, etc., which are part of the work group activities. Some group requirements should be taking into account: (1) Support carrying out group tasks from the individual level continuously throughout the global level: individual, within groups, for the group as a whole, among groups, within the organization, and among organizations, (2) Support multiple ways to carry out a group task: in principle, there should not be a unique way to carry out a single group task, but several mechanisms should be offered for this purpose. If a mechanism is no longer available, another one should be selectable, (3) Support the group evolution over time: when the group evolves over time, the workflow definition should be easily maintained and reflected in the system, (4) Provide multiple ways of interaction: group members need multiple interaction methods such as electronic mail, audio, written, verbal, and visual, (5) Sustain several behavioral characteristics: the reaction of a group is always difficult to analyze, the dynamism of a group can

be chaotic (Mandviwalla & Olfman, 1994).

A virtual community is a social network with a common interest, idea, task or goal that interacts in a virtual society across time, geographical and organizational boundaries and is able to develop personal relationships. The Web had become a privileged platform for implementing workflow systems. The Web provides ubiquitous access to information, supports inherent distribution of business process, and consists of platform-independent UIs. A Web community is simply a community that happens to exist online, rather than in the physical world (Kim, 2000).

Taking advantage of this type of communities, it is possible to coordinate work, improve remote communication, keep inform and formed all the members of the group, facilitate problems resolution in the group; despite of some inconvenient as to differentiate who is working for the group and who is been benefited from the group or the resistance to change from resources.

Creating an information system to support work group and that evolves with the organization involves the design of UIs with appropriate widgets to cover the requirements of each group member.

METHOD FOR DEVELOPING THE UI OF A WORKFLOW SYSTEM

To design UIs it is necessary a User Interface Description Language (UIDL), which consists of a high-level computer language for describing characteristics of interest of a UI with respect to the rest of an interactive application; it helps define user interfaces linguistically with a general trend to do so in an XML-complaint way. Many UIDLs have been conceived that contain different features and focus on different levels of granularity; also, a language definition consists of three components: Semantic, syntax, and stylistic. The USer Interface eXtensible Mark-up Language (UsiXML) (Limbourg & Vanderdonckt, 2004; Vanderdonckt, 2005) has been selected as the UIDL to be used in the remainder of this work, because of its capabilities of extensiveness, availability, central storage of models, and its transformational approach.

UsiXML is explicitly based on the Cameleon Reference Framework (Calvary, Coutaz, Thevenin, Limbourg, Bouillon, & Vanderdonckt, 2003). Its simplified version, reproduced in Figure 2, structures development processes for contexts of use into four development steps:

- **Task & Concepts (T&C):** Describe the various user's tasks to be carried out and the domain-oriented concepts as they are required by these tasks to be performed.

- **Abstract UI (AUI):** Defines abstract containers and individual components, two forms of Abstract Interaction Objects by grouping subtasks according to various criteria, a navigation scheme between the containers and selects abstract individual component for each concept so that they are independent of any modality. An AUI abstracts a CUI into a UI definition that is independent of any modality of interaction (e.g., graphical interaction, vocal interaction, speech synthesis and recognition, video-based interaction, virtual, augmented or mixed reality). An AUI can also be considered as a canonical expression of the rendering of the domain concepts and tasks in a way that is independent from any modality

of interaction. An AUI is considered as an abstraction of a CUI with respect to interaction modality. At this level, the UI mainly consists of input/output definitions, along with actions that need to be performed on this information.

- **Concrete UI (CUI):** Concretizes an abstract UI for a given context of use into Concrete Interaction Objects (CIOs) so as to define widgets layout and interface navigation. It abstracts a final UI into a UI definition that is independent of any computing platform. Although a CUI makes explicit the final Look & Feel of a final UI, it is still a mock-up that runs only within a particular environment. A CUI can also be considered as a reification of an AUI at the upper level and an abstraction of the final UI with respect to the platform.

- **Final UI (FUI):** Is the operational UI i.e. any UI running on a particular computing platform either by interpretation or by execution.

UsiXML is a collection of models (small rectangles in Figure 2) for specifying a UI:

- **taskModel**: Is a model describing the interactive task as viewed by the end user interacting with the system.

- **domainModel**: Is a description of the classes of objects manipulated by a user while interacting with a system.

- **mappingModel**: Is a model containing a series of related mappings between models or elements of models.

- **transformationModel**: Graph Transformation (GT) techniques were chosen to formalize explicit transformations between any pair of models, except from the FUI level.

- **contextModel**: Is a model describing the three aspects of a context of use in which a end user is carrying out an interactive task with a specific computing platform in

Figure 2. The simplified Cameleon Reference Framework and UsiXML

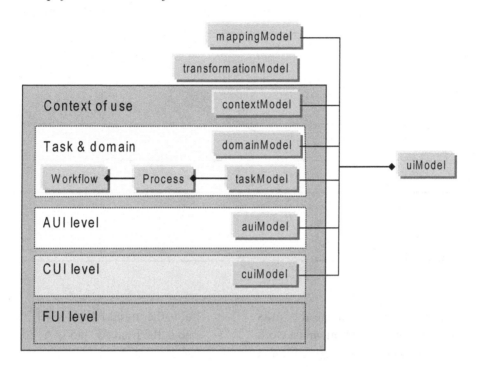

a given surrounding environment. Consequently, a context model consists of a *user model*, a *platform model*, and an *environment model*.

- **auiModel:** Is the model describing the UI at the abstract level as previously defined.
- **cuiModel:** Is the model describing the UI at the concrete level as previously defined.
- **uiModel:** Is the topmost super class containing common features shared by all component models of a UI.

Continuing with the language definition one can say that *syntax* deals solely with the form and structure of symbols in a language without any consideration given to their meaning. The *abstract syntax* is defined as the hidden structure of a language, its mathematical background. FlowiXML uses *directed graph* as abstract syntax. A *concrete syntax* is an external appearance; the *visual syntax*

consists of boxes and arrows, a somewhat classic representation for a graphical structure. This visual syntax will be mainly used to in this work as an expression means for the transformation rules that are going to be developed in a future. The *textual syntax* is described using an XML-based language. The objective of *stylistics* is to provide a representation of a set of defined objects in order to facilitate their understanding and manipulation in tools. The representation can be of different types (e.g., graphical, textual); this representation is reflected in a workflow editor tool.

After having defined the UIs involved in the workflow, we need now to link all the UIs: the ones for the workflow management and the ones for the workflow tasks. This will be achieved thanks to the *user Interface flow* (see Figure 3). During the execution of work, information passes from one resource to another as tasks are finished or delegated; in FlowiXML we use an agenda

Figure 3. User interfaces flow

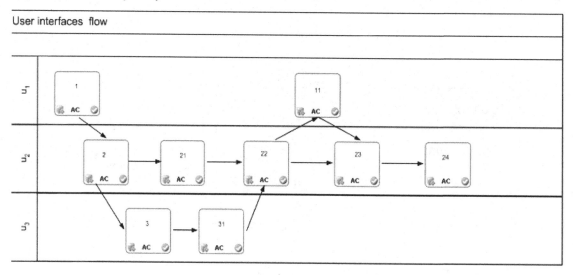

assigned to each resource to manage the tasks that are allocated/offered to her/him, and a work list that allows to workflow manager views and manages the tasks that are assigned to resources. By linking UIs we expect to solve the problem of synchronizing the communication among them. The flow of User Interfaces is an octuple UIF (A, Σ, U, T, δ, ω, ai, ao) where

- A is a nonnegative finite set of Abstract Containers (AC)
- Σ is a set of input events [set of events occurring in AC]
- U is a nonnegative set of user stereotypes, such that $\forall$ a $\in$A:$\exists$! u $\in$U † is used by (a,u) [unique] or $\exists$ u_1, u_2... u_n $\in$U † is used by {a, u_1, u_2... u_n} [a is shared among u_1, u_2... u_n]
- T is a set of output transitions [output transitions means a navigation from starting AC to a final one, we do not want to commit ourselves to a particular type or representation]
- δ is a transition function, $\delta : A \times \Sigma \rightarrow A$ [a transition is AC + abstract event occurring in one AC]
- ω is an output function, $\omega : A \rightarrow T$

- ai is the initial AC [ai $\in$ A]
- ao is the final AC [ao $\in$ A, ao $\neq$ ai]

CASE STUDY AND TOOL SUPPORT

Considering that virtual communities are formed and exploited by a variety of social and professional groups interacting via the Internet, we want to illustrate how the methodology proposed above allows a research group to collaborate using a blog on a Web site.

Tool support: In order to support the development of UIs from a workflow model to a task model, a workflow editor has been developed. This editor allows modeling the general workflow defining processes and tasks models, defining organizational units, jobs and resources involved, allocation of tasks to resources, and to manage the flow of tasks.

Case study: A research group, working in the same university but in different departments, needs to keep in touch in order to change information due to they are working in a specific project to be submitted to get founding. A good option to help them is creating a collaborative blog (a Web site where publishes posts are written by multiple users, called co-bloggers). Thus, it is necessary to create a blog, to select the users, to invite them to participate and collaborate through the blog posting, adding comments or just reading publishes posts and comments.

We might start to specify what we want to do:

- **What?** *Workflow specification*: the workflow specification, depicted in the process model, takes place inside the organizational units' framework. This part of the graphical notation of the workflow is based on Petri nets notation (van der Aalst, 1998). Process definition gives the paths that may be followed by a particular item through the set of tasks. In our example (Figure 4), the first step is to *log in*, and then registered users can *create a blog*, and/or *edit* an existing blog. Once the blog has been created, co-bloggers need to log in to edit the blog. Also it is possible to create another blog. However, thanks to the post-condition attribute of the task log in, it is mandatory that the blog exists to be edited.

- **How?** *Task models specification*: for each task a task model is specified to describe in detail *how* the task is performed. Task models do not impose any particular implementation so that user tasks can be better analyzed without implementation constraints.

In order to accomplish the task *log in*, it is necessary to execute a series of steps (Figure 5) which are: to *register* to the Web site, there are two options: type user's account directly if there is already an account or to provided personal information to get a new account. After the system *verifies* the *information* received, in case information is wrong the system *sends a message* to notify the user. Finally, the user could continue with the next task or not.

Then, the user proceeds to create the blog (Figure 6). The first step it to *assign a name* for the blog, after *select the URL*, then *select a template*, finally the system validates and provides feedback to the user, who *receives a message* with the results of its creation.

Once the blog has been created, it is possible to edit it (Figure 7). In this part of the design users *create an entry, edit a created entry, configure and modify* the blog. To create an entry, it is advisable to *assign a title*, to *type the text*,

Figure 4. Workflow to create a blog

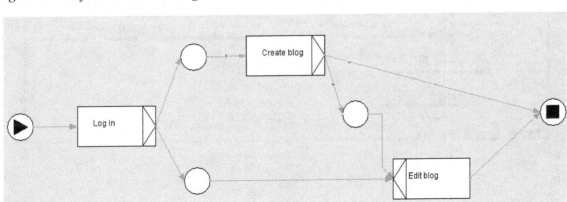

Figure 5. Log in task model

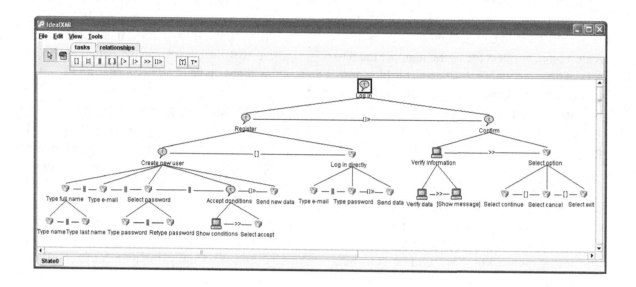

Figure 6. Create blog task model

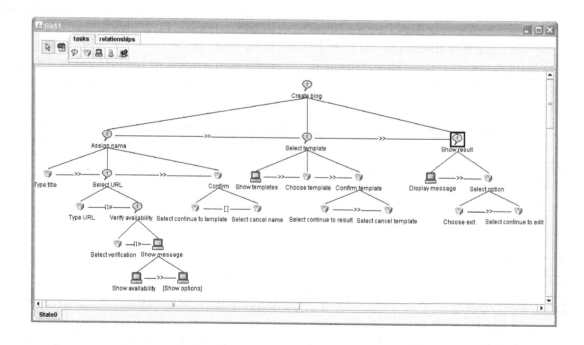

Figure 7. Edit blog task model

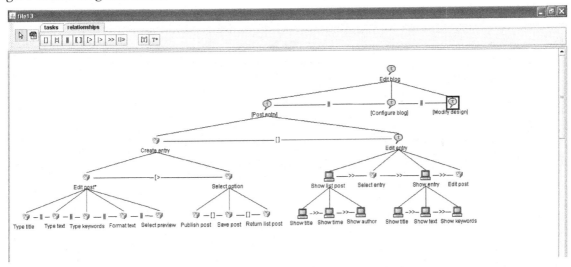

Figure 8. Configure basic elements task model

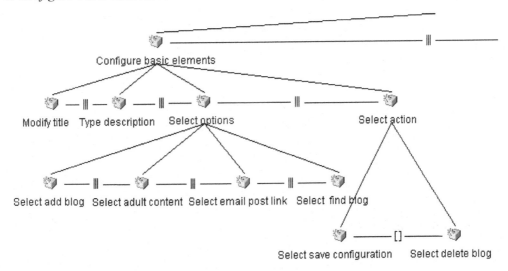

to *format* it (e.g. highlight some words), *specify keywords*, *have a pre-view* of the entry, *save* the entry. Once the entry was published, it is feasible to edit it in order to make corrections, or add new information, etc.

It is important to specify that as an attribute of the task *edit entry*, it has as a precondition that an entry was created.

As part of *blog configuration* (second task in Figure 7), it is possible to *modify title* of the blog, *write* a brief *blog description*, specify if the blog will be added to a list of commercial blogs, specify if the content is just for adults, specify if the email post links let visitors easily email posts from your blog to their friends, specify if the blog will be included in blog search engines, or *delete* the blog (Figure 8).

Also one significant aspect is to configure the comments (Figure 9), in this case they can be visualized or not and, most important, it is pos-

Figure 9. Configure comments task model

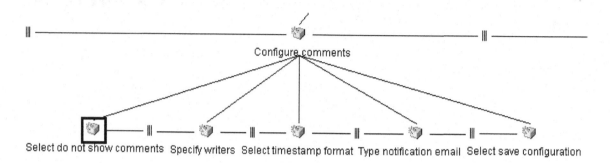

Figure 10. Configure email task model

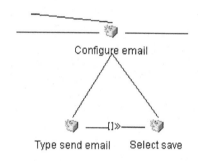

Figure 11. Configure permissions task model

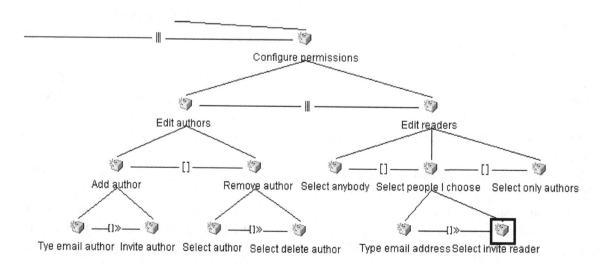

sible specify who can add a comment and how the users can know that a comment was added thanks to the notification by email.

In addition, it is relevant notify to the users each time that a new posting was made (Figure 10), so in this case different email addresses are specified.

Furthermore, it is necessary to configure the permissions of the blog (Figure 11), thus specifying which users will be playing the job of co-blogger (write and read entries and comments) and readers (read entries and write comments or just read).

Now, as part of *modify the blog design* (third task in Figure 7), it refers principally to the selection of fonts and colors, and the possibility to change the template.

- **Where?** : Once the specification of what we want to do and how it will be done, we continue with the workflow model, so the next step is defining where the work will be execute, in this case the participants belong to different departments in the same university, thus we can say that in each department involved the users can be accessing to the blog. However, we are talking about a virtual space where the communication and collaboration will be taken place.

- **Who?** *Specification of jobs and users*: this step consists on describing who will be involved in the performance of tasks. Jobs are ways to structure the crew of people inside the organization. It involves the complete collection of knowledge and practices needed by a definite human resource to perform a task. The jobs specified in the definition of the current case study are: a blog designer, a blog manager, authors and users.

Once jobs are defined it is possible to incorporate workers able to carry out tasks of a particular job. Workers are defined in terms of attributes (name, experience, hierarchy level) and the list of jobs they can perform. Once the work and workers were added to the workflow, they can be linked with the tasks.

- **Whom?** *Assigning tasks to resources*: one characteristic of workflow is to determine the right person for the right task at the right moment; for that purpose, we use workflow resource patterns (Russell, van der Aalst, ter Hofstede, & Edmond, 2005) to specify who will perform tasks realization inside organizational units. We already determine the range of resources available in the different organizational units. Now, we go further by adding rules defining the way work will be undertaken. For each process in the workflow model it is possible to define one or several allocation or offering relationships: Distribution, Managing, Deviation, Auto-start, Visibility, or Multiple resources. In our case study, the task *create blog* is allocated to *Steve Geller* who has experience as *blog designer*.

As a result of these steps, we can visualize the complete workflow in our editor (Figure 14).

Generating UIs, *from task model to UI.* This step is achieved by relying on the UsiXML method that progressively moves from a task model to a final user interface (Figure 15). This approach consists of three steps: deriving abstract user interfaces from a task model, deriving concrete user interfaces from each abstract one, and producing the code of the corresponding final user interfaces. To ensure these steps, transformations are encoded as graph transformations performed on the involved models expressed in their graph equivalent. For each step, a graph grammar gathers relevant graph transformations for accomplishing the sub-steps. For instance, applying this method

Figure 12. Specification of jobs and users in the workflow

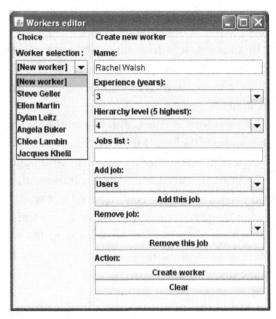

Figure 13. Assigning tasks to resources in the workflow

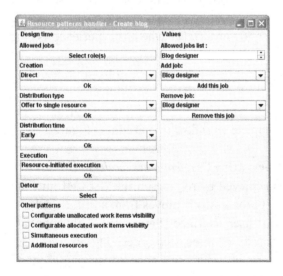

to the task model *Log in* we obtain its correspondent UI. Figure shows the four levels to develop UIs (Figure 2).

Then by analogy we can obtain the complete set of UIs corresponding to a workflow model.

Selecting the option to send emails to users we can assure the notification of new posts/comments that are published on the blog.

Figure 14. Workflow editor

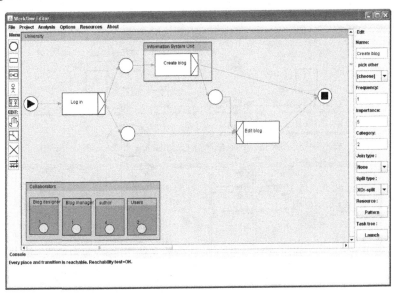

FUTURE TRENDS

Until recently, workflow information systems, as well as their supporting UIs, have been condemned to stay pre-defined and fixed along most dimensions. In the near future, we expect that these constraints will be relaxed progressively so as to give rise to a new series of open questions including, but not limited to:

- **User variation:** Not only a worker could evolve dynamically over time, after all human being is very adaptable, but also a worker could be replaced by another for the same job as people are asked to become more flexible in their job positions. Consequently, a workflow UI should accommodation multiple user stereotypes over time, but also variations of a given user stereotype over time.
- **Task variation:** Most of the time, the processes and their underlying tasks are defined at design time, thus preventing the workflow from supporting new tasks or evolving tasks, unless the engineer applies the required

modification. Moreover, if there is needs for incorporating dynamic tasks that are know only at run-time, perhaps without the support of the workflow manager, appears a need for end-user definition of a new task.

- **Workplace variation:** As workers are requested to become more and more mobile, they are confronted with tasks and processes that are no longer executed in their traditional stationary contexts of use, but in new contexts. These tasks and processes are then redefined depending on the workplace where they are achieved. Consequently, the supporting UIs should support this variation. Task migration or redistribution is likely to appear as well. A UI could for instance be decomposed into smaller pieces, some of them being detached from the main UI and attached to another workplace, even if the main system remains at the same workplace.
- **Platform variation:** As a consequence of the previous variation or independently of that, the worker may want to use another computing platform at run-time because it

Figure 15. Generating UIs

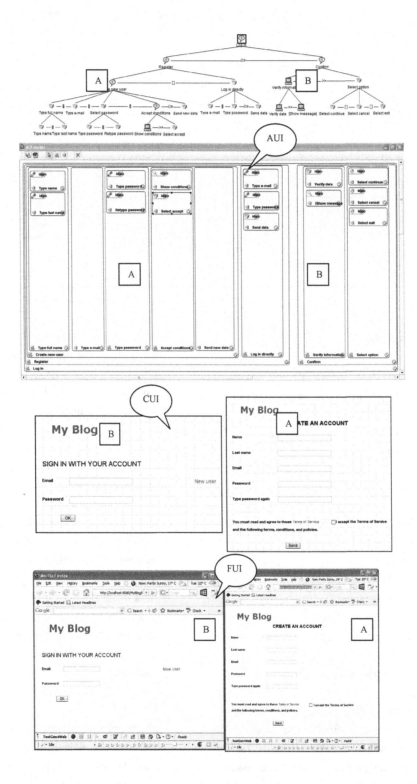

Figure 16. Some final user interfaces

is more convenient for her. Therefore, the supporting UIs should support the same task on different computing platforms and accommodate their variations.

CONCLUSION

Virtual communities are formed around different disciplines to bring together people sharing a common interest, concern or desire. One important aspect to consider is the design of the user interfaces of the system that will be used by the community to foster collaboration. Ideally, such a design should be freed from the specificities of platforms, access terminals and local workflow bindings. To this effect, it is important to generate user interface software for community-oriented workflows in a manner which platform independent, customizable and extensible.

In this chapter we have introduced a model-driven engineering method that provides designers with methodological guidance on how to systematically derive user interfaces of workflow information systems from a model of workflow, which is decomposed into processes to end up with

tasks. Based on workflow patterns, it is possible to model an entire workflow with high-level mechanisms and automatically generate the workflow specifications and their corresponding UIs.

All models are uniformly expressed in the same XML-based specification language so that mappings between models are preserved at design-time and can be exploited at run-time in needed. Then, the different *steps* of the approach have been properly defined based on the underlying models and a *workflow editor-manager tool* has been developed to support the method enactment. The major benefit of the above method is that all the design knowledge required to progressively move from a workflow specification to its corresponding UIs is expressed in the model and the mapping rules. The method preserves continuity (all subsequent models are derived from previous ones) and traceability of its enactment (it is possible to trace how a particular workflow is decomposed into processes and tasks, with their corresponding user interfaces). In this way, it is possible to change any level (workflow, process, task, and UI) and to propagate the changes throughout the other levels by navigating through the mappings established at design time.

This method has been so far validated on 4 real-world case studies (e.g., a hospital dept., a triathlon organization, a cycling event, and personalized order of compression stockings over Internet).

RESOURCES

All resources related to this workflow UI development method can be found at: http://www.usixml. org/index.php?mod=pages&id=40. On this Web page, the FlowiXML software can be downloaded, along with its user's manual, and case studies with examples. A video demonstrating the system could be also downloaded.

ACKNOWLEDGMENT

We gratefully acknowledge the support of the CONACYT program (www.conacyt.mx) supported by the Mexican government and the SIMILAR network of excellence (http://www.similar. cc), the European research task force creating human-machine interfaces similar to human-human communication of the European Sixth Framework Programme (FP6-2002-IST1-507609).

REFERENCES

Calvary, G., Coutaz, J., Thevenin, D., Limbourg, Q., Bouillon, L., & Vanderdonckt, J. (2003). A Unifying reference framework for multi-target user interfaces. *Interacting with Computers, 15*(3), 289-308.

Guerrero, J., Vanderdonckt, J., & Gonzalez, J. M. (2008). FlowiXML: A step towards designing workflow management systems. *International Journal of Web Engineering and Technology, 4*(2), 163-182.

Guerrero, J., Vanderdonckt, J., Gonzalez, J. M., & Winckler, M. (2008, March). Modeling user interfaces to workflow information systems. Paper presented in *4th International Conference on Autonomic and Autonomous Systems ICAS'2008*, Gosier, Guadeloupe.

IBM. (2005). *IBM WebSphere MQ Workflow V3.6 expands support for large enterprise workflow integration solutions.* Retrieved April 19, 2005, from http://www-01.ibm.com/common/ssi/cgi-bin/ssialias?infotype=an&subtype=ca&appname=GPA&htmlfid=897/ENUS205-096

Kim, A. J. (2000). *Community building on the Web: Secret strategies for successful online communities.* PeachPit Press. From http://www.naima.com/community

Kitta, T. (2007). *Professional windows workflow foundation.* Indianapolis, IN: Wiley Publishing, Inc.

Limbourg, Q., & Vanderdonckt, J. (2004). UsiXML: A user interface description language supporting multiple levels of independence. In M. Matera & S. Comai, (Eds.), *Engineering advanced Web applications*, (pp. 325-338). Paramus, NJ: Rinton Press.

Mandviwalla, M., & Olfman, L. (1994). What do groups need? A proposed set of generic groupware requirements. *ACM Transactions on Computer-Human Interaction, 1*(3), 245-268.

Paternò, F. (1999). *Model based design and evaluation of interactive applications.* Berlin: Springer Verlag.

Rheingold, H. (2000). *The virtual community: Homesteading on the electronic frontier.* London: MIT Press.

Russell, N., ter Hofstede, A. H. M., Edmond, D., & van der Aalst, W. M. P. (2004). *Workflow data patterns* (Tech. Rep. FIT-TR-2004-01). Brisbane, Australia: Queensland University of Technology.

Russell, N., van der Aalst, W. M. P., ter Hofstede, A. H. M., & Edmond, D. (2005). Workflow resource patterns. In O. Pastor & J. Falcao e Cunha, (Eds.), *17th Conference on Advanced Information Systems Engineering (CAiSE'05): Vol. 3520 of Lecture Notes in Computer Science* (pp. 216-232). Berlin: Springer-Verlag.

Stavness, N. (2005) *Supporting flexible workflow process with a progression model*. Unpublished master's thesis. University of Saskatchewan, Saskatoon.

van der Aalst, W. M. P. (1998). The application of Petri nets to workflow management. *Journal of Circuits, Systems, and Computers, 8*(1), 21-66.

van der Aalst W. M. P., ter Hofstede, A. H. M., Kiepuszewski, B., & Barros, A. P. (2003). Workflow patterns. *Distributed and Parallel Databases, 14*(3), 5-51.

van der Aalst, W. M. P., & ter Hofstede, A. H. M. (2005). YAWL: Yet Another Workflow Language. *Information Systems, 30*(4), 245-275

Vanderdonckt, J. (2005). A MDA-compliant environment for developing user interfaces of information systems. In O. Pastor & J. Falcao & Cunha, (Eds.), *17th Conference on Advanced Information Systems Engineering (CAiSE'05): Vol. 3520 of Lecture Notes in Computer Science* (pp. 16-31). Berlin: Springer-Verlag.

van Welie M., van der Veer, G. C., & Eliëns, A. (1998). An ontology for task world models. In *Proceeding of the 5th International Eurographics Workshop on Design, Specification, and Verification of Interactive Systems* DSV-IS98 (pp. 57-70). Abingdon, UK.

van Welie, M., van der Veer, G. C., & Koster, A. (2000). Integrated representations for task modeling. In *Proceedings of the Tenth European Conference on Cognitive Ergonomics* (pp. 129-138) . Linköping, Sweden.

Verbeek, H. M. W., Hirnschall, A., & van der Aalst, W. M. P. (2002, May). *XRL/Flower: Supporting inter-organizational workflows using XML/petri-net technology*. Paper presented at *Web Services, e-Business, and the Semantic Web (WES): Foundations, Models, Architecture, Engineering and Applications, held in conjunction with CAiSE 2002* [The Fourteenth International Conference on Advanced Information Systems Engineering], Toronto, Ontario, Canada.

Visual Paradigm International Ltd. (2007). *Business Process Visual ARCHITECT, User's guide*. Retrieved January 2, 2007, from www.visual-paradigm.com/product/bpva/bpvadocuments.jsp

Workflow Management Coalition (1999). *Workflow management coalition terminology & glossary*. Document Number WFMC-TC-1011. Document Status – Issue 3.0.

KEY TERMS

Aui Model: It is the model describing the UI at the abstract level.

Collaborative Blog: Also known as a group blog. It is a web log (blog) written by multiple people and based on a single unifying theme.

Context Model: It is a model describing the three aspects of a context of use in which a end user is carrying out an interactive task with a specific computing platform in a given surrounding environment. Consequently, a context model consists of a user model, a platform model, and an environment model.

Cui Model: Is the model describing the UI at the concrete level.

Domain Model: It describes the real-world concepts, and their interactions as understood by users and the operations that are possible on these concepts.

FlowiXML: It is a methodology for developing the various UI of a Workflow Information System, which are advocated to automate processes, following a model-centric approach based on the requirements and processes of the organization.

Mapping Model: It is a model containing a series of related mappings between models or elements of models. A mapping model serves to gather a set of intermodel relationships that are Semantically related. It expresses reification, abstraction, and translation.

Petri Net: Also known as a place/transition net or P/T net, is a directed bipartite graph, in which the nodes represent transitions (i.e. discrete events that may occur), places (i.e. conditions), and directed arcs (that describe which places are pre- and/or post conditions for which transitions).

Process: It is a collection of tasks linked by relationships. The definition of a process indicate which tasks must be performed and in what order.

Task: An activity performed to reach a certain goal.

Task Model: It is a model describing the interactive task as viewed by the end user interacting with the system. A task model represents a decomposition of tasks into sub-tasks linked with task relationships. Therefore, the decomposition relationship is the privileged relationship to express this hierarchy, while temporal relationships express the temporal constraints between sub-tasks of a same parent task.

Ui Model: It is the topmost superclass containing common features shared by all component models of a UI. A uiModel may consist of a list of component model sin any order and any number, such as task model, a domain model, an abstract UI model, a concrete UI model, mapping model, and context model. A user interface model needs not include one of each model component. Moreover, there may be more than one of a particular kind of model component.

UsiXML: It stands for USer Interface eXtensible Markup Language, a XML-compliant markup language that describes the UI for multiple contexts of use such as Character User Interfaces (CUIs), Graphical User Interfaces (GUIs), Auditory User Interfaces, and Multimodal User Interfaces. In other words, interactive applications with different types of interaction techniques, modalities of use, and computing platforms can be described in a way that preserves the design independently from peculiar characteristics of physical computing platform.

User Interface (UI): The user interface is the aggregate of means by which people (the users) interact with a particular machine, device, computer program or other complex tool (the system).

Workflow: It is the automation of a business process, in whole or part, during which documents, information or tasks are passed from one participant to another for action, according to a set of procedural rules.

Workflow Information Systems (WIS): It refers to the application of information technology to business problems. Its primary characteristic is the automation of process involving combinations of human activities with information technology applications.

Section E
Practice Domains and Case Studies

Chapter XVII
Virtual Communities in Health and Social Care

Manolis Tsiknakis
Institute of Computer Science, FORTH, Greece

ABSTRACT

This chapter provides an overview and discussion of virtual communities in health and social care. The available literature indicates that a virtual community in health or social care can be defined as a group of people using telecommunications with the purposes of delivering health care and education, and/or providing support. Such communities cover a wide range of clinical specialties, technologies and stakeholders. Examples include peer-to-peer networks, virtual health care delivery and E-Science research teams. Virtual communities may empower patients and enhance coordination of care services; however, there is not sufficient systematic evidence of the effectiveness of virtual communities on clinical outcomes. When practitioners utilize virtual community tools to communicate with patients or colleagues they have to maximize sociability and usability of this mode of communication, while addressing concerns for privacy and the fear of de-humanizing practice, and the lack of clarity or relevance of current legislative frameworks. Furthermore, the authors discuss in this context ethical, legal considerations and the current status of research in this domain. Ethical challenges including the concepts of identity and deception, privacy and confidentiality and technical issues, such as sociability and usability are introduced and discussed.

INTRODUCTION

Health care is a sector which today experiences a number of pressures, both from inside and outside. The continuing innovation in medicine and health care technologies expands the methods and tools available in health care. Combined with citizen empowerment the demographic changes of an ageing European population stretch the limits of what countries can afford to offer as services within their national health systems.

Governments are confronted by the urgent need to find means to contain the rise in health care expenditure without compromising quality, equity and access. Consequently, new ways to organise and deliver health services are being investigated and experimented with. Public-private partnerships in care delivery are emerging. Citizens and patients are given more responsibility in the management of their own health and chronic illnesses (World Health Organisation, 2002).

As a result of these developments, an important trend throughout Europe and globally is a move towards more involvement of patients or citizens in informed decision making of any choice and responsibility for their own health. The vision behind this work is comprised of two components: new innovative services to the citizens and networking services and care across organisational boundaries. Within such a context, virtual communities, despite their infant stage, have already shown the potential to provide new virtuality in the collaboration and communication-intensive paradigm that progressively emerges.

The Changing Environment

Considering the dynamics in health care, the traditional system model of health care has emphasized hierarchical structures with strict separation of organisational responsibilities within the framework of health care. This hierarchy can be seen through the following points:

- Strict organisational division of responsibilities between primary care (e.g., municipal GP-led health centres) and secondary care (e.g. regional or specialist-led hospitals).
- Geographical separation of patient care responsibility (e.g., within primary and secondary care).
- Separation of duties between different health care professional groups (i.e., physicians and nurses) and specialties as well as separation of patients from the care process.

- Separation between public and private care providers within the different levels.

In the healthcare information and communication technology (ICT) context, these hierarchical divisions can be seen in the implementation and scope of information and communication systems used by care facilitators. Separation is actually amplified when exchange of information is considered. Conventional health ICT systems, supporting overall service provision, are centralized and follow these boundaries closely, while system interoperability is often minimal. Furthermore, direct patient access to electronic patient record information is typically minimal or non-existent. Similarly for professionals, the use of integrated ICT systems and services is restricted to their primary working facility.

This traditional system model faces several challenges and structural changes are unavoidable (Tsiknakis & Saranummi, 2005). For example, aging populations, limited resource allocations, increasing specialization in medicine requiring convenient consultation tools, and trends towards patient and non-physician empowerment drive the system towards the breaking down of strict organizational and other boundaries, i.e. towards process-orientation and ad-hoc networking in the search for better results. As a result we witness a movement towards shared or integrated care in which the single doctor–patient relationship is giving way to one in which an individual's healthcare is the responsibility of a team of professionals across all sectors of the healthcare system. This is being accompanied by a very significant growth in home care, which is increasingly viable even for seriously ill patients through sophisticated eHealth services facilitated by intelligent sensors, monitoring devices, hand-held technologies, and the Internet.

In parallel to this organizational restructuring of the care system, enabled by current information and communication technologies, citizens in developed countries are already making more decisions about their own treatment. The informed, knowledgeable and increasingly demanding patients are moving into the heart of the healthcare system. Preventive and personalized medicine, which fundamentally requires the active engagement, understanding and involvement of the citizen or consumer, is gradually shifting the emphasis towards promoting wellness rather than treating illness.

Patient Empowerment and Personalized Medicine

As discussed earlier, two key drivers are shaping the healthcare delivery model of the future (see *Figure 1*); patient empowerment and personalized medicine. Patient empowerment is a concept that has emerged in the health care literature in the last few years. It is based on the principle that patients are entitled to access health information and determine their own care choices. Feste & Anderson (1995) argue that the empowerment model introduces "*self-awareness, personal responsibility, informed choices and quality of life*". Empowerment can be perceived as an enabling process through which individuals or groups take control over their lives and the management of disease.

Advances in telecommunication technologies have introduced new ways to enhance and supplement communication between health care professionals and patients. The implication is a shift of focus for system designers who had primarily focused on designing information technology applications that addressed the needs of health care providers and institutions only. As a result, the data models included episodic patient encounters as one group of health care related transactions, but did not aim to evolve around the life course of the individual patient or ensure continuity of care. New technologies and advancements in informatics research call for the development of informatics tools that will support patients as active consumers in the health care delivery system. Virtual communities are one of the tools that enable a shift from institution-centric to patient-centric information systems.

On the other hand, doctors have long known that people differ in susceptibility to disease and response to medicines. But, with little guidance for understanding and adjusting to individual differences, treatments developed have generally been standardized for the many, rather than the few. Human DNA contains more than 20,000 genes, all of which are stored in our cells' nuclei. Each person's overall blueprint is basically the same,

Figure 1. The gradual transformation of the healthcare delivery model form a "reactive" to a "predictive" one with emphasis on patient empowerment & personalized healthcare delivery

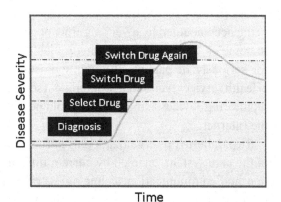
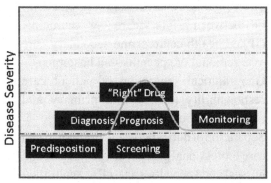

made up of about 3 billion "letters" of code, each letter corresponding to a chemical subunit of the DNA molecule. But subtle variants in about 1 percent of our DNA—often the result of just a single chemical letter being different—give humans their individual identities. Beyond physical appearance, genes give rise to distinct chemistries in various realms of the body and brain. Such differences sometimes predispose people to particular diseases, and some dramatically affect the way a person will respond to medical treatments.

Ideally, doctors would be able to diagnose and treat people based on those individual differences, a concept commonly referred to as *personalized medicine*. At its core, personalized medicine is about combining genetic information with clinical data to optimally tailor drugs and doses to meet the unique needs of an individual patient. "Personalized medicine", writes L. Lesko (2007) of the U.S. Food and Drug Administration,

can be viewed… as a comprehensive, prospective approach to preventing, diagnosing, treating, and monitoring disease in ways that achieve optimal individual health-care decisions.

VIRTUAL COMMUNITIES IN HEALTH AND SOCIAL CARE

Virtual communities are *"social aggregations that emerge from the Net when enough people carry on ... public discussions long enough, with sufficient human feeling, to form Webs of personal relationships in cyberspace"* (Rheingold, 1993). Virtual communities are therefore social networks formed or facilitated through electronic media (Wellman, 1997). The term "virtual" implies properties that, unlike those of a traditional community, i.e. assumption of geographic proximity, are based on the utilization of advanced technologies enabling interactions and exchange of information between members

who may not have a face-to-face interaction at any point in time.

A report resulting from the workshop held at the ACM Computer Human Interaction (CHI) conference on the theory and practice of physical and network communities identified several core attributes of virtual communities, such as a shared goal or interest among members that provides the main reason for forming and maintaining a community, repeated and active member participation, access to shared resources, defined policies for the type and frequency of access and reciprocity of information, support and services (Whittaker, Issacs, & O'Day, 1997).

A virtual community in health care refers to a group of people and the social structure that they collectively create that is supported by information and communication technologies (ICT) with the purposes of collectively conducting activities related to health and disease management as well as education. Such activities can include actual delivery of health care services, staff or patient education, provision of support, discussions on health and treatment related issues and problems, sharing of documents, consulting with experts and sustaining relationships beyond face-to-face events. The stakeholders and participants of such communities can be a mix of health care providers and educators, patients and caregivers. More specifically, these communities could be networks including:

- Health care professionals (providers and researchers) only
- Patients/informal caregivers only
- Health care professionals and their patients and family members/informal caregivers
- Members of the general public

Examples of virtual communities that include only healthcare professionals can be virtual care delivery and research teams. Such teams can ensure continuity of care as they utilize a common platform for exchange of messages, opinions and resources. Virtual teams are considered essential to successful disease management and to providing continuity of care for the patients.

Virtual communities involving only patients and their family members include applications that function as self-help groups of individuals diagnosed with the same medical condition or undergoing the same treatment. One study (Finn, 1999) found that virtual self-help groups could provide many of the processes used in face-to-face self-help and mutual aid groups. The emphasis in such virtual communities is on mutual problem solving, information sharing, expression of feelings, mutual support and empathy.

Virtual communities involving both health care providers and patients include applications that enhance disease management or provide alternative ways of communication between providers and patients beyond face-to-face meetings. Finally, virtual communities open to the general public may include educational services, discussion forums and other activities without requiring that their members assume an official role in the care delivery process and identify themselves as such (Burnett, Besant, & Chatman, 2001).

This Chapter provides an overview and discussion of virtual communities in health and social care and specifically, patient and caregiver-centric support groups, peer-to-peer networks and virtual research teams. In this context, we analyze the concept of patient empowerment as well as issues of identity and deception in a virtual health care community. Furthermore, we aim to discuss ethical and legal considerations, as well as related privacy and security issues.

A TAXONOMY OF VIRTUAL COMMUNITIES IN eHEALTH

In the following, we discuss the types of virtual communities (classified by intended type of membership, i.e. health care providers, researchers,

patients and caregivers) and the ethical and legal challenges associated with this concept.

Virtual Health Care Delivery Teams

Chronic illnesses require specialized and complex treatment protocols that involve a team of healthcare professionals and disciplines to address the multiple dimensions of care and social, psychosocial and clinical needs of patients. Such teams are essential to effective care provided to ensure continuity and to improve the patient's quality of life. However, there are often practical constraints, such as time conflicts, geographic distances, other coordination challenges and limited resources that limit the type and frequency of interactions among health care professionals. The use of advanced ICT technologies provides an opportunity to bridge geographic distance and create "virtual" health care teams.

In order to understand the concept of a "virtual team" we first need to examine how a team is defined and what dimensions it encompasses. Lorimer and Manion(1996) define a team as a

small number of consistent people committed to a relevant shared purpose, with common performance goals, complementary and overlapping skills, and a common approach to their work.

The physical presence of team members at the same place and time is not an inherent requirement for the creation of a team. Rather, it is the nature of the interactions, namely the interdisciplinary character of the information exchange that becomes essential to an effective team. Health care providers of different disciplines (such as physicians, nurses, social workers, physical therapists, etc.) can create a team in which they combine their knowledge and expertise to develop and deliver a comprehensive plan of care.

Heinemann (2002) describes four domains of team function that can guide interdisciplinary team development: (1) structure (composition of team members and representation of disciplines); (2) context (relationship to the larger institution); (3) process (of team functioning, hierarchy and communication) and (4) productivity. In this context, the third domain referring to the process is the one that would be defined differently for virtual teams. The communication in this case could on the one hand be Web-based synchronous interaction or video-mediated or on the other be asynchronous interaction using message boards and discussion forums. It can be argued that such an asynchronous mode of communication could lead to increased overall productivity of the team as professionals contribute at their own discretion and convenience, having the opportunity to review the files, notes and records carefully before communicating a message to the rest of the team.

Several examples of such systems are reported in the literature. WebOnCoLL (Chronaki et al., 1997) is a Web-based collaboration infrastructure designed to support both synchronous and asynchronous collaboration of virtual healthcare teams. WebOnCOLL manages Teleconsultation Folders (TCFs) as shared virtual workspaces. Each collaborative teleconsultation session is associated with a TCF that includes relevant medical multimedia documents, such as reports, digitized x-rays, biosignals, ECGs, progress notes, etc. In a synchronous teleconsultation mode it also involves video conferencing. The use of XML combined with terminology standards promotes reuse and standardization, while facilitating efficient search of archived teleconsultation records (Chronaki et al., 2001).

A system reported by Pitsillides et al. (2004) aims to support the *"dynamic creation, management and coordination of virtual medical teams for the continuous treatment"* of home care patients. The team in this project includes oncologists, family physicians, home care nurses, physiotherapists, psychologists, social workers and the patient. The system architecture utilized the Internet and included a centralized electronic

medical record system and mobile agents and devices distributed to members of the team.

Good pain and symptom management for patients at the end of their life requires the intervention of all disciplines in a holistic approach (Mazanec et al., 2002). This mandates an interdisciplinary approach to managing care at the end-of-life. The Telehospice Project at the University of Missouri utilizes commercially available videophones that operate over regular phone lines to enable patients at home and their caregivers to interact with hospice providers at the clinical site (Demiris et al., 2004). This interaction enables the "virtual" participation of patients in interdisciplinary team meetings and allows for them and their caregivers to interact with hospice providers.

Virtual Disease Management

The concept of disease management refers to "… a set of coordinated healthcare interventions and communications for populations with conditions in which patient self-care efforts are significant" (Disease Management Association of America, 2002). These interventions aim to enhance the care plan and the provider–patient relationship while emphasizing prevention of deterioration and complications using evidence-based practice guidelines. In addition, further goals include the improvement of outcomes, decrease of costs, patient education and monitoring. The concept of "virtual disease management" is defined by the utilization of Internet based technologies in allowing patients suffering from chronic conditions to stay at home and be involved in the care delivery process. Such technologies can link home care with hospital and ambulatory care, and facilitate information exchange and communication between patients, family members and care providers.

Patient education is an essential component of disease management and can be supported by the transmission of tailored health information or automated reminders to patients or their caregivers. The integration of commercially available household items, such as television sets, mobile phones, videophones, medication dispensing machines, and handheld computers introduces new communication modes and patient empowering tools.

The Internet has been used as a platform for several disease management applications and in different clinical areas. Disease management for asthma patients, for example, has the potential of early detection and timely intervention as demonstrated by the home asthma telemonitoring (HAT) system (Finkelstein, O'Connor, & Friedmann, 2001) which assists patients in the daily routine of asthma care with personalized interventions and alerts health care providers in cases that require immediate attention. Internet technologies and mobile communications have been used in a study reported in (Pascual et al., in print) with the objective to evaluate in real-life settings the effect of services for the follow-up and control of hypertensive patients, with particular emphasis on the virtual team roles, tasks and resources involved. In a study by Basch et al. (2005), 80 patients with gynaecologic malignancies beginning standard chemotherapy regimens were enrolled and encouraged to log in and report symptoms at each follow-up visit, or alternatively, to access the system from home. Numerous toxicities entered from home prompted clinician interventions. Patients were capable of reporting symptoms experienced during chemotherapy and their reporting often led to clinical interventions and changes in the care plan indicating that the use of virtual disease management technologies can be beneficial for the treatment and monitoring of home patients diagnosed with cancer.

Leimeister et al (2007) reports that adolescent cancer patients have to deal with many dependencies and obligations. Very often they are torn out of their social environment and become isolated because of changing therapy cycles and different treatment locations. This causes significant social

and economic damage. The article presents the first steps of an empirical exploration of the possibilities of mobile IT support for communication and coordination for this target group during treatment and aftercare. Special emphasis is put on the effects of mobile systems on the patient's perceived quality of life.

Morlion et al (2002) reports on the use of a Web-based telemonitoring system providing direct transmission of home spirometry to the hospital. The study demonstrates that home monitoring of pulmonary function in lung transplant recipients via the Internet is feasible and accurate. Another application utilizing commercially available monitoring devices and Web-based technologies was developed within the HYGEIAnet project at the region of Crete aiming to enable patients at home, who were diagnosed with congestive heart failure (Chiarugi et al., 2003) or chronic obstructive pulmonary disease (Traganitis et al., 2001), to interact—synchronously and/or asynchronously—with health care providers at secondary or tertiary healthcare facilities.

More recently, a study reported by Rubinelli et al (2008) discusses the organisation of a virtual community composed of health professionals and patients affected by chronic low back pain. The community was created as part of a pilot study for promoting self-management of the disease. The study deals with the social and theoretical framework behind the development of the community, as well as with the way health professionals and patients interact on a Web site specifically designed for the project. Finally, the first virtual community of practice specifically designed for nursing has been developed in Canada, as stated in http://www.canarie.ca/funding/ehealth/projects.html. This Virtual Nurse Website provides health professionals and the general public with important information about heart disease, heart health and local services. The project gathered cardiovascular care information from nurses who are experts in the field, and tested new forms of professional collaboration and knowledge sharing.

Patient and Caregiver Peer-to-Peer Applications

A peer-to peer system enables any unit within a network to communicate with and provide services to another unit within the network. All peers are of the same importance to the system; no single peer is critical to the functionality of the system and the application functions without the control or authorization of an external entity. Peers can be assumed to be of variable connectivity and can join and leave the system at their own discretion. The widespread diffusion of the Internet has enabled the creation of electronic peer-to-peer communities for people with common interests, clinical conditions or health care needs to gather "virtually" to ask questions, provide support and exchange experiences.

One such application in the health care field is PeerLink (Schopp et al., 2004) designed for people with disabilities. Persons with disabilities have high need for timely and complex information coordination and resource sharing. Most of the existing Web-based structures and applications rely heavily on third parties to maintain and update information, resulting in high maintenance costs and limited direct control by users with disabilities. PeerLink is an information management system that allows users to share information instantaneously with others, and to selectively share personal and local community resource information according to their own specifications.

Sharf (1997) studied the communication taking place at Breast Cancer List, an online discussion group which continues to grow in membership and activity. Three major dimensions of communication were identified: exchange of information, social support and personal empowerment. The study concluded that the list fulfils the functions of a community, with future concerns about information control and the potential to enhance patient–provider understanding.

Hoybye, Johansen, & Tjornhoj-Thomsen (2005) used ethnographic case-study methodology to explore how support groups on the Internet can break the social isolation that follows cancer and chronic pain. They studied the Scandinavian Breast Cancer List and using participant observation and interviews, followed 15 women who chose the Internet to battle social isolation. Study findings indicate that these women were empowered by the exchanges of knowledge and sharing experiences within the support group.

Tate, Jackvony, & Wing (2003) conducted a randomized trial to compare the effects of an Internet weight loss program and concluded that adding e-mail counselling to a basic Web-based weight loss intervention program significantly improved weight loss in adults at risk of diabetes. Another study by Houston, Cooper, & Ford (2002) focused on the characteristics of users of Internet-based depression support groups and found indications that Web-based support groups can play a positive role in the treatment of depression.

In a recent study (Eysenbach et al., 2004), researchers compiled and evaluated the evidence on the effects on health and social outcomes of computer-based peer-to-peer communities and electronic self-support groups. The study conclusions were that no robust evidence exists, as of yet, of consumer led peer-to-peer communities, partly because most of these communities have been evaluated only in conjunction with more complex interventions or involvement with health professionals. However, given the great amount of non-moderated Web-based peer-to-peer groups, further research is needed to assess when and how electronic support groups can be effective.

Finally, new Internet based collaboration environments may assist individuals in coping with the challenges and isolation of caring for a chronically ill family member as reported in http://www.canarie.ca/funding/ehealth/projects.html. Developed by the Baycrest Centre for Geriatric Care in Toronto, this online caregiver support network has received positive reviews from the 72 caregivers from Alberta and Northern Ontario who participated in the trial. The Web site uses video conferencing and other interactive tools to provide support and disease-specific information to people caring for stroke victims, or those with Alzheimer's or Parkinson's. The Web site will be particularly useful for caregivers living in rural and remote areas, and can be adapted for use by other caregiver groups.

Virtual eScience Teams

Significant engineering challenges lie ahead of the scientific community in realizing the potential of personalised medicine, discussed earlier. One engineering challenge is developing better systems to rapidly assess a patient's genetic profile; another is collecting and managing massive amounts of data on individual patients; and yet another is the need to create inexpensive and rapid diagnostic devices such as gene chips and sensors able to detect minute amounts of chemicals in the blood.

Many Internet pioneers believe that the next generation of Internet will emerge using Semantic Web technologies to transform the way the Web is used. Taking the Computer-Supported Collaborative Learning (CSCL) community as an example, methods are explored for analysing and cultivating scientific communities of practice. The current research focus is on continuity of membership, geographical distribution and international connectivity. Design principles for cultivating scientific communities and requirements for a platform to support their analysis and cultivation are reported in (Kienle & Wessner, 2006).

In addition to collaboration, Semantic publishing could revolutionise scientific research. Tim Berners-Lee predicted in 2001 that the Semantic Web

will likely profoundly change the very nature of how scientific knowledge is produced and shared, *in ways that we can now barely imagine* (Berners-Lee & Hendler, 2001).

Revisiting the Semantic Web in 2006, he and his colleagues assert that the Semantic Web "*could bring about a revolution in how, for example, scientific content is managed throughout its life cycle*" (Shadbolt, Berners-Lee, & Hall, 2006). One simple idea that may radically change scientific communication is for researchers to directly self-publish their experimental data in Semantic format on the Web. One can easily imagine how many new possibilities will open up if most research data are available on the Web as units or single experiments, which can be searched by everyone and consumed by computers.

Looking into the domain of clinical research on cancer, as an example, one observes that recent advances in research methods and technologies have resulted in an explosion of information and knowledge about cancers and their treatment. Exciting new research on the molecular mechanisms that control cell growth and differentiation has resulted in a quantum leap in our understanding of the fundamental nature of cancer cells and has suggested valuable new approaches to cancer diagnosis and treatment.

The ability to characterize and understand cancer is growing exponentially based on information from genetic and protein studies, clinical trials, and other research endeavors. The breadth and depth of information already available in the research community at large, present an enormous opportunity for improving our ability to reduce mortality from cancer, improve therapies and meet the demanding individualization-of-care needs (Sotiriou & Piccart, 2007).

While these opportunities exist, the lack of a common infrastructure is preventing clinical research institutions from being able to mine and analyze disparate data sources. As a result, very few cross-site studies and multi-centric clinical trials are performed and in most cases it is not possible to seamlessly integrate multi-level data (from the molecular to the organ and individual levels). Moreover, clinical researchers often find it hard to exploit each other's expertise due to the absence of a collaborative environment which enables the sharing of data, resources or tools for comparing results and experiments, and a uniform platform supporting the seamless integration and analysis of disease-related data at all levels. This inability to share technologies and data developed by different organisations is therefore severely hampering the research process.

A number of flagship research projects and initiatives are currently in progress exploring these ideas of virtual eScience teams and self-publishing of research data. One such pioneering initiative in the US is the effort to create a virtual

community of cancer researchers with access to a vast array of previously unavailable scientific data (Buetow, 2005). The Cancer Biomedical Informatics Grid (caBIG - https://cabig.nci.nih.gov/) focuses on the creation of a virtual community that shares resources and tackles the key issues of cyber infrastructure. It is an open infrastructure striving to achieve computational Semantic interoperability. The caBIG's infrastructure is a grid supported Semantic service-based architecture. Within its framework it supports Semantic resource discovery and distributed queries.

Similarly, the EU has funded an integrated project under the 6th Framework Programme called Advancing Clinico-Genomic Trials on Cancer (ACGT) (www.eu-acgt.org). Its objec-

Figure 2. The ACGT Semantic grid infrastructure, allowing the creation of dynamic Virtual Organisations (VOs) and the coordinated and secure sharing of scientific data and tools

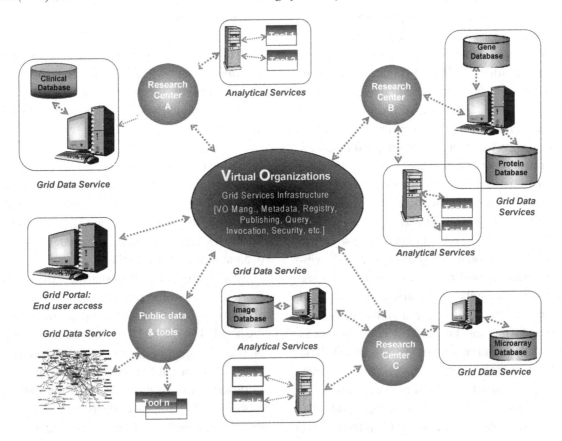

tive is to contribute to the resolution of these problems by developing a Semantically rich grid infrastructure in support of multi-centric, post-genomic clinical trials (CTs), and thus enabling for discoveries in the laboratory to be quickly transferred to the clinical management and treatment of patients (Tsiknakis et al., 2008). ACGT's vision is to become a pan-European voluntary network connecting individuals and institutions, thus creating and supporting scientific communities, and enabling their efficient collaboration and the sharing of data and tools (see Figure 2) and thereby creating a European Wide Web of cancer clinical research.

Use of Grid Technologies and Semantic Web Technologies in Support of Virtual Communities

Both these two key initiatives, on both sides of the Atlantic, build their technical architectures on open software frameworks based on WS-Resource Framework (WSRF) and Open Grid Service Architecture (OGSA), the de facto standards in Grid computing. Building on concepts and technologies from both the Grid and Web services communities, OGSA defines uniform exposed service Semantics (the Grid service) and standard mechanisms for creating, naming, and discovering transient service instances; provides location transparency and multiple protocol bindings for service instances; and supports integration with underlying native platform facilities.

A Grid based computational infrastructure couples a wide variety of geographically distributed computational resources, storage systems, data sources, databases, libraries, computational kernels and presents them as a unified integrated resource which can be shared by communities as they tackle common goals (Foster, 2005). Grid technology has several distinguishing features. First, as a consequence of the widespread use of the Globus Toolkit in various settings, grid technology is increasingly mature. Grid technology

can support virtual communities through sharing of computational and data resources. Access and identity control are fundamental components of the architecture. The technology supports deterministic queries across a distributed, common schema. Its fundamental architecture also supports stateful processes important to the concept of eScience workflows.

The way in which data at different levels of the Grid can be effectively acquired, represented, exchanged, integrated and converted into useful knowledge is an emerging research field known as "Grid Intelligence" (Roure, Jennings, & Shadbolt, 2003). The term indicates the convergence of Web service, grid and Semantic Web technologies and in particular the use of ontologies and metadata as basic elements through which intelligent Grid services can be developed. An example of this convergence is the Semantic Grid that came into existence as an effort to introduce the Semantic Web technologies into the grids. Semantic Grid is usually defined as

an extension of the current grid in which information and services are given well-defined meaning, better enabling computers and people to work in cooperation (Roure, Jennings, & Shadbolt, 2003).

Semantic Grid focuses on the systematic adoption of metadata and ontologies to describe Grid resources, to enhance and automate service discovery and negotiation, application composition, information extraction, and knowledge discovery (Cannataro & Talia, 2003).

In a "grid enabled" data sharing Virtual Community, datasets may not be well known amongst all participants of the community. To integrate the highly fragmented and isolated data sources, one needs Semantics to answer higher-level questions. Therefore, it becomes critically important to describe the context in which the data was captured. This contextualization of the data is usually referred to as "metadata" (data about data). Associating appropriate metadata to the grid services is vitally important to both the caBIG and ACGT initiatives, discussed earlier.

WHAT IS THE EFFECT OF VIRTUAL COMMUNITIES ON WELL-BEING AND HEALTH OUTCOMES?

Increasingly virtual communities and communities of practice are moving beyond face-to-face exchanges, to interact in online environments, shared Web spaces, email lists, discussion forums, and synchronous chats. Not surprisingly, the support of these environments demands both financial and technological resources. These demands force organizations to invest with caution while trying to capture the value that communities ultimately deliver to their core business. As with any other significant investment in IT and human capital, managers are naturally interested in understanding the impact these communities have on individual performance, team effectiveness, and overall productivity.

To address the challenge of how organizations can begin to analyze these financial tradeoffs the benefits and costs of communities of practice within large, geographically dispersed organizations need to be quantified and the challenges inherent in justifying the corporate investment in such communities need to be discussed. For a thorough analysis the interested reader is referred to (Millen, Fontaine, & Muller, 2002) and the references therein.

In the domain of health and social care, virtual communities are probably the one Internet application area with the greatest effect on persons with cancer. Anecdotal reports from patients support the notion that they can benefit enormously from these interactions (Penson et al., 2002; Winzelberg et al., 2003).

There is an ongoing debate on whether electronic communities in fact lead to social isolation and reduced well-being rather than a strengthening of social support. These concerns are based mainly on the controversial "Internet paradox" publication reporting results from a longitudinal study of the effect of the HomeNet project at Carnegie Mellon University, where 169 persons were provided free computers and Internet access and followed for a period of 1 to 2 years. The study provided alarming evidence of the possible harmful effects of Internet use (Kraut et al., 1998). The paradox was that a "social technology" (e-mail, newsgroups, and chatrooms) used primarily for interpersonal interaction apparently increased social isolation and decreased mental health and psychological well being among its users. Heavy Internet use was associated with increases in loneliness and depression and tended to increase stress. To explain the paradox, the researchers reasoned that superficial relationships (weak ties) formed online displaced meaningful relationships (strong ties) in the real world.

It should be noted that the HomeNet study was conducted with healthy participants and not with patients. However, in a cross-sectional study looking at persons living with cancer in an electronic support group (14 men with prostate cancer, 2 of whom were receiving active treatment) and a face-to-face group (26 men and women with "different cancer diagnoses," 14 of whom were undergoing active treatment), Klemm and Hardie (2002) noted a significant higher proportion of depressed persons with cancer in ESGs (92%) compared with no depressed participants in face-to-face cancer support groups.

Does this mean that ESG participation causes depression? Or that face-to-face groups reduce depression, whereas ESGs do not? Or only that depressed persons are turning primarily to electronic groups while staying away from face-to-face groups? Obviously, an association does not tell us anything about the causal sequence, and the latter explanation (selection bias of the study participants) might be the most plausible explanation for this finding. Longitudinal studies or randomized trials are needed to investigate this question further.

Conversely, there are many patient narratives (Penson et al., 2002; Fogel et al., 2003) and studies reporting benefits for persons with cancer that are incompatible with the notion that Internet use leads to depression. Fogel, et al. (2002; 2003) reports that Internet use in persons with breast cancer is associated with increased perceived social support and decreased loneliness. The most impressive study to date, to my view, a randomized controlled trial with recipients of a breast cancer mailing list, suggests that a Web-based support group can be useful in reducing depression and cancer-related trauma as well as perceived stress (Winzelberg et al., 2003).

In summary, all these studies show that the benefits or harms cannot be stated without considering context; the impact of virtual communities is mediated by computer skills, psychological type, and possibly numerous other contextual factors. High quality controlled trials will probably disaggregate such contextual influences (Klemm et al., 2006).

ETHICAL CHALLENGES

The development and administration of virtual communities in health and social care faces challenges as such communities often include members from countries around the world. One of the main concerns relates to the so-called "progressive dehumanization" of interpersonal relationships, namely the conduct of not only professional but also personal interactions online or via communication technologies with a decreasing number of face-to-face interactions.

Virtual support groups, while having the potential to bring people together from all over the world and allow for anonymity that might be desired for a specific medical condition, might

be lacking the sense of touch and inter-human close contact that occurs in face-to-face meetings. Virtual communities represent a physically disembodied social order. While this virtual order exists in parallel with social structures in physical space, some argue (Winner, 1990) that it will eventually compete with a structure or network of entities, which occupy spatial locations. It is often stated that

the fabric of human relationships and communities rests on real presences, real physical meetings and relationships (Horner, 2001).

It remains to be investigated whether the conventional notions of a social contract, personal rights, justice and freedom survive in a virtual world.

The concept of virtual health care communities is relatively new and there are no specific guidelines or regulations addressing some of these ethical considerations. The American Medical Informatics Association (AMIA) has provided guidelines for the electronic communication of patients with health care providers (Kane & Sans, 1998). For the conduct of virtual visits using videoconferencing technologies in home care, the American Telemedicine Association (2003) has produced a set of clinical guidelines for the development and deployment of such applications. These guidelines refer to patient, technology and provider criteria.

Such guidelines by professional organizations address some important concerns and provide an appropriate framework for the integration of virtual health care communities in the care delivery process. However, many issues, such as licensing, accreditation or concerns of identity deception and dependency discussed later, have not been fully addressed yet by legislative or professional entities.

Identity and Deception

Identity is an essential component of members of virtual communities. Being aware of the identity of those with whom one interacts is essential for understanding and evaluating the interactions. Determining one's identity in the "disembodied" world of a virtual community becomes a challenge as many of the basic cues about personality and social role one is accustomed to in the physical world, are absent (Donath, 1998).

Members of virtual communities become attuned to the nuances of communication styles. Members are being distinguished by their own "voice" and language. There are specific identity clues that refer to the location or the hardware of the member (such as the IP address, domain name and browser type) and more general clues that refer to the writing style, tone and language used by the member. However, these identity cues are not always reliable. Members of a virtual community who have the intention to deceive the community about their identity could deliberately misuse such clues.

Another dimension of identity deception is impersonation, namely a case where one user pretends to be another member of the virtual community providing false identity cues that lead other members of the community to believe that he/she is the member the impersonator is portraying to be.

While the issue of identity deception has been often studied in online communities where members share common hobbies or cultural interests, the impact of this behavioural pattern has not been studied extensively in the context of health and social care related virtual communities. In such cases, the impact of deception can go beyond impacting the trust among members of the community and lead to a damaging effect on members' health care status.

Numerous cases of deception in virtual communities have been reported in the media and scientific literature (O'Brien, 1999). Feldman (2000) reports several cases where people in online support groups falsely claim to suffer from specific medical conditions.

The identity issue of virtual community members becomes obviously essential in the context of virtual medical teams – that is online communities that aim to enhance continuity of care or peer-to-peer communities where members exchange experiences and advice for a specific clinical condition.

Privacy and Confidentiality

The healthcare sector is facing many challenges in regard to the privacy and confidentiality of individual health information in the information age. Information privacy is the patient's right to control the use and dissemination of information that relates to them. Confidentiality is a tool for protecting the patients' privacy.

For disease management applications that are Web-based, ownership of and access to the data have to be addressed. In many vitrual care delivery teams in home care, patients record monitoring data and transmit them daily to a Web server owned and maintained by a private third party that allows providers to login and access their patients' data. This type of application calls for discussion and definition of the issue of data ownership and patients' access rights to parts or all of their records. The implications are not only possible threats to data privacy but extend to ethical debates about the restructuring of the care delivery process and introduction of new key players.

Advanced information technology is being employed to protect information transactions from unauthorized third parties. However, it remains largely unexplored how to safeguard a consumer's consent to view their private information in a virtual environment. Coiera and Clarke (2004) propose a framework for obtaining and determining electronic consent (e-consent) within health care. They argue that an electronic system should permit access to confidential patient information by checking "that patient consent exists for the information request by invoking methods that check for explicit, inferred or implied consent". While this concept of e-consent has been introduced as a theoretical framework, it addresses the privacy concerns associated with virtual communities and as such it should be integrated into the design of systems so that they are equipped with a mechanism that documents and employs the specific inclusion and exclusion criteria pertaining to patients' consent intentions.

DISCUSSION AND CONCLUSION

Discussion

Virtual communities, despite their infant stage, have already shown the potential to provide new virtuality in the collaboration - and communication-intensive paradigm that progressively emerges. Such virtual constructions are already prominent in various applications domains. Moreover, there is evidence to suggest that they will continue to prevail, re-shaping the conduct of computer-mediated human activities in the future.

Virtual communities are also emerging in many health care related domains. Such communities aim to support patients, caregivers, families and health care providers and facilitate information exchange, provide support and enhance communication among people who do not have to be physically present at the same time at one location. Whether such communities are based on moderated or non-moderated discussions, it is important to have a clear, published and easily accessible set of rules and regulations or code of conduct for the members of the virtual community.

Virtual communities have the potential to bring people together bridging geographic distance; thus, the Internet and other advanced telecommu-

nication technologies can cross national borders and link people from different countries for the purposes of health care delivery and education. In these cases the premise that electronic health care data protection depends on national laws is insufficient in providing a clear framework for the definition of a data privacy violation. As Kluge (2000) argues, it is important to define "*ethical guidelines for the protection of electronic health care data that must focus solely on fundamental ethical principles*" and not on national laws.

As the number of vitrual communities in health care increase and institutions exchange information on a global level, a code of ethics for the protection of patient records needs to be developed to address this new reality based on the notion, as Kluge (2000) puts it, that the "*action domain of health information professionals assumes global dimensions*".

Conclusion

Powerful technologies and trends are emerging in the health care field. Advanced technologies that enable people to communicate and form virtual teams and communities can revolutionize the health care field and support a paradigm shift, namely the shift from institution-centric to patient-centric or consumer-centric systems. Policy, ethical and legal issues associated with virtual health care communities will have to be addressed.

Furthermore, extensive research initiatives are needed that will determine the impact of virtual health care communities on clinical outcomes, the overall process and quality of and access to care. Such initiatives should go beyond pilot-testing an innovative application and employ experimental design methods to investigate the utility of virtual health care communities and the extent to which they empower patients and their caregivers. As advanced Web-based applications continue to emerge and grow, system designers, health care settings, organizations and policy makers need to be prepared to properly adopt these technologies and develop the capacity to evaluate and make informed decisions about their appropriate use.

When practitioners utilize virtual community tools to communicate with patients or colleagues they have to maximize sociability and usability of this mode of communication, while addressing concerns for privacy and the fear of de-humanizing practice, and the lack of clarity or relevance of current legislative frameworks.

In conclusion, Virtual communities have the potential to become powerful tools for practitioners; however, extensive research is needed to document the effectiveness of this mode of communication.

REFERENCES

American Telemedicine Association (2003). *ATA adopts Telehomecare clinical guidelines.* Retrieved on 15 June 2005 from http://www.americantelemed.org/icot/hometelehealthguidelines.htm

Basch, E., Artz, D., Dulko, D., Scher, K., Sabbatini, P., Hensley, M., Mitra, N., Speakman, J., McCabe, M., & Schrag, D. (2005). Patient online self-reporting of toxicity symptoms during chemotherapy. *Journal of Clinical Oncology, 23*(15), 3552–3561.

Berners-Lee, T., & Hendler, J. (2001). Scientific publishing on the 'Semantic Web'. *Nature, 410,* 1023-1024.

Buetow, K. H. (2005). Cyberinfrastructure: Empowering a "third way" in biomedical research. *Science Magazine, 308*(5723), 821-824.

Burnett, G., Besant, M., & Chatman, E. A. (2001). Small worlds: normative behaviour in virtual communities and feminist bookselling. *Journal of American Society for Information Science and Technology, 52*(7), 536-537.

Cannataro, M., & Talia, D. (2003). KNOWLEDGE Grid - An architecture for distributed knowledge discovery. *Communications of the ACM, 46*(1), 89-93.

Chiarugi, F., Trypakis, D., Kontogiannis, V., Lees, P. J., Chronaki, C., Zeaki, M., Giannakoudakis, N., Vourvahakis, D., Tsiknakis, M., & Orphanoudakis, S. C. (2003). Continuous ECG monitoring in the management of pre-hospital health emergencies. In *Proceedings of the IEEE Computers in Cardiology 2003 (CIC'2003) Conference, 30,* 205-208, 21-24 September, Chalkidiki, Greece.

Chronaki, C., Katehakis, D., Zabulis, X., Tsiknakis, M., & Orphanoudakis, S. C. (1997). WebOnCOLL: Medical collaboration in regional healthcare networks. *IEEE Transactions on Information Technology in Biomedicine, 1*(4), 257-269.

Chronaki, C., Lees, P. J., Antonakis, N., Chiarugi, F., Vrouchos, G., Nikolaidis, G., Tsiknakis, M., & Orphanoudakis S. C. (2001). Preliminary results from The deployment Of integrated teleconsultation services in rural Crete. In *Proceedings of the IEEE Computers in Cardiology,* (pp. 671-674), Rotterdam, Sept 21-25.

Coiera, E., & Clarke, R. (2004). e-Consent: the design and implementation of consumer consent mechanisms in an electronic environment. *Journal of the American Medical Informatics Association, 11*(2), 129-40.

Demiris, G., Parker Oliver, D., Fleming, D., & Edison, K. (2004). Hospice staff attitudes towards "Telehospice". *American Journal of Hospice and Palliative Medicine, 21*(5), 343-347.

Disease Management Association of America (2002). *Definition of disease management.* Retrieved on 6/10/2005 from http://www.dmaa.org/definition.html

Donath, J. S. (1998). Identity and deception in the virtual community. In P. Kollock & M. Smith (Eds.), *Communities in cyberspace.* London: Routledge.

Eysenbach, G., Powell, J., Englesakis, M., Rizo, C., & Stern, A. (2004). Health related virtual communities and electronic support groups: Systematic review of the effects of online peer to peer interactions. *British Medical Journal, 328*, 1166–1172.

Feldman, M. D. (2000). Munchausen by Internet: Detecting factitious illness and crisis on the Internet. *Southern Medical Journal, 93*(7), 669-672.

Feste, C., & Anderson, R. M. (1995). Patient empowerment: From philosophy to practice. *Patient Education and Counselling, 126*, 139-144.

Finkelstein, J., O'Connor, G., & Friedmann, R. H. (2001). Development and implementation of the home asthma telemonitoring (HAT) system to facilitate asthma self-care. In V. Patel, R. Rogers, & R. Haux (Eds.), *MedInfo 2001 proceedings*, Amsterdam: IOS Press.

Finn J. (1999). An exploration of helping processes in an online self-help group focusing on issues of disability. *Health and Social Work, 24*(3), 220-231.

Fogel, J., Albert, S. M., Schnabel, F., Ditkoff, B. A., & Neugut, A. I. (2002). Internet use and social support in women with breast cancer. *Health Psychology, 21*, 398-404.

Fogel, J., Albert, S. M., Schnabel, F., Ditkoff, B. A., & Neugut, A. I. (2003). Racial/ethnic differences and potential psychological benefits in use of the Internet by women with breast cancer. *Psychooncology, 12*, 107-117.

Foster I. (2005). Service oriented science. *Science, 308*(5723), 814-817.

Heinemann, G. Z. A. (2002). Team performance in health care—assessment and development. In G. Stricker (Ed.), *Issues in the practice of psychology*, (p. 400). New York: Kluwer Academic/Plenum Publishers.

Horner, D. S. (2001). The moral status of virtual action. In T. W. Bynum (Ed.), *Proceedings of the Fifth International Conference on the Social and Ethical Impacts of Information and Communication Technologies*.

Houston, T. K., Cooper, L. A., & Ford, D. E. (2002). Internet support groups for depression: A 1-year prospective cohort study. *American Journal of Psychiatry, 159*, 2062-2068.

Hoybye, M. T., Johansen, C., & Tjornhoj-Thomsen, T. (2005). Online interaction: Effects of storytelling in an Internet breast cancer support group. *Psychooncology, 14*(3), 211-220.

Kane, B., & Sans, D. (1998). Guidelines for the clinical use of electronic mail with patients. *Journal of the American Medical Informatics Association, 5*, 104-111.

Kienle, A., & Wessner, M. (2006). Analysing and cultivating scientific communities of practice. *International Journal of Web Based Communities, 2*(4), 377-393.

Klemm, P., & Hardie, T. (2002). Depression in Internet and face-to-face cancer support groups: a pilot study. *Oncology Nursing Forum, 29*(4), E45-51.

Klemm, P., Bunnell, D., Cullen, M., Soneji, R., Gibbons, P., & Holecek, A. (2006). Online cancer support groups: A review of the research literature. *Computers, Informatics, Nursing, 21*, 136–142.

Kluge, E. W. (2000). Professional codes for electronic HC record protection: Ethical, legal, economic and structural issues. *International Journal of Medical Informatics, 60*(2), 85–96.

Kraut, R., Patterson, M., Lundmark, V., Kiesler, S., Mukopadhyay, T., & Scherlis, W. (1998). Internet paradox: A social technology that reduces social involvement and psychological well-being? *American Psychologist, 53*(9), 1017-1032.

Leimeister, J. M., Knebel, U., & Krcmar, H. (2007). Exploring mobile information systems for chronically ill adolescent patients. *International Journal of Web Based Communities, 3*(4), 404-415.

Lesko, L. J. (2007). Personalized medicine: Elusive dream or imminent reality? *Clinical Pharmacology & Therapeutics, 81*(6), 807-816.

Lorimer, W., & Manion, J. (1996). Team-based organizations: Leading the essential transformation. *PFCA Rev*, (pp. 15–19).

Mazanec, P., Bartel, J., Buras, D., Fessler, P., Hudson, J., Jacoby, M., Montana, B., & Phillips, M. (2002). Transdisciplinary pain management: a holistic approach. *Journal of Hospice & Palliative Nursing, 4*(4), 228-234.

Millen, D. R., Fontaine, M. A., & Muller, M. J. (2002). Understanding the benefit and costs of communities of practice. *Communications of the ACM, 45*(4), 69-73.

Morlion, B., Knoop, C., Paiva, M., & Estenne, M. (2002). Internet-based home monitoring of pulmonary function after lung transplantation. *American Journal of Respiratory and Critical Care Medicine, 165*(5), 694-697.

O'Brien, J. (1999). Writing in the body: gender (re)production in online interaction. In M.A. Smith, & P. Kollock (Eds.), *Communities in cyberspace*, (pp. 76–106), London: Routledge.

Pascual, M. M., Salvador, C. C. H., Sagredo, P. P. G., Marquez-Montes, J. J., Gonzalez, M. M. A., Fragua, J. J. A., Carmona, M. M., Garcia-Olmos, L. L. M., Garcia-Lopez, F. F., Munoz, A. A., & Monteagudo, J. J. L. (in print). Impact of patient-general practitioner short messages based interaction on the control of hypertension in a follow-up service for low-to-medium risk hypertensive patients. A randomized controlled trial. *IEEE Transactions on Information Technology in Biomedicine.*

Penson, R. T., Benson, R. C., Parles, K., Chabner, A. B., & Lynch, J. T. Jr. (2002). Virtual connections: Internet health care. *Oncologist, 7*(6), 555–568.

Pitsillides, A., Pitsillides, B., Samaras, G., Dikaikos, M., Christodoulou, E., Andreou, P., & Georgiadis, D. (2004). DITIS: A collaborative virtual medical team for home healthcare of cancer patients. In R. H. Istepanian, S. Laxminarayan, & C. S. Pattichis (Eds.), *M-Health: Emerging mobile health systems*. New York: Kluwer Academic/Plenum Publishers.

Rheingold, H. (1993). *The virtual community.* New York: Harper Perennial Library.

Roure D. d., Jennings, N. R., & Shadbolt, N. (2003). The Semantic Grid: A future e-Science infrastructure. In F. Berman, A. J. G. Hey, & G. Fox (Eds.), *Grid computing: Making the global infrastructure a reality*, (pp. 437-470). John Wiley & Sons.

Rubinelli, S., Schulz, PJ., & Vago, F. (2008). Designing and evaluating online communities for promoting self-management of chronic low back pain. *International Journal of Web Based Communities*, 4(1,2), 80-97.

Schopp, L. H., Hales, J. W., Quetsch, J. L., Hauan, M. J., & Brown, G. D. (2004). Design of a peer-to-peer telerehabilitation model. *Telemedicine Journal and e-Health, 10*(2), 243-251.

Shadbolt, N., Berners-Lee, T., & Hall, W. (2006). The Semantic Web revisited. *IEEE Intelligent Systems, 21*(3) 96-101.

Sharf, B. F. (1997). Communicating breast cancer on-line: support and empowerment on the Internet. *Women Health, 26*(1), 65-84.

Sotiriou, C., & Piccart, MJ. (2007). Taking gene-expression profiling to the clinic: When will molecular signatures become relevant to patient care? *Nature Reviews, 7*, 545-553.

Tate, D. F., Jackvony, E. H., & Wing R. R. (2003). Effects of Internet behavioural counseling on weight loss in adults at risk for type 2 diabetes: a randomized trial. *Journal of the American Medical Association, 289*(14), 1833-1836.

Traganitis, A., Trypakis, D., Spanakis, M., Condos, S., Stamkopoulos, T., Tsiknakis, M., & Orphanoudakis, S. C. (2001, October 25-28). Home monitoring and personal health management services in a regional health telematics network. In *Proceedings of EMBC 2001, 23rd Annual International Conference of the IEEE Engineering in Medicine and Biology Society,* Istanbul.

Tsiknakis, M., & Saranummi, N. (2005). Lessons learned from PICNIC. In N. Saranummi, D. Piggott, D. G. Katehakis, M. Tsiknakis, & K. Bernstein (Eds.), *Regional health economies and ICT services,* (pp. 215-228), ISBN: 1-58603-538-x.

Tsiknakis, M., Brochhausen, M., Nabrzyski, J., Pucacki, J., Sfakianakis, S. G., Potamias, G., Desmedt, C., & Kafetzopoulos, D. (2008). A Semantic Grid infrastructure enabling integrated access and analysis of multilevel biomedical data in support of post-genomic clinical trials on Cancer. *IEEE Transactions on Information Technology in Biomedicine, 12*(2), 205-217.

Wellman B. (1997). An electronic group is virtually a social network. In S. Kiesler (Ed.), *Cultures of the Internet,* (pp. 179–205), Mahwah, NJ: Lawrence Erlbaum.

Whittaker, S., Issacs, E., & O'Day, V. (1997). Widening the net. Workshop report on the theory and practice of physical and network communities. *SIGCHI Bulletin, 29,* 27–30.

Winner, L. (1990). Living in electronic space. In T. Casey, & L. Embree (Eds.), *Lifeworld and technology,* (pp. 1-14). Lonham, MD: Center for Advanced Research on Phenomenology and University Press of America.

Winzelberg, A. J., Classen, C., Alpers, G. W., Roberts, H., Koopman, C., Adams, E. R., Ernst, H., Dev, P., & Taylor, B. (2003). Evaluation of an Internet support group for women with primary breast cancer. *Cancer, 97*(5), 1164–1173.

World Health Organisation (2002). Innovative care for chronic conditions: building blocks for action (No. WHO/NMC/CCH/02.01). France: World Health Organization.

KEY TERMS

Consumer Participation: The term refers to the transformation gradually taking place in developed countries. Citizens in developed countries are already making more decisions about their own treatment. The informed, knowledgeable and increasingly demanding patients are moving into the heart of the healthcare system.

Disease Management: Disease management is the concept of reducing healthcare costs and/or improving quality of life for individuals with chronic disease conditions by preventing or minimizing the effects of a disease, usually a chronic condition, through integrative care.

Patient Empowerment: Patient empowerment is a concept that has emerged in the health care literature in the last few years. It is based on the principle that patients are entitled to access health information and determine their own care choices. Empowerment can be perceived as an enabling process through which individuals or groups take control over their lives and the management of disease.

Virtual Communities in Healthcare: A virtual community in health care refers to a group of people and the social structure that they collectively create that is supported by information and communication technologies (ICT) with the purposes of collectively conducting activities related to health and disease management as well as education.

Virtual eScience Teams: The term eScience is used to describe computationally intensive science that is carried out in highly distributed network environments, or science that uses immense data sets that require grid computing; the term sometimes includes technologies that enable distributed collaboration, such as the Access Grid.

Chapter XVIII
Research Communities in Context:
Trust, Independence, and Technology in Professional Communities

Dimitrina Dimitrova
York University, Canada

Emmanuel Koku
Drexel University, USA

ABSTRACT

This chapter examines a community of professionals, created by a government agency and charged with conducting country-wide, cross-disciplinary, and cross-sectoral research and innovation in the area of water. The analysis describes the structure of the community and places it in the context of existing project practices and institutional arrangements. Under challenging conditions, the professionals in the area recruit team members from their trusted long-term collaborators, work independently on projects, use standard communication technologies and prefer informal face-to-face contacts. Out of these practices emerge a sparsely connected community with permeable boundaries interspersed with foci of intense collaboration and exchange of ideas. In this community, professionals collaborate and exchange of ideas with the same colleagues. Both collaboration and exchanges of ideas tend to involve professionals from different disciplines and, to a lesser extent, from different sectors and locations.

VIRTUAL COMMUNITIES OF PRACTICE IN RESEARCH WORK

In the past few decades, when knowledge and innovation have been identified as the key to economic development and competitive advantage, governments worldwide have made considerable efforts to encourage knowledge creation and transfer (Drucker, 1993; Quintas, 2002). The Canadian federal government is no exception. Its

Networks of Centres of Excellence (NCE) program targets strategic areas of scientific development. In each area, the program forges private-public partnerships and fosters multidisciplinary and nation-wide collaborative research. Since traditional bureaucracies are not conducive to knowledge generation and transfer, the program creates flexible organizational forms of the type of "invisible colleges" based on informal ties and permeable boundaries (Heckscher & Donnovan, 1994). A small NCE agency in each strategic area develops a network of stakeholders – leading researchers, government decision-makers, private companies and NGO staff, that serves as a catalyst for research and innovation. In essence, the program creates communities with distinctive characteristics: they are geographically dispersed, connected to some extent by technology, and include participants who have shared interests but diverse disciplinary and institutional background. There is an inherent tension in the mandate of the NCE agencies and in the communities they create: on the one hand, they connect professionals bound by their expertise in a particular area and their interest in collaborative solutions; on the other, they aim to foster connections across sectoral, disciplinary, and organizational boundaries to ensure innovation and novel solutions.

This chapter examines the Canadian Water Network (CWN) – the community representing the NCE program in the area of water. CWN is seen as a Virtual Community of Practice (VCoP), which gets its distinctive qualities by the tension between the shared interests and the diverse background of its participants. The analysis departs from such common research issues in the study of VCoPs such as technology, information sharing, or relational characteristics of the community. Instead, its objectives are to map the structure of the community using Social Network Analysis (SNA) and to explain how these structural characteristics emerge out of the institutional arrangements in the area of water and the practices of the participants in the community.

BACKGROUND, RESEARCH QUESTIONS AND DATA

Literature Review

At the centre of the study is a dispersed community of professionals engaged in applied collaborative research. Given this, literature in three areas contribute to the framing of the research questions and the interpretation of the results: learning and knowledge processes, scientific research, and social networks.

Unlike early research on learning and knowledge processes, which overlooks the embedded nature of knowledge, recent studies interpret knowledge as collaborative and socially embedded. Knowledge processes can only be understood in the context of the groups that create knowledge, the practices they employ, and the situation in which they function (Wenger, 2000; Brown and Duguid, 1991). The central concept in the literature is CoP, defined as informal self-selected communities of learners bound by shared expertise and joint enterprise. CoPs are the centres of knowledge creation and the building blocks of larger learning systems (Wenger & Snyder, 2000; Wenger, 2000; Brown & Duguid, 2000; Lesser and Prusak, 1999). With the increasing importance of knowledge processes in society, however, comes the proliferation of knowledge creating groups. Learning and information exchange processes on the level of organizations and beyond are captured in terms such as social learning systems, Networks of Communities of Practice (NCoPs), and Virtual Communities of Practice (Wenger, 2000; Brown & Duguid, 2000). In their typology of collaboration among researchers, Bos and his colleagues (2007) add newer organizational forms supporting the creation and sharing of knowledge such as Virtual Learning Communities and Distributed Research Centres.

Among all these forms, Virtual CoPs are distinguished by their dispersed nature, the use of technology, and the common interests, goals, needs or practices of their participants (Chiu et al., 2006; Bos et al., 2007). In reality, such communities differ widely: participants range from professionals in the same area working for various organizations to employees of the same global organization; they might work together on a common project or just share news of common interest; their technology might involve anything from bulletin boards to sophisticated collaborative web technologies (Restler and Woolis, 2007; Chiu et al., 2006). In all of them, however, distant participants benefit from online information exchanges.

As usually with new phenomena, practitioners drive the research agenda of VCoPs. The main concern is what factors affect knowledge sharing. Some studies examine variables reminiscent of the knowledge management literature: appropriate technology, support by senior management, commitment to the organization, and organizational support for the knowledge processes (Restler and Woolis, 2007). Other studies follow closely traditional CoPs research. They focus on the concept of social capital, i.e. on the resources embedded in the interpersonal ties or in a community (Daniel et al., 2003; Chiu et al, 2006). This stream of research links information sharing with trust, reciprocity, or identification with the community – characteristics difficult to achieve in the environment of VCoPS, characterised by physical separation (Chiu, 2006; Wellman and Gulia, 1998; Daniel et al., 2007; Bos et al., 2007). Notably, these are all relational properties. Although researchers recognize the structural dimension of social capital, few studies actually explore it (Lesser and Prusak, 1999; Daniel et al., 2007). The structural characteristics of VCoPs such as density or direction of ties is not yet systematically studied and its impact on information flows - not well understood.

The systematic study of the structural characteristics of a community is best done using SNA. SNA is an analytical and substantive approach, which focuses on the connections among people (or other actors) and views sets of actors as networks. Among other characteristics, it shows the actual rather than the prescribed or desired exchanges among participants, describes who is connected to whom and what exchanges bind them together, identifies internal groupings and distinct positions in a community. Applied to CoPs and VCoPs, SNA offers a number of advantages. By capturing the actual interactions and the informal rather than formal ties, it can reliably identify a CoP or a VCoP. Next, it captures the interactions, ties and the information flows within a community, including the points of intense exchanges. It thereby provides a more specific and precise picture of the structure of CoPs and VCoPs and the way in which the communities function. Finally, SNA can offer further insights about boundary interactions, brokering in its various forms, or learning loops between functional groups and project teams (Wenger, 2000, 235, 237). In the words of Cross and his colleagues (2002), SNA makes invisible interactions visible and actionable.

SNA shows the ties and the information flows they support but it does not usually explain why people interact the way they do and create the ties researchers observe. Understanding the network structure of a community requires understanding the context in which the community is embedded. The interactions and ties of the community of experts, involved in applied research on water in Canada, are shaped by the institutional context, in which they act, and the practices, in which they engage (or the immediate context). This is where existing studies of scientific research can contribute to the background of this research. Today, scientific research is the domain of large collaborative projects, which are typically dispersed and often cross-organizational and multidisciplinary. Among the key concerns of the literature on science are: the factors which assist or impede collaborative research, the collaborative practices of researchers, project management, and scholarly networks. A number of findings refer to the conditions, under which researchers create VCoP, and clarify their practices in the community.

Researchers in this area have devoted considerable attention on the difficulties of collaborative research. Researchers, Bos and his colleagues argue (2007), do not make good distant collaborators because they like working independently. Further, they prefer informal one-to-one collaboration and face-to-face interactions to the formal procedures and technology mediated communication of dispersed teams (Bos et al., 2007). Multi-disciplinary research projects are particularly hard to launch: their initiation is hampered by university environment which still emphasizes functional boundaries (Caruso and Rhoten, 2001; Rhoten, 2003). When researchers do collaborate, their collaboration might be limited. Haythornwhate and her colleagues (2003) distinguish between integrative and additive collaboration of scholars; in the first case collaborators constantly negotiate their goals and results, in the second they simply ensure that their independent pieces of work fit together. Learning is much stronger in integrative collaboration (Haythornwhaite et al., 2003).

Many studies examine the challenges of managing dispersed teams with members from many organizations and diverse disciplinary backgrounds (Cummings and Kiesler, 2005; Bos et al, 2007; Olson and Olson, 2003; Zheng et al., 2002). Cummings and Kiesler (2005) argue that such teams require managing of both tasks and relationships. In multi-disciplinary teams, differences in training, scientific forums, and publication channels weaken social bonds and make management especially difficult (Caruso and Rhoten, 2001; Rhoten, 2003; Cummings and Kiesler, 2005; Shrum et al., 2001).

To summarize, this review suggests that VCoPs vary yet in all cases their participants have shared expertise, interests and joint enterprises. Applied to the network of professionals cultivated by the CWN agency, the concept of VCoP highlights the similarities of participants as well as their

dispersal and their use of technology. Compared to other VCoPs, CWN is characterized by a distinctive tension between similarity and diversity: the members of this community have shared expertise in water issues and common interest in collaborative solutions, but they come from different disciplines and sectors. The interactions and ties among participants are likely to be weaker. Further, the numerous challenges which existing research of scientific collaboration uncovered suggest that this distinctive community is likely to have complex structure with internal sub-groups. The precise shape of its structure and the nature of exchanges in it are shaped by the institutional arrangements and the practices of the professionals working in the area.

Research Questions and Methods

This research sets out to examine the structure and the information flows in the communities operating at three distinct levels. First, it examines the broader community of professionals working in the area of water (the professional community). Second, it investigates the community of professionals involved in the work of the NCE Agency in the area (the Insiders). This is the VCoP which the Agency directly cultivates. While the activities of the Agency often target key individuals from the outsiders that can contribute their reputation and social capital to the community, it is the Insiders that the Agency directly supports. The Insiders are a segment of the broader professional community in the area of water. Finally, the analysis examines the internal groupings within the broader professional community. Such groupings are centres of intense collaboration and exchanges of ideas and can be interpreted as CoPs.

The study is guided by the three sets of questions:

- What are the institutional arrangements in the area of water that serve as barriers and enablers for the connections among professionals? What are the practices of these professionals and how do these practices shape the interactions among them?

- What are the structural characteristics of the Insider community and the broader professional community in the area of water? What are the boundaries between them?

- What are the internal sub-groups in the broader communities? What do they tell us about the information flows among the professionals in the area?

The data for this chapter was collected as part of a larger study of the Agency working under the NCE program in the area of water. This analysis draws directly on the results of a web-based national survey (N=173) and semi-structured interviews (N=65); it is also informed by the review of numerous documents as well as the results of a limited citation analysis (N=31). Both the survey and the interviews include not only Insiders but also members of the broader professional community and thus provide insights for both communities.

Data for the primary focus of this analysis is derived from two questions in the social network survey focusing on collaboration and exchanges of ideas. In the first question, participants were asked to list the colleagues with whom they have collaborated; in the second question, they indicated with whom they shared innovative ideas. The analysis of the network survey data used three SNA analytic measures to capture community structure:

- **Network composition:** e.g. percentage of ties who are academics. This measure shows various characteristics of network members.
- **Network density measures:** e.g. the percentage of ties that are actually present in a network, relative to those that are possible. Such a measure reveals the connectivity in

the network and can show the boundaries around various sub-groups within the network.

- **Clique analysis:** Cliques are sub-groups, in which members interact directly and are more strongly connected to each other than they are to the rest of the network. Thus, clique analysis provides a measure of internal sub-groups in the network. Further, such a sub-group analysis also helps identify bridges (cut-points) within the network.

The analysis uses a social network program - UCINET 6.0, to compute all our social network measures and graphical representations.

THE SOCIAL CONTEXT OF COLLABORATIVE RESEARCH

Barriers and Enablers for the Emergence of Professional Community

Diversity

Professionals in the area of water face particular challenges in connecting to each other. In any research area, exchanges among professionals occur naturally in course of their life. Individuals work and discuss ideas with coworkers, students, or supervisors; meet like-minded individuals at professional events; and become aware of others working on similar issues by following publications or best practices. Professionals working on water issues are no exception yet the exchanges among them are more difficult. As a rule, ties tend to follow organizational, sectoral, and disciplinary boundaries. It is an axiom in network literature that people meet and associate with people like them; their ties fold back within their own group. However, water issues are "everybody's concern"[1]; water issues cannot be understood or resolved within a single discipline or organization. Stakeholders in the area are diverse in terms of sector, discipline, work responsibilities, and specific interests. Academics from a wide range of disciplines – from biology to engineering and management, contribute to water issues. The responsibility for policy making and the management of water is shared by several government agencies at all levels of government. The NGOs and industries involved are also quite different. To summarize, the solutions of water issues require diversity; beyond their expertise in water issues and their shared interests in collaborative solutions, the points of common interests among such diverse professionals are few. Thus, it is likely that they have limited connections and their professional community is fragmented along disciplinary, sectoral and organizational lines.

Institutional Arrangements

These characteristics are further enhanced by existing institutional arrangements. Government agencies and universities, which are most heavily involved in water issues, each presents its own challenges for connections among professionals in the area. By and large, government organizations function as bureaucracies, which are not known for sharing information and ideas. Political concerns may also discourage risky undertakings and collaboration with outsiders. On their part, universities emphasize disciplinary divisions and act as "exemplars of Fordist theories of production" (Caruso and Rhoten, 2001). Traditionally, the evaluation of academics is based on the number of publications and the prestige of the journals in which they publish—the 'publish or perish' criteria. However, multidisciplinary and applied (or cross-sectoral) research is not conducive for these traditional outcomes. Working with non-academic partners does not necessarily generate opportunities for scholarly publications: its outcomes are manuals, software tools, or website information — "very informative but not peer-reviewed publications." Writing academic papers from multidisciplinary research is difficult since it requires integrating results based on different methods, theories, or even scale of empirical research. Yet few journals publish multidisciplinary articles and they are not highly valued in universities. In short, the interview data shows that the institutional arrangements in government and academia do not reward complex collaborative research and discourage the connections among professionals interested in such research.

On the other hand, the Agency acts as an important enabler for connections among the professionals in the area. First, it funds multidisciplinary, cross-sectoral, and country-wide research. The applicants for its funding have to meet rigorous criteria for the applicability of the outcomes, knowledge and technology transfer plans, partners from government, industry or NGOs, and collaborators from other institutions. The resulting projects are complex, often organized in several sub-projects, with team members from across the country. Ideally, working on such a project enables professionals to meet new colleagues and fosters the exchange ideas. In other words, teams are focal points for both collaboration and networking.

Second, the Agency organizes networking events such as workshops, retreats, or annual meetings; it also supports similar events of partner organizations. Such events enable the exchanges of ideas, raise awareness of others working in the area, and foster the creation of ties outside the boundaries of research projects. The goal is to expand the ties among the Insiders and indeed among professionals in the areas as a whole, to attract key individuals from the broader professional community that are currently outsiders, and ultimately create a strong community of like-minded individuals, which in the future will become self-sustaining. The networking events of the Agency specifically focus on ties crossing spatial, sectoral and disciplinary boundaries, which are outside one's immediate interests;

such ties are hard to create, especially in a more traditional institutional environment. This focus on boundary-crossing ties is what creates the tension between similarity and diversity in the community nurtured by the Agency.

The individuals involved in the work of the Agency are considered 'members' or 'Insiders' of a professional network. These are academics funded by the agency, non-academic researchers, or practitioners who are involved in a variety of roles in the research projects or networking events organized by Agency. Being an Insider is not a strictly formal designation yet it puts individuals on the distribution list of the Agency and gives them online access to the profiles of other Insiders, thereby facilitating networking. The Agency maintains a website with information on funding, jobs, or a variety of events in the area of water. Besides using the website, many of the Insiders contact directly the staff of the Agency to seek information, advice, or help with professional networking.

Under these conditions, it is reasonable to expect relatively few connections among the professionals in the area and the existence of sub-groups along sectoral, disciplinary and organizational lines. Further, as a result of the networking and funding activities of the Agency Insiders are expected to be better connected. Finally, if project funding is the great motivator for cross-boundary ties, this means that we can expect significant differences between collaboration and exchanges of ideas for Insiders. This is because collaborative ties will follow formal projects and will cross disciplinary, sectoral and organizational lines; on the other hand, professionals will share ideas only with trusted colleagues and confidantes who are similar to themselves. The collaboration and the exchanges of ideas may therefore illustrate the learning loops between projects and CoPs Wenger (2000) envisioned.

Team Recruitment, Organization of Work and Technology Use on Projects

While funding from the Agency can jumpstart collaborative projects, it cannot eliminate the challenges faced by their participants. The same diversity and institutional arrangements, which hampers the connections among professionals, generates a number of difficulties in coordinating and managing projects. Among Insiders, the projects funded by the Agency are known for having "high transaction cost" and bringing "much frustration."

By definition, such projects are multidisciplinary, cross-sectoral, cross-organizational, and most often dispersed. Project participants include some combination of academic and government researchers, policy and decision-makers at various levels and from different agencies of the government, industry researchers and managers, as well as NGO staff. Such participants work under different timelines, priorities, funding procedures, and decision-making cycles; their attitudes and practices vary. When diverse team members start working together, often the first order of the day is to establish common practices for work and communication: ways to format the data, interpret results, or confirm the delivery of samples. Such informal agreements decrease the risks of miscommunication and incompatible results. Team members, further, need to develop trust in their colleagues. They have to be confident that the lab work of their colleagues is up to par, the data are properly formatted, "the numbers make sense", and their colleagues can be trusted to return email and phone calls and send their reports on time. "Waiting for other people to get their stuff in" is perceived as a lack of commitment and a personal working style that eliminates any chances for future collaboration.

Team Recruitment

Such difficulties lead to a recruitment strategy that minimizes problems by creating teams of long-term collaborators. In science, reputation and a proven track record have always attracted potential collaborators. Our interview data shows that to find such desirable collaborators, researchers and practitioners rely on their personal experience and contacts. The single most common strategy for team recruitment is utilizing personal networks and inviting long-term collaborators; those invited first to a project recommend and bring in their own collaborators and partners. In short, recruitment utilizes social capital. Typically, researchers have a few close long-term collaborators—sometimes only one, sometimes three or four. They swap ideas, consult each other, identify together research opportunities, secure funding from partners, and work together on various teams. In virtually all projects, project leaders put a team together by first inviting their core group of collaborators. The interviews show that a number of respondents have worked together with some of their team members on previous projects; at any given moment, they collaborate with them on several different projects. Most professionals have "many years of intensive collaboration" with their team members. This preference for long-term collaborators holds true for academic and practitioners alike: practitioners also prefer to work with people they know. They want academics who are a "known quantity" and can be trusted to produce tangible outcomes rather than abstract reports; they also want academics sensitive to the political constraints under which practitioners are labouring.

As a result of this recruitment strategy, teams include mostly long-term collaborators who know each other well. In such teams, members do not have to develop common practices and trust: these have been already developed in previous collaboration. Recruitment, therefore, goes a long way in preventing problems and smoothing down the work on a project. In addition, the same practices mean that it is not the funding of the Agency that creates a project team; it is the group of long-term collaborators that applies for funding. When a team receives funding, most often members transform their informal collegial ties into formal project ties.

Independent Work

The second common strategy for coping with the coordination and communication challenges on a project is organizing project work in a way that minimizes the need for coordination and maximizes the independence of the researchers. The organization of work on projects differs. Some projects are relatively integrated: their components, or subprojects, feed into each other, participants exchange data and analytical results, and project leaders constantly monitor work. Communication is to a great extent lateral, among team members, and extensive. Integrated project are more difficult because the team spends a lot of time communicating and coordinating work. They are also riskier - the delays, bad work or lack of commitment of a single member might endanger the whole project. Among Insiders, such projects are known as "suicide" projects. That is why most of the projects are independent. They are like the additive projects Haythornthwaite (2003) described: team members handle segments of the work that only fit together at the end of the project. The components, or sub-projects, are nor interdependent. Members work independently, although they may coordinate work within their own sub-project. Communication is limited and vertical: project leaders act as the hub of the team but team members do not contact each other directly. The key to coordination is a clear division of labour. Independent projects rarely have team-wide meetings and members may never meet. In such projects, coordination and communication are easier and the risks of failure are minimized. Because independent practices minimize the formal workflow interactions on projects, project interactions in them are likely to follow pre-existing informal ties.

Technology

In turn, the organization of work is related to the use of collaborative technologies. In geographically dispersed projects, technology is indispensable for coordination and communication. The professionals in this community do not employ sophisticated technology, although there are some differences in the type of technology and the patterns of use between independent and integrated projects. In independent projects, team members make do with emails, phone calls and voice conferences. Typically, project leaders use email to broadcast updates and requests or keep in touch with separate team members. Phone calls, which are more intrusive, are used only when team members know each other well. In turn, phone conferences are reserved for important discussions such as the division of work at the beginning of the projects or the planning of field studies. More integrated projects tend to rely on more sophisticated technology such as internal servers and websites. Team-wide meetings, including face-to-face meetings, are also more common. Finally, regardless of the project type, many team members have extensive informal face-to-face meetings with colleagues. When some of the team members are collocated, a lot of discussions are done in hallway meetings and locker room chats. Since professionals much prefer informal face-to-face contacts, they strive hard to ensure them: they coordinate going to the same conferences, join the same advisory groups, sit on the thesis committees of their students, visit each other for dinner or spend weekends together. The extent of face-to-face contacts is surprising for dispersed teams. However, it fits well with existing research: such contacts enable the development of trust and their importance is consistent with

the importance of trust and prior ties uncovered in the interviews (Bos et al., 2007).

These practices of recruitment, work organization and technology use not only shape project team composition and the interactions on a project but also affect the characteristics of the Insider community. The most salient pattern is the prominence of long-term informal professional ties. In many cases, the formal ties created by membership in project teams and the ties in the Insider community, are just superimposed over these informal ties. The long-term informal ties of each individual member thus buttress and become the backbone of the Insider community.

The same prominence of long-term informal ties suggests that the initial expectation of significant differences between collaborative ties and ties supporting the exchanges of ideas may prove wrong. SNA literature postulates that with time, interpersonal ties tend to become stronger, support additional activities, and carry additional resources. It is therefore possible that long-term colleagues working on projects both collaborate and exchange ideas; collaborative ties and exchanges of ideas may overlap. What kind of community emerges out of these strategies is the subject of the next section.

STRUCTURAL CHARACTERISTICS OF THE PROFESSIONAL COMMUNITY

This section presents the results of several SNA techniques describing the connections among the professionals working in the area of water. Following the actual ties uncovered by SNA techniques, the analysis presents both the Insider community fostered by the Agency and the broader community of professionals that includes Insiders and outsiders. The discussion examines the connectivity, the boundaries, and the internal subgroups of these communities.

Throughout the section, the analysis draws on the patterns of two types of ties: those supporting collaboration and those supporting exchanges of ideas. Collaborative ties show who collaborates with whom in the community. The exchanges of ideas, in turn, show who shares ideas with whom. In different communities, these two types of ties may overlap or they may be very different. Our analysis indicates that in the community under investigation, professionals collaborate and share ideas with the same people. Their collaborative ties and those ties supporting exchanges of ideas are significantly correlated[2] and have very similar patterns. This can be explained by the dominance of long-term collegial ties, which over time take new functions and support both collaboration and exchanging of ideas. To avoid repetition, in the subsequent sections collaboration and exchanges of ideas are in most cases discussed together.

Connectivity and Boundaries

The most salient finding is that professionals in the area have very few ties in the community[3]. In SNA language, ties are sparse and connectivity in the community is low. In sparse networks, ideas do not travel quickly, resources are not mobilized easily, and members do not influence each other strongly. This connectivity reflects the diversity of the professionals and their institutional environment. These patterns are illustrated by Fig. 1 - a sociogram that visually represents the collaborative ties among all professionals working in the area of water.

To further understand the connections among the Insiders and the dynamic of the exchanges among them, we disaggregated the broader professional network into two components: Insiders component, or the community the Agency cultivates, and outsiders component. The second component includes only professionals who work in the area of water but are not involved in the work of the Agency. Not surprisingly, the sociogram representing the ties among the Insiders is strik-ingly different from the sociogram representing the ties among outsiders. While the Insiders are connected among themselves and form their own network (Fig. 2), outsiders are largely disconnected from each other (Fig. 3).

What comes as a surprise are the strong connections between Insiders and outsiders. Figure 1 shows numerous ties between Insiders and outsiders. Further, connectivity is higher in the broader professional community (Fig. 1) than it is in the Insider community (Fig. 2)[4]. This means that Insiders are less connected among themselves than they are to outsiders. To put it differently, collaboration and exchanges of ideas are most active in the broader professional community. This finding is reinforced by the fact that ties also cross formal project boundaries; most collaboration ties connect members of different projects. These patterns are similar for collaboration and for exchanges of ideas. The sociograms representing the exchanges of ideas in the broader professional community (Fig. 4), in the Insider community (Fig. 5), and among outsiders (Fig. 6) are very similar to the corresponding sociograms representing collaborative ties (Fig. 1, Fig. 2, Fig. 3).

This is, at a first glance, unexpected given the work of the agency and the formal project ties that link Insiders to their own Insider community. Formal project ties, the recruitment practices suggest, are based on long term collegial ties. Yet this pattern is not illogical. When funding is available, long-term collaborators become members of the formal project team. This "conversion" cannot include all close collaborators in a single project team: collaborators have different specialization and can contribute to different projects, they are not always available to join a team, or they join teams funded by different agencies. Further, the Agency is not the single organization to fund research in the area. At any given moment, Insiders collaborate with long-term colleagues on numerous projects, some of which are funded by the Agency and others are not. On each project, further, professionals work independently from

Figure 1. Collaborative ties in the broader professional community

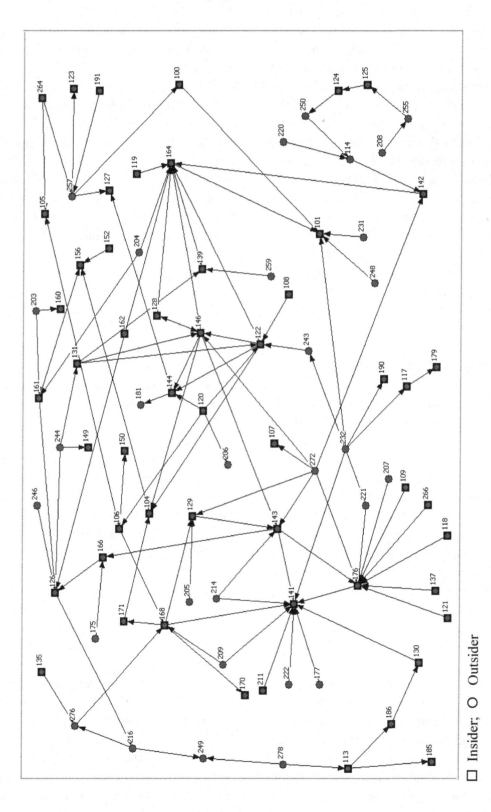

□ Insider;   ○ Outsider

Figure 2. Collaborative ties among insiders

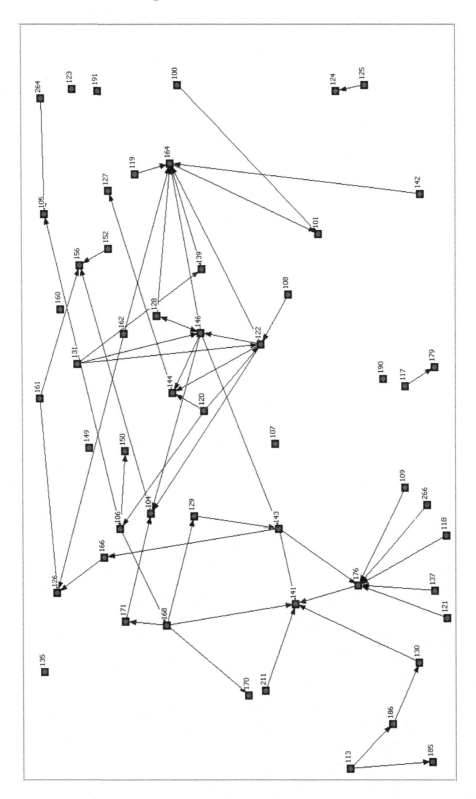

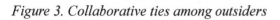

Figure 3. Collaborative ties among outsiders

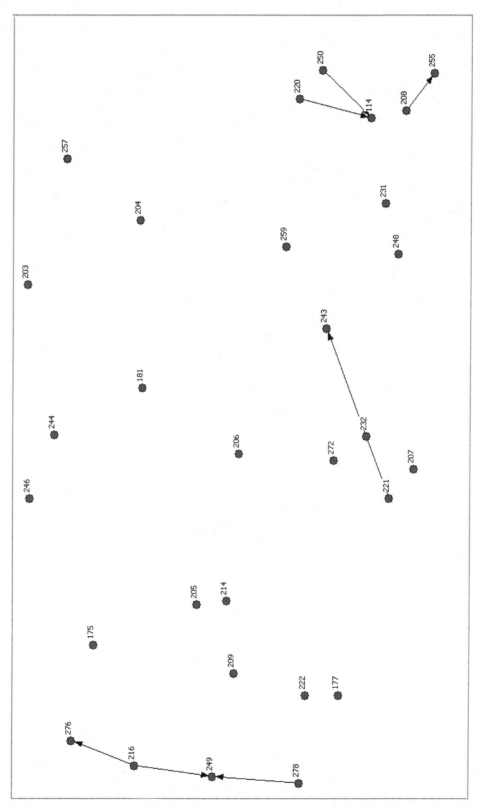

Figure 4. Exchanges of ideas ties in the broader professional community

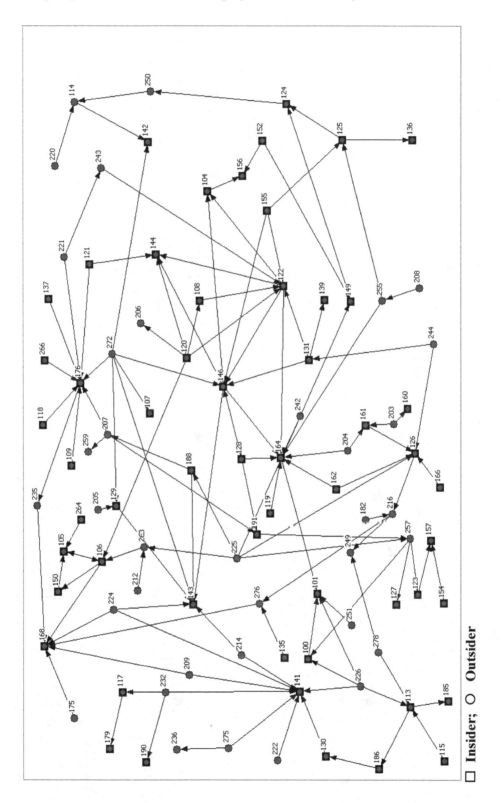

□ **Insider;** ○ **Outsider**

Figure 5. Exchanges of ideas ties among insiders

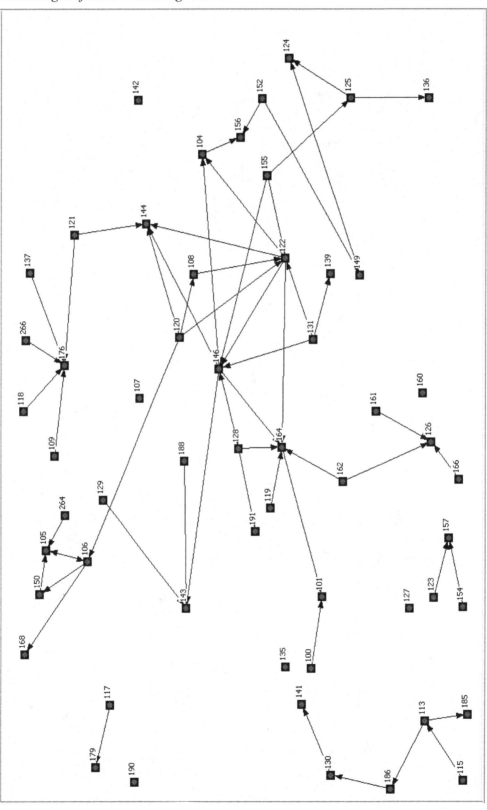

Figure 6. Exchanges of ideas ties among outsiders

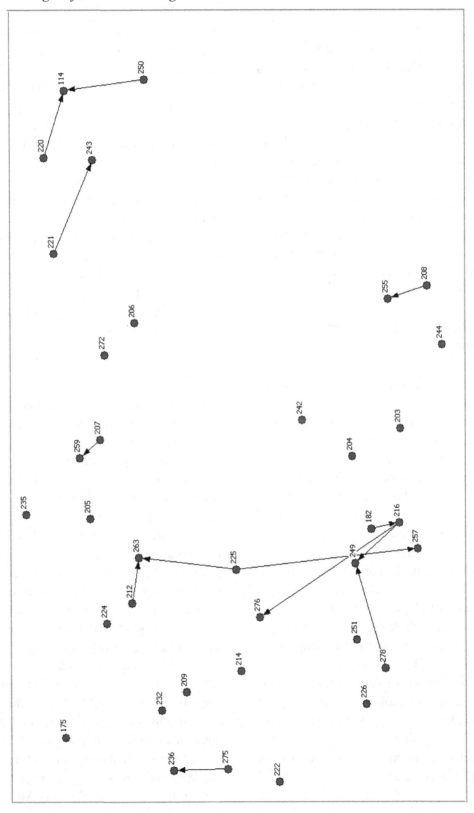

most of the team members; if they have long-term collaborators on the team they are likely to interact only with them. As a result, the ties of collaboration and exchanges of ideas cut across the formal boundaries of the projects funded by the Agency and criss-cross the broader professional community.

This suggests that the Agency has not created a densely knit bounded community. Yet Insiders are better connected among themselves and within the broader professional community; the Agency has either expanded the ties of its members or has attracted the most well connected professionals. However, the formal boundaries of Insiders community remain permeable; it is nested into and connected to the broader professional community.

Cliques of Collaborators and Confidants

How do information and resources travel in this community? In other words, where do intense collaboration and exchanges of ideas take place? The centres of interaction and active exchanges in a network can be made visible, in the words of Cross, by finding its internal sub-groups (Cross et al., 2002). Given the strong connections between Insiders and outsiders, it is possible that internal sub-groups cross Insider - outsider boundary. Hence, the analysis looks for sub-groups on the level of the broader professional community. The investigation of the internal structure identified about a dozen of cliques of professionals, who closely collaborate (Table 1), and another dozen of cliques, where members actively exchange ideas among themselves (Table 2). Much can be gleaned about the way information and resources flow in the community by looking at characteristics such as whether cliques are contained within the Insider community, do they draw their members from project teams, or do close collaborators and close confidants coincide.

Background

Not everyone in the water community has a group of close collaborators and confidants. Most of the respondents don't belong to a clique; they might have close colleagues outside the water community, or have just one close colleague, or their close colleagues simply did not fill in the survey. Those professionals who are indeed members of cliques tend to be older and have longer work experience than other community members so they have had time to develop their professional ties. The most numerous among them are academics, who are more likely to do research than government and industry employees, although clique members come from a variety of sectors. The overwhelming majority of clique members are Insiders, who have probably benefited from the networking activities of the Agency (Table 1; Table 2).

Trust

Given this, it is not surprising that within each single clique members tend to come from the Insiders community (Table 1; Table 2). In two thirds of the cliques, all the members are Insiders. The remaining cliques consist of two Insiders working with an outsider. Cliques, this result shows, tend to remain bound within the confines of the Insider community. This shows that while Insiders are well connected to the broader professional community, their close collaborators and confidants come from the Insiders community. In other words, when it comes to intense professional exchanges that require trust, Insiders find trust within their own community.

This finding might be interpreted not as trust but as the result of formal project membership. Such an interpretation will be at odds with further patterns. First, cliques do not follow project boundaries. In terms of project membership, the typical composition of a clique is three Insiders, two of whom work on the same project and a third person outside this shared project. Most likely, the members of such a clique collaborate on several research projects and not all of their projects are funded by the Agency. It is their informal rather than formal ties that bind the professionals in these intense exchanges.

This fits well with the recruitment strategy discussed in the previous section. In addition, the organization of project work with its discontinuities encourage participants to fall back on informal social process and, it can be added, on informal ties (Brenan et al., 2003). This characteristic of the cliques simultaneously validates the importance of the Insiders network in facilitating trust and confirms that formal project boundaries do not coincide with the informal boundaries of intense exchanges.

Overlap of Collaboration and Exchanges of Ideas

The processes of collaborating, presumably taking place within formal projects, and exchanges of ideas, free of the impact of projects, to a great extent overlap. In SNA language, collaborative ties overlap with the ties supporting the exchanges of ideas. The analysis identified 12 small three-member cliques of close collaborators, who work together (Table 1), and 12 equally small cliques, in which members discuss ideas with each other (Table 2). These two types of cliques largely coincide: two thirds of them have identical members. To a great extent, then, the professionals in the community collaborate and exchange ideas with the same people; their close colleagues are both collaborators and sounding boards. Cliques serve 'double duty' as centres of collaboration and exchanges of ideas – a characteristic that can be expected of researchers and is consistent with the long-term nature of their ties.

Disciplinary and Sectoral Diversity

Perhaps a more interesting characteristic, from the viewpoint of VCoP literature, is the question who participates with whom in a clique. The main pattern of clique composition is their diversity in terms of discipline and, to a great extent, sector. The pattern is similar for collaboration and exchanges of ideas (Tables 1; Table 2). The background of the clique participants shows that they come from different disciplines. None of the cliques draws its members from a single discipline; instead, all of them have members from two or more disciplines. Sectoral diversity is less pronounced. Nonetheless, over half of the cliques include some combination of academics and practitioners from either industry or government.

The disciplinary and sectoral diversity of the cliques is significant, especially when considered together with the overlap of collaboration and exchanges of ideas. Wenger (2000) argues that by their very diversity, cross-functional projects encourage learning and innovation; the new ideas they generate are then synthesized and spread through the homogeneous home communities of the participants. Yet the professionals in this community both collaborate and exchange ideas across disciplines; the complex multi-disciplinary nature of water issues seems to break down disciplinary boundaries. Shared expertise might involve understanding water issues from the viewpoints of different disciplines. The boundaries that still matter are sectors: about half of the cliques draw participants within a single sector. It is the differences in institutional context rather than the differences in the subject matter of disciplines that still separate professionals. There is a slight difference between the sectoral composition of the collaboration cliques and cliques for exchanging ideas: slightly more of the cliques for exchanging ideas are homogeneous and draw members from one single sector. This difference is admittedly minor, yet it confirms an overall pattern: the professionals collaborate across sectors as needed but are still more comfortable discussing ideas with colleagues in their own sectors.

Table 1.

Collaborative Cliques by Sector, Discipline, Membership and Location Combination				
Work Clique Members (ID #)	**Sector combination**	**Discipline combination**	**Membership**	**Location (Cities)**
1: 214	Local government	Environmental Science/Geology	Outsider	12
141	Academic	Civil Engineering	Insider	14
143	Academic	Epidemiology	Insider	7
2: 141	Academic	Civil Engineering	Insider	14
143	Academic	Epidemiology	Insider	7
177	Academic	Environmental Science/Geology	Outsider	13
3: 209	Local government	Economics	Outsider	11
141	Academic	Civil Engineering	Insider	14
168	Academic	Microbiology	Insider	14
4: 104	Academic	Environmental Science/Geology	Insider	1
122	Academic	Biology/Microbiology	Insider	1
146	Academic	Animal Biology/Zoology	Insider	1
5: 120	Prov Govt	Animal Biology/Zoology	Insider	6
122	Academic	Animal Biology/Zoology	Insider	1
144	Academic	Environmental Science/Geology	Insider	3
6: 122	Academic	Animal Biology/Zoology	Insider	1
144	Academic	Environmental Science/Geology	Insider	3
146	Academic	Animal Biology/Zoology	Insider	1
7: 122	Academic	Animal Biology/Zoology	Insider	1
131	Academic	Geography	Insider	2
146	Academic	Animal Biology/Zoology	Insider	1
8: 122	Academic	Animal Biology/Zoology	Insider	1
146	Academic	Animal Biology/Zoology	Insider	1
164	Academic	Biology/Environmental Science	Insider	1
9: 128	Federal government	Animal Biology/Zoology	Insider	7
146	Academic	Animal Biology/Zoology	Insider	1
164	Academic	Biology/Environmental Science	Insider	1
10: 129	Academic	Economics	Insider	10
143	Academic	Epidemiology	Insider	7
272	Federal government	Civil Engineering	Outsider	11
11: 143	Academic	Epidemiology	Insider	7
146	Academic	Animal Biology/Zoology	Insider	1
272	Federal government	Civil Engineering	Outsider	11
12: 143	Academic	Epidemiology	Insider	7
177	Academic	Environmental Science/Geology	Outsider	13
272	Federal government	Civil Engineering	Outsider	11

Fed Govt = Federal Government;   Loc Govt = Local Government;   Prov Govt = Provincial Government

Table 2.

Innovation Clique Members (ID #)	Sector combination	Discipline combination	Membership	Location (Cities)
Exchanges of Ideas Cliques by Sector, Discipline, Membership and Location Combination				
1: 122	Academic	Animal Biology/Zoology	Insider	1
131	Academic	Geography	Insider	2
146	Academic	Animal Biology/Zoology	Insider	1
2: 122	Academic	Animal Biology/Zoology	Insider	1
144	Academic	Environmental Science/Geology	Insider	3
146	Academic	Animal Biology/Zoology	Insider	1
3: 104	Academic	Environmental Science/Geology	Insider	1
122	Academic	Animal Biology/Zoology	Insider	1
146	Academic	Animal Biology/Zoology	Insider	1
4: 122	Academic	Animal Biology/Zoology	Insider	1
146	Academic	Animal Biology/Zoology	Insider	1
155	Academic	Human Health/Medicine/Epidemiology	Outsider	4
5: 122	Academic	Animal Biology/Zoology	Insider	1
146	Academic	Animal Biology/Zoology	Insider	1
164	Academic	Biology/Environmental Science	Insider	1
6: 108	Fed Govt	Biology/Microbiology	Insider	5
120	Prov Govt	Animal Biology/Zoology	Insider	6
122	Academic	Animal Biology/Zoology	Insider	1
7: 120	Prov Govt	Animal Biology/Zoology	Insider	6
122	Academic	Animal Biology/Zoology	Insider	1
144	Academic	Environmental Science/Geology	Insider	3
8: 100	Industry	Civil/Chemical Engineering	Insider	7
101	Academic	Earth/Env. Science/Geology/Ecology	Insider	7
226	Industry	Earth/Env. Science/Geology/Ecology	Outsider	4
9: 105	Local Govt	Geography/Law/Social Science	Insider	7
106	NGO	Geography/Law/Social Science	Insider	8
150	NGO	Business/Administration/Economics	Insider	9
10: 128	Fed Govt	Animal Biology/Zoology	Insider	7
146	Academic	Animal Biology/Zoology	Insider	1
164	Academic	Biology/Environmental Science	Insider	1
11: 129	Academic	Economics	Insider	10
143	Academic	Epidemiology	Insider	7
272	Fed Govt	Civil Engineering	Outsider	11
12: 143	Academic	Epidemiology	Insider	7
146	Academic	Animal Biology/Zoology	Insider	1
272	Fed Govt	Civil Engineering	Outsider	11

Fed Govt = Federal Government;   Loc Govt = Local Government;   Prov Govt = Provincial Government

Distance

Further, the cliques depart from the patterns expected in collaboration and CoP literature in their spatial characteristics. Intense collaboration and communication are easier done face-to-face; collaborative teams and CoP are often local. Yet the clique members in this community are not necessarily local. In the typical clique, two of the members are academics in the same university while the third member is distant (Table 1; Table 2). In about half of the cliques, all three members are in distant locations. Only a few of the cliques have three collocated members. The pattern holds for collaboration and exchanges of ideas. Despite their preference for informal face-to-face interactions, evident in the interviews, clique members collaborate and conduct at least some of their intense exchanges from a distance. In other words, the Agency has succeeded in fostering cross-organizational ties.

Size

These findings of disciplinary and sectoral diversity as well as distance between clique members are all the more significant given the size of the cliques (Table 1; Table 2). They are very small: without exceptions, all cliques have only three participants. Such patterns fit well into the existing recruitment and work organization strategies: the professionals in the community do not work closely in large groups and have just a few long-term close collaborators. The small clique size suggests that close collaboration and exchanges of ideas are selective processes. Professionals collaborate and share their ideas in small groups of trusted colleagues.

In short, even though the professionals in the area are sparsely connected, their community is interspersed with a number of sub-groups, which are centres of intense collaboration and exchanges of ideas. Only a small number of the professionals in the community are involved in them and

these professionals are in turn very selective in their interactions. The exchanges remain within the Insider community, suggesting the existence of trust in it. Further, both the collaboration and exchanges of ideas in the community cut across disciplinary boundaries and, to a great extent, across sectors and distance. They bring together diverse resources and ideas considered crucial for innovation. The tension in the work of the Agency has therefore brought about a community with somewhat unusual characteristics.

CHALLENGES AND SOLUTIONS

For practitioners interested in designing VCoPs, several findings suggest some important challenges in their work and possible solutions. First, while knowledge creation and knowledge transfer processes benefit from participants with diverse background, complex communities of practice, in which ties not only stretch over distance but also cut across sectors, disciplines and organizational affiliations, face significant challenges in their development. Current institutional arrangements discourage them and the natural processes of developing ties tend to fold back within the circle of one's immediate interests. That is why organizations such as the Agency under investigation are critical enablers. Through funding research, networking events, and even informal introductions of professionals to each other, the Agency fosters the most difficult to develop ties. Its success is reflected in the fact that cliques – the foci of intense collaboration and exchanges of ideas, are multidisciplinary, dispersed, and to a great extent cross-sectoral.

At the same time, the Agency neither replaces nor overrides the existing processes of tie development. In the community of professionals working in the area of water, ties and activities are not entirely dependent on the Agency. That is why the formal boundaries of the community of Insiders are permeable. For the same reason, the informal ties among Insiders continue to play an important role in the processes of collaboration and exchanges of ideas. This permeability and interplay of formal and informal ties provide the maximum flows of work resources and ideas. Attempts to "close off" the boundaries of the Insiders community might be counterproductive for the knowledge processes in the community.

The same key role of informal ties means that it is people with social capital that contribute most to the network. When they join the Insider community, they bring their ties with them and enhance the overall connectivity among Insiders.

Further, the collaboration and exchanges of ideas among the professionals in the area of water proved highly selective processes based on trust and shared experience. This selective nature is reflected in the team recruitment strategy targeting long-term collaborators. Both on the level of the overall Insider community and on the level of teams and cliques this leads to the dominance of participants that are mature senior professionals. That CoPs require trust is not unexpected. Yet the obvious corollary - the maturity and seniority of participants, is often overlooked.

These patterns raise some concerns about the effectiveness of the information exchanges in the community. If researchers and practitioners tend to work and exchanges ideas with long-term collaborators and use project funding to simply formalize their existing ties, new collaborators and their new ideas will be hard to come by. On their part, young researchers and practitioners may find it very difficult to participate in the collaboration and exchanges of ideas in the community. Outsiders will also have difficulties entering the Insider community if they do not have prior informal ties to Insiders. In other words, the formal boundaries between Insiders and outsiders are highly permeable and no barrier for collaboration and exchanges; it is the long term-informal ties among participants that separate them. For all these reasons, the Agency and similar organizations need to offer incentives in order to encourage

their participants to go out of their comfort zone and take risks with new collaborators. They might also want to consider networking events targeting outsiders and junior professionals.

Finally, the professionals in the community tend to work in small groups or independently: their project work tends to be limited to the few members of their sub-project. Cliques – for those who have cliques, are very small. Given how closely the exchanges of ideas follow work, this is a worrisome. This means, for example, that project teams do not fully utilize the opportunities for networking and for exchanges of ideas on a project. Funding criteria, including a specific communication plan and setting funding aside for project wide meetings, may encourage project networking and communication to offset such work practices.

CONCLUSION

The analysis above suggests that government initiatives such as the NCE program can be understood from the perspective of communities of practice. However, such formally initiated VCoPs have to be placed within the institutional context, in which they were created, and the practices of the participants.

The NCE Agency set out to deliberately forge a community of professionals with shared expertise in water and shared interest in collaborative solutions yet from diverse disciplinary and sectoral backgrounds. The resulting community is inevitably sparsely connected, fragmented, with only a small core of active participants. Yet the goal of diversity and boundary-crossing connections is achieved. Such deliberately engineered communities my trade off quantity for quality and have fewer but more difficult to achieve under normal conditions interactions.

Next, the community with its semi-formal membership relies heavily on pre-existing informal ties and has highly permeable boundaries.

Informal ties among long term collaborators are the backbone of the community. They shape both collaboration and knowledge exchanges. Indeed, the overlap between collaborate and knowledge exchange relations might partly be due to their mutual reliance on the same core sets of long-term ties. It is informal ties that shape the composition of the community, possible closure processes, and the exchanges among the participants.

Finally, our analysis has shown that SNA approach is indispensable for the study of such complex collaborative communities. While existing research on CoPs focus on the social capital (i.e. resources) inherent in interpersonal exchanges in the community, this study underscores the fact that social capital is equally embedded in network structures composed of diverse ties. An examination of such a structure has enabled us to explore its boundaries, find its internal grouping and thus pinpoint the location of the active exchanges in the community, and describe important characteristics of the collaboration and exchanges of ideas in the community. SNA tools have thus demonstrated their value in contributing to our understanding of the role of social capital in learning processes and knowledge generation.

REFERENCES

Borgatti, S. P., Everett, M. G., & Freeman, L. C. (2002). *Ucinet for Windows: Software for social network analysis.* Harvard, MA: Analytic Technologies.

Bos, N., Gergle, D., Olson, J., & Olson, G. (2001). Being there versus seeing there: Trust via video, *Proceedings of CHI. Retrieved September, 2007 from* http://www.crew.umich.edu/publications. html

Bos, N., Zimmerman, A., Olson, J., Yew, J., Yerkie, J., Dahl, E., & Olson, G. (2007). From shared databases to communities of practice: A taxonomy of collaboratories. *Journal of Computer-Mediated Communication, 12*(2), 318-338.

Bresnen, M., Edelmanb, L., Newellb, S., Scarbrough, H. & Swana, J. (2003), Social practices and the management of knowledge in project environments. *International Journal of Project Management, 21*(3), 157-166.

Brown, J. S., & Duguid, P. (1991). Organizational Learning and Communities-of-Practice: Toward a Unified View of Working, Learning, and Innovation. *Organization Science, 2*(1), 40-57.

Caruso, D. & Rhoten, D. (2001). *Lead, follow, get out of the way: Sidestepping the barriers to effective practice of interdisciplinarity.* Report for the Hybrid Vigor Institute, Retrieved October 2005 from http://www.hybridvigor.net/publications. pl?s=interdis&d=2001.04.30#

Chiu, C., Hsu, M., & Wang, E. (2006). Understanding knowledge sharing in virtual communities: An integration of social capital and social cognitive theories. *Decision Support Systems., 42*, 1872-1888.

Cross, R., Borgatti, S. P., & Parker, A. (2002). *Making invisible work visible: Using social network analysis to support strategic collaboration.* The Network Roundtable at the University of Virginia. Retrieved December 2007 from https://webapp.comm.virginia.edu/SnaPortal/ portals%5C0%5Cmaking_invisible_work_visible.pdf

Cross, R., Parker, A. Prusak, L. & Borgatti, S. P. (2001). Knowing what we know: Supporting knowledge creation and sharing in social networks. *Organizational Dynamics, 30*(2), 100-120.

Cummings, J., & Kiesler, S. (2005). Collaborative research across disciplinary and organizational boundaries. *Social Studies of Science, 35*(5), 703-722.

Daniel, B., Schwier, R. A., & McCalla, G. (2003). Social capital in virtual learning communities and distributed communities of practice. *Canadian Journal of Learning and Technology*, 29(3). Retrieved May 2007 from http://www.cjlt.ca/content/vol29.3/cjlt29-3_art7.html

Drucker, P. (1993) *Post-capitalist society*. Oxford: Butterworth-Heinemann.

Haythornthwaite, C. et al. (2003). *Challenges in the practicce and study of distributed, interdisciplinary, collaboration*. GSLIS Technical Report No.: UIUCLIS--2004/1+DKRC. Retrieved September, 2006 from http://www.lis.uiuc.edu/~haythorn/hay_challenges.html

Heckscher, C. (1996). Defining the post-bureaucratic Types. In Heckscher & Donnellon (Eds.), *The Post-Bureaucratic Organization*. Sage.

Lesser, E., & Prusak, L. (1999). *Communities of practice, social capital and organizational knowledge*. White Paper, IBM Institute for Knowledge Management. Retrieved May 10th, 2007 from http://www.providersedge.com/docs/km_articles/Cop_-_Social_Capital_-_Org_K.pdf

Cross, R., Borgatti, S. P., & Parker, A. (2002). *Making invisible work visible: Using social network Analysis to Support Strategic Collaboration*. Virginia Institute Roundtable December 2007. Retrieved May 10th, 2007 from https://webapp.comm.virginia.edu/SnaPortal/portals%5C0%5Cmaking_invisible_work_visible.pdf

McLure Wasko, M., & Faraj, S. (2000). "It is what one does": Why people participate and help others in electronic communities of practice. *The Journal of Strategic Information Systems*, 9(2-3), 155-173.

Olson, G., & Olson, J. (2003). Mitigating the effects of distance on collaborative intellectual work. *Economic Innovation and New Technologies*, 12(1), 27-42.

Quintas, P. (2002) Managing Knowledge in a New Century. In S. Little, S., P. Quintas, & T. Ray (Eds.), *Managing knowledge*. London; Thousand Oaks, CA: Sage.

Restler, S., & Woolis, D. (2007). Actors and factors: Virtual communities for social innovation. *The Electronic Journal of Knowledge Management, 5*(1), 89-96.

Rhoten, D. (2003). *National Science Foundation BCS-0129573: A multi-method analysis of the social and technical conditions for interdisciplinary collaboration*. Report for the Hybrid Vigor Institute. Retrieved October 2005 from http://hybridvigor.net/interdis/pubs/hv_pub_interdis-2003.09.29.pdf

Shrum, W., Chompalov, I., & Genuth, J. (2001). Trust, conflict and performance in scientific collaborations. *Social Studies of Science, 31*(5), 681-730.

Walsh, J., & Bayama, T. (1996). Computer networks and scientific work. *Social Studies of Science, 26*(3), 385-405.

Wellman, B., & Gulia, M. (1998). Net surfers don't ride alone: Virtual communities as communities. In Smith and Kollock (Eds.) *Communities in cyberspace*, (pp.163-190). Berkley:University of California Press.

Wenger, E. C., & Snyder, W. M. (2000). Communities of practice: The organizational frontier. *Harvard Business Review, 78*(1), 139-45.

Wenger, E. C. (2000). Communities of practice and social learning systems. *Organization, 7*(2), 225-246.

Zheng, J., Veinott, E., Bos, N., Olson, J., & Olson, G. (2002). Trust without touch: Jumpstarting long-distance trust with initial social activities. *Proceedings of CHI, Retrieved September 2007 from* http://www.crew.umich.edu/publications.html

KEY TERMS

Collaborative Research: This is research involving a group of scientists, institutions or organizations working together on a project, often bringing perspectives from different disciplines.

Knowledge Networks: A loosely organized network of people or virtual communities of professional staff and collaborating centers who share common interests. Primarily, knowledge networks represent informal interactions among people, with the objective of collecting and distributing information. The informality of knowledge networks implies that its structure tends to shift and change as people meander in and out in search of information. Broadly defined, knowledge networks encompass the interactions among people, documents, data, analytical tools, and interactive collaborative spaces such as forums and wikis.

Knowledge Transfer (KT): The term, often used in the fields of organizational learning and knowledge management, is not merely about the communication of knowledge. This is because knowledge in organizations is tacit, residing in / among organizational members and their interpersonal networks, tools (such as databases) and tasks. Hence it is essential to articulate a more elaborate process to capture, organize and distribute this knowledge. Knowledge transfer accomplishes this task. By definition, knowledge transfer refers to the process and challenges of creating, organizing, capturing and distributing knowledge, transferring knowledge from one part of an organization to the other parts.

Multidisciplinary Research: This type of research, usually associated with academics, occurs at the edges/frontiers of traditional disciplines and across traditional subject boundaries. Thus, multidisciplinary research involves partners from more than one discipline.

Scholarly Networks: A term referring to a social network in which the nodes are scholars/academics, engaged in both formal collaboration and exchange of scholarly ideas, and informal ties of friendship.

Social Capital: Social capital is a concept used in many disciplines (sociology, business, economics, organizational behaviour, political science, public health) to denote the value of the connections within and between social networks. It is the sum of the actual (and also potential) resources/values embedded within, available through and derived from the network of relationships possessed by an individual or social unit (Nahapiet and Ghoshal 1998, p. 243). Thus, a person has social capital to the extent that she/he has the ability to mobilize and secure benefits by virtue of membership in social networks or other social structures.

Social Network Analysis: Social network analysis is the scientific study of social structure and its relationships. Social network analysis views social structure in terms of nodes and ties/relationships. Nodes are the individual actors within the network (such as people, groups, organizations, institutions, computers, web sites), tied by one or more relationships (such as exchange ideas, friendship, kinship, sex, dislike, conflict, trade). Thus, social network analysis involves the mapping and measurement of the relationship or ties between the nodes being studied.

Virtual Communities Of Practice (Virtual CoPs): These are similar to Communities of Practice (CoP) in the sense that they comprise an informal self-selected communities of learners bound by shared expertise and joint enterprise. However, Virtual CoPs are distinguished by their dispersed nature, the use of technology, and the common interests, goals, needs or practices of their participants. Examples of such communities range from professionals in the same area working for various organizations, to employees of the same global organization. Participants in Virtual CoPs might work together on a common project or just share news of common interest; their technology might involve anything from bulletin boards to sophisticated collaborative web technologies.

ENDNOTES

[1]   All the text in double quotation marks comes from interview data.

[2]   QAP correlation coefficient=0.74, $p < 0.05$.

[3]   The particular number of average ties reported in the analysis is influenced by the response rate of the study, the size of the community studied and the sampling utilized (convenience), as well as the nature of the tie the data captures. This number should not be interpreted as the exact number of collaborators but as an indication of overall connectivity.

[4]   The average number of ties is higher in the all professional community than it is in the Insider community.

Chapter XIX
Enabling Virtual Music Performance Communities

Chrisoula Alexandraki
Technological Educational Institute of Crete, Rethymnon Branch, Greece

Nikolas Valsamakis
Technological Educational Institute of Crete, Rethymnon Branch, Greece

ABSTRACT

The chapter provides an overview of virtual music communities focusing on novel collaboration environments aiming to support networked and geographically dispersed music performance. A key objective of the work reported is to investigate online collaborative practices during virtual music performances in community settings. To this effect, the first part of the chapter is devoted to reviewing different kinds of communities and their corresponding practices as manifested through social interaction. The second part of the chapter presents a case study, which elaborates on the realization of virtual music communities using a generic technological platform, namely DIAMOUSES. DIAMOUSES was designed to provide a host for several types of virtual music communities, intended for music rehearsals, live performances and music learning. Our recent experiments provide useful insights to the distinctive features of these alternative community settings as well as the practices prevailing in each case. The chapter is concluded by discussing open research issues and challenges relevant to virtual music performance communities.

INTRODUCTION

Undoubtedly, music forms a popular application domain for diverse application and services. Although collaboration has always been a key element in music expression, however the social interaction in virtual music communities is mostly circumferential to music creation or music expression itself. In their majority, these communities are concerned with information exchange of existing music works. The collaborative tasks in these communities are concentrated on file sharing, information exchange on news, events and releases, popularity monitoring, information retrieval of music trends etc (Poblocki, 2005). In contrast with these well developed music communities of practice, this chapter presents recent achievements in the area of Network Music Performance (NMP) and attempts to portray virtual communities in which music content is dynamically created on the fly and shared among remotely located music associates.

Although there is a large debate on the origins of dislocated music performance, it appears that the first attempts in performing music through computer networks dates back in the late 1970s and are associated with the commercialization of personal computers in the United States (Barbosa 2003). Due to the technological constraints presented in network music performance, the advancement of music performance communities has been somewhat belated. However, current advances in network technologies have encouraged a variety of novel applications and services that are related to performing music through the network. A number of systems have emerged both in research as well as in commercial contexts. These systems raise the issue of community oriented behaviour throughout network music performance. In these communities the collaborative purpose may range from professional stage performances to social music making, such as music improvisation and jamming.

The main objective of this chapter is to elaborate on the collaboration practices supported across music performance communities and to propose new techniques for enhancing the publicity of these communities. Clearly, the most outstanding constraint that hinders the evolution of virtual music performance communities is the technological barrier of the unavailability of appropriate network infrastructures to support them. However, progress of the last few years in this area of research shows that performing music through networks is becoming feasible in the near future.

The rest of this chapter is structured as follows. The next section presents an overview of the currently and near future supported virtual communities of practice in music. A classification of these communities is attempted on the basis of the purpose of their collaboration. This classification is followed by a discussion on the modes of collaboration and the diverge requirements for supported practices in the different types of music communities. The section that follows provides insights on realizing music performance communities, based on the recent outcomes of an ongoing R&D project, namely DIAMOUSES. Finally, the chapter concludes with a discussion on open issues and prominent perspectives in virtual music performance communities.

VIRTUAL COMMUNITIES OF PRACTICE IN MUSIC

This section provides an overview of the state of the art research on virtual music communities and the practices prevailing in different scenarios and collaborative settings. It attempts to provide a classification of these communities based on their purpose, or more precisely, on the expected outcome. The proposed classification is based on the assumption that social interaction in music communities varies depending on the purpose of collaboration. Therefore the practices supported by the corresponding virtual environment should be different depending on the type of the community they aim to support.

Types of Music Communities

Investigating the purpose set for virtual music communities, five distinct types of music communities may be discerned, namely, music sharing communities, audience communities, performance communities, learning communities and music composers' communities. At present, each of these virtual community types has reached a different stage of popularity and growth, as technological constraints severely restrict the possibility to support the various social interaction practices that are required by different community settings. Thus, one may contrast the high popularity of music sharing communities, with the exemplary case of the Napster community, against the infant state of music instrument learning communities that are yet in a preliminary experimental stage. The main technological requirement of the first community type is the availability of a reliable network protocol for fast transfer of multimedia files, whereas the second type of community requires synchronous collaboration and social interaction not only based on file transfer but also on physical co-presence and communication through sound, vision and corporal movement. The affect of the technological requirements on the development of music communities is further confirmed by the fact that the well established music sharing communities, started to evolve with the invention of the MP3 sound file format, which may give acceptable sound quality in relatively low bit-rates and therefore may be easily exchanged through standard network connections.

Music Sharing Communities

Music sharing communities are communities that share music, sounds, MIDI files, or music playlists. Typically, the music sharing practices of these communities are asynchronous. Napster was the first widely used peer-to-peer online music file sharing community. It allowed community members to share music files and it was freely available during the years 1999 to 2001. The music industry accused Napster for massive copyright violations, a phenomenon taking place in many music-sharing communities, which led the service to terminate its operation by court order (Oberholzer & Strumpf, 2004). Historically, Napster made a major impact on the next generation decentralized peer-to-peer file-sharing communities. Presently, most music sharing communities are licensed under the Creative Commons Sampling License (2008), which reserves certain rights to composers and grants certain other rights to licensees, thus expanding the range of sounds and music to legally share.

In addition to Napster-type communities, music sharing communities have also aimed at introducing independent composers to the general public. The web applications that promote these communities provide facilities for aspiring artist to access millions of people on a daily basis (Sellers, 2008; Siwal, 2008). MySpace (http://www.myspace.com) is one of the most popular social networking music communities which offers its members the possibility to build their own music artistic profile, interact with a community group of 'friends' and upload up to six of their own compositions.

Among the various music-sharing communities, there are communities dedicated to sharing sound material of specialized interest. Such a community is 'The Freesound Project' (http://freesound.iua.upf.edu/) targeting communities interested in soundscape recordings and sound effects. The project provides its community members the possibility to collaboratively create and manage file tags which annotate and classify the available sound material. Freesound is a project offered by the Music Technology Group of Pompeu Fabra University Free Cultural Works and the shared files are licensed under the Creative Commons Sampling Licenses.

A notably large music community is developed around Last.fm (http://www.last.fm) Internet radio website. One of the features of Last.fm is that it builds the music profile of its members automatically, based on the radio stations streamed and reproduced on their personal computer or their portable music device. Last.fm uses a music recommendation system, which implements a collaborative filtering algorithm that allows community members to browse a list of artists that appear on the profile of members with similar musical preferences. Recommendations based on similarities can also be made directly by the members of the community.

An example of a music community that is specialized exclusively in sharing MIDI files is the one supported by MIDISharing (http://www.midisharing.cn). Supplementary specialized music communities are based on podcasts. Podcasts are distributed to community members using syndication feeds that facilitate protocols such as RSS or Atom and notify interested members whenever new content is made available. Podcasting allows community members to share their own radio-style shows or education communities to share school lessons.

Table 1, summarises the elements of practice in music sharing communities. Apparently there are only two activities that are synchronous, namely chatting and monitoring file exchange.

Audience Communities

There is a debate on whether music aesthetics should be assessed based on the composer's incentive or on the listener's interest (Garnett, 2001), although listener's interest and excitement may be guided by the creator's motivational drive. Nevertheless, music, like any artwork deduces its endurance from human excitement and human delight.

In the context of remote music performance systems, current advancements in network infrastructures such as the advent of broadband networking and the Internet2 have allowed live internet multicasts of onstage performances. Examples of such live network transmission are the Global Concert Series of the Philadelphia Orchestra ("The Philadelphia Orchestra", 2008) and the live broadcasts of the telematic concerts of the SoundWIRE research group of the Stanford University (SoundWIRE, 2008).

These recent attempts for live network multicasts are, from a technological point of view, more affordable than distributed music performances, even in high-quality audiovisual stream transferring. The reason for this is that the bandwidth demanding communication channel from the stage to the audience is unidirectional. Moreover network latency is not crucial in this type of communication. The tolerable latency in collaborative network performance is of the order of 20msec (Chafe, Gurevich, Leslie & Tyan, 2004), whereas in live broadcasts a latency of the order of 1-2 sec may be acceptable.

Aspects of social interaction in audience communities are not yet fully supported. In order to more actively support audience involvement and enhance community oriented behaviour in

Table 1. Collaboration practices in music sharing communities

Elements of practice	Synchronous	Asynchronous
Share audio and MIDI file		✓
Tag file content		✓
Use preference recommendations based on profiles and similarities		✓
Monitor independent artist promotion		✓
Vote for music chart		✓
Get news update through syndication feeds		✓
Participate in discussion forums		✓
Participate in chat rooms	✓	
Monitor file exchange in peer-to-peer community networks	✓	

audience communities both synchronous and asynchronous interaction techniques may be employed without significantly raising the technological requirements. Similarly to Interactive TV, in order to provide audience interactivity the communication requires a return path. However, this path may be a low bandwidth connection since audience interaction is communicated through typical stateless requests instead of bandwidth demanding multimedia streams. Moreover, as proposed in the DIAMOUSES case study presented in the next sections, the return channel may be entirely decoupled from the forward channel by allowing a separate server to dispatch audience requests.

True audience interactivity is supported when the audience may actually alter the flow of the performance. Altering the flow of the performance may be desirable only in cases of theatrical improvisation ("Stanford Center for", 2003) or in algorithmically controlled interactive performances, such as performances of electroacoustic music exploiting gesture based interaction. Table 2 presents a number of the possibilities for providing audience interaction throughout a live stage performance broadcast or multicast.

Music Performance Communities

The term 'music performance communities' is used to refer to virtual communities whose main purpose is to perform music across different interaction scenarios. Such scenarios may include geographically displaced music rehearsals, network group improvisations, dislocated jamming sessions, remote collaborative music compositional sessions, network music master classes, network enabled music learning sessions and several variations of the above.

Different application scenarios pose different requirements both on the efficiency of the underlying technological infrastructure as well as on the tools provided for interaction. In general, music performance communities are more difficult to implement due to various technological constraints, with the most outstanding being the latency in audio signal transition from one network node to another. Specifically, performing music has strict requirements for timely and accurate delivery of audible streams. The term audible, is used here instead of audio in order to take into account forms of sound representation that are alternative to audio, such as MIDI streams or communication through the OpenSound Control protocol (Schmeder, 2008). Timely delivery of audible streams refers to latency minimisation

Table 2. Suggested collaboration practices in audience communities

Elements of practice	Synchronous	Asynchronous
Selection of video viewing angle (i.e. preferred camera)	✓	
Participate in live interviews with musicians	✓	
Participate in algorithmically controlled interactive performances	✓	
Use video/audio on demand services		✓
Participate in discussion forums		✓
Vote for preferred music works to be multicast (polls, questions or comments)	✓	✓
Retrieve metadata about performances	✓	✓

concerns and synchronisation requirements on the exchanged resources, whereas accurate delivery of audible streams conveys high requirements in the quality of audible sound which demand increased network bandwidth and eliminated network jitter and packet loss.

A number of systems supporting live music performance over the network have been implemented and referred to as Network Music Performance or NMP systems. Renault et al. (2007) provided an overview of the state of the art research in NMP systems and classified existing efforts in three categories, namely:

- The Realistic Jam Approach (RJA)
- The Latency Accepting Approach (LAA)
- The Remote Recording Approach (RRA)

RJA refers to systems aiming at latency and audio quality optimization. These systems appear feasible only in the context of the Internet2 backbone. Systems of the Latency Accepting Approach are NMP systems which conform to the inevitable latencies in the transmission of signals and attempt to investigate performance under circumstances of high latencies (of the order of 200msec) in the communication of audible signals. Finally, RRA involves systems in which the bandwidth demanding channel is unidirectional. RRA systems are based on the idea of remote recording sessions. These systems require high quality in the transmitted audio streams; however latency issues are less significant.

Regarding the collaborative tasks in music performing communities, both synchronous and asynchronous activities are necessary as summarized in Table 3.

Music Learning Communities

Although music learning involves performance on behalf of the teacher, the student or both, music learning communities are discerned as a separate type of community due to the fact that research on music learning environments has considerably different priorities than in music

Table 3. Community practices in virtual music performance communities

Elements of practice	Synchronous	Asynchronous
Maintain community awareness (i.e. connected participants)	✓	
Specify communication channels (audio, video, MIDI)	✓	
Establish connection to performing sessions	✓	
Control reproduction of the receiving signals (i.e. volume, mute, solo)	✓	
Perform music	✓	
Communicate through chat	✓	
Communicate through speech	✓	
Manipulate shared/synchronised objects (e.g. scores metronomes, virtual instruments)	✓	
Share electronic resources (audio, video files, electronic scores, etc)	✓	✓
Participate in discussion forums		✓
Post and view public announcements		✓
Schedule performance events		✓

performance. The outstanding requirement in distributed environments that support distant music learning is not the timely and accurate delivery of audible streams, but instead, suitable methods for learning and appropriate pedagogical paradigms. Since simultaneous performance from remotely located peers is not a common practice in music learning, the systems developed to support music education are sufficiently supported by videoconferencing platforms for the audiovisual communication (Anderson & Ellis, 2005). These platforms are originally targeted to speech signal exchange. When discussing, latency is not as crucial as when performing music with others over the network. Moreover, the signal quality and therefore the required bandwidth capacity are much lower in speech signals (the spectral bandwidth of speech goes up to 4 kHz, whereas the spectral bandwidth of CD quality audio goes up to 22050 Hz). Clearly, distant music learning can considerably benefit from the advancements in network music performance systems, since the quality of sound in the connection of the teacher and the student, although not a priority is significant when it comes to learning music interpretation.

Music learning may involve learning the theory of music (this may range from notation and dictation to advanced theory such as music morphology), learning to play a certain music instrument (which involves music interpretation and physical technique) or learning to compose (from basic harmony lessons to advanced orchestration and composition). It is interesting to observe that platforms targeting learning communities are oriented towards specific learning subjects. In particular, platforms developed for music instrument learning are concerned with a specific music instrument. For example the MAV framework (Koerselman, Larkin & Ng, 2007), which has been implemented in the context of the i-maestro project (http://www.i-maestro.net/), aims to support cello lessons through gesture analysis and gesture following techniques. On the other hand, the systems VEMUS and IMU-TUS (Fober, Letz, Orlarey, Askenfeld, Hansen & Schoonderwaldt 2004) are targeted towards learning wind instruments. It appears that most of these systems invest quite a lot of their research efforts in providing the possibility for automatic evaluation of student's individual practice (Percival, Wang & Tzanetakis, 2007). Table 4 outlines some of the collaboration practices that take place in music learning communities.

Table 4. Community practices in music learning communities

Elements of practice	Synchronous	Asynchronous
Perform simultaneously the same piece of music (play along)	✓	
Listen to the instructor's performance and repeat (repeat after)		✓
See student's movements and correct through spoken instructions	✓	
Manipulate shared/synchronised objects (e.g. annotate electronic scores, set electronic metronomes, interact on virtual instruments)	✓	
Chat	✓	
Use software for automatic evaluation during home practice		✓
Share electronic resources (e.g. audio, video, electronic scores)		✓

Music Composers' Communities

This type of community refers to virtual communities whose purpose is to allow members to collectively create a music work of art. The outcome of this collaboration may be either in the form of a set of instructions in a certain notation (i.e., a score) or in the form of a recorded music track. This type of community is not concerned with any type of music creation other than composing a piece of music to be later performed or broadcasted. Therefore improvisation, as a form of music creation does not apply to this type of community but rather to music performance communities.

Conventionally, the activity of composing involves the transcription of music into some form of a symbolic musical notation. The simplest form of collaborative composition in a virtual community is the process of editing a shared music score between remotely located composers. The shared music score can be in the format of a MIDI file or the file format of some specialised score editing application, such as Finale or Encore. This simple form of collaboration, typically, takes place asynchronously through email exchange or file sharing among members of a community. An early example of such a virtual community is the Netjam community (Latta, 1991). More recent implementations of composing communities provide the possibility to edit scores on-line and share them with other composers though a dedicated server application, such as the one provided by the WikiComposer website (http://www.wikicomposer.com).

Nowadays, the composition activity in addition to online score editing may involve synthesis, processing, assembling and mixing of sound material. Specialised applications like ProTools, Digital Performer, Logic, Ardour, Audacity, Sonar or Cubase provide a multi-track audio and score editing compositional framework. Composers in collaboration may work and exchange complex multi-track sessions produced in such environ-ments. The Open Media Framework (OMF) is a handy, platform-independent file format intended for transfer of digital media and multi-track sessions between different software applications. A sophisticated platform that provided online collaboration on an audio and score multi-track graphical environment was the Res Rocket Surfer Project (Mühlhäuser, Welzl, Borchers, & Gutkas, 2001), which supported the additional option of importing and exporting multitrack sessions for some of the most popular of the aforementioned software. DigiDelivery by Digidesign is today the successor of the Res Rocket Surfer project and it is used by many professional studios and individuals in the music industry ("DigiDelivery Overview", 2008).

In more advanced scenarios, composers apart from working with music material in the form of note events or sounds, additionally develop their own compositional tools that create or transform music material through algorithmic processes. The compositional tools may be developed in music programming environments (i.e. Csound, SuperCollider, MaxMSP, Pure Data, Common Lisp Music, Nyquist, OpenMusic, etc.), in mathematical and signal processing environments (e.g. Matlab, Mathematica) or by the direct use of a programming language. In such cases, composers may share code and data produced in the above environments. The collaboration in this case is carried out mainly asynchronously and offline. An exception was the no longer available online studio (Wöhrmann, 1999) of the Institut de Recherche et Coordination Acoustique/Musique (IRCAM), which provided online access to some sophisticated sound synthesis algorithms and processing tools as well as to the IRCAM sound databases.

In summary Table 5 depicts some of the key practices prevailing in virtual music composition communities with indication of their collaborative nature.

Table 5. Community practices in virtual music composing communities

Elements of practice	Synchronous	Asynchronous
Chat	✓	
Edit electronic scores	✓	✓
Share multi-track sessions		✓
Share other electronic resources (audio, photos, video)		✓
Share composition algorithms		✓

Consolidation

The classification of music communities presented in this chapter shows that, like any form of co-located physical collaboration, virtual collaboration involves both synchronous as well as asynchronous practices. These practices may take place either in private (locally) or in public space. In fact, practices that take place in the public space may concern the entire community, specific groups of the community or certain individuals. The target members of specific collaborative practices may be negotiated through a so called 'notification policy'.

Figure 1, shows the synchronous and asynchronous community practices that can take place in computer mediated collaboration in music performance communities. In contrast with some virtual music communities where asynchronous practices dominate, in music performance communities the prevailing practices are mostly synchronous; in fact asynchronous practices are actually marginal. Moreover, Figure 1 indicates that asynchronous practices in music performance communities take place only in the public space. Although music performance may take place in private, this type of performance is typically not computer mediated, thus only indirectly influenced by online activity. This may be contrasted with music learning communities in which a key research issue is computer-mediated music instrument practicing, which is an asynchronous practice taking place in private space.

CASE STUDY AND REFLECTIONS

The above have motivated developments in the DIAMOUSES project which set out to provide a generic platform for experimenting with various virtual music community settings. The primary goal of DIAMOUSES was to provide a platform in which the audio communication among remotely connected peers would be carried out with the minimum possible latency and the maximum possible audio quality. Although this is the primary requirement for music performance communities, DIAMOUSES is implemented as a generic platform, thus able to host additional types of music communities, as portrayed in the previous section. The following subsections aim to: (a) describe some of the system's generic components facilitating virtual music communities, (b) report on a number of empirical findings concerning the collaborative features of the DIAMOUSES platform and (c) present the possibilities for extending the platform so as to support both synchronous and asynchronous collaboration for different types of communities.

The DIAMOUSES Platform

DIAMOUSES, distributed interactive communication environment for live music performance, provides an integrated virtual environment which allows musicians to perform the same piece of music through the network, while distributed

Figure 1. Computer mediated collaboration practices in music performance communities

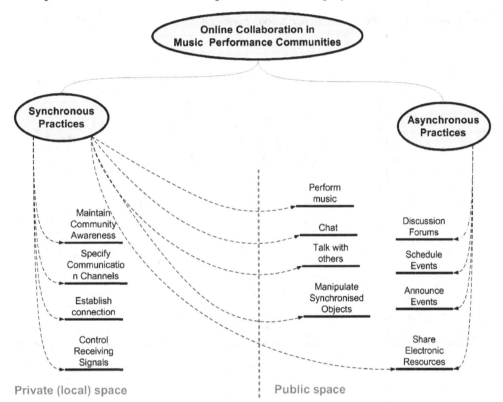

in remote geographical locations. Musicians-members of an orchestra, whilst geographically spread, are able to simultaneously perform the same piece of music. At the same time, this 'network-performance' can be witnessed by an audience located elsewhere, breaking the barriers set by geographical distance, thus resulting in a new network collaborative community.

Figure 2, depicts the overall architecture of the DIAMOUSES platform. The central entities of the distributed environment are the DIAMOUSES Streaming Server, the DIAMOUSES Collaboration Server and DVB-T broadcasting center. Users may interact with these entities as portal users via an internet browser (appearing at the left area of the diagram), as performers (appearing at the center area of the diagram) or as the audience of a digital TV transmission (appearing at the right area of the diagram).

During collaborative performance, each performer is equipped with a set of hardware devices (i.e. microphone and speakers or headphones, camera, possibly some MIDI controllers and a personal computer). The primary communication channels among the performers are based on audio, video and MIDI streams. An additional communication channel is offered through chat, in case audio connection cannot be facilitated. Performers communicate through the network connection of their personal computers, where a two-layered software application is executed. The component at the bottom layer, denoted as 'stream processing', is responsible for fast and reliable data (audio, video, MIDI) capturing, data transmission and reception from the network and data reproduction. The top-layer component, denoted as 'collaboration & GUI', is the graphical user interface.

Figure 2. The overall architecture of the DIAMOUSES platform

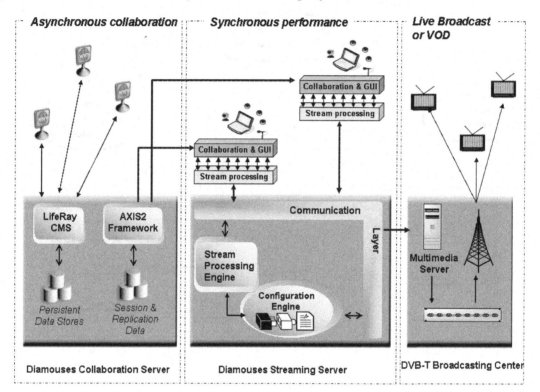

The DIAMOUSES GUIs include shared objects, such as music scores, acoustic or visual metronomes, etc., which require the awareness of the state of a performing session. This information is exchanged through the DIAMOUSES Collaboration Server. The DIAMOUSES Collaboration Server, apart from maintaining session information in the course of a performing session, it additionally serves the asynchronous collaboration services offered through a dedicated portal. For the digital TV broadcast, DIAMOUSES exploits an existing platform for digital terrestrial transmission, DVB-T. In order to broadcast the combined performance of the distributed performers, the incoming audio and video streams of the performers are multiplexed in the stream processing engine and they are sent to the 'Multimedia Server' of the DVB platform as a single stream. The Multimedia Server de-multiplexes

the stream and supplies the resulting individual streams to the rest of the DVB platform. These streams are then encoded to the appropriate formats and transmitted to the network of the digital TV subscribers.

The entire system is implemented for the Linux operating system in order to eliminate problems related to clock inaccuracy and further latencies introduced by the audio device drivers.

Pilot Application Scenarios and Empirical Findings

Three pilot application scenarios were selected for evaluating the DIAMOUSES platform. The evaluation was concerned with objective and subjective measures of signal transition (e.g. real and perceived latency and distortion due to network jitter and packet loss or insufficient network bandwidth), as well as with the experience of the users (both performers and audience) in participating in the three scenarios. This subsection describes the setup of each scenario and reports on the user experience during performance. Musician experience is presented in terms of the capability of the connected musicians to socially interact with each other as compared with their social interaction when co-located.

The three scenarios were specified in the early phases of the project. The choice of the specific scenarios was made on the basis of four criteria: (a) to present the interaction in different collaboration activities (i.e. rehearsal, live performance, lesson), (b) to allow for exploring the differences in the interaction through different music types (i.e. jazz, electroacoustic, classical), (c) to allow experimentation with different network infrastructures (e.g. wired and wireless, Local Area Networks, Wide Area Networks) and finally (d) to be scalable. The implementation carried out in the context of the DIAMOUSES project (both server and client implementations) is fully scalable. Scalability, in the context of the DIAMOUSES environment, refers to the ability

of the platform to expand the scenarios both in terms of the number of connected peers as well as in terms of their geographical spread.

Jazz Rehearsal Scenario

The first scenario concerns the rehearsal of a Jazz duet (double bass and electric piano) performing through a 100Mpbs LAN. The communication among musicians, shown in Figure 3, was based on high quality audio and low quality video streams. The experience of the two musicians is outlined in Table 6. The same experiment was carried out with three musicians, distributed within a LAN. The three musician experiment was done with the music genres of pop/rock and Greek modern music. The participation of three musicians did not change the efficiency in the communication among performers. An additional finding relating to the collaborative performance of three or more musicians is that during sound-check performers want to be able to control the individual levels of each musician participating in the performing session and occasionally use the functionalities 'mute' and 'solo' for one of them.

Figure 3. The jazz rehearsal scenario

Table 6. Empirical findings regarding the jazz rehearsal scenario

1	The double bass player preferred to listen to the pianist through headphones, because he claimed that his performance (reproduced in physical space) was disturbing him to concentrate on the pianist performance, which was reproduced on a stereo speaker system. There was no such requirement from the pianist.
2	When the audio quality was raised from CD quality (44100kHz, 16-bit resolution, stereo) to 48kHz 32-bit resolution, stereo, both felt that the sound quality was noticeable, and in particular the bass player reported that he felt that there was more brightness in the sound of the piano.
3	The two musicians did not find necessary to communicate through video. As they explained, this is due to the fact that they rehearse with each other on a daily basis and the communicate through
4	The main problem in the communication of the two musicians was that when video communication was activated in addition to audio communication there were occasional dropouts in the sound coming from the network, which disturbed them in their rhythmic attacks. It is believed that these dropouts were caused due to network packet loss due to insufficient bandwidth.

Figure 4. Network diagram for the live performance scenario

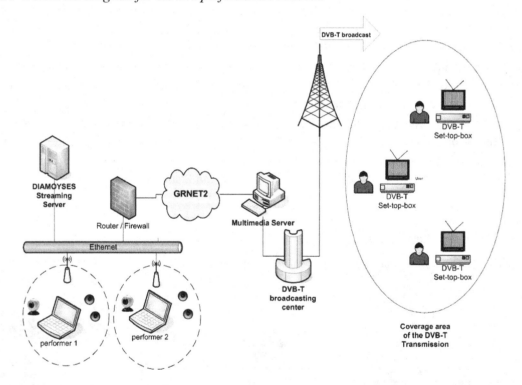

Live Electroacoustic Music Performance Scenario

This scenario involves a live performance of two musicians of electroacoustic music connected through Wireless LAN and a simultaneous live broadcast an audience of DVB-T viewers. Musicians were communicating through the use of MIDI streams and through low quality video. As shown on Figure 4, the communication with the DVB-T broadcasting center was unidirectional carrying two MIDI streams and two high quality video streams. These four streams were multiplexed in a single stream before sent to the DVB-T platform in order to avoid the need for stream synchronisation at the receiving end. The connection was based on GRNET2 (http://www.grnet.gr), which is a high speed (reaching 1-2.5 Gbps) optical fibre network connecting various research and academic institutions in Greece.

Figure 5, shows a snapshot of the video displayed on the TV receiver. It can be seen that in order to receive DVB-T streams the receiver was equipped with a DVB-T set-top box. Due to the fact the terrestrial transmission of digital TV does not inherently offer a return path viewers could not interact with the content of the broadcast stream. In order to make the video content more interesting, an application was developed which allowed for alternatively switching to either or both of the received video streams displaying the performers. This application was running on the 'Multimedia Server' (on Figure 4) during the live broadcast. The qualitative results in this experiment are outlined in Table 7.

Piano Lesson Scenario

This scenario concerns a piano lesson performing through the Internet. The communication between the music teacher and her student was based on a 34Mbps optical fibre Internet connection, though which CD quality audio and low quality video was transmitted from each network node to the other. The qualitative results in this experiment are outlined in Table 8.

DIAMOUSES Communities

Although currently aiming at music performance communities, DIAMOUSES is implemented as a generic platform allowing for hosting a broad range of virtual music communities and a variety of synchronous and asynchronous collaboration practices. This section elaborates on some of the features of the DIAMOUSES platform which are explicitly related to community management and asynchronous/synchronous collaborative practicing using examples of a recent case study.

Figure 5. Live DVB-T broadcast of the electro acoustic performance

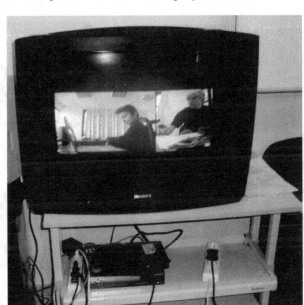

Table 7. Empirical findings regarding the live electroacoustic music performance scenario

Performers' feedback	The video communication did not appear to be of much help to the communication among the two performers due to the following reasons:
	The coverage of the camera was small
	They both felt that visual communication through video would be more effective if the video display would be projected on the wall, instead of a small window of the computer screen.
	Their video communication was broadcast to the audience, which did not allow for private visual communication among performers. They reported that visual communication among performers must be done in private without the audience being aware of inter-performer communication.
	The performers felt that they were not able to communicate as well as when they are located in the same physical space.
	The fact that the audience was located elsewhere destructed them from having the feeling of a live performance. Performer's need the audience feedback in order to express themselves.
	One of the performers was feeling insecure whether the other was listening what she was playing and if she was listening to what the other performer was playing.
	They both felt that they could adapt to this type of dislocated performance if they would have the possibility to do it again.
Audience feedback	The audience that was invited to watch the performance were not familiar with electro acoustic music and they had a difficulty to assess the event. Overall they were excited with the idea of dislocated performances.

Figure 6. The piano lesson scenario

Table 8. Empirical findings regarding the piano lesson scenario

Teacher & student feedback	Both teacher and student found it difficult to communicate visually due to the small video display size.
	Both teacher and student had synchronization problems when performing simultaneously in fast tempo. They couldn't figure out if this was due to the latency of the system or due to the student's difficulty to follow a constant tempo.
Teacher feedback	The teacher had a difficulty directing the student since she wanted two video displays, one for the student's hand positions and one for the student's face.
	The teacher found the option of an electronic metronome as necessary
Student feedback	The student had a difficulty reading the score and watching her teacher at the same time. She suggested that two parallel windows on the same screen, one with the electronic score and one with the teachers' video, would be more suitable.
	The student suggested that electronic score scrolling in the computer screen would be a helpful feature.

Realization of Asynchronous Activities

A dedicated portal has been implemented in order to support the asynchronous collaboration practices. In this portal, users may register either as general public or as music performers (see Figure 7).

Once registered, users may post announcements, participate in discussion forums and get informed forthcoming events. Additionally, portal users may register to participate in a live performance as members of the audience (Figure 8).

When registered as a musician, a member of the DIAMOUSES community may create 'virtual rooms'. DIAMOUSES 'virtual rooms' correspond to synchronous sessions of music performances, rehearsals, etc. Figure 9, shows the process of scheduling and participating in DIAMOUSES virtual rooms. The button labelled 'Launch Application', allows users who wish to participate in a synchronous session, to download and launch the application supporting synchronous DIAMOUSES sessions. The GUI of this application is depicted on Figure 10.

Realization of Synchronous Activities

In DIAMOUSES, synchronous sessions are distributed performing sessions. The term 'virtual room' is facilitating the room metaphor to indicate performing collaboration in a distributed environment similarly to performers' collaboration when they are located in the same room.

The graphical user interface of the application supporting synchronous performance sessions is the one depicted on Figure 10. It can be easily confirmed that this application supports all the synchronous collaborative activities reported on Table 3. Specifically, video communication with each performing peer may be started/stopped at any time, some basic mixing functionalities are supported (i.e. level control, mute and solo), the metronome may be activated/deactivated to reproduce a predefined tempo and rhythm and finally chat is supported in order to allow communication when all the other communication channels (audio/video/MIDI) are inactive.

The metronome has been implemented as a shared collaborative object in this application. Due to the fact that the particular object is extremely sensitive to synchronization offsets, the

Figure 7. Registration to the DIAMOUSES portal as simple user and as music performer

Figure 8. Announcement of forthcoming events and requesting to view a live event

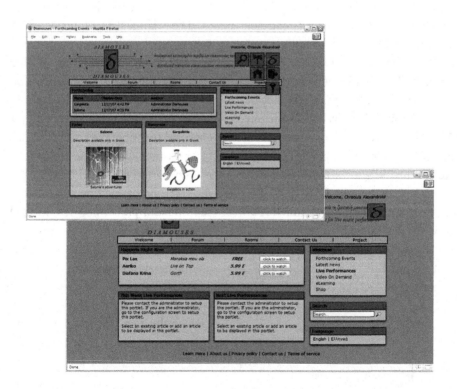

Figure 9. Scheduling and participation in DIAMOUSES 'virtual rooms'.

Figure 10. The 'virtual room' of a DIAMOUSES performance

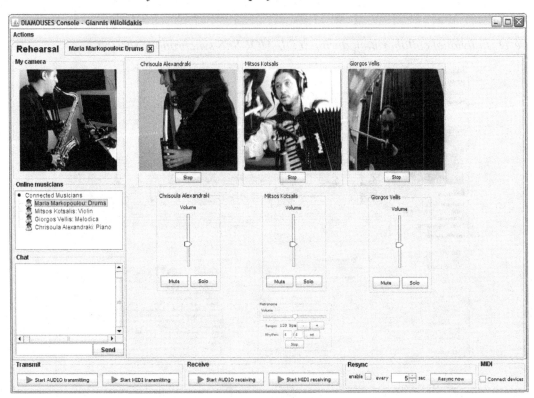

metronome can be started from one performer at a time. Once the metronome is started at the site of a certain performer it is then propagated to the other participants, through the DIAMOUSES streaming server in the form of an audio or a MIDI stream. Obviously, the metronome may be muted by participants not wishing to listen to the rhythmic beats.

In addition to this collective collaboration, individual collaboration is allowed through the use of separate panels activated through the tabs shown on Figure 10. The content of these tabs is depicted on Figure 11. Individual collaboration among two members of a synchronous performing session, allows for viewing and editing each musician's part, chatting and exchanging resources as a synchronous collaborative activity. The score, similarly to the metronome is a synchronized shared object in the sense that the state of each score—retained in the DIAMOUSES collaboration server—is available to all the member of a synchronous session.

OPEN ISSUES AND FUTURE PERSPECTIVES

The majority of musicians become skeptic in the idea of network collaborative music performance, as in their opinion, musicians should be able to see, feel, touch and smell each other during a collaborative performance. Clearly, network music performance systems do not intend to substitute conventional live performance; on the contrary they aim to support musicians when real co-presence is not possible and to furthermore enable novel forms of music expression that are more appropriate for virtual environments as such. Moreover, musicians' claims convey that in order to enhance the feeling of co-presence in these systems, multimodal interaction methods must be incorporated.

It is being said that composers create music depending on the hall that their music is to be performed. So for example, the music composed for orchestral performance (e.g. fast note attacks)

Figure 11. Individual collaboration during a DIAMOUSES synchronous session

is dramatically different than the music composed for church (e.g. long notes) and of course very different than the music composed for small music groups such as string quartets. Furthermore the name 'chamber music' is intentional as it defines the type of music to be performed in small music chambers. In respect with the above, two possibilities appear: to either try to artificially simulate the physical space of a performance depending on the music performed, or to encourage the composition of music that will be appropriate for 'virtual performance rooms', i.e. for the network. Both approaches may be further enhanced by utilising multi-channel audio for sound immersion (Sawchuck, Chew, Zimmermann, Papadopoulos & Kyriakakis, 2003).

A significant aspect of music creation through virtual music performance communities is related to the fact that the Internet allows for merging the cultural traditions of different populations. Especially when it comes to art and music in particular, merging multicultural traditions may lead to surprisingly interesting results, especially for music traditions that are inherently improvisational. Examples of this multicultural merging may be the combination of Indian music with electronic music or the combination of Jazz with European folk and so on. Merging different cultures in music expression through the advancement of virtual music performance communities will have a considerable impact on the aesthetics of new music.

CONCLUSION

This chapter has attempted to investigate the collaboration practices that take place in different types of music communities. The main focus of the chapter is on virtual music performance communities which, although in preliminary stage, are increasingly becoming the focus of various research and development efforts. Due to the restricted availability of network infrastructures

able to support live distributed music performances, the social interaction taking place in these communities is not yet fully understood.

Clearly, different application scenarios for music performance raise different requirements on the supporting technological infrastructure. However, the requirements in such scenarios are complementary rather than contradictory. Therefore combining research achievements and practical experience from different types of virtual music communities will encourage unforeseeable practices, thus redefining the entire concept of music performance and music expression.

ACKNOWLEDGMENT

The DIAMOUSES project is being implemented in the context of the Regional Operational Programme of Crete and it is co-funded by the European Regional Development Fund (ERDF) and the Crete Region, coordinated by the General Secretariat for Research and Technology, of the Ministry of Development of Greece. The partners of the DIAMOUSES consortium are: Department of Music Technology and Acoustics, Technological Educational Institute (TEI) of Crete – Project Coordinator; Department of Applied Informatics and Multimedia, TEI of Crete; Department of Electronics, TEI of Crete; Department of Computer Engineers and Informatics, University of Patras; FORTHnet S.A.; AKMI, School of Vocational Training.

REFERENCES

Anderson, A., & Ellis, A. (2005), Desktop video-assisted music teaching and learning: New opportunities for design and delivery, Colloquium. *British Journal of Educational Technology*, *36*(5), Retrieved May 10, 2008, from http://www.blackwell-synergy.com/doi/abs/10.1111/j.1467-8535.2005.00496.x?journalCode=bjet

Chafe, C., Gurevich, M., Leslie, G., & Tyan, S. (2004). Effect of time delay on ensemble accuracy. In *Proceedings of the International Symposium on Musical Acoustics*, Nara, Japan.

Creative Commons Sampling Licenses (2008), "*The Sampling Licenses*", Retrieved May 19, 2008, from http://creativecommons.org/about/sampling

DigiDelivery Overview. (2008). Retrieved May 19, 2008, from http://www.digidesign.com/index.cfm?langid=100&navid=38&itemid=4782&action=news_details

Fober, D., Letz, S., Orlarey, Y., Askenfeld, A., Hansen, K., & Schoonderwaldt, E. (2004). IMUTUS - An interactive music tuition system. *Proceedings of the Sound and Music Computing conference (SMC04)*, Paris, France

Garnett, G. (2001). The aesthetics of interactive computer music. *Computer Music Journal, 25*(1), 21-33.

Koerselman, T., Larkin, O, & Ng, K., (2007), The MAV framework: Working with 3D motion data in Max MSP / Jitter. In *Proceedings of the 3rd International Conference on Automated Production of Cross Media Content for Multi-channel Distribution (AXMEDIS 2007)*. Barcelona, Spain

Latta, C. (1991). Notes from the NetJam Project. *Leonardo Music Journal, 1.*

Mühlhäuser M., Welzl M., Borchers J., & Gutkas R. (2001). GlobeMusic: The Internet scale of eMusic-making. In *Proceedings of the International Conference on Web Delivery of Music (Wedelmusic)*, Florence, Italy.

Oberholzer, F., & Strumpf, K. (2007). The effect of file sharing on record sales: An empirical analysis. *Journal of Political Economy, 115*(1).

Percival, G., Wang, Ye, & Tzanetakis, G. (2007), Effective use of multimedia for computer-assisted musical instrument tutoring. *ACM Workshop on Educational Multimedia and Multimedia Education (EMME-07)*, Augsburg, Germany.

Poblocki, K. (2005), The Napster network community. *First Monday, 10*(7), Retrieved May 10, 2008, from URL: http://www.firstmonday.org/issues/issue6_11/poblocki/

Renaud, A., Carôt, A., & Rebelo, P. (2007), Networked music performance: State of the art. In *Proceedings of the AES 30th International Conference*, Saariselkä, Finland

Sawchuk, A. A, Chew, E., Zimmermann, R., Papadopoulos, C., & Kyriakakis C. (2003). From remote media immersion to distributed immersive performance. *Proceedings of the ACM SIGMM 2003 Workshop on Experiential Telepresence*, Berkeley, California, USA

Schmeder, A. (2008). *Everything you ever wanted to know about open sound control* (Tech. Rep.). Berkeley, USA: Center for New Music and Audio Technologies, University of California.

Sellers, P. (2008). *MySpace cowboys*. retrieved May 19, 2008, from http://money.cnn.com/magazines/fortune/fortune_archive/2006/09/04/8384727/index.htm

Siwal A. (2008). *Facebook,Myspace Statistics.* retrieved May 19, 2008, from http://techradar1.wordpress.com/2008/01/11/facebookmyspace-statistics/

SoundWIRE Research Group at CCRMA, Stanford University (2008). Retrieved May 10, 2008, from http://ccrma.stanford.edu/groups/soundwire/

Stanford Center for Innovations in Learning: News: CyberSImps. (2003). Retrieved May 10, 2008, from http://scil.stanford.edu/news/CyberSImps.html

The Philadelphia Orchestra - Global Concert Series. (2008). Retrieved May 10, 2008, from http://www.philorch.org/internet2_3.html

Wöhrmann, R. (1999). Design and architecture of distributed sound processing and database systems for Web based computer music applications. *Computer Music Journal. 23*(3).

KEY TERMS

Asynchronous Collaboration Activity: A collaboration activity which does not require immediate response from collaborating parties.

Audible Data: Any form of digital data that encompasses or may be converted to meaningful sound or music. Apart from audio data the term includes alternative representations of sound and music such as MIDI or OSC data.

Collaborative Music Performance: Joint music performance by several peers / partners or performers.

Dislocated Music Performance: Music performance by geographically dispersed performers.

Network Music Performance (NMP): A dislocated music performance in which the communication among performers is accomplished through the use of computer networks and media tools.

Podcasts: Podcasts allow users to subscribe RSS Feeds of files containing audio or other media content. A podcasting client running in the background of a portable device periodically checks for updates and, if new content is available, downloads it automatically to the client device.

Synchronous Collaboration Activity: A collaboration activity which requires immediate response from collaborating parties.

Virtual Music Community: A group of people who share common interests, knowledge and expertise related to music, and use computer networks for communication, interaction and collaboration.

Virtual Music Performance Room: The virtual host for activities taking place during a network music performance.

Chapter XX
Sustainable E-Learning Communities

Chris Stary
University of Linz, Austria

ABSTRACT

Knowledge acquisition in E-Learning environments requires both, individualization of content, and social interaction based on relevant learning items. So far few E-Learning systems support an integrated didactic and social perspective on knowledge transfer. Intelligibility Catchers (ICs) are E-Learning components designed for establishing sustainable communities of E-Learning practice. They encapsulate didactic and communication-centered concepts for effective collaborative and reflective generation and exchange of knowledge. Due to their open nature, they can be created dynamically, for any domain and on different levels of granularity. By intertwining content and communication, context can be kept for learning and exploration, even bound to specific community members.

INTRODUCTION

As adaptation, experimentation, and innovation have been identified essential for sustainable organizational success, learning and knowledge creation have to be considered as primary forces of self and organizational development (cf. Bennet et al., 2003). Communities of Practice describe social settings where knowledge can be exchanged and generated effectively (cf. Laudon et al., 2005). In order to enable a sustainable E-Learning community the respective processes should be structured according to learning support (Dijkstra et al., 1997). In this chapter, the Scholion developments, a long-term project and learning support system are utilized as a case study, constructing a context-sensitive concept for this endeavor. Initiated about 12 years ago by students of the Johannes Kepler University in Linz, it aims at meeting learning requirements for today's dynamically changing organizations, and thus, knowledge demands.

The learning process itself is considered as a combination of content handling, instructional services, and self-management activities (cf. Schulmeister, 1996, Reigeluth, 1998). It links users to domain-specific information sources in collaboration spaces designed for positive knowledge transfer and knowledge generation. With the advent of E-Learning ontologies (Meder, 2000, Leidig, 2001) the didactical value of the conveyed content has moved to the center of interest in development. Today, the didactic value of content has to be considered as a decisive factor for empowering self-management in E-Learning. In this way, the context of subject items has become a challenge for learner-centered education. Active (re-)construction is seen particularly beneficial for learners as they can pursue their individual interests, while they are motivated to communicate their understanding to others. The situated and public nature of any construction activity has been identified as important for positive knowledge transfer (cf. Farmer et al., 2005).

In the following we report and reflect on a structural improvement to E-Learning platforms providing communication, collaboration, and content facilities, termed Intelligibility Catcher (IC). It tackles both, the content and the social aspects of transfer and learning, in a mutually tuned way. It can be shown that effective learning support in this way requires substantial conceptual and technical effort. Besides the didactic categorization of content elements and processing (according to their role in transfer), linking categorized elements to communication items directly is crucial for knowledge generation.

We review the Scholion developments towards a community platform and show how the addressed development and support challenges can be met. After providing insights into the features and situations of use we discuss the community aspect of the supported learning processes. We reflect how learners can benefit from a sustainable E-Learning community driven by dedicated transfer structures such as Intelligibility Catchers.

A PLATFORM COUPLING CONTENT AND SOCIAL INTERACTION

Computer technologies for learning have opened up new avenues for designing content, triggering active learner participation in transfer processes, and coupling communication to content (cf. Koschmann, 1996). To meet the requirements for computer-mediated context-sensitive and collaborative learning, it must be possible for learners to explore different categories of information in virtual environments and to communicate, so that meaningful learning of a domain can proceed in tandem with establishing communities of learning. Still, the ultimate goal is to create personally meaningful mental representations (cf. LaJoie, 1998, Stary, 2001).

The significance of being able to treat learning as a socially valid exploratory activity, rather than a linear, planned activity, has been recognized by coaches and developers step-by-step. One appreciation has been gained through looking at deeper issues than domain-specific structures of knowledge, web-design of user interfaces, or domain-specific methods. Such an endeavor addresses context from different perspectives:

- The didactic knowledge that drives the transfer of knowledge – developers have to look for a corresponding engineering process of content,
- Communication channels utilized for learning and transfer processes – developers have to look for links of communication entries to content items, and
- Information beyond the core of domain content, such as cultural issues like ethno-computing in computer science education – developers have to look for additional information to facilitate comprehensive understanding of a topic.

Our research so far has not only been targeting towards didactically effective content development, but also towards context-rich transfer and situation-sensitive learning (cf. scholion.ce.jku. at, www.mobilearn.at, www.schule.suedtirol. it/blikk). Our work is grounded on a corresponding frame of reference displayed in Figure 1. This conceptual frame reflects the required decomposition of learning material (termed information in the left upper corner of Figure 1) into so-called blocks. These blocks represent didactic information types, such as 'definition'. As they are also encoded into different media (text blocks, graphic elements, videos etc.) multiple (re)presentations of content (termed polymorph content in the figure) may exist. Hyperlinks between blocks and media are common in E-Learning (bottom left of the figure).

In addition, in Scholion (cf. Auinger et al., 2002; Stary, 2007) different levels of detail (LOD) for each block can be specified, e.g., providing a slide for a definition on the top level (LOD 1) based on

the full text of the definition on LOD 2 (representing a textbook). Annotations constitute individual views on content items by commenting, linking, or highlighting items block elements, or enriching content blocks (Fürlinger et al., 2004). Some of those annotations can be links to communication entries of the SCHOLION communication components (chat, forum, infoboard etc.). In this way communication elements are directly linked to content blocks and *vice versa* (middle bottom to right in the figure). Communication needs to be established among peers for learning, as well as between learners and coaches. The latter, in the role of quality managers, are responsible for improving content and settings based on learner input and feedback.

In Scholion the content (see Figure 2) is arranged according to the aforementioned didactic information types (see bottom of hierarchy in the figure). Currently, 15 generic types of this sort

Figure 1. The SCHOLION frame of reference

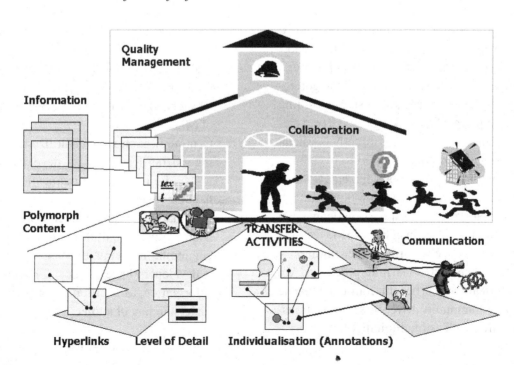

Figure 2. IMS-conform derivation of didactic content-element types

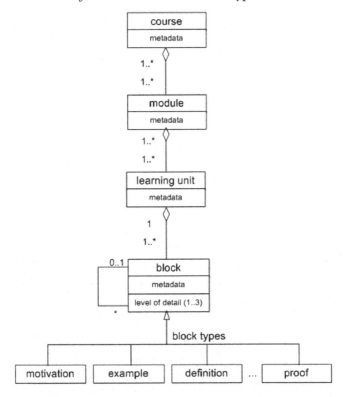

are available as part of an XML scheme (see also Table 2). They comprise definition, motivation, background, directive, example, self test, and other didactically relevant content structures. Some domain-specific block types have been added to support domain-specific applications, such as proof for mathematics. Each block type can be visualized in Scholion through a certain layout, e.g., colored background. Block types allow learners to scan the entire learning content for specific categories of information using a filter function. The workspace then shows only selected block types. In this way learners might follow their interests and habits, such as starting to learn with studying background information.

Figure 3 shows a sample content area at two different levels of granularity. The navigation area in form of a tree view on the left side of the screen reflects the didactic value of each block element accordingly. The shown didactic block types are 'definition', 'explanation', and 'theorem'. In the sample screen shots, the sense of moving is defined. Seeing as one of the modalities for interaction is explained, and guidance for developers is provided to display only relevant information for users.

The bar on top of the content area allows for annotating the information of a learning unit according to individual needs. The users might select particular content elements, such as 'examples' for problem-based learning, using the filter function. They also might switch between various levels of detail, using the LOD function besides the filter in the function bar. With respect to content manipulation, in addition to marking content elements users might link blocks to internal or Internet-based sources of information, as well as to entries of discussion forum or other Scholion communication elements. All annotation activities are stored in user-specific views that

Figure 3. Level of Detail 1 (presentation slides) and 2 (full text) in a Scholion application for HCI

might be shared and cascaded, using the view functionality located on the utmost left side in the function bar ('neu').

User-specific views are key features for collaboration, as they allow individuals, either learners or coaches, to document their mental map in terms of markers, links, comments, questions etc.. Members of view-empowered communities share a common pool of domain-specific content items (definitions, motivations, examples etc.) as well as individual views. The content elements serve as points of reference whereas the individual views are parts of active or passive collaboration. The latter can be kept private and pop up in group work indirectly, e.g., as an argument in an entry of the discussion forum. They also might be set public by users to be shared among community members, and to be enriched with additional items (annotations). Such scenarios of communication and collaboration define learning technologies as social technologies.

Consequently, knowledge generation is supposed in environments like Scholion to occur in a context-sensitive way. In particular, awareness about the learning process itself should be provided, in order to implement self-management. Within the context of sharing knowledge in collaborative processes, awareness can be considered as 'keeping people informed of certain objects' (Bentley et al., 1992). As Hawryszkiewycz (1997) pointed out, the process of maintaining awareness has to be grounded on a systematic and dynamic basis. It is awareness in terms of knowledge about the objects that leads actors to an understanding of various aspects of their collaborative processes they are part of. These aspects include

- The role that an actor plays within the collaboration process,
- The roles played by other collaborating actors,
- Various tasks performed by the collaborating actors in certain roles, and finally
- Knowledge artifacts that are used (e.g., shared, created, exchanged, etc.) by these actors.

Typical roles in E-Learning activities are 'coach' and 'student'. Before transfer the coaches' task is to provide didactic content elements. It reveals his/her mental model. Using the Scholion features for individualization and communication further information might either be generated in terms of

- Content, e.g., as attachment to a forum entry
- Links, e.g., coupling prepared examples with additional ones
- Views, e.g., marking relevant information of the provided content.

Communication plays a crucial role for knowledge generation. Besides the exchange of views content can be attached to asynchronous communication entries in a forum or the infoboard. Information might also be generated via synchronous communication, such as chatting. Due to the direct links between communication entries and content elements in Scholion, information generated through communication can be kept in its original setting - Scholion provides context for communication, collaboration and private learning phases.

Figure 4 shows a Scholion application for media- and bio informatics as prototyped in the MobiLearn project, enabling web access via PC and PDA (www.mobiLearn.at). Community building and context-sensitive E-Learning requires displaying content ('Kurse') semantically close to communication elements. In that application, two different media for communication are provided per default. The infoboard allows broadcasting of information relevant for all users, e.g., organizational details of a course. The discussion forum allows thematic discussion among peers and between coaches and students. Communication media might be dedicated to user groups, either assigned to courses or work tasks. In this way,

Figure 4. Entry screen *Figure 5. Discussions* *Figure 6. Sample Forum Entry*

learning communities are established. Figure 5 shows themes of interest that are grouped according to their relevance, e.g., media informatics. The users might switch between communication, learning, and administration, as the options of the bar located above the theme list shows. Figure 6 shows a sample content for discussing multimedia data compression. The user-interface logic for PDA and PC web access is identical, although compression techniques and screen splitting have to be used due to PDA space limits.

The features shown so far are essential for social interaction, and consequently for establishing E-Learning platforms as social technologies. However, learners need to be trained in applying those features according to their demands and interests. In addition, coaches need to develop skills to design the use of these features, i.e. to prepare transfer settings according to formal and informal education requirements. To facilitate this task and to setting up sustainable learning communities we have designed mediating structures. They are termed Intelligibility Catchers (ICs), as they should allow learners to 'catch' the idea of the subject and develop individual skills to its respect (Stary, 2007; Eichelberger et al., 2008). They should rather understand the prepared content and its use in problem solving situations than replicate prefabricated chunks of information. According to our design ICs reflect the social nature of learning. ICs do not only trigger the creation of views, but also trigger community development and active participation in collaboration. They will be discussed in the subsequent section.

MEDIATE STRUCTURES FOR COLLABORATIVE CAPACITY BUILDING

They overall goal in (e-)learning is to empower learners in active problem solving and knowledge generation. This process of capacity building requires a domain-specific content preparation for individualization and sharing, as well as community support features. The latter characterize E-Learning Communities of Practice (e-CoPs), as the push for informal social networking. They can be established within or across organizational (formal) boundaries. In general, CoP members have similar interests, work on similar items or accomplish similar tasks (Wenger et al., 2002). CoPs can be distinguished from formal structures, such as teams, project organization. Membership of individuals in CoPs is fluent. Persons often switch between various CoPs according to their interests and (temporary) profiles. Such a setting is typical for E-Learning. For instance, students form peer groups for certain tasks, in order to mutually benefit from different problem-solving strategies.

e-CoP members are not regulated by formal positions or particular locations. They have no direct responsibility for products or processes, they rather share perspectives, concerns or challenges for a certain period of time. Typical activities in e-CoPs are trainings for individuals or groups, conferences, thematic get-togethers, on-line news, and periodical exchange of experiences, techniques or ideas to solve problems or accomplish tasks. In E-Learning settings, coaches might train a group of students to catch up with the others in a course.

CoPs are also of crucial importance for E-Learning when established in educational institutions:

- They facilitate knowledge reuse. Individuals might refer to relevant and shared documents within the community.
- Members mentor individuals and start discussions and discourse.
- Members might enforce learning curves for newcomers, either through mentoring or referring to experts and contacts for particular themes. They might even facilitate the access to best practices and well-established methods, tools and procedures.

- The serve as breeding force for novel ideas, techniques, and decision making.

For positive transfer of knowledge and active learning support Intelligibility Catchers have been designed. As mediate structures they serve as media for bringing about learning results. They should do that by conveying the subject area, in terms of their content elements, requiring communication among the e-CoP members. When applied in formal educational settings, such as universities, they also form a contract between coaches and learners. As such they do not only facilitate learning, but also establish sustainable learning communities. The contract remains transparent together with the documented learning process and the results.

ICs have been implemented as assignments that are made available through the information or bulletin board in Scholion. After our first positive experiences in the European EISWeb project (cf.

Eichelberger et al., 2006) we concluded with the structure as shown in Table 1 (item 1-7). The table exemplifies the promotion of historical context to understand a specification language for software engineers. The example stems from a learning unit on object-oriented modeling with the UML (Unified Modeling Language).This IC has been used in a class for distributed systems development at the University of Linz. It has been prepared by the lecturer for the section dealing with foundations of software specification using UML. Following the steps given in the IC the learners should gain insights into the development of the language, and thus, understand the type of diagrams that exist for software specification. All students could access that IC, but did not have to complete it to pass the exam. The IC has been designed as intelligibility driver which effect could be measured in terms of in-depth knowledge in exams by the lecturer. As such, the UML-IC was a contract learners only enter when they like to develop a complete

Table 1. A sample Intelligibility Catcher

1 – Preface / Orientation	Modelling is a core activity in system and software development. So far the demand for modelling has been motivated. Now a specific modelling technique is introduced. The assignment helps exploring UML, a modelling language for system construction.
2 – Objectives	Understand UML 2.0 from a modelling perspective, including the UML rationale.
3 – Tasks	- Capture the development of UML 2.0 - Apply UML 2.0 for interactive distributed systems design - Discuss your results with peers in the course-specific discussion forum
3.a Documented Work	• Filter content for 'background information' • Develop view[1] ,UML 0.x/1.x' for each type of UML diagram • Search for historical background for each diagram, such as UML 1.0 • Supplement (annotate) each type of diagram with the information found • Annotate each diagram with a practical example in a separate view • Make views public • Describe your results in dedicated linked entries of the discussion forum • Compare and reflect results in topic-specific chats
3.b Intellectual Challenge	• (Re-)Construction of material • Develop individual position
4 – Conferences	Continuous feedback by peers and coaches
5 – References	http://www.omg.org
6 – Bulletins	Infoboard@Scholion.ce.jku.at
7 – Departmental Cuts	This assignment should take you no longer than 20 hours.

picture of UML by reflecting a historical perspective on the language and its development. Those students who committed themselves and worked on the IC formed an e-CoP. They shared views and used the communication forum for group reflection. The CoP rules were either triggered by the structure of setting views public and the structure of the discussion forum, or developed in face-to-face discussions.

For IC generation the coach has to define content for 7 items. Besides that he/she has to recognize the added value of view definition and the coupling content items to communication entries for learning support. Both should play a major role in IC design. The didactic content elements should serve as focus of interaction, as they allow not only supporting different types of learners, but also various styles of teaching in a virtual environment.

The *orientation* section addresses the stage of capacity building the IC should be used and what learners can expect when accomplishing the IC tasks. The *objectives* set the scope in terms of the topics that are addressed and the understanding that should result from exploring

and processing topic information. It reflects the didactic value of that learning unit. The *task* section comprises a documented and an intellectual work part. It encourages active information search and processing, communication, and personality development. The *conference* section sets the minimal rules for the community of practice that should evolve on that topic. The *reference* section provides links to material that helps to accomplish the tasks. The *bulletins* can be dynamically created and are available in the infoboard. Finally, the *departmental cuts* reveal the estimated individual effort to meet the objectives.

The structure combines organizational with subject-specific information arranged from a didactic perspective. For instance, the orientation section in the beginning informs coaches and learners when to use this IC addressing competencies, the content involved, and the rationale for exploring this content and co-constructing mental representations. Initially, the learners are encouraged to identify those blocks of the learning unit where historic context is already available, i.e. part of the prepared content. Then they are asked to complement particular content items,

Table 2. Didactic block types in Scholion

Didactic Categories of Content	Markings
Motivation	Underline
Definition	Definition
Explanation	Formula
Background information	Mathematical equation
Content	Proof
Theorem	Citation
Directive	Remark
Example	Source code
Case Study	Acronym
Training Unit	Reference
Test	
Interactive element	
Summary	

namely UML diagrams, having no information about their origin so far. After practical modeling, all results should be shared with peers, enabled by dedicated views and focused, since content-related discussion items. All results are validated by the coach through feedback, in order to ensure correct learner representations.

As already mentioned, points of reference for exploration and communication are the content types listed in the previous subsection. The table lists these most commonly used in the context of the sample IC. The categories developed so far range from traditional ones in different disciplines, such as explanation, to specific ones, such as T-account for accounting (cf. www.jku.at/BuKoLab). Markings (right row of Table 2) are used to denote important elements within block types. For instance, in case an explanation contains a term's definition, this part should be marked, in order to grasp the definition part at a glance. The block types can be arranged according to access or learning patterns. As such different didactic settings and learning styles can directly be represented and supported in their variety of occurrence.

In Figure 7 the motivation serves as entry point to a summary, followed by a definition or explanation. Tests might be taken immediately after that, or after handling a case study and/or an example. From a paradigmatic E-Learning perspective, the network reveals a cognitivist teaching and learning scheme (in contrast to constructivist and behaviorist ones): Before examples or case studies are addressed, explanations or definitions have to be accessed. Such an understanding of teaching and learning is often revealed when looking at text books used in traditional learning environments. In some cases, even linear progression of learning is assumed, represented by a network without any connector.

In self-managed or constructivist settings, learning would start with an OR- or XOR split, eventually preceded by a motivation. With respect to the example in Figure 7 such an approach would learners guide to follow either the case study/example/test path before going to defini-

Figure 7. Sample content structure and navigation paths

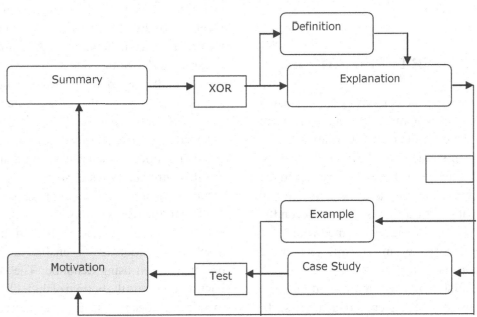

tions or explanations, depending on their learning style and situational preferences. The latter should guide knowledge acquisition and generation (cf. Lehrer, 1993, Euler, 2005).

For IC-design, besides guiding learners to use filtering of content to select specific content elements, the use of OR-connectors is highly recommended, since they allow learners to reach certain levels of competence in a variety of ways. It depends on the IC designer whether predefined learning paths as given through a network structure are directly incorporated into ICs. The more possibilities to achieve learning results are available the more likely parts of the network might become part of section 3. In any case, the generation and sharing of views or other collaboration elements have still to be added for coherent IC design.

In a completely self-managed learning environment learners might develop ICs themselves. Basically, ICs are mediate structures reflecting a certain perspective for a certain topic. Learners might initiate an e-CoP in this way, with the coach intervening on individual or collective demand. Following this scenario might require self-explaining domain ontologies, in order to enable the acquisition and positive transfer of correct knowledge.

MEETING USER EXPECTATIONS

The Scholion developments have been associated with continuous field work and user testing. With respect to the embodiment of ICs into Scholion two empirical studies have been performed. In the course of designing ICs we have checked the expectations of coaches and learners already working with E-Learning systems. Secondly, qualitative tests have been performed with users when preparing for exams. In this section we briefly report on both of them.

For the first study we tried to find out user expectations (before implementing the ICs). In contrast to traditional user and knowledge testing learners were asked independently from dealing with ICs how they would like to build capacities when using E-Learning systems. In addition, coaches were asked how capacity building could occur effectively in E-Learning environments from their perspective. We then were able to check in how far ICs could meet the elicited user expectations in the course of design, and later on, in the second study.

We have used the repertory grid technique for eliciting expectations (see also Stary, 2007). In contrast to highly structured acquisition techniques, such as questionnaires, it does not impose representational restrictions on elicitation, but rather let structures emerge according to the individual mental models of users. The technique provides a procedure for eliciting individual mental models with respect to a specific range of convenience. Repertory grids have been successfully applied in various software-development domains, most of all in expert system development, but also in requirements engineering, and instructional design.

In order to check whether ICs could meet user expectation in E-Learning we asked 4 coaches and 4 learners well experienced in E-Learning. As elements 4 different E-Learning scenarios were identified (A,B,C,I in Table 3 – 'I' encoding ideal transfer or learning situations). A sample grid of a learner is shown in Table 3.

The qualitative data are expressed pair wise through constructs and contrasts – note that the individual value systems of interviewees might not correspond to traditional thinking in pros or cons. The collected data can now be compared to the structure and types of scenarios of ICs. For instance, the top construct-contrast pair of Table 3 refers to the IC capability to provide transparent background – a visually marked block type 'background information' enables to meet this objective when using Scholion. The construct-contrast entries at the bottom of the table also refer to didactic block types, as they enable coaches to arrange content properly for user empowerment, such as sequencing theorem and proof in mathematics. Finally, the second entry reveals the need of social contact and situational context that can be promoted in ICs as shown in Table 1.

The elicited grids have been analyzed qualitatively. The content analysis for all grids allowed us the conclusion that ICs could be considered as valuable and effective means for learners. Most of the coaches and learner have identified those elements that were expected to build capacity in E-Learning environments. Typical statements supporting the design have been marked in *italics* in the table.

After implementation of the ICs these data have been confirmed in a second empirical study performed in 2007 in a course in Business Process Modeling. In this course we used a blended learning and transfer setting. An IC similar the one shown for UML in Table 1 has been prepared and made available to the learners via the Scholion infoboard, in order to practice modelling of business processes in an accurate and coherent way. Some of the students have used this IC for training purposes, and to prepare for the final course exam. 8 of them have been interviewed and tested with respect to their competence and understanding of process modelling. All of the showed not only a deep understanding, but also appreciated the features for setting up and running the virtual learning community. They reported the direct link between didactic content elements and communication entries in the discussion forum motivated them to contribute to information sharing and discourse.

Overall, the results match those traditionally achieved in E-Learning studies (cf. Elliot et al., 2005). On one hand, self-management requires adaptation facilities of content and proper interaction mechanism, on the other hand, context-sensitive communication facilitates collaboration.

CONCLUSION

Sustainable E-Learning communities require dedicated mediate structures. As such, Intelligibility Catchers (ICs) provide not only the capability to improve self-managed capacity building in E-Learning environments, but also the set-up and establishment of learning communities. However, they require a bundle of adaptation activities of existing E-Learning systems. First, didactic block types, such as background information, have to be considered as inherent part of the content. Secondly, filtering block types has to be considered crucial to support individual learner types, since they allow selecting content of didactic value for individualized or group studying. Finally, individual and public views allow the creation and

Table 3. Sample entries of a learner grid (italics denote positive transfer characteristics)

Construct					Rated Element				Contrast		
1 (= high)		2 (= medium)		3 (= low)	A	B	C	I	4 (= low) 5 (= medium) 6 (= high)		
Transparent representation and context-sensitive transfer of background information					4	3	1	1	Jump into details too early, it is before the entire context is transparent		
Coach and peers can be contacted anytime, and they know what I am currently working on					2	5	2	1	Transfer does not recognize individual learner requirements – no sensitivity for learning situation		
Sequence of content presentation does not fit my way of approaching content – I receive a patchwork of information that I cannot reassemble myself					6	2	2	6	*Each content part should neatly fit to the others like in a puzzle - it enables individual recapturing, it utilizes structure as a means to convey meaning*		
Structure of content allows step-by-step acquisition					1	2	5	1	A mess!		

sharing of annotations and have to be considered as integral part of sustainable cooperation and collaboration.

REFERENCES

Auinger, A., & Stary, Ch. (2002). Embedding self-management and generic learning support into courseware structures. In *Proceedings of the HICSS-35*, IEEE, 465-474.

Bennet A., & Bennet D. (2003). The partnership between organizational learning and knowledge management. In C. W. Holsapple (Ed.), *Handbook on knowledge management, 1*, (pp. 439-455). New York: Springer.

Bentley, R., Bentley J. A., Hughes D., Randall T., Rodden P., Sawyer, D., Shapiro, D., & Sommerville, I. (2002). Ethnographically-informed systems design for air control In *Proceedings of the Conference on Computer-Supported Cooperative Work*, (pp. 123-129).

Dijkstra, S., Seel, N., Schott, F., Tennyson, R. D. (Eds.) (1997). *Instructional design: International perspectives,* Vol. 2. Mahaw, NJ: Lawrence Erlbaum.

Eichelberger, H., & Laner, Ch. (2006). *Internet(t)e Schulentwicklung auf SCHOLION*, Pädagogisches Institut Bozen, ISBN 9783 0001 8836-7.

Eichelberger, H., Kohlberg, H.-D., Laner, Ch., Stary, Ch., & Stary, E.(2008). *Reformpädagogik goes E-Learning*, Oldenbourg, München.

Elliot, A. J., & Dweck , C. S. (eds.) (2005). *Handbook of competence and motivation*. Guilford, NY.

Euler, D. (2005). *Forschendes Lernen. Universität und Persönlichkeitsentwicklung*, Campus, Franfurt/Main.

Farmer, R. A., & Hughes, B. (2005). A situated learning perspective on Learning Object Design. In *Proc. ICALT'05*, IEEE.

Fürlinger, St., Auinger, A., & Stary, Ch. (2004). Interactive annotations in Web-based learning environments. In *Proceedings of the ICALT'04*, IEEE, (pp. 360-364).

Gücker, R. (2007). *Wie E-Learning entsteht. Untersuchung zum Wissen und Können von Medienautoren*, kopaed, München.

Hawryszkiewycz, I. (1997). *Designing the networked enterprise*. Boston: Artech House Inc.

Koschmann, T. (ed.) (1996). *CSCL: Theory and practice of an emerging paradigm*. Mahaw, NJ: Lawrence Erlbaum.

LaJoie, S P. (ed.) (1998). *Computers as cognitive tools: The next generation*. Mahaw, NJ: Lawrence Erlbaum.

Laudon, K.-C., & Laudon, J. P. (2005). *Essentials of management information systems: Managing the digital firm*, 6th edition. Upper Saddle River, NJ: Pearson.

Lehrer, R. (1993). Authors of knowledge: Patterns of hypermedia design. In S.P. LaJoie, S.J. Derry, (Eds.), *Computers as cognitive tools*. Mahaw, NJ: Lawrence Erlbaum.

Leidig, T. (2001). L3-Towards an open learning environment. *ACM J. Educ. Res. in Computing, 1*(1), Art. 5.

LSDA (2004). *Mobile Learning and m-learning*. http://www.lsda.org.uk/research/ResearchCentres/RFSTechEnhanceLearn.asp?section=8

Meder, N. (2002). Didaktische Ontologien, In *Globalisierung und Wissensorganisation: Neue Aspekte für Wissen, Wissenschaft und Informationssysteme*, Vol. 6: Fortschritte in der Wissensorganisation, eds Ohly, G.R.H.P.; Siegel, A., Ergon Verlag, Würzburg, pp. 401-406.

Reigeluth, C. M. (ed.) (1998). *Instructional design theories and models: The current state-of-the-art*, 2nd edition. Mahaw, NJ: Lawrence Erlbaum.

Schulmeister, R. (1996). *Grundlagen hypermedialer Lernsysteme. Theorie – Didaktik – Design.* Bonn: Addison Wesley.

Stary, Ch. (2001). Exploring the concept of virtuality: Technological approaches and implications from tele-education. In A. Riegler, F.-M. Peschl, K. Edlinger, G., Fleck, & W. Feigl (Eds.), *Virtual reality - Cognitive foundations, technological issues & philosophical implications* (pp. 113-128). Peter Lang, Frankfurt/Main..

Stary, Ch. (2007). Intelligibility Catchers for Self-Managed Knowledge Transfer. *Proceedings ICALT07*, IEEE.

Wenger, E., McDermott, R., & Snyder, W. (2002). *Cultivating Communities of Practice – a Guide to Managing Knowledge*. Harvard Business School Press.

KEY TERMS

Annotation: Marking, enriching, complementing or linking of content elements to other content elements or communications entries in E-Learning applications.

Community of Practice: Group of people with common interest and dynamically changing roles and active memberships.

E-Learning Environment: A socio-technical systems enabling knowledge acquisition and generation for learners guided by coaches

Intelligbility Catcher: Mediate structure facilitating the process of understanding as integral part of E-Learning environments

Individualization: Way of personalization of content and facilities of an E-Learning environment

View: Taking a particular perspective, expressed through individual annotations in E-Learning applications.

ENDNOTE

[1]   As already mentioned, in Scholion a view is a virtual overhead slide put on top of content items containing all annotations. It can be made public to share annotations with other users, or remain private for further learning.

Chapter XXI
Cross–Organization Virtual CoPs in E–Tourism:
Assembling Information–Based Products

Nikolas Vidakis
*Technological Education Institution of Crete,
Greece*

Anargyros Plemenos
*Technological Education Institution of Crete,
Greece*

Dimitrios Kotsalis
*Technological Education Institution of
Crete, Greece*

Emmanouela Robogiannaki
*Technological Education Institution of Crete,
Greece*

Giannis Milolidakis
*Technological Education Institution of Crete,
Greece*

Kyriakos Paterakis
*Technological Education Institution of Crete,
Greece*

George Vellis
*Technological Education Institution of Crete,
Greece*

Demosthenes Akoumianakis
*Technological Education Institution of Crete,
Greece*

ABSTRACT

This chapter describes recent work and experience in setting up and supporting cross-organization virtual communities of practice to facilitate new product development. The authors' reference domain is tourism and the community's joint enterprise is assembly of vacation packages. The chapter contrasts existing practices involved in building vacation packages against the computer-mediated practices flourishing in an electronic village of local interest on regional tourism. The electronic village is considered as an aggregation of thematic virtual communities (i.e., neighborhoods) each with own rules, policies and primitive offerings covering tourism services such as accommodation, transportation, cultural resources, etc. Electronic squads are formed as cross-neighborhood communities of practice to engage in computer-mediated assembly of vacation packages. The chapter presents key tasks involved in managing both electronic squads and the workflows through which the shared resources are combined and transformed into new collective offerings.

INTRODUCTION

Recently, a wide range of technologies have given rise to new business models, such as e-shop, e-mall, e-auction, e-procurement, e-marketplace, e-communities, e-brokers and other commerce-support e-intermediaries (Timmers, 1998), which increasingly catalyze information-based industries. In the majority of the cases, the distinction between these new virtualities is drawn around functional rather than technological characteristics. Moreover, although frequently non-homogeneous and seemingly different, these efforts tackle a variety of issues such as global marketing, 24/7 operations, quick responses, competitive pricing, multimedia and hypermedia information, interactive search and navigation process, personalized and customized services, innovative products and services, push and pull marketing mechanisms, thus establishing a new context for electronic commerce and practice.

Inevitably, the travel and tourism industries have also faced new challenges that pushed them to adopt more innovative Internet-based strategies and technologies (Yu, 2002; Stockdale & Borovica, 2006; Connell & Reynolds, 1999; Hjalager, 2002; Palmer & McCole, 2000; Werthner & Ricci, 2004).

A virtuality, which has recently received substantial attention, is the electronic village of local interest which represents a tight coupling between a virtual space and a corresponding physical space. In the literature, there are various examples of electronic villages / cities (e.g., Carroll et al., 2001) acting as catalysts to local community social and economic life.

In the context of on-going collaborative research and development, we are developing technology and tools for building local electronic villages as unified collaborative spaces for managing electronic services of local interest / scale towards new product development. This definition makes a sharp distinction between an electronic village of local interest and the notion of the 'global electronic village'. The distinction amounts to the fact that the former concept emphasizes a tight coupling between virtual and local physical activities, while it affords opportunities to develop alternative forms of productive social relations between members. Some of the design issues confronting the construction of electronic villages are common to other types of virtual communities of practice and include community visualization, awareness, social interaction, collaboration and knowledge persistency. However, as electronic villages need to function as catalysts towards added-value products and services, there are additional issues to be addressed, pertaining to a variety of organizational aspects.

To this end, eKoNEΣ is a collaborative R&D project, which seeks to extend the conventional connotation of an electronic village so as to provide an operational model of a virtual organization fostering strong social links between members of inter-organizational partnerships and an explicit focus on performing tasks to yield added-value products and services. The project's pilot application domain is in the area of tourism where it has set up and operates eKoNEΣ-Tourism, a regional electronic village on local tourism. In its basic form eKoNEΣ seeks to facilitate community problem solving by fostering tight collaboration between multi-sector community groups, frequently referred to as coalitions or collaboratives. Such coalitions may be permanent or temporal depending on the set targets. For example, in the tourism sector coalitions may be formed to facilitate transportation, local accommodation and entertainment for a group of people interested to visit archaeological sites in a region for a specified period of time.

The distinctive characteristics of such services are that they have a 'local' character (i.e. they are regionally bound and can be assembled and offered by locals), they typically have short life cycles (i.e., a few days), are targeted to specific customer groups (i.e., visitors of a specific destination within a particular age group), while they are orthogonal to other services (i.e., tourist destination packages) offered by established mainstream tourism actors. The rationale for creating such services is often based on purely circumstantial factors depending of foreseen or unforeseen events taking place in the wider social environment. Consequently, assembling and packaging such services (on-demand) yields added-value for all parties concerned including the end user. A necessary precondition for effective and efficient compilation of such services is that they need to be dynamically created through the collaboration between members who appreciate the value of virtual networking, participation and collaboration in virtual community settings. In turn, such services are owned by the coalition for as long as the service is offered. Nevertheless, participation in the coalition is discretionary.

The project is currently in its deployment phase where basic concepts have been formed and an operational system is available (http://www. e-kones.teiher.gr/). In this chapter, we present consolidated outcomes of the initial operation of eKoNEΣ-Tourism, its underlying organizational model and the corresponding architectural underpinnings of the virtual organization. To facilitate illustration of concepts we also present one of the working scenarios.

The next section reviews current and emerging trends in the tourism sector and positions our work in the landscape of technical developments taking place and characterizing e-Tourism in general. Then, we describe the research questions relevant to this work, the methodology employed to address them and key findings. Subsequently, eKoNEΣ-Tourism is elaborated focusing on both the community management functions and the vacation package assembly practices. In the final section, we draw some conclusions and discuss pending issues and on-going research and development activities.

TECHNOLOGY AND COMMUNITY TRENDS IN TOURISM

Tourism is a networked industry containing a set of interrelated businesses, involving travel companies, accommodation facilities, catering enterprises, tour operators, travel agents, providers of recreation and leisure facilities, to name a few. It represents a highly fragmented reality with a large number of actors—with different culture and background—operating according to different business models. Accordingly, there are a variety of information systems, keeping their services and data in different formats, thus creating an interoperability gap across actors and services. In the past, there have been various initiatives aiming to enhance cooperation by providing solutions based on standards and common interchange formats (i.e., the United Nations rules for Electronic Data Interchange for Administration, Commerce and Transport – Travel Tourism & Leisure, the Hospitality Industry Technology Integration Standards – HITIS, omnis-online, International Air Transport Association – IATA, Travel Technology Initiative – TTI), and more recently Semantic Web technologies (Dell'Erba et al., 2005; Antoniou et al., 2005). These trends progressively transform tourism from a leading application in B2C e-commerce into an information business. Since customers (i.e. tourists) in the vast majority of cases are not able to test the product in advance, information is the only means which can close this gap. In turn, the customer base of the tourism sector necessitates new business models and improved quality of services. Specifically, recent evidence indicates an increase of demand for customized services, which implies that customers prefer to compile their own packages rather than purchase prepackaged offers.

The above have stimulated a variety of developments leading to new technologies as well as novel e-business models. We will briefly review representative efforts related to the present work in an attempt to sketch the trends and challenges in this industry. Specifically, we will concentrate on emerging technologies such as dynamic packaging, tourism ontologies and service-oriented architectures, as well as the promises offered by business-sponsored community models.

Dynamic Packaging Systems

Dynamic packaging technology helps online travel customers to build and book vacation packages. The primary function of a dynamic packaging application is to allow consumers or travel agents to bundle trip components. The range of products and services to be bundled varies widely from guider tour, entertainment, event/festival, shopping, activity, accommodation, transportation, food and beverage, etc. In their basic form, dynamic packaging solutions allow a customer to put together elements of vacation so as to assemble the mostly preferred package, given the customer's requirements and preferences. Traditionally, packages of this type are put together by tour operators. New technology offers a more engaging and interactive medium for assembling a customizable reservation, handled seamlessly as one transaction and requiring only one payment from the consumer, hiding the pricing details of individual components. On the other hand, dynamic packages differ from traditional packages in that the pricing is always based on current availability of subsuming services.

Despite its promise, dynamic packaging at present offers a solution which tends to be more of a response to the interoperability challenge, rather than an economically feasible business model. Specifically as currently practiced, dynamic packaging amounts to interfacing across various systems, allowing interoperability of decentralized, autonomous, and heterogeneous tourism information systems. Although success stories have been reported in the relevant literature, the whole concept seems to fall short from

the intended target of catalyzing customized package development.

Ontologies and SOAs

Ontologies and service-oriented architectures (SOA) are critical to dynamic packaging engines (Fodor & Werthner, 2004-5), although they represent alternative philosophies. Ontologies are important because they provide a shared and common understanding of tourism data and services, allowing interoperability and integration of information systems. In recent years a variety of efforts have been devoted to attaining some sort of harmonization using tourism ontologies. The Harmonise (http://www.harmonise.org) is an EU Tourism Harmonisation Network promoting an ontology-based mediation and harmonization tool for establishing bridges between existing and emerging online marketplaces. The approach followed allows participating tourism organizations to keep their proprietary data format and use ontology mediation while exchanging information (Missikoff et al., 2003). In the Satine project, a secure Semantic-based interoperability framework was developed for exploiting Web service platforms in conjunction with P2P networks in the tourist industry (Dogac et al., 2004). Semantic Web methodologies and tools for the intra-European sustainable tourism were also developed in the Hi-Touch project (Hi-Touch Working Group, 2003). Common characteristic across these projects is the availability of tools to store and structure knowledge on customers' expectations and tourism products.

Ontology-based approaches are often contrasted with service-oriented architectures (SOA). The argument is that whereas the ontology enforces a common global view upon content and its interoperability, the SOA approach does not enforce a global view, but rather it makes use of Web services and languages (i.e., WSDL, SOAP, etc) to provide an environment for dynamic discovery and use of loosely independent component services. Services in SOA represent coarsely-grained expertise from an application (business) domain. In many cases, the two technologies are used synergistically (Tsai et al., 2007) with ontology engineering complementing service discovery and management in a SOA. For instance, considering composition from a software architecture standpoint, a common ontology enables the identification of the common characteristics of services that fall into a particular category. These characteristics affect the architecture and design of the SOA-based solution from the individual service level up to the entire composite application. Categorization supports composability by clarifying the roles of the different components, thus helping reason about component interrelationships. Categorization also assists with the discoverability of services (for example, searching for existing services by using a service repository), which can further promote reuse.

Community Models

Another important trend, catalyzing several industries including tourism and travel, is the business-sponsored on-line community model. Recently, several tourism players have revisited customer relationship management by exploiting business-sponsored online community models. By developing and maintaining online communities, firms can foster relationships between customers, reinforce brand recognition, use customer feedback to develop products and services more effectively, accumulate customer information, improve pre and post transaction services and test new products (McWilliam, 2000; Walden, 2000). Innovative tourism actors have exploited online tourism communities quite successfully. There are several such travel communities now evident on the Web (e.g. Travelocity.com, Lonely Planet and Fodors.com) and few studies examining their underlying model and philosophy. Specifically, Hagel (1999) used the online travel community developed by Travelocity to illustrate his argu-

ments for the adoption of the virtual community as a business model. Stockdale and Borovica (2006) studied the adoption of this model by Lonely Planet to establish one of the most successful online travel communities.

RESEARCH FOCUS, METHODOLOGY AND FINDINGS

The rationale for the present work is to be found in the cumulative effect the above trends have on the tourism industry. Specifically, it is argued that the emerging business environment in tourism is increasingly catalyzed by new products and services of non-material (intangible) nature, while knowledge is central to gaining competitive advantage. In this context, new e-business models have been exploited primarily as tools for improved marketing and customer-relationship management. The more challenging issues related to novel product development, cross-industry collaborations and the involvement of creative end users are seldom addressed.

Context

The eKoNEΣ project set out to investigate new methods for strengthening the ties between members of a local industry and its intended customer base, by appropriating the promises of virtual networking and communities of practice towards assembling novel vacation packages. We have chosen to investigate a particular type of vacation packages which are not widely supported at present. These are packages tightly linked to a geographic region and independent of the pre-packaged solutions available to customers through modern destination management systems. Typically, these packages have short durations (i.e., a few days) and high added value resulting from their locality. They are made up from primitive components such as transportation to and from a designated site, food & beverage, entrance fees, local accommodation (if needed), etc., all blended into one transaction. Such primitive services should be tailorable so as to reflect special requirements and optional offerings. Packages of this sort may be considered either as peripheral supplements of a pre-packaged vacation or as factors stimulating the ultimate choice of destination and /or pre-packaged solution. They are created by responding to informal customer requests, circumstantial incidents or foreseen events taking place within a designated geographic region. These characteristics necessitate that such vacation packages must be innovative 'collective' offerings, quickly compiled (if possible by reusing assets) and adaptable so as to suit different needs and requirements of the customer base. The qualification 'collective' is used to convey that no single business actor can provide the vacation package effectively and efficiently by account of own resources. It can then be argued that creating such packages is a knowledge management task of a dedicated community of practice.

Research Questions and Methods

Having outlined the general issue relevant to eKoNEΣ, we will attempt to briefly elaborate on some key research questions. These can be broadly grouped into three constituents, namely:

- Practice related questions such as what are the elements of current practices involved in the compilation of vacation packages; what activities are involved and how they are socially instituted into practices
- Technological questions such as how are practices manifested (i.e., on-line versus off-line practices) and what type of technologies are used for on-line practices
- Collaboration context-related questions aiming to unfold sense of community albeit the medium used or the community support system, drives for participation and behaviors emerging from the community setting

It is perhaps worth mentioning that our understanding of practice in general is in line with recent proposals framing it in relation to processes and tools used as well as social interaction (Turner et al., 2006). Consequently, practice is conceived of as subsuming activities on objects (see Chapter XV) in this volume where the notion is further elaborated and explained).

To address the above questions, a variety of research methods were used to collect data and envision new capabilities for improved practices. Specifically, a non-experimental descriptive survey was conducted utilizing interviews, on-site visits and scenarios to provide the insights required. As our intention was to unfold hidden or implicit elements of community practice, interviews and on-site visits were tailored so as to feed envisioning of new (improved) practices. In turn, these were contextualized using scenarios and rapid prototyping. The scenarios included detailed description of the actions taken for a task to be performed by all actors involved in building vacation packages. Prototypes, cognitive walkthroughs and interviewing of tour operators and travel agencies provided further insights and feedback. In the next section, we elaborate on the findings of the survey focusing on the vacation package development workflows.

Findings

Our survey was directed to tour operators, travel agencies and was complemented by documented materials i.e., "Tour Operators Initiative" (GRI, 2002). The findings can be analyzed into practices employed and technologies used for the development of a vacation package in a conventional way of making business. Table 1 summarizes the current practices encountered. Specifically, the survey identified 7 conventional practices used for the development of vacation packages. Some of them are enacted individually (i.e., they are performed by one actor alone) such as "Define Package Abstract Details" or Define Package

Services" and others are cooperative (i.e., they are performed by a group of collaborators) such as "Discuss Service Details" or "Package Service Finalization". Depending on the nature of the vacation package the enactment of a designated practice may vary in terms of effort and scope. For instance, "Package Dissemination / Promotion" implicates different set of activities for overseas packages requiring travel documents than inland traveling where the promotion is performed exclusively by the tour operator. In this sense, the community (actors) involved or implicated may vary accordingly.

Table 2 provides a summary of the survey's outcomes in terms of technologies used for the development of a vacation package. As shown, there are practices which are manifested as offline local activities performed using traditional tools and artifacts such as notebook, drawing board etc. As for community support systems and media, our survey revealed a blend of conventional means such as telephone, fax, e-mail, etc., as well as more advanced tools and collaboration technologies such as portals, bulletin boards, Web pages, legacy software such as reservation systems (CRS) and costumer relationship management (CRM) systems.

Framing practices around such tools reveals that the vast majority of them are 'local' practices bound to an organizational setting with some of them driving subsequent on-line social practices. For example, when the "Package Retail" practice is performed the travel agency uses the reservation system to perform a 'local' practice (i.e. to book a package) followed by computer-mediated feedback and/or feed through using telephone or email. These findings indicate that practices are institutions of interrelated (local or social) activities with some being manifested electronically.

Summarizing our analysis of the current situation leads to the following conclusions. First of all, vacation packages undergo distinct stages from conception to population and marketing, with a fair

amount of iteration. In each stage there are specific issues to be addressed with clear milestones and outcomes. Ownership is solely with the creator of the package, not the contributing partners. Thus the contributor's liability amounts to executing part of the plan as delegated to him/her by the owner. Communities exist to facilitate customer-relationship management and less frequently inter-organizational alliances. In the later case, community formation is largely opportunistic, based on personal contacts and making use of traditional community support media. Community membership does raise implications on local practices, but only marginal. Interaction between community members, if existent, is on a need-driven basis and purely informative (i.e., one member informs another about an event). Entering or opting out from a community is dissertational and seldom follows specific rules. Consequently, sense of community is weak and it can, by no means, be considered a catalyst for new or differentiated vacation packages.

Requirements for New Practices

In an effort to gain insight to potential improvements, we have also presented the experts with a tentative scenario of a cross-organization community of practice specializing on vacation package assembly and analyzed their response and feedback. It turns out that the envisioned scenario establishes a new practice for building vacation packages of a particular type and scope. This new fully computer-mediated institution of practices results from transforming / expanding existing practices and establishing new elements as needed. For instance, the practice "Find appropriate partners" is expanded and subsumes the on-line practices "Invite appropriate partners" and "Formation of community of practice". In the existing status quo there are previous agreements between the tour operators and service suppliers and thus there is no need for invitations. Instead,

Table 1. Conventional practices

Title	Description	Personal / Social
Define Package Abstract Details	Sketch the original package skeleton and define basic details such as package duration, destination, package type, etc.	Personal Practice *(Tour Operator)*
Define Package Services	Analyze the abstract package details and come up with the necessary services for the development of the package. Such services are: Transport Services Air, Rail, Coach, Taxi, Ferry, Train, etc. Accommodation Services Hotels, Self-catering, Pension/Bed & Breakfast, Holiday house/villa/chalet, Campsites, etc. Leisure Services natural and cultural excursions, Guiding Services, Catering Services, Retailers, etc.	Personal Practice *(Tour Operator)*
Find Appropriate Service Supplier	Following the definition of the services possible suppliers are located (from business lists) and a possible supplier list is created. Suppliers are categorized per service. One supplier may offer more that one service (e.g. catering and accommodation). Typical Supplier Categories include: Transport Suppliers Airlines, Taxi providers, Coach companies, etc. Accommodation Suppliers Hotels, Self-catering, Pension/Bed & Breakfast, Holiday house/villa/chalet, Campsites. etc Leisure Suppliers Sport and adventure tourism service providers, Guide providers, etc.	Personal Practice *(Tour Operator)*
Discuss Service Details	Discuss service details to be provided. Agree on service details according to package necessities and peculiarities	Social Practice *(Tour Operator & Service Supplier)*
Package Service Finalization	Refinement of service issues, final agreement with supplier and contract signature	Social Practice *(Tour Operator & Service Supplier)*
Package Dissemination / Promotion	Create Brochures, Promotion Material in general and Travel Documents	Personal or Social Practice *(Tour Operator, Marketing Professionals & State Bureaus)*
Package Retail	Package is ready for retail through appropriate channels (usually a travel agency cooperating with the tour operator)	Social Practice *(Travel Agency & Customers)*

tour operators typically choose from a list according to the needs of the package. Another example is "Discuss Activity Specifics" which subsumes "Issue detection", "Issue resolution proposal" and "Solution Selection". At present, when tour operators face a problem they resolve it by formal or informal communication (i.e., telephone, fax or email). However, in a computer-mediated environment an issue is raised and addressed through dedicated tools (i.e., asynchronous forums, bulletin boards, issue management systems, etc) and in a totally different manner.

Synthesizing a new practice out of the pool of empirical evidence entails decisions on two primary constituents, namely the package development workflows and community management. In terms of package development workflows four distinct stages have been identified representing intertwining activities in the development of a vacation package. These are initiation, elaboration, deployment and tailoring, each hosting separate institutions of practice. Specifically, the definition of the package, its duration and the required activities are designated in the initiation phase.

Table 2. Conventional practices vs. technology used

Practice \ Technology	Define Abstract Package Details	Define Package Activities	Find appropriate partners	Discuss Activity details	Activity Finalization	Package Dissemination / Promotion	Package Retail
Offline Practice Artifacts							
Drawing board, Note book, etc.	✓	✓			✓		
Communication Media & Artifacts							
E-mail			✓	✓	✓	✓	✓
Telephone			✓	✓	✓	✓	✓
Fax			✓	✓	✓	✓	✓
News Papers						✓	
Leaflets, Brochures						✓	
Computer-mediated Practices & Legacy Software							
Agency Web						✓	
Bulletin Boards						✓	
Reservation Systems							✓
CRMs	✓					✓	✓

Package elaboration entails commitment of resources on behalf of the partners for the activities each can support. This may involve discussion and reflection upon tentative proposals as well as negotiation of details of one or more activities. The deployment stage gathers all contributions and packages them into a concrete offering which can be disseminated. Finally the tailoring stage is concentrated on the package retail allowing prospective customers to request changes and modifications so as to suit own requirements and preferences.

The second constituent relates to the community management. For our purposes, the community of practice is conceived of as a mission-specific electronic squad. The mission is the development of the vacation package so as to meet designated constraints. The electronic squad is the cross-organization community of practice involved in the vacation package development workflows. In this context, three distinct roles are identified, namely the squad moderator, the squad member and the customer. Table 3 contrasts these roles against the traditional setup for building vacation packages. As shown a typical squad established in the traditional practice environment comprises the tour operator, the travel agent, the service provider and the end-customer. In contrast, an electronic squad is made up from one moderator, several members representing the inter-organizational alliance and the customer (or villager).

In terms of squad lifecycles, our survey informally confirmed existing sociological accounts rooted in dynamic group stabilization theories (Tuckman, 1965) indicating four basic lifecycle stages, namely forming, storming, norming and performing. As described in the next section, these four stages were used to track and classify social interaction taking place between members of an electronic squad.

Table 4 summarizes the scope of the computer-mediated practice environment for assembling vacation packages and defines the boundaries of the envisioned scenario. The side by side presentation of the practices serves to illustrate how conventional activities are encapsulated into institutions of on-line practice. As shown, a squad is formed once the abstract package is defined. Squad re-formation continues through the initiation workflow and up to the end of the elaboration workflow to allow candidates to opt out from a squad either due to lack of resources or other reasons. At this point the squad is stabilized and not likely to change until the end of the package lifecycle. The storming stage starts when initial activities are defined and the squad has taken its principal form. Storming is about reaching consensus on the specific mission and subsuming activities. The stage ends once all relevant issues have been addressed. Devising a common agenda with respect to the issues raised is the objective of the norming stage which is in partial overlap with the package elaboration workflow lasting until the end of the deployment workflow. Finally, the performing stage is in full temporal overlap with the package tailoring workflow.

eKoNEΣ Framework

This section describes constituents of the computer mediated practice environment which facilitates vacation package assembly in the context of the eKoNEΣ project. It is worth noticing that eKoNEΣ is not aiming to establish yet another business-sponsored virtual community. Instead, it concentrates on building an environment for managing distributed collective practices in an information-based industry such as tourism. To this end, the project exploits the state of the art in Web-based technologies and tools and the promise of 'social' experience factories (for details see Chapter VI in this volume) to support integrated management of families of packages of local interest.

A package family is considered as a codified abstract representation which is progressively transformed to a concrete offering through social interaction / mediation between prospective customers and a virtual organization (i.e., the eKoNEΣ electronic village on regional tourism). Communities of practice represent electronic squads with one moderator responsible for guiding, mentoring and reflecting upon the squad's collaborative work efforts. A squad's mission is to elaborate a new information-based product within the scope of a product line specification.

Community Constituents

Figure 1 provides a logical view of the constituents of an eKoNEΣ electronic village, following the online community framework proposed in (de Souza & Preece, 2004). It follows that an eKoNEΣ electronic village is an aggregation of virtual communities each representing a thematic neighborhood. Neighborhoods support specific goals, such as maintaining a neighborhood directory, a catalogue of pool of primitive services, depending

Table 3. Squad member mapping

Traditional squads	Electronic squads
Tour Operator	Administrator / Moderator
Travel Agency	Administrator / Moderator
Service Supplier	Business Partner
Customer	End-Customer

Table 4. Practices vs. package lifecycle and squad lifecycle

Package Development Stages	Practices				Squad Lifecycle Stages
	Conventional		Computer Mediated		
	Title	Qualification (Personal / Social)	Title	Qualification (Personal / Social)	
Initiation	Define Package Abstract Details	Personal *(Tour Operator)*	Choose Package Family	Social *(Moderator)*	Forming
			Define Package Abstract Details		
	Define Package Activities	Personal *(Tour Operator)*	Instantiate Package Template		
			Define service neighborhoods		
Elaboration	Find appropriate partners	Personal *(Tour Operator)*	Invite partners according to neighborhoods	Social *(Moderator)*	
			Squad Formation	Social *(All squad members)*	
	Discuss Activity specifics	Social *(Tour Operator & Service Supplier)*	Issue Detection	Social *(Moderator)*	Storming
			Issue Solution proposals	Social *(All squad members)*	
			Solution Selection	Social *(All squad members)*	
	Activity Finalisation	Social *(Tour Operator & Service Supplier)*	Consolidate solved issues into norms & rules	Social *(All squad members)*	Norming
			Compilation package protocol agreement	Social *(All squad members)*	
			Activity Finalization	Social *(All squad members)*	
Deployment	Package Dissemination / Promotion	Personal or Social *(Tour Operator, Marketing Professionals & State Bureaus)*	Choose Package Presentation Template	Social *(All squad members)*	Performing
			Assemble Package Dissemination Data	Social *(All squad members)*	
			Disseminate / Promote Package	Social *(All squad members)*	
Tailoring / Personalization	Package Retail	Social *(Travel Agency & Customers)*	Respond to tailoring requests	Social *(All squad members)*	
			Support execution of Package	Social *(All squad members)*	

Figure 1. Constituents of the eKoNEΣ local village

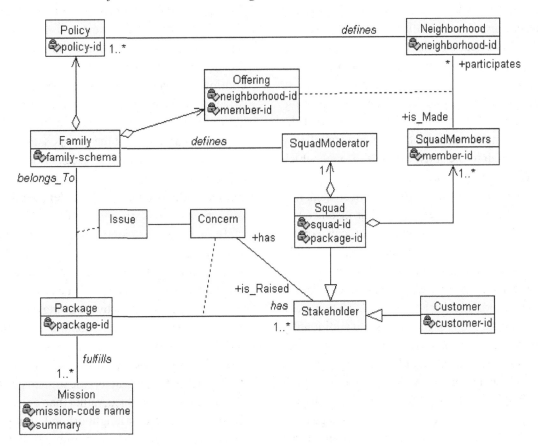

on the needs of its members or the expectations of the wider market / economic environment. Neighborhood-specific goals are pursued by registered members undertaking distinct roles and providing contributions governed by policies and rules of engagement. For instance, there are neighborhoods which do not allow participation of candidates already registered in another neighborhood. In general, such policies are embedded into processes covering registration and access, acceptance of new members, rules of acceptable behavior, security, privacy, freedom of speech/ act and moderation. Examples of such rules and corresponding practices will be described in subsequent sections, providing insight to the design of the community software platform.

eKoNEΣ supports primary and secondary roles. Primary community roles include the vil-

lager (a registered user who has access to specific eKoNEΣ neighborhood services but does influence their private contents) and the partner (service providers registered in a neighborhood). Villagers have access to information published in the neighborhood virtual spaces and may contribute to the public forums by posting requests for new products / services or by depositing experiences with a particular service. The secondary or 'implied' role is that of a 'squad'. This is a composite role comprising one moderator and several partners (i.e., neighbors) registered in the village's neighborhoods. Squads are virtual groups operating from a mission-driven perspective. Their mission focuses on a defined (sub) problem (i.e., assembly of a vacation package) and either succeeds or fails. For example, an eKoNEΣ squad may be formed to facilitate the creation of a vacation package involving designated neighborhood services (i.e., transportation, local residence, feeding and entertainment) intended for people interested to visit a historical site (i.e., a city) for a specified period of time. eKoNEΣ squads follow distinct lifecycle stages representing typical stages in group stabilization such as forming, storming, norming and performing. These stages and the interactions allowed in each of them are explicitly embedded into the software tools through which squads attain their missions.

For each community role, there are designated tasks which can be performed. For instance villagers have access to their account, can explore available information published through the neighborhoods and take part in asynchronous discussions (forums) operating either at the level of the village or individual neighborhoods. The partner's role assumes the villager's tasks and additionally it allows declaration of deposited resources and access to the dedicated tools allowing squads to accomplish their mission. The moderator's role is assumed by a user competent in a particular area / thematic domain such as vacation packages. We will show later that the moderator is in charge of several critical tasks carried out by squad members towards the assembly of a collaborative artifact. The other participants of a squad are partners offering designated services required to complete the squad's mission. Thus, if such a mission is the compilation of a three-day package including transportation, local residence, feeding and entertainment then squad members are all partners registered under these neighborhoods. Of course, initial squad formation may vary as the virtual group proceeds to accomplish its task. At any time, tasks performed by squad members are distinct and of a private character. They are embedded into software tools which are the only means for participating in the social life of a squad. These tools are downloadable components made available to members completing successfully their registration to neighborhoods.

Rules of engagement declare responsibilities assumed by the various roles. Some of them are explicitly stated and presented during registration, while others are assumed in the design of the dedicated software tools. Specifically, becoming a villager involves explicit acceptance of rules detailing access rights and content liability. On the other hand, becoming a partner requires guarantee that the user possesses and is able to deliver primitive services of one of more designated neighborhoods. In general, eKoNEΣ supports rules of engagement under the following general categories summarized in Table 5.

In such a setting, community practices evolve around the assembly of information-based, mission-specific, collaborative artifacts. In the tourism sector such artifacts are vacation packages assembled on demand or by assessing circumstantial factors (i.e., an international event, cultural activity, etc). A new package represents the shared responsibility of the squad which has assembled it. The distinctive characteristic of such packages is that they are assembled, rather than constructed from scratch, from neighborhood component services (i.e,. transport, accommodation, food & beverage, entertainment) in factory-type set-up. This implies dedicated tools and models representing software assembly lines. Moreover, they constitute added-value services both for the end users and the coalition (squad) members since none of them could offer the new package by themselves, cost effectively. Consequently, services of this type are the prime measurable outcome of a conscious effort towards appropriating the benefits of virtual networking.

To assemble added-value services virtually, through integrating and customizing generic components, and negotiating their details, eKoNEΣ proposes a kind of domain specific 'software factory' (Aaen et al., 1997) namely the social experience factory (SEF) described in Chapter VI. The SEF integrates dedicated tools (i.e., domain-specific design languages, authoring tools, product-line specifications, etc) in a collaborative

Table 5. Rules of engagement

Rule category	Villager	Partner	Squads
Registration and access	✓	✓	✓
Acceptance of new members		✓	✓
Rules of acceptable behavior	✓	✓	✓
Security		✓	✓
Privacy	✓	✓	✓
Freedom of speech/act		✓	✓
Moderation			✓

platform which is downloadable upon successful registration to a neighborhood and geared towards coordinating and performing tasks, rather than simply exchanging information.

Vacation Package Workflows and Assembly Practices

To illustrate the concepts and to provide insight into the technical features of eKoNEΣ, we will briefly describe a representative scenario. Let us assume that Bob has just purchased a package for a two-week vacation in a popular resort in Greece. As he is interested in the region of Peloponnesus and especially in history, culture and archaeology, he would like to spend a few days visiting archaeological sites. Looking around for possible solutions he comes across the eKoNEΣ-Tourism portal. By searching and exploring the available offerings (see Figure 2) Bob realizes that there is nothing close to his request. Nevertheless, the system allows Bob to register with the system and specify a request for a new vacation package which would satisfy his requirement. Indeed, Bob creates an account with eKoNEΣ and subsequently registers his request for a four day cultural tour around the Peloponnisos. In a few seconds, the system returns back with a message confirming the registration of the request and an indication of an approximate date in which a possible vacation package is to be compiled and made available.

Once such a request is registered, eKoNEΣ-Tourism triggers several parallel activities to create an eKoNEΣ resource to fulfill the demand. It is useful to consider these activities as asynchronous / synchronous knowledge management tasks assigned to designated workflows.

Asynchronous Tasks

Package Initiation Workflow

In the package initiation phase the moderator selects an appropriate package family (i.e., XML template) from the community experience data store and encodes the high-level details of the new package:

- **Start Date:** 3 / 9 / 2008, End Date: 6 / 9 / 2008
- **Day 1:** Visit Achaia
- **Day 2:** Visit Olympia and the Archaeological Museum
- **Day 3:** Visit Arcadia
- **Day 4:** Visit Messinia
- Requested Services: Transportation, Accommodation, Food, Entertainment

This results in the automatic compilation of an instance of the designated package family (see Figure 3) and the creation of a virtual workroom (see Figure 4) in which this new package is to

Figure 2. eKoNEΣ search engine

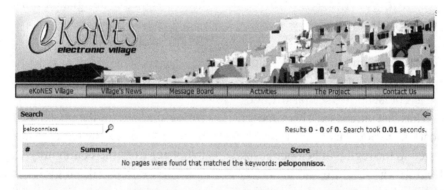

Figure 3. Abstract package initiation dialogue   *Figure 4. Package initial parameters*

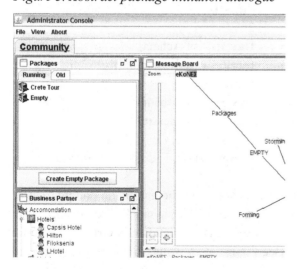   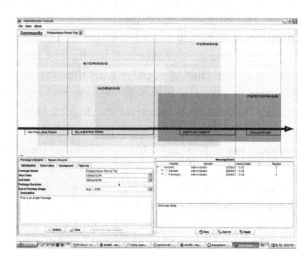

be further articulated. Every package family includes mandatory and optional fields. Mandatory fields, such as title, start date, duration and brief description define the vacation package as an instance of the designated package family, while optional fields are populated in the course of assembling the package. As shown in Figure 4, the package's work room offers a variety of tools for manipulating the package as well as a dedicated message board where social interactions between the corresponding squad take place. Finally, it should be noted that the initiation stage does not entail any involvement on behalf of the registered members. Rather, it may be considered as a 'local' practice enacted by the moderator and resulting in a consolidated statement of a mission to be undertaken by a squad (i.e., a community of practice).

Package Elaboration Workflow

In the elaboration phase, the objective is to populate the package by defining specific activities and elaborating a tentative proposal to be negotiated by a corresponding squad. Figure 5 provides an instance of an interactive package elaboration scenario. As shown for each day of the package, the administrator assigns the activities to take place. All activities in a designated day are represented as selectable objects differentiated by color depending on their type. Once a proposal is compiled, the moderator publishes the package as an internal private virtual asset. Registered business partners offering services in the packages designated activities are notified and invited to commit resources to this new package. Business partners obtain access to the package through their own software suite which is downloaded upon successful registration to at least one eKoNEΣ-Tourism neighborhood. The electronic registration system, which is omitted from this discussion, is a separate community support component built on top of the basic LifeRay setup allowing prospective actors to register

their resources as shared virtual assets, articulate their virtual presence through eKoNEΣ, access neighborhood private resources, contribute to the neighborhoods' contents and obtain access to the suite of tools which will allow them to contribute as members of prospective squads.

Figure 6 depicts how business partners obtain access and contribute to a new package. The upper part of the user interface visualizes the package in development. It is worth noticing the slightly different view of the package which this time is presented as a sequence of activities in a timeline. Moreover, partners have variable access to the package's resources according to their registered capabilities. Thus, a partner in the accommodation neighborhood can view the entire package but s/he can only manipulate those activities for which s/he is registered. This role-based access mechanism is supported by the software in a manner transparent to the user.

The lower part of the user interface in Figure 6 depicts the squad's collaborative message board which is a separate application making persistent

Figure 5. Package activities definition

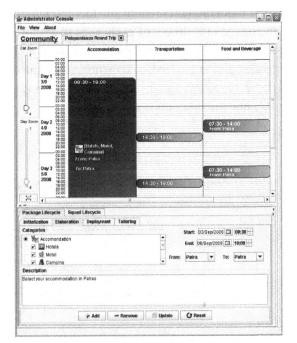

Figure 6. Business partners' view of collective resources

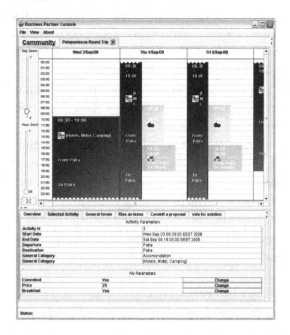

The moderator's view of the message board is different (see Figure 9), as its prime goal is to depict in a structured manner how the squad members contribute towards the accomplishment of the mission. In this view, the message board lists the content of the asynchronous forum (lower part in Figure 9) and renders it in a graphical manner (upper part in Figure 9) depicting contributions per squad lifecycle stage. This makes it possible for the moderator to assess posts made during the forming, storming, norming and performing stages of the designated squad. This graphical view of the posts is fully synchronized with its flat counterpart depicted in the lower dialogue of Figure 9.

Package Deployment Workflow

In the deployment phase the vacation package is finalized in terms of presentation details and supporting content, thus becoming a concrete offering with clear illustration of package options, alternatives and offers per activity. A key decision is the presentation template to be used which determines the type of content to be included in the published package. There are templates requiring marginal input of textual information and others which are media-specific requiring visual artifacts, video, sound, etc. A typical template is depicted in Figure 10. As shown in this example, the package supplementary information includes an informative title, short description, representative photo, title and brief outline for each day.

all social interactions and facilitating the partner's accumulation of situational and mission-specific knowledge. Such knowledge will ultimately result in the partner's commitment or withdrawal of interest from the package (by a certain date set by the moderator). Through this tool, members can engage in a variety of exchanges to explore package details, pose questions, rise issues, and express opinion and feedback. Figure 7 and Figure 8 depict representative instances of this message board and the tasks users can initiate.

Figure 7. Business partners' view of message board (general forum)

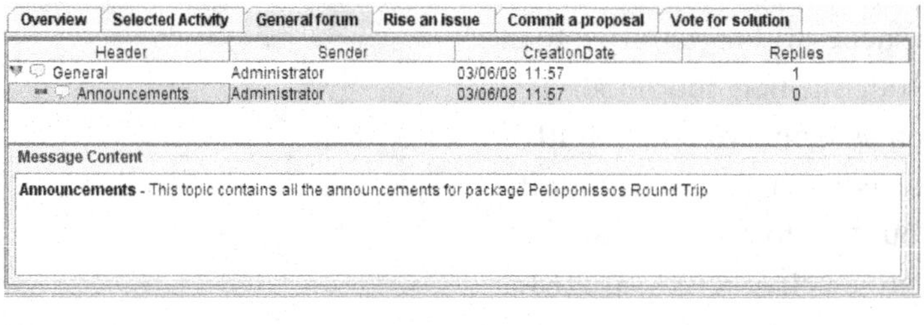

Overview	Selected Activity	General forum	Rise an issue	Commit a proposal	Vote for solution
Header		Sender		CreationDate	Replies
General		Administrator		03/06/08 11:57	1
Announcements		Administrator		03/06/08 11:57	0

Message Content
Announcements - This topic contains all the announcements for package Peloponissos Round Trip

Figure 8. Business partners' view of message board (rise an issue)

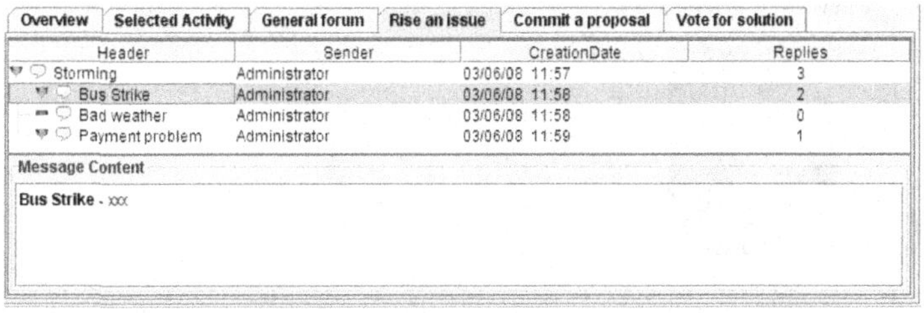

Overview	Selected Activity	General forum	Rise an issue	Commit a proposal	Vote for solution

Header	Sender	CreationDate	Replies
Storming	Administrator	03/06/08 11:57	3
Bus Strike	Administrator	03/06/08 11:58	2
Bad weather	Administrator	03/06/08 11:58	0
Payment problem	Administrator	03/06/08 11:59	1

Message Content

Bus Strike - xxx

Figure 9. Moderators' view of message board

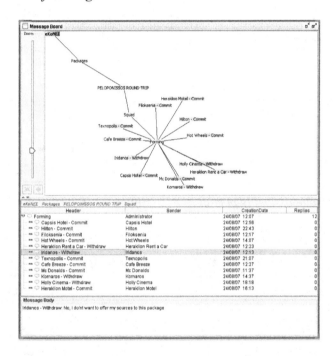

As terms and conditions are optional, there have been none assigned to the package.

If an existing template is deemed as insufficient, the squad may decide to prepare a new one. Moreover, there may be more than one template layouts assigned to a package so as to facilitate package multi-platform presentation (e.g., desktop using Java or HTML, PDA or a cellular phone). Once the details of the package are agreed and finalized, it is published as a new resource (see Figure 11) in a portlet context through the eKoNEΣ

portal (see Figure 12), while all registered villagers having expressed an interest in the package are notified through the eKoNEΣ multi-channel notification service. The distinctive characteristic of the vacation package assembly portlet depicted in Figure 11 is that it extracts from the database all package-related data and renders it in a device-specific markup language. The example in Figure 12 depicts such a rendering in HTML in a portlet context.

Figure 10. Package deployment

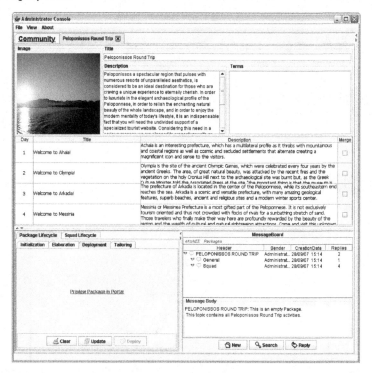

Figure 11. Vacation package assembly portlet

Figure 12. Package rendering

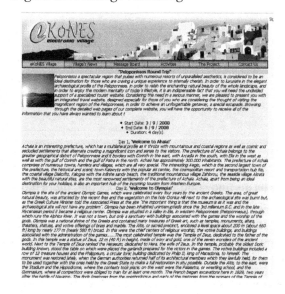

Package Tailoring and Personalizing Workflow

As soon as the package is deployed, prospective customers may request further details, elaboration of certain parts of the package or decide to make a reservation (see Figure 13). In this stage eKoNEΣ acts either as an information service, presenting options to the customer and processing further requests s/he may have or as a B2C mediator

Figure 13. Package tailoring

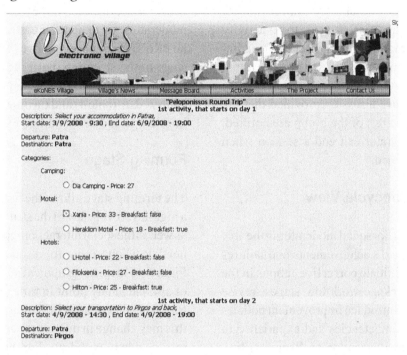

undertaking transaction-oriented services (e.g., booking, payment clearance, etc). Specifically, once the package is published end users can register their interest in the package. Since the package is fully populated, end users can access it through a variety of devices with clear indication of the tailoring that the user can undertake. The user may request further modifications of the package by submitting requests through the message board and asking the eKoNEΣ moderator and the package squad to consider specific issues. This process may be iterated until a personalized package is created to suit specific user needs and preferences.

Synchronous Sessions

There may be details of the package which require resolution by all committed members in the context of synchronous collaborative sessions (virtual meetings). This is supported by a domain-specific groupware toolkit. A synchronous deliberation is initiated by the squad moderator, either as part of the package elaboration phase or as a result of customer requests posted during the package's tailoring phase. Initiation of a synchronous session entails a schedule and the definition of the agenda of collaboration. The agenda specifies the relevant part of the package (i.e., the neighborhoods) and the phase of the package. Thus, a synchronous session may be scheduled so as to address 'accommodation' and 'transportation' activities or indeed the entire package in a designated stage such as elaboration (see Figure 14).

Upon the session's initiation the designated part of the package is assembled from the database and rendered using the templates of the elaboration phase. An object replication mechanism is used to facilitate synchronized rendering of the content across different templates (i.e., the moderators and the business partners') as shown in Figure 15 and Figure 16 respectively. In terms of control, a floor manager undertakes access rights management by maintaining a queue of recent requests. In a synchronous session, members have access to their own resources which they can manipulate by requesting/suggesting changes to an activity through direct manipulation, inserting annotations, making comments, etc. All these are transparent to the registered partners. Participant may also decide to leave a session provided that the moderator and the rest of the group are notified. Finally, the moderator can end a session when consensus is reached.

The Squad Lifecycle View

It is very important for squad moderators to be able to review the squad's achievements and failures and accordingly initiate corrective actions in the course of the package workflow stages, revise marketing plans, introduce improvement policies and build new competencies and experience in the form of targeted vacation package families. All these are knowledge-intensive tasks requiring dedicated support and tools for moderators to engage in knowledge management. The current version of eKoNEΣ integrates several tools for

Figure 14. Collaboration agenda definition

managing knowledge across different squad lifecycle stages. In effect, these tools aim to facilitate moderators in articulating social dynamics of an eKoNEΣ squad as it moves from the forming stage to the storming, norming and performing (i.e., contributing to the package development as analyzed in Table 4) and turning them into useful knowledge and new codified experiences.

Forming Stage

The forming stage allows the moderator to obtain a high-level overview of the structure of the squad as well as the social interactions justifying the partners' decision to commit resources. For instance Figure 16 depicts graphically the composition of a squad at any point in time (either prior to or following the package initiation phase). However, this may change in due course as certain partners may decide to withdraw. For the moderator, it is useful to know why this has happened and what implications it may have on the package. This implies a two-stage squad formation. The first stage is automatically executed by the system by classifying as squad members all the business partners that belong to the neighborhoods involved. The second stage includes only the committed members – those who have reviewed the tentative package and its demands, expressed opinion and decided to commit resources. A squad is stabilized only after the second stage in the squad formation. Figure 16 illustrates the graphical depiction of a stable squad as seen by the moderator during the forming stage. Colour is used to depict search results by neighborhood or type of squad member.

Storming Stage

The storming stage is more demanding as it requires management of the squad's social interactions as members attempt to make sense of the requirements of the package being developed by requesting clarification, expressing opinion

Figure 15. Moderator's (upper) and business partners' (lower) view of the shared object in a synchro-nous session

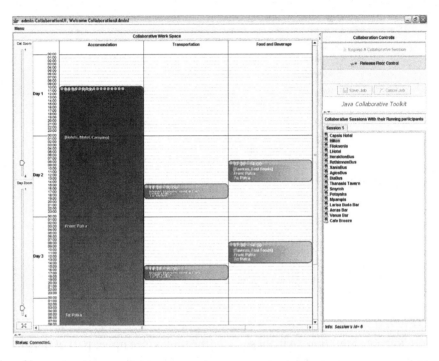

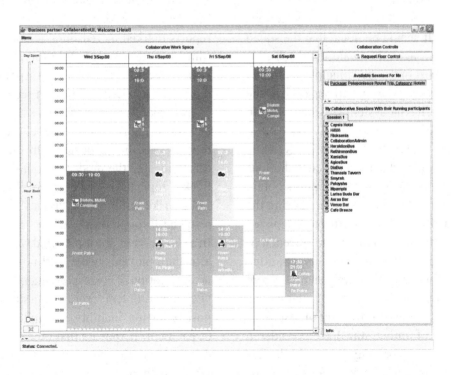

Figure 16. Moderator's view of the forming stage of an eKoNEΣ squad

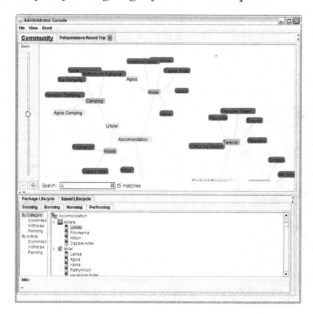

and raising issues for consideration. All these are persistent exchanges enacted through the squad's message board in the client applications (see Figure 6). It should be noted that the squad members are not actually aware that such contributions are part of the storming phase. In fact the squad lifecycle stages are transparent to the squad members. It is the system's responsibility to classify the contributions and the moderator's task to make sense of such data and accordingly define issues to be addressed and solicit contributions towards resolving the issues. Moderators obtain detailed insight to the state of affairs during the storming phase through a dedicated tool depicted in Figure 17. This tool visualizes the current topics and issues raised and the proposals submitted for consideration in a temporal fashion. From the system's point of view, all social interactions taking place after the commitment of resources (i.e., end of the forming stage) are considered as contributions to storming. Figure 17 depicts graphically the results of such an asynchronous discussion as viewed and articulated by the moderator. As shown, the moderator can see all

the topics (see upper part of the graph titled "topics") identified by squad members in the message board and assess their popularity (i.e., number of reports marked as red line), temporal sequence (time runs from top to bottom) and corresponding issues. Decoding the information presented to the moderator in Figure 17 we can see that the topic "Bus Strike" has started before the other topics and has a high degree of popularity as several reports have being posted. On the grounds of this evidence, the moderator qualifies the "Bus Strike" topic as an issue (see oval artifact titled "Bus strike issue" at the "issues" section) to be resolved through proposals by squad members. In a similar vein, the topic "Bad weather" started after the topic "Bus strike" with no popularity (i.e., no declaration of corresponding issue). The topic "Payment problem" represents a squad member's post reporting inability to handle certain type of payment. It appears that other partners share this problem, thus the topic's relative popularity which justifies its qualification as an issue (see oval artifact titled "Payment issue" at the "issues" section). It is also useful to notice that issues are

Figure 17. Moderator's view of the storming stage

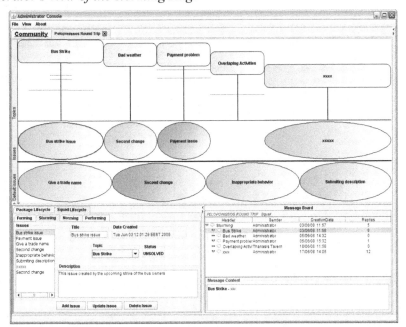

color coded to reflect their solution state. Thus green color (see "Payment issue") means that there is a solution, while yellow color (see "Bus strike issue") means that there is still ongoing discussion about the solution. Apart from the topics raised by squad members, moderators are also allowed to raise issues as needed (see lower left hand side dialog in Figure 17). These issues are depicted at the "Default Issues" section of the graph. Color code follows the same pattern as with issues raised by squad members.

Norming Stage

In this stage the squad reaches agreement on how the mission is to be executed by consolidating all issues raised and codifying them into norms and rules covering global quality attributes or constraints of the package (i.e., discount policies per neighborhood, temporal constraints for neighborhood activities). Collectively, these norms constitute the agreed protocol for compiling the package, thus binding conditions for all

squad members engaged in the assembly of the specific package. To reach such agreements, the moderator needs overviews of collective social behavior. Figure 18 depicts graphically the ongoing asynchronous discussion concerning the raised issues. This discussion takes the form of voting upon solutions proposed by the moderator. Proposals are managed by the moderator, trough the norming tab interface (see lower left part of Figure 18). The tool gives moderator the ability to add a new proposal, remove an existing proposal and set a proposal as the chosen solution to the raised issue according to the voting results. Voting results are depicted graphically (see upper part of the tool) to the moderator and are color coded, green means support, red means opposed and grey means indifferent to the proposal. Graphical presentation can take the form of tree, a pie chart or a bar chart. Moderator can alter the graphical presentation with use of the chart artifacts at the lower left corner of the graph.

Squad members can express their opinion on the issues raised by voting positively, negatively

Figure 18. Moderator's view of the norming stage

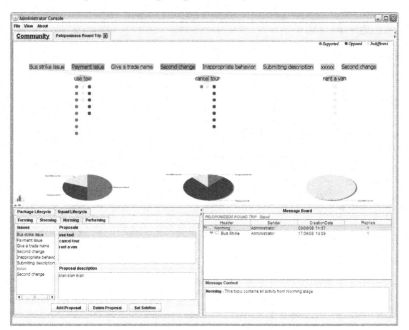

or indifferently to a given proposal. Voting is performed through the "Voting for solution" tab (see Figure 19) of the business partner client toolkit. Solution proposals, as created by the moderator, are presented in a list (see middle part of the tool) and squad members vote using the appropriate "vote selection" control. Squad members are also presented with information on how other members have voted (see right middle part of the tool) both in textual and graphical form. Finally, it is important to mention that the result achieved in this stage or the squad members behavior is package-specific and does not bind the member's actions in future packages. This allows, amongst other things, cross-package analysis and may be useful for understanding the behavior of members across different missions.

Performing Stage

The performing stage is mainly concerned with the squad members' undertaking of local practices which will enable them to support the activities assigned to them by the package. This entails making local arrangements and reserving the resources demanded by the package as well as informing the squad on progress made. Specifically, the performing stage in a squad's lifecycle is in full temporal overlap with the tailoring workflow in the vacation package development. For instance, reserving a room for a customer who has chosen a specific accommodation option is a local practice carried out by the squad member in a manner transparent to the rest of the squad. On the other hand, feeding back to the squad details on progress made regarding this activity is a social practice useful to the entire squad.

SUMMARY, CONCLUSIONS AND OPEN ISSUES

The work presented in this chapter represents an effort in the direction of facilitating new virtual practices in cross-organization alliances. The new practice entails assembly of vacation packages

Figure 19. Business partner voting

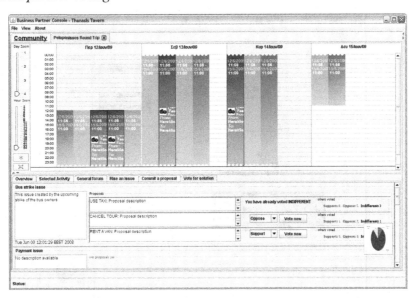

using a dedicated practice-oriented toolkit. The toolkit constitutes the shared asset through which registered community members engage in the joint enterprise of assembling vacation packages. Initial evaluation of this new practice was planned and executed in the context of the eKoNES project using standard formative techniques such as prototype walkthroughs, laboratory testing and analysis of break downs in the execution of hypothetical scenarios. Further analysis of operational details was obtained through virtual ethnographic studies with the researchers acting as moderators of electronic squads. The results today constitute an evolving experience base providing useful insight to the actual practice of vacation package assembly and how the computer-mediated environment introduced changes in the habits, routine work and culture of the community members. Despite the fact that the results of these evaluations have been very positive it is strongly believed that the actual value is to be found from observing operating squads over large periods of time. This will give sufficient data to answer critical questions about eKoNES relating to the conditions for establishing

and sustaining community ties, understanding the knowledge management that takes place, the way such communities are cultivated as well as behavioral patterns which emerge as a result of the members' social interactions and / or the customers' purchasing behavior and its impact on individual and community levels.

In addition to on-going evaluations, a complementary line of development is targeted to providing interactive mechanisms for obtaining analytic insight to squad collective memories and thus understanding factors which determine both the squad's level of stabilization and the corresponding outcomes per lifecycle stage. The idea is to establish measurable quality metrics by assessing the social interactions taking place through the squad's message board. Figure 20 provides an illustrative example of exploration-based access to a squad's archive indicating the type of analysis supported at present. As shown, the tool allows squad-level knowledge management at various levels. The query interface (left-hand side component) allows users to specify queries by manipulating graphical components.

Figure 20. The CommonsBoard graphical user interface

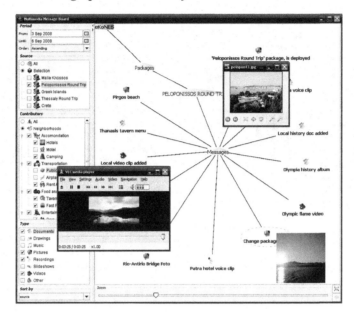

In turn, the query results are mapped to a customized interactive display (right hand side of the display), which can be used to either reach specific data or refine the original query by direct manipulation of the nodes. In this manner, it is possible to extract the rationale behind a vacation package (by analyzing the contributions of the corresponding squad), the collective resources of the package (i.e., contributions of a particular type such as documents, videos, images, made by members), etc. It is also possible to extract useful information regarding the behavior of representatives of a particular neighborhood in a designated package, or all packages within a specified period. This can be done by selecting a package, one or more neighborhoods of interest and accordingly specifying the type and range of data to be displayed.

REFERENCES

Aaen, I., Bøtcher, P., & Mathiassen, L. (1997). Software factories. *In Proceedings of the Twentieth Information Systems Research Seminar* in Scandinavia, Oslo.

Antoniou, G., Skylogiannis, T., Bikakis, A., & Bassiliades, N. (2005). A Semantic brokering system for the tourism domain. *Information Technology & Tourism, 7*, 183–200.

Cardoso, J., & Lange, C. (2007). A framework for assessing strategies and technologies for dynamic packaging applications in e-tourism. *Information Technology & Tourism, 9*, 27–44.

Carroll J., Rosson M-B., Isenhour, P., Ganoe, C., Dunlap, D., Fogarty, J., Schafer, W., & Van Metre, C. (2001). Designing our town: MOOsburg. *International Journal of Human-Computer Studies, 54*, 725-751.

Connell, J. & Reynolds, P. (1999). The implications of technological Ddevelopments on tourist information centres. *Tourism Management, 20*(4), 501-509.

Davidow, W. H., & Malone, M. S. (1992). *The virtual corporation: Structuring and revitalizing the corporation for the 21ˢᵗ century*. New York: Harper Collins.

de Souza, C., & Preece, J. (2004). A framework for analyzing and understanding on-line communities. *Interacting with Computers, 16*, 579-610.

Dell'Erba, M., Fodor, O., Hopken, W., & Werthner, H. (2005). Exploiting Semantic Web technologies for harmonizing e-markets. *Information Technology & Tourism, 7*, 201–219.

Dogac, A., Kabak, Y., Laleci, G., Sinir, S., Yildiz, A., & Kirbas, S. (2004). Semantically enriched Web services for the travel industry. *ACM Sigmod Record, 33*(3), 21-27.

Dustdar S., & Gall, H. (2003). Pervasive software services for dynamic virtual organizations. In *Processes and foundations for virtual organizations* (PRO-VE' 03), Kluwer Academic Publishers, ISBN 1-4020-7638-x: 281-208.

Fodor, O., & Werthner, H. (2004-5). Harmonise: A step toward an interoperable e-tourism marketplace. *International Journal of Electronic Commerce, 9*(2), 11-39.

GRI, (2002). *Tour operators' sector supplement*. Presented at GRI 2002 Sustainability Reporting Guidelines,

Hagel, J. (1999). Net gain: Expanding markets through virtual communities. *Journal of Interactive Marketing, 13*(1), 55-65.

Hi-Touch Working Group (2003). *Semantic Web methodologies and tools for intra-European sustainable tourism*. Retrieved from http://www.mondeca.com/articleJITT-hitouch-legrand.pdf

Hjalager, A.M. (2002). Repairing innovation defectiveness in Tourism. *Tourism Management, 23*(5), 465-474.

Jarvenpaa, S. L. & Leidner, D. E. (1998). Communication and trust in global virtual teams. *Journal of CMC, 3*(4), 1-38.

Lethbridge, N. (2001). An I-based taxonomy of virtual organizations and the implications for effective management. *Informing Science: Developing Effective Organizations, 4*(1), 17-24.

McWilliam, G. (2000). Building stronger brands through online communities. *Sloan Management Review, 41*(3), 43- 54.

Missikoff, M., Werthner, H., Hopken, W., Dell'Ebra, M., Fodor, O., & Formica, A. (2003). HARMONISE: Towards interoperability in the tourism domain. In *Proceedings of information and communication technologies in tourism 2003, ENTER 2003*, (pp. 58–66). Helsinki: Springer.

Palmer, A. & McCole, P. (2000). The role of electronic commerce in creating virtual tourism destination marketing organizations. *International Journal of Contemporary Hospitality Management, 12*(3), 198-204.

Stockdale, R., & Borovicka, M. (2006). Developing an online business community: A travel industry case study. In *Proceedings of the 39th Hawaii International Conference on System Sciences*, (pp. 134-143), IEEE Computer Society.

Timmers, P. (1998). Business models for electronic markets. *Electronic Markets, 8*(2), 3-8.

Tsai, W. T., Qian Huang, Xu, Chen, Y., & Paul, R. (2007). Ontology-based dynamic process collaboration in service-oriented architecture. In *IEEE International Conference on Service-Oriented Computing and Applications (SOCA'07)*, (pp. 39-46), IEEE Computer Society.

Tuckman, B., (1965). Developmental sequence in small groups. *Psychological bulletin, 63*, 384-389.

Turner, W. (2006). Information infrastructures for distributed collective practices. *Computer Supported Cooperative Work, 15*(2-3), 93-110.

Vartiainen, M. (2001). The functionality of virtual organizations. In Suomi (Ed.), *Proceedings of Workshop on t-world 2001*, Helsinki, (pp. 273-292).

Walden, E. (2000). Some value propositions of online communities. *Electronic Markets, 10*(4), 244-249.

Wenger, E., & Snyder, W. M. (2000). Communities of practice: The organizational frontier, *Harvard Business Review*, (January-February), (pp. 139-145).

Werthner, H., & Ricci, F. (2004). E-commerce and tourism. *Communications of the ACM, 47*(12), 101-105.

Yu, C. C. (2002). Designing a Web-based consumer decision support system for tourism services. In *Proceedings of the 4th International Conference on Electronic Commerce*.

KEY TERMS

Electronic Squads: An electronic squad is a virtual cross-organization community of practice involved in computer-mediated assembly of vacation packages.

Information-Based Product Development: A product development process which assembles intangible (software-based) products whose value results from the information encoded into or surrounding the product.

Moderated Virtual Communities of Practice: A virtual community of practice whose members are assigned distinct roles (upon registration) which in turn, determine access to the community's shared repertoire of resources.

Practice-Oriented Toolkit: A software suite allowing members of a virtual community of practice to engage in the practice the community is about

Virtual Cross-Organization Community of Practice: Inter-organization virtual alliances operating as moderated communities of practice and comprising representative organizations of different sectors of an industry.

Virtual Practice: A practice encoded, enacted and transmitted using a dedicated practice-oriented toolkit

Chapter XXII
Social Interactive Media and Virtual Community Practices:
Retrospective and an R&D Agenda

Demosthenes Akoumianakis
Technological Education Institution of Crete, Greece

ABSTRACT

This chapter attempts to consolidate concepts, ideas and results reported in this volume in an effort to synthesize an agenda and sketch a roadmap for future research and development on virtual community practices facilitated by synergistic combination of social interactive media. In this endeavor, the author revisits the notions of new media, communities and social practice, in the light of the preceding chapters and with the intention to pickup seemingly heterogeneous concepts and sketch the puzzle of social interactive media and virtual community practice. The ultimate target is to make inroads towards a reference model for understanding and framing online social practice under the different regimes constituted by new media and social computing.

INTRODUCTION

In this volume we have been concerned with the design of virtual community practices as enabled or facilitated by a broad range of new media (i.e., social software, collaborative practice toolkits and emerging infrastructures such as Grids and Web 2.0) and performed by human collaborators in a variety of community settings (i.e., online communities, virtual communities of practice, cross-organization communities of practice, etc). In this effort, three key concepts stand out very promptly as primary challenges motivated by a variety of theoretical and / or engineering perspectives. These are the concepts of 'new media', 'community' and 'social practice'. As discussed in the introductory tutorial (Chapter I in this volume), these concepts continue to pose numerous challenges since common ground is yet to be established, despite years of study. Furthermore, it is also striking that very few studies have explicitly addressed how these three constituents are intertwined to shape new virtualities in a networked-society.

In light of the above, this final chapter of the volume, is concerned precisely with such an interplay between the constituents of the triad – new media, community and social practice – assuming that it is this interplay and tight intertwining that facilitates more enlightening accounts of a variety of novel forms of human communication and interaction across a broad range of community settings. Consequently, our intention in this chapter is to consider, in light of the preceding contributions, what are the prominent characteristic tensions shaping virtual community practices and how these can be conceptualized in a prescriptive frame of reference. In doing so, there are several challenges lying ahead of us.

Firstly, new media, communities and social practices are three concepts widely discussed and researched by scholars of various theoretical traditions, using however different frames of reference and units of analysis. This volume is just one example indicative of the breadth of perspectives and approaches followed by researchers. Consequently, there are no standard definitions, unified theories or consolidated engineering frameworks which holistically and exhaustively prescribe these phenomena per se, or the tensions between their constituent parts. For instance, we cannot explain with the required scientific rigor or empirical knowledge how different community settings or types emerge, how new media facilitate their formation and what practices are likely to emerge along the way.

Secondly, it seems that no single theoretical stand or engineering perspective is equipped with the necessary tools to provide the required insight. For example, pure engineering analysis of the new

social media and applications may offer useful insight into technical and architectural abstractions, but fail to explain why some of them are more successful as social software applications than others. On the other hand, social science perspectives and practice-based analysis into the new virtual practices go as far as explaining retrospectively the new status quo, rather offering means and tools for proactive design. For instance, there are social theories explaining prominent differences between interpersonal off-line practices and on-line practices, but no such theory could actually anticipate or foresee or motivate some of the new virtual practices through innovative design insights or guidelines.

Finally, it may be that aiming to investigate the intertwining between new media, community and social practice is useless effort, bound to fail. It may be that, as in many other domains of human endeavor, evolution and progress are processes grounded purely on biological events and phenomena rather than conscious theorizing or engineering practice.

In spite of the constraints and the danger sketched above, the chapter will attempt to bring some insight to the relationship between new social media, communities and social practice, in an attempt to contribute to a better understanding of their intertwining and its implications. In this effort, we will assume that the reader is aware of the contextual definitions, orientation and premises presented in Chapter I. This will allow the present chapter to concentrate on synthesizing common ground rather than analyzing the concepts per se.

Thus, the next section attempts to formulate an integrative view by discussing the 'Community-media-Practice' (CmP) grid – an instrument for assessing the existing status quo and envisioning future developments. Then, we use the CmP to gain further insight to the design of practice-oriented toolkits. To this end, we explore useful concepts such as 'linguistic domains' and how they are related to engaging in online virtual practices. Finally, the chapter is concluded by briefly commenting on the role design can play to facilitate novel practicing using new media so as to foster creative endeavors in virtual communities of various types.

TOWARDS AN INTEGRATIVE FRAME OF REFERENCE

In the introductory tutorial on new media, communities and social practice presented in Chapter I our intention was to clarify for the reader variations in the terms' connotation and engineering base, as well as to briefly review some of the relevant implications. Subsequently, different parts of the volume presented useful insights to these concepts concentrating on community types and models (Section B), social media and tools (Section C), practice toolkits and design techniques (Section D) as well as practice and experience in different application domains (Section E). It is therefore not only appropriate but also necessary to attempt a consolidation of the findings

presented in an effort to address a dual goal: (a) synthesize an integrative framework for analyzing existing systems and institutions of practice, and (b) sketch a roadmap for understanding and envisioning future developments. To this end, we will briefly discuss a synthetic view of what has already been presented in the various chapters and then explore how such synthesis can lead to an improved model for understanding design of practices in virtual community settings.

One plain message which is hopefully derived from our analysis so far is that a key issue of the intertwining between communities, new media and social practice is evolution, seen as transition within a three-dimensional space. This space is depicted in Figure 1 which illustrates schematically the 'Community-Media-Practice' grid (CmP), a normative tool that encapsulates issues raised in this volume but also in the relevant literature. Such a conceptualization may help us understand the various concepts introduced so far and the challenges posed when designers plan transitions along the three dimensions. Each dimension represents a continuum towards more

Figure 1. The virtual community practices

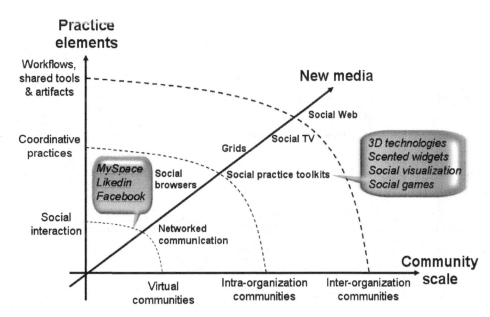

complex structures and states. Transitions in each dimension should be seen more as desirable 'states of affairs' defined in terms of qualitative properties rather than discrete, quantifiable or even measurable units.

The 'practice elements' dimension defines a continuum representing the scale in which elements of practice may be framed. It is argued that in virtual community settings in which dialogue practices prevail, elements of practice may be framed more in interpersonal and social interactions than in coordinative and/or linguistic acts (i.e., workflows, shared tools and artifacts). In contrast, in boundary spanning and workflow-oriented virtual communities of practice, it is expected that boundary objects (i.e., inanimate brokers and translators between constituencies and communities of practice) will be increasingly required to facilitate negotiation and making sense of collaborative praxis framed in domain-specific workflows, tools and artifacts. Consequently, the location of each state in the axis presents a measure of design complexity – an issue to be addressed later on.

The 'new media' dimension aims to capture evolution in technology generations, with emerging technologies and new media located farthest away from the center of the axis in order to depict the need for providing tools and mechanisms for hosting boundary objects, coordinative practices and practices framed in workflows, shared tools and artifacts.

Finally, the 'community scale' dimension represents different community models as introduced in Chapter I (i.e., online communities, business-sponsored community models, distributed communities of practice, cross-organizational virtual communities of practice, etc). Again the farthest away a community model, the more complex and demanding it is to support it and its associated practices.

The CmP grid is best interpreted by combining transitions in more than one dimension. For instance, it would suggest that to support cross-organization virtual communities of practice, designers will increasingly need to design suitable media encapsulating more advanced practices manifested increasingly through boundary objects. In this context, boundary objects are

Table 1. The CmP grid design space

		Virtual communities	Communities of practice		Knowledge communities
			Intra-organization	Inter-organization	
Elements of practice	Social interaction	*Networked communication*	*Networked communication*	*Networked communication*	*Networked communication*
		Social software	*Social visualization*	*Web conferencing*	*Social visualization*
	Coordinative action	*Not applicable*	*Not applicable*	*Computational grids*	*Computational grids*
					Data grids
	Workflows, tools and artifacts	*Tool-specific*	*Collaboratories*	*Practice toolkits*	*Social Semantic web*
			Groupware		
			Organizational memory systems & archives		

conceived as elements of a practice which are both plastic enough to adapt to local needs of the member employing them, yet robust enough to maintain a common identity across members' sites (Star & Griesemer, 1989; Star, 1989). In terms of our referent states in the 'practice elements' dimension, boundary objects are meaningful when used to foster coordinative practices, or to facilitate making sense of the workflows, the shared tools and the collective artifacts of the community. This is generalized in Table 1 which describes the CmP grid design space.

THE CmP AND THE DESIGN OF PRACTICE-ORIENTED TOOLKITS

The CmP grid as briefly introduced above brings to the forefront the notion of practice-oriented toolkits. In the broader sense of the term, these may be conceived of as artificial languages through which members of a virtual community engage in the practice the community is about. In this volume, the reader has been presented to a broad range of such artificial languages designed to facilitate collaborative practicing in applications domains such learning, music performance, building information-based products and services, etc. There at least two high level design issues relevant to building practice-oriented toolkits; the first amounts to understanding what is to be designed, namely the toolkit as opposed to the community, while the second is related to the technological regime which determines the choice of social media and the intended informational / social scope of design. The CmP offers useful insight to both these issues and facilitates an improved understanding of the distinct role of practice-oriented toolkits in virtual community settings.

Practice Toolkits as Tools for Communicating in Linguistic Domains

Designing artificial languages for communication is a long-standing goal of many engineering disciplines. Software engineers have a long tradition in constructing procedural, declarative and object-oriented languages for computer programming. Similarly, industrial designers have been concerned with guidelines and artificial languages of various sorts (i.e., specification languages, simulation languages, visual design languages) to cope with engineering design problems and their ergonomic, aesthetic, usability and economic constraints. Furthermore, Human-Computer Interaction designers are also keen to building graphical design languages (Rheinfrank & Evenson, 1996) and visual metaphors to hide the complexities of computer-based operations.

In all these cases, the language comes as a bridge to the gap between two distinctively different worlds – the symbolic world of humans and the numerical world of computers (Akoumianakis & Stephanidis, 2003). However, this widely appreciated perspective is not necessarily an appropriate metaphor for building practice-oriented toolkits i.e., artificial languages through which members of a community engage in the practice the community is about. Specifically, in community settings the important gap to be bridged is not so much that between humans and computers as that between members of the community as well as the virtual space.

In this section, we revisit this challenge from a slightly different perspective in order to support the argument that designing a practice-oriented toolkit amounts to designing the interaction vocabulary of a 'linguistic domain'. The term 'linguistic domain' is borrowed from Maturana and Varela (1998) where it is defined as

... system of learned communicative behaviors that arise between organisms as the result of their 'particular history of co-existence (p. 207).

In practical terms this implies facilitation of recurrent interactions between members that lead to an act of communication. The notion is best illustrated by means of an example. Consider the hypothetical situation of driving on the motorway in a foreign country. In such a setting, the driver is concurrently engaged in two distinct linguistic domains, each having its own language for communication. One linguistic domain is between the driver and the macro-context of the motorway as manifested by the local 'culture' of driving on a motorway, the available sign posts, the motorway's state and condition, the allowable speed limits, etc. Yet another linguistic domain is between the driver and the micro-context of the vehicle involving the 'local' actions subsumed by the practice of driving.

There are two issues worth noticing. The first relates to the duality of boundary and locality as related to the driving practice. The macro-context of the motorway is almost entirely characterized by boundary objects whereas the micro-context of the vehicle entails locality. The boundary objects of the macro-context are robust enough to maintain a common identity across different micro-contexts (i.e., users driving their own cars) as well as plastic enough to adapt to local needs of a micro-context. It then stands to argue that driving safely on the motorway entails the drivers' engagement in intertwining boundary and local practices characterizing the macro- and micro-context of the driving practice respectively. The second issue worth mentioning is that in both contexts of practice, communication is through some sort of artificial language and takes the form of learned communicative behavior that arises between inhabitants as the result of their 'particular history of co-existence'. Moreover, it is the binding of communication to linguistic domains which distinguishes one artificial language from another and both from traditional language.

By analogy, virtual practice-oriented toolkits provide the means of communication in linguistic domains which are established and sustained virtually. As each distinct linguistic domain may have its own language, the toolkit should be designed as the interactive encapsulation of elements of this language. Then members operate in a designated linguistic domain by learning its language and interacting using it. Different genres of social software may be seen as interactive vocabularies aiming to support the virtuality of members' engagement in designated linguistic domains. For instance, a 'blog' can be considered as a linguistic domain supporting the practice of providing one's diary or regular commentary via a 'Web-log' Web site (Denning & Dunham, 2006). To operate in such a linguistic domain there are two prerequisites corresponding to elements of the designated practice, namely a means to create 'Web-log' Web site and a browser for managing contributions. Today open source software has provided a variety of tools for bloggers to create Web sites and readers to manage their subscriptions. Similarly, mySpace can be understood as the means of communicating in the linguistic domain of virtual presence or social networking. Generalizing the concept, it may then be argued that designing the virtuality of more complex practice domains such as engineering of consumer products or the design of information-based artifacts amounts to designing the means of communications in the corresponding linguistic domains so as to allow members to engage in the practice the community is about.

Having framed community virtuality as communication in linguistic domains using some sort of language, we now turn to the link between language and community practices. In general, language is used to transmit a practice. However, practice, conceived of as learnt behavior which is manifested as embodied recurrent actions taken without conscious thought, is itself a constituent of a linguistic domain. Thus, the language of a linguistic domain should be designed so as to transmit its underlying practice, allowing interactions between members, sharing or adhering to this practice. In virtual settings, such interaction

Figure 2. A linguistic domain

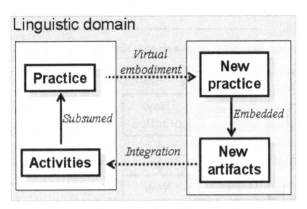

has a strong evolutionary character resulting from the reproduction of the basic practice of the linguistic domain in a virtual setting.

This is depicted schematically in Figure 2 which indicates the cyclical reconstruction of elements of a practice through their virtual embodiment in social practice toolkits. It is worth noticing that this cyclical reformulation of practice is useful for understanding both variation in practice enactment as well as new behaviors arising in a virtual community setting and incrementally becoming part of the community's culture. Often, such behaviors may not have offline counterparts. For instance there is no such thing as civic inattention in the virtual practice of presence. Thus, virtual practices should not be seen as mere interactive embodiments of offline practice reproduced virtually, but as learnt communicative behaviors that induce innovative changes of habit by offering and supporting new tools or processes perceived as high value by adopters. This raises the question as to what are the intrinsic elements that drive new practices in virtual settings, which is further explored below.

Practice Toolkits and the Macro- and Micro-Contexts of Practice

Clearly, interactions in virtual settings are catalyzed by the new media and the social practice toolkits and applications. However, it is not clear how this is done and why. To gain the required insight we will revisit our reference example of driving on the motorway in a foreign country to remind ourselves of a key issue; the fact that practice occurs in macro-contexts that provide broad commonalities of action, but also in micro-contexts in which action is highly localized. Additionally, the macro-context is likely to influence the reconstruction of practice at the micro-context, leading to continuous adaptation of its elements. This distinction has implications for the technical design of practice-oriented toolkits which should be compliant to a prevailing macro-context while supporting a designed micro-context practice. The macro-context represents the current technological trajectory or paradigm (i.e., the Web), while micro-context relates to domain-specific elements of practice.

We can now reconstruct our schematic depiction of a linguistic domain (see Figure 2) to arrive at a general model for building virtual community practice-oriented toolkits. This model is illustrated in Figure 3. As shown, the macro-context represents the prevalent technological trajectory or paradigm within the new media dimension which is broad enough to facilitate several genres of micro-contexts or localized action facilitated by dedicated practice toolkits. Consequently, different genres or types of community, such as

Figure 3. Practice evolution in macro- and micro-contexts

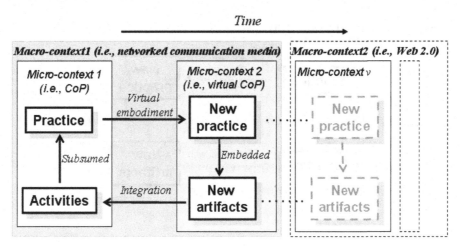

traditional communities of practice, virtual communities of practice or virtual cross-organization communities of practices, may be viewed as evolutionary transitions of micro-contexts within the same or across consecutive macro-contexts.

It is also evident that micro-contexts do not exist in isolation; indeed there is a tight feedback loop which incrementally enriches a practice with new elements resulting from the practice's virtual embodiment. This may be linked to the practice grid and the pathways of innovation (see Chapter I in this volume) to explain why for instance mySpace can be seen as an evolution of the practice of presence or social networking in virtual settings, as well as why the new virtual practice has redefined elements of the traditional practice (i.e., no civic inattention, etc).

The above analysis highlights the dual role of practice toolkits which should be reflected by their design. Specifically, practice-oriented toolkits act either as facilitators of established practices (at micro-level) or as change enablers (at macro-level) leading to the progressive establishment and attainment of new capabilities. In their role as practice facilitators, toolkits are designed so as to encapsulate existing and well established

practices. As change enablers, toolkits should be designed to establish new practice.

Practice Toolkits and Informational / Social Connectivity

The last but equally important dimension of designing practice oriented toolkits, either as facilitators or change enablers of (macro- or micro-context) practice relates to their intended social impact. A useful variable to understand a toolkit's social impact is the type and degree of connectivity to be facilitated. Connectivity may be conceived as either sharing information or a social value, thus it may be classified as information connectivity and social connectivity respectively. Using this two scale-variable of connectivity, we can classify the macro-contexts of practice as evolutionary transitions representing the paradigm shift in collaborative computing. Figure 4 summarizes these paradigms shifts and the micro-contexts in which practice occurs in each paradigm.

Specifically, in terms of macro-contexts, four broad maturity levels are identified progressively leading to the social Semantic web as the ultimate

Figure 4. Technological trajectories & new social media

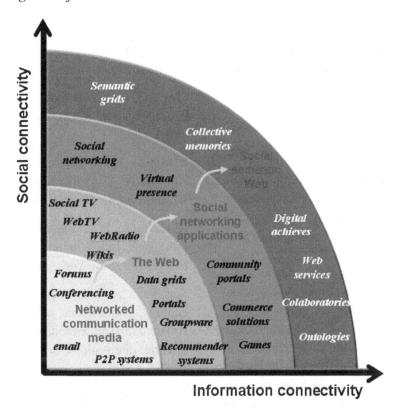

macro-context for knowledge sharing and high utilization of resources. Each maturity level builds on the previous one and extends micro-practices in both scales of connectivity. Furthermore, each maturity level is characterized by genres of social practice toolkits designed to attain different goals and functions. Thus, for instance, in the networked communication media maturity level there are practice-oriented toolkits, such as P2P music sharing systems with high informational connectivity (i.e., they have the capacity to share large amounts of information) but low social connectivity (i.e., the size of the appropriators of the benefits of the innovation is comparatively small).

SUMMARY AND CONCLUSION

This chapter has attempted to provide a consolidated overview of the intertwining nature of new media, communities and social practice in an effort to sketch a roadmap for future research and development likely to drive forthcoming innovations in virtual community practices. From our discussion, several conclusions may be drawn which make inroads to a better understanding of the issues at stake.

Firstly, social software as widely experienced today is the virtual (interactive) embodiment of a social practice in micro-contexts. Their high popularity and innovative character is rooted in the fact that they reproduce widely accepted social practices such as presence, dating and networking in virtual settings, eliminating physical proximity and space and time constraints which traditionally confine the enactment of these practices in offline settings. Due to intrinsic properties of the new media, such applications do not only facilitate variation in the transmission and enactment of a practice. More importantly, they induce changes in the basic practice, thus leading to a new virtual culture.

Secondly, as new technology matures, more practice domains other than presence, dating and social networking are likely to have virtual reconstructions leading to new virtualities such as knowledge communities, distributed virtual communities of practice, cross-organization practice networks which will dominate how collective knowledge is shared, produced, articulated and enriched. A useful construct to understand these developments is to frame them as interactions in linguistic domains. Linguistic domains defined as systems of learnt communicative behaviors arising between members of a community as a result of their history of co-existence, form the unit of analysis for studying practice, its offline boundaries as well as its expansion or enrichment in virtual settings. Then, virtual practicing becomes synonymous to communicating and interacting in linguistic domains such as new product development, distributed and networked music composition, gaming, medical diagnosing, etc.

Finally, practice-oriented toolkits will progressively provide the means of communicating and practicing in novel linguistic domains. The corresponding virtual practices will be framed both in the social interactions between the members as well as in the processes, tools and artifacts embedded in the practice-oriented toolkit. Consequently, it is these practice-oriented toolkits that are the subject of future design, not their respective communities.

REFERENCES

Akoumianakis, D., & Stephanidis, C. (2003). Multiple Metaphor|Environments: Designing for diversity. *Ergonomics*, *46*(1-3), 88 – 113.

Denning, P., & Dunham, R. (2006). Innovation as language action. *Communications of the ACM*, *49*(5), 47-52.

Maturana, H., & Varela, F. (1998). *The Tree of Knowledge: The Biological Roots of Human Understanding.* Boston, MA: Shambala.

Rheinfrank, J., & Evenson, S. (1996). Design Languages. In T. Winograd (Ed.), *Bringing design to software.* New York: Addison-Wesley.

Star, S. L., & Griesemer, J. (1989). Institutional ecology, translations' and boundary objects: Amateurs and professionals in Berkeley's museum of vertebrate zoology. *Social Studies of Science*, *19*, 387-420.

Star, S. L. (1989). The structure of ill-structured solutions: Boundary objects and heterogeneous distributed problem solving. In M. N. Huhns & L. Gasser (Eds.), *Distributed Artificial Intelligence 2.* Morgan Kaufmann.

KEY TERMS

New Media: The tools and/or artifacts allowing users to engage in some sort of collaborative practice.

Social Practice: The collective wisdom (habits, rules of thumb and socially-defined modes of acting) through which a community negotiates meaning and articulates common ground.

Virtual Community: The virtual space in which a community's (social) practice is interactively manifested using computer-mediated tools and processes.

Compilation of References

3DTV Network of Excellence. (2005). *Display techniques: A survey.* Retrieved from http://www.3dtv-research.net/

3DTV Network of Excellence. (2006). *Technical report on 3DTV potential applications.* Retrieved from http://www.3dtv-research.net/

Aaen, I., Bøtcher, P., & Mathiassen, L. (1997). Software factories. *Proceedings of the 20th Information Systems Research Seminar in Scandinavia*, Oslo. Retrieved May 13 from http://www.cin.ufpe.br/~in953/lectures/papers/Software_Factories_17.pdf

Abreu, J., Almeida, P., & Branco, V. (2001). 2Be on – Interactive television supporting interpersonal communication. In *Proceedings of the 6th Eurographics workshop on Multimedia.*

Ackerman, M. S. (1998). Augmenting organizational memory: A field study of Answer Garden. *ACM Transactions on Information Systems, 16*(3), 203-24.

Ackerman, M. S., & Halverson, C. (2004). Organizational memory as objects, processes, and trajectories: An examination of organizational memory in use. *Computer Supported Cooperative Work, 13*, 155-189.

Ackerman, M. S., & Palen, L. (1996). The Zephyr help instance: Promoting ongoing activity in a CSCW system. *ACM Conference on Human Factors in Computing Systems (ACM CHI '96)*, (pp. 268-275). New York: ACM Press.

Agamanolis, S. (2006). At the intersection of broadband and broadcasting: How ITV technologies can support Human Connectedness. In *Proceedings of the 4th Euro iTV Conference* (pp. 17-22). Athens, Greece.

Agarwal, R., & Prasad, J. (1997). The role of innovation characteristics and perceived voluntariness in the acceptance of information technologies. *Decision Science, 28*(3), 557-582.

Ahonen, A., Turkki, L., Saarijärvi, M., Lahti, M., & Virtanen, T. (2006). Guidelines for designing easy-to-use interactive television services: Experiences from the ArviD Programme. In *Proceedings of the 4th Euro iTV Conference* (pp. 225-233). Athens, Greece.

Akoumianakis, D., & Stephanidis, C. (2003). Multiple Metaphor |Environments: Designing for diversity. *Ergonomics, 46*(1-3), 88-113.

Akoumianakis, D., Vellis G., Milolidakis I., Kotsalis D., & Alexandraki, C. (2008). Distributed collective practices in collaborative music performance. *In Proceedings of 3rd ACM International Conference on Digital Interactive Media in Entertainment and Arts (DIMEA 2008)*, (pp. 368-375), New York: ACM Press.

Akoumianakis, D., Vidakis N., Vellis G., Milolidakis G., & Kotsalis D. (2008). Interaction scenarios in the 'social' experience factory: Assembling collaborative artefacts through component reuse and social interaction. In D. Cunliffe (Ed.), *IASTED-HCI'2008 Human Computer Interaction*, (pp. 611-068), Anaheim: Acta Press.

Akoumianakis, D., Vidakis, N., Vellis, G., Milolidakis G., & Kotsalis, D. (2007). Experience-based social and collaborative performance in an electronic village of local interest: The eKoNEΣ framework. In J. Cardoso,

J. Cordeiro, & J Filipe (Eds.), *ICEIS'2007 - 9th International Conference on Enterprise Information Systems, Volume HCI* (pp. 117-122), Funchal, Madeira, Portugal: INSTICC.

Allen, C. (1993). Reciprocal evolution as a strategy for integrating basic research, design, and studies of work practices. In D. Shuler and A. Namioka (Eds.), *Participatory design* (pp. 239-253). Hillsdate, NJ: Lawrence Erlbaum Assoicates.

American productivity and quality center (2000). *Building and sustaining communities of practice.* Final Report. APQC, USA.

American Telemedicine Association (2003). *ATA adopts Telehomecare clinical guidelines.* Retrieved on 15 June 2005 from http://www.americantelemed.org/icot/hometelehealthguidelines.htm

Amin, A., & Roberts, J. (2008). Knowing in action: Beyond communities of practice. *Research Policy, 37*(2), 353-369.

Amonashvili, S. A. (1984). Development of the cognitive initiative of students in the first grades of elementary education. *Voprosy Psychologii, 5*, 36-41 (in Russian).

Anderson, A., & Ellis, A. (2005), Desktop video-assisted music teaching and learning: New opportunities for design and delivery, Colloquium. *British Journal of Educational Technology, 36*(5), Retrieved May 10, 2008, from http://www.blackwell-synergy.com/doi/abs/10.1111/j.1467-8535.2005.00496.x?journalCode=bjet

Anderson, B. (1991). *Imagined communities* (Second ed.). New York: Verso.

Andrews, P. L. (1986). *Behave: Fire behavior prediction and fuel modeling system - BURN* Subsystem Part 1. USDA Forest Service General Technical Report INT-194.

Antoniou, G., Skylogiannis, T., Bikakis, A., & Bassiliades, N. (2005). A Semantic brokering system for the tourism domain. *Information Technology & Tourism, 7*, 183–200.

Appadurai, A. (1996). *Modernity at large: Cultural dimensions of globalization.* Minneapolis, MN: University of Minnesota Press.

Argyris, C. (1993). *Knowledge for action: A guide to overcoming barriers to organizational change.* San Francisco: Jossey-Bass.

Argyris, C., & Schon, D. A. (1978). *Organisational learning: A theory of action perspective.* Reading: Addison-Wesley.

Auer, S., Bizer, C., Kobilarov, G, Lehmann, J., Cyganiak, R., & Ives, Z. (2007). DBpedia: A nucleus for a Web of open data. *The 6th International Semantic Web Conference (ISWC 2007).*

Auinger, A., & Stary, Ch. (2002). Embedding self-management and generic learning support into courseware structures. In *Proceedings of the HICSS-35*, IEEE, 465-474.

Ayers, D. (2007). Evolving the link. *IEEE Internet Computing, 11*(3), 94-96.

Baca, M., & Holtzman, H. (2008). Television meets Facebook: Social networks through consumer electronics. In *Adjunct Proceedings of the 6th Euro iTV Conference* (pp. 35-36). Salzburg, Austria.

Bajjaly, S. T. (1999). *The community networking handbook.* Chicago and London: American Library Association.

Ball, S. J. (2000). Performativities and fabrications in the education economy: Towards the performative society. *Australian Educational Researcher, 27*(2), 119-129.

Ball, S. J. (2003). *Class strategies and the education market: The middle classes and social advantage.* London, New York: Routledge Falmer.

Barab, S. A., Mackinster, J. G., & Scheckler, R. (2003). Designing system dualities: Characterizing a Web-supported professional development community. *Information Society, 19*(3), 237-257.

Barbera, R., Falzone, A., & Rodolico A. (2003). *The GENIUS Grid Portal, Computing in High Energy and Nuclear Physics.* La Jolla, California.

Barnes, B. (2001). Practice as collective action. In T. Schatzki, K. K. Cetina, & E. Von Savigny (Eds.), *The practice turn in contemporary theory* (pp. 17-28). London: Routledge.

Barth, F. (1981). *Process and form in social life.* Boston: Routledge & Kegan Paul.

Bartle, R. (2004): *Designing virtual worlds.* New Riders.

Basch, E., Artz, D., Dulko, D., Scher, K., Sabbatini, P., Hensley, M., Mitra, N., Speakman, J., McCabe, M., & Schrag, D. (2005). Patient online self-reporting of toxicity symptoms during chemotherapy. *Journal of Clinical Oncology, 23*(15), 3552–3561.

Basili, V. R. (1993). The Experience Factory and its relationship to other improvement paradigms. In I. Somerville, & M. Paul, (Eds.), *4th European Software Engineering Conference (ESEC), Lecture Notes in Computer Science 717,* (pp. 68-83), London: Springer-Verlag.

Basili, V. R., Lindvall, M., & Costa, P. (2001). Implementing the Experience Factory Concepts as a Set of Experience Bases. *International Conference on Software Engineering and Knowledge Engineering (SEKE '01) – Conference Proceedings,* Buenos Aires, Argentina. Retrieved May 13 from http://www.cs.umd.edu/~basili/publications/proceedings/P90.pdf

Bastanlar, Y., Grammalidis, N., Zabulis, X., Yilmaz, E., Yardimci, Y., & Triantafyllidis, G. (2008). 3D reconstruction for a cultural heritage virtual tour system. In *Proceedings of the International Society for Photogrammetry and Remote Sensing,* ISPRS 2008, Beijing, China.

Bauman, Z. (2000). *Liquid modernity.* Cambridge: Polity Press, Malden, MA: Blackwell.

Baym, N. K. (1995). The emergence of community in computer-mediated communication. In S. Jones (Ed.), *CyberSociety* (pp. 138-163). Newbury Park, CA: Sage.

Becerra-Fernandez, I., & Sabherwal, R. (2001). Organizational knowledge management: A contingency perspective. *Journal of Management Information Systems, 18*(1), 23-55.

Beck, U. (1992). *Risk society: Towards a new modernity.* (Translated by Mark Ritter). London, Newbury Park: Sage Publications.

Beck, U., & Beck-Gernsheim, E. (2002). *Individualization: Institutionalized individualism and its social and political consequences.* London: Thousand Oaks: SAGE.

Beck, U., Giddens, A., & Lash, S. (1994). *Reflexive modernization: Politics, tradition and aesthetics in the modern social order.* Stanford: Stanford University Press.

Beckett, D., & Berners-Lee, T. (2008). Turtle - Terse RDF triple language. *W3C Team Submission.* Latest version available at http://www.w3.org/TeamSubmission/turtle/

Bedny, G., & Meister, D. (1997). *The Russian Theory Of Activity Current Applications To Design.* London: Lawrence Erlbaum Assoc.

Bell, D. (1996). *The cultural contradictions of capitalism.* New York: Harper Collins Publishers.

Benford, S., Greenhalgh, C., Brown, C., Walker, G., Regan, T., Rea, P., Morphett, J., & Wyver, J. (1998). Experiments in inhabited TV. In *Proceedings of CHI' 98* (pp. 289-290). New York: ACM.

Benkler, Y. (2003). The Political Economy of Commons. *UPGRADE: European Journal for the Informatics Professional, 4*(3), 6-9.

Bennet A., & Bennet D. (2003). The partnership between organizational learning and knowledge management. In C. W. Holsapple (Ed.), *Handbook on knowledge management, 1,* (pp. 439-455). New York: Springer.

Bentley, R., Bentley J. A., Hughes D., Randall T., Rodden P., Sawyer, D., Shapiro, D., & Sommerville, I. (2002). Ethnographically-informed systems design for air control In *Proceedings of the Conference on Computer-Supported Cooperative Work,* (pp. 123-129).

Berners-Lee, T., & Hendler, J. (2001). Scientific publishing on the 'Semantic Web'. *Nature, 410,* 1023-1024.

Berners-Lee, T., Bray, T., Connolly, D., Cotton, P., Fielding, R., Jeckle, M., et al. (2004). *Architecture of the World Wide Web, Volume One.* W3C, Retrieved 15 June 2008, from http://www.w3.org/TR/webarch/

Berners-Lee, T., Hendler, J., & Lassila, O. (2001). *The Semantic Web. Scientific American, 284*(5), 28-37

Bernstein, B. (1996). *Pedagogy, symbolic control, and identity : Theory, research, critique.* London, Bristol, PA: Taylor & Francis.

Bimber, B., Flanagin, A. J., & Stohl, C. (2005). Reconceptualizing collective action in the contemporary media environment. *Communication Theory, 15*(4), 365-388.

Bizer, C., Heath, T., Idehen, K., & Berners-Lee, T. (2008). *Linked data on the Web (ldow2008). In WWW '08: Proceeding of the 17th International Conference on World Wide Web (pp. 1265-1266). New York: ACM.*

Blizzard (n.d.). Glossary. Retrieved 2 July 2006, from http://www.worldofwarcraft.com/info/basics/glossary.html

Blumer, H. (2004). Society in action. In S.E.Cahill. (Ed.). *Inside social life: Readings in sociological psychology and microsociology* (4th ed., pp.320-324). Los Angeles: Roxbury Publishing Company.

Boaler, J., & Greeno, J. G. (2000). *Identity, agency, and knowing in mathematical worlds.* In J. Boaler (Ed.), *Multiple perspectives on mathematics teaching and learning* (pp. 171-200). Stamford, CT: Ablex.

Bodker, S. (1991). *Through the interface: A human activity approach to user interface design.* Hillsdale, NJ: Lawrence Erlbaum.

Boersma, J. S. K. T., & Stegwee, R. A. (1996). Exploring the Issues in Knowledge Management. *Information Technology Management in Europe, Track of the 1996 Information Resources Management Association International Conference.*

Boertjes, E. (2007). ConnecTV: Share the experience. In *Proceedings of the 5th Euro iTV Conference* (pp. 139-140). Amsterdam.

Bojars, U., Breslin, J., & Moller, K. (2006). *Using Semantics to enhance the blogging experience. In Proceedings of 3rd European Semantic Web Conference, ESWC 2006,* (pp. 679-696).

Bollier, D. (2003). The rediscovery of the Commons. *Upgrade, 4*(3), 10-12.

Borgatti, S. P., Everett, M. G., & Freeman, L. C. (2002). *Ucinet for Windows: Software for social network analysis.* Harvard, MA: Analytic Technologies.

Bos, N., Gergle, D., Olson, J., & Olson, G. (2001). Being there versus seeing there: Trust via video, *Proceedings of CHI. Retrieved September, 2007 from* http://www.crew.umich.edu/publications.html

Bos, N., Zimmerman, A., Olson, J., Yew, J., Yerkie, J., & Dahl, E. (2007). From shared databases to communities of practice: A taxonomy of collaboratories. *Journal of Computer-Mediated Communication, 2*(2), article 16. Retrieved May 13 from http://jcmc.indiana.edu/vol12/issue2/bos.html

Bos, N., Zimmerman, A., Olson, J., Yew, J., Yerkie, J., Dahl, E., & Olson, G. (2007). From shared databases to communities of practice: A taxonomy of collaboratories. *Journal of Computer-Mediated Communication, 12*(2), 318-338.

Bouras, C., Igglesis, V., Kapoulas, V., & Tsiatsos, T. (2005). A Web-based virtual community. *International Journal of Web Based Communities, 1*(2), 127-139.

Bourbonnais, S., Gogate, V. M., Haas, L. M., Horman, R. W., Malaika, S., Narang, I., & Raman, V. (2004). Towards an information infrastructure for the grid. *IBM Systems Journal, 43*(4), Grid Computing.

Bourdieu, P. (1977). *Outline of a theory of practice.* Richard Nice, Trans. New York, NY: Cambridge University Press.

Bourdieu, P. (1980). *The logic of practice.* Stanford, CA: Stanford University Press.

Bourdieu, P., & Wacquant, L. J. D. (1992). *An invitation to reflexive sociology.* University of Chicago Press.

Bouwen, J., Vanderlinden, K., & Staneker, T. (2005). Communication meets entertainment: Community television. *Alcatel Telecommunications Review*, 1ˢᵗ Quarter.

Bradner, E., Kellogg, W. A., & Erickson, T. (1998). Babble: Supporting conversation in the workplace. *SIGGROUP Bull., 19*(3), 8-10.

Bradner, E., Kellogg, W. A., & Erickson, T. (1999). *The adoption and use of 'BABBLE': A field study of chat in the workplace.* Paper presented at the Sixth conference on European Conference on Computer Supported Cooperative Work, Copenhagen, Denmark.

Breakwell, G. M., & Beardsell, S. (1992). Gender, parental and peer influences upon science attitudes and activities. *Public Understanding of Science, 1*, 183-197.

Breslin, J., & Decker, S. (2007). The future of social networks on the Internet: The need for Semantics. IEEE Internet Computing, (pp. 86-90).

Breslin, J., Harth, A., Bojars, U., & Decker, S. (2005). Towards Semantically-interlinked online communities. In Proceedings of the 2nd European Semantic Web Conference (ESWC05), Heraklion, Greece, LNCS, 3532, 500-514.

Bresnen, M., Edelmanb, L., Newellb, S., Scarbrough, H. & Swana, J. (2003). Social practices and the management of knowledge in project environments. *International Journal of Project Management, 21*(3), 157-166.

Brickley, D., & Guha, R. (2004). RDF Vocabulary description language 1.0: RDF schema. W3C Recommendation 10 February 2004. World Wide Web Consortium.

Broadbananas (2005). http://www.broadbandbananas.com

Brown, J. S., & Gray, E. S. (1995, November). The people are the company. *Fast Company Magazine*.

Brown, J. S., & Duguid, P. (1991). Organizational Learning and Communities of Practice: Toward a Unified View of Working, Learning, and Innovation. *Knowledge and Communities, 2*(1), 40-57.

Brown, J. S., & Duguid, P. (1998). Organizing knowledge. *California Management Review, 40*, 90–111.

Brown, J. S., & Duguid, P. (2000). *The social life of information*. Boston: Harvard Business School Press.

Browne, J., Sacket, P. J., & Wortmann, J. C. (1995). Future manufacturing systems – Towards the extended enterprise. *Computers in Industry, 25*, 235-254.

Bruner, J. (1986). *Actual minds, possible worlds*. Cambridge, MA: Harvard University Press.

Buchel, B., & Raub, S. (2002). Building Knowledge-creating Value Networks. *European Management Journal, 20*(6), 587–596.

Buetow, K. H. (2005). Cyberinfrastructure: Empowering a "third way" in biomedical research. *Science Magazine, 308*(5723), 821-824.

Burnett, G., Besant, M., & Chatman, E. A. (2001). Small worlds: normative behaviour in virtual communities and feminist bookselling. *Journal of American Society for Information Science and Technology, 52*(7), 536-537.

Bushe, G. R. (1995). Advances in appreciative inquiry as an organization development intervention. *Organization Development Journal, 13*(3), 14-22.

Byrne, J. A., Brandt, R., & Port, O. (1993). The virtual corporation. *BusinessWeek*, February 8, (pp. 36-41).

Calvary, G., Coutaz, J., Thevenin, D., Limbourg, Q., Bouillon, L., & Vanderdonckt, J. (2003). A Unifying reference framework for multi-target user interfaces. *Interacting with Computers, 15*(3), 289-308.

Calzada, I. (2004). Una forma organizativa para intervenir en las organizaciones: comunidad de prácticas (CoP). *MIK, S. Coop.*

Camarinha-Matos, L. M., Afsarmanesh, H., Garita, C., & Lima, C. (1997). Towards an architecture for virtual enterprises. *Journal of Intelligent Manufacturing, 9*(2), 189-199.

Cannataro, M., & Talia, D. (2003). KNOWLEDGE Grid - An architecture for distributed knowledge discovery. *Communications of the ACM, 46*(1), 89-93.

Cappe, E. (2008). *Conditions D'émergence Et De Développement Des Communautés De Pratique Pour Le Management Des Connaissances.* Unpublished PhD, Universite Pierre Mendes, Grenoble, France.

Cardoso, J., & Lange, C. (2007). A framework for assessing strategies and technologies for dynamic packaging applications in e-tourism. *Information Technology & Tourism, 9,* 27-44.

Carroll J., Rosson M-B., Isenhour, P., Ganoe, C., Dunlap, D., Fogarty, J., Schafer, W., & Van Metre, C. (2001). Designing our town: MOOsburg. *International Journal of Human-Computer Studies, 54,* 725-751.

Carroll, J. M., Neale, D. C., Isenbour, P. L., Rosson, M. B., & McCrickard, D. S. (2003). Notification and awareness: Synchronizing task-oriented collaborative activity. *International Journal of Human–Computer Studies, 58,* 605-632.

Carroll, J. M., Rosson, M. B., Convertino, G., & Ganoe, H. C. (2006). Awareness and teamwork in computer-supported collaborations. *Interacting with Computers, 18,* 21-46.

Cartwright, D., & Zander, A. (1968). *Group dynamics: Research and theory.* New York: Harpercollins College Division.

Caruso, D. & Rhoten, D. (2001). *Lead, follow, get out of the way: Sidestepping the barriers to effective practice of interdisciplinarity.* Report for the Hybrid Vigor Institute, Retrieved October 2005 from http://www.hybridvigor.net/publications.pl?s=interdis&d=2001.04.30#

Castells, M. (1996). *The rise of the network society.* Cambridge, MA: Blackwell Publishers.

Cauberghe, V., & De Pelsmacker, P. (2006). Belgian advertisers' perceptions of interactive digital TV as a marketing communication tool. In *Proceedings of the 4th Euro iTV Conference* (pp. 371-381). Athens, Greece.

Cayzer, S. (2004). *Semantic blogging and decentralized knowledge management. Communications of the ACM, 47(12), 47-52.*

Chafe, C., Gurevich, M., Leslie, G., & Tyan, S. (2004). Effect of time delay on ensemble accuracy. In *Proceedings of the International Symposium on Musical Acoustics,* Nara, Japan.

Checkland, P. B., & Casar, A. (1986). Vicker's concept of an appreciative system: A systematic account. *Journal of Applied Systems Analysis, 3,* 3-17.

Checkland, P., & Holwell, S. (1998). *Information, systems and information systems: making sense of the field.* New York: John Wiley & Sons Ltd.

Chen, H., & Duh, H.B.L. (2007). Understanding Social Interaction in World of Warcraft. In *Proceedings of the International Conference on Advances in Computer Entertainment Technology, 203,* 21-24.

Chen, V.H.H., Duh, H.B.L., Phuah, P.S.K., & Lam, D.Z.Y. (2006). Enjoyment or Engagement? Role of Social Interaction in Playing Massively Multiplayer Online Role-playing Games (MMORPGS). *Lecture Notes in Computer Science, 4161,* 262-267.

Cheng, W. (1996*). The virtual enterprise: Beyond time, place and form.* Economic Bulletin, Singapore International Chamber of Commerce, 5-7 February.

Cherny, L. (1999). *Conversation and community: Chat in a virtual world.* Stanford, CA: CSLI Publications.

Cheshire, C. (2007). Selective incentives and generalized information exchange. *Social Psychology Quarterly, 70*(1), 82-100.

Cheshire, C., & Antin, J. (2008). The social psychological effects of feedback on the production of Internet information pools. *Journal of Computer-Mediated Communication, 13*(3), 705-727.

Cheung, C. M. K., Lee, M. K. O., & Chen, Z. (2002). *Using the Internet as a learning medium: An exploration of gender difference in the adoption of FaBWeb.* Paper presented at the 35th Hawaii International Conference on System Science.

Chia, R., & Robin, H. (2006). Strategy as practical coping: A Heideggerian perspective. *Organization Studies, 27,* 635–655.

Chiarugi, F., Trypakis, D., Kontogiannis, V., Lees, P. J., Chronaki, C., Zeaki, M., Giannakoudakis, N., Vourvahakis, D., Tsiknakis, M., & Orphanoudakis, S. C. (2003). Continuous ECG monitoring in the management of prehospital health emergencies. In *Proceedings of the IEEE Computers in Cardiology 2003 (CIC'2003) Conference, 30*, 205-208, 21-24 September, Chalkidiki, Greece.

Chin, A. (1998). Future visions. *Journal of Organization and Change Management.*

Chin, G., Jr., & Lansing, C. S. (2004). Capturing and supporting contexts for scientific data sharing via the biological sciences collaboratory. *Proceedings of ACM CSCW Conference*, (pp. 409-418), New York: ACM Press.

Chiu, C., Hsu, M., & Wang, E. (2006). Understanding knowledge sharing in virtual communities: An integration of social capital and social cognitive theories. *Decision Support Systems., 42*, 1872-1888.

Chronaki, C., Katehakis, D., Zabulis, X., Tsiknakis, M., & Orphanoudakis, S. C. (1997). WebOnCOLL: Medical collaboration in regional healthcare networks. *IEEE Transactions on Information Technology in Biomedicine, 1*(4), 257-269.

Chronaki, C., Lees, P. J., Antonakis, N., Chiarugi, F., Vrouchos, G., Nikolaidis, G., Tsiknakis, M., & Orphanoudakis S. C. (2001). Preliminary results from The deployment Of integrated teleconsultation services in rural Crete. In *Proceedings of the IEEE Computers in Cardiology*, (pp. 671-674), Rotterdam, Sept 21-25.

Chuah, M. (2002). Reality instant messenger. In *Proceedings of the 2nd Workshop on Personalization in Future TV (TV02)*. Malaga, Spain.

Clear, T., & Kassabova, D. (2005). Motivational patterns in virtual team collaboration. In A. Young, & D. Tolhurst (Eds.), *Proceedings of Australasian Computing Education Conference 2005*, Newcastle, Australia, conferences in *Research and Practice in Information Technology*, Vol. 42.

Cobb, P. & Hodge, L. L. (2003 April 23). *Students' construction of identities as doers of mathematics in the context of statistical data analysis.* Talk presented as part of the session Identity, Equity and Mathematical Learning in the Context of Statistical Data. Chicago, IL. American Educational Research Association.

Cobb, P., & McClain, K. (2003, April 24). *Situating teachers instructional practices in the institutional setting of the school and school district.* Talk presented as part of the session, Supporting and Sustaining the Learning of Professional Teaching Communities in the Institutional Setting of the School and School District. Chicago, IL. American Educational Research Association.

Cohen, A. (1985). *The symbolic construction of community.* London: Tavistock Publications.

Cohill, A. M., & Kavanaugh, A. L. (1997). *Community networks: Lessons from Blacksberg, Virginia.* Norwood, MA: Artech House.

Coiera, E., & Clarke, R. (2004). e-Consent: the design and implementation of consumer consent mechanisms in an electronic environment. *Journal of the American Medical Informatics Association, 11*(2), 129-40.

Cole, M. (1990). Cultural Psychology: A once and future discipline? In J. J. Berman, (Ed.), *Cross-cultural perspectives, Nebraska Symposium on Motivation, 37*, 279-335. Lincoln: University f Nebraska Press.

The Complete Oxford English Dictionary. (1971). Oxford: Oxford University Press.

Connell, J. & Reynolds, P. (1999). The implications of technological Ddevelopments on tourist information centres. *Tourism Management, 20*(4), 501-509.

Cooperrider, D. (1986). *Appreciative inquiry: Toward a methodology fo understanding and enhancing organizational innovation.* Unpublished doctoral dissertation. Case Western Reserve University, Cleveland, Ohio.

Cooperrider, D. L., & Srivastva, S. (1987). Appreciative inquiry in organizational life. In W. Pasmore & R. Woodman (Eds.), *Research in organization change and development, 1*, 129-169. Greenwich, CT: JAI Press.

Cooperrider, D. L., & Whitney, D. (2005). *Appreciative inquiry: A positive revolution in change.* San Francisco: Berrett-Koehler.

Coppens, T., Trappeniers, L., & Godon, M. (2004). AmigoTV: Towards a social TV experience. *In Proceedings of the 2nd Euro iTV Conference,* Aalborg, Denmark.

Cortada, J. W., & Woods, J. A. (2000). *The Knowledge Management Yearbook 2000-2001.* Butterworth-Heinemann.

Cox, A. (2005). What are communities of practice? A comparative review of four seminal works. *Journal of Information Science, 31*(6), 527–540.

Cragin, M., & Shankar, K. (2006). Scientific data collections and distributed collective practice. *Computer Supported Cooperative Work, 15*(2-3), 185-204.

Creative Commons Sampling Licenses (2008), "*The Sampling Licenses*", Retrieved May 19, 2008, from http://creativecommons.org/about/sampling

Cross, R., Borgatti, S. P., & Parker, A. (2002). *Making invisible work visible: Using social network analysis to support strategic collaboration.* The Network Roundtable at the University of Virginia. Retrieved December 2007 from https://webapp.comm.virginia.edu/SnaPortal/portals%5C0%5Cmaking_invisible_work_visible.pdf

Cross, R., Parker, A. Prusak, L. & Borgatti, S. P. (2001). Knowing what we know: Supporting knowledge creation and sharing in social networks. *Organizational Dynamics, 30*(2), 100-120.

Cubranic, D., Murphy, C. G., Singer, J., & Booth, S. K. (2004). Learning from project history: A case study for software development. *ACM Conference on Computer Supported Cooperative Work (CSCW '04),* (pp. 82-91), New York: ACM Press.

Cullinan, C., & Agamanolis, S. (2002). Reflexion: A responsive virtual mirror. *Conference Companion, UIST 2002 Symposium on User Interface Software and Technology.*

Cummings, J., & Kiesler, S. (2005). Collaborative research across disciplinary and organizational boundaries. *Social Studies of Science, 35*(5), 703-722.

Curran, M. (1991). Appreciative inquiry: A third wave approach to organization development. *Vision/Action,* December, (pp. 12-14).

Cusumano, F. M. (1989). The software factory: A historical interpretation. *IEEE Software, 6*(2), 23-30.

D'Andrade, R. (1995). *The development of cognitive anthropology.* Cambridge: Cambridge University Press.

Dahan, E., & Hauser, J. (2002). The virtual customer. *Journal of Product Innovation Management, 19*(5), 332-353.

Daniel, B., Schwier, R. A., & McCalla, G. (2003). Social capital in virtual learning communities and distributed communities of practice. *Canadian Journal of Learning and Technology, 29*(3). Retrieved May 2007 from http://www.cjlt.ca/content/vol29.3/cjlt29-3_art7.html

Davenport, T. H., & Prusak, L. (1998). *Working knowledge: How organizations manage what they know.* Boston: Harvard Business School Press.

Davidow, W. H., & Malone, M. S. (1992). *The virtual corporation – Structuring and revitalizing the corporation for the 21st century.* New York: HarperCollins.

Davis, B. H., & Brewer, J. (1997). *Electronic discourse: Linguistic individuals in virtual space.* Albany: State University of New York Press.

Davis, F. D. (1989). Perceived usefulness, perceived ease of use and user acceptance of information technology. *MIS Quarterly, 13*(3), 319-340.

Davis, F. D. (1993). User acceptance of information technology: System characteristics, user perceptions and behavioral impacts. *International Journal of Man-Machine Studies, 38*(3), 475-487.

Davis, F. D., Bagozzi, R. P., & Warshaw, P. R. (1989). User acceptance of computer technology: A comparison of two theoretical models. *Management Science, 35*(8), 982-1003.

Davydov, V. V. (1988). Problems of developmental teaching: The experience of theoretical and empirical psychological research. *Soviet Education, Part I: 30*(8), 15-97; Part II: 30(), 3-38; Part III: 30(10), 3-77.

Davydov, V. V. (1990). *Types of generalisation in instruction: Logical and psychological problems in the structuring of school curricula.* Reston: National Council of Teachers of Mathematics.

De Angelis, M. (2006). *On the "tragedy of the commons" (that is, the tragedy of commons without communities).* Retrieved 4 December, 2006, from http://www.commoner.org.uk/blog/?p=79

de Souza, C., & Preece, J. (2004). A framework for analyzing and understanding on-line communities. *Interacting with Computers, 16*, 579-610.

Dean, M., Schreiber, G., et al. (2004). *OWL Web ontology language reference. W3C Recommendation, 10.*

Deaux, K., & Lafrance, M. (1998). Gender. In D. T. Gilbert, S. T. Fiske & G. Lindzey (Eds.), *Handbook of social psychology* (Vol. 4, pp. 788-827). New York: Random House.

Decker, S (2006). *The social Semantic desktop: Next generation collaboration infrastructure. Information Services & Use, 26(2), 139-144.*

Defense Department of USA (2004) Information technology (IT) community of practice. *Defense & AT-L, 33*(5), 79-80.

Dell'Erba, M., Fodor, O., Hopken, W., & Werthner, H. (2005). Exploiting Semantic Web technologies for harmonizing e-markets. *Information Technology & Tourism, 7*, 201–219.

Demiris, G., Parker Oliver, D., Fleming, D., & Edison, K. (2004). Hospice staff attitudes towards "Telehospice". *American Journal of Hospice and Palliative Medicine, 21*(5), 343-347.

Denning, P., & Dunham, R. (2006). Innovation as language action. *Communications of the ACM, 49*(5), 47-52.

Denzin, N. K. (1974). The methodological implication of symbolic interactionism for the study of deviance. *The British Journal of Sociology, 25*(3), 269-282.

Detienne, F. (2006). Collaborative design: Managing task interdependencies and multiple perspectives, *Interacting with Computers, 18*, 1-20.

Dewey, J. (1938). *Experience and education.* New York: The Macmillan Company.

Dewey, J. (1957). E*xperience and education.* New York: MacMillan.

Dewhurst, F. W., & Cegarra Navarro, J. G. (2004). External communities of practice and relational capital. *The Learning Organization: The International Journal of Knowledge and Organizational Learning Management, 11*(4/5), 322-31.

Dibb, S., Simkin, L., Pride, W. M., & Ferrell, O. C. (2006). *Marketing – Concepts and strategies.* 5th Ed. New York: Houghton Mifflin.

Dick, B. (2003, 4-5 may 2003). *What Can Action Researchers Learn from Grounded Theorists.* Paper presented at the Australia and New Zealand ALARPM/SCAIR Conference, Gold Coast, Australia.

Dierkes, M., Marz, L., & Teele, C. (2001). Technological visions, technological development, and organizational learning. In M. Dierkes, A.B. Antal, et al. (Eds.), *Handbook of Organizational Learning and Knowledge* (pp. 282-304). Oxford University Press.

DigiDelivery Overview. (2008). Retrieved May 19, 2008, from http://www.digidesign.com/index.cfm?langid=100&navid=38&itemid=4782&action=news_details

Dijkstra, S., Seel, N., Schott, F., Tennyson, R. D. (Eds.) (1997). *Instructional design: International perspectives,* Vol. 2. Mahaw, NJ: Lawrence Erlbaum.

Disease Management Association of America (2002). *Definition of disease management.* Retrieved on 6/10/2005 from http://www.dmaa.org/definition.html

DiSessa, A. A., & Minstrell, J. (1998). Cultivating conceptual change with benchmark lessons. In J. G. Greeno

& S. Goldman (Eds.), *Thinking practices* (pp.155-187). Mahwah, NJ: Lawrence Erlbaum.

Division of Health Promotion, World Health Organisation. (1998). Health promotion glossary [Data file]. Available from World Health Organisation Web site, http://www.who.int/hpr/NPH/docs/hp_glossary_en.pdf

Dogac, A., Kabak, Y., Laleci, G., Sinir, S., Yildiz, A., & Kirbas, S. (2004). Semantically enriched Web services for the travel industry. *ACM Sigmod Record, 33*(3), 21-27.

Donath, J. S. (1998). Identity and deception in the virtual community. In P. Kollock & M. Smith (Eds.), *Communities in cyberspace*. London: Routledge.

Donath, S. J. (2002). A Semantic approach to visualizing online conversations. *Communications of the ACM, 45*(4), 45-49.

Drucker, P. (1993) *Post-capitalist society*. Oxford: Butterworth-Heinemann.

Drucker, P. F. (1988). *The coming of the new organization* (pp. 53-65). Harvard Business Review, Summer.

Drucker, P. F. (1990). *The emerging theory of manufacturing*. Harvard Business Review (May/June), (pp. 94-102).

du Plessis, M. (2008). The strategic drivers and objectives of communities of practice as vehicles for knowledge management in small and medium enterprises. *International Journal of Information* Management, *28*(1), 61-67.

Ducheneaut, N., & Moore, R. J. (2004, April). *Gaining more than experience points: Learning social behavior in multiplayer computer games*. Position paper for the CHI2004 workshop on Social Learning Through Gaming, Vienna, Austria.

Ducheneaut, N., & Moore, R. J. (2004, November). *Let me get my alt: digital identiti(es) in multiplayer games*. Position paper for the CSCW2004 Workshop on Representation of Digital Identities, Chicago, IL.

Ducheneaut, N., & Moore, R.J. (2004). The social side of gaming: a study of interaction patterns in a massively multiplayer online game. In *Proceedings of the 2004 ACM conference on Computer Supported Cooperative Work*, 360-369.

Ducheneaut, N., Moore, R.J., & Nickell, E. (2004). Designing for sociability in massively multiplayer games: an examination of the 'third places' of SWG.' In J.H. Smith and M. Sicart (Eds.), *Proceedings of the Other Players conference*. Copenhagen: IT University of Copenhagen.

Ducheneaut, N., Moore, R.J., Oehlberg, L., Thornton, J.D., & Nickell, E. (2008). SocialTV: Designing for distributed, social television viewing. *International Journal of Human-Computer Interaction, 24*(2).

Ducheneaut, N., Yee, N., Nickell, E., & Moore, R.J. (2006). Alone together? Exploring the social dynamics of massively multiplayer games. In *Proceedings of the SIGCHI Conference on Human Factors in Computing Systems*, 407-416.

Duguid, P. (2005). The art of knowing: Social and tacit dimensions of knowledge and the limits of the community of practice. *The Information Society, 21*, 109-18.

Dustdar S., & Gall, H. (2003). Pervasive software services for dynamic virtual organizations. In Camarinha-Matos, L., & Afsarmanesh, H. (Eds.), *PRO-VE'03 – Processes and Foundations for Virtual Organizations, IFIP TC5/WG5.5 Fourth Working Conference on Virtual Enterprises* (pp. 201-208). Kluwer Academic Publishers.

Eccles, J. S. (1994). Understanding woman's educational and occupational choices: Applying the Eccles et al. model of achievement-related choices. *Psychology of Women Quarterly, 18*(4), 585-609.

Eccles-Parsons, J. (1984). Sex differences in mathematics participation. In M. W. Steinkamp & M. L. Maehr (Eds.), *Advances in motivation and achievement: Women in science* (Vol. 93-137). Greenwich, CT: JAI Press.

Ehin, C. (2000). *Unleashing intellectual capital*. Boston, MA: Butterworth-Heinemann.

Ehn, P. (1989). *Work-oriented design of computer artifacts*. Stockholm: Arbetslivscentrum.

Eichelberger, H., & Laner, Ch. (2006). *Internet(t)e Schulentwicklung auf SCHOLION*, Pädagogisches Institut Bozen, ISBN 9783 0001 8836-7.

Eichelberger, H., Kohlberg, H.-D., Laner, Ch., Stary, Ch., & Stary, E.(2008). *Reformpädagogik goes E-Learning*, Oldenbourg, München.

Elliot, A. J., & Dweck , C. S. (eds.) (2005). *Handbook of competence and motivation*. Guilford, NY.

Engeström, Y. (1999). Activity theory and individual and social transformation. In Y. Engeström, R. Miettinen & R. L. Punamäki (Eds), *Perspectives on activity theory* (pp. 19-38). Cambridge, MA: Cambridge University Press.

Engestrom, Y. (2001). Expansive learning at work: Toward an activity theory reconceptualization. *Journal od Eduaction and Work, 14*, 133-156.

Engstrom, Y. (1987). *Learning by expanding: An activity-theoretical approach to developmental research.* Orienta-Konsultit, Helsinki.

Engstrom, Y., Miettinen, R., & Punamaki, R-L. (1999). *Perspectives on activity theory.* Cambridge University Press, UK.

,Erickson, T. (2003). *Designing visualizations of social activity: Six claims.* Paper presented at the CHI '03 Human factors in computing systems, Ft. Lauderdale, Florida, USA.

Erickson, T., & Kellogg, W. (2001). Knowledge Communities: Online Environments for Supporting Knowledge Management and its Social Context. In M. Ackerman, P. Volkmar, and V. Wulf (Eds.), *Beyond Knowledge Management: Sharing Expertise*, (pp. 299-325), Cambridge, MA: MIT Press.

Erickson, T., & Kellogg, W. A. (2000). Social translucence: An approach to designing systems that support social processes. *ACM Trans. Comput.-Hum. Interact., 7*(1), 59-83.

Erickson, T., & Laff, M. R. (2001). *The design of the 'Babble' timeline: a social proxy for visualizing group activity over time.* Paper presented at the CHI '01 Human factors in computing systems, Seattle, Washington.

Erickson, T., Smith, D. N., Kellogg, W. A., Laff, M. R., Richards, J. T., & Bradner, E. (1999). Socially translucent systems: Social proxies, persistent conversation, and the design of Babble. In *ACM Conference on Human Factors in Computing Systems* (pp. 72-79). New York: ACM Press.

Euler, D. (2005). *Forschendes Lernen. Universität und Persönlichkeitsentwicklung*, Campus, Franfurt/Main.

Eysenbach, G., Powell, J., Englesakis, M., Rizo, C., & Stern, A. (2004). Health related virtual communities and electronic support groups: Systematic review of the effects of online peer to peer interactions. *British Medical Journal, 328*, 1166–1172.

Farmer, R. A., & Hughes, B. (2005). A situated learning perspective on Learning Object Design. In *Proc. ICALT'05*, IEEE.

Farnham, S., et al. (2003): Personal Map: Automatically Modeling the User's Online Social Network, *Human–Computer Interaction* (INTERACT 03), (pp. 567-574), Amsterdam: IOS Press.

Feier, C., Roman, D., Polleres, A., Domingue, J., Stollberg, M., & Fensel, D. (2005). Towards intelligent Web services: The Web service modeling ontology (WSMO). *International Conference on Intelligent Computing (ICIC)*.

Feldman, M. D. (2000). Munchausen by Internet: Detecting factitious illness and crisis on the Internet. *Southern Medical Journal, 93*(7), 669-672.

Ferlie, E. F. L., Wood, M., & Hawkins, C. (2005). The nonspread of innovations: The mediating role of professionals. *Academy of Management Journal 48*(1), 117-134.

Fernback, J. (2007). Beyond the diluted community concept: a symbolic interactionist perspective on online social relations. *New Media & Society, 9*(1), 49–69.

Fernstrom, C., Narfelt, H. K., & Ohlsson, L. (1992). Software factory principles, architecture and experiments, *IEEE Software, 9*(2) pp. 36-44.

Feste, C., & Anderson, R. M. (1995). Patient empowerment: From philosophy to practice. *Patient Education and Counselling, 126*, 139-144.

Fielding, R. T., & Taylor, R. N. (2002). Principled design of the modern Web architecture. *ACM Transactions on Internet Technology (TOIT), 2*(2), 115-150

Figallo, C., & Rhine, N. (2002). *Building the knowledge management network.* New York: John Wiley & Sons.

Finchman, R., & Clark, T. (2006). Within and beyond communities of practice: Making sense of learning through participation, identity and practice. *Journal of Management Studies, 43*(3), 641-53.

Fink, M. (2006). Social and interactive television: Applications based on real-time ambient – audio identification. In *Proceedings of the 4th Euro iTV Conference* (pp. 138-146). Athens, Greece.

Finkelstein, J., O'Connor, G., & Friedmann, R. H. (2001). Development and implementation of the home asthma telemonitoring (HAT) system to facilitate asthma self-care. In V. Patel, R. Rogers, & R. Haux (Eds.), *MedInfo 2001 proceedings*, Amsterdam: IOS Press.

Finn J. (1999). An exploration of helping processes in an online self-help group focusing on issues of disability. *Health and Social Work, 24*(3), 220-231.

FireLib. (2008). *FireLib software implementation.* Retrieved May 10, 2008, from http://www.fire.org/n=content&task=category&sectionid=2&id=11\&Itemid=29

Fischer, C. S. (1992). *America calling: A social history of the telephone to 1940.* Berkeley: University of California Press.

Fishbein, M., & Ajzen, I. (1975). *Belief, attitude, intention, and behavior: An introduction to theory and research.* Reading, MA: Addison-Wesley.

Fober, D., Letz, S., Orlarey, Y., Askenfeld, A., Hansen, K., & Schoonderwaldt, E. (2004). IMUTUS - An interactive music tuition system. *Proceedings of the Sound and Music Computing conference (SMC04),* Paris, France

Fodor, O., & Werthner, H. (2004-5). Harmonise: A step toward an interoperable e-tourism marketplace. *International Journal of Electronic Commerce, 9*(2), 11-39.

Fogel, J., Albert, S. M., Schnabel, F., Ditkoff, B. A., & Neugut, A. I. (2002). Internet use and social support in women with breast cancer. *Health Psychology, 21*, 398-404.

Fogel, J., Albert, S. M., Schnabel, F., Ditkoff, B. A., & Neugut, A. I. (2003). Racial/ethnic differences and potential psychological benefits in use of the Internet by women with breast cancer. *Psychooncology, 12*, 107-117.

Fokker, J., Brinke, M., Ridder, H., Westendorp, P., & Pouwelse, J. (2007). A demonstration of Tribler: Peer-to-peer television. In *Adjunct Proceedings of the 5th Euro iTV Conference* (pp. 185-186), Amsterdam, Netherlands.

Foster I. (2005). Service oriented science. *Science, 308*(5723), 814-817.

Foster, I. (2002). *What is the Grid? A three point checklist.* Argonne National Laboratory and University of Chicago.

Foster, I., & Kesselman, C. (1998). *The Grid: Blueprint for a new computing infrastructure*, San Francisco: Morgan Kaufmann Publishers Inc.

Foster, R., Daymon, C., & Tewungwa, S. (2002). Future reflections: Four scenarios for television in 2012. *Condensed Report for the Future Reflections Conference* led by Bournemouth Media School.

Fox, G., Pierce, M., Gannon, D., & Thomas, M. (2003). *Overview of Grid computing environments.* GFD-I.9. The Global Grid Forum.

Fox, H. S. A. (1981). Approaches to the adoption of the midland system. In T. Rowley (Ed.), *The origins of open field agriculture.* London: Croom Helm.

Franke, N., & Piller, F. (2004). Value creation by toolkits for user innovation and design: The case of the watch market. *The Journal of Product innovation management, 21*, 401-415.

Franke, N., & Shah, S. (2001). How communities support innovative activities: An exploration of assistance and sharing among innovative users of sporting equipment. *Sloan Working Paper #4164.*

Franklin, C. (2008). *How 3-D graphics work.* Retrieved May 10, 2008, from http://computer.howstuffworks.com/3dgraphics.htm

Frenkel, S., Korczynski, M., donoghue, L., & Shire, K. (1995). Re-constituting work: Trends towards knowledge work and info-normative control. *Work, Employment and Society, 9*(4), 773-796.

Fukui, K., Jacob, B., Brown, M., & Trivedi, N. (2005). Introduction to Grid computing. *IBM Redbooks.*

Fuller, J., Bartl, M., Ernst, H., & Muhlbacher, H. (2006). Community based innovation: How to integrate members of virtual communities into new product development. *Electronic Commerce Research, 6*, 57–73.

Fürlinger, St., Auinger, A., & Stary, Ch. (2004). Interactive annotations in Web-based learning environments. In *Proceedings of the ICALT'04*, IEEE, (pp. 360-364).

Gagliardi, F. (2006). *Production Grids: General overview.* Production Grid Session at Global Grid Forum 2006, Athens, Greece.

Garnett, G. (2001). The aesthetics of interactive computer music. *Computer Music Journal, 25*(1), 21-33.

Garratt, B. (1987). *The learning organization: And the need for directors who think.* Aldershot, Hampshire, England: Ashgate.

Garvin, D. A. (1993). Building a learning organization. *Harvard Business Review, 71*(4), 78-91.

Gasser, L., & Ripoche, G. (2003, December 3-4). Distributed collective practices and free/open source software problem management: Perspectives and methods. *2003 Conference on Cooperation, Innovation & Technologie (CITE'03)* (Université de Technologie de Troyes, France).

Gawlinksi, M. (2003). *Interactive television production.* Oxford: Focal Press.

Gee, J. P. (2002). Literacies, identities, and discourses. In M. J. Schleppegrell & M. C. Colombi (Eds.) *Developing advanced literacy in first and second languages: Meaning with power.* Mahwah, NJ: Lawrence Erlbaum Associates.

Geerts, D., Harboe, G., & Massey N. (2007). *Overview of social TV workshop, 5th Euro iTV Conference,* Amsterdam, Netherlands.

Gergen, K. J. (1990). Affect and organization in post-modern society. In S. Srivastva, D.L. Cooperrider, & Associates (Eds.), *Appreciative management and leadership: The power of positive thought and action in organizations* (1st ed., pp. 289-322). San Francisco, CA: Jossey-Bass Inc.

Ghittino A., Iatrino A., Modeo S., & Ricchiuti F. (2006). Living@room: A support for direct sociability through interactive TV. In *Adjunct Proceedings of the 5th Euro iTV Conference* (pp. 131-132). Amsterdam, Netherlands.

Gibson, J. J. (1966). *The senses considered as perceptual systems.* Boston: Houghton Mifflin.

Giddens, A. (1979). Central problems in social theory: Action, structure and contradiction in social analysis. Berkeley: University of California Press.

Giddens, A. (1984). *The constitution of society, Outline of the theory of structuration.* Cambridge: Polity Press.

Giddens, A. (1990). *The consequences of modernity.* Stanford, Calif.: Stanford University Press.

Giddens, A. (1991). *Modernitet og selvidentitet*, Kobenhavn Hans Reitzels Forlag. As transferred by Rasmussen, T.A. and Christensen, L.H. (2006), from user generated content and community communication for television. In *Proceedings of the 4th Euro iTV Conference* (pp. 27-31). Athens, Greece.

Giddens, A., Duneier, M., & Applebaum, R. P. (2005). *Introduction to sociology.* W.W. Norton & Company: College Books.

Gifford, B. R., & Enyedy, N. D. (1999, December 12-15). Activity centered design: Towards a theoretical framework for CSCL. *In proceedings of Computer Supported*

Collaborative Learning, (pp. 189-196). Palo Alto, CA. Lawrence Erlbaum Associates.

Girgensohn, A., & Lee, A. (2002). Making Web sites be places for social interactions. In *Proceedings of ACM 2002 Conference of Computer Supported Cooperative Work* (pp. 136-145): ACM Press.

Gochenour, H. P. (2006). Distributed communities and nodal subjects. *New Media & Society, 8*(1), 33-51.

Goffman, E. (1963). *Stigma: Notes on the management of spoiled identity.* Englewood Cliffs, NJ: Prentice-Hall.

Goffman, E. (2004). The presentation of self. In S.E. Cahill. (Ed.), *Inside social life: Readings in sociological psychology and microsociology* (pp.108-116). Los Angeles, California: Roxbury Publishing Company.

Goldin, R., Rochat, A., & Anderson, G. (2008). Pluralizing the screen: Converging gesture, environment & interface. In *Adjunct Proceedings of the 6th Euro iTV Conference* (pp. 138-141). Salzburg, Austria.

Goldman, S., Nagel, R., & Preiss, K. (1995). A*gile competitors and virtual organizations: Strategies for enriching the customer.* New York: van Nostrand Reinhold.

Gongla, P., & Rizutto, C. R. (2001). Evolving communities of practice: IBM Global Services experience. *IBM Systems Journal, 40*(4), 842-853.

Gongla, P., & Rizzuto, C. R. (2004). Where did that community go? Communities of practice that "disappear". In P. Hildreth & C. Kimble (Eds.), *Knowledge networks: Innovation through communities of practice* (pp. 295-307): Idea Group Publishing.

Google Earth software. (2008). Retrieved May 10, 2008, from http://earth.google.com/

Goro Otsubo (2007). Goromi-TV browsing for thousands of videos at will. In *Adjunct Proceedings of the 5th Euro iTV Conference* (pp. 187-188). Amsterdam, Netherlands.

Gourlay, S. (2002, April). *Tacit knowledge, tacit knowing or behaving?* Paper presented at the Third European conference on organizational knowledge, learning and capabilities.

Gourlay, S. (2003). The Seci Model of knowledge creation: Some empirical shortcomings. *4th European Conference on Knowledge Management,* 377-385.

Gourlay, S. (2004). 'Tacit knowledge': The variety of meanings in empirical research. *Fifth European Conference on Organizational Knowledge, Learning and Capabilities Innsbruck.*

Gourlay, S. (2006). Conceptualizing knowledge creation: A critique of Nonaka's Theory. *Journal of Management Studies, 43*(7), 1415-1436.

Graham, W., & Osgood, D. (1998). A real-life community of practice. *Training & Development,* 52(5), 34-38.

Greaves, Mark (2007). Semantic Web 2.0. IEEE Intelligent Systems, 22(2), 94-96

Greenfield, J., & Short, K. (2004). *Software Factories - Assembling Applications with Patterns, Frameworks, Models & Tools.* New York: John Wiley & Sons.

GRI, (2002). *Tour operators' sector supplement.* Presented at GRI 2002 Sustainability Reporting Guidelines,

Griffiths, M. D., Davies, M. N. O., & Chappell, D. (2003). Breaking the stereotype: The case of online gaming. *CyberPsychology and Behavior, 6,* 81–91.

Gruber, T. (2007). *Collective knowledge systems: Where the social Web meets the Semantic Web.* To appear in Journal of Web Semantics, 2007; http://tomgruber.org/writing/CollectiveKnowledgeSystems.htm

Guba, E. (1981). Criteria for assessing the trustworthiness of naturalistic inquiries. *Education Communication and Technology Journal, 29*(2).

Guba, E., & Lincoln, Y. (1998). Competing paradigms in qualitative research. In N. Denzin & Y. Lincoln (Eds.), *The landscape of qualitative research.* California: Sage Publications.

Gücker, R. (2007). *Wie E-Learning entsteht. Untersuchung zum Wissen und Können von Medienautoren,* kopaed, München.

Guerrero, J., Vanderdonckt, J., & Gonzalez, J. M. (2008). FlowiXML: A step towards designing workflow management systems. *International Journal of Web Engineering and Technology, 4*(2), 163-182.

Guerrero, J., Vanderdonckt, J., Gonzalez, J. M., & Winckler, M. (2008, March). Modeling user interfaces to workflow information systems. Paper presented in *4th International Conference on Autonomic and Autonomous Systems ICAS'2008*, Gosier, Guadeloupe.

Gulliksen, J., Göransson, B., Boivie, I., Blomkvist, S., Persson, J., & Cajander, A. (2003). Key principles for user-centred systems design. *Behaviour & Information Technology, 22*(6), 397-409.

Gutwin, C., Greenberg, S., & Roseman, M. (1996). Workspace Awareness in real-time distributed groupware: Framework, widgets, and evaluation. In A. Sasse, R. J. Cunningham, & R. Winder (Eds.), *People and computers XI,* (pp. 281-298).Berlin: Springer-Verlag.

Haakonssen, K. (1995). *Republicanism: A companion to contemporary political philosophy.* Cambridge: Blackwell.

Hackbarth, G., & Grover, V. (1999). The knowledge repository: Organization memory information systems. *Information Systems Management, 16*(3), 21-30.

Hagel III, J., & Armstrong, A.G. (1997). *Net gain: Expanding markets through virtual communities.* Boston: Harvard Business School Press.

Hagel, J. (1999). Net gain: Expanding markets through virtual communities. *Journal of Interactive Marketing, 13*(1), 55-65.

Hakken, D. (2002). Building our knowledge of virtual community: Some responses. In K. A. Renninger & W. Shumar (Eds), *Building virtual communities: Learning and change in Cyberspace* (pp. 355-367). Cambridge, UK: Cambridge University Press.

Hammann, R. B. (2000) Computernetze als verbindendes Element von Gemeinschaftsnetzen. In U. Thidecke, (Ed.), *Virtuelle Gruppen: Charakteristika und Problemdimensionen,* (pp. 221-243). Wiesbaden.

Handley, K., Sturdy, A., Fincham, R., & Clark, T. (2006). Within and beyond communities of practice: making sense of learning through participation, identity and practice. *Journal of Management Studies, 43*(3), 641-53.

Haque, R. S. (2008). Social TV: Lean-in versus lean-out. In *Adjunct Proceedings of the 6th Euro iTV Conference* (pp. 142-143). Salzburg, Austria.

Hardin, G. (1968). The Tragedy of the Commons. *Science, 62,* 1243-1248.

Harman, W. W. (1990). Shifting context for executive behavior: Signs of change and re-evaluation. In S. Srivastva, D. L. Cooperrider, & Associates (Eds.), *Appreciative management and leardership: The power of positive thought and action in organizations* (1st ed., pp. 37-54). San Francisco, CA: Jossey-Bass Inc.

Harper, M. F., Frankowski, D., Drenner, S., Yuqing, R., Yuqing, Kiesler, S., Terveen, L., et al. (2007). Talk amongst yourselves: inviting users to participate in online conversations. In *12th international conference on Intelligent user interfaces* (pp. 62-71). Honolulu, Hawaii, USA: ACM.

Harré, R., & Van Langenhove, L. (1991). Varieties of positioning. *Journal for the Theory of Social Behavior, 21*(4), 393-407.

Harrington, J. (1991). *Organizational Structure and Information Technology.* Hertfordshire, U.K.: Prentice-Hall International.

Harrison, C., & Amento, B. (2007). CollaboraTV – Making TV social again. In *Adjunct Proceedings of the 5th Euro iTV Conference* (pp. 137-138). Amsterdam, Netherlands.

Hartwick, J., & Barki, H. (1994). Explaining the role of user participation in information system use. *Management Science, 40*(4), 440-465.

Hawryszkiewycz, I. (1997). *Designing the networked enterprise.* Boston: Artech House Inc.

Haythornthwaite, C. et al. (2003). *Challenges in the practicce and study of distributed, interdisciplinary, collaboration.* GSLIS Technical Report No.: UIUCLIS-

-2004/1+DKRC. Retrieved September, 2006 from http://www.lis.uiuc.edu/~haythorn/hay_challenges.html

Heckscher, C. (1996). Defining the post-bureaucratic Types. In Heckscher & Donnellon (Eds.), *The Post-Bureaucratic Organization*. Sage.

Hedberg, B., Dahlgren, G., Hansson, J., & Olve, N. (1997). *Virtual organizations and beyond: Discover imaginary systems*. John Wiley & Sons Ltd.

Hedegaard, M. (1986). Instruction of evolution as a school project and the development of pupils' theoretical thinking. In M. Hildebrand-Nilshon & G. Ruckreim, (Eds.), *Workshop contributions to selected aspects of applied research. Proceedings of the 1st International Congress on Activity Theory* (Vol. 3). Berlin: System Druck.

Hedegaard, M. (1987). Methodology in evaluative research on teaching and learning. In F. J. van Zuuren, F. J. Wertz, & B. Mook (Eds.), *Advances in qualitative psychology: Themes and variations* (pp. 53-78). Lisse, Swets & Zeitlinger.

Hedegaard, M. (1990). The zone of proximal development as basis for instruction. In L. Moll (Ed.), *Vygotsky and education: Instructional implications and applications of sociohistorical psychology* (pp. 349-371). Cambridge: Cambridge University Press.

Heinemann, G. Z. A. (2002). Team performance in health care—assessment and development. In G. Stricker (Ed.), *Issues in the practice of psychology*, (p. 400). New York: Kluwer Academic/Plenum Publishers.

Held, D., & McGrew, A. (2003). *The global transformations reader: An introduction to the globalization debate*. Cambridge: Polity Press in association with Blackwell Pub.; Malden, MA: Distributed in the USA by Blackwell Pub.

Hemlin, S., Allwood, C. M., & Martin, B. R. (2004). *Creative Knowledge Environments: The influences on creativity in research and innovation*. Northampton, MA, USA: Edward Elgar.

Herr, P. M., Kardes, F. R., & Kim, J. (1991). Effects of word-of-mouth and product-attribute information on persuasion: An accesibility-diagnosticity perspective. *Journal of Consumer Research, 17*(March), (pp. 454-462).

Herring, S. (1996). Posting in a different voice: Gender and ethics in computer-mediated communication. In C. Ess (Ed.), *Philosophical approaches to computer-meidated communication* (pp. 115-145). Albany: SUNY Press.

Herzberg, F., Mausner, B., & Snyderman, B. B. (1959). *The motivation to work*. New York: John Wiley & Sons.

Hesselman, C., Derks, W., Broekens, J., Eertink, H., Gülbahar, M., & Poortinga, R. (2008). An open service infrastructure for enhancing interactive TV experiences. In *Adjunct Proceedings of the 6th Euro iTV Conference* (pp. 23-24). Salzburg, Austria.

HHI Fraunhofer. (2008). *Free2C autostereoscopic display*. Retrieved May 10, 2008, from http://www.hhi.fraunhofer.de/en/departments/im/products-services/interaction-modules/free2c.html

Hildreth, P., & Kimble, C. (2000). Communities of practice in the international distributed environment. *Journal of Knowledge Management, 4*(1), 27-38.

Hiltz, S. R., & Turoff, M. (1993). *Network Nation: Human Communication Via Computer (Revised Edition)*: The MIT Press.

Hi-Touch Working Group (2003). *Semantic Web methodologies and tools for intra-European sustainable tourism.* Retrieved from http://www.mondeca.com/articleJITT-hitouch-legrand.pdf

Hjalager, A.M. (2002). Repairing innovation defectiveness in Tourism. *Tourism Management, 23*(5), 465-474.

Hoadley, C., & Pea, R. D. (2002). Finding the ties that bind: Tools in support of a knowledge-building community. In K. A. Renninger & W. Shumar (Eds), *Building virtual communities: Learning and change in Cyberspace* (pp. 321-354). Cambridge, UK: Cambridge University Press.

Hoegl, M., & Schulze, A. (2005). How to support knowledge creation in new product development: An investigation of knowledge management methods. *European Management Journal, 23*(3), 263-273.

Hoffman, D. L., & Novak, Th. P. (1996). Marketing in hypermedia computer-mediated environments: Conceptual foundations. *Journal of Marketing, 60*(July), 50-68.

Holland, D., Lachicotte, W. Jr., Skinner, D., & Cain, C. (1998). *Identity and agency in cultural worlds.* Cambridge, MA: Harvard University Press.

Hoof, B. van den, Ridder, J. de & Aukema, E. (2004). *The eagerness to share: Knowledge sharing, ICT and social capital.* Working Paper, Amsterdam School of Communication Research, University of Amsterdam, The Netherlands.

Horner, D. S. (2001). The moral status of virtual action. In T. W. Bynum (Ed.), *Proceedings of the Fifth International Conference on the Social and Ethical Impacts of Information and Communication Technologies.*

Houston, T. K., Cooper, L. A., & Ford, D. E. (2002). Internet support groups for depression: A 1-year prospective cohort study. *American Journal of Psychiatry, 159*, 2062-2068.

Hoybye, M. T., Johansen, C., & Tjornhoj-Thomsen, T. (2005). Online interaction: Effects of storytelling in an Internet breast cancer support group. *Psychooncology, 14*(3), 211-220.

Hubbard, B. M. (1998). *Conscious evolution: Awakening the power of our social potential.* Novato, CA: New World Library.

Hudson, E. S., & Smith, E. I. (1996). Techniques for addressing fundamental privacy and disruption tradeoffs in awareness support systems. In *Proceedings of the 1996 ACM conference on Computer Supported Cooperative Work,* (pp. 248-257). New York: ACM Press.

Hummel, J., & Lechner, U. (2002). Social profiles of virtual communities. In *Proceedings of the 35th Hawaii International Conference on System Sciences.*

Humphrey, M. (2004). *Grid computing using .NET and WSRF.NET.* Tutorial at GGF11, Honolulu.

Iatrino, A., & Modeo, S. (2006). Text editing in digital terrestrial television: A comparison of three interfaces. In *Proceedings of the 4th Euro iTV Conference* (pp. 198-204). Athens, Greece.

Iatrino, A., Modeo, S., & CSP - ICT Innovation (2007). Living@room: A support for direct sociability through interactive TV. In *Adjunct Proceedings of the 5th Euro iTV Conference* (pp.131-132). Amsterdam, Netherlands.

IBM. (2005). *IBM WebSphere MQ Workflow V3.6 expands support for large enterprise workflow integration solutions.* Retrieved April 19, 2005, from http://www-01.ibm.com/common/ssi/cgi-bin/ssialias?infotype=an&subtype=ca&appname=GPA&htmlfid=897/ENUS205-096

Igbaria, M. (1999). The Driving Forces in the Virtual Society. *Communications of the ACM, 42*(12), 64-70.

Igbaria, M., Zinatelli, N., Cragg, P., & Cavaye, A. L. M. (1997). Personal computing acceptance factors in small firms: A structural equation model. *MIS Quarterly, 21*(3), 279-305.

Iverson, J. O. (2003). *Knowing volunteers through communities of practice.* Arizona State University. Arizona, USA.

Jagers, H., Jansen, W., & Steenbakkers, W. (1998). Characteristics of virtual organizations. In P. Sieber and J. Griese (Eds.), *Organizational Virtualness*, Proceedings of the VoNet-Workshop, April 27-28, Simowa Verlag, Bern.

Jakob Nielsen's Alertbox (1997). *WebTV Usability Review.* Retrieved May 13 (2008) from http://www.useit.com/alertbox/9702a.html

Jakobsson, M., & Taylor, T.L. (2003). The Sopranos meets EverQuest. Social networking in massively multiplayer online games. In *Proceedings of Digital Arts and Culture Conference,* 81-90.

Jarvenpaa, S. L., & Leidner, D. E. (1998). Communication and trust in global virtual teams. *Journal of Computer-Mediated Communication, 3*(4), 1-38.

Jarvenpaa, S., & Leidner, D. (1998). Communication and trust in global virtual teams. *Journal of Computer Mediated Communication, 3.*

Jarzabkowski, P. (2003). Strategic practices: An activity theory perspective on continuity and change. *Journal of Management Studies, 40*(1), 23-56.

Jarzabkowski, P. (2004). Strategy as practice: Recursiveness, adaptation, and practices-in-use. *Organization Studies, 25*(4), 529–560.

Jarzabkowski, P. (2005). *Strategy as practice: An activity-based approach.* London: Sage.

Jayasinghe, N. (May 2006), *Spannerworks White Paper.* Retrieved from http://www.spanerworks.com

Jensen, J. F. (2005). Interactive television: New genres, new format, new content. In *Proceedings of the Second Australasian Conference on Interactive Entertainment* (pp. 89-96). Sydney, Australia.

Jin, Y., & Hong, P. (2007). Coordinating global inter-firm product development. *Journal of Enterprise Information Management, 20*(5), 544-561.

Jones, Q. (1997). Virtual communities, virtual settlements & cyberarcheology: A theoretical outline. *Journal of Computer-Mediated Communication,* (3). Available at http://www.ascusc.org/jcmc

Jorna, R. (1998). Managing knowledge, *Semiotic Review of Books* (9 ed., Vol. 9, pp. 5-8).

Juriado, R., & Gustafsson, N. (2007). Emergent communities of practice in temporary inter-organisational partnerships. *The Learning Organization: The International Journal of Knowledge and Organizational Learning Management, 14*(1), 50-61.

Kakadadse, N. K., Kakadadse, A., & Kouzmin, A. (2003). Reviewing the knowledge management literature: Towards a taxonomy. *Journal of Knowledge Management, 7*(4), 75-91.

Kane, B., & Sans, D. (1998). Guidelines for the clinical use of electronic mail with patients. *Journal of the American Medical Informatics Association, 5,* 104-111.

Karkosi, K. (2006). *Hurricane Katrina Changed People in Uncommon and Unknown Ways.* Retrieved 16 January 2007, 2007, from http://www.associatedcontent.com/article/59042/hurricane_katrina_changed_people_in.html?page=2

Katz, J. (1998). *Luring the lurkers* [Electronic Version]. Retrieved 09.04.2008, from http://slashdot.org/features/98/12/28/1745252.shtml

Kavanaugh, A., Carroll, J. M., Rosson, M. B., Zin, T. T., & Reese, D. D. (2005). Community networks: Where offline communities meet online. *Journal of Computer-Mediated Communication, 10*(4), article 3. Retrieved May 13 from http://jcmc.indiana.edu/vol10/issue4/kavanaugh.html

Kazzak does Stormwind (n.d.). Retrieved 2 July 2006, from http://video.google.com/videoplay?docid=-982380251124231965

Kern, E-M., & Kersten, W. (2007). Framework for Internet-supported inter-organizational product development collaboration. *Journal of Enterprise Information Management, 20*(5), 562-577.

Kienle, A., & Wessner, M. (2006). Analysing and cultivating scientific communities of practice. *International Journal of Web Based Communities, 2*(4), 377-393.

Kim, A. J. (2000). *Community building on the Web: Secret strategies for successful online communities.* PeachPit Press. From http://www.naima.com/community

Kim, D. (1993). The link between individual and organizational learning. *Sloan Management Review,* (Fall), (pp. 37-50).

Kim, P., & Sawhney, H. (2002). A machine-like new medium - Theoretical examination of interactive TV. *Media, Culture and Society, 24,* 217-233.

Kimberly, T., Greenberg, S., & Gutwin, C. (2006). Providing artifact awareness to a distributed group through screen sharing, In *Proceedings of the ACM CSCW'06 conference* (pp. 99-108), New York: ACM Press.

Kimble, C. (2006). *Communities of Practice: Never Knowingly Undersold.* Paper presented at the EC-TEL 2006 Workshops, Crete, Greece.

Kimble, C., & Hildreth P. (2005). Dualities, Distributed Communities of Practice and Knowledge Management. *Journal of Knowledge Management, 9*(4), 102-113.

Kimble, C., & Hildreth, P. (2002). The Duality of Knowledge. *Information Research, 8*(1).

Kimble, C., & Hildreth, P. (2005). Dualities, Distributed Communities of Practice and Knowledge Management. *Journal of Knowledge Management, 9*(4), 102 - 113.

King, W. R. (1996). IS and the learning organization. *Information Systems Management, 13*(3): 78-80.

Kiss, J. (2008). Web 3.0 is all about rank and recommendation. *The Guardian*, February 4 2008, Retrieved 15 May 2008, from http://www.guardian.co.uk/media/2008/feb/04/web20?gusrc=rss&feed=media

Kitta, T. (2007). *Professional windows workflow foundation*. Indianapolis, IN: Wiley Publishing, Inc.

Klein, J. H. (2008). Some directions for research in Knowledge Sharing. *Knowledge Management Research and Practice, 6*, 41-46.

Klein, J. H., Connell, N., & Meyer, E. (2005). Knowledge characteristics of communities of practice. *Knowledge Management Research and Practice, 3*, 106-114.

Klemm, P., & Hardie, T. (2002). Depression in Internet and face-to-face cancer support groups: A pilot study. *Oncology Nursing Forum, 29*(4), E45-51.

Klemm, P., Bunnell, D., Cullen, M., Soneji, R., Gibbons, P., & Holecek, A. (2006). Online cancer support groups: A review of the research literature. *Computers, Informatics, Nursing, 21*, 136–142.

Kluge, E. W. (2000). Professional codes for electronic HC record protection: Ethical, legal, economic and structural issues. *International Journal of Medical Informatics, 60*(2), 85–96.

Koerselman, T., Larkin, O, & Ng, K., (2007), The MAV framework: Working with 3D motion data in Max MSP / Jitter. In *Proceedings of the 3rd International Conference on Automated Production of Cross Media Content for Multi-channel Distribution (AXMEDIS 2007)*. Barcelona, Spain

Kolo, C., & Baur, T. (2004). Living a virtual life: social dynamics of online gaming. *Game Studies: International Journal of Computer Game Research, 4* (1). [online journal], viewed 15 July 2005, http://www.gamestudies.org/0401/kolo/.

Kopecký, J., Vitvar, T., Bournez, C., & Farrell, J. (2007). SAWSDL: Semantic annotations for WSDL and XML schema. *IEEE Internet Computing*, (pp. 60-67).

Koschmann, T. (ed.) (1996). *CSCL: Theory and practice of an emerging paradigm*. Mahaw, NJ: Lawrence Erlbaum.

Kose, K., Grammalidis, N. Yilmaz, E. E., & Cetin, E. E. (2008). 3D wildfire simulation system. In *Proceedings of the International Society for Photogrammetry and Remote Sensing, ISPRS 2008*, Beijing, China.

Koutsonanos, D., Moustakas, K., Tzovaras, D., & Strintzis, M.G. (2004). Interactive cloth editing and simulation in virtual reality applications for theater professionals. In *5th International Symposium on Virtual Reality, Archaeology and Cultural Heritage* (Eurographics), Brussels.

Kraut, R., Patterson, M., Lundmark, V., Kiesler, S., Mukopadhyay, T., & Scherlis, W. (1998). Internet paradox: A social technology that reduces social involvement and psychological well-being? *American Psychologist, 53*(9), 1017-1032.

Kuhn, S., & Muller, M. J. (Eds.). (1993). *Participatory design: Special issue of the communications of the ACM* (Vol. 36): Associated Computing Machinery.

Kuhn, T. S. (1996). *The structure of scientific revolutions*. Chicago and London: University of Chicago Press.

Kurlander, D., Skelly, T., & Salesin, D. (1996). Comic Chat. In *Proceedings of the ACM SIGGRAPH 96*, (pp. 225-236). New York: ACM Press.

Kuutti, K. (1994). *Information systems, cooperative work and active subjects: The activity-theoretical perspective*. Doctoral thesis. (Research papers Series A 23, Department of Information Processing Science, University of Oulu, Finland).

LaJoie, S P. (ed.) (1998). *Computers as cognitive tools: The next generation.* Mahaw, NJ: Lawrence Erlbaum.

Land, F. (1985). Is an information theory enough? *The Computer Journal, 28*(3), 211-215.

Lassila, O., Swick, R., et al. (1999). Resource description framework (RDF) model and syntax specification. *W3C Recommendation, 22*, 2004-03.

Latour, B. (1987). *Science in action: How to follow scientists and engineers through society.* Cambridge, MA: Harvard University Press.

Latour, B. (1994). *We have never been modern.* Harvest Wheatsheaf, Hertfordshire.

Latta, C. (1991). Notes from the NetJam Project. *Leonardo Music Journal, 1.*

Lau, A., Yen, Y., & Chau, P. Y. K. (2001). Adoption of online trading in the Hong Kong financial market. *Journal of Electronic Commerce Research, 2*(2), 58-65.

Laudon, K.-C., & Laudon, J. P. (2005). *Essentials of management information systems: Managing the digital firm, 6*[th] edition. Upper Saddle River, NJ: Pearson.

Laure, E. (2006). *EGEE – A large scale production Grid infrastructure.* Production Grid Session at Global Grid Forum 2006, Athens, Greece.

Lave, J. (1993). The practice of learning. In S. Chaiklin & J. Lave (Eds.), *Understanding practice: Perspectives on activity and context.* New York: Cambridge University Press.

Lave, J. (1997). The culture of acquisition and the practice of understanding. In D. Kirschner & J. A. Whitson (Eds.), *Situated cognition: Social, semiotic and psychological perspectives.* Mahwah, NJ: Lawrence Erlbaum Associates, Inc.

Lave, J., & Wegner, E. (1991). *Situated Learning – Legitimate peripheral participation.* Cambridge, MA: Cambridge University Press.

Lazar, J., & Preece, J. (1998). *Classification schema for online communities.* Paper presented at the 1998 Association for Information Systems, Americas Conference.

Lazar, J., & Preece, J. (2002). Social considerations in online communities: Usability, sociability, and success factors. In H. van Oostendorp (Ed.), *Cognition in the digital world* (pp. 127-152). Mahwah: NJ: Lawrence Erlbaum Associates Inc. Publishers.

Lee, A., Girgensohn, A., & Zhang, J. (2004). Browsers to support awareness and social interaction. *IEEE Computer Graphics and Applications*, September/October, (pp. 66-75).

Lee, A., Girgensohn, A., & Zhang, J. (2004). Browsers to support awareness and social interaction. *IEEE Computer Graphics and Applications, 24*(5), 66-75.

Lee, H., et al. (2008). Balancing simplicity and functionality in designing user-interface for an interactive TV. In *Adjunct Proceedings of the 6*[th] *Euro iTV Conference* (pp. 277-278). Salzburg, Austria.

Lee, J. (2003). Building successful communities of practice: CoPs are networks of activities. *Information Outlook.*

Lehrer, R. (1993). Authors of knowledge: Patterns of hypermedia design. In S.P. LaJoie, S.J. Derry, (Eds.), *Computers as cognitive tools.* Mahaw, NJ: Lawrence Erlbaum.

Leidig, T. (2001). L3-Towards an open learning environment. *ACM J. Educ. Res. in Computing, 1*(1), Art. 5.

Leidner, D., & Jarvenpaa, S. (1995). The use of information technology to enhance management school education: A theoretical view. *MIS Quarterly*, Sept.

Leimeister, J. M., Knebel, U., & Krcmar, H. (2007). Exploring mobile information systems for chronically ill adolescent patients. *International Journal of Web Based Communities, 3*(4), 404-415.

Lektorsky, V. A. (1984). *Subject, object, cognition.* Moscow: Progress.

Leonard-Barton, D. (1995). *Wellsprings of knowledge: Building and sustaining the sources of innovation.* Boston: Harvard Business School Press.

Leont'ev, A. N. (1978). *Activity, consciousness, and personality.* Engelwood Cliffs, NJ: Prentice-Progress.

Leont'ev, A. N. (1981). *Problems of the development of the mind.* Moscow: Progress.

Lesko, L. J. (2007). Personalized medicine: Elusive dream or imminent reality? *Clinical Pharmacology & Therapeutics, 81*(6), 807-816.

Lesser, E., & Everest, K. (2001). Using communities of practice to manage intellectual capital. *Ivey Business Journal, 65*(4), 37-42.

Lesser, E., & Prusak, L. (1999). *Communities of practice, social capital and organizational knowledge.* White Paper, IBM Institute for Knowledge Management. Retrieved May 10th, 2007 from http://www.providersedge.com/docs/km_articles/Cop_-_Social_Capital_-_Org_K.pdf

Lethbridge, N. (2001). An I-based taxonomy of virtual organizations and the implications for effective management. *Informing Science, 4*(1), 17-24.

Levine, L. (2001). Integrating knowledge and processes in a learning organization. *Information Systems Management,* (Winter), (pp. 21-32).

Levine, P. (2002). Symposium: Democracy in the electronic era. *The Good Society, 11*(3), 3-9.

Lewin, K. (1951/1997). *Field theory in social science.* Walhsington, DC: American Psychological Association.

Lewis, S., Passmore, J., & Cantore, S. (2008). *Appreciative inquiry for change management: Using AI to facilitate organizational development.* London: Kogan Page.

Library of Congress. (2003). *American Folklife Center at the Library of Congress to House the Storycorps Archive.* Retrieved 18 April, 2006, from http://www.loc.gov/today/pr/2003/03-168.html

Liedtka, J. (1999). Linking competitive advantage with communities of practice. *Journal of Management Inquiry, 8*(1), 5-17.

Lifton, R. J. (1993). *The protean self: Human resilience in an age of fragmentation.* New York: Basic Books.

Limbourg, Q., & Vanderdonckt, J. (2004). UsiXML: A user interface description language supporting multiple levels of independence. In M. Matera & S. Comai, (Eds.), *Engineering advanced Web applications,* (pp. 325-338). Paramus, NJ: Rinton Press.

Lindkvist, L. (2005). Knowledge Communities and Knowledge Collectivities: A Typology of Knowledge Work in Groups. *Journal of Management Studies, 42*(6), 1189-1210.

Ling, K., Beenen, G., Ludfort, P., Wang, X., Chang, K., Li, X., et al. (2005). Using social psychology to motivate contributions to online communities. *Journal of Computer-Mediated Communication, 10*(4), article 10.

Linn, M. C. (2000). Designing the knowledge integration environment: The partnership inquiry process. *International Journal of Science Education, 22* (8), 781-796.

Lipnack, J., & Stamps, J. (1997). *Virtual teams: Reaching across space, time, and organizations with technology.* New York: Wiley & Sons Ltd.

Livingstone, S., & Bovill, M., (1999). Young people, new media. *Summary report of the research project: Children, Young People and the Changing Media Environment.* As accessed on http://www.lse.ac.uk/Depts/Media/people/slivingstone/young people report.pdf

Lorimer, W., & Manion, J. (1996). Team-based organizations: Leading the essential transformation. *PFCA Rev,* (pp. 15–19).

Lounsbury, M., & Crumley, T. E. (2007). New Practice Creation: An Institutional Perspective on Innovation. *Organization Studies, 28,* 993-1012.

Loyarte, E., & Rivera, O. (2007). Communities of practice: A model for their cultivation. *Journal: Journal of Knowledge Management, 113,* 67-77.

LSDA (2004). *Mobile Learning and m-learning.* http://www.lsda.org.uk/research/ResearchCentres/RFSTechEnhanceLearn.asp?section=8

Lueg, C. (2001). Information dissemination in virtual communities as challenge to real world companies. In *Towards the E-Society: E-Commerce, E-Business and E-Government, 74*, 261-270.

Lueg, C. (2003). Knowledge sharing in online communities and its relevance to knowledge management in the e-business era. *International Journal of Electronic Business, 1*(2), 140-151.

Lull, J. (1990). *Inside family viewing: Ethnographic research on television's audiences.* London: Routledge.

Lundkvist, A. (2004). User Networks as Sources of Innovation. In P. Hildreth & C. Kimble (Eds.), *Knowledge Networks: Innovation through Communities of Practice* (pp. 96-105): Idea Group Publishing.

Luyten, K., Thys, K., Huypens, S., & Coninx, K. (2006). Telebuddies: Social stitching with interactive television. *CHI 2006*, Montreal Canada. Available at: http://research.edm.uhasselt.be/kris/research/projects/telebuddies/

Lyotard, J-F. (1984). *The postmodern condition: A report on knowledge.* Minneapolis: University of Minnesota Press.

MacInnes, I. (2006). Property rights, legal issues, and business models in virtual world communities. *Electronic Commerce Research, 6*(1), 39-56.

Mackay, W. (1999). Media spaces: Environments for informal multimedia interaction. In Beaudouin-Lafon (Editor), *Computer supported cooperative work* (pp. 55-82). New York: John Wiley & Sons Ltd.

Macklin, B. (2002). What every marketer needs to know about iTV. *eMarketer*, http://www.broadbandbananas.com/wem.pdf

Malhotra, Y. (2000). Knowledge management and new organization forms: A framework for business model innovation. In Y. Malhotra (Ed.), *Knowledge management and virtual organizations* (pp. 2-19). Hershey, PA: Idea Group Publishing.

Malone, D. (2002). Knowledge management: A model for organizational learning. *International Journal of Accounting Information Systems, 3*(2), 111-124.

Mandviwalla, M., & Olfman, L. (1994). What do groups need? A proposed set of generic groupware requirements. *ACM Transactions on Computer-Human Interaction, 1*(3), 245-268.

Mantzari, E., & Vrechopoulos, A., (2007), "My Social Tube": User fenerated content and communication on interactive digital television. In *Adjunct Proceedings of the 5th European Interactive TV Conference*, (pp. 241-246). Amsterdam.

Marks, M., Mathieu, J., & Zaccaro, S. (2001). A temporally based framework and taxonomy of team processes. *Academy of Management Review, 26*, 356-376.

Martin, D., Paolucci, M., McIlraith, S., Burstein, M., McDermott, D., McGuinness, D., et al. (2004). Bringing Semantics to Web Services: The OWL-S Approach. In *Proceedings of the First International Workshop on Semantic Web Services and Web Process Composition (SWSWPC 2004)*, (pp. 6-9).

Marx, K., & Engels, F. (1968). *The German ideology.* Moscow: Progress.

Mas, J. (2005). *Software libre: técnicamente viable, económicamente sostenible y socialmente justo.* Zero Factory, S.L. Barcelona.

Masthoff, J. (2004). Group modelling: Selecting a sequence of television items to suit a group of viewers. *User Modelling and User-Adopted Interaction, 14*, 37-85. Kluwer Academic Publishers, Netherlands.

Mathieson, K. (1991). Predicting user intentions: comparing the technology acceptance model with the theory of planned behavior. *Information Systems Research, 2*(3), 173-191.

Maturana, H., & Varela, F. (1998). *The Tree of Knowledge: The Biological Roots of Human Understanding.* Boston, MA: Shambala.

Mawasha, P. R., Lam, P. C., Vesalo, J., Leitch, R., & Rice, S. (2001). Girls entering technology, science, math and research training (GET SMART): A model for preparing girls in science and engineering disciplines. *Journal of Women and Minorities in Science and Engineering, 7*(1), 49-57.

Mazanec, P., Bartel, J., Buras, D., Fessler, P., Hudson, J., Jacoby, M., Montana, B., & Phillips, M. (2002). Transdisciplinary pain management: a holistic approach. *Journal of Hospice & Palliative Nursing, 4*(4), 228-234.

McDermott, R. (1999). Learning across teams: How to build communities of practice in team organizations. *Knowledge Management Review, 2*(2), 32.

McDermott, R. (1999). Nurturing three dimensional communities of practice: How to get the most out of human networks. *Knowledge Management Review, 2*(5), 26.

McDermott, R. (2000). Critical success factors in building communities of practice. *Knowledge Management Review, 3*(2), 5.

McGregor, D. (1960). *The human side of enterprise.* New York: McGraw Hill.

McIlraith, Sheila A., Cao Son, Tran, & Zeng, Honglei (2001). Semantic Web Services. *IEEE Intelligent Systems, 16*(2), 46-53

McLure Wasko, M., & Faraj, S. (2000). "It is what one does": Why people participate and help others in electronic communities of practice. *The Journal of Strategic Information Systems, 9*(2-3), 155-173.

McQuail, D. (1998). *Mass communication theory: An introduction.* London: Sage Publications.

McWilliam, G. (2000). Building stronger brands through online communities. *Sloan Management Review, 41*(3), 43- 54.

Mead, G. H. (1938). *The philosophy of act.* Chicago: University of Chicago Press.

Meder, N. (2002). Didaktische Ontologien, In *Globalisierung und Wissensorganisation: Neue Aspekte für Wissen, Wissenschaft und Informationssysteme*, Vol. 6: Fortschritte in der Wissensorganisation, eds Ohly, G.R.H.P.; Siegel, A., Ergon Verlag, Würzburg, pp. 401-406.

Michinov, N., Michinov, E., & Toczek-Capelle, M.-C. (2004). Social identity, group processes, and performance in synchronous computer-mediated communication. *Group Dynamics, 8*(1), 27-39.

Middleton, M., & Lee, J. (2007). *Cultural institutions and Web 2.0.* Eveleigh, New South Wales: Smart Internet Technology CRC.

Miles, R. E., & Snow, C. C. (1986). Organizations: New concepts for new forms. *California Management Review, 28*, 62-73.

Millen, D. R., Fontaine, M. A., & Muller, M. J. (2002). Understanding the benefit and costs of communities of practice. *Communications of the ACM, 45*(4), 69-73.

Missikoff, M., Werthner, H., Hopken, W., Dell'Ebra, M., Fodor, O., & Formica, A. (2003). HARMONISE: Towards interoperability in the tourism domain. In *Proceedings of information and communication technologies in tourism 2003, ENTER 2003*, (pp. 58–66). Helsinki: Springer.

Moller, K., Bojars, U., & Breslin, J. (2006). Using Semantics to enhance the blogging experience. In I*3rd European Semantic Web Conference (ESWC2006), LNCS, 4011*, 679-696.

Mollison, B. (1990). *Permaculture: A practical guide for a sustainable future.* Washington, DC: Island Press.

Moore, T. D., & Serva, M. A. (2007). *Understanding member motivation for contributing to different types of virtual communities: A proposed framework.* Paper presented at the ACM SIGMIS CPR conference on Computer personnel doctoral consortium and research conference: The global information technology workforce, St. Louis, Missouri, USA.

Morlion, B., Knoop, C., Paiva, M., & Estenne, M. (2002). Internet-based home monitoring of pulmonary function after lung transplantation. *American Journal of Respiratory and Critical Care Medicine, 165*(5), 694-697.

Moustakas, K., Koutsonanos, D., Tzovaras, D., & Strintzis, M.G. (2005). Enhancing costume designer creativity utilizing haptic interaction in cloth editing applications. In *HCI International Conference*, Las Vegas USA.

Moustakas, K., Tzovaras, D., & Nikolakis, G. (2007). Simulating the use of ancient technology works using advanced virtual reality technologies. *International Journal of Architectural Computing, Special Issue on Cultural Heritage, 02*(05), 255-282.

Mowshowitz, A. (1997). Virtual organization. *Comm. ACM, 40*(9), 30-37.

Mühlhäuser M., Welzl M., Borchers J., & Gutkas R. (2001). GlobeMusic: The Internet scale of eMusic-making. In *Proceedings of the International Conference on Web Delivery of Music (Wedelmusic)*, Florence, Italy.

Mutch, A. (2003). Communities of practice and habitus: A critique. *Organization Studies, 24*(3), 383-401.

Nardi, B., Whittaker, S., & Bradner, E. (2000). Interaction and outeraction: Instant messaging in action. In *Proceedings of the ACM CSCW Conference* (pp. 79-88). New York: ACM Press.

NIIIP. (1996). *The NIIIP reference architecture*. National Industrial Information Infrastructure Protocols. Retrieved from: http://www.niiip.org.

Nikolakis, G., Moustakas, K., Tzovaras, D., & Harissis, T. (2004). Interactive simulation of ancient technology works. In *5th International Symposium on Virtual Reality, Archaeology and Cultural Heritage* (Eurographics).

Nonaka, I. (1991). The Knowledge-Creating Company. *Harvard Business Review*(69), 96-104.

Nonaka, I. (1994). A dynamic theory of organizational knowledge creation. *Organization Science, 5* (1), 14-37.

Nonaka, I., & Takeuchi, H. (1995). *The Knowledge creating company: How Japanese companies create the dynamics of innovation.* Oxford University Press.

Nonaka, I., Umemoto, K., & Senoo, D. (1996). From information processing to knowledge creation: A paradigm shift in business management. *Technology in Society, 18*(2), 203-218.

Nonnecke, B., & Preece, J. (2000). *Lurker demographics: Counting the silent. Proceedings of CHI 2000. 73-80. The Hague, Netherlands: ACM.* Paper presented at the CHI, The Hague, Neatherlands.

Nonnecke, B., & Preece, J. (2001). *Why lurkers lurk.* Paper presented at the Americas Conference on Information Systems, Boston, MA.

O'Brien, J. (1999). Writing in the body: gender (re)production in online interaction. In M.A. Smith, & P. Kollock (Eds.), *Communities in cyberspace*, (pp. 76–106), London: Routledge.

O'Leary, D. E. (1998). Enterprise knowledge management. *IEEE Computer, 31*(3), 54-61.

O'Reilly, T. (2005). *What is Web 2.0: Design patterns and business models for the next generation of software.* Retrieved 15 May 2008, from http://www.oreillynet.com/pub/a/oreilly/tim/news/2005/09/30/what-is-web-20.html

Oberholzer, F., & Strumpf, K. (2007). The effect of file sharing on record sales: An empirical analysis. *Journal of Political Economy, 115*(1).

Ochsner, K. N., & Lieberman, M. D. (2001). The emergence of social cognitive neuroscience. *American Pyschologist, 56*(9), 717-734.

Oehlberg, L., Ducheneaut, N., Thornton, J. D., Moore, R. J., & Nickell, E. (2006). Social TV: Designing for distributed, sociable television viewing. In *Proceedings of the 4th Euro iTV Conference* (pp. 251-259). Athens, Greece.

Ogaming.com (n.d.). WoW specific slang. Retrieved 2 July 2006, from http://wow.ogaming.com/data/1679~WoWSpecifcSlang.php

Olson, G., & Olson, J. (2000). Distance matters. *Human-Computer Interaction, 15*(2-3), 139-178.

Olson, G., & Olson, J. (2003). Mitigating the effects of distance on collaborative intellectual work. *Economic Innovation and New Technologies, 12*(1), 27-42.

Olson, M. (1965). *The logic of collective action.* Cambridge: Harvard University Press.

Orbist, M. (2007). My Home: Let users design their own social TV. In *Adjunct Proceedings of the 5th European Conference of Interactive Television* (pp. 133-134). Amsterdam, Netherlands.

Orem, S. L., Binkert, J., & Clancy A. L. (2007). *Appreciative coaching: A positive process for change.* San Francisco, CA: Jossey-Bass.

Orlikowski, J. W. (2002). Knowing in practice: Enacting a collective capability in distributed organizing. *Organization Science, 13*(3), 249-273.

Orlikowski, W. (2000). Using technology and constituting structure: A practice lens for studying technology in organizations. *Organization Science, 12*, 404–428.

Packard, B. W.-L. (2003). Web-based mentoring: Challenging traditional models to increase women's access. *Mentoring & Tutoring, 11*(1), 53-65.

Packard, B. W.-L., & Hudging, J. A. (2002). Expanding college women's perceptions of physicists' lives and work through interactions with a physics careers Web site. *Journal of College Science Teaching, 32*(3), 164-170.

Palmer, A. & McCole, P. (2000). The role of electronic commerce in creating virtual tourism destination marketing organizations. *International Journal of Contemporary Hospitality Management, 12*(3), 198-204.

Papadogiorgaki, M., Grammalidis, N., Sarris, N., & Strintzis, M.G. (2004). Synthesis of virtual reality animations from SWML using MPEG-4 body animation parameters. In *Workshop on the Representation and Processing of Sign Languages, 4th International Conference on Language Resources and Evaluation LREC 2004*, Lisbon, Portugal.

Pascual, M. M., Salvador, C. C. H., Sagredo, P. P. G., Marquez-Montes, J. J., Gonzalez, M. M. A., Fragua, J. J. A., Carmona, M. M., Garcia-Olmos, L. L. M., Garcia-Lopez, F. F., Munoz, A. A., & Monteagudo, J. J. L. (in print). Impact of patient-general practitioner short messages based interaction on the control of hypertension in a follow-up service for low-to-medium risk hypertensive patients. A randomized controlled trial. *IEEE Transactions on Information Technology in Biomedicine*.

Paternò, F. (1999). *Model based design and evaluation of interactive applications*. Berlin:Springer Verlag.

Peltier, S., et al. (2003). The Telescience Portal for Advanced Tomography Applications. *Journal of Parallel and Distributed Applications, Special Edition on computational Grids, 63*(5), 539-550.

Penson, R. T., Benson, R. C., Parles, K., Chabner, A. B., & Lynch, J. T. Jr. (2002). Virtual connections: Internet health care. *Oncologist, 7*(6), 555–568.

Percival, G., Wang, Ye, & Tzanetakis, G. (2007), *Effective use of multimedia for computer-assisted musical instrument tutoring. ACM Workshop on Educational Multimedia and Multimedia Education (EMME-07)*, Augsburg, Germany.

Perry, E., & Donath, J. (2004). *Anthropomorphic visualization: A new approach for depicting participants in online spaces.* Paper presented at the CHI '04 Human factors in computing systems, Vienna, Austria.

Pesce, M. (2005). The human use of human networks. Presented at *Designing the Future*, ISOC Australia.

Pew Internet Project. (2003). Let the games begin: Game technology and entertainment among college students. Available: http://www.pewinternet.org/pdfs/PIP_College_Gaming_Reporta.pdf [2008, Jan 1]

The Philadelphia Orchestra - Global Concert Series. (2008). Retrieved May 10, 2008, from http://www.philorch.org/internet2_3.html

Pitsillides, A., Pitsillides, B., Samaras, G., Dikaikos, M., Christodoulou, E., Andreou, P., & Georgiadis, D. (2004). DITIS: A collaborative virtual medical team for home healthcare of cancer patients. In R. H. Istepanian, S. Laxminarayan, & C. S. Pattichis (Eds.), *M-Health: Emerging mobile health systems*. New York: Kluwer Academic/Plenum Publishers.

Plale, B. D., Gannon, J., Brotzge, K., Droegemeier, J., Kurose, D., McLaughlin, R., Wilhelmson, S., Graves, M., Ramamurthy, R. D., Clark, S., Yalda, D. A., Reed, E., Joseph, V., & Chandrasekar (2006). CASA and LEAD: Adaptive cyberinfrastructure for real-time multiscale weather forecasting. *IEEE Computer (special issue on System-Level Science), 39*(11), 56-63. Retrieved May 10, 2008, from http://doi.ieeecomputersociety.org/10.1109/MC.2006.375

Poblocki, K. (2005), The Napster network community. *First Monday, 10*(7), Retrieved May 10, 2008, from URL: http://www.firstmonday.org/issues/issue6_11/poblocki/

Powell, A., Piccoli, G., & Ives, B. (2004). Virtual teams: A review of current literature and directions for future research. *The DATA BASE for Advances in Information Systems, 35*(1), 6-36.

Preece, J. (2000). *Online communities: Designing usability, supporting sociability.* Chichester, England: John Wiley & Sons.

Preece, J., Nonnecke, B., & Andrews, D. (2004). The top five reasons for lurking: Improving community experience for everyone. *Computers in Human Behavior, 20*(1), 201-223.

Price, L. L., & Feick, L. F. (1984). The role of interpersonal sources and external search: An informational perspective. In Th.C. Kinnear, (Ed.), *Advances in Consumer Research, 11*, 250-255. Provo, UT: Association for Consumer Research.

Prudhommeaux, E., & Seaborne, A. (2008). *SPARQL query language for RDF. W3C Recommendation 15 January 2008.* Available from http://www.w3.org/TR/rdf-sparql-query/

Putnam, R. D. (2000). *Bowling alone: The collapse and revival of American community.* New York: Simon and Schuster.

Putnik, G. D., & Cunha, M. M. (Eds.) (2005). *Virtual enterprise integration: Technological and organizational perspectives.* Hershey, PA: Idea Group Publishing.

Quan-Haase, A., & Wellman, B. (forthcoming). How does the Internet affect social capital? In M. Huysman, & V. Wulf, (Eds.), *IT and social capital.*

Quico, C. (2003), Are communication services the killer applications for Interactive TV? Or "I left my wife because I am in love with the TV set". In *Proceedings of the 1st European Conference on Interactive TV,* (pp. 99-107). Brighton, UK.

Quinn, J. B. (1990). *The intelligent enterprise.* New York: The Free Press.

Quintas, P. (2002) Managing Knowledge in a New Century. In S. Little, S., P. Quintas, & T. Ray (Eds.), *Managing knowledge.* London; Thousand Oaks, CA: Sage.

Rafaeli, S., Raban, D., & Ravid, G. (2007). How social motivation enhances economic activity and incentives in the Google answers knowledge sharing market. *International Journal of Knowledge and Learning, 3*(1), 1-11.

Rainie, L. (2006), Life online: Teens and technology and the world to come. In *Proceedings of the Annual Conference of Public Library Association.*

Rama, O., & Hilton, J. (2006). Securing the virtual organization – Part 1: Requirements from Grid computing, *Network Security, 4,* 7-10.

Ramakrishnan, R., & Tomkins, A. (2007). Toward a peopleweb. *Computer, 40*(8), 63-72.

Rashid, A. M., Ling, K., Tassone, R. D., Resnick, P., Kraut, R., & Riedl, J. (2006). *Motivating participation by displaying the value of contribution.* Paper presented at the Conference on Human Factors in computing systems, Montréal, Québec, Canada.

Rasmussen, T. A. (2005), The sociability of interactive television. In J.F. Jensen (Ed.), *User-centred ITV systems, Programmes and Applications, Proceedings of the 3rd Euro iTV Conference,* Aalborg.

Rasmussen, T. A., & Christensen, L. H. (2006). User generated content and community communication for television. In *Proceedings of the 4th Euro iTV Conference* (pp. 27-31). Athens, Greece.

Reed, J. (2007). *Appreciative inquiry: Research for change.* London: Sage Publications.

Reichling, T., Veith, M., & Wulf, V. (2007). Expert recommender: Designing for a network organization, *Computer Supported Cooperative Work, 16*(4-5), 431-465.

Reigeluth, C. M. (ed.) (1998). *Instructional design theories and models: The current state-of-the-art,* 2nd edition. Mahaw, NJ: Lawrence Erlbaum.

Renaud, A., Carôt, A., & Rebelo, P. (2007), Networked music performance: State of the art. In *Proceedings of the AES 30th International Conference,* Saariselkä, Finland

Renninger, K. A. (2000). Individual interest and its implications for understanding intrinsic motivation. In C. Sansone & J. M. Harackiewicz (Eds.*), Intrinsic and extrinsic motivation: The search for optimal motivation and performance* (pp. 373-404). New York: Academic.

Renninger, K. A., & Shumar, W. (2002). Community building with and for teachers: *The Math Forum* as a resource for teacher professional development. In K. A. Renninger & W. Shumar (Eds.), *Building virtual communities: Learning and change in cyberspace.* New York: Cambridge University Press.

Renninger, K. A., & Shumar, W. (2004). The centrality of culture and community to participant learning at and with The Math Forum. In S. Barab, J. Grey, & R. Kling, (Eds.), *Designing Virtual Communities.* New York: Cambridge University Press.

Restler, S., & Woolis, D. (2007). Actors and factors: Virtual communities for social innovation. *The Electronic Journal of Knowledge Management, 5*(1), 89-96.

Rheinfrank, J., & Evenson, S. (1996). Design Languages. In T. Winograd (Ed.), *Bringing design to software.* New York: Addison-Wesley.

Rheingold, H. (1993). *The Virtual Community: Homesteading on the Electronic Frontier.* Reading, MA: Addison-Wesley Pub.

Rheingold, H. (2001), Mobile virtual communities. *The Feature,* July 2001, Tapscott. Available at: http://www.thefeature.com/index.jsp? url=article.jsp?page id=12070

Rheingold, H. (2002). *Smart mobs: The next social revolution.* Cambridge: Perseus Books Group.

Rhoten, D. (2003). *National Science Foundation BCS-0129573: A multi-method analysis of the social and technical conditions for interdisciplinary collaboration.* Report for the Hybrid Vigor Institute. Retrieved October 2005 from http://hybridvigor.net/interdis/pubs/hv_pub_interdis-2003.09.29.pdf

Ridings, C. M., & Gefen, D. (2004). Virtual community attraction: Why people hang out online. *Journal of Computer-Mediated Communication, 10*(1), Arcticle 4.

Riemenschneider, C. K., Harrison, D. A., & Mykytyn, P. P. J. (2003). Understanding it adoption decisions in small business: integrating current theories. *Information & Managemeint, 40*(4), 269-285.

Ripeanu, M., Singh, P. M., & Vazhkudai, S. S. (2008). Virtual organizations. *IEEE Internet Computing, 12*(2), 10-12.

Roberto, M., Fer, A., & Botelho, C. (2008). iTV Project: An authoring tool for MHP based on a Web environment. In *Adjunct Proceedings of the 6th Euro iTV Conference* (pp. 214-216). Salzburg, Austria.

Roberts, J. (2006). Limits of communities of practice. *Journal of Management Studies, 43*(3), 623-639.

Roberts, P. (1998). Rereading Lyotard: Knowledge, commodification and higher education. *Electronic Journal of Sociology* 3(3) Special issue, April 1998, http://www.sociology.org/content/vol003.003/roberts.html

Roberts, P., & Henderson, R. (2000). Information technology acceptance in a sample of government employees: A test of the technology acceptance model. *Interacting with Computers, 12*(5), 427-443.

Roberts, T. L. (1998). *Are newsgroups virtual communities?* Paper presented at the CHI 98, Los Angeles.

Rogers, C. (1980/1995*). A way of being.* Boston: Houghton Mifflin.

Roure D. d., Jennings, N. R., & Shadbolt, N. (2003). The Semantic Grid: A future e-Science infrastructure. In F. Berman, A. J. G. Hey, & G. Fox (Eds.), *Grid computing: Making the global infrastructure a reality,* (pp. 437-470). John Wiley & Sons.

Rubinelli, S., Schulz, PJ., & Vago, F. (2008). Designing and evaluating online communities for promoting self-management of chronic low back pain. *International Journal of Web Based Communities,* 4(1,2), 80-97.

Runge, C. F., & DeFrancesco, E. (2006). Exclusion, inclusion, and enclosure: Historical commons and modern intellectual property. *World development, 34*(10), 1713-1727.

Russell, N., ter Hofstede, A. H. M., Edmond, D., & van der Aalst, W. M. P. (2004). *Workflow data patterns* (Tech. Rep. FIT-TR-2004-01). Brisbane, Australia: Queensland University of Technology.

Russell, N., van der Aalst, W. M. P., ter Hofstede, A. H. M., & Edmond, D. (2005). Workflow resource patterns. In O. Pastor & J. Falcao e Cunha, (Eds.), *17th Conference on Advanced Information Systems Engineering (CAiSE'05): Vol. 3520 of Lecture Notes in Computer Science* (pp. 216-232). Berlin: Springer-Verlag.

Sack, W. (2000). Conversation Map: A Content-Based Usenet Newsgroup Browser. In *Proceedings of the 5th International Conference on Intelligent User Interfaces (IUI 2000)*, (pp. 233-240), New York: ACM Press.

Saint-Onge, H., & Wallace, D. (2003). *Leveraging communities of practice for strategic advance.* Butterworth & Heinemann, USA.

Sandrock, J., & Tobin, P. (2007). *Critical success factors for communities of practice in a global mining company.* Nr Reading, Academic Conferences Ltd.

Sassen, S. (1998). *Globalization and its discontents: Essays on the new mobility of people and money.* New York: New Press.

Sassen, S. (2000). Spatialities and temporalities of the global: elements for a theorization. *Public Culture, 12*(1), 215-232.

Sawchuk, A. A, Chew, E., Zimmermann, R., Papadopoulos, C., & Kyriakakis C. (2003). From remote media immersion to distributed immersive performance. *Proceedings of the ACM SIGMM 2003 Workshop on Experiential Telepresence,* Berkeley, California, USA

Scacchi, W. (2005). Socio-technical interaction networks in free/open source software development processes. In Silvia T. Acuna & Natalia Juristo (Eds), *Software process modelling* (pp. 1-27). New York: Spinger.

Scacchi, W., Feller, J., Fitzgerald, B., Hissam, S., & Lakhani, K. (2006). Understanding free/open source software development processes. *Software Process – Improvement and Practice, 11*(2), 95-105.

Scardamalia, M., & Bereiter, C. (1994). Computer support for knowledge-building communities. *Journal of the Learning Sciences, 3*(3), 265-283.

Schaert, S. (2006). IkeWiki: A Semantic Wiki for collaborative knowledge management. In *Proceedings of the 15th IEEE International Workshops on Enabling Technologies: Infrastructure for Collaborative Enterprises,* (pp. 388-396).

Schatzki, T. R., Knorr-Cetina, K., & von Savigny E. (2001). *The practice turn in contemporary theory.* London: Routledge.

Schepers, J., & Wetzels, M. (2007). A meta-analysis of the technology acceptance model: Investigating subjective norm and moderation effects. *Information & Managemeint, 44*(1), 90-103.

Schewen, T. M. & Hara, N. (2003). Community of practice: A metaphor for online design? *Information Society, 19*(3), 257-271.

Schibelsky, L., Piccolo, G., Menckie Melo, A., & Calani Baranauskas, M. C. (2007). A convergent proposal for accessible interactive TV applications development. In *Adjunct Proceedings of the 5th European Conference of Interactive Television* (pp. 259-264). Amsterdam, Netherlands.

Schimke, D., & Stoeger, H. (2007). Web-basierte Teilnahme an SchülerInnenwettbewerben als Möglichkeit der Förderung begabter Mädchen im mathematisch-naturwissenschaftlichen Bereich [Web based Competitions for Students as a Way to Promote Talented Girls in the Field of Natural Sciences]. *Journal für Begabtenförderung, 2007*(1), 21-28.

Schlager, M. S., & Fusco, J. (2004). Teacher professional development, technology, and communities of practice: Are we putting the cart before the horse? In S. A. Barab, R. Kling, & J. H. Gray (Eds.), *Designing for virtual communities in the service of learning* (pp. 120-153). New York: Cambridge University Press.

Schmeder, A. (2008). *Everything you ever wanted to know about open sound control* (Tech. Rep.). Berkeley,

USA: Center for New Music and Audio Technologies, University of California.

Schmidt, K. (2000, September 19-22). Distributed collective practices: A CSCW perspective'. *Invited Talk, Conference on Distributed Collective Practices,* Paris, France 2000.

Schmidt, K. (2002). The problem with 'awareness'. *Computer Supported Cooperative Work, 11,* 285-298.

Schmidt, K., Wagner, I., & Tolar, M. (2007). Permutations of cooperative work practices: A study of two oncology clinics. In T. Gross, et al. (Eds.), *GROUP 2007: Proceedings of the International Conference on Supporting Group Work, (*pp. 1-10). New York: ACM Press.

Schon, D. A. (1983). *The reflective practitioner.* New York :Basic Books, Inc.

Schopp, L. H., Hales, J. W., Quetsch, J. L., Hauan, M. J., & Brown, G. D. (2004). Design of a peer-to-peer telerehabilitation model. *Telemedicine Journal and e-Health, 10*(2), 243-251.

Schuler, D. (1996). *New community networks: Wired for change.* New York: ACM Press.

Schuler, D., & Namioka, A. (Eds.) (1993). *Participatory design: principles and practices.* Hillsdale, New Jersey: Lawrence Erlbaum Associates.

Schulmeister, R. (1996). *Grundlagen hypermedialer Lernsysteme. Theorie – Didaktik – Design.* Bonn: Addison Wesley.

Schultz, F., & Pucher, H. F. (2003). www.deck - Wissensmanagement bei Volkswagen. *Industrie Management, 19*(3), 64-66.

Schultz, F., & Pucher, H. F. (2003). www.deck - Wissensmanagement bei Volkswagen. *Industrie Management, 19*(3), 64-66.

Schutz, W. (1958). *Firo: A three-dimensional theory of interpersonal behavior.* New York: Holt, Rinehart, and Winston.

Seaman, B. C., Mendonca, G. M., Basili, R. V., & Kim, Y-M. (2003). User interface evaluation and empirically-based evolution of a prototype experience management tool. *IEEE Transactions on Software Engineering, 29*(9), 838-850.

Seifert, T. (2004). Understanding student motivation. *Educational Research, 46,* 137-149.

Sellers, P. (2008). *MySpace cowboys.* retrieved May 19, 2008, from http://money.cnn.com/magazines/fortune/fortune_archive/2006/09/04/8384727/index.htm

Senge, P. (1990*). The fifth discipline: The art and practice of the learning organization.* London: Currency Doubleday.

Shadbolt, N., Berners-Lee, T., & Hall, W. (2006). The Semantic Web revisited. *IEEE Intelligent Systems, 21*(3) 96-101.

Sharf, B. F. (1997). Communicating breast cancer online: support and empowerment on the Internet. *Women Health, 26*(1), 65-84.

Sherry, J. F., & Kozinets, R. V. (2000). Qualitative inquiry in marketing and consumer research. In D. Iacobucci (Ed.), *Kellogg on marketing* (pp. 165-194). New York: John Wiley & Sons.

Shore, B. (1996). *Culture in mind: Cognition, culture and the problem of meaning.* New York: Oxford University Press.

Shrum, W., Chompalov, I., & Genuth, J. (2001). Trust, conflict and performance in scientific collaborations. *Social Studies of Science, 31*(5), 681-730.

Shumar, W., & Renninger, K. A. (2002). On community building. In K. A. Renninger & W. Shumar (Eds.), *Building virtual communities: Learning and change in cyberspace.* New York: Cambridge University Press.

Shumar, W., & Sarmiento, J. (2008). Communities of Practice at the Math Forum: Supporting teachers as professionals. In P. Hildreth, & C. Kimble, (Eds.), *Communities of practice: Creating learning environments for educators,* (pp. 223-239). Hershey, PA: IGI Global Publishing.

Sigala, M. (2007). Investigating the Internet's impact on interfirm relations: Evidence from the business travel management distribution chain. *Journal of Enterprise Information Management, 20*(3), 335-355.

Siwal A. (2008). *Facebook,Myspace Statistics.* retrieved May 19, 2008, from http://techradar1.wordpress.com/2008/01/11/facebookmyspace-statistics/

Smeds, R., & Alvesalo, J. (2003). Global business process development in a virtual community of practice. *Production Planning & Control, 14*(4), 361-372.

Smith, A., M., & Fiore, T. A. (2001). Visualization Components for Persistent Conversations. In *Proceedings of the ACM SIGCHI Conference on Human Factors in Computing Systems* (CHI 2001), (pp. 136-143), New York: ACM Press.

Sotiriou, C., & Piccart, MJ. (2007). Taking gene-expression profiling to the clinic: When will molecular signatures become relevant to patient care? *Nature Reviews, 7*, 545-553.

Soto, J. P., Vizcaino, A., Portillo-Rodriguez, J., & Piattini, M. (2007). Applying trust, reputation and intuition aspects to support virtual communities of practice. In *Knowledge-Based Intelligent Information and Engineering Systems*: Kes 2007 - Wirn 2007, Pt Ii, Proceedings, (pp. 353-360).

SoundWIRE Research Group at CCRMA, Stanford University (2008). Retrieved May 10, 2008, from http://ccrma.stanford.edu/groups/soundwire/

Spannerworks (2006). *What is social media?, an e-book.* Available at: http://www.spannerworks.com/ebooks

Sproull, L. S., & Kiesler, S. B. (1992). *Connections: New Ways of Working in the Networked Organization*: MIT Press.

Stalk, Jr., G., Evans, E., & Shulman, L. E. (1992). *Competing on capabilities: The new rules of corporate strategy.* Harvard Business Review, March-April.

Stanford Center for Innovations in Learning: News: CyberSImps. (2003). Retrieved May 10, 2008, from http://scil.stanford.edu/news/CyberSImps.html

Star, S. L. (1989). The structure of ill-structured solutions: Boundary objects and heterogeneous distributed problem solving. In M. N. Huhns & L. Gasser (Eds.), *Distributed Artificial Intelligence 2*. Morgan Kaufmann.

Star, S. L., & Griesemer, J. (1989). Institutional ecology, ,translations' and boundary objects: Amateurs and professionals in Berkeley's museum of vertebrate zoology. *Social Studies of Science, 19*, 387-420.

Starks, M., (1996). *3D for the 21st century-The Tsukuba Expo & beyond.* Retrieved May 10, 2008, from www.3dmagic.com/pdf/21ST-CEN.PDF

Stary, Ch. (2001). Exploring the concept of virtuality: Technological approaches and implications from tele-education. In A. Riegler, F.-M. Peschl, K. Edlinger, G., Fleck, & W. Feigl (Eds.), *Virtual reality - Cognitive foundations, technological issues & philosophical implications* (pp. 113-128). Peter Lang, Frankfurt/Main..

Stary, Ch. (2007). Intelligibility Catchers for Self-Managed Knowledge Transfer. *Proceedings ICALT07*, IEEE.

Statistisches-Bundesamt. (2006). Im Blickpunkt: Frauen in Deutschland 2006 [In the Spotlight Women in Germany 2006] [Electronic Version]. Retrieved 30.12.2007, from https://www-ec.destatis.de/csp/shop/sfg/vollanzeige.csp?ID=1018095

Stavness, N. (2005) *Supporting flexible workflow process with a progression model.* Unpublished master's thesis. University of Saskatchewan, Saskatoon.

Steinkuehler, C. A. (2004). A Discourse analysis of MMOG talk. In J. H. Smith & M. Sicart (Eds.), In *Proceedings of the Other Players Conference*, Copenhagen: IT University of Copenhagen.

Stewart, J. (2004). Interactive television at home: Television meets the Internet. *The Future of TV*, v.4.2, March (Published in Cathy Toscan - Jens Jensen eds. 1999, Aalborg University Press).

Stewart, T. A. (1997). *Intellectual capital: The new wealth of organizations.* New York: Doubleday.

Stockdale, R., & Borovicka, M. (2006). Developing an online business community: A travel industry case study. In *Proceedings of the 39th Hawaii International Conference on System Sciences*, (pp. 134-143), IEEE Computer Society.

Stoeger, H. (2007). Berufskarrieren begabter Frauen [Careers of talented Women]. In K. A. Heller & A. Ziegler (Eds.), *Begabt sein in Deutschland [Being Gifted in Germany]* (pp. 265-293). Berlin: LIT.

Stoeger, H., Ziegler, A., & David, H. (2004). What is a specialist? Effects of the male concept of a successful academic person on the performance in a thinking task. *Psychology Science, 46*(4), 514-530.

Stopford, J. M. (2001). Organizational learning as guided responses to market signals. In M. Dierkes, A.B. Antal, et al. (Eds.), *Handbook of Organizational Learning and Knowledge* (pp. 264-281). Oxford University Press.

Strader, T. J., Lin, F. R., & Shaw, M. J. (1998). Information infrastructure for electronic virtual organization management. *Decision Support Systems, 23*(1), 75-94.

Strauss, C. & Quinn, N. (1997). *A cognitive theory of cultural meaning.* New York: Cambridge University Press.

Suchman, L. A. (1987). *Plans and situated actions: The problem of human-machine communication.* Cambridge: Cambridge University Press, .

Sun, L. (2004). *Motivational visualization in peer-to-peer systems.* CS Dept, University of Saskatchewan.

Sun, L., & Vassileva, J. (2006). *Social visualization encouraging participation in online communities.* Paper presented at the CRIWG 2006, Medina del Campo, Spain.

Surowiecki, J. (2005). *The wisdom of crowds.* Anchor. Paperback.

Swan, J. A., Scarbrough, H., & Robertson, M. (2002). The construction of communities of practice in the management of innovation. *Management Learning, 33*(4), 477-497.

SWSI (2004). *Semantic Web services initiative* (SWSI). Retrieved 15 May 2008, from http://www.swsi.org/

Tajfel, H. (1978). *Differentiation between social groups: Studies in the social psychology of intergroup relations.* London: Academic Press.

Tajfel, H., & Turner, J. C. (1986). The social identity theory of intergroup behavior. In S. Worchel & W. G. Austin (Eds.), *Psychology of Intergroup Relations* (pp. 7-24). Chicago: Nelson Hall.

Tate, D. F., Jackvony, E. H., & Wing R. R. (2003). Effects of Internet behavioural counseling on weight loss in adults at risk for type 2 diabetes: a randomized trial. *Journal of the American Medical Association, 289*(14), 1833-1836.

Taylor, S., & Todd, P. A. (1995). Understanding information technology usage: A test of competing models. *Information Systems Research, 6*(2), 144-176.

Thatchenkery, T. (2005). *Appreciative sharing of knowledge: Leveraging knowledge management for strategic change.* Chagrin Falls, OH: Taos Institute Publishing.

Thatchenkery, T., & Chowdhry, D. (2007). *Appreciative inquiry and knowledge management.* Northampton, MA: Edward Elgar.

Thomke, S., & von Hippel, E. (2002). Customers as innovators: A new way to create value. *Harvard Business Review, 80*(2), 74-81.

Thompson, M. (2005). Structural and epistemic parameters in communities of practices. *Organizational Science, 16*(2), 151-164.

Thorson, K. S., & Rodgers, S. (2006). Relationships between blogs as eWOM and interactivity, perceived interactivity and parasocial interaction. *Journal of Interactive Advertising, 6*(2), 39-50. Spring Eds. Published at: http://jad.org/vol6/no2/thorson

Tichi, C. (1991). *Electronic hearth: Creating an american television culture.* New York: Oxford University Press.

Timmers, P. (1998). Business models for electronic markets. *Electronic Markets, 8*(2), 3-8.

Traganitis, A., Trypakis, D., Spanakis, M., Condos, S., Stamkopoulos, T., Tsiknakis, M., & Orphanoudakis, S. C. (2001, October 25-28). Home monitoring and personal health management services in a regional health telematics network. In *Proceedings of EMBC 2001, 23rd Annual International Conference of the IEEE Engineering in Medicine and Biology Society*, Istanbul.

Travica, B. (2005). Virtual organization and electronic commerce. *The DATABASE for Advances in Information Systems, 36*(3), 45-68.

Tsai, W. T., Qian Huang, Xu, Chen, Y., & Paul, R. (2007). Ontology-based dynamic process collaboration in service-oriented architecture. In *IEEE International Conference on Service-Oriented Computing and Applications (SOCA'07)*, (pp. 39-46), IEEE Computer Society.

Tsakiris, A., Filippidis, I., Grammalidis, N., Tzovaras D., & Strintzis, M. G. (2005). VRLAB: Remote experiment laboratories using virtual reality technologies: The VR-Lab Project. In *Proceedings of the ICTAMI-International Conference on Theory and Applications in Mathematics and Informatics*, Alba Lulia, Romania.

Tsiknakis, M., & Saranummi, N. (2005). Lessons learned from PICNIC. In N. Saranummi, D. Piggott, D. G. Katehakis, M. Tsiknakis, & K. Bernstein (Eds.), *Regional health economies and ICT services,* (pp. 215-228), ISBN: 1-58603-538-x.

Tsiknakis, M., Brochhausen, M., Nabrzyski, J., Pucacki, J., Sfakianakis, S. G., Potamias, G., Desmedt, C., & Kafetzopoulos, D. (2008). A Semantic Grid infrastructure enabling integrated access and analysis of multilevel biomedical data in support of post-genomic clinical trials on Cancer. *IEEE Transactions on Information Technology in Biomedicine, 12*(2), 205-217.

Tsoukas, H. (1996). The firm as a distributed knowledge system: A social constructionist approach. *Strategic Management Journal, 17*(Winter Special Issue), 11-25.

Tuckman, B. (1965). Developmental sequence in small groups. *Psychological Bulletin,* 63, 384-389. Retrieved May 13 from http://dennislearningcenter.osu.edu/references/GROUP%20DEV%20ARTICLE.doc

Turkle, S. (1995). *Life on the Screen: Identity in the Age of the Internet.* New York: Touchstone.

Turner, W. (2006). Information infrastructures for distributed collective practices. *Computer Supported Cooperative Work, 15*(2-3), 93-110.

Turner, W., Bowker, G., Gasser, L., & Zacklad, M. (2006). Information infrastructures for distributed collective practices. *Computer Supported Cooperative Work, 15*(2-3), 93-110.

Tzovaras, D. (2006). *INCOVIS: An intelligent configurable electronic shop platform based on 3D Visualisation.* Retrieved May 10, 2008, from http://avrlab.iti.gr/HTML/Projects/recent/INCOVIS.htm

Tzovaras, D. (2006). *POLEIS: Virtual cultural visits.* Retrieved May 10, 2008, from http://avrlab.iti.gr/HTML/Projects/recent/POLEIS.htm

Tzovaras, D. (2006). *VRLAB: Experimental remote control laboratories using virtual reality technologies.* Retrieved May 10, 2008, from http://avrlab.iti.gr/HTML/Projects/recent/VRLAB.htm

Urquhart, C., Yeoman, A., & Sharp, S. (2002). *NeLH communities of practice evaluation report.* University of Wales Aberystwyth, England.

Uschold, M., & Gruninger, M. (1996). Ontologies: Principles, methods and applications. *Knowledge Engineering Review, 11*(2).

Utz, S. (1999). *Soziale Identifikation mit virtuellen Gemeinschaften - Bedingungen und Konsequenzen. [Social identification with virtual communities - causes and consequences].* Lengerich: Pabst.

Utz, S. (2008). Social identification with virtual communities. In E. Konijn, S. Utz & S. Barnes (Eds.), *Mediated interpersonal communication.* New York: Routledge Taylor & Francis Group.

Vaast, E. (2004). O brother, where are thou? From communities to networks of practice through intranet use. *Management Communication Quarterly, 18*(1), 5-44.

van der Aalst W. M. P., ter Hofstede, A. H. M., Kiepuszewski, B., & Barros, A. P. (2003). Workflow patterns. *Distributed and Parallel Databases, 14*(3), 5-51.

van der Aalst, W. M. P. (1998). The application of Petri nets to workflow management. *Journal of Circuits, Systems, and Computers, 8*(1), 21-66.

van der Aalst, W. M. P., & ter Hofstede, A. H. M. (2005). YAWL: Yet Another Workflow Language. *Information Systems, 30*(4), 245-275

van House, A., N. (2003). Digital libraries and collaborative knowledge construction. In Ann Peterson Bishop, Nancy A. Van House, & Barbara P. Buttenfield (Eds), *Digital library use: Social practice in design and evaluation* (pp. 271-296). Cambridge, MA: MIT Press.

van Welie M., van der Veer, G. C., & Eliëns, A. (1998). An ontology for task world models. In *Proceeding of the 5th International Eurographics Workshop on Design, Specification, and Verification of Interactive Systems* DSV-IS98 (pp. 57-70). Abingdon, UK.

van Welie, M., van der Veer, G. C., & Koster, A. (2000). Integrated representations for task modeling. In *Proceedings of the Tenth European Conference on Cognitive Ergonomics* (pp. 129-138) . Linköping, Sweden.

Van Zolinger, S. L., Sreumer, J. N., & Stooker, M. (2001). Problems in knowledge management: A case study of a knowledge-intensive company. *International Journal of Training & Development, 5*(3), 168-185.

Vanderdonckt, J. (2005). A MDA-compliant environment for developing user interfaces of information systems. In O. Pastor & J. Falcao & Cunha, (Eds.), *17th Conference on Advanced Information Systems Engineering (CAiSE'05): Vol. 3520 of Lecture Notes in Computer Science* (pp. 16-31). Berlin: Springer-Verlag.

Vartiainen M. (2001). The functionality of virtual organizations. In Suomi (Ed.) *Proceedings of Workshop on t-world* (pp. 273-292).Helsinki.

Vassileva, J., & Sun, L. (2007). *An improved design and a case study of a social visualization encouraging participation in online communities.* Paper presented at the CRIWG 2007, Bariloche, Argentina.

Venkatesh, V., & Davis, F. D. (2000). A theoretical extension of the technology acceptance model: Four Longitudinal Field Studies. *Management Science, 46*(2), 186-204.

Venkatesh, V., Morris, M. G., Davis, G. B., & Davis, F. D. (2003). User acceptance of information technology: Toward a unified view. *MIS Quarterly, 27*(3), 425-478.

Venkatraman, N., & Henderson, J. C. (1998). Real strategies for virtual organizing. *Sloan Management Review, 40*(1), 33-48.

Venters, W., & Wood, B. (2007). Degenerative structures that inhibit the emergence of communities of practice: A case study of knowledge management in the British Council. *Information Systems Journal, 17*(4), 349-368.

Verbeek, H. M. W., Hirnschall, A., & van der Aalst, W. M. P. (2002, May). *XRL/Flower: Supporting inter-organizational workflows using XML/petri-net technology.* Paper presented at *Web Services, e-Business, and the Semantic Web (WES): Foundations, Models, Architecture, Engineering and Applications, held in conjunction with CAiSE 2002* [The Fourteenth International Conference on Advanced Information Systems Engineering], Toronto, Ontario, Canada.

Vickers, G. (1965). *The art of judgment.* New York: Basic Books.

Vickers, G. (1968). *Value systems and social process.* New York: Basic Books.

Vickers, G. (1972). Communication and appreciation. In Adams et al (Eds.), *Policymaking, Communication and Social Learning: Essays of Sir Geoffrey Vickers.* New Brunswick, NJ: Transaction Books.

Viegas, B., F., & Donath, S., J. (1999). Chat Circles. In *Proceedings of the ACM SIGCHI Conference on Human Factors in Computing Systems* (CHI 99), (pp. 9-16), New York: ACM Press.

Visual Paradigm International Ltd. (2007). *Business Process Visual ARCHITECT, User's guide.* Retrieved January 2, 2007, from www.visual-paradigm.com/product/bpva/bpvadocuments.jsp

Völkel, M., Krötzsch, M., Vrandecic, D., Haller, H., & Studer, R. (2006). Semantic Wikipedia. *Proceedings of the 15th international conference on World Wide Web*, (pp. 585-594).

von Hippel, E. (1988). *The sources of innovation.* New York: Oxford University Press.

von Hippel, E. (2001). Perspective: User toolkits for innovation. *The Journal of product innovation management, 18*(4), 247.

von Hippel, E., Katz, R. (2002). Shifting innovation to users via toolkits. *Management Science, 48*(7), 821-833.

Vorderer, P. (2000). Interactive entertainment and beyond. In D. Zillman & P. Vorderer (Eds.), *Media entertainment: The psychology of its appeal.* Mahwah, NJ: Lawrence Earlbaum.

Vygosky, L. S. (1978). *Mind in society.* Cambridge, MA: Harvard University Press.

Vygotsky, L. S. (1981). The genesis of higher mental functions. I J. V. Wertsch (Ed.), *The concept of activity in Soviet psychology,* (pp. 144-188), Armonk: M.E. Sharpe.

Walden, E. (2000). Some value propositions of online communities. *Electronic Markets, 10*(4), 244-249.

Walsh, J., & Bayama, T. (1996). Computer networks and scientific work. *Social Studies of Science, 26*(3), 385-405.

Wang, J., Pouwelse, J., Fokker, J., & Reinders, M. J. T. (2006). Personalization of a peer-to-peer television system. In *Proceedings of the 4th Euro iTV Conference* (pp. 147-155). Athens, Greece.

Wasko, Molly M., & Faraj, S. (2005) Why should I share? Examining social capital and knowledge contribution in electronic networks of practice. *Management Information Systems Quarterly, 29*(1), 35–57.

Watkins, J. M., & Cooperrider, D. L. (1996). Organization inquiry model for global social change organizations. *Organization Development Journal, 14*(4), 97-112.

Wellman B. (1997). An electronic group is virtually a social network. In S. Kiesler (Ed.), *Cultures of the Internet,* (pp. 179–205), Mahwah, NJ: Lawrence Erlbaum.

Wellman, B. (2001). Physical place and CyberPlace: The rise of personalized networking. *International Journal of Urban and Regional Research, 25.*

Wellman, B., & Gulia, M. (1998). Net surfers don't ride alone: Virtual communities as communities. In Smith and Kollock (Eds.) *Communities in cyberspace,* (pp.163-190). Berkley:University of California Press.

Wellman, B., Quan-Haase, A., Boase, J., & Chen, W. (2002). *Examining the Internet in everyday life.* Keynote address given by B. Wellman to the Euricom Conference on e-democracy. Nijmegen, Netherlands, October, 2002.

Wellman, B., Salaff, J., Dimitrova, D., Garton, L., Gulia, M., & Haythornthwaite, C. (1996). Computer networks as social networks: Collaborative work, telework, and virtual community. *Annual Review of Sociology, 22*, 213-238.

Wenger, E. (1998). *Communities of practice: Learning, meaning and identity.* Boston: Cambridge University Press.

Wenger, E. (1998b). Communities of practice: Learning as a social system. *Systems Thinker.*

Wenger, E. (2006). Communities of Practice - a Brief Introduction.   Retrieved 10/11/2006

Wenger, E. C. (2000). Communities of practice and social learning systems. *Organization, 7*(2), 225-246.

Wenger, E. C., & Snyder, W. M. (2000). Communities of practice: The organizational frontier. *Harvard Business Review, 78*(1), 139-45.

Wenger, E., McDermott, R., & Snyder, W. (2002). *Cultivating communities of practice: A guide to managing knowledge.* Boston: Harvard Business School Press.

Werthner, H., & Ricci, F. (2004). E-commerce and tourism. *Communications of the ACM, 47*(12), 101-105.

Wertsch, J. V. (1990). *Voices of the mind.* Cambridge, MA: Harvard University Press.

White, T. W. (1996). Working in interesting times. *Vital Speeches of the Day, LXII*(15), 472-474.

Whitney, D., & Trosten-Bloom, A. (2003). *The power of appreciative inquiry: A practical guide to positive change.* San Francisco, CA: Berrett-Koehler Publishers, Inc.

Whittaker, S. (1996). *Talking to strangers: An evaluation of the factors affecting electronic collaboration.* Paper presented at the ACM conference on Computer supported cooperative work, Boston, Massachusetts, United States.

Whittaker, S., Issacs, E., & O'Day, V. (1997). Widening the Net. Workshop report on the theory and practice of physical and network communities. *SIGCHI Bulletin, 29*, 27–30.

Wikipedia. (2008). *3D computer graphics.* Retrieved May 10, 2008, from http://en.wikipedia.org/wiki/3D_computer_graphics

Wikipedia. (2008). *3D modelling.* Retrieved May 10, 2008, from http://en.wikipedia.org/wiki/3D_modeling

Wilkinson, D. M., & Huberman, B. A. (2007, 20 February 2007). *Assessing the value of cooperation in Wikipedia.* Retrieved 12 February, 2007, from http://www.hpl.hp.com/research/idl/papers/wikipedia/wikipedia.pdf

Willett, W., Heer, J., & Agrawala, M. (2007). Scented Widgets: Improving Navigation Cues with Embedded Visualizations. *IEEE Transactions on Visualization and Computer Graphics, 13*(6), 1129-1136.

Williamson, T. (1987). Common land. In J. Eatwell, M. Milgate & P. Newman (Eds.), *The new Palgrave: A dictionary of economies* (Vol. 1). London: MacMillan.

Winner, L. (1990). Living in electronic space. In T. Casey, & L. Embree (Eds.), *Lifeworld and technology,* (pp. 1-14). Lonham, MD: Center for Advanced Research on Phenomenology and University Press of America.

Winograd, T. (ed.) (1996) *Bringing design to software.* New York: Addison Wesley.

Winzelberg, A. J., Classen, C., Alpers, G. W., Roberts, H., Koopman, C., Adams, E. R., Ernst, H., Dev, P., & Taylor, B. (2003). Evaluation of an Internet support group for women with primary breast cancer. *Cancer, 97*(5), 1164–1173.

Wisker, G., Robinson, G., et al. (2007). Postgraduate research success: Communities of practice involving cohorts, guardian supervisors and online communities. *Innovations in Education and Teaching International, 44*, 301-320.

Wittgenstein, L. (1953). *Philosophical investigations.* London: Basil Blackwell.

Wöhrmann, R. (1999). Design and architecture of distributed sound processing and database systems for Web based computer music applications. *Computer Music Journal. 23*(3).

Wolton, D. (1997). *Penser la communication.* Paris: Flammarion.

Workflow Management Coalition (1999). *Workflow management coalition terminology & glossary.* Document Number WFMC-TC-1011. Document Status – Issue 3.0.

World Health Organisation (2002). Innovative care for chronic conditions: building blocks for action (No. WHO/NMC/CCH/02.01). France: World Health Organization.

Wyeld, T. G., Prasolova-Førland, E., & Chang, T-W. (2006, July 5-7). Virtually collaborating across cultures: A case study of an online theatrical performance in a 3DCVE spanning three continents. *In proceedings of the International Conference on Advanced Learning Technologies,* Kerkrade, Netherlands.

Xiong, R., & Donath, J. (1999). *PeopleGarden: Creating data portraits for users.* Paper presented at the 12th annual ACM symposium on User interface software and technology, Asheville, North Carolina, United States.

Yee, N. (2006). The Psychology of MMORPGs: Emotional Investment, Motivations, Relationship Formation, and Problematic Usage. In R. Schroeder & A. Axelsson (Eds.), *Avatars at Work and Play: Collaboration and Interaction in Shared Virtual Environments* (pp. 187-207). London: Springer-Verlag.

Yee, N. (2006). The Demographics, Motivations and Derived Experiences of Users of Massively-Multiuser Online Graphical Environments. *PRESENCE: Teleoperators and Virtual Environments, 15*, 309-329.

Yu, C. C. (2002). Designing a Web-based consumer decision support system for tourism services. In *Proceedings of the 4th International Conference on Electronic Commerce.*

Zabulis, X., Grammalidis, N., Bastanlar, Y., Yilmaz, Y., Cetin, Y.Y. (2008). *3D scene reconstruction based on robust camera motion estimation.* 3DTV-CON2008, Istanbul, Turkey.

Zajonc, R. B. (1965). Social facilitation. *Science, 149*(3681), 269-274.

Zheng, J., Veinott, E., Bos, N., Olson, J., & Olson, G. (2002). Trust without touch: Jumpstarting long-distance trust with initial social activities. *Proceedings of CHI, Retrieved September 2007 from* http://www.crew.umich.edu/publications.html

Ziegler, A., & Stoeger, H. (2004). Evaluation of an attributional retraining to reduce gender differences in chemistry instruction. *High Ability Studies, 15*(1), 63-81.

Ziegler, A., & Stoeger, H. (2008). Effect of role models from films on short-term ratings of intent, interest, and self-assessment of ability by high school youth: A study of gender-stereotyped academic subjects. *Psychological Reports*, in press.

About the Contributors

Akoumianakis, Demosthenes (PhD) – Editorial Advisory Board Member & Reviewer is an associate professor at the Department of Applied Information Technology & Multimedia, Technological Education Institution of Crete. He is also the founder and director of the *Interactive Software and Systems Engineering Laboratory* (iSTLab, http://www.istl.teiher.gr/). He received a BA (Hons) in computing in business from The University of Huddersfield (1990) and MSc and PhD degrees in human computer interaction from the University of Kent at Canterbury, UK in 1995 and 1999 respectively. His work on his final year dissertation was awarded the 1st IBM prize from the Department of Computing & Mathematics of the University of Huddersfield. Prof Akoumianakis has published widely in referred archival scientific journals, international conferences and workshops and is the author of a textbook on human computer interaction (in Greek). He also serves as a member of the scientific committee for various established archival journals, international conferences and national / international standards bodies.

* * *

Chrisoula Alexandraki (MSc) is a software engineer and an active researcher in the field of Music Technology with special interest in the areas of: network music performance, distributed environments for music collaboration, multimedia streaming technologies, multimodal interaction techniques based on sound and music, sound representation in multichannel and spatial audio systems and games technology. She received an MSc degree in Music Technology from the University of York (UK) in 1998, and a Degree in Physics from the University of Athens (Greece) in 1996. Additional studies include piano performance and music theory. She is a Lecturer at the Department of Music Technology & Acoustics of the Technological Educational Institute of Crete, where she teaches the subjects 'Music Communication Protocols' and 'Audio Programming'. She has participated in various R&D projects and is currently the primary investigator of the DIAMOUSES research project and a member of the research team of the eKoNES consortium.

Ioannis Barbounakis (PhD) is a lecturer at the Department of Electronics, Technological Educational Institute of Crete. He received an electrical engineering degree from The Aristotelian University of Thessaloniki, Greece (1991) and MSc and PhD degrees in digital communications from the Technical University of Crete, Greece and the University of Bradford, UK in 1993 and 2000 respectively. His dissertation thesis was in the area of error correction techniques for the general class of correlative encoded continuous phase modulation signals. He is actively involved in various national and European collaborative research and development projects, with emphasis on service quality, wireline/wireless network aspects and Grid tTechnologies. Dr. Barbounakis has published in referred archival scientific journals, international conferences and workshops and is co-author of a chapter of the textbook on *"Wireless local Loops Theory and Applications"* ISBN: 0471-49846-7, June 2001, Wiley & Sons, England. He also serves as a member of the scientific community for various established archival journals

Henry Been-Lirn Duh (PhD) is currently an assistant professor in the Department of Electrical and Computer Engineering, Interactive and Digital Media Institute, and NUS-KEIO CUTE joint research center at National University of Singapore. He received degree from psychology, design and engineering respectively. His current research interests include human-computer interaction, usability engineering, mobile computing, user experiences and interaction design, and game effects in advanced display and mobile systems. His work periodically appear in the prestigious conferences such as ACM CH, ACM ACE, MobileHCI, and journals such as *PRESENCE*. He is a senior member of ACM, member of IEEE and FAA certified PPL and AGI.

Hsueh-hua Vivian Chen (PhD) is currently an assistant professor in Wee Kim Wee School of Communication and Information at Nanyang Technological University in Singapore. She is trained in the area of culture and communication. Her current research interest is socio-cultural impact of new media technology such as digital games, blogs, and internet. Research topics include issues of relationship building, social interaction, lifestyle and popular culture. Previously, she looks at the interplay between culture and communication medium as well as human communication behaviors. She has been awarded several research grants to conduct research on the impact of gaming and the gaming culture constructed. She has published papers on social interaction in gaming in prestigious conferences and journals.

Dima Dimitrova (PhD) - Reviewer holds a PhD from the University of Toronto and works in the areas of work, new technologies and social networks. She has almost 20 years of research experience in a range of areas, including remote work and workplace and knowledge networks. Among her recent projects are a study of a nation-wide network of researchers and a project on the role of public-private consortia for innovation. Her work has been published independently or in collaboration in the *New Technology, Work and Employment, Annual Review of Sociology, Business Value Directions, Telektronikk, Notiziario Del Lavoro, Human Resource Management in Europe,* and elsewhere. She teaches organizational studies at York University and is a research associate with NetLab at the University of Toronto and with the Ontario Metropolis Centre. She has a research and consulting business and volunteers at Scadding Court Community Centre.

Juan Manuel Gonzalez Calleros (MSc) is a researcher assistant of the University catholic of Louvain (UCL). He is member of the Belgian Lab of Human Computer Interaction and of the UsiXML consortium. Having received a scholarship award, he came to Belgium and completed his DEA in computer Science from UCL. He received a master degree in Computer Sciences at National Institute of Astrophysics, Optics and Electronic (Mexico). Juan Manuel Gonzalez Calleros is pursuing a PhD in computer sciences with the thesis *Model driven engineering of 3D User Interfaces* at UCL, Louvain School of Management (IAG-LSM). Her research interests include workflow models, model-driven engineering for developing user interfaces, in general, and 3D user interfaces, in particular

Nikos Grammalidis (PhD) is a senior researcher (Researcher C') with the Informatics and Telematics Institute. He received the BS and PhD degrees in electrical and computer engineering from the Aristotle University of Thessaloniki, in 1992 and 2000, respectively. His PhD dissertation was titled *"Analysis, coding and processing of multi-view image sequences using object-based techniques"*. Prior to his current position, he was a researcher on 3D Imaging Laboratory at the Aristotle University of Thessaloniki. His main research interests include computer vision, 3D data processing, virtual reality, multimedia image communication, stereo and multi-view image sequence coding. His involvement with those research areas has led to the co-authoring of 16 articles in refereed journals, two book chapters and more than 40 papers in international conferences. Since 1992, he has been involved in more than 10 projects, funded by the EC and the Greek Ministry of Research and Technology. He has served as a regular reviewer for a number of international journals and conferences.

Josefina Guerrero García (MSc) is doing her PhD research in the domain of management sciences, option "Information Systems" at Université catholique de Louvain (Belgium), Louvain School of Management (IAG-LSM). She received a DEA (Diplôme d'Etudes Approfondies) in management sciences from the same university in 2006 and a Master's Degree in management at Instituto de Estudios Universitarios (Mexico) in 2001. She is a member of the Belgian Laboratory of Computer Human Interaction (BCHI) and the UsiXML Consortium. Her research interests include workflow models, computer supported cooperative work, and information systems.

Chris Kimble (PhD) – Editorial Advisory Board Member is an associate professor of Information Systems at Euromed Marseille École de Management, France. Prior to that, he was a lecturer in information systems at the University of York and the University of Newcastle upon Tyne in the UK. His research focuses on communities of practice, knowledge management and distributed collaborative working. He has published articles in several journals and has also published two collections of edited papers on Communities of Practice as books.

Emmanuel Koku (PhD) is an assistant professor of sociology in the Department of Culture and Communication at Drexel University, Philadelphia, USA. He is a graduate of the University of Ghana, Legon, Queen's University (Canada), and the University of Toronto (Canada). His research interests are social network analysis, virtual communities, sociology of development, sociology of health, research methods/social statistics. His current research examines the lived-experiences of persons living with HIV in Africa and US, as well as analysis of professional and informal networks of academic researchers and policy makers.

Dimitrios Kotsalis received a BSc in applied informatics & multimedia from the Technological Education Institution of Crete in 2007. In the past, he has worked for Forthnet S.A (Greece) and the Technological Education Institution of Crete (Greece). During this period he has been involved in a few Research and Technological Development projects, funded by national and European organizations. Kotsalis, since May 2006, is an Associated Researcher in istlab (research laboratory of the Technological Educational Institution of Crete) and since February 2008, is an Associated Lecturer in the Department of Applied Informatics & Multimedia, Faculty of Applied Technologies at the Technological Education Institution of Crete. His current research interests are in the areas of HCI, DSM and VCoP.

George Lekakos (PhD) is an assistant professor in e-business at the Department of Information and Communication Systems, University of the Aegean, Greece. He leads the Intelligent Media Lab (IML), which is a research group within the ELTRUN Research Center (http://www.eltrun.gr) at the Athens University of Economics and Business (AUEB), Greece. He also teaches in AUEB at undergraduate and postgraduate courses (e-business). He is also teaching staff at the Greek Open University. During the previous three years he worked in adjunct and visiting teaching posts at the Department of Computer Science, University of Cyprus, and the Department of Technology Education and Digital Systems, University of Piraeus, Greece. He holds a BSc in Mathematics (University of Thessaloniki, Greece), MSc in Formal Methods in Software Engineering (University of London, UK), and PhD in Interactive Television (Athens University of Economics and Business, Greece). He has published more than thirty-five papers in international journals and conferences, he is co-editor of books and conference proceedings, and he serves as editorial board member of international journals. He is member of the EuroiTV steering committee and the IFIP TC14 working group on interactive television (WG 14.6). For the last 8 years, he has been working in several EU funded projects and has been appointed as project reviewer by the European Commission and the General Secretariat of Research and Technology in Greece.

Edurne Loyarte (PhD) is the financial and quality manager of VICOMTech, a technological centre of computer graphics located in San Sebastian. She received her Bachelor's degree in business management and administration from the University of Deusto with a speciality master in strategy. She is PhD in economics and business administration from the University of Deusto (San Sebastian) with the thesis called "*A model of cultivation and integration of Communities of Practice for organizations in the Basque Country*". Therefore, she has published some articles in the field of communities of practice.

Evangelia Mantzari is a PhD candidate at Athens University of Economics and Business, in the Department of Management Science and Technology (AUEB, DMST). She is part of ELTRUN, the e-Business Research Center of Athens University of Economics and Business, and she is actively engaged in projects relating to Interactive Digital Television, Consumer Behavior, e-Business and e-Government. Also, she is currently member of the coordinating committee for the Greek eBusiness Forum for Interactive Digital TV, which aims in evaluating the conditions for the media market's transition. Mantzari holds an International MBA degree (AUEB, DMST) and a first degree in economics from the University of Piraeus. Besides her research activity, she is employed as a financial consultant for the National Bank of Greece and as a trainer in the field of electronic business and marketing for the national program of lifelong learning of the Greek Ministry of Education. During her post-graduate studies, she has been involved in the joined research of the Greek Ministry of Internal Affairs and Athens University, Department of Informatics for "E-Government Applications around the world".

Giannis Milolidakis is on the Ecricome PhD Programme at the Euromed Management School. He obtained his BSc in information yechnology and multimedia from the Department of Applied Information Technology and Multimedia of the Technological Educational Institution of Crete in 2007. The last two years he has been working as an associated researcher in the Interactive Software Technologies & System Engineering Laboratory which is a research unit of the Technological Educational Institution of Crete. During this time he participated in various local and large scale research and development projects. His current research interests are in the areas of human computer interaction and virtual communities and in particular communities of practice.

Natalie Pang - Reviewer is a PhD candidate in Monash University's Faculty of Information Technology. Her research focuses on the knowledge commons in the contemporary media environment, and cases of cultural institutions engaging community participation. Her teaching interests include information management, usability evaluations, peer to peer technologies and approaches, and digital libraries. A graduate of Melbourne University and Nanyang Technological University in Singapore, Pang has worked in Singapore, Malaysia, and Australia. Other than her involvement in ongoing research with communities from China, Italy, Australia, Singapore and Malaysia, she has also previously served as an honorary research associate of Museum Victoria in Australia and a visiting scholar at the School of Communication and Information, Nanyang Technological University in Singapore. Pang is currently a contributing member of the Foundation for Peer to Peer Alternatives, with interests in participatory technologies in Web 2.0, social networks and discourse on open content licenses applicable in the digital environment.

Kyriakos Paterakis received a BSc from the Information Technology and Multimedia department at the Technological Education Institution of Crete in 2008. Since January 2008, he is an associate researcher at the iSTLab research laboratory, Technological Education Institution of Crete.

Anargyros Plemenos was born in Melbourne, Australia. He received a BSc from the Information Technology and Multimedia department at the Technological Education Institution of Crete in 2008. Since January 2008, he is an associate researcher at the iSTLab research laboratory: Technological Education Institution of Crete.

Ekaterina Prasolova-Førland (PhD) obtained her PhD degree in computer science from the Norwegian University of Science and Technology (NTNU) in 2004. She is currently an associate professor at the Program for Learning with ICT (LIKT) at NTNU. Her research interests include educational and social aspects of 3D Collaborative Virtual Environments and augmented environments as well as virtual universities, mobile learning and educational games. Dr. Prasolova-Førland has published more than 30 papers in refereed conference proceedings and journals. She is currently involved in two EU-financed projects focusing on educational games in 3D virtual worlds.

Richard Ribeiro (MSc) - Reviewer was trained as an electrical engineer and has a Master's degree in electrical engineering. He worked as lecturer in computer science in Brazil for twelve years and is now a PhD student in the department of Computer Science at University of York where his research is focused on communities of practice and knowledge management.

Olga Rivera (PhD) is a professor in organization and business policy and Head of the team on Innovation and Knowledge Management at the University of Deusto (San Sebastian). She is also a member of Orkestra, Basque Institute for Competitiveness and part of the MOC (Microeconomics of Competitiveness) Network, launched by the Institute of Strategy and Competitiveness of the University of Harvard. Professor Rivera has worked on clusters, Learning Organizations and Learning Networks, focusing in these last years on the interaction between Knowledge Sharing and Innovation Capability.

Emmanuela Rombogianaki (BSc) received a BSc in applied information technology and multimedia from the Department of Applied Information Technology and Multimedia, Technological education Institution of Crete. From December 2007 to May 2008, she was an associate researcher at the iSTLab research laboratory at the Technological Education Institution of Crete.

Diana Schimke studied computer science with a minor in psychology at Ulm University and is currently pursuing her PhD in computer science. Her research interests lie in virtual communities and evaluating strategies for virtual communities to function properly. She is currently working at the University of Regensburg where she coordinates the CyberMentor project.

Stelios Sfakianakis (MSc) received his BSc in computer science in 1995 and his MSc with highest distinction in advanced information systems in 1998 from the University of Athens. In January 2000 he joined the ICS-FORTH's Biomedical Informatics Laboratory (BMI). His interests include the Semantic integration and composition of services in state of the art computational environments such as the Grid and the Semantic Web. Additionally he in interested in the design of programming languages and their various paradigms, such as functional, object and data oriented, and concurrent.

Wes Shumar (PhD) – Editorial Advisory Board Member is an associate professor of anthropology at Drexel University, USA. His research focuses on higher education, ethnographic evaluation in education, virtual community, the semiotics of mass culture, and the self in relation to contemporary personal and political issues of identity and globalization. Since 1997, Prof. Shumar has worked as an ethnographer at the Math Forum, a virtual math education community and resource center. Currently he is involved in various NSF-funded projects, including the projects 'The Virtual Math Teams (VMT)' and 'Leadership Development for Technology Integration: Developing an Effective NSDL Teacher Workshop Model'. Prof. Shumar is co-editor of *Building Virtual Communities: Learning and Change in Cyberspace*, published by Cambridge University Press.

Chris Stary (PhD) is currently a full professor and the head of the department of Business Information Systems – Communications Engineering at the University of Linz. His interest is in model-based and user-oriented application design. Areas of application include articulation work, modelling, multimedia systems, e-learning, organisational development and adaptive systems engineering.

Heidrun Stoeger (PhD) is a full professor at the University of Regensburg. She holds the chair for school research, school development and evaluation. Her main research fields are learning and instruction, gender issues and evaluation. She is project leader of CyberMentor at the University of Regensburg.

Georgios Triantafyllidis (PhD) was born in Thessaloniki, Greece, in 1975. He received the Diploma degree in electrical engineering and the PhD degree in image/video processing from Aristotle Univ. of Thessaloniki, Greece, in 1997 and 2002, respectively. From 1997 till 2000 he worked as a research assistant at the Information Processing Lab of the Aristotle Univ. of Thessaloniki. From 2000 to 2008 he joined the Informatics and Telematics Institute in Thessaloniki as an associate researcher and since 2003 as a senior researcher. From 2005 to 2008 he was also with the Electrical and Computer Eng Dept of the Aristotle Univ. of Thessaloniki as a visiting lecturer. Since 2008, he has been assistant professor in the Applied Information Technology and Multimedia Dept of the

Technological Educational Institute of Crete, Greece. He has been involved in several national and international research projects, where he conducted research in various fields of image/video processing and coding, computer vision and computer graphics and published more than 50 referred research papers.

Manolis Tsiknakis (PhD) – Editorial Advisory Board Member received the BEng degree in electronic engineering, in 1983, the MSc degree in microprocessor engineering, in 1985, and the PhD degree in control systems engineering from the University of Bradford, Bradford, U.K., in 1989. Since 1992, he has been with the Institute of Computer Science, Foundation for Research and Technology–Hellas, Greece, where he is currently a principal researcher. He is the head of the Center of eHealth Technologies, and has been the technical coordinator of the development of HYGEIAnet, the regional health information network of Crete. He is the initiator and co-chair of the ERCIM Biomedical Informatics Working Group. He is the scientific coordinator of the Advancing Clinico-Genomic Trials on Cancer EU funded integrated project and also involved in a number of R&D projects in the domain of cancer biomarker discovery and translational medicine. His current research interests include biomedical informatics, component-based software engineering, biomedical information integration, ambient intelligence in eHealth and mHealth service platforms, and IT adoption related issues.

Dimitrios Tzovaras (PhD) is a senior researcher in the Informatics and Telematics Institute. He received the Diploma in electrical engineering and the PhD in 2D and 3D image compression from Aristotle University of Thessaloniki, Greece in 1992 and 1997, respectively. Prior to his current position, he was a leading researcher on 3D imaging at the Aristotle University of Thessaloniki. His main research interests include image compression, 3D data processing, virtual reality, multimedia image communication, 3D motion estimation, stereo and multiview image sequence coding. His involvement with those research areas has led to the co-authoring of over twenty articles in refereed journals and more than 50 papers in international conferences. He has served as a regular reviewer for a number of international journals and conferences. Since 1992, Dr Tzovaras has been involved in more than 20 projects, funded by the EC and the Greek Ministry of Research and Technology.

Nikolas Valsamakis (MSc) is a composer and performer of electroacoustic music. He studied music with D.Kamarotos and S.Vasiliades in the Center of Contemporary Music research in Athens, Greece and Music Technology (Msc) with Simon Emerson in City University in London, England. He is especially interested in the directions of algorithmic composition, microsound, nonstandard synthesis, interactive systems, live electronics and soundscape composition. He explores and applies computer technology and electronics in the creation of his own meta-tools for music composition as well as in the construction of musical meta-instruments for live performance. In 2004 was invited composer in residence in the Center de Creation Musicale Iannis Xenakis (CCMIX) in Paris. He is a founding member and President of the Hellenic Electroacoustic Music Composers Association (ΕΣΣΗΜ - HELMCA) and founding member of the Hellenic Society of Acoustic Ecology (EEAE - HSAE). He is lecturer in the Music Technology & Acoustics Department of TEI of Crete, in Rethymnon, Greece.

Jean Vanderdonckt (PhD) is full professor in computer science at Université Catholique de Louvain (Belgium), Louvain School of Management (IAG-LSM) where he leads the Belgian Laboratory of Computer-Human Interaction (BCHI). This laboratory is conducting research, development, and consulting services in the domain of user interface engineering, a domain that is located midway between software engineering, human-computer interaction, and usability engineering. Vanderdonckt is the founder and the coordinator of the UsiXML Consortium that structures activities towards the definition and the usage of UsiXML (User Interface eXtensible Markup Language) as a common User Interface Description Language. He is the coordinator of HCI activities within the Similar network of excellence (The European research taskforce creating human-machine interfaces SIMILAR to human-human communication). He is also a member of the European COST n°294 Action MAUSE on usability engineering and of the SESAMI Working Group. He is a senior member of IEEE, ACM, and SIGCHI. He is also co-editor in chief of Springer HCI Series of books.

Kam Hou Vat - Reviewer is currently a lecturer in the Department of Computer and Information Science, under the Faculty of Science and Technology, at the University of Macau, Macau SAR, China. His current research interests include learner-centered design with constructivism in Software Engineering education, architected applications developments for Internet software systems, information systems for learning organization, information technology for knowledge synthesis, and collaborative technologies for electronic organizations and virtual communities.

Goerge Vellis is an associated researcher at the istLab, Technological Education Institution of Crete. He received a BSc in applied informatics & multimedia from the Technological Education Institution of Crete in 2007. In the past, he has worked for Forthnet S.A (Greece) and the Technological Education Institution of Crete (Greece). During this period he has been involved in a few research and technological development projects, funded by national and European organizations. Since September 2008, he is an associated lecturer in the Department of Applied Informatics & Multimedia, Faculty of Applied Technologies at the Technological Education Institution of Crete. His current research interests are in the areas of user interface software technologies and collaborative computing.

Nikolas Vidakis (PhD) - Reviewer received a BSc(Hons) in computing in business from the University of Northumbria at Newcastle in 1993 and obtained his PhD degree from the Technical University of Vienna in 1997. In the past, he has worked for the Technical University of Vienna (Austria), Minoan Lines S.A. (Greece) and the Technological Education Institution of Crete (Greece). During his work at Minoan Lines and the Technological Education Institution of Crete he has been involved in a few research and technological development projects, funded by national and European organizations. Since October 2005, Dr Vidakis has been a lecturer in the Department of Applied Informatics & Multimedia, Faculty of Applied Technologies at the Technological Education Institution of Crete. His current research interests are in the areas of software engineering, virtual communities of practice, and in particular electronic villages, on-line communities, as well as 3D interactive artifacts.

Adam Vrechopoulos (PhD) is an assistant professor at the Athens University of Economics and Business (AUEB), Department of Management Science and Technology and Scientific Coordinator of the Interactive Marketing and Electronic Services (IMES) research group at the ELTRUN Research Center at AEUB. His research interests are digital marketing, electronic retailing and consumer behaviour in multichannel retailing. He holds a PhD from Brunel University at UK, an MBA from ALBA, and a BSc in information systems from AUEB. He has participated in many funded research projects and acted as researcher at the Electronic Business Interaction Research Group at Brunel University and at the

ELTRUN Research Center at AUEB. He has published more than 70 papers in peer reviewed journals and academic conferences, and has acted as a reviewer for several international journals, member of conferences' scientific committees and books' editor. He is the 2002 "Gold Award" winner of the ECR Europe Academic Partnership Award. Before starting his academic career he worked in the industry in marketing, sales and project management positions.

Theodor Wyeld - Reviewer has a background in architecture and planning, and games development and is widely published in these fields. He has given keynote lectures on the topics of information visualisation, cultural heritage knowledge communication, and virtual environments as cross-cultural classrooms. He currently lectures in interaction design and user evaluation at Flinders University, Adelaide, Australia.

Michael Zervakis (PhD) holds a PhD degree from the University of Toronto, Department of Electrical Engineering, since 1990. He joined the Technical University of Crete on January 1995, where he is currently full professor at the department of Electronic and Computer Engineering. Prof. Zervakis is the director of the Digital Image and Signal Processing Laboratory (DISPLAY) and is involved in research on modern aspects of signal processing, including estimation and constrained optimization, multi-channel and multi-band signal processing, wavelet analysis for data/ image processing and compression, biomedical imaging applications, neural networks and fuzzy logic in automation applications. He has been involved in more than 20 international projects and has published more than 90 papers in related areas of image/signal processing.

Albert Ziegler (PhD) is a full professor at the Ulm University. He holds the chair for educational psychology. His main research fields are giftedness, gender studies, and learning and instruction with new media. He is project leader of the CyberMentor project at Ulm University.

Index

D

E